Concepts for Corporate Strategy

Concepts for Corporate Strategy
Readings in Business Policy

John W. Bonge
Graduate School of
Business Administration
Michigan State University

Bruce P. Coleman
Graduate School of
Business Administration
Michigan State University

1972

The Macmillan Company, New York
Collier-Macmillan Limited, London

To Our Wives

Printed in the United States of America

THE MACMILLAN COMPANY
866 THIRD AVENUE, NEW YORK, NEW YORK 10022

COLLIER-MACMILLAN CANADA, LTD., TORONTO, ONTARIO

Library of Congress catalog card number: 70–165578

First Printing

preface

This book has been compiled to assist in the teaching of corporate strategy (or more popularly, business policy) and to enhance the understanding of strategy formulation as a distinct managerial activity. The objective has been to provide (1) a basic rationale and focus for the entire subject of corporate strategy; (2) key conceptual ideas for policy formulation and implementation; and (3) current and emerging issues having strategy implications.

The book is designed to fit a variety of approaches to the teaching of business policy. The usual approaches consist of case analysis and reporting, business games, lecture and discussion, or some combination of these. This book is intended to strengthen any of the preceding approaches in policy courses at both the undergraduate and graduate levels. Specifically, it can be used (1) as a supplement to a case course, (2) as a supplement to cases and text material, (3) as background for use with computerized business games, or (4) as text material for lecture and discussion. In addition, it may be highly useful for the practicing manager in bringing to him the administrative policy viewpoint on a number of key issues of importance in the management of his firm.

Business policy may be viewed as having two major components. The first is strategic—having to do with the choice of purpose, molding of organization character, and formulation of broad plans for guiding the direction of the enterprise. Decisions are strategic in nature and aim at integrating the interests of the organization and those of its environment. The second component of policy is administrative or executive—having to do with the implementation actions to mobilize resources, to carry out strategic decisions, and to achieve organization goals.

These components of policy are interdependent and constitute a continuous system or flow of activities differing in range and specificity as decisions go from strategic to executive. Of necessity, these are matters of concern to top management. Put succinctly, policy is the study of the functions and responsibilities of general managers and higher-level executives.

In addition to developing an understanding of the strategic and administrative components, courses in business policy have other objectives. The more significant of these are (1) integrating knowledge gained in separate business fields and utilizing it in the analysis of complex business problems; and (2) developing the ability to appraise situations within which the enterprise operates, to analyze pertinent variables bearing on the problem at hand, and to formulate goals, strategies, and plans for implementing decisions reached on the basis of appraisal.

The view of business policy described approaches to teaching policy courses, and course objectives were dominant criteria for the selection of articles in this book. They were selected for their contribution to an understanding of the concept of corporate strategy as a field of study in business administration.

The articles vary in conceptual difficulty. A particular set of articles can be selected for use in an undergraduate course. A different set can be used for graduate study. A third grouping would be appropriate for a more theoretical discussion of the nature and scope of the problems of corporate management.

Policy courses are based on a knowledge of the business functions of marketing, accounting and finance, operations, and personnel, as well as fundamental concepts of economics, decision making, organization and administration, and the behavioral sciences. Although knowledge of those areas is essential background for the study of policy, such topics do not constitute the field of corporate strategy and consequently are not treated separately in this book. The emphasis here is on the interdepartmental aspects of the management of complex organizations. It is up to the student and instructor to recall concepts and to fill in gaps, because curricula do not usually provide all the background knowledge assumed for the study of policy.

Most of the articles have been used in our graduate and undergraduate policy courses. The articles have had to survive tests of relevance to the courses and particularly the specific criticism of student evaluation with respect to contribution of knowledge and understanding.

Numerous constraints—internally imposed and externally generated—have operated in the formation of this book. Many trade-offs have been necessary in the selection of articles. Consequently, at the beginning of each part references are provided for suggested further readings.

The book is in four parts. The basic rationale is to pursue the logical development of issues pertinent to a comprehensive coverage of corporate strategy formulation and implementation. The part introductions define the scope of each major topic area, integrate it with other materials of major importance, and indicate the relationship of the readings to the topic area. The introductory sections, taken as a total unit, constitute an identification of a concept of corporate strategy and a basis for teaching and studying it.

Part One (Sections 1 and 2) contains articles that relate to the over-all perspective of the organization. It is appropriate to begin by establishing the attitude necessary for the integrative approach required if policy decisions are to be made for the achievement of corporate goals. Section 1 focuses on the total systems nature and informational requirements of the organization. An understanding of these concepts has the greatest potential for freeing policy-makers from the narrow confines of a single functional discipline and for fostering a recognition of the interdependencies of policy issues. In Section 2 the characteristics of top management as a primary policy-making group are investigated. By looking at personal values, social responsibility, behavioral characteristics, and the responsibilities of the managers and board of directors, the reader is prepared to begin the actual process of developing corporate strategy.

Part Two (Sections 3 and 4) focuses on issues relating to the assessment of the situation within which the enterprise operates and to the development of broad strategies for the firm. In Section 3 a general framework is established for goal setting, strategy formulation, and the establishment of long-range plans. Given an over-all picture of the policy formulation process, in Section 4 the critical variables that must be considered in strategy formulation are investigated, such as environmental and internal conditions, opportunities, resource evaluation, and risk assessment.

The development of goals and policies is only part of the concern of the corporate strategist. To be successful, the plans must be implemented. Accordingly, Part Three (Sections 5 and 6) deals with activities and concepts of implementation. Section 5 is concerned with the translation of corporate strategy into short-range plans and budgets and the necessary control over these plans, methods of organization appropriate to various strategies, and the basic processes of coordination and communication. Emphasis is placed on coordination, because it is at this point that interdepartmental and inter-organizational problems must be resolved. Section 4 is concerned with the implementation of growth strategies and deals with issues of corporate expansion and contraction.

Part Four (Sections 7 and 8) deals with selected issues of current and emerging, but continuing, importance to the management of corporations and having major policy implications. Section 7 contains articles dealing with policies for international operations. The articles focus on variables that, in a broad sense, have been covered previously, but which in the context of a multinational operation are sufficiently different in their application to warrant separate examination. Section 8 contains articles covering a variety of issues having an impact on the dynamic role of the corporation in a rapidly changing social, political, and technological environment. Articles have been selected to stimulate discussion of corporate power, involvement in social problems, the social effect of corporations on employees and consumers, and challenges for influencing the community's quality of life.

We would like to express our appreciation to the authors whose contributions are reprinted in this book and to both them and their publishers for granting permission to reprint the articles. We are also indebted to those several individuals who offered constructive criticism of the early drafts of the manuscript. Finally, we greatly appreciate the assistance of Mrs. Pat Linderman and Mrs. Mary Palacino in the typing of the manuscript, and of Miss Jane Glowacki in preparing the materials for publication.

J. W. B.
B. P. C.

contents

perspectives for strategy formulation

part one

The consideration of problems of corporate policy and the formulation of strategies to increase the viability and profitability of an organization require the consideration of many variables and the assessment of many alternatives. The variables that are identified, the sensing of their interrelationships, and the recognition of strategies that are related to those variables are often influenced by the particular problem solver's point of view. Thus, a marketing-oriented person may see customer satisfaction and pricing policies as key issues, whereas a financially oriented individual may focus on cash budgets and cost controls as primary areas requiring attention. When corporate goals, policies, strategies, and allocation of scarce resources are under consideration, this multiplicity of viewpoints complicates the decision-making process. Unless there is some agreement among participants as to the relevant variables and their ranking, corporate strategy can be established and implemented only with great difficulty.

An approach to alleviating the effects of the conflict of multiple viewpoints is to adopt a corporate perspective, a focus on the goals and activities of the total organization and the role of top management. Such an orientation does not eliminate concern for the programs of functional areas. Instead, the over-all view permits departmental activities to be understood in terms of their contribution to corporate goals and their impact on the activities of other departments. The integrative nature of a corporate perspective assists the strategist in dealing with the variety and number of variables operating in situations and the different orientations of decision makers.

The formulation of corporate strategy is the task of decision makers at levels of the organization which permit them access to information necessary for effective and intelligent decisions. Usually those decision makers are at the top levels of the organization. Regardless of precise level, those charged with strategy formulation must have a perspective of the entire organization, access to needed information, and an integrative viewpoint. The process is facilitated if an organization (structure and procedure) exists for strategy formulation.

The readings in this part have been selected to help establish an understanding of and appreciation for a corporate perspective, or the environment within which strategy formulation can effectively take place. The readings are grouped in two sections: (1) the systems view of the organization and (2) the roles and perspectives of top-level decision makers. The selections in the systems section are designed to develop ideas and concepts related to an integrative and over-all viewpoint of the firm, information availability and flow for strategic decision making, and a structure or system to facilitate strategy formulation. The readings in the second section concentrate on the decision makers and aim at developing an understanding of their role and perspective, including the effect of values on their decisions. Each of these topics is presented to "set the stage" for the discussions of strategy formulation and implementation which follow in subsequent sections.

The Systems Approach

The systems approach is a highly useful one for designing organizations, managerial activities, information flow, and decision systems for strategy formulation. It highlights interrelations among variables and facilitates decision making. In short, it permits the construction of models of the organization for a number of purposes, including corporate strategy formulation.

To view an organization as a system, one needs a number of general concepts. Such topics as control and feedback elements, sensing and decision-making activities, inputs, outputs and processes, and adaptation can be arranged in various combinations to construct a model of the organization. The focus of the model developed from these concepts may vary.

First, at the broadest level, the model may consider the organization as one element interacting with components of the total society. These components might include regulatory agencies, suppliers, stockholders, customers, and competitors. This "social system" focus may be applied to the consideration of the corporation and its social responsibilities or to consideration of proper goals or directions.

A second and more restricted model might focus on the corporation as the system and consider departments or functions as subsystems. Elements outside the corporation might be considered but would generally be taken as given. Viewing the organization as the system to be studied permits the analyst to consider questions of the relationships among departments, the allocation of resources among competing units, and the proper activities of departments for optimization of corporate objectives.

A third focus may be a single process, such as materials flow, order processing, cash transactions, or manpower planning and development. These activities are typically interdepartmental and may bear little resemblance to the formal organizational structure. Their study can be facilitated by a systems approach.

Each of these levels of analysis has merit for the consideration of policy questions. Used in combination, they may help in resolving conflicts or in isolating inconsistencies in goals and programs through the application of different viewpoints. On the other hand, some situations may demand only one approach, as in the case of materials flow analysis.

The articles in Section 1 outline the general concepts of systems and equip the reader with a perspective of the corporation which will be productive in strategy formulation. Richard Johnson, Fremont Kast, and James Rosenzweig describe the systems concept and its relationship to managing, and set forth a practical model for the design of management systems to implement the concept. Their article is particularly useful for understanding the basic concept and language it utilizes as well as the practical problems of effective implementation. Stanley Young considers the organization as a total adaptive system of flows, information, men, material, and behavior in which time and change are critical aspects. Rather than viewing the design of an organization structurally, he views it as a process conducive to the full utilization of new managerial techniques. His illustrations of the use of such an approach provide a basis for a fuller understanding of the perspective for corporate strategy formulation. Robert Stich discusses some misconceptions of the systems concept and in so doing provides insight into the strength and applications of systems management. The focus of Robert Johnson and Irwin Derman is on the corporate information system. Working within the framework of the systems concept, they discuss the value of systems design for collecting data, processing data into information, and converting it into intelligence suitable for goal setting and strategy formulation.

The Role and Perspective of Top Management

The suggestion that the formulation of effective policy relies heavily on the adoption of a corporate perspective implies an understanding of the executive role. The president, board of directors, and vice presidents of a corporation ordinarily must make the decisions which give direction to and coordinate the activities of the organization. Although these top-level personnel presumably have achieved their positions through skill in decision making and in dealing with people, their actions may not always be based on conscious motives. The understanding of policy formulation can be enhanced by examining the executive role.

Although all levels of management can benefit from using the broad viewpoint discussed previously, such an approach is mandatory for top management in strategy formulation. Unfortunately, it is difficult to perceive what exactly a broad point of view means in terms of the executive's job. The tasks of the executive (and to some extent those of the middle manager) cannot be categorized into mutually exclusive divisions of activity. Nor is the individual manager's job precisely defined and supplied with clearly specified authorities and responsibilities which preclude conflicting relationships. Such variables as personal values and personalities must be considered as essential elements of the strategic decision-making process. In the face of this great complexity the executive group must work together to establish corporate strategy.

The articles in Section 2 have been selected to identify the role and perspective of top-level decision makers and to raise some issues which bear on the definition or nature of that role as it relates to effective strategy formulation and action. Seymour Tilles provides a linkage with the articles in Section I by describing the manager's job in systems terms. Not only does he examine the executive's key tasks, but he also identifies some of the significant elements of strategy formulation that are discussed explicitly in Part Two. Lee Grossman discusses the perspective of the company president, including some problems with which he must cope. Mayer Zald, largely utilizing a theoretical approach, discusses the role of boards of directors. Although little empirical insight is provided on the operations of boards, Professor Zald does provide a basis for understanding the functions of boards of directors and the way in which they may contribute to the strategic decision process. William Guth and Renato Tagiuri examine the relationship between personal values of executives and the determination of corporate strategy. Building upon the position that personal values are important determinants in the choice of corporate strategy, they discuss some of the relationships and how to resolve conflicts arising between them. In a theoretical vein, Abraham Zaleznik examines interpersonal behavior, its relation to the manager's job, and the best means for achieving competent interpersonal behavior. His article will challenge the reader to examine behavioral aspects of the executive task and help him understand further the role of values and personality styles and characteristics in decision processes. The final article in this section was included as a challenge for the reader to consider, if he has not already done so, some issues which have a profound effect on the determination of business values of executives. James Patterson attacks the problem of ethical responsibilities of business, which clearly is a major factor in strategic decision making. Other issues of this type are presented in the final section of the book.

Part One. References for Further Study

Section 1: The Organization As a System

Boulder, James B., and Elwood S. Buffa. "Corporate Models: On-line, Real-time Systems." *Harvard Business Review,* **48**, 4 (July-August 1970), 65–83.

Discusses the manner in which advanced computer application programs have created a valuable tool for managerial decision making at the corporate systems level.

Brooker, W. M. A. "The Total Systems Myth." *Systems and Procedures Journal,* July–August 1965, 28–32.

Critically examines the total systems concept in light of general systems theory and lists advantages and disadvantages of systems thinking in business.

Cleland, David I., and William R. King. *Systems Analysis and Project Management.* New York: McGraw-Hill Book Company, 1968.

Discusses in Parts I and II the basic concepts of systems and some techniques involved in using systems thinking in problem solving.

Crowley, William J. "Can We Integrate Systems Without Integrating Management?" *Journal of Data Management,* August 1966, 14–18, 23–24.

Argues that top management must work closely with EDP specialists to effect an efficient information system in various kinds of control situations.

Harvey, Allan. "Systems Can Too Be Practical." *Business Horizons,* **7**, 2 (Summer 1964), 59–69.

Discusses the requirements for successful application of systems analysis in business and the pitfalls of systems management that can lead to failure.

Hofer, Charles W. "Emerging EDP Pattern." *Harvard Business Review*, **48**, 2 (March–April, 1970), 16–18ff.

Discusses the results of a study on computer applications, including predictions of future effects from various observers and findings of other researchers.

Katz, Daniel, and Robert L. Kahn. "Organizations and the Systems Concept." Chapter 2 in *The Social Psychology of Organizations.* New York: John Wiley and Sons, Inc., 1966, pp. 14–29.

Discusses characteristics of organizations as a special class of open systems and contrasts this approach with views of organizations as closed systems.

Zani, William M. "Blueprint for MIS." *Harvard Business Review,* **48,** 6 (November–December 1970), 95–100.

Proposes a framework that focusses on key tasks and decisions as a basis for the design of an effective management information system.

Section 2: The Role and Perspective of Top Management

Bernthal, Wilmar F. "Value Perspectives in Management Decisions." *Academy of Management Journal,* **11**, 4 (December 1968), 190–196.

Develops awareness by the executive of his responsibilities through the establishment of a hierarchy of values and argues for inclusion of this hierarchy in decisions and actions.

"The Board: It's Obsolete Unless Overhauled." *Business Week,* 2177 (May 22, 1971), 50–58.

Surveys current practices and problems of boards, with discussion of various trends in composition and operation of boards.

Carr, Alber Z. "Can an Executive Afford a Conscience?" *Harvard Business Review*, **48**, 4 (July-August 1970), 58–64.

The problems of ethics in business, and some tactical suggestions for selling ethical decisions.

Holden, Paul E., Carlton A. Pederson, and Gayton E. Germane. *Top Management.* New York: McGraw-Hill Book Company, 1968.

The findings of an extensive study of top management practices in dealing with internal and external problems of a corporation. 248 pp.

Mautz, R. K., and F. L. Neuman. "The Effective Corporate Audit Committee." *Harvard Business Review,* **48**, 6 (November–December 1970), 57–65.

Discusses the functions of the director's audit committee in preventing financial disaster, and the necessary conditions for its staffing and operation.

McDonald, John. "How the Men at the Top Avoid Crises." *Fortune*, **LXXXI**, 1 (January 1970), 121 ff.

Discusses the need to blend and balance the different and sometimes conflicting interests of various parties, including the executive's own values.

Zaleznik, Abraham. "Power and Politics in Organizational Life." *Harvard Business Review*, **48**, 3 (May–June 1970), 47–60.

Discusses the quality of organizational life as a function of the importance of personality factors and the sensitive use of strengths and limitations of people in decisions on power distributions.

the organization as a system

section 1

1

Designing Management Systems

Richard A. Johnson, Fremont E. Kast, and
James E. Rosenzweig

The vast growth in size, complexity, and diversity of operations of the modern business organization has made the managerial function exceedingly difficult, but even more essential to the success of the enterprise.

During the past few years there have been many new concepts advanced for improving management; e.g., organization theory, decision theory, planning theory, and the behavioral theory of the firm. Each of these philosophies has helped to sharpen management skills; however, there is still a need for an operative theory of management—a theory which provides a conceptual framework of better business design and operation. It is our contention that today's large-scale business enterprise could apply the systems concepts to meet the growing complexities and proliferation of operations, for systems theory provides a conceptual framework within which the manager can integrate his operations effectively.

We are concerned here with design—the key activity in implementing the systems concept. This function is the means for establishing subsystems and

Source: Reprinted with permission from *The Business Quarterly*, Summer 1964, pp. 59–63.

larger systems into a composite, integrated whole. However, for completeness of presentation we will review general systems concepts briefly. Specifically, we will:

- Show the relationship between the systems concept and managing,
- Set forth a practical model using the systems concept,
- Discuss the scope of the design function,
- Introduce flow concepts in systems design,
- Discuss systems design as the implementation of the systems concept and
- Appraise some of the constraints on the design function.

Systems Concepts and Management

A system is "an organized or complex whole; an assemblage or combination of things or parts forming a complex or unitary whole." The term system covers an extremely broad spectrum of concepts. For example, we have mountain systems, river systems, and the solar system as part of our physical surroundings. The body itself is a complex organism including the skeletal system, the circulatory system, and the nervous system. We come into daily contact with such phenomena as transportation systems, communication systems (telephone, telegraph, etc.), and economic systems.

The systems concept is a useful way of thinking about the job of managing. It provides a framework for visualizing internal and external environmental factors as an integrated whole. It allows recognition of the proper place and function of subsystems. The systems within which businessmen must operate are necessarily complex. However, management via systems concepts fosters a way of thinking which, on the one hand, helps to dissolve some of the complexity and, on the other hand, helps the manager recognize the nature of the complex problems and thereby operate within the perceived environment. It is important to recognize the integrated nature of specific systems, including the fact that each system has both inputs and outputs and can be viewed as a self-contained unit. But it is also important to recognize that business systems are a part of larger systems—possibly industry-wide, or including several, perhaps many, companies and/or industries, or even society as a whole.[1]

The theory of systems is not new, for much of it has been developed and used in the natural sciences for many years. Further, it is being used to some degree in business. For example, systems theory is used in administering certain military programs where specification and time requirements are critical, and in some single-venture programs, e.g., construction projects. There is no reason, however, why this concept is not equally applicable to appliance manufacturing, retailing, or banking.

[1] For a more comprehensive discussion of these concepts see R. A. Johnson, F. E. Kast, and J. E. Rosenzweig, *The Theory and Management of Systems*, McGraw-Hill Book Company, Inc., New York, 1963.

A Model of the Systems Concept

Traditionally, business firms have not been structured to utilize the systems concept. In adjusting the typical business structure to fit within the framework of management by systems, certain organizational changes will be required. The following Model illustrates *one* arrangement which would implement the systems concept. We do not imply that this Model is the most effective arrangement, only that it illustrates the use of "systems thinking" in managing a business.

Referring to Exhibit 1, a master planning council engages in high-level design activity and establishes guidelines for the entire organization. This council would make decisions relative to the products or services the company supplied. Further, it would establish the limits of an operating program, decide on general policy matters relative to the design of operating systems and

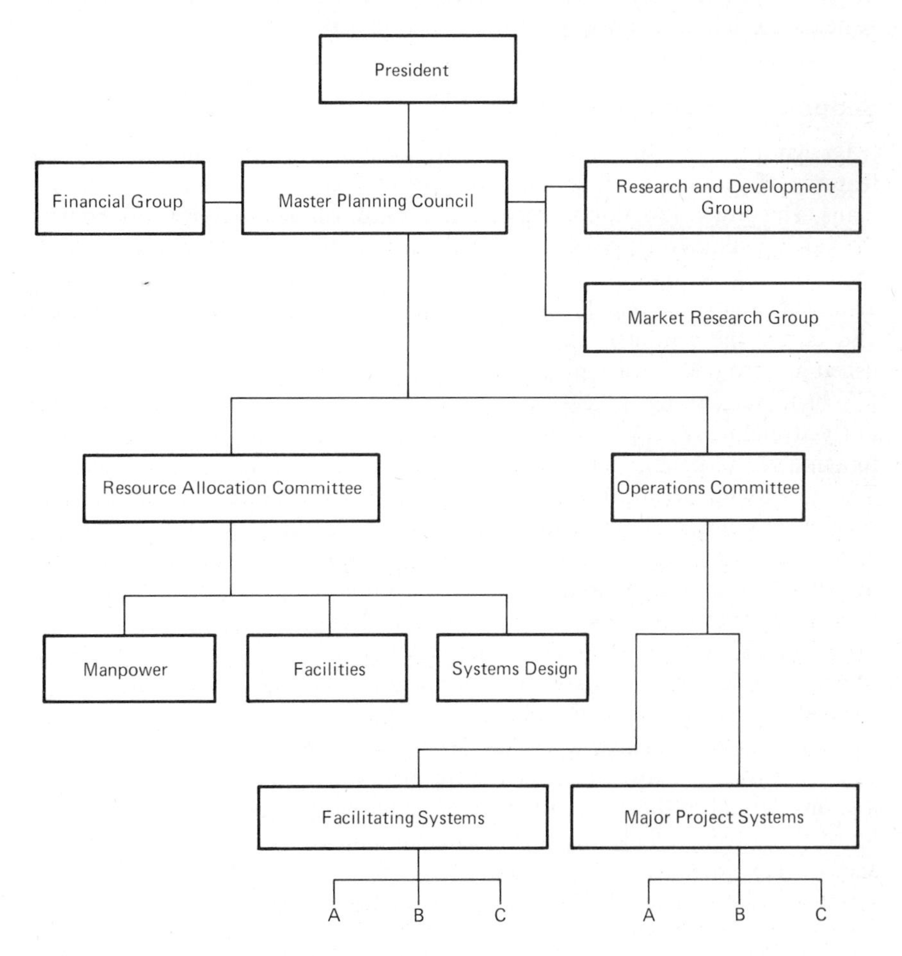

Exhibit 1. A Systems Model: Top Management

select the director for each new product. New-project decisions would be made with the assistance and advice of the product research and development, market research, and financial groups.

Within that framework, design activity is carried on by the resource-allocation planning group—a group which combines manpower and facilities to form working systems designed to accomplish given objectives. In both facilitating systems[2] and major project systems, additional design activity—systems review—is necessary to maintain working systems on a current basis.

The master planning council must have a definite approach to developing premises which serve as the basis for systems design. Meaningful information must be translated from environmental data on such questions as economic activity, political developments, and social trends. It is important that top management develop clear-cut systems of such information flow which will provide inputs for planning and decision making. In most companies such systems are left to chance, or at best, periodic review.

Scope of the Design Function

Design means to "mark-out, designate, or indicate." It includes combining features or details and often calls for preparation of preliminary sketches or plans. The design function is important in establishing a relationship between the various stages or phases of a system, linking them together, and outlining the composite whole. For business systems the design function includes the arrangement of physical facilities for production and auxiliary activities. It also covers the arrangement of people and communication networks established to provide information concerning the process.

When establishing a new business operation, the design function seems fairly straightforward. However, the scope of systems design also covers the function of "redesign," assessing existing systems with an eye toward change. This activity has received considerable attention over the years under headings such as systems and procedures, work simplification, systems analysis, or systems engineering. Of these terms, *work simplification* seems to have the narrowest connotation in that it applies primarily to simple man-machine operations or clerical activity. However, as with most tools and techniques, its practitioners have proclaimed its applicability to a wide range of problems. In any case, it applies to existing systems rather than to the establishment of new systems.

Systems and procedures work has been pointed up as an all-encompassing activity, covering many facets of the business operation. However, implicitly it seems limited to the office, the flow of paper work, and the design of forms. Since the advent of electromechanical equipment, systems and procedures activity has included the designing and programming of data-processing systems. Unfortunately, EDP has been overemphasized in recent years to the

[2] Facilitating systems are those designed to serve major project systems, e.g., a computer center.

exclusion of broader concepts of systems design. The specific aspects of programming, form design, and routing of paper work—as a part of the information-decision system—should be fitted into the over-all systems design.

Another term used in describing this general sphere of activity is systems analysis. It also is focused on existing systems rather than on the design of new systems. Systems analysis often has a connotation of application primarily to information flow in the office and does not seem as applicable to a production or processing environment. This is not to say that it is not feasible; rather, most of the literature on the subject deals with information-processing problems.

Systems engineering implies the creation of systems as well as the analysis of existing systems. Systems engineering sometimes is assumed to deal only with physical components; that is, it deals with the integration of components and subcomponents into a total product such as a computer or missile. Using the definition of engineering as "the art and science by which the properties of matter and the sources of power in nature are made useful to man in structures, machines, and manufactured products," there is systems implication. Moreover, systems engineering can be defined as "making useful an array of components designed to accomplish a particular objective according to plan." This approach implies the interaction of more than equipment. It suggests the development of a man-machine system which could function as a task-oriented assemblage. Systems engineering comes closest to implying design activity. In many cases the systems-engineering function involves "starting from scratch" to develop subsystems, larger systems, and a composite whole.

Flow Concepts in Design

One general approach to systems design involves identification of material, energy, and information flow. These three elements are part of every system and subsystem. Consideration of them plus the use of flow concepts facilitates thinking about systems of systems.

Material. The material aspects of any system include both the facilities involved and the raw material, if any, which flows through the process. A system must be designed to ensure the *acquisition* of raw materials and/or components necessary for processing into finished products. The systems design would include identification or transportation means required to move the raw material to the processing location.

The processing operation needs to be designed in terms of constructing new facilities or realigning existing facilities. Questions of plant layout and materials-handling equipment would be a vital part of the systems-design function for in-plant processing and in-plant material flows. Industrial engineers have considered problems of this nature for many years and have developed detailed methods and techniques for optimizing layout and material handling. The trend toward automation has been evident in many material-processing operations.

Much attention also has been focused on distribution of finished goods. Where items become raw material or components in additional processing operations, the distribution problem is often straightforward. In such cases the material flow would be considered part of the flow of raw materials for a subsequent processing operation. Physical-distribution management, for items moving from producer to ultimate consumer, can be a much more difficult problem. In this case, channels of distribution vary from direct producer to consumer to a myriad of combinations of middlemen. Inventory management, at various points along the distribution channel, must be considered, as well as modes of transportation. In many cases transportation costs have been isolated for analysis without reference to the impact of such decisions on stocks of material in the pipeline. Systems design, in this sphere, would concern itself with identifying the flow of materials and with the development of an explicit network of distribution, recognizing *all* the costs involved—handling, inventory, and transportation costs. Increased effort is being devoted to the design of explicit material-flow systems from a raw-material stage through the production process and to the final consumer.[3]

Whenever the operation in question involves the flow and processing of material, appropriate systems can be designed. For business operations such as insurance companies or other commercial institutions, there may be no flow of material per se. Rather, the material in these systems is represented by the facilities and equipment involved. Regardless of whether there is any material flow, all business operations, whether processing a product or service, contain elements of energy and information.

Energy. Some source of energy is present in any operating system. It may be electricity obtained from available sources or generated by a firm's own power plant. The process may require natural gas, petroleum, coal or other fuel for production. A business usually requires electrical energy for operating facilitating systems, if not for the main processing operation itself.

Another obvious source of energy is people. Both physical and mental energy are required to operate business systems. People represent a renewable source of energy, at least for the short run. As an energy source, people are quite variable as individuals. However, *in toto*, the group represents a reasonably stable source of energy for the system.

Electricity, natural gas, or petroleum can be described in terms of flow concepts. Energy flows are under continual inspection by systems designers. However, they are concerned primarily with the energy or power system itself, not the integration of the energy system with other subsystems and the whole. It is somewhat more difficult to visualize people, or the work force, in terms of flow concepts. However, in a very real sense, this is entirely appropriate. There may be a continual flow of workers in terms of shifts where 24-hour, 7-day weeks are scheduled. Even for 5-day, 40-hour weeks there is a systematic

[3] See Stanley H. Brewer and J. Rosenzweig, "Rhochrematics and Organizational Adjustments," *California Management Review*, Spring 1961, pp. 52–71.

flow of worker energy into the operation. In a larger sense, a business operation maintains a flow of worker energy throughout its life—from the recruiting, hiring, and orientation stages, all the way to retirement. Thus all energy can be considered as a flow process both in and of itself and as a part of other systems.

Information. Another basic element in any system is information. It facilitates interrelationships among subsystems and provides the linkage necessary to develop systems of systems. Information flow may be developed to flow along with the routing of material. Requisitions, orders, bills of lading, packing slips, receiving information, inspection reports, accounts payable, and cheques might represent the information flow connected with the acquisition of raw material. The information flow appropriate to production control is another example. In this case production instructions, material requirements, processing information, inspection requirements, routing, and scheduling would be developed from engineering drawings and/or other specifications. The information would flow through the system along with the material necessary to accomplish the planned objectives.

The accounting system requires a flow of information toward the development of income statements and balance sheets for tax purposes or stockholder reports or both. While many data-processing systems have developed on the basis of periodic batch processing, more and more systems are being developed which call for flow concepts approximating real-time activity; that is, the action or activity to be considered is recorded at the time it happens and action is taken at that time.

Information flow is the primary focus of attention for systems designers in many cases. If manufacturing facilities are fixed and if layout requirements are rigid, then the only variables remaining are raw materials (which may be uniform), energy (in the form of power and/or people), and information (in the form of plans and instructions). Systems design in such cases must concentrate on the arrangement of people and the use of information flow to optimize decision making within the system under observation. For many other systems where manufacturing and material flow are not present—service, commercial, and many governmental organizations—flow of information is the critical element. Information must flow to key decision points where action is taken with regard to a service to be performed by the organization in question. In such cases the system can be defined primarily on the basis of the flow of information to appropriate decision points. Subsystems can be identified on this basis, and they in turn can be interrelated to define the total system.

Unfortunately, most present-day systems of this nature have been established on the basis of people relationships and organization charts without regard for project systems or task-oriented groups. In many cases these organizations function primarily on the basis of informal relationships and informal communications systems. One of the main points in systems design is the necessity of recognizing the natural relationships of informal subsystems in developing a total system. It is by means of these flow concepts that the total system can be conceptualized as a system of systems. Particular emphasis will be placed on the design of information-decision systems. Such systems are integral parts of any operating system, whether it is designed to yield a product or service.

Integrating Flow Concepts

Basic to the theory of systems is the premise that given certain inputs, the processor will give certain outputs or operate within established limits. However, the business firm, as a whole, is not a structured or predictable system. Its equilibrium cannot be determined by equation, and it will change, within limits, as the components of the system are rearranged or as the inputs are reallocated.

In more advanced form, a system will include some means of control, i.e., a sensor for measuring output or related characteristics, a means of comparing the measurement with a standard, and an activating group to adjust inputs to correct the indicated deficiencies. The objective is to control variables so the system will tend to stabilize near the ideal equilibrium point. This objective is possible only if the ideal standard can be determined and if the operating values can be measured. A complete system, including control, is illustrated in Exhibit 2.

It shows the flow of planning information as it releases resources of materials, energy, and processing information. A record of the plan is stored where it can be used as a standard for control purposes. The resources are released by an activating group. For example, detailed schedules are planned (processing information), workers are assigned to specific tasks (energy), and the necessary raw materials or purchased parts are provided (materials). The combination of these inputs into the system results in the performance of a task (processing), and output is produced.

Sensory devices are placed at strategic points in the system flow to measure performance or output. These measurements are fed back to a control group, and this information is compared with the standard. As significant deviations from plan are recognized, information to correct the situation is released to the activating group, which in turn will change the release of resources or information, energy, or materials.

Designing Operating Systems

Operating systems have one thing in common: they should all use a common language for communicating among themselves and with higher levels. In addition, of course, each system designed should be structured in consideration of company-wide policies. Other than these limits, each operating system can be created to meet the specific requirements of its own product or service.

The operating system is structured to (1) direct its own inputs, (2) control its own operation, and (3) review and revise its own system design as required. Input is furnished by three different groups: technical information is generated as input into the processing system, and in addition, technical information is

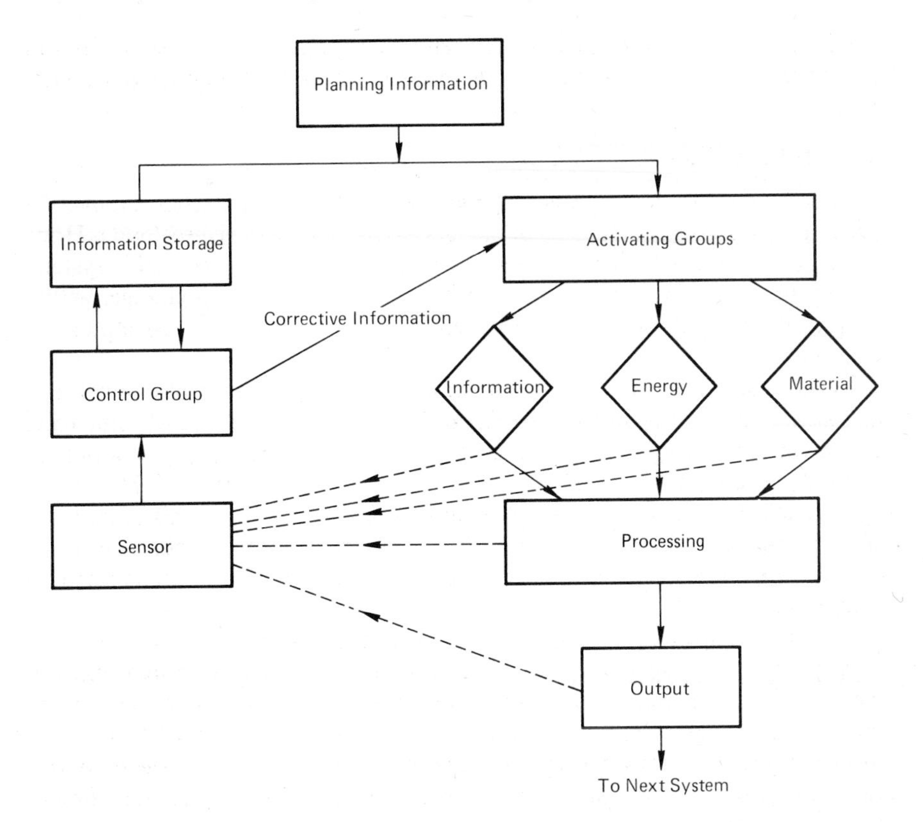

Exhibit 2. An Operating System

the basis for originating processing information. Both technical and processing information are used by the material input system to determine and supply materials for processing. The operating system has its own control unit, which measures the inputs and outputs of system. However, corrective action, when necessary, would be activated by input allocation.

This model of an operating system can be related to any business situation. For example, if it represents a system to produce television sets, the technical information would refer to the design of the product, processing information would include the plan of manufacture and schedule, and the material input would pertain to the raw materials and purchased parts used in the processing. These inputs of information and material would be processed and become output. Process control would measure the output in comparison with the standard (information storage) obtained from input allocation and issue corrective information whenever the system failed to function according to plan. The design of the system would be reviewed continually, and the components rearranged or replaced when these changes would improve operating efficiency.

A systems-review function is an integral part of each project system. The system as a whole should be reviewed periodically by means of a thoroughgoing analysis and synthesis of the system and its components. The system should be broken down into its individual subsystems, and each of these should be evaluated in terms of the likelihood of continuing efficiency. Adjustments can be made on the basis of the results of such analysis. Then a process of synthesis must take place in order to restructure an integrated whole.

Why is it that subsystems and/or project systems must be reviewed and adjusted continually? One obvious reason was mentioned above; system requirements change over a period of time, and hence the system must be redesigned in the light of evolutionary trends. Static systems design goes out of date almost immediately. In fact, the battle cry of some systems analysts and designers is, "If it works, it must be obsolete!" As a particular project progresses through its life cycle, the product mission may change, as may other environmental or competitive conditions. Organizational adjustments may be required, or technological advancements may allow improvements in handling of either material or information flow.

Some systems are built around individuals within an organization. If identification of decision points is based on strong or dominant personalities, the information-decision system may be disrupted completely whenever key-personnel changes are made. Hence systems must be redesigned in order to accommodate the changes in managerial personnel.

The original allocation of resources may have been temporary in the sense of availability of necessary elements either internally or externally. Makeshift systems have a way of perpetuating themselves regardless of inefficiencies. It is important to reappraise the situation often enough to make sure that such temporary arrangements are revised when conditions allow.

Another typical problem is the tendency toward empire building, the accumulation of more than enough material, manpower, and facilities to accomplish given objectives. The project manager must resist the tendency toward bigness for the sake of prestige or status. A semi-detached, hopefully objective systems-review group can help nurture such a point of view.

Continuing attention must be devoted to systems review and the implementation of proposed changes. Follow-up is necessary because of the seemingly inherent resistance to change on the part of people involved in the system. Unless such resistance can be overcome, poor systems may be prolonged. Once the atmosphere is established for continual analysis and review, implementation of change becomes progressively easier.

Constraints on the Design Function

In order to place the systems-design function in proper perspective it is important to consider the various constraints on this activity. Policy decisions on the part of the master planning council not only provide guidelines for systems design at lower levels, they also provide boundaries. If top management does not embrace the systems concept as a managerial philosophy, systems design cannot be implemented. The proper atmosphere must be created at all levels in order for this approach to be utilized.

Other limiting factors include the amounts and kinds of facilities available as well as the work force and its skill mix. Elaborate and sophisticated systems designs might be forthcoming which could not be implemented because of lack of facilities and/or manpower. However, we suggest that the systems-design group start with designs for systems that are needed rather than those which obviously can be implemented. The organization will progress if it is forced to strain toward goals and objectives. If the design proves too much of a "cloud nine" approach, the system can always be scaled back to meet existing resources.

The resource-allocation council places constraints on the system-review function in terms of policy decisions with regard to allocation of the resources between major projects systems and facilitating systems. It may be that systems analysts within major project systems have designed optimal arrangements for their own operation without regard to other project systems. The resource-allocation planning group may decide that certain facilitating systems common to several or all project systems should be set up to serve the entire group. Thus policy decisions throughout the total system provide constraints within which systems designers must operate.

Along with policy decisions and equipment and facility limitations, another constraint which must be taken into consideration by systems designers is people. The remark "It would be a great system if it weren't for the people involved" is appropriate here. Problems of resistance to change or of out-and-out antagonism are evident throughout the literature describing impacts of automation and electronic data processing. Similar reaction is often evident when designing information decision systems which call for realignment of people and equipment according to the systems concept. These human factors are important variables in systems design and must be given consideration.

Conclusion

Systems design is the key activity in implementing the systems concept. This function provides an over-all framework by establishing subsystems, larger systems, and a composite, integrated whole.

We cannot overemphasize the fact that, first and foremost, the systems concept is a frame of mind. Management must be receptive to this approach and develop a philosophy in which planning, organizing, controlling, and communication are accomplished in terms of subsystems integrated into a composite whole. Once there is acceptance of the systems concept and the feasibility of organizing on the basis of a master planning council, a resource-allocation planning group, and an operations planning group (with facilitating and project systems reporting to it), the systems-design function can be carried out in a progressive atmosphere. The atmosphere created is all-important; it fosters creativity and innovation on the part of systems designers.

2

Organization As a Total System

Stanley Young

Increasingly, organizations are being considered from a systems point of view in both descriptive and normative context.[1] Ashby's work would exemplify some of the descriptive work. Systems Development Corporation, Strategic Air Command, and Lockheed are effectively using the systems concept to redesign major phases of organizations in an operational and normative sense.[2] Many companies have expanded similar efforts to certain subsystems, such as steel-rolling mills, oil refineries, and so on.[3]

Our conception of the organization is changing from one of structure to one of process. Rather than visualizing the organization in its traditional structural, bureaucratic, and hierarchical motif, with a fixed set of authority relationships, much like the scaffolding of a building, we are beginning to view organization as a set of flows, information, men, material, and behavior. Time and change are the critical aspects. When we consider the organization from a normative point of view, we find another reason for this trend which is of more immediate concern. This is the working hypothesis of my article. Only when the organization is designed (organization planning) from a systems engineering orientation will it be able to take full advantage of the new and emerging managerial technologies, such as quantitative methods, the computer, information sciences, and the behavioral sciences. The engineering sciences have illustrated unusual success in the rapid creation and application of new technology and will, therefore, represent the guiding model of this analysis.

However, before taking up my thesis, let us note the current problems concerning the effective utilization of managerial technology. One problem relates to the absence of a construct as to how this new technology is to be used in an integrated and systematic manner; or consider it as the absence of a meaningful gestalt, or whole, into which such a technology would logically fit. What does exist might be categorized as a tool chest or "bits and pieces" state.

For example, let us suppose that a personnel manager has a problem of excessive absenteeism. Given the external and internal environment of the

Source: Copyright 1968 by The Regents of the University of California. Reprinted from *California Management Review*, Vol. X, No. 3, pp. 21–32, by permission of The Regents and the author. Portions of this article were presented at the Midwest Academy of Management, Spring Meeting, 1966, Lexington, Kentucky.

[1] For example, see Joseph Litterer, *Analysis of Organizations* (New York: John Wiley & Sons, Inc., 1965); Claude MacMillian and Richard Gonzales, *Systems Analysis* (Homewood: Richard D. Irwin, Inc., 1965), Chaps. 11–14; Ross Ashby, *An Introduction to Cybernetics* (New York: John Wiley & Sons, Inc., 1958), Chaps. 10–14.

[2] For example, see Donald G. Malcolm, et al., *Management Control Systems* (New York: John Wiley & Sons, Inc., 1960).

[3] See Cornelius Leondes, *Computer Control Systems Technology* (New York: McGraw-Hill Book Company, Inc., 1961), Chaps. 15–20.

firm, the organizational constraints he has as a manager, and a set of behavioral information and managerial tools that he has acquired, how does he reduce the absenteeism rate? He knows something about psychology—perception, cognition, learning, and motivation theory. From social psychology, he should be aware of theories of attitude formation and resistance to change. From sociology, he recalls the implication of group theory. He can calculate the median, mean, and mode, run a correlation, and find a derivative. He is a qualified MBA student. Yet, what specifically should he do to reduce the absenteeism rate? Students and practitioners are given a tool chest filled with some mathematics, some psychology, and so on, and the manager is then admonished to build a better house.

Although one can appreciate the value of these various approaches, one is still confronted with the problem of their integrated application in order to be relatively assured of achieving a desired result. What is missing is the bridge or discipline between tools and organizational results. The engineering sciences represent such a discipline.[4]

Although one can raise many serious questions as to the reality, validity, predictability, and effectiveness of the classical principles approach, nevertheless it can be said that it roughly holds together as a whole or single unit, and its parts are related in logical fashion. Starting with the concept of private property and the delegation of authority, the organizational chart is drawn; authority is allocated; a division of labor is specified; and the functions of management, planning, organizing, and staffing are outlined. A certain internal logic is present, not unlike the economist's model of perfect competition. The parts are related to each other in a particular manner. Viewed as a single construct, the traditional model is understandable and operational to students and practitioners alike.

A Systems Approach

The same cannot be said for the newer managerial technology. The general management or organization theorist's domain is the whole. One is concerned with the problem of organization space or the distance between subfunctions, subprocesses, tools, and techniques—the interface problems. To those who are concerned with the whole, the partial approach of the new technology is disconcerting. Where and how do all these parts fit together, and what is the relationship between one and another? Sprinkling behavioral and quantitative courses about a business curriculum is of questionable effectiveness. Therefore, as far as the newer technologies are concerned, a gestalt, or general, model has been missing which will integrate all the parts meaningfully. What is being suggested is that the systems approach will provide this model.

[4] See Arthur D. Hall, *A Methodology for Systems Engineering* (Princeton: D. Van Nostrand Company, Inc., 1962); and Harry E. Goode and Robert E. Machol, *System Engineering* (New York: McGraw-Hill Book Company, Inc., 1957).

Another problem which has emerged, which requires that the organization be designed as a total system, is that all too frequently the organizational context into which the newer technologies are inserted tends to be inappropriate. We are attaching sophisticated techniques to a primitive vehicle—the bureaucratic structure. Organizations should be designed around the technology; technology should not be forced to fit an existing structure. Thus, some corporations, to be fashionable, have created operations research departments which in fact have been given little or nothing to do. One case was reported in which the primary duty of the O.R. official was to solve the school mathematics problems of the corporate president's daughter!

In the history of innovation, one frequently finds that when a new device is invented it is attached to the existing model. For example, when the gasoline motor was first invented, it was connected to a buggy. However, as additional innovations occurred, the vehicle itself eventually had to be modified. If advantage was to be taken of additional improvements, obviously one could not unite a 300-horsepower motor to a light wooden shay. If innovation follows its usual course, we can expect the new managerial techniques to force a modification in the traditional organizational arrangements. This, indeed, has been taking place. The exploitation of the computer has led to a weakening or abolishment of the traditional divisional or departmental lines of authority. Improvements in the control and measurement of operations have the same consequences.

The differences between administrative and engineering analyses that will be taken up are:

- The engineering sciences view of the operation to be analyzed as a system or subsystem.
- The design and implementation of such systems as a sequential analysis of a team effort composed of appropriate specialized personnel.

Research, development, hardware specifications, and pilot and field studies are conducted with at least one purpose: to create and apply an improved technology to the functional operations being considered. Further, historically, the engineering sciences have incorporated the basic sciences of physics, chemistry, and quantitative methods into their analyses.

To demonstrate how the organization may be treated from an engineering point of view, it will first be analyzed as a system, and then the design process will be briefly outlined. In the presentation of the organization as a system, the approach will be analytical—a successive breakdown of the whole into increasingly smaller parts.

Organization as a Total System. In Figure 1, the business organization is presented in its most simplified form. The basic input is economic resources, the organization is the process, and the output is economic welfare. Other organizations can be represented by changing the inputs and outputs. For example, the hospital has a human input (sick patient) and a healthy patient as the output.

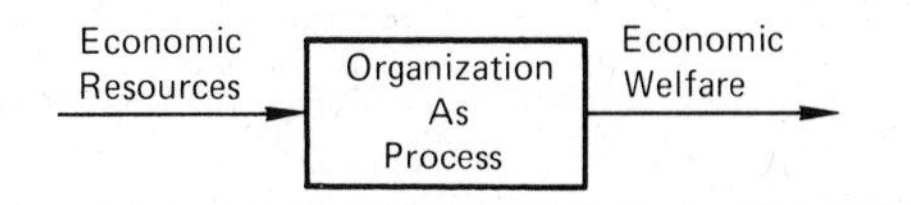

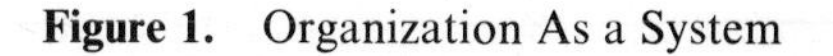

Figure 1. Organization As a System

In Figure 2, the control or feedback mechanism is added to the organization, which is represented by management. Or, in terms of control theory, the management segment constitutes the basic control element of the organization. Thus, given a certain welfare objective or expected welfare output (a profit increment), actual welfare is measured against expected welfare. If a difference exists, then a problem is indicated. This information is sent to the management segment which formulates a solution that is then input into the organization process. This feedback device will operate until the actual and expected welfares are approximately equal.

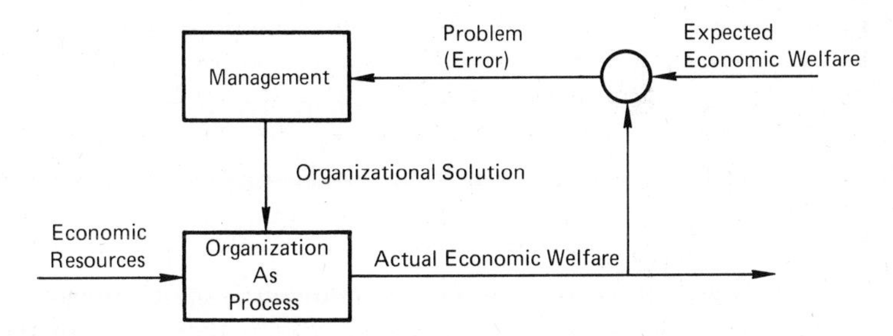

Figure 2. Organization with Control Unit

In Figure 3, the control unit is further broken down into a series of parts, in order to provide an adaptive capability for the organization.[5] Given a change

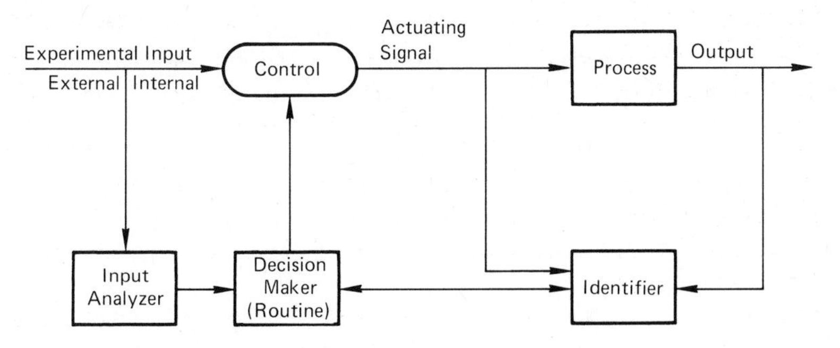

Figure 3. Organization As an Adaptive System

[5] For a review of adaptive systems, see El. Mishkin and Ludwig Braun, Jr., *Adaptive Control Systems* (New York: McGraw-Hill Book Company, Inc., 1961); and J. H. Westcott, *An Exposition of Adaptive Control* (New York: The Macmillan Company, 1962).

in certain environmental inputs, one initially has an input analyzer, which indicates the nature of such changes. This is an information-gathering or sensory device; somewhat analogously, market research might be so categorized in terms of sensitizing the organization to some of the external variables, as accounting functions for the internal changes. One has also a display device, the identifier, which indicates the state of the organization or any of its subprocesses at any given time.

Hence, if the subprocess were a production plant, the identifier at a given time could indicate the productive capacity, current running capacity, order backlog, inventory conditions, orders in process, production lines in operation, and machine breakdown. Such information is fed to a decision-making unit along with the information from the environment. We assume that a set of rules has been programmed, one of which will be selected for a particular environmental input and a given process point to achieve a certain output.

For example, if the initial input is a large order with a required completion date, the rule may be to go to overtime. This information is called a control signal and is sent to the control unit. The control unit is that element which actually changes the input before it enters the system, or the process itself. The order could have been put into a queue. Such information is simultaneously sent to the identifier. Therefore, at any given time, the identifier tells us what inputs have entered the process, the state of the process, and its outputs.

Because the control signal and the control unit are frequently confused, the difference between the two should be explained. The example that is usually given is the driving of an automobile. If one wants to stop an automobile by depressing the brake pedal, information is relayed to the brakes of the car. It is not the brake pedal that stops the car, but the brakes, which constitute the control unit. Similarly, in a man-to-man system, the control signal and the control unit would appear as shown in Figure 4.

Let us suppose that the total employee population is the basic system, and we want a higher work output. Further, assume that we know exactly what the relationship is between need satisfaction input and expected work output. Given the figure for expected work output, the decision maker will increase or decrease the amount of need satisfaction (for example, money) via a control

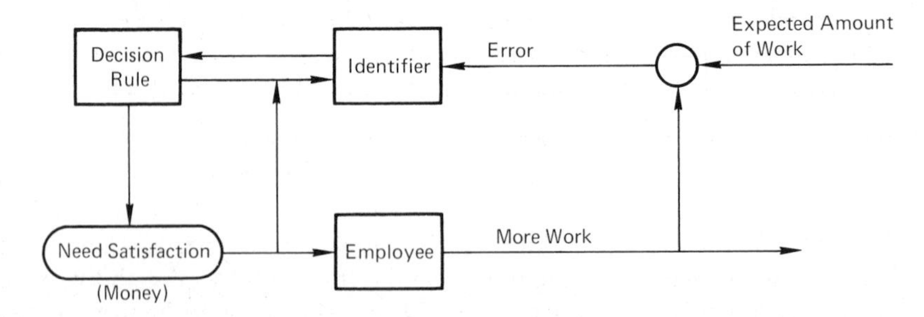

Figure 4. The Control Signal and the Control Unit

signal to the financial department, where need satisfaction is stored in the form of money. This department would release funds until the expected work output was achieved. It is not the decision to increase work output or its relay to the employee that constitutes the control element or even the decision to augment wages and salaries, but the reservoir and release of funds that is the control element. In other words, a salary may be to the employee what brakes are to an automobile. For our particular purposes, those subparts of the organizational control mechanism—input analyzer, and so on—give the process an adaptive capability or the ability to adapt to changing inputs so as to maintain a desired or expected output.

In Figure 5, the organization is further broken down into a series of major subprocesses: marketing, production, and so on, with its own adaptor. The adaptor consists of an input analyzer, decision rules, identifier, and control for each subprocess. Moreover, it is assumed that each of these subprocesses can be identified and separated from other subprocesses. A super-adaptor applies a series of decision rules for subdecision makers, to assure appropriate adjustment between processes. It is further assumed that each subsystem's adaptor has this same capability concerning subprocesses. Consequently, the the production system may have subsystems of purchasing, inventory control maintenance, and so forth. The inputs and outputs of these subsystems would have to be controlled appropriately with the proper decision rules.

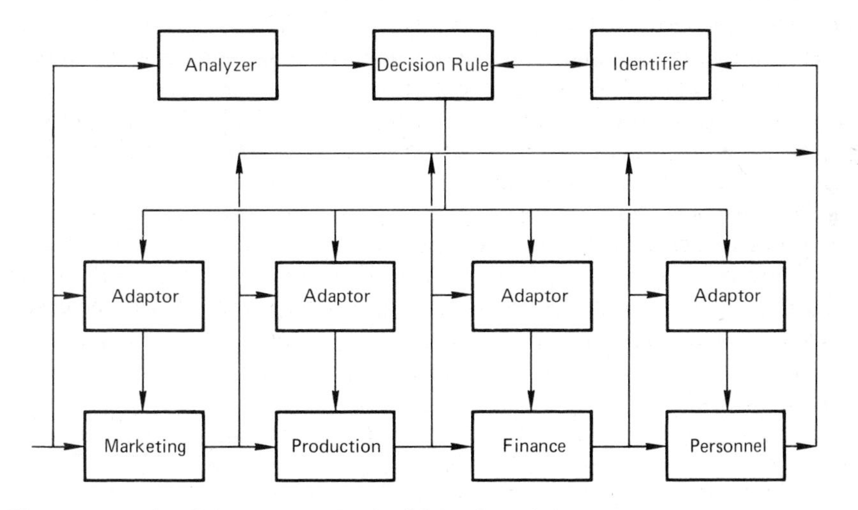

Figure 5. Major Subprocesses, Each with Its Own Adaptor

In Figure 6, a learning capability in the form of a designer is added to the adaptive system. A learning capability can be thought of as the ability of the system to redesign itself or learn from past mistakes so as to improve system performance. Given the environmental state of the system and the application

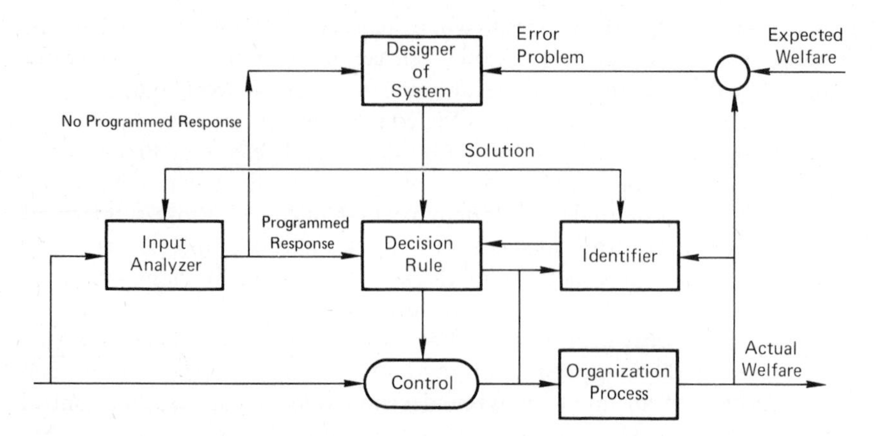

Figure 6. Adaptive System with Learning Capability

of what is thought to be the correct rule, the expected output may still not be produced. This indicates design problems.

The designer would receive information as to system performance. Then, to increase welfare output, he would attempt to improve the adaptive mechanism: by formulating more effective decision rules for the decision-making routine, by improving the identifier in terms of more and better information, by achieving a more rapid response in information from the input analyzer, by improving the sensory devices, and by improving the control mechanism.

In Figure 7, we now see the total system in some detail. We have our environmental inputs on the left, both external and internal (psychological, sociological, etc.). *Two basic subsystems* are shown: marketing and production, in which the marketing output becomes a production input. Each of these subsystems has its own adaptor, and although not shown, a coordinating adaptor to integrate the two. Further, each subsystem has its own design capability.

The only new feature of the schematic is the box at the top: Design of System Design. This particular function would integrate the work of subdesigners. For example, if the organization is viewed as an aircraft, the design of which is generally broken down into such areas as weight and structures, air frame, power, information system, and so on, design coordination is required. Moreover, this function would also advise as to design technique and strategy, and, ideally, one should be able to reach a stage in which the design itself of subsystems could be programmed.

Thus, in looking at Figure 7, we see in some detail the organization as a total system which is self-regulating and self-learning, at least partially closed, in which the environment can be detailed and in which subsystems are integrated. Further, the adaptor provides for appropriate internal adjustments between subsystems. In other words, the organization without too much difficulty can be considered as a total system. All of its essential elements can be

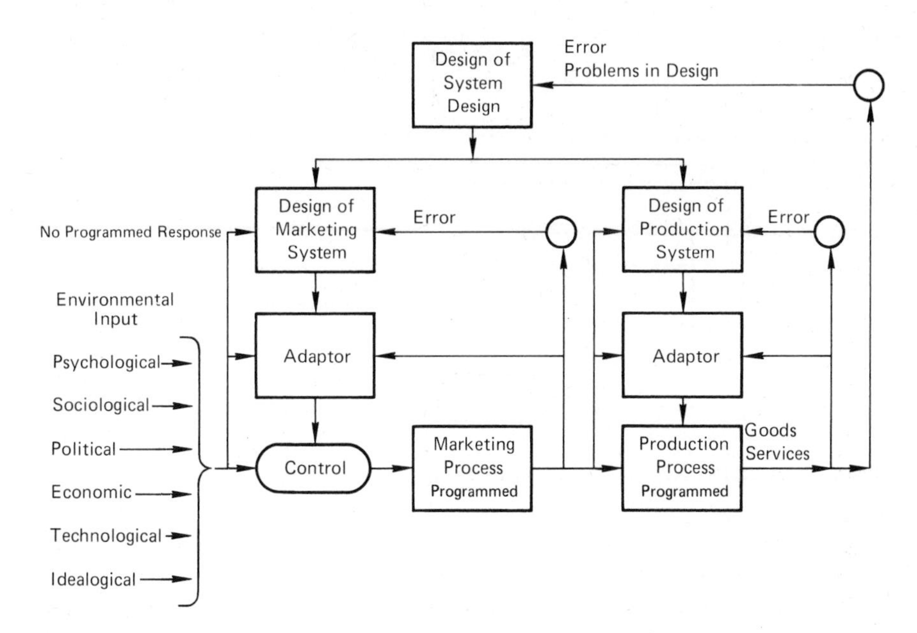

Figure 7. Organization As a Total Adaptive System

incorporated into a design. Also, with an appropriate index, one can detail the subsystems. Each subsystem can be broken down into its subsystems, and so forth. The indexing of the system's subparts is a complex but not an insurmountable problem. For example, it is estimated that the blueprints for a new aircraft may finally weigh two or three tons—more than the aircraft itself!

System Design. In Figure 8, we can briefly go through the design process, which further analyzes the function of the designer. Given a statement of the problem or the type of system with which one is concerned, the next, and key, step is the construction of a model of the system. Such a model would be essentially stochastic in nature and would stipulate the output or mission of the sytem and the inputs, of which there are three:

- The input upon which the process is to operate or that input which enters the system.
- Environmental inputs which affect the process.
- Instrumental or control inputs which modify the operation of the process or the process itself—and here we are concerned with the technology of processing the load inputs. For example, in a marketing subsystem, if the initial input is a potential customer, he has to be processed through the subsystem so that a sale will result.

The system's logic relates to the set of decision rules or, given certain inputs, the state of the system and a certain control capability, such as more or less advertising—what particular decision rule should be utilized to achieve some expected output? Information requirements relate to the classification,

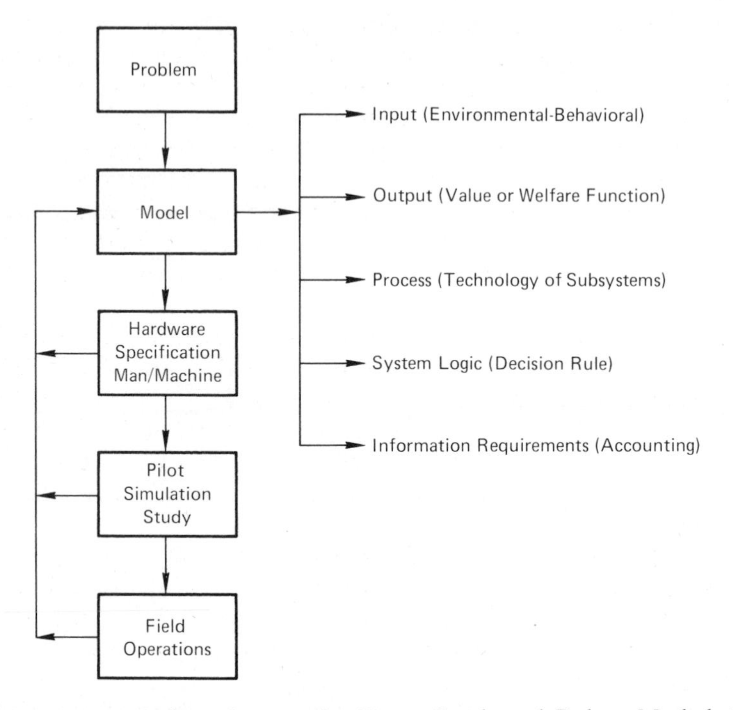

Figure 8. System Design Source: See Harry Goode and Robert Machol, *System Engineering* (New York: McGraw-Hill Book Company, 1957)

amount, and timing of information, so that the system will operate as expected. Hence, concerning the environmental variables, what information about which variables should be gathered? How often? How much? And how soon would this information have to reach the decision rule?

At the outset, it would be a highly worthwhile investment to construct a complete stochastic model of the system with which one is concerned, in which output is the dependent variable, and inputs, environmental and instrumental, are the independent variables. For example, one might be concerned with a personnel selection subsystem in which the output is a certain number of qualified employees. The environmental inputs might be the labor demand for certain occupations, amount of unemployment, the number of graduates, and so on; the instrumental variables might be the recruiting budget, the number of recruiters, the training program, etc.

It is more efficient to construct one model to which various decision rules can be applied than to construct a new model every time a new decision rule is formulated. With the latter approach, one would always be reconstructing the model, given a change in tools. Once the model is constructed, the research and development begins. One can experiment—try different decision rules and different hardware specifications—in terms of devising appropriate controls and measuring devices.

Experimentation requires a certain ingenuity. A grocery chain may have to set aside one of its representative stores for research purposes. It would not only be important to establish the consequences of various pricing strategies, but if possible, the causes for such consequences or, at least, the ability to predict their outcome. Given a new rule on a pilot basis, one can apply it to actual hardware. Naturally, one has to be sure that the data from pilot studies are meaningful in terms of the total system with which one is concerned. Research and development represent the essence of the engineering effort. Experimentation is costly and uncertain, but there is little doubt that the payoff is greater than using an intuitive approach.

If it is successful, the new rule can be applied, and data can be fed back regularly to the designer, so that he can continually improve and refine his initial model. Although one may begin with a relatively unrefined model, with successive experimentation and field experience, hard data will constantly flow back to the designer. This will enable him to improve his model in terms of the nature of the variables, the preciseness of the parameters, and the model's predictability.

Over time, an improvement in the state of the art should occur, if research development is effectively executed. Our grocery chain should have an ever-improving pricing strategy. As for hardware specifications, apart from the consideration of costs, one is concerned with providing components that will execute the operations as specified.

In terms of Figure 8, of particular concern is the problem of how to convert what is essentially a paper model into something that approaches operating reality. We can construct reasonably good stochastic or econometric models which can be used to simulate different decision rules, but the conversion of these into operating reality with appropriate hardware is a different matter. In an operating context, the stochastic model or identifier becomes an information panel for a decision or rulemaker. In terms of hardware, information collection or sensory devices are needed which survey the environment and send such data to a central location, so that the values of the variables of the model can be displayed. An example is the control room in a public utility, in which the operator watches continually the changing values of significant variables. Only with such a display can appropriate action be taken. However, wiring such a system is a particularly difficult task.

For example, as a member of a team that has been given the responsibility of designing a metropolitan poverty program as a total system, the primary inputs are poverty families, and the outputs are supposed to be self-sufficient economic units. Although there exists some technical assurance that a stochastic model can be constructed, we have not yet been able to reach this design step, because we are at the initial stage of inventing a sensory machine that will give us some running idea of the nature of our changing inputs which, in this instance, is the changing mix of the characteristics of our poverty families. This program appears in Figure 9.

Another area that requires additional work is the control element, which

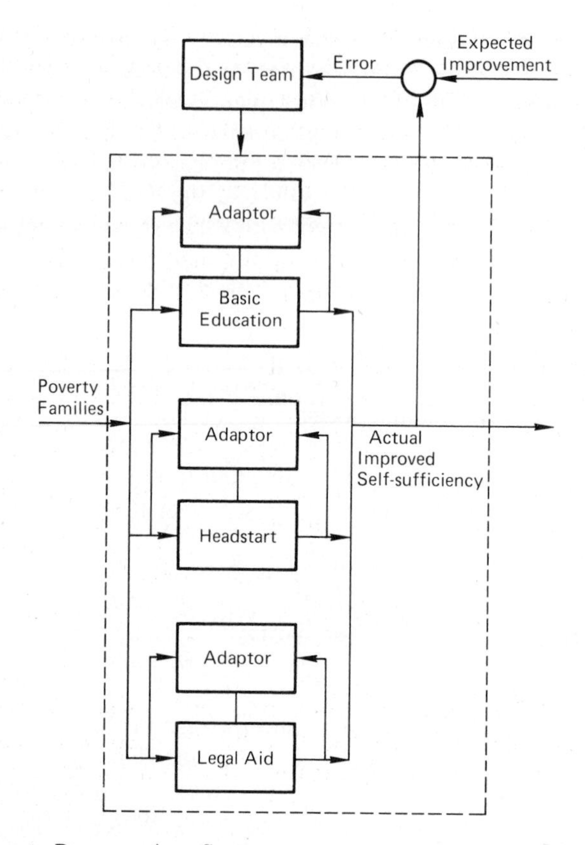

Figure 9. Poverty Program As a System

actually modifies the operation of the system. In a man-to-man system, we do not have sufficient information about which variables to vary and by how much, in order to achieve the desired human behavior. The crude reward and punishment system that we have all too often gives us dysfunctional results. Presumably, in the design process, when serious deficiencies arise, research and development should be directed to those areas.

Managerial Technology as Utilized in System Design. Although this view of the organization as a total adaptive system and the design process has been brief, it has been sufficient to indicate how one can take advantage of the newer managerial techniques in the use of system analysis.[6] In terms of the system presented, where and how do these techniques fit? As for the behavioral sciences, our environmental inputs or variables are behavioral in nature. To build a model and eventually a display panel, such knowledge is essential. In the decision box, we would utilize our various decision rules, such as Linear Programming, Game Theory, Dynamic Programming, PERT, and so forth.

[6] For a more complete review, see Goode and Machol, op. cit.

Because system design requires one to deal eventually with a total subsystem such as marketing, in all likelihood we will become increasingly concerned with the problem of combining various decision rules. For example, Gerald Thompson has indicated that we must combine appropriate decision rules to achieve the most satisfactory system output. Under what conditions is it advisable to move from Linear Programming to rule of thumb, and then back to Linear Programming? As Professor Thompson has noted,

> We need to develop heuristics about using heuristics. That is, an executive program that would accept a problem and then decide which of a list of heuristics (decision rules) should be employed to give its solution.[7]

The information sciences relate to the input analyzer and the collection, manipulation, and relay of information. Here we have all our data collection and processing problems. The control element relates to the area of control theory, specifically, the direction of human effort. Finally, in designing a specific subsystem, such as personnel or marketing, one should have some knowledge with regard to the technology of these systems; for example, one should be able to use employment tests correctly in the selection process.

In designing the organization as a total system, it would appear rather apparent that one would not only have to be familiar with but also be able to use a wide array of sophisticated managerial techniques and knowledge. The understanding and use of managerial techniques is an integral part of the design process. This is distinctly counter to the bureaucratic structure, which merely attaches such techniques to it with little purpose or place.

Design Criteria. Design criteria are rules which are utilized to evaluate designs as to their acceptability. Given a number of designs, which one is the best? Although there are numerous rules, the most widely used are : *measurability, feasibility, optimality, reliability, and stability.* We will consider only the first three.

Measurability is the system's ability to evaluate its performance. If its performance cannot be measured, a system's desirability or undesirability cannot be established. Its particular excellences or deficiencies cannot be known. When models are measurable, the superior system can be inferred from the specific measuring devices used in each. In the model that has been suggested, the identifier as a display panel is the primary measuring mechanism, in that we would know the actual inputs, process, outputs, and decision rules. If the model is not working as expected, the errors would be fed to the designer on a more or less continual basis, so that the system could be redesigned for more effective results.

One of the most serious weaknesses of the bureaucratic design as a management system is that it lacks measurability. When the bureacratic system is redesigned, for example, from a product to a functional arrangement or when the line of command is lengthened by the introduction of additional levels of

[7] Gerald L. Thompson, "Some Approaches to the Solution of Large Scale Combinatorial Problems," Carnegie-Mellon University, Pittsburgh, working paper, p. 25.

managers, no measuring devices exist either in the previous or subsequent design that will indicate what improvements, if any, have occurred.

Feasibility relates to the question of whether or not the model will operate as planned. As the model must be realistic, it must be capable of being installed, of achieving expected payoff, and of performing its task requirements within the environment of the system. If a particular quantitative decision-making tool is suggested, can we be reasonably certain that it can be employed in an operational context? The use of pilot studies or experimental models relates to the question of feasibility.

Given any managerial device, we of course want to know if it will increase organizational payoff when it is utilized; will stockholders, employees, and consumers be better off than before? Organizations are normative systems. All too often, the student and practitioner are exposed to quantitative manipulations and behavioral research that are interesting, but either no directions are provided as to how these findings are to be incorporated into the operations of the firm or no measuring devices are suggested that will establish the quantity of welfare that the research results will actually produce.

The end purpose of the manager, as it is viewed in this analysis, is to design subsystems which will actually increase human well-being. The manager is not, per se, a mathematician, statistician, sociologist, or psychologist. However, he must rely on these disciplines in much the same way that the engineer has to rely on physics. This does not mean that continuous research is not required in these disciplines, if designs are to improve. However, such research will not automatically lead to improvements. It is only when the designer is able to incorporate findings into an operating reality that he can achieve the full value of the research.

A corollary to the feasibility criterion relates to the question of balance between the parts of the system. All parts of the system must not only be integrated, but they must also be mutually consistent. One would not put into practice a primitive input analyzer and follow this with a complex regression analysis in the identifier. The final system output will be no more productive than the least productive part of the system. Each part acts as a constraint on all other parts. Consequently, the identifier can never be any better than the input analyzer, and so on. The absence of integration and/or balance is self-defeating.

For example, we frequently find information systems personnel providing voluminous data; that is, the input analyzer is well developed. However, the rest of the system may be missing; there is no identifier or set of decision rules. In other instances, we may have analyses of the use of a single decision rule, linear programming, but nothing else.

As long as we find this type of analysis, managers will always revert, out of necessity, to the most primitive part of the total system, because this part represents the primary constraint. In such a context, increasing sophistication will not meet the criterion of feasibility. Even if it is used, no increment in organizational payoff will result.

For example, in the design of the poverty program system that was mentioned earlier, the staff's initial impulse was to design an econometric model of the program including exogenous variables. We immediately ran into the constraints of the rest of the system and realized that, until we had a relatively effective input analyzer, a set of decision rules, and a control element, we could not move to the sophisticated model we wanted. In other words, when one designs a total system, he is generally forced to start with a fairly elementary model. Then, when all the parts are developed, he can progress to a more complex system.

The management sciences may be overly concerned with the *optimality* criterion and ignore such other criteria as measurability and feasibility, on the assumption that if one has an optimal solution there is little else that has to be done. But unless all criteria are considered, we will not get the hoped-for results. To have a solution that is optimum but nonfeasible is meaningless. Obviously, a solution has to be measurable, feasible, and reliable, before we can consider its optimality.

For the most part, operating managers stress the feasibility criterion. At the outset, they want something that will work and actually function and are not overly concerned with optimality. In dealing with a complex system, I am not sure what constitutes an optimal solution. Russell Ackoff has said:

> One of the things Operations Research has learned about putting results to work is having considerable effect on its methods. This means the team must either translate elegant solutions into approximations that are easy to use or side step the elegance and move directly to a quick and dirty decision rule. Operations Research is learning that an approximation that is used may be a great deal better than an exact solution that is not.[8]

Because design methodology imposes a specific discipline on the designer, we can be assured that new techniques will be effectively utilized.

Conclusions

Some Implications. Although this has been a rather broad treatment of the organization as a total system, certain implications can be inferred.

1. On a normative basis, organizations should be viewed as a *total system* if we are to increase organizational output. Different organizations, corporations, universities, poverty programs, and so on can be categorized. Further, although this is by and large an article of faith, nevertheless some empirical evidence does exist (certainly in the area of complex weapons systems) that, if organizations are viewed as a total system, better results will be obtained. We are in the initial stages of this development, and, at this time, we can only block out the basic characteristics of total systems.

[8] Russell L. Ackoff, "The Development of Operations Research," *Scientific Decision Making in Business*, Abe Shuchman, ed. (New York: Holt, Rinehart and Winston, Inc., 1963), pp. 59–60.

2. There has been an attempt to demonstrate that the systems approach is a highly conducive vehicle for the *incorporation of current managerial technologies*, unlike the bureaucratic structure. Irrespective of the developing managerial concepts, the bureaucratic structure itself represents such a serious constraint that only minimal advantages would accrue.

3. When viewed in this context, the *essential role of the manager is that of designer of organizational or behavioral systems*, just as the engineer is the designer of machine systems. The design of a large complex system, however, will necessitate a team effort: mathematicians, psychologists, and information specialists. But, as in large machine systems, system specialists will be required to integrate the team effort. There is little reason why efforts cannot be organized to design a marketing system in the same fashion as the F-111 aircraft was designed.

In conclusion, the engineering and management sciences face the same fundamental problem—the creation of improved systems. Both suggest that quantitative modeling be performed, based on their respective underlying sciences, physical and social. However, in the engineering sciences the design and implementation of machine-to-machine systems tends to be organizationally highly systematic, whereas such a development is yet to occur with respect to the management sciences in their designs of man-to-man systems.

3

Pitfalls to Systems Management

Robert S. Stich

The term "systems management" is a relatively new phrase that has gained immense popularity within recent years with businessmen and teachers alike. To the teacher it conjures up words such as "simulation of cognitive processes," "business games" and "heuristic approaches to control." To the businessmen, it connotes words such as "data processing," "real-time and time-shared control systems" and "management information systems." It is almost unthinkable to suggest that decision-making cannot be improved through the use of "the systems approach." And it has become almost impossible to pick up any magazine, journal or book in any subject without reading about the systems approach, whether it be applied to business organization, city planning, defense planning or hospital design.

While systems management may still mean many different things to different

Source: Reprinted with permission from *Management International Review*, Vol. 1, 1970, pp. 19–22.

people, it has become obvious to some of us who teach the subject and apply it in business that there are several misconceptions surrounding the systems approach that are fairly widespread—these I have labeled "the pitfalls to systems management." They are pitfalls in the sense that they are either misunderstandings on the part of those trying to apply the approach, or that they are problems that should be understood by practitioners and theorizers alike. Let us take a look at what these common problems are.

The Systems Approach Is Nothing More Than Scientific Management.

The feeling that applying the principles of scientific management is synonymous with practicing systems management is a fallacy. The two concepts differ radically in several important respects. First of all, scientific management is concerned with the analysis of individual tasks. Systems management focuses on integration of the various functions making up a business enterprise. Secondly, systems management recognizes the *role of time* within the process of management; scientific management has little concern with a time dimension other than how it applies to individual effort. Thirdly, while both concepts attempt to quantify the variables seen as relevant, scientific management is essentially empirical in nature, while systems management begins with some type of postulate that it believes is normal or expected.

These differences could rightfully be construed as suggesting that the systems approach and scientific management are direct opposites, and in many ways they are. While both are tools useful in making a business more understandable and manageable, scientific management is concerned primarily with the *job* itself, whereas the systems approach focuses on the entire operation or process. The two concepts are very much related in the sense that we have learned about the systems approach by studying scientific management. In practice, the followers of scientific management have established a logical process for evaluating work and making decisions. With the systems approach, the scope of decision-making has increased to the point where many of its proponents are postulating a model of the firm that includes all internal operations as well as many external constraints.

The Application of Systems Management Necessitates Using a Computer

Another common pitfall of systems management is the thought that, "If we are going to follow the systems approach in this company, then we are going to have to get a computer." This misunderstanding stems from (1) a misconception of the concept of systems management and (2) a misunderstanding of what computers do or what they are supposed to do.

The Concept of Systems Management. At the heart of the misconception is the thought that systems management is an analytical process. In this type of process, one tries to break work down into its component parts so as to better understand it. As has already been pointed out, systems management requires a synthesis of the information that has already been analyzed. In other words, systems management is, as its name signifies, a *systemic* process that attempts to put work together into a meaningful whole.

The application of systems management in a plant is a good example of the differences between analysis and synthesis. A typical manufacturing facility would include the following management tasks: production planning, production scheduling, inventory of raw materials, inventory of finished products, warehousing, and distribution. It was through *analysis* that one is able to break the manufacturing job down into these several parts. But, a systems management approach would cause one *not* to organize the plant by setting up separate departments for each of these tasks, each reporting to the plant manager. Through synthesis, system management would guide one to the insight that they are all part of a larger task—that of materials management. The systems approach would lead you to consider establishing only one department and have the various required tasks coordinated so as to better improve the effectiveness of the facility.

What Do We Want the Computer to Do? It is typical of businessmen to ask the question, "What do we want the computer to do for us?" but in reality it is the wrong question to ask. What we need to ask is, "What do we want the manager to do?" and given this, "What are the best tools we can put at his disposal?"

One large-scale computer in the United States was programmed in an effort to assist doctors in making diagnoses. The doctor would query the computer after he had performed. In one case the computer came back and said, "It's probably diphtheria." The doctor looked over the computer output, thought about the patient, and stated that it probably wasn't that disease at all. At this point in time there was no use going back and asking the computer to try again, for without additional data and information it could only reply with the same answer.

The reason that the doctor could not go back to the computer for some more advice centers around the misconception concerning the computer; i.e., that it can synthesize information. All the computer can do is to *analyze* the data by comparing it with recognized symptoms that have been stored in its memory. To ask it to come up with a more learned answer would be to assume that it can synthesize information—a process still beyond the computer's capability.

The Systems Approach Requires Highly Trained Mathematicians

When the systems approach was first being promoted in the United States, I had the experience of working with a management consulting firm specializing in the field of systems management. In interviewing perspective clients and doing research in the field, I noticed that it was a commonly held idea that mathematicians and logicians would make the best systems managers; the thought being that in order to implement the concept, these types of backgrounds were essential. When it came down to it, what top managers were really hiring were people to man their computers.

Interestingly enough, one computer company found that their best computer programmers were not mathematicians. Instead, the people who seemed to be the best programmers were music majors and people interested in poetry. It was the latter who thought in terms of integration and synthesis, rather than the mathematicians. From a practical standpoint, however, it was difficult to convince a musician or some prospective poet that programming was an acceptable job substitute.

What has happened over the years since is the realization that what is really needed is not mathematicians, but simply *people who understand the business.* An example of this will help to make the point.

A large television broadcaster was sold the idea of automating his broadcasting procedures. A systems study performed by a mathematician showed that it was possible to design a system whereby a computer could be used to (1) integrate all program and commercial elements making up a television broadcast, and (2) produce, automatically, documents that would indicate where each program and commercial element would be broadcast and the facilities required for the actual broadcast. From a technical standpoint the proposed system was thought to be quite feasible, and with an economic benefit to boot. The people who were responsible for the broadcasts fought the idea, but were never able to convince their management that the proposed system would not be workable. Their objections were interpreted as a desire to maintain the status quo. In addition, they could not prove that the proposed system would not work.

When the new system was installed, however, trouble began. Because the people responsible for the system did not understand the needs of the business, the actual operation of the broadcast function was impaired. The system demanded that each element going into the broadcast be known and predictable. However, the minute a special news broadcast came along, or a late change in commercials by the advertiser, the system broke down. Changes required computer programming with the necessary checks and rechecks of input, and all this took time. The trouble was the broadcast people didn't have the time—they had to react quickly to meet the needs of the business. What was lacking in the system was the understanding that a successful broadcast function was a flexible one that could adapt to the changing needs.

Given the choice of training the mathematician to understand the business or training the businessman in the use of tools required to do a good systems job, I would prefer the latter, although it is not without its problems. The reason for my choice, of couse, is that systems management requires a thorough understanding of the business itself, and skill in the tools needed to implement systems management is more easily acquired.

Systems Management Is a Middle-Management Tool

Another common misunderstanding concerning systems management is that it is considered a middle-management tool. The thought here is that systems applications make more sense at the middle-management level because the work of top management is unstructured and, therefore, not subject to programming. The problem with this approach to systems management is that it does not recognize that the only way top management can evaluate the contribution of middle management is to ask itself the question, "What are they doing to contribute to our work?" and *not* "What are they doing to contribute to their own department?" In other words, a middle manager's contribution can only be measured by focusing upward and appraising what he is doing for his boss. Given this concept, systems management becomes a vital top management tool; top management must ask itself what benefits *it* can reap from the application of systems management at all levels of the enterprise.

One large manufacturing company bent on implementing systems management went out and bought a large-scale computer and ordered the controller to spearhead the project in conjunction with the other company officers in an effort to systematize the operations of the company. Three years and over a million dollars later they asked themselves how systems management and the computer helped them make their own decisions. The answer was that it didn't. With the help of outside consultants they finally began to ask themselves what systems management could contribute to their jobs. This made them think through what their own needs were. Once this was done, it was possible to design and implement systems that would contribute to top management.

Systems Management Should Result in Lower Costs

The last major pitfall of systems management stems from the thought that the application of the concept should result in lower costs for an enterprise. Behind this thought is the assumption that systems management should focus on increasing operating efficiency. Actually, though, the real benefit of systems management is not increased efficiency but, rather, increased effectiveness of a company's management. The concepts of "efficiency" and "effectiveness" are quite different. Efficiency asks the question, "How best can I use the resources that I have available to me?" Effectiveness asks quite a different question, namely, "How can I better accomplish my objectives?"

A large watch manufacturer was convinced that his manufacturing costs were out of line with companies producing similiar products. Systems studies were initiated with the objective of reducing these costs. The studies did point out where waste and duplication were taking place, and actions were taken to streamline the manufacturing function. Costs were reduced by over 10 per cent, but the company soon found itself in financial difficulty. The real problems the company were experiencing were design and marketing of their products.

If they had applied systems management to the entire process, they would have focused on the real problems and not on the peripheral ones.

Of course, management should focus its attention on both efficiency and effectiveness, but the real payoff is not in doing the job right, but in doing the right job. Efficiency, unfortunately, only focuses on the former. Focusing on doing the right job requires management to analyze whether or not the jobs it currently performs need to be performed at all. If the answer is in the affirmative, then it can pay attention to efficiency; i.e., making the best possible use of the resources it has to allocate to the task.

The Road Ahead

Just as today's managers take scientific management for granted, the manager of tomorrow may very well take systems management for granted, for he would have been educated in its use. The advantages that accrue from systems management will no longer be thought of as added benefits, but as integral to managing an enterprise successfully. The pitfalls of systems management outlined in this article are major ones but they in no way negate the value of the systems management approach. And that approach becomes even more valuable as a rational way of coherently organizing our increasingly complex businesses.

4

How Intelligent Is Your "MIS"?

Robert L. Johnson and Irwin H. Derman

Business organizations provide for the accomplishment of corporate objectives through the delegation of accountability and authority. The organizational hierarchy represents a network for the flow of communications without which such delegation and reporting activities would be impossible. Except for such institutions as the press and schools, few organizations have been formed with the objective of producing and utilizing information. Few businesses, in fact, consider themselves in the information business, yet none could long exist without information and effective distribution channels.

"Totality of Information" Concept

Since most organizational activity is centered around the acquisition, production, or transfer of information in various forms, employees are the

Source: Reprinted from *Business Horizons*, February 1970, pp. 55–62. Copyright 1970 by the Foundation for the School of Business, at Indiana University. Reprinted by permission.

targets of a conglomeration of data, information, and intelligence. Decisions are communicated by passing information to those with the delegated authority and responsibility for performance. Standards are established against which product quality, cost, and completion time are measured; evaluation procedures are developed for checking performance against the standards. The entire operation is continually monitored by a reporting system that communicates performance information to the manager, who uses a control system to feed back instructions to correct or prevent deviations from planned performance.

Within the operational framework, the words, "data," "information," and "intelligence" do not represent the same entity. The distinction lies more in usage than in format. Data represent facts catalogued according to a retrieval scheme, maintained either by computer or manually, and, as elements of knowledge at the statistical level, are passive. Information, on the other hand, represents data to which the need to satisfy a requirement has been added. In other words, information consists of data combined with direction. In contrast to data, information pertinent to the understanding of a situation or to forming the basis for action is active and has a limited useful life expectancy. Finally, in the business communications hierarchy there is intelligence resulting from the analysis of organized information that provides the decision maker with a preferred course of action after having evaluated available alternatives.

Businessmen are subjected to a barrage of data—organized and random—that impinge on their conscious as well as their subconscious minds. These data may be meaningless or pertinent at either level, and only a small amount relates generally to work interests or specifically to work projects. That which is relevant comes from a variety of sources, not exclusively through a formalized information transfer structure. From the entire universe of data, a finite amount is applicable to a specific decision. Because a decision maker never has all the data needed to guarantee the correctness of an action, decisions ultimately must be based on imperfect intelligence made up of a combination of data, experience, opinions, and intuition.

Information As a Resource. A resource is an entity that has present or potential utility. Until recently, information was neither recognized nor appreciated as a corporate resource valuable to management when used to effect the operation of an organization. Without information, day-to-day or long-range organizational functions cannot be carried out. The executive commands a higher salary than the janitor because he has learned to use information more profitably for the organization; the more scarce the possessors of knowledge on a given subject, the more valuable is the master of that information.

Information has many of the characteristics of material resources. It can be produced, stored, and distributed; it is perishable to the extent that it has no utility beyond the time it is needed; yet it is not consumable in the sense that it can be used up. As for its worth, the less a decision maker knows about a problem and its possible solutions, the higher the cost he must pay for potentially useful information. The greater the potential value of information, the larger the investment management must be willing to make for its acquisition.

Information Resource Management. Since information has value as a resource, it must be treated like other valuable resources. Because of the costs associated with procurement, transfer, storage, and conversion, information should receive consideration similar to that given such corporate resources as materials and facilities. To estimate the worth of a piece of information, its cost-value factors must be carefully examined, including the cost of acquisition and conservation, and the cost of not having it available when needed. In the latter case, the cost of raw data depends on the cost consequences of making a decision without that data.

The cost of the procurement of information on an *ad hoc* basis is high and sometimes intolerable. Nevertheless, most information needed for top management decision making is procured in this manner, since the formal management information system rarely is responsive to the special needs of the corporate executive. When gathering data, he must either search for, find, and exploit an external source or assign the task to a staff information specialist. Consequently, the search for, and isolation of, required data from the available universe and the conversion to information and intelligence results in the consumption of another valuable resource—time.

In short, an information system designed for the orderly and systematic procurement, transfer, storage, and conversion of data will reduce time, effort, and cost, and increase the utility of information. The cost of developing and implementing such a system must be weighed against the cost of searching for, finding, and handling data on an *ad hoc* basis or, worse, the consequences of making a decision without pertinent information.

Impact on Top Management

Executive Awareness. The executive often feels he is deluged with data, but rarely feels he is receiving enough information. To replace intuition and opinion, he sifts a mass of data to satisfy his information needs; nevertheless, he must often intuitively evaluate the risks of a poor decision in the absence of perfect information about the probable consequences of his actions.

All modern corporations have some form of information system that is supposed to reduce the cost of decision making and lower the probability of making poor decisions because relevant information is lacking. These systems have been designed to provide information to support corporate studies. Typically, however, they lack the essential elements of an intelligence system required to support top management marketing and investment decision making and so imperil the very survival of the corporation. Even detailed information about company resources and activities is of limited value to top management for planning corporate response to major technological, political, or economic shifts. A class of facts relating to the environment in which the corporation operates is what is really required by top management.

Today's top executives are aware of this knowledge gap in decision making. Information systems have proved their worth in supporting operating level activities by assuring a steady flow of tools, materials, and information essential for production and distribution of goods. Existing data processing systems also do a reasonable job of helping top managers get a general indication of corporate efficiency from accounting summary reports, from which financial and market reports can be extrapolated. The top executive must know that these information systems, efficient and useful as they may be to the functional managers, are not much help in making those decisions on which corporate prosperity or even survival depend.

The Problem. Too much of the executive's time is spent searching for the technical, economic, and political intelligence needed to make policy and strategy decisions. Existing information systems, generally, cannot tell him the potential impact of industry, government, and corporate threats and opportunities; he lacks, therefore, the essential elements of intelligence required for evaluating the risks and rewards associated with various options. An executive cannot obtain, remember, or retrieve all available facts pertinent to a strategic situation.

Because of the differences in the needs for facts at various levels, the corporate information system has rarely been designed to satisfy upper management requirements. Appeals by top management for more pertinent information usually bring the same data—a summary of what has happened or what is happening—not what is likely to happen "if," or how the firm can exploit an opportunity or cope with a threat, or what cost or profit may result from a future action.

To perform their tasks, top management planners need intelligence on threats, opportunities, risks, and information about future resource requirements and sources (both economic and technological), investment-payoff criteria, and techniques for evaluation of alternatives. A complete system designed to collect data, process them into information, and convert them to intelligence suitable for goal setting and strategy determination would indeed be costly. Weighed against the value of such intelligence in terms of competitive advantage, however, the investment may well be warranted. If the cost of getting and processing the information top mangement now uses is considered, the investment may be even more justified.

Unfortunately, few executives are aware of how much it is costing them to get strategic intelligence. They do not consider the cost of consultants, corporate staff planners, and economic analysts; business periodical and services subscriptions; and the expenditure of their own time in searching for and processing information in the same way they might calculate the costs and benefits from the operational support of management information systems.

Information Economics. The value of information to a business is a function of timeliness and the hierarchical position of the user in the organizational structure. With regard to production work, the value of an instruction, job order, or job sheet is the profit obtained from the sale of a product. If the sale is forfeited because of mistiming or incomplete information, the cost to the firm is more than just the worker's wages; it is also the lost profit from the potential sale. It is obvious that the potential loss will exceed the cost of having provided the worker with necessary information. Therefore, management willingly commits the required funds to establish a system to provide job-related data to the operating level personnel.

People in resource management, on the other hand, have different requirements for data than do production workers. It is more difficult, for example, to justify economically such long lead time activities as an information system where the purpose is to facilitate resource management data acquisition, processing, and reporting. These systems generally begin with the limited objective of developing an operational management data base and a reporting system to account for the expenditure of time and materials. Where time is especially valuable, as in managing high cost, potentially automatic processes, the extension of the system to real time monitoring might even be justified.

Sharing of repetitive resource and program management information can justify a high investment in a computer-based information processing system, relieving the manager of *ad hoc* data collection and processing. A computer system has an obvious advantage—its ability to "remember" facts useful to a number of mangement problem solvers. Inventory management, for example, may be systematized to monitor stock levels to optimize the time and effort of production control, purchasing, and stock control personnel. With a computer monitoring out-of-control conditions, the inventory manager is free to devote more time to research, creative planning, managing, and communication, the work he is best qualified to perform. Having the computer provide the manager with exception reports removes him from the normal crisis management loop to which he now devotes much of his day-to-day activity.

The computer, then, can make planners out of managers instead of forcing them to "plan on the fly." The computer, with its ability to remember rules and recall stored transaction data, introduces elements of predictability, reliability, and capability that go far towards establishing a true management environment. Since the computer is not under pressure to do "more important things," there is little danger that priorities could develop that would result in the postponement of decisions vital to production efficiency.

Limited Utility of Operating Activity Data. A look at the business oriented activities performed by computers shows that day-to-day applications predominate. Payroll, accounts receivable, accounts payable, inventory control, and tax processing—all activities that involve simple manipulations of data—comprise the major portion of business data processing. This is because of the ease in identifying potential cost savings that result from automating such operating activities. Since computers can handle simple, repetitive tasks, the overwhelming majority of past design activity has been directed toward installing operating level information systems.

Although the survival of the firm is rarely threatened by operating level decisions, the financial consequences of a poor decision can easily exceed the cost of reducing the probability of making such a decision. With the development of computer programs to systematize operating procedures, it was expected that the data base would provide information pertinent to long-range business activities. Planning was to be facilitated by the use of modeling techniques and simulation routines that operate on the data to identify preferable courses of action. The computer capability to recall, manipulate, and integrate large masses of data was supposed to ease the problem of handling data required for top management activity.

What has happened, though, is that top management has found operating data no more than vaguely useful for executive decision making. Therefore, those companies that went the computer/data base route have discovered information systems have had little effect on middle and upper management activities.

If the information system is not providing sufficient data to allow management to carry out planning activities, what kinds of information are lacking? It is difficult, at best, to make a definitive list of information required to run a company. First, industry considerations are important in determining the kinds of information needed to carry out all kinds of activity. Next, such factors as the size of the company, its market share, objectives, interest in acquisitions, and growth pace strongly influence the establishment of a comprehensive information base. In general, certain classes of information can be identified as potentially useful to a manager during a study or planning activity.

Fact-Opinion Dichotomy. Executives are paid for their knowledge, the relative use made of that knowledge, and their decision-making guts. Knowledge, in this case, consists of some combination of factual information, insight, and opinion. Even though some decisions must be made on the basis of insight and intuition in the face of data contradicting such judgments, the executive should have the integrity to examine pertinent facts when they are available. In other words, he must be aware of the dichotomy of fact and opinion. The information system should provide for this dichotomy by separating fact from opinion, and making the collected mass available to the manager in the form of information or intelligence.

An intelligence system for top management then can provide both data and opportunities to use those data in testing probable consequences by use of simulation prior to actual decision making. Such simulations can provide a feedback of more information to improve the odds of making a good decision.

Types and Sources of Information

Some kinds of information are not now included in corporate information system data bases. Although such information is available in some form, it is the ability to retrieve a fact within a specified time frame that is crucial. A key piece of information needed to make the optimum decision, but not available at the right time or not known to be in existence, may make the difference between success and failure. Certain information classes, if included in the corporate data base, will upgrade operational capabilities of computer systems into true corporate-wide information systems.

Middle Management Information Sources. Although it is the function of a company library to maintain a complete file of *general business publications* like the *Wall Street Journal, Forbes, Business Week,* and *Fortune,* imagine a situation in which the index of these publications is stored in the corporate data base. When a manager needs information relevant to a particular topic, he would use a computer terminal to communicate his request for citations to a retrieval program that would scan all indexes to produce a list of pertinent articles. A simple approach to the scanning problem would be the use of a KWIC (Key Word in Context) program to scan the indexes. Information retrieval would then be reduced to a document retrieval problem. The importance of this step lies more in focusing the power of the computer on the speed-of-retrieval problem than in the replacement of the manual search of a card file.

Trade association publications constitute a source of information relevant to particular industries. Besides maintaining an index of available material in the computer, it would be well to monitor selected association publications and data releases for industry wide information that could be included in the company data base as support material.

Because of the difficulty of obtaining proprietary information about competitors, a structured data format for *competitive information* would be hard to specify and maintain. Certainly there are sources of information on such matters as competitor sales, long-range plans, research activities, and plant location announcements that have a direct effect upon company plans. Although most information would be of a qualitative nature, some form of structure, including retrieval codes, could be imposed, and the data base could be designed to accommodate such qualitative information.

The *federal government* publishes a wealth of statistics on a wide range of subjects. Although most of this is unrelated to the interests of a particular company, general categories of material, besides specific industry-oriented publications, can be invaluable in supporting planning activities. For example, reports of pending legislation can be used to determine the effect of laws on the conduct of business on a nationwide basis. The same would be true, of course, for state and local communities passing legislation directly affecting manufacturing, distribution, or sale of company products. For example, federal legislation on truth-in-packaging is of immediate interest to product planning and manufacturing activities.

A general class of information published by the Bureau of Labor Statistics is also useful. Information such as salary surveys in selected areas would be of interest to personnel managers for salary comparisons or to planning managers for new facility location determinations.

Consumer purchasing behavior is, after all, the final determinant of company success. Even companies not selling consumer products are affected by the percentage of the consumer dollar remaining after purchases of necessities and conveniences, leisure services, and savings. It is in the long-range interest of a company to monitor closely shifts in consumer preferences, not only to protect future profitability in existing product lines, but also to guide potential development of related or diverse products and services. In addition to reports of trends that can be found in magazines and newspapers, the federal government is a potential source of long-range information; a government staff, headed by the Special Assistant for Consumer Affairs, could be a valuable source of consumer related facts.

Closely related to consumer expenditure statistics is the information on the *gross national product* published by the government. Many companies look to this information to help establish trends for consumer and industrial purchases. Research has attempted to relate the trends of certain key indicators to company sales. By isolating leading and lagging indicators in the components of GNP, a firm would be able to predict sales based on the over-all activity of the economy. GNP information could supplement the data normally contained in the company data base to assist management in the conduct of predictive studies and economic simulations.

With the federal government sponsoring so much *research*, it is reasonable to assume that discoveries will be made outside a company's R & D activity that will affect the future course of the firm. In the medical field, for example, research is conducted not only at the National Institute of Health but also in universities and private laboratories. The results of these projects will shape the activities of companies directly and indirectly allied to the health field. Although such results may be "far out," some kind of project directory with supporting descriptive information should be available to planning managers who must predict future health developments. The same is true in other fields of commercial interest in which there is government supported R&D.

Predictions are being made constantly, with varying degrees of supporting material, that can be used to plot the course of future company activities. Even qualitative information gleaned from these reports and included in a supportive section of the data base would be of assistance to company planners. What effect will a coming election have on the business and consumer climate for the following period? What are the weather predictions by the U.S. Weather Bureau for the coming year? What is the extent and duration being forecast for a flu epidemic that may hit the United States? (How many employees will probably miss work and how long will they be out?) These are examples of questions that have a direct bearing on every business.

Top Management Information Sources. What has been examined is a class of information, not normally formalized for inclusion in a company data base, that should be useful to management—especially middle managers—in planning beyond day-to-day company activities. Were such information to be included in a company information base with ready access provided to middle managers, there would be a marked improvement in the coverage and completeness of studies performed at the middle management level.

Yet this is not the whole story. An existing data base stands in relation to operating personnel as the preceding information stands to middle management in fulfilling its missions. That does not complete the evaluation of information for the firm as a whole. There is a class of activities, performed primarily by top management, that must also be considered. Here, the act of management must be viewed more nearly as an art. Consequently, it is significantly more difficult to isolate the data needed by top managers to carry out their roles successfully. Whereas middle managers have a more clearly defined set of information requirements, top management needs are seen as a series of dimensions to the art of management. Several kinds of activities are representative of top management interests.

Threats to the firm encompass such areas as the political climate of the firm in relation to governmental agencies and consumers. There are also the internal problems such as organizational structure, labor constraints, and individual executive power plays, as well as external threats—competitive action, substitute product development, and natural disasters, for instance. Where possible, the data base should contain information pertinent to all forms of threat to organizational integrity.

Risks include such areas as resource allocation, setting priorities for undertaking new projects, research and development decisions, new product development and integration, and investment decision making.

Top management must be aware of *future resource cost*. This calls for knowledge of developments in the money market; keeping a satisfactory debt-to-equity ratio, given the varying conditions of the investment community and awareness of general stock market trends as well as the effects of particular actions on the company stock in order to protect stockholders' interests. *Future resource technology* is a top management interest. Product development of competitive firms must be monitored, and the effects of developing technology must be projected to ensure that current products and production processes are not made obsolete by competitive action. This includes a continuing need to evaluate the cycle time from development to implementation of a process, product, or service.

Top management must take the lead in *concept developments*—determining the nature of the firm and its policy. Where is the expertise of the firm and how can it be best exploited?

What are the *goals* of the business? Is the effort of the firm to be directed toward maintaining the highest return on investment, the highest return on sales, the highest earnings per share? What are the short-term goals and the long-term goals, assuming they differ?

Strategy determination is required. Given the goals of the firm, what steps must be taken to implement them? In the short run? In the long run? In the growth area alone, a range of strategies might be followed. Growth could come from existing product lines; diversification into complementary lines or unrelated services; product and facilities acquisition in either complementary or competing industries; acquisition of an entire subsidiary; the sale of the firm to another company; or liquidation, if the assets are deemed more valuable than the going concern.

Company Posture. A company is more than a production and distribution entity. In the complex society of today, a company must have a posture on public issues. It must be able to react to consumer pressures, be aware of pending legislation as it may affect the firm, be prepared to handle the problems of minority employment, and know the dimensions of the government interface.

The preceding list is neither exhaustive nor set out in any order of priority. Items were selected to point out the areas of concern for top management decision making. In each of these areas, some combination of experience and available information must be used to arrive at the optimum answer for the firm. Although operating daily activities can be carried out by operating personnel using a maximum of data and a minimum of "creative art," the opposite is true of the kinds of decisions made by top management. Even though it is more difficult to isolate those items of information that top management must have, the requirement that they be available when needed is critical. *A lack of information at the operating level may cost the firm some money or time. A lack of information at the top management level may cost the firm its entire existence.*

Information technology, associating the power of the computer and advanced techniques for management planning and control, has significantly improved the practice of management in the past fifteen years. The phrase "management information system" is widely understood in business and government organizations. Many corporations are installing computer-based systems to support operating managers with the information needed for effective planning and control of resources and programs; some provide varying levels of opportunity for the manager to interact with the computer.

Current operating systems provide for status and performance accounting, with a variety of detail from a high level of summarization and consolidation to a mass of operational level data. Because such data have been recognized as a corporate resource, management generally is aware of its value and the wisdom of investing in systems for its economical production and distribution.

Top management, and middle management to a lesser degree, has not yet reaped similar benefits from the information revolution. The bulk of knowledge relevant to major corporate decisions is still a personal resource; decisions with life-or-death impact on the corporation are often made more on the basis of intuition and guts than on valid information. The cost of collecting and processing the information currently used is high, especially in the use of executive time. The "typical" management information system with its operation-oriented data base is of low utility in major decision-making situations, since the character of data needed for internal operations differs significantly from that used in policy making and strategic planning.

Top management is aware of its need for strategic information and is frustrated by the failure of existing systems to satisfy that need. It is apt to be unaware of the low investment required, relative to the cost of maintaining present intelligence gathering methods, to develop a strategic intelligence capability as a logical extension of an existing or planned system. Corporate management must first recognize the utility of a strategic intelligence system, then consider the options for development of such a system appropriate to the corporate and industry environments. It must consider the investment and payoff implications of the viable options; then, with that imperfect information plus its intuition and guts, the investment decision can be made. Implementation of a strategic intelligence system should prove of significantly greater value to top management than current management information systems to middle management.

the role and perspective of top management

section **2**

5

The Manager's Job: A Systems Approach

Seymour Tilles

"What does a manager do?" I once asked a group of foremen. Here are two typical answers I received:

- He's the guy who gives orders to people.
- He sits in a plush office at the corner of the building and drives a large automobile.

Naturally, when I related such answers to the top officials of the company, they were derisive. However, when I asked the executives to answer the question themselves, they did not do nearly as well. At least the foremen based their responses on reliable firsthand observation. The managers themselves could only provide responses that were nothing more than secondhand clichés. For example, they said that—

- They "organize things"—but not one could remember who designed the existing structure, or explain how it contributed to the achievement of corporate objectives.

Reprinted from *Harvard Business Review*, Vol. 41, No. 1 (January–February 1963), pp. 73–81, by permission of the publisher.

• Their job is "getting things done," but there was little agreement concerning *which* things were meant.

At the end of the discussion, we were no closer to solving the riddle of the manager's job than when we began.

The question, "What does a manager do?" is a vital one. Its significance is recognized on both sides of the Iron Curtain. And yet we still lack an answer which would prove helpful to managers in deciding whether they are, in fact, doing what they ought to be doing.

The unfortunate result of not having a comprehensive concept of the manager's job is that many executives become so preoccupied with issues which are not really critical to their company's success that they ignore other issues of truly vital significance. One management team, for example, was justifiably proud of the data-processing system it had installed. Meanwhile, however, its labor relations had deteriorated to a point where a long strike made the high-speed computer output extremely dour reading. A second management group prided itself on its high return on investment and continuous dividend record. Meanwhile, however, competitors were ensuring the company's demise by plowing money into research.

Part of the problem of developing a comprehensive concept of the manager's job is that we do not yet have a theory which covers the whole expanse of the problem. One distinguished student of management recently put it this way:

> [The manager's] predicament is that he is an involved member of an open-ended system through which he is trying to secure results. So far as I know, no scientist has come up with a satisfactory theory of and for this predicament. Most theories I know tell him how to escape from rather than how to cope with it.[1]

Of course, we do have a lot of very good theories which explain limited aspects of management. Specifically:

• Social scientists and personnel executives theorize that "the firm is really a *social system*." Starting from this point of view, they have developed a large body of knowledge concerning the manager's function in the social system.

• Data-processing specialists, as well as company controllers, have been saying that "the firm may be considered as a *data-processing system* and *decision network*." From this theory they have accumulated a considerable amount of information about the manager's role in decision making.

• Financial people hold that "the firm is really a system of funds flows." This concept has led them to compile a store of knowledge about the manager's use of financial resources.

How do we go about fusing all of these separate theories into a meaningful and integrated concept of the manager's job? In my opinion, the most prom-

[1] F. J. Roethlisberger, talk given to the Harvard Business School Association, 32nd National Business Conference, Boston, June 8, 1962.

ising approach to such a synthesis stems from the emerging field of systems theory. Therefore, in this article, I will attempt (a) to describe the manager's job in systems terms, and (b) to show how the manager, once he understands the full range of his responsibilities as revealed by a systems approach, is enabled to do a better job.

Systems Approach

The basic notion of a system is simply that it is a set of interrelated parts. Thus, a molecule may be thought of as a system of atoms, a person as a system of organs, and a group as a system of individuals. Implicit in these concepts is a degree of "wholeness" which makes the whole something different from, and more than, the individual units considered separately.

While it is convenient to introduce the concept of a system as an entity in itself, any attempt to deal with actual systems, whether atoms, people, or companies, immediately reveals that such things do not exist in themselves. They are intimately connected with a wider variety of other units which cannot really be ignored if meaningful statements about systemic behavior are to be made.

Of course, we could say, "Let us look at the company as if it existed all by itself," but this has been the trouble with so many statements that have been made about management in the past. In fact, it is precisely because the concept of "system" involves an understanding of the relationships among things that it has so much to offer as a basis for thinking about the problems that face the general manager. For the general manager must constantly be concerned about how things relate to each other. This is true both of the relationship between his company and a wide variety of external entities (competitors, customers, government, and so on) and among groups within the company itself.

Suppose we turn now to an examination of just what the manager's job really is—if we look at it from a systems point of view. Considered this way, the manager's work divides into four basic tasks:

1. Defining the company as a system.
2. Establishing system objectives, which can be further broken down to:
   - Identifying wider systems.
   - Setting performance criteria.
3. Creating formal subsystems.
4. Systemic integration.

As with any other breakdown of the management task, the parts are really meaningless in themselves—for each aspect necessarily involves all the others. So I will ask readers to suspend their questions until each of these tasks has been individually discussed.

Defining the Company

One of the most common errors which general managers commit—especially in smaller companies—is that of equating (1) the notion of viewing things in their totality with (2) doing everything oneself. Both, however, are clearly incompatible. In fact, the strongest argument against failure to delegate is that it prevents the general manager from thinking about his primary responsibility: How do things all fit together? This, of course, leads to the question, "What is the company as a system?" While the answer to this may appear ridiculously simple from a conventional point of view, every systems engineer will testify that this is one of the most fundamental, and most difficult, issues to be resolved in any serious project. In management terms, this question may be further subdivided into two critical issues:

1. Who is the company (the business as a group of people, or a social system)?
2. What is the company (the business as an integrator of markets and products)?

Who is the company? Systems theory contributes importantly to this seemingly academic question by saying: "Hold on a moment—don't just claim that the company consists of everyone on the payroll, period. The boundaries of a company are not so simply and narrowly defined." Chester Barnard, whose brilliant analysis of management is still a classic, showed that he recognized this long ago when he wrote:

> In industrial organizations the group is commonly regarded as "officers and employees," but from some points of view stockholders, the terms of whose participation are radically different, are included. At other times, or in other contexts, creditors, suppliers, and customers must be included. . . .[2]

Thus, when a company is defined from a systems point of view, no single group—customers, stockholders, or anybody else—is, for all purposes, considered to be the "insiders." There are times when it is tactically wise to include within the company's boundaries people who would never conventionally be thought of as being within it. The justification for this is quite simply that, since their cooperation is essential to the success of the enterprise, they should be explicitly included in any model of the real situation that is created. Otherwise, their significance may well be overlooked.

Two areas where this becomes particularly important are cost reduction and managerial assistance. Cost reduction can be achieved to a very limited extent if the scope of investigation is restricted only to those factors which are completely within a company's exclusive control. In many cases, the big payoff comes from cooperative action with individuals in other organizations.

[2] *The Functions of the Executive* (Cambridge, Harvard University Press, 1938), p. 69.

Thus:

—After a careful analysis of its costs, one company concluded that one of the major cost reduction opportunities was in its relationship with suppliers. It therefore enlisted their cooperation and reduced its cost considerably.

—Another organization, a newspaper, found its operations hampered by the manner in which it received copy from some of its major advertisers. Joint action was instituted and resulted in both improved service to the customer and better efficiency of the paper.

Many organizations have a management team that includes individuals—auditors, lawyers, bankers, brokers, and a variety of other specialists—who never appear on the organization chart. In some cases, these outside experts are consulted with such regularity that they are really a part of the management system. In fact, the extent of the management system is frequently an indication of the manager's ability.

What is the Company? A highly important contribution the general manager makes to any company is, first, in getting it committed to a concept of itself; and, secondly, in forcing it to re-examine the appropriateness of that concept as conditions change.

As has been pointed out previously in an HBR article,[3] the company is essentially the device which integrates the customer's requirements and the products which will fulfill them economically. But once we have said this, the concept of the business has not been settled; in fact, it has barely begun to be recognized. Immediately many questions arise:

- What customers are we interested in?
- What specific customer needs do we wish to satisfy?
- Which products will we include in our line?

These issues are intimately related to each other; answering one immediately limits the freedom with which we may answer the others. However, there has to be some consistency of pattern among the answers to these questions if the company is to operate successfully.

For example, the McGraw-Hill Publishing Company has built its magazine business around the concept of providing vocationally useful information to narrowly defined groups of readers. It therefore publishes such magazines as *Business Week, Chemical Engineering, Gasoline Retailer, American Machinist/Metalworking Manufacturing,* and *Textile World.* On one occasion it attempted to publish a general circulation periodical called *Science Illustrated.* This was not successful.

There are numerous other illustrations of this: the attempt of the publishers of *Playboy* to put out *Show Business Illustrated,* the effort of Packard Motors to introduce a small car, and the attempts of Underwood and Royal McBee to enter the computer business. Each enterprise individually discovered that

[3] Theodore Levitt, "Marketing Myopia," HBR July–August 1960, p. 45.

when it tried to go beyond some consistent pattern of customers, needs, and products—some definition of itself—it ran into trouble.

An organization is never finished dealing with the problem of self-definition. The caustic observation of Mark Twain about life being "just one damned thing after another" holds just as true for corporate affairs as for people. Take, for example, two organizations which are readily recognized as outstanding in their respective fields: International Business Machines and *The New York Times.* While each organization may be considered currently successful, each faces critical developments at present which will determine its future:

- IBM, today the acknowledged leader in the field of data processing, is directly influenced by the tremendous technological developments sweeping the whole electronics industry. One result of this technological revolution has been to force IBM to integrate into the component field, after years of depending almost entirely on outside sources for supply of components. Thus, despite decades of success, this company is still in the process of redefining itself. This is not only the price of leadership; it is essential to survival. Like dinosaurs, modern corporations die when they become too big to change in the face of environmental demands.
- *The New York Times* is one of the great newspapers of the world. Today the clear tendency in the United States for many reasons is for fewer and fewer newspapers. The combination of the movement of advertisers to television and the movement of readers to the suburbs has resulted in there being fewer and fewer newspapers each year. One result of this has been the appearance of newspapers which are no longer limited to a single community. The recent decision of *The New York Times* to publish a West Coast edition and an International edition may well make national or even international journalism the rule, rather than the exception. In any case, the *Times,* like IBM, has found that greatness does not provide immunity from a continuing concern with the issue: "What are we now, and what should we become?"

Setting System Goals

The general state of the art of setting corporate objectives is an appalling one. By and large, the terms in which managers state their official aspirations are oversimplified deceptions: profit, market share, or return on investment. Each of these indicators still has great appeal to management, despite the extent to which scholars have rejected them as valid bases for performance evaluation.[4] Their appeal lies primarily in the fact that each one sounds simple, since its inherent ambiguities are not obvious; each can be expressed in numbers, and thereby endowed with an aura of objectivity and utility; and each one can be claimed to be a logical measure of past performance.

[4] See, for example, Robert N. Anthony, "The Trouble with Profit Maximization," HBR November–December 1960, p. 126.

The trouble with these criteria is that they entice the general manager to focus his attention where it does not belong: on the company itself, rather than on the relationship between the firm and the broader systems of which it is a part. This is vividly reflected in the design of the information systems which ultimately produce the quantitative criteria listed above. Looking at these systems, one sees a great deal of money and effort devoted to analyzing what went on within the organization itself and very little, if anything, devoted to an analysis of environmental trends. Managers, too, frequently lose sight of the fact that corporate performance is the result of a company interacting with its environment, rather than the result of factors wholly within the company itself.[5]

This preoccupation with events taking place inside the company, rather than with the company's relationship to a wider environment, is reflected in many aspects of managerial action. For example, much that has been written about the relationship between managers and subordinates is quite misleading, because it has been built on an implicit assumption that the behavior of subordinates would be influenced only by the way the manager behaved toward them. Thus, the manager has been exhorted to be a "benevolent autocrat," a "participative leader," and a variety of other subordinate-oriented roles.

One advantage of a systems view of the manager's job is that it broadens the area of relationships that a manager properly should consider. It encourages him to think seriously about looking outward and upward, instead of being continually preoccupied with looking down the ladder at his subordinates. Many managers rivet their attention on their subordinates, despite the fact that meddling in the affairs of competent assistants is likely to do much more damage than good. Actually, the major contribution the general manager can make to his unit lies in the area of his relationship with individuals over whom he does *not* exercise direct control, his peers, his superiors, or persons who are completely outside the company—customers, stockholders, bankers, lawyers, politicians, or labor leaders. Without their cooperation, it is unlikely that the business will be successful.

Moreover, subordinates are likely to be influenced at least as much by a manager's attitude toward the environment as by his attitude toward them. The manager who is adventurous, entrepreneurial, dynamic—even though he may be discourteous to his employees—will generate fierce loyalties. And, conversely, the stagnant company which treats its employees well usually winds up with an executive team that is either incompetent, dissatisfied, or both. The following quote from a young executive about to switch jobs is typical:

> I have no complaint about being unfairly treated—he's been very fair about everything; and he pays me a pretty good salary. I just don't want to get tied down to a firm that isn't going anywhere.

[5] See Robert B. Young, "Keys to Corporate Growth," HBR November–December 1961, p. 51.

Similarly, in the case of profit, it is not so much the reported profit itself that must be the focus of management's concern, but rather *what the reported figure implies for the company's relationships with the various systems of which it is a part.* One such system will be the network of investors and creditors who provide the organization with funds. Clearly, their confidence must be preserved, and they must be compensated for the risks they assume. However, profit is not an automatic indicator of the extent to which either is accomplished. Conversely, the business which says that its only objective is to enhance the stockholders' equity implies that no other system of which it is a part—neither market, nor community, nor nation—can be considered as deserving of equal priority.

Of course, the traditional significance which attaches to profit as a prerequisite for corporate survival is important. But for most companies it can well be claimed that the achievement of a reported profit is less a test of the quality of management than of how its funds are distributed.

It can be established that many companies have faced their most critical tests of survival in precisely those years when they were reporting the highest net profits in their history—mainly because these were being achieved at the price of not keeping up with competitors in research, equipment renewal, and management development.

If, then, criteria such as profit are to be rejected as the measures of performance, what will take their place? It follows from the preceding arguments that what must be substituted is *sets of criteria,* each corresponding to some wider system of which the company is a part. One implication of this is that the general manager must be concerned both with the identification of relevant wider systems and with an assessment of the relative obligation the organization owes each of them.

Identifying Wider Systems. In order to survive, an organization must achieve what is called "symbiosis" (i.e., the mutually beneficial living together of two dissimilar organisms) with a variety of external systems, and it is the responsibility of the general manager to be concerned with all of these systems. The first step in discharging this responsibility is the identification of those broader or, to use a more technical term, those superordinate systems of which the company is a part. For example, we can think of an enterprise as being part of an industry, a community, a market, an economy, and a variety of other superordinate systems. But each of these systems is really only a nebulously defined abstraction, and yet each of these abstractions poses a set of highly significant issues for management.

Let us take the notion of an "industry," which may appear to be a fairly obvious and unambiguous superordinate or wider system. No doubt it once was—when specializations were clearly defined, broad, and stable—but not in today's changing world. Consider these examples:

- Petroleum used to be quite a precise description of an industry. Today, the rapid advances in petrochemistry and the development of a variety of energy sources (from fuel cells to thermoelectricity) have presented petroleum companies with a greater variety of alternatives concerning industry definitions as well as more knotty problems of strategic choice. Now it is crucial for a petroleum company to decide whether it is in the petrochemical industry, or the petroleum industry, or both.

• In the aircraft industry the necessity for redefining superordinate systems arises as missiles are rapidly replacing manned aircraft for military use. This is a dramatic illustration of the basic issue that confronts management in every industry.

Another important superordinate system involves the federal government. To an ever-increasing extent, the federal government and the individual firm have to be thought of as parts of the same system; the recent furor over steel pricing is an excellent example of this. But the tendency toward a government and business being parts of the same system is apparent in numerous other aspects of business life, ranging from tariff policy and depreciation allowances to research expenditures and production contracts.

It is unfortunate that this issue of government and business has so often been posed in terms of freedom versus control. This point of view leads to conceptualizing the situation in terms of two antagonists—as only black and white. It is more in tune with the times to think of business and the federal government as part of the same system, and to explore the effect that each may have on the other by pursuing a particular course of action. Today in the free countries of Western Europe, joint government-industry activities are well advanced. Their experience has made clear that enlightened management can no longer refuse to accept the existence of the federal government within the same system as the company. Of course, approving the over-all system does not completely solve the question of the relationship between the parts of the system. But some consideration of that issue will benefit a business much more than will simply resenting "interference from Washington."

A final example of a superordinate system is that which embraces a business and the communities in which it operates. This issue appears in its most acute form when the company is large and the community small; for, under this set of circumstances, the mutual relationship between the two systems is apparent. Certainly the issue is most dramatic in this context, as has been demonstrated again and again in now nearly deserted New England textile communities and neglected Pennsylvania mining towns. However, from an ethical point of view, the issue over the relationship between the business and the community becomes no less significant merely because the relative size of each is different.

Setting System Criteria. Once the broader systems of which the company is a part have been identified, some criteria must be adopted which will determine how well the company has performed with respect to each system. One set of performance criteria which reflects the broad range of management concern is shown in Exhibit 1.

Exhibit 1. Systems Criteria for Judging Company Performance

Superordinate System	*Criteria*
Stockholders	Price appreciation of securities Dividend payout
Labor force	Wage levels Stability of employment Opportunity
The market: consumers	Value given
The market: competitors	Rate of growth Innovation
Suppliers	Rapidity of payment
Creditors	Adherence to contract terms
Community	Contribution to community development
Nation	Public responsibility

It should be clear, for example, from the criteria listed in Exhibit 1 that improved short-run payouts with respect to any particular system can only be achieved in three ways: (1) by immediately raising the level of performance of the whole organization, (2) by paying out now what might be saved for the future, or (3) by raising the payouts to one superordinate system at the expense of another. Consequently, the wise general manager should never be concerned with a *single* objective and with a single superordinate system. Rather, he must be concerned with a *set* of objectives; and thus the trade-off of one good against another is a critical aspect of his responsibility.

He must decide whether short-run profits (so dear to the "stockholder system") are obtained at the expense of long-range profits (within the same system) or at the expense of payouts to other systems. For example, short-run profits may stem from actions which will reduce the company's effectiveness in coping with future competition (the "market/competition system") or with future labor demands (the "labor system"). He must decide whether his company's contribution to the "nation system" is sufficient to warrant risks of loss to the "stockholder system." In short, he is concerned with how the organization relates to *all* who contribute to it; and unless he can formulate a meaningful set of objectives which cover all such relationships, he is in danger of running into difficulty in some area.

Many other sets of criteria are of course possible. However, each should be considered in terms of (1) which superordinate systems have been explicitly included, and (2) what criteria will best serve as reliable indicators of how well the company is achieving its objectives in relationship to the included systems.

Creating Subsystems

One of the most significant ways in which managerial ability expresses itself is in the creation and change of formal subsystems. The term "formal subsystem" is used here to refer to the officially established groups and entities which are created to carry on the company's activities. These include such units as divisions, departments, and regions which are reflected on the conventional organization chart. Also included are the committees, boards, and groups which have official status but are frequently not shown on the organization chart, despite the fact that decisions concerning which committees shall be established, what their membership will be, and how long they will be permitted to operate are at least as significant to the operation of a company as is its formal structure.

Thinking of the company as a set of formal subsystems offers two benefits:

1. It focuses attention on the essential relatedness of activities carried on by specific individuals.
2. It emphasizes the fact that to meet the particular requirements of a specific business, the subunits of which the organization is composed must be as carefully designed as the subunits of any other system.

One of the tragedies frequently suffered by people who fall in love with such traditional organizational techniques as job descriptions and organization charts is that after a while they become far more concerned with specialization than with coordination. Somehow the inevitable result of boxes and lines appears to be the *division* of tasks, rather than merely their *delineation*. As a result, the neat little lines on the chart, which were originally intended to be boundaries, always seem to become fences.

This is so universal and unfortunate a tendency that it would not be too wild a statement to claim that *most organizations would probably contribute enormously to their own progress if they burned their existing organization charts and manuals*. Then management would be free to think about how the employees might be grouped together to form meaningful systems, rather than being concerned with which particular bits and pieces of a total activity should be set aside as the exclusive preoccupation of a single individual.

Most serious company problems call for cooperative action, rather than for individual decisions. And yet not one job description in a hundred tells what an individual contributes to a broader system or how he cooperates with his colleagues. The net effect has been to hinder cooperation, stifle creativity, and restrict change. Indeed, it is not accidental that formal organizational arrangements are played down by those companies which are most dynamic and most creative.

This idea should not be construed to mean that organization charts of a different type might not prove to be of value and importance. However, if they are to be of more help than hindrance, charts should be drawn in terms of systems, rather than in terms of *individual components*. And they should be viewed as blueprints—as the expression of a design—and not as the photograph of a jungle.

When an engineer looks at formal organizational arrangements, he is immediately struck by how seldom such arrangements have been "designed"—in the sense of matching specific groups and structures to the objectives and resources of a particular business. In most companies, the organizational structure is merely the result of a haphazard process of evolution, and, as such has no particular relationship to the needs, aspirations, or competencies of the people in it—and even less relationship to the company's external strategy.

Unfortunately, there are no ready rules for the design of a set of subsystems which will meet the requirements listed in Exhibit 1. In the field of formal organization we are still very much at the level of amateur mechanics. At present, we know a good deal more about breaking tasks apart than about putting them together in new and imaginative ways. This task, then, is one which has to be performed by the effective chief executive on the basis of his own judgment and intuition, rather than as a result of a set of precise principles. The great managers have made impressive and lasting improvisations in this way.[6]

Systems Integration. The chief executive is the focal point of many different worlds. His desk is the point of contact between a bewildering variety of groups, issues, pressures, and values. His major responsibility, therefore, is to maintain some degree of *consistency* between the demands imposed by the many systems which are part of his organization's life. This is what is meant by systems integration, a process that involves two different kinds of activities: (1) the integration of the systemic hierarchy; (2) the integration of systemic models. Both of these are essential parts of the manager's job.

It cannot be emphasized enough that the essence of the manager's job is not simply that of understanding broader and broader superordinate systems, but rather of achieving some measure of integration between the broader superordinate systems and the smallest subsystems which form his organization. Thus, an economist or a market researcher on the corporate staff will certainly be more intimately concerned with some broad superordinate system than the chief executive should be. But what distinguishes the executive's job from theirs is the range of systems which he must integrate. Specifically, the general manager must be able to:

—Translate the broadest abstractions into the most detailed aspects of company operations.

—See what implications major industry trends hold for the kind of worker recruitment that he expects to do over the next few years, for the kinds of machines he may expect to buy, and for the materials which may be available.

—Translate the broad trends which are transmuting our society into specific

[6] See Alfred D. Chandler, *Strategy and Structure* (Cambridge, MIT Press, 1962); also James W. Culliton, "Age of Synthesis," HBR September–October 1962, p. 36.

decisions concerning new products, the development of salesmen, and many other detailed issues.

—Recognize the strategic implications of the ostensibly humdrum event. For example:

- A small shift in the market performance of a product may presage a major movement.
- The introduction of a minor change in office methods can be the key to a whole data-processing installation.
- A whole new social structure may eventually emerge from an act as seemingly insignificant as moving a coffee machine.

A second aspect of systemic integration is that concerning the various models of corporate life. A manager must understand thoroughly how an organization behaves if he is to influence it, and the key to such understanding lies in an awareness of the various models which may be used to explain its operation. Such an awareness is not only essential to the manager's perception of the company; it is also essential to the manager's perception of himself.

What happens in an organization may often be explained by the use of a particular "model." For example, a company may be regarded as:

1. A *social system*—where the many and varied tools of the social scientists may be used to reveal the patterns and significance of the way the members behave.
2. An *economic system*—where the insights afforded by classical economics may be highly useful in explaining a wide range of occurrences.
3. A *data-processing system*—where a knowledge of information-handling technology is required in order to analyze communication needs.

Each of these analogies is extremely useful to the manager, for each is often the key to a valid explanation of what goes on inside the company. Consequently, the more models a manager can bring to bear on particular problems, the more he will be able to understand why specific events take place, and what he ought to do about them. Conversely, a manager may easily damage his organization by assiduously behaving in accordance with an inappropriate model. A frequent illustration of this is the reliance on economic incentives to remedy deficiencies in the social system.

This still happens often, despite the amount of research that has been done on the social determinants of output levels. One would think that more than 20 years after the publication of *Management and the Worker*[7] exclusive reliance on economic means to deal with performance would no longer be common. However, a panacea frequently resorted to by managers who wish to raise output is a sweetened bonus program for individuals. Here is one example:

[7] F. J. Roethlisberger and W. J. Dickson (Cambridge, Harvard University Press, 1939).

• A manufacturer of custom-built machinery, eager to improve output per man-hour, installed a wage incentive plan. All that it did was cost the company money, since the key individuals turned out to be highly skilled senior mechanics whose work could not be measured. Only by cancelling the incentive plan, by conscientiously improving communications within the plant, and by transferring greater responsibility to its foremen did the company begin to solve its problems. Its mistake, obviously, was that it was trying to cure ills in its social system by applying economic measures. If the top management of this company had considered a broader variety of models, it might well have avoided this costly error.

Of course, no single model or conceptual scheme embraces the whole breadth and complexity of reality, even though each in turn may be useful in particular instances. This is why management remains an art, for the practitioner must go beyond the limits of theoretical knowledge if he is to be effective. As soon as the manager begins to think "scientifically," he has already made an abstraction from reality. This abstraction may be based on economics, sociology, psychology, or engineering—but it is only a part of reality. The real challenge to the manager is to see and to understand the whole situation.

Conclusion

In this atomic age too many managers are thinking of themselves and of their companies in buggy-whip terms. They have a concept of management which rests on a point of view that has remained largely unchanged since it was formulated by Henri Fayol just after World War I. In the meantime, however, a deluge of important new ideas has swept across the business scene. Whole new fields of critical importance to management have emerged: cybernetics, integrated data processing, systems engineering, and a variety of others ranging from social psychology to Bayesian statistics. The impact of all these new ideas on management has been so fundamental that new ways of thinking about the manager's job are long overdue.

The modern manager needs a new approach to his job for three reasons:

1. He must have a way of thinking about management that permits him to take account of the tremendous amount of new knowledge that is appearing.
2. He has to have a framework that permits him to relate one specialty with another in his work.
3. He must be able to raise his sights above the hurly-burly of current in-company operations and understand how his company relates to its complex environment—to the other great systems of which it is a part.

A systems approach to management promises to do this, as I have tried to demonstrate in this article. I have also attempted to indicate the kinds of questions that come up when a manager tries to think of his job in systems terms. One of the most important of these is: "Have I been concerned with those things that I, as a manager, must be concerned with?" This is a very disconcerting question for a manager to ask. But if there is some suspicion that the answer is *no,* isn't it better for a manager to reach that conclusion himself?

6

How to Think Like a Company President

Lee Grossman

At a recent seminar for company presidents, two executives were discussing their various presidential duties. One represented a firm with over 3,000 employees. His company was highly centralized and decisions were made at the top. The other represented a company with only 500 employees, but decision making was decentralized and decisions were made at the lowest level possible.

The president of the 3,000 employee firm complained that his job was difficult because he was directly responsible for the activities of over 3,000 people. The president with only 500 employees disagreed. "Although you are responsible for 3,000 people," he argued, "I am responsible for '500 presidents.'"

The significance of the remark should not be lost. This president was saying he had an organization of 500 who, because they were decision makers, thought like they were presidents. Although this meant he had a lot of competition, it also meant he had a lot of people who were very much concerned about the welfare of the company.

Busy Throwing Rocks

It's not easy to get people to think like a company president. Often they are too busy throwing rocks at the guy on the top of the heap.

Throwing rocks at the guy on top does have some value. The company president is not unlike the abominable snowman to many people in his organization. Particularly in large companies, he rarely gets the opportunity to meet and talk with the people doing the work or even the people managing those who do the work. They may see him at the company picnic or the Christmas party, but for the most part he's almost mythical and legends of his abilities and failings constantly circulate through the organization.

To change the organization from one which throws rocks to one where

Adapted from the October 1970 issue of *Business Management* magazine, pp. 36–38, by permission of the publisher.

everybody thinks they're at the top of the heap is a difficult matter. To do this requires understanding of what makes a company president tick and what pleases or displeases him. Such understanding enables executives reporting to the president to practice "anticipative management."

If you know how your president thinks, you can react in advance to what he will require even before he knows he needs it. Attempts at such understanding give an executive "presidential perspective."

Presidential Perspective

Viewing the world from the president's perch can be a heady experience. From this vantage point it's amazing how quickly organizational conflicts and functional bias disappear. Responsibility and authority disputes between groups (even one in which you play a part) somehow pale in comparison to the awesome responsibility of running the company. A seemingly important decision fades to nothing in comparison to the weight of much larger decisions and their implications.

Without even knowing your company president there are some things anyone can say about him. Many are as different as from night to day. Some grew from a sales background and retain their sales orientation. Others came from production, retain their production orientation and are more at ease and familiar with the technical side of their business. Still others came from accounting and maintain the "scorekeeper" orientation with which they are most familiar. Technical specialists tend to favor their particular backgrounds.

Some presidents never successfully complete the transition. They strongly retain their old interests and bias and stubbornly refuse to grow into their new roles. Growth companies need growth presidents and perhaps the degree of company growth can be measured in some part by the degree of presidential growth.

Something else happens when a man becomes a company president. Presidents become a breed unto themselves, not unlike the early pioneers and their outward manifestations of rugged individualism. The breed tends to exhibit the characteristics of the typical business entrepreneur. This is not hard to understand for they both share the total and ultimate responsibility for risk taking.

There are other almost universal presidential characteristics, attitudes, abilities and disabilities. But the "profile" of an individual company president varies. The value in the profile is not that our president fits at all points, but what we learn from it in those areas where he does fit.

The common denominator of the presidential profile is business problems. All company presidents share them. While many of these problems appear to be different, close examination reveals that they tend to cluster or focus on specific management areas and are more common than one would suspect.

Let's examine and categorize typical problems. At the outset let's understand that a president's inability to solve particular problems doesn't necessarily mean failure for his company. Problem solving is never-ending; some will never be solved. Others are solved by diligence, hard work and sometimes sheer luck.

Success as a company president doesn't require solving all problems that arise, but an inability to solve some of the basics goes a long way toward presidential downfall. Obviously, those problems related to company profits are of utmost importance to most company presidents. Frequently, you don't know the problem is solved until some time after corrective action is taken. Sometimes problems appear to be solved but in reality they've shifted elsewhere; the company has traded one set of problems for another. Many presidents liken their own company to a piece of putty. Solving one problem is like pushing a bulge in the putty to make it fit the mold. But the putty just bulges elsewhere.

A basic problem for the typical company president is using his time—a precious commodity—effectively. Presidents have more things to do than they can possibly get to on any given work day. As a result, most presidents, contrary to popular belief, work longer and harder hours than most of their employees.

Still, he is plagued by the unfinished work and the unsolved problem, the lost production, lower morale and widespread confusion. The "pressure cooker" causes rush decisions and actions taken with inadequate evaluation of all the facts—and frequently the results show it.

Paradoxically, presidents lack time for important matters because their time is squandered on detail work that could have been accomplished easier and better by others. Too often he works on things he likes to do rather than things he should do.

At one time or another, most presidents experiment with devices that claim to save time. A would-be president should look into such things as special dictating equipment, memory joggers and files, electronic communication equipment and push button desks. Another device that claims to save time is the computer. Company presidents subconsciously identify the computer as a time-saving machine; therefore, the company should have one. Others just feel it's the thing to do. If a decision to go computer is based on such limited views then the company and the president are surely skating on thin ice.

Fact gathering and analysis may be delegated, but which facts to gather and how to analyze them? Irrelevant information frequently clouds decision making. Therefore, presidents strongly respect and reward any light-shedding ability they find in their organizations. This capability is a highly desirable prerequisite for presidential assistant or anyone hoping to fill the president's shoes.

Language Explosion

As business becomes more complex and specialized the president finds himself surrounded by functional technicians, each one speaking a separate language. From the president's view it's a tower of Babel. The production vice president speaks of productive capacity, production control, equipment and raw material specifications. The marketing vice president speaks about market share, product life cycles and competitors' marketing strategies. The controller speaks of ratio analysis, costs and profits and balance sheets. The R&D vice president speaks of exotic materials, new product generation and increased budgets for pure research. The data processing manager speaks of hardware, software and programing.

This "language explosion" is growing. Each functional specialist speaks, to some degree, a technical jargon understandable only to those of his own ilk. As the organization and language explosion expands a "language barrier" develops.

The language barrier creates some of the most difficult problems the president has to face. Although the specialists talk to the president (they have to), they do not talk to each other in a common language. Part of the problem is, of course, in the listening device. Too often the president is called upon as arbitrator in a dispute that has its origins in semantic misunderstanding.

Communication problems are increasing for the president because business more and more is scientifically managed. Some presidents recognize there is a point of diminishing return for specialization within their organization. Getting too technical too fast can be just as bad, or worse, than operating by the seat of your pants. The optimum change rate for the organization has to be ascertained and carefully controlled.

A difficult problem for many company presidents is adjusting to the fact that he has to get things done through other people. Frequently, he does the work himself because he doesn't know how to get other people to do it for him. More than one company president has overcome this difficulty by saying, "Don't do yourself what you can get somebody else to do."

The company president must learn to be a tutor, planner, counselor, disciplinarian and mediator. He must learn the skills of asking effective questions and the gentle art of listening. A successful president proposes objectives, suggests alternatives, breaks bottlenecks and smooths out organizational conflict. His real job is developing people, not doing "things."

To get people to do things requires an effective organization that operates in a systematic manner. Finding, training, stimulating and motivating key executives is a never-ending presidential task. Yet many company presidents feel that all or just about all of their employees are slightly incompetent. They feel they can do every job better than any of their employees. Moreover, they're probably right.

As president, they have perspective that no other employee could possibly have. They understand the "big picture" and therefore know to what degree jobs should be completed. A clerk, for example, may do things that are unnecessary for the proper operation of the business. A president would take shortcuts that the clerk never has the option to take.

Presidents who display this impatient "know it all" attitude create an unhealthy organizational environment. Each function becomes dependent upon the president for decisions, since no one wants the responsibility of making mistakes.

Moreover, people tend to take the role we ascribe to them. If we think of them as incompetent they become incompetent. If on the other hand, we stretch them to their full potential they will develop their capabilities and do a better job. Developing their talents and encouraging their growth causes them to respond in a like manner. During a period of organizational growth and development the president has to stand on the sideline and bite his tongue when he sees mistakes being made. It's temporary, and in the long run, for the good of the company. Only in this way can the president assure the future of any organization that, at some point in time, has to continue without him.

Balancing the Organization

Often you hear the statement from the sales-oriented: "If we can just sell more, everything would be fine." The company president who ascribes to that philosophy is surely in trouble. One firm that wholeheartedly believed in this selling philosophy recently went bankrupt. Their business methods and systems were so inadequate and costly that the more they sold, the more money they lost. Theirs was the philosophy: "We lose a little on each sale, but we make it up in the volume."

Profit is not made by simply selling more. It results from a careful balancing of sales with the cost of those sales. Developing an organizational philosophy that properly balances each contribution is the best way to assure control and maximum profit.

Business would be better off if managers could be trained to think like company presidents.

7

The Power and Functions of Boards of Directors: A Theoretical Synthesis[1]

Mayer N. Zald

Such broad-scale metaphors as "The Managerial Revolution" (Burnham 1941) or "The Power Elite" (Mills 1957) direct our attention to the control of major decisions both at the level of the total society and of large-scale

Reprinted from *American Journal of Sociology*, July 1969, pp. 97–111 by permission of the publisher and author.

[1] This paper was begun during a study of the Young Men's Christian Association of Metropolitan Chicago, supported by a grant (GM-10777) from the Institute of General Medical Sciences,

organizations. Although these metaphors and their associated underlying variables lead to hypotheses that may be testable in long historical perspective, they are too gross for short-run analysis. In formulating hypotheses about the control of organizations, for instance, we must specify a range of variables and conditions under which elites or managers may or may not influence important decisions.

Analysis of the functions and conditions of power of boards of directors provides intellectual leverage on this question of the control of organizations. The board of directors of a corporate organization has formal and legal responsibility for controlling and maintaining organizational operation and effectiveness (Lattin 1959, pp. 211–78). The corporate form with its board of directors (governing boards) has been applied to many types of organizations, for example, businesses, voluntary welfare associations, private schools, public school systems, hospitals, and governmental agencies with "autonomous" or independent functions.[2]

Yet as the size and scope of organizations have increased, some scholars have doubted whether the formal system of board control does any more than provide lip service to the law. Those who argue that boards of directors are merely a legal and coopted appendage believe organizations are controlled by the full-time managers (Gordon 1945, chaps. 5 and 6). They believe boards are at the mercy of the managers who control information, definitions of alternatives, the nominating process, and, indeed, the very agenda of decision making.[3] On the other hand, some students—especially those looking at welfare organizations and the American stratification system, note that boards have ultimate power to hire and fire executives, which shapes executives' decision premises (Hunter 1963, pp. 231–36; Baltzell 1958, pp. 364–83).[4]

NIH, USPHS. At a later point, a grant from the Vanderbilt University Research Council and a Career Development Award (K-34, 919) NIMH, USPHS, aided in its completion. It is a revised version of a paper delivered at the 1968 Annual Meetings of the American Sociological Association, Boston, Massachusetts. Mark S. Massel, Nicholas Mullins, and James Price gave astringent criticism to earlier versions.

[2] It should be noted that the earliest corporations were religious orders (see Davis 1961).

[3] "I've been concerned and at the same time both amused and somewhat guilty about the fact that the Board of Directors makes policy decisions, both by authority of the by-laws and in the actual voting they do; yet actually in the present day family casework agency the staff has to "educate" the Board constantly and persistently and it certainly does choose the elements of education which lead toward the conclusions of which the staff approves. In other words, we tell them how to vote and they vote and we call that process 'the Board sets the policies of the agency. . . .' I can frankly cite very few instances when Board opinion has influenced my judgment about policy and practices during the (many) years I have been Executive of this agency, although the Board has made every important policy decision and has been 'informed' ad nauseum before every decision." This is from a letter written by the executive of a family service agency in 1956 (see Wilensky and Lebeaux 1965, p. 273).

[4] Heffernan (1964) shows how social work executives moderate their political activities to keep in the good graces of their boards.

The pervasiveness of the corporate form in America and the disagreement over the importance of boards of directors relates not only to sociological questions but to policy ones as well. Although this essay does not deal directly with policy issues, it is worth noting that questions of the proper and improper activities of boards of directors preoccupy several arms of government.

In this theoretical synthesis of propositions about the power and influence of boards of directors our general orientation is that, in the relationships among boards (as collectivities), individual board members, and executives, each party brings to bear "resources." These resources may be based in legal rights, in monetary control, in knowledge, or even in force of personality and traditions. Resources may be crudely classified as "detachable" resources, personal characteristics, and strategic contingency situations. It is the balance of resources for specific situations and decisions that determines the attribution of relative power in the encounter between boards and executives.

It must be noted that the power of boards of directors or of individual board members does not refer to their formal voting rights. As in so many voting situations, formal voting may be irrelevant to many (though not all) of the crucial decisions. Instead, the power of board members relates to their service on and control of key committees and the extent to which other members and the management (who may also be board members) find it necessary to be bound by their perspectives and ideas.

The corporation form (as we have come to know it) was created as a means of accomplishing "desirable" ends that were beyond the capabilities of individuals. Boards of directors were created and recognized in law in order to insure continuity in the management of organizations and to fix a locus of responsibility for the control of "independent" organizations.[5] Boards are charged with the proper use of resources in pursuit of organizational goals. Directors are not personally responsible for organizational losses, but they are responsible for prudent action in behalf of the "owners" (whomever that might be).

Prudent action includes appointing and perpetuating effective management of the organization and overseeing the work of such management. This control function of the boards of directors is inward looking; the board operates as the agent of the corporation at the request of the owners (members) to oversee organizational activity.[6]

Because of their formal position of responsibility and their involvement in the organization, boards also develop an outward-looking function; they promote and represent the organization to major elements of the organiza-

[5] Although much of our discussion is applicable to governmental organizations, most of it is framed in terms of nongovernmental ones. Governing boards and organizations in the "public" sector tend to have less autonomy of organizational operation. Mainly discussing private organization gives our propositions a greater specificity and concreteness.

[6] We usually think of boards of directors as agents of the "owners," but legally they are servants of the corporation vested with corporate control. On the ambiguities here, see Marris (1964, pp. 12–13).

tional set, for example, customers, suppliers, stockholders, interested agencies of the state, and the like. That is, they defend and support the growth, autonomy, and effectiveness of their agencies vis-à-vis the outside world.

Obviously, boards differ in the extent to which they perform either the external representation or internal control functions. For instance, it is likely that boards of prosperous manufacturing firms, in a competitive industry, and with unproblematic governmental relations, have less of an external representation function than welfare agencies heavily dependent on wealthy donors or on the community fund. Similarly, in small organizations in which board members have intimate knowledge, they may decide all nonroutinized expenditures, major personnel changes, markets, and types of product. In other organizations they may be restricted to formal appointment of the executive and the auditor and to setting executive salaries.

Although there is this variety, there are some relatively standard activities in which boards engage and which have implications for their potential power. First, a major concern of boards tends to be personnel. At the very least, boards usually must choose a chief operating officer and decide on his salary (if there is one). Second, boards that are not "paper boards," that actually hold meetings and discuss organizational affairs, usually review the financial condition of the organization and set financial policy (dividend rates, capital indebtedness, etc.). In some cases the rules and bylaws of the board require formal approval for all nonroutine expenditures over a stipulated amount. Finally, many boards review organizational output, its "product," markets, and comparative operating efficiency. Which of these activities are performed, and to what extent, depends on the structure of the organization, its environmental interrelations, and the sources of board member power vis-à-vis executives.

Detachable Resources a Power Base

A resource is "detachable" if it is not closely tied to the person, that is, if it is transferable. Utilizing a cross-sectional approach, we examine gross variables between organizations and between board members causing differences in the relative power of boards and individual board members.

There are two main bases of power considered. First, the relative power of board members can be based on their access to and control of relevant external resources. Second, knowledge relevant to the ongoing operations of the organization may be considered an internal organizational base of power differentially distributed between boards and executives.

External Bases of Power. The members of a board of directors may serve largely on the sufferance of the executive or they may "represent" salient blocs of shareholder votes, sources of financial material support, or of community legitimation and representation. In general, *to the extent that board members control or represent salient external "resources," they are more powerful than if they do not control such resources.* (For this and all other propositions, *read* "everything else being equal.")

Stockownership. Stockownership in a corporation is an external basis of power because it is completely dependent on definitions of legal rights attached to shares. The owner of common stock does not own a "piece" of the corporation, but a right to a certain *proportionate* share of voting power on a restricted list of issues (including the election of board members), declared dividends, and, in the extreme case, the distribution of the corporation's assets. Board member power is related to the relative dispersal of stockownership. *Where stockownership is widely dispersed, board members have low power; where board members represent major blocs of stock, they have high to moderate influence; where shareownership is highly concentrated, only the board members representing the dominant group of owners have high influence.*

Under high dispersion conditions, the incumbent management (chairman and/or the president) controls the solicitation and voting of proxies. nominates all committee chairmen, assigns them to their duties, and controls the internal process of the board. New board members are appointed at the discretion of the nominating committee, which in turn is a creature of the chairman's. In this situation, the board and individual board members are relatively weak.

By possession of a large enough share of votes, a shareowner (or group of shareowners) can press for a seat on the board.[7] Often such representation is equivalent to partial control, for the management wishes to avoid proxy fights and open conflicts. Therefore, the perspectives of the voting block get incorporated in management's decision premises. However, there may be several such blocs.

When one person or family controls a major bloc of stock or even a majority,[8] the power of the board, as a whole, and management declines. Here power is centralized as in the case of the widely dispersed ownership situation, but now it is centralized in the hands of the representatives of the owning family or person. While the "forms" of board action are maintained to satisfy legal requirements, the board serves at the discretion of the controlling owners.

At least since Berle and Means (1932) it has been assumed that the historical trend is toward the dispersal of ownership. This particular generalization has served the interests of those arguing "everyone a capitalist," and it has led to a gross oversimplification of the extent of ownership dispersion. It has also encouraged many scholars to assume that boards are powerless. Villarejo's (1961, pp. 51–52) painstaking analysis indicates that of the largest 232 (out of 250 on the 1960 *Fortune* list) industrial corporations

[7] The ability to "press" for a seat on the board is related to the ability to wage proxy fights and to command the loyalty of other stockholders. The insurgents are more likely to gain other stockholders' loyalties if the company has been unsuccessful in making profits relative to its profit potential. For a dramatic rendering of a proxy fight, see Nizer (1961, pp. 427–524). The ability to press for a seat is also related to the voting rules required by the state. Cumulative voting aids minorities in electing directors (see Williams 1951).

[8] I have been purposefully vague about the percentage of stocks that must be owned by a dominant family. If all other stocks are widely dispersed or held by nonactive groups (e.g., insurance companies, trust accounts in banks, pension funds) even 5 or 6 percent may represent a dominant bloc (see the discussion in Villarejo 1961, pp. 54–55).

for which data were available, the directors as a group owned 5 percent or more of the stock in seventy-six of them. Furthermore, since this does not include stocks of corporations held by other corporations represented on the board, there is no question but that there is even more concentration.[9] Lundberg's (1968, App. B) more impressionistic, but historically rich, analysis would indicate that about two-thirds of the largest 200 corporations have "large" family holdings. Although direct family ownership of a majority of shares may have declined, the control of stock in beneficial trusts combined with direct ownership remains a significant control base.

External Funding and Facilities Control. The general proposition about the external resource base of board members also applies to control of capital and facilities. For many corporations, profit and nonprofit alike, a major source of board member control and influence stems from their control of crucial inputs of capital, raw materials, or "market."

Control of external resources serves as a lever for board power when the organization finds it difficult to secure these facilities from other sources and requires this resource. We would expect greater dependency on the board members representing banks during depressions than during times of prosperity. Furthermore, industries that are debt ridden would be more likely than others to have representatives of lenders on their boards; the railroads, which are a high debt ratio industry, are reported by Newcomer (1955, p. 54) to have a higher proportion of bankers on their boards than other industries she studied. To the extent that organizations can raise money from ongoing operations, both the money market and the money lender become less important to the organization, and external dependency is decreased.[10]

The proposition about external dependency also applies to nonprofit and voluntary agencies. The historic pattern of raising funds has seen a shift from the support of agencies by a few wealthy philanthropists to mass campaigns and community funds. When agencies were the "agents" of one or two families, or a small circle, the policies and procedures were sharply governed by these members of the board and by the chief funders. As funding shifts to the community fund or to mass drives, the power of the board *as funders*

[9] Villarejo (1962, pp. 53–54) also studied the distribution of ownership *among* the directors in these 232 corporations. Of 2,784 directors (individuals, some holding multiple directorships), ninety-nine "propertied rich" (those who inherited their shares or who were wealthy before becoming attached to the company in question) owned 73 percent of the shares owned by all directors. Furthermore, 12 percent of *total* shares could be traced to the propertied rich.

[10] Commentators of the Berle and Means school have argued that as corporations have grown larger their policy of retaining a large proportion of earnings rather than distributing them as dividends (most of the larger corporations distribute less than half of net earnings) leads to the corporations becoming divorced from the money market, and to the decline of importance of the role of bankers and especially investment bankers. A word of caution is in order. Littner (1959, pp. 166–201) has summarized his studies of the rate of borrowings, bond flotation, and the like. His findings suggest that the rate of corporate borrowings has not declined over time—instead it fluctuates inversely with the cost of money. Furthermore, he concludes that even among the largest nonfinancial corporations there is no long-range trend for increased reliance on internal funds.

may decrease. Two corollary hypotheses can be stated for voluntary agencies: (1) *The more agencies receive contributions in small amounts from many givers, the less the likelihood of board members having power vis-à-vis the executives.* (2) *To the extent that fund-raising campaigns are based more on a sharp image of need and less on interpersonal relations of board members and fund raisers, we would expect the influence of the board member to be diminished.*

The growth of community funds has a complex relation to the structure of individual boards. The fund represents a centralized source of financial support, and the amount received from the fund can be crucial to the agencies involved.

The funds themselves allocate money through committees made up of businessmen, housewives, and professionals. To the extent that professionals dominate the funds, we would expect the boards of the agencies to become less important in interceding for the organization. However, students of these organizations suggest that there is a correlation between the prestige of the boards of agencies and their likelihood of having their requests granted a respectful hearing. Auerbach (1961) suggests that the settlement house serving a slum neighborhood but having an unknown board is less likely than the middle-class agency having a prestige ("power") board to receive a favorable hearing. The high-prestige board member may not only be generally respected but may control significant financial contributions to the fund. If Auerbach is correct, the maintenance of a prestige board facilitates relations with the community fund.

Community Legitimation. Board members may control neither shares nor tangible external facilities and yet "control" an important external resource, a segment of community legitimation. They control community legitimation in that they "represent" diverse groups or interests which can be mobilized to affect the organization. Such organizations as boards of education and government commissions have boards either elected directly by the voters or appointed by the political executive. In general, *the more closely board members are linked to external groups, the more they "represent" community legitimation and, therefore, the more powerful they are vis-à-vis the administrative leadership.* Board members may be elected or appointed and yet not represent group interests if, for instance, appointment is "nonpartisan" and if board membership is largely symbolic. The more diverse and intense the interests in a given organization, however, the more likely the organization is to be politicized and the more likely board members are to represent community segments.

All three of the external bases of power discussed above provide opportunities for factions to arise as groups commanding different resources contend for the definition of organizational goals and directions and for control of the organization. *The larger the number of board members having external bases of power, the more likely are coalitions of board members to arise.* Furthermore, given a number of board members with external bases of power, *the more divergent the definitions of organizational goals and policies, the more likely are the coalitions to resemble factions.*

Even if board members do represent external interests, ownership, or sources of funding, factions need not arise and board members need not attempt to influence managerial decision premises. An ideology of professionalism may lead to an effective abrogation of the role of the board. In such cases, the board serves to provide a mantle of legitimation and community justification (Kerr 1964). Only when a given issue is defined as outside of legitimate professional competence will board members' attitudes and perspectives begin to influence decisions. Thus, Crain and Street (1966) note that, in large cities, on the issue of school policy toward desegregation, it is the board and its attitudes, not the school superintendents' professional or personal perspectives, that predict the outcome of policy debate.

Internal Resources: Knowledge. Knowledge is a "detachable" resource in that it can be acquired and lost. Detailed knowledge of the organization and its problems is a *sine qua non* of decision making. The board member or executive without knowledge has difficulty influencing the decision process, especially when there are agreed-upon goals. Knowledge can come from detailed familiarity with the specific organization or from general expertise about a given technical process.

Several conditions of organizational size, complexity, and technology condition the ability of boards to have sufficient knowledge to challenge and/or formulate lines of action. At the most general level, sufficient knowledge is a function of the degree of complexity of the organization and the technicality of its knowledge base. *The greater the complexity of the organization and the more technical its knowledge base, the lower the influence of board members.* The proposition leads us to expect, for instance, that larger organizations, with many product lines or task domains and geographically dispersed units, would have a less well-informed board than smaller, more concentrated organizations.

When an organization is small, with few plants, products, and markets, the directors can have independent knowledge of the plants, contact with the staff at several levels, and detailed acquaintance with the community and market situation. As the organization grows larger, the board member becomes increasingly dependent on the staff for his information. Furthermore, the organization is usually structured to channel information to and through the president or chief operating officer. Thus, the board becomes dependent on the executive, and one of their few outside checks becomes the balance sheet, subject to independent audit. Even accounting reports may become so complex that a high degree of familiarity and expertise is needed for their interpretation.

Of course, as the organization becomes larger and more complex, the chief operating officers also become more dependent on *their* staff. But the staff's conditions of work are directly dependent on the executive, and to some extent he is able to use them as his eyes. Even though the executive is formally appointed by the board, his greater knowledge of the full range of organizational concerns allows him to shape the kinds of information they receive and the kinds of matters they discuss.

Boards may be adapted to this imbalance in knowledge by being required to spend more time on organizational affairs (Brown and Smith 1957, pp. 57–59). Sometimes, the appointment of "inside" board members (full-time executives) is recommended as a solution, but the independence of the officer from the chief executive cannot be assured.[11]

The relevance of knowledge to power becomes even clearer if we examine organizations in which various kinds of professionals and scientists furnish the key services of the organization. For instance, we would expect boards of directors of hospitals to be concerned mainly with financial matters while boards of educational institutions might have a greater say in personnel matters, though not curriculum matters, and finally, boards of such organizations as YMCAs might be involved in decisions about all phases of organizational activity. Where the knowledge base is esoteric, the board is not able to evaluate the requirements of the organization for new lines of endeavor, or to evaluate lines of action and personnel except in terms of fiscal matters.

Again there are adaptive solutions to the imbalance. Boards may delegate to internal committees the evaluation of projects involving technical decision criteria. Second, they may add to the board members with technical knowledge. General expertise, acquired outside of the organization, becomes a base for power.

To this point, I have offered propositions about bases of power which increase or decrease the board members' potential to influence the policies of large-scale organization, focusing on external resource control and the relative imbalance of knowledge. However, this cross-sectional approach is limited in at least two ways. First, I have played down the identities or characteristics of board members that may influence their role in boards. Second, I have ignored the process and phasing of boards that lead them to be more or less important and powerful at different times.

Personal Characteristics and Participation

Attributes attached to persons such as social status, sex, and personality are very general factors influencing how an individual will relate to others and how others will respond. While they are not "detachable" resources (at least to the same extent) as were those discussed in the last section, they are external characteristics brought into the board-executive relation from the larger society, and they affect the participation and influence of board members.[12]

[11] Questions about the functions of inside directors pervade the policy-oriented literature. Wiley (1967) shows that among large corporations there is a slight tendency over time for them to have a greater proportion of outside board members. His findings are at variance with popular stereotypes.

[12] Goffman (1961, p. 30) distinguishes between "external resources" and "realized resources" to discuss the exactly parallel phenomena of how external resources become determinants of interaction locally realized.

Socioeconomic Status. Given the structure of American society and the function of boards in controlling property, in legitimating voluntary agencies, and in linking the activities of diverse institutions, it is not surprising that members of boards of directors tend to be selected from the higher reaches of the stratification system. While some organizations, such as YMCAs and settlement houses may dip into the middle-middle class[13] for a few board members, most board members will be drawn from the higher reaches of the socioeconomic pyramid.

The prestige and status of the board member gives him a reputation which affects others' reactions to him, and it gives him a set of expectations of how others should react to him. In general, *the higher the prestige and status of the member, the more likely other board members and staff are likely to defer to his opinions.*

Of course, reputation and generalized status do not fully determine influence. Strodtbeck, James, and Hawkins (1957) have presented data from jury deliberations indicating that the higher-status jury members are more likely to be chosen as foremen and have high rates of initial participation and, presumably, influence. However, they also note that, over time, the correlation between SES, participation, and influence declines. Generalizing from the findings of Strodtbeck et al., we might expect that, *if the only criteria for allocating influence is participation and knowledgeability, the low-status members who participate highly and are knowledgeable will become equal to the higher-status board members, even though officers will be more likely to be drawn from higher-status members.*

However, if the functions of boards involve more than just deliberation (as in the jury), the external resources of votes controlled, access to funds, and prestige which can be used in interorganizational relations will guarantee to the higher-status board members a greater share of influence. (See the above discussion of the role of "power" boards.) Furthermore, if we compare boards composed of people of different status levels, those in higher-status boards are likely to expect a higher level of deference and influence than boards composed of people from the middle ranks (Moore 1961).

The comments above also apply to the relation of executives *to* boards as well as *among* board members. Some boards employ executives whose salaries and status may be equivalent to or higher than that of the board members (e.g., in some YMCAs and in school boards). If so, executive influence is enhanced.

Sex. Societal role definitions associated with sex also influence board member participation. Babchuk, Marsey, and Gordon (1960) found that, in a middle-sized community, women are more likely to be on boards of smaller and low prestige organizations than on the boards of the larger voluntary agencies—the hospitals and universities. Not only do women have less command of

[13] In our study of the Chicago YMCA, less than 10 percent of the almost 1,000 board members of the thirty-seven local departments were rated in 1961 as earning less than $8,000 a year.

external resources—they rarely represent major bureaucratic organizations—but, on the average, they are socialized to more passive role taking. In boards with male executives, we would expect women to have less influence than men, to participate less freely in discussion, to be less assertive, and to be taken seriously to a lesser degree.

Other personal characteristics also influence board-executive interaction. The range of personality and self-presentation variables that are relevant is well known. Instead of pursuing them, the discussion turns to phases of organizational growth and change that implicate board power. In these last two sections resources have attached to the individual role occupant. But now we turn to power resources attached to the situation, that is, to the role expectations and definitions created by the ongoing social system.

Strategic Contingencies Situations

Examination of the functioning of a board over long periods of time would reveal an ebb and flow of board functions, importance, and power during different phases of organizational development and activity. Organizational phases affect the power of boards in several ways. First, at some points in the history of an organization, the formal requirements of board ratification and action require at the very least that managers get the approval of the board. Even if the board is but a rubber stamp, such periods allow some reinforcement of the image of board power. Furthermore, at such times dissident board members have a chance to crystallize board discontent with management and to express such discontent. At other times, the absence of meetings and debated issues prohibits such expression. Second, the phases of organizational development require the board to perform activities in the service of the organization—such as fund raising—that give it power over the managers. Thus some of our "cross-sectional" propositions (above) may also be implicated in the phase development of organizations.

Let us specify a number of broad organizational problems that not only require board action but also seriously implicate the responsibility of board members to debate and decide organizational matters.

The general proposition is that *it is during the handling of major phase problems, or strategic decision points, that board power is most likely to be asserted.* It is at such times, too, that basic conflicts and divisions both within the board and between the managers and the board are likely to be pronounced. Three types of broad-phase problems are discussed: life-cycle problems, choosing of successors, and fund-raising and facilities expansion.

Life-cycle Problems. Life-cycle problems are those of organization genesis, character formation and transformation, and basic identity.

Organization Genesis. When a corporate organization is newly established, or when the board as a responsible agent is being formed, a great deal of attention is likely to be paid to the formulation of policy, the roles of managers and boards, and the formulation of guidelines for actions. *Boards will meet regularly and often, and it is likely that board power and influence will be continuously used and called upon.*

But qualification is in order; many business corporations develop out of individually owned firms or partnerships. If the new board does not control ownership certification, the power of the board may be relatively restricted during this period.

Character Crises and Transformation. Organizations develop characters which become institutionalized in procedures and modes of handling problems. Organizational character, a term used by Selznick (1957), is the standard pattern developed for resolving recurring and basic problems and conflicts within the organization and with the organization's environment. These include such aspects of organization environment and intraorganization relations as labor policy, major product emphases, market strategies, relation to competitors, and quality-quantity emphases.

Pressures to change these aspects of character almost inevitably become issues for the board of directors. First, both legal requirements and the standard functions of boards in policy setting become obviously implicated when the major dimensions of the organization are subjected to change. Second, if these aspects of character have developed qualities of the sacred and traditional, as so often happens, changing them is likely to develop conflict. The managers will be forced both by divisions among the managers and by the awareness of concerned board members to bring such matters to the board.

In general, *the more routine and stable the organization in all its aspects—for example, labor, market, financing, etc.—the less likely are crises of character to occur and the less likely are boards to be mobilized.*[14]

Moreover, *character crises are likely to be more difficult to solve in organizations without computational criteria*[15] *for choosing among alternatives.* For instance, voluntary welfare agencies with their ambiguous goals and unproven means are likely to have more prolonged debate on such matters than are businesses.

Identity Crises.[16] Large-scale organizations have identity crises of several kinds. One is the crisis of mergers in which the existence of the organization as an organization is threatened, even though there is perpetuation of the function and the capital of the organization. A second is the threat to vanish entirely. A third identity crisis is involved in joint undertakings with other organizations. Such joint undertakings partially restrict the autonomy and independence of organizations.

Because there are often clear benefits to be gained through organizational mergers or joint undertakings, it is possible that business corporations, as a

[14] See an interview with Cordiner (1967), former president of General Electric, for a discussion of the role of the board during GE's internal transformation of organizational structures.

[15] The phrase "computational criteria" refers to known means to agreed-upon goals (see Thompson and Tuden 1958, pp. 195–216).

[16] Identity crises are subcases of character crises—i.e., those subcases in which an organization's social recognition as an entity are at stake.

class of organizations, have a higher rate of identity crises than other kinds of organizations. However, YMCAs, orphanages, settlement houses, ethnic-based community centers, religious denominations, universities, governmental commissions, and others have all faced identity crises—problems of fission and fusion. Again, it is when issues like these are debated that boards are most fully involved and likely to have influence.

Choosing a Successor. Often the only real contact board members have with the organization is through the chief executive, and one of the prime responsibilities of boards is the choice of effective managerial leadership. In some organizations the board chooses only the chief executive, but in others the board may take an active part in appointing most upper executives. The amount of active participation in appointing upper executives is probably a good index of its power. More important here, *it is at the time of choosing a successor that board power is most mobilized* (Zald 1965).

Succession processes can vary greatly. Of course, if a dominant executive or controlling group creates a "crown prince" or appoints the successor, then the board as such only ratifies the appointment. A crown prince appointment by a chief executive (not by a controlling ownership group) can only be effective when a retiring chief has been seen as successful. Thus, just as we suggested that the board is more likely to be active when an organization is involved in crises, so too *is it more likely to be active in choosing a successor when the organization is facing a crisis.*

The choosing of a successor often allows the basic questions of organizational mandate, character, and identity to come to the fore. Since the choice of the executive is so closely linked to decisions about organizational directions, it is natural to have a period of stock taking at that time.

Since the mobilization of board influence occurs around the time of succession, the periodicity of succession becomes of great importance. Because of deaths, age, and career patterns, some boards may be confronted fairly often with questions of succession, while others may only confront this question once in a generation. (Some Protestant denominations appoint their ministers yearly, while many larger business corporations try to arrange for ten-year terms for their chief executives.)

Conclusions

Such phrases as the "managerial revolution" or the "power elite" call to mind great forces and processes in society. Some of the propositions implied by the metaphors are patently true. For instance, it is clear that large bureaucratic organizations are hallmarks of modern society, and, consequently, the heads of these organizations are in a position of potential power. Nevertheless, detailed investigation is required to spell out the conditions of their power and their relative power in different situations. Eventually, a complex theory of power and control in modern society will be required.

Without directly attacking the global questions posed by Burnham (1941) and Mills (1957) we have dealt with one aspect of the phenomena they discuss—the control of major bureaucratic organizations. In particular we have suggested a range of external detachable resources, personal characteristics, and strategic contingency situations that affect the conditions of board power. Many of the hypotheses presented appear fairly obvious. Nevertheless, taken together, this presentation, I believe, demolishes the cavalier approach to boards taken by both economists and sociologists. Boards of directors may sometimes be impotent, and they may sometimes be all-powerful. The question is: In what kinds of organizations under what conditions?

Furthermore, more complex theoretical treatments are possible. Boards may be most implicated in decisions when the unified chain of command is broken up. For instance, as hospitals have come to look more like pluralistic polities, boards may reenter the power arena either at the invitation of the contending parties (Perrow 1963, pp. 112–46)[17] or on their own accord. Furthermore, the stance of the manager may lead to great variation in board involvement and power. Chief executives range from those that are obsequious to their boards, to those that are Machiavellian—manipulating consensus—to those that are disdainful or at least unconcerned with their boards. Executives help to develop traditions of board consultation and influence, and these traditions can become binding upon the organization. Social-psychological variables of interest and commitment are also important, for it may be that lack of interest is a basic cause of the diminishment of board influence.

This work has been largely theoretical. At this point, there is a scarcity of meaningful data, and only at a few points have I been able to tie my arguments to evidence. Boards of directors are hard to study. Often they conduct their business in secret; their members are busy people; the processes themselves are sometimes most effectively described by novelists. Nevertheless, study is possible, and pieces of evidence can be brought to bear. The difficulty of study is more than compensated for by the theoretical and practical importance of the problem.

References

Auerbach, Arnold J. 1961. "Aspirations of Power People and Agency Goals." *Social Work* 6 (January):66–73.

Babchuk, Nicholas, N. R. Marsey, and C. W. Gordon. 1960. "Men and Women in Community Agencies: A Note on Power and Prestige." *American Sociological Review* 25:399–403.

Baltzell, E. Digby. 1958. *Philadelphia Gentleman, the Making of a National Upper Class.* Glencoe, Ill.: Free Press.

Berle, A. A., Jr., and Gardner C. Means. 1932. *The Modern Corporation and Private Property.* New York: Macmillan.

Brown, Courtney C., and E. Everett Smith. 1957. *The Director Looks at His Job.* New York: Columbia University Press.

Burnham, James. 1941. *The Managerial Revolution: What Is Happening in the World.* New York: Van Rees.

[17] Perrow traces out the changing context of board power and involvement in hospital affairs.

Cordiner, Ralph. 1967. An Interview with Ralph Cordiner. *Forbes* 100 (October 15): 30–37.

Crain, Robert L., and David Street. 1966. "School Desegregation and School Decision-making." *Urban Affairs Quarterly* 2 (September): 64–83.

Davis, John P. 1961. *Corporations.* New York: Capricorn Books.

Goffman, Erving. 1961. *Encounters.* Indianapolis: Bobbs-Merrill.

Gordon, Robert A. 1945. *Business Leadership in the Large Corporation.* Washington, D.C.: Brookings Institute.

Heffernan, W. Joseph. 1964. "Political Activity and Social Work Executives." *Social Work* 9 (April): 18–23.

Hunter, Floyd. 1963. *Community Power Structure,* Garden City, N.Y.: Anchor Books.

Kerr, Norman. 1964. "School Board as an Agency of Legitimation." *Sociology of Education* 38 (Fall): 34–59.

Lattin, Norman D. 1959. *The Law of Corporations,* Brooklyn: Foundation Press.

Littner, John. 1959. "The Financing of Corporations." In *The Corporation in Modern Society,* edited by Edward Mason. Cambridge, Mass.: Harvard University Press.

Lundberg, Ferdinand. 1968. *The Rich and Super-Rich.* New York: Lyle Stuart.

Marris, Robin. 1964. *The Economic Theory of 'Managerial' Capitalism.* New York: Free Press.

Mills, C. Wright. 1957. *The Power Elite.* New York: Oxford University Press.

Moore, Joan A. 1961. "Patterns of Women's Participation in Voluntary Associations." *American Journal of Sociology* 66 (May): 592–98.

Newcomer, Mabel. 1955. *The Big Business Executive: The Factors that Made Him.* New York: Columbia University Press.

Nizer, Louis E. 1961. *My Life in Court.* Garden City, N.Y.: Doubleday.

Perrow, Charles. 1963. "Goals and Power Structure: A Historical Case Study." In *The Hospital in Modern Society,* edited by Eliot Friedson. New York: Free Press.

Selznick, Philip. 1957. *Leadership in Administration.* New York: Harper & Row.

Strodtbeck, Fred L., Rita N. James, and Charles Hawkins. 1957. "Social Status in Jury Deliberations." *American Sociological Review* 22 (December): 713–19.

Thompson, J. D., and Arthur Tuden. 1958. "Strategies, Structures and Processes of Organizational Decision." In *Comparative Studies in Administration,* edited by J. D. Thompson et al. Pittsburgh: University of Pittsburgh Press.

Villarejo, Don. 1961. "Stock Ownership and the Control of Corporations." Pts. 1 and 2. *New University Thought,* vol. 2 (Autumn).

———. 1962 "Stock Ownership and the Control of Corporations." Pt. 3. *New University Thought,* vol. 2 (Winter).

Wilensky, Harold L., and Charles N. Lebeaux. 1965. *Industrial Society and Social Welfare.* New York: Free Press.

Wiley, James A. 1967. "Trends in Board of Directors Structure in Industry." Unpublished paper, Vanderbilt University.

Williams, Charles. 1951. *Cumulative Voting for Directors.* Cambridge, Mass.: Graduate School of Business Administration, Harvard University.

Zald, Mayer N. 1965. "Who Shall Rule: A Political Analysis of Succession in a Large Welfare Organization." *Pacific Sociological Review* 8 (Spring): 52–60.

8

Personal Values and Corporate Strategy

William D. Guth and Renato Tagiuri

Some managers may feel that their choices of corporate strategy are entirely objective. This may well be so *if* they include their personal values among the elements they take into account in their analyses and decisions. For it is quite clear, on the basis both of observation and of systematic studies of top management in business organizations, that *personal values are important determinants in the choice of corporate strategy.*

Need for Examination

Unfortunately, our values are so much an intrinsic part of our lives and behavior that we are often unaware of them—or, at least, we are unable to to think about them clearly and articulately. Yet our values, along with other factors, clearly determine our choices, as can be proved by presenting men with equally "reasonable" alternative possibilities and comparing the choices they make. Some will choose one course, others another, and each will feel that his election is *the* rational one.

Problem in Strategy. In early 1961 the four top executives of U.S. Research, Inc. (disguised name), a large research and development company with a high proportion of its business in government work, were considering possible strategies for the future. Three major alternatives had been identified:

1. Attempt to triple, over the next three to five years, the company's volume of business by broadening its base of research "products" and thus capturing a larger share of the then growing government expenditures for space exploration.
2. Aim for the same growth objective, but achieve it through the development of commercially exploitable hardware products generated in the research activity.
3. Aim for a slower rate of growth, continuing the business along the lines in which it had achieved its present position.

The president, convinced that each top executive of the company needed to be personally committed to the strategy finally chosen, held a number of meetings directed at achieving consensus on one of the alternatives. The meetings proved fruitless. All three possibilities were strongly favored by one or more of the officers, each of whom justified his choice as the only "objectively" feasible alternative.

The president believed, on the basis of the evidence available, that all three

Reprinted from *Harvard Business Review,* Vol. 43, No. 5 (September–October 1965), pp. 123–132 by permission of the publisher.

alternatives were equally feasible. It occurred to him that further progress might be made in achieving a personal commitment from each manager if attention were focused on the relationship of the managers themselves to the nature of the alternatives. Using knowledge about *personal values,* he was able to identify differences between himself and the other three top officers which seemed to account for their choices among the strategic alternatives:

- The vice president who favored the first alternative—tripling the volume of business through broadening the company's base of research products—was seen by the president as having the values of a businessman-scientist whose involvement in the company was motivated by a desire to earn as much money as possible while at the same time being associated with the intellectual stimulation of a research "atmosphere." He wanted the company to grow rapidly and become more profitable, but he also wanted it to remain exclusively a research company.
- The vice president who favored rapid growth through the development of commercially exploitable hardware products was seen by the president as having the value orientation of a businessman whose involvement with the company was predominantly motivated by an interest in economic progress as measured by growth and profitability. Rapid growth and increased profitability for the company were his prime interests, along with efficiency and orderliness in the company's day-to-day operations. He believed that the company would, by getting into commercial production, grow rapidly and increase its profitability. Also he believed that competition in the commercial field would create additional concern for efficiency and orderliness in the company's day-to-day operations.
- The third vice president, favoring continuation of the present activity aimed at achieving a slower rate of growth, was seen by the president as having the values of a scientist who joined the company with the principal objective of working on research projects with practical applicability. This vice president viewed the possibility of getting into commercial production with alarm, believing such activity would disturb the company's research climate. In addition, he believed that substantial company growth in any field might lead to bureaucratic organizational practices also potentially inimical to creative research.
- The president saw *his own* values as an almost equally balanced combination of economic, scientific, and human-relations concerns. His involvement in the company reflected not only economic and scientific objectives, but also an interest in working closely and productively with a tightly knit group of men who were all personally involved in the company's efforts.

On the basis of these insights, the president switched from favoring the first alternative to favoring a modification of the third alternative, which called for attempting to double the company's growth in the next five years through continuing the business along the lines in which it had achieved its present position. He believed this new alternative matched the values of the *group* of top executives better than any of the three previously identified alternatives. Armed with this analysis, he was able to lead the group toward consensus on the modified third alternative. The strategy chosen has proved itself successful, and the top executive group of the company remains very satisfied with the choice.

Few of us make the effort of studying our own values to the point of being able to be explicit and articulate about them. The busy executive is no exception. Indeed, being primarily a man of action, he may spend less time over this matter than other people do. Thus many top-level managers do not have an explicit and useful way of thinking about personal values and about the influences these have on the strategic choice processes of the company. As a result, this important element is often left unexamined.

Nature of Values

For our purposes a value can be viewed as a conception, explicit or implicit, of what an individual or a group regards as *desirable,* and in terms of which he or they select, from among alternative available modes, the means and ends of action.

Values are such an intrinsic part of a person's life and thought that he tends to take them for granted, unless they are questioned or challenged. He acquires them very early in life. They are transmitted to him through his parents, teachers, and other significant persons in his environment who, in turn, acquired their values in similar fashion. Child-rearing practices are expressions of a family's values, and of the values of the social group to which the family belongs.

Although there are dramatic cases of deviation from values acquired early in life, an adult's values are usually the result of the interplay of (a) what he learned from those who reared him, and (b) his particular individuality and "times." Undoubtedly, this is not a simple process of faithful transmission from one generation to another. However, much of the process takes place early in life, and this portion of it affects the possibilities for later modifications and acquisitions of values.

As is the case with most important characteristics acquired in the first few years of life, we have difficulty identifying values until we come face to face with situations that force us to recognize their presence in our makeup. Parents themselves, often not being articulate about their own value systems, transmit them and teach them to their children more by means of examples, rewards, and punishments than by the use of words and labels that would make the children explicit about alternative value systems. Nevertheless, language helps and delimits the development of values. Indeed, the value system of a society and its language are often closely related, the language having developed special mechanisms useful for conveying the value alternatives chosen by that society. This sometimes makes it difficult for people to understand the values of other cultures where the language system is quite different.

Values are closely related to personality; indeed, they are part of it. If we say that a man decides among alternatives on the basis of whether the choice will maximize his usefulness to others, rather than on the basis of considerations of personal gain, we are describing his values as well as his personality. Values can be thought of as the guidance system a personality uses when faced with choices of alternatives. They are a very stable feature of his personality, especially if some values clearly dominate over others.

Values may be identified by noting differences between individuals or groups in dealing with similar problems. Naturally, not all differences can be accounted for by variations in values; for instance, some variations are produced by differences in accumulated knowledge and intellectual skills. Yet there appears to be an interdependence among knowledge, skills, and values. Sometimes, a change in the first two will lead to a change in the third.

Contrasting Profiles

Individuals express their value systems in any number of ways: some very abstract, with word labels attached to them, others in unselfconscious, concrete ways, mostly in terms of specific situations and behaviors. In order to treat the subject of values in a way useful to the present task of seeing how they enter into the process of choosing between alternative strategies, we need a scheme that will help us distinguish, classify, and compare values and value systems of individuals, groups, or cultures. Let us look at one such conceptual scheme and at the differences it illuminates in different groups' values.

Classification Scheme. Much has been written on values, on classifications of values, and on the value differences among people, cultures, professions, and generations. One classification of values that should prove quite useful to us was developed by a German philosopher, Eduard Spranger, for the purpose of distinguishing among types of men.[1] He found it helpful to identify six kinds of value orientations:

1. The *theoretical* man is primarily interested in the discovery of truth, in the systematic ordering of his knowledge. In pursuing this goal he typically takes a "cognitive" approach, looking for identities and differences, with relative disregard for the beauty or utility of objects, seeking only to observe and to reason. His interests are empirical, critical, and rational. He is an intellectual. Scientists or philosophers are often of this type (but they are not, as we shall see, the only ones).

2. The *economic* man is primarily oriented toward what is useful. He is interested in the practical affairs of the business world; in the production, marketing, and

[1] *Types of Men,* translated by P. Pigors (Halle, Germany, Niemeyer, 1928). For other instances of classifications and discussions of values, see C. Kluckholn, "Values and Value-Orientations in the Theory of Action," in *Toward a General Theory of Action,* edited by Talcott Parsons and Edward A. Shils (Cambridge, Massachusetts, Harvard University Press, 1951); and Florence R. Kluckholn and F. L. Strodtbeck, *Variations in Value Orientations* (Evanston, Illinois, Row, Peterson and Company, 1961).

consumption of goods; in the use of economic resources; and in the accumulation of tangible wealth. He is thoroughly "practical" and fits well the stereotype of the American businessman.

3. The *aesthetic* man finds his chief interest in the artistic aspects of life, although he need not be a creative artist. He values form and harmony. He views experience in terms of grace, symmetry, or harmony. Each single event is savored for its own sake.

4. The essential value for the *social* man is love of people—the altruistic or philanthropic aspect of love. The social man values people as ends, and tends to be kind, sympathetic, unselfish. He finds those who have strong theoretical, economic, and aesthetic orientations rather cold. Unlike the political type, the social man regards love as the most important component of human relationships. In its purest form the social orientation is selfless and approaches the religious attitude.

5. The *political* man is characteristically oriented toward power, not necessarily in politics, but in whatever area he functions. Most leaders have a high power orientation. Competition plays a large role in all life, and many writers have regarded power as the most universal motive. For some men, this motive is uppermost, driving them to seek personal power, influence, and recognition.

6. The *religious* man is one "whose mental structure is permanently directed to the creation of the highest and absolutely satisfying value experience." The dominant value for him is unity. He seeks to relate himself to the universe in a meaningful way and has a mystical orientation.

Averages for Executives. Spranger's value classification served as the theoretical underpinning for a questionnaire designed to measure quantitatively the *relative* strength of each of the six value orientations in an individual.[2] Recently we gave the questionnaire to high-level U.S. executives attending the Advanced Management Program at the Harvard Business School.[3] The following average value profile resulted:

Value	*Score*
Economic	45
Theoretical	44
Political	44
Religious	39
Aesthetic	35
Social	33
	240

(The questionnaire was designed so as to yield a total of 240 points, distributed over the six value dimensions.)

[2] G. W. Allport, P. E. Vernon, and G. Lindzey, *The Study of Values* (Boston, Houghton Mifflin Company, 1960).

[3] See Renato Tagiuri, "Value Orientations and the Relationships of Managers and Scientists," *Administrative Science Quarterly,* June 1965, pp. 39–51.

Thus the major orientation of these men is a combination of economic, theoretical, and political values. The economic and political orientations are clearly in line with our stereotypes of businessmen. The theoretical value may surprise us, but for a moment only. The high-level executive needs to have theories and cognitive and rational approaches to his work in order to satisfy his economic and political values. He works with and through others; he has to explain, teach, express, be explicit, be rational. And he also has to be abstract, since he is removed from direct operations and has the function of integrating human and material resources. In short, the executive shows up here as a bit of a theoretician while we suspect he likes to think of himself as a man of action.

The values just reported are averages. There are, among executives, enormous individual variations, and it is these that lead to diverse choices among alternatives. Exhibit 1 shows, in order of importance, the values of four individuals, all high-level managers, included in our sample. Each of these cases differs greatly from the average value configuration of the group; yet each man is an effective member of some top-flight team.

Exhibit 1. Value Profiles of Four Top Executives

Mr. A		*Mr. B*		*Mr. C*		*Mr. D*	
Value	*Score*	*Value*	*Score*	*Value*	*Score*	*Value*	*Score*
Religious	57	Theoretical	65	Aesthetic	48	Economic	58
Political	41	Aesthetic	45	Social	44	Political	49
Theoretical	36	Religious	37	Economic	43	Theoretical	37
Economic	36	Political	33	Theoretical	36	Religious	37
Aesthetic	35	Economic	32	Political	35	Social	31
Social	35	Social	28	Religious	34	Aesthetic	28

Such individual differences notwithstanding, our study indicates that the values of executives, *on the average,* are different from the values of men in other professions. In the field of religion, for example, a sample of ministers had values in the following order of decreasing importance: religious, social, aesthetic, political, theoretical, economic.[4] This pattern is virtually opposite to that of the executives.

[4] Adapted from G. W. Allport, P. E. Vernon, and G. Lindzey, *Manual for the Study of Values* (Boston, Houghton Mifflin Company, 1960), p. 14.

Effect on Strategy

How, exactly, do an executive's values affect his thinking about strategy? First, bear in mind that a corporate strategy is an explicit and shared set of goals and policies defining what the company is to achieve and become in the future and how it must operate in order to reach its goals.

Not all companies have corporate strategies. Most executives, however, have personal concepts of what their company's corporate strategy is or ought to be. In the absence of a viable degree of consensus on a particular set of goals and policies, each executive will tend to behave in accordance with his own concept and, in turn, his own values.

Should there be great divergence in the unstated concepts of corporate strategy among company executives, there will tend to be conflict and disorganization in the company's operations, possibly without clear recognition of the source of the difficulty.

Criteria for Strategy. The process by which an individual's concept of or feel for his company's strategy is formulated includes assessment of environmental opportunities and risks and of company resources. Such an assessment results in reasoned or intuitive judgments as to what the company might achieve and become over some period of time if it operates in certain particular ways. The individual's system of values is then applied to these judgments, and a choice among the alternative corporate strategies is made.

Until this last step is taken, the man is not really engaged with strategy. He remains uncommitted, uninvolved in the key choices affecting the company's future and determining its basic character. Since his personal values are such an intrinsic part of his life and behavior, however, he will eventually have to use them as criteria in making his conscious choices. If he is not very conscious or articulate about his personal values, they will impose themselves no less forcefully on his actual choices, i.e., those evidenced by his behavior.

Thus, consciously or unconsciously, personal values are one of the determinants of a manager's concept of what his company's strategy ought to be. For example:

- If economic values clearly dominate his other values, he will be more inclined to emphasize opportunities for growth and profitability and to make strategic decisions which call for stretching or adding to present resources to attain these goals.
- If, on the other hand, other values dominate his personality, he will match his company's opportunities, risks, and resources in terms of the values he does emphasize, possibly at the sacrifice of growth and profitability. Thus, an executive with strong and dominant political values may tend to choose among alternative strategies the particular one which maximizes his opportunity to gain additional power.

Values in Action. The role and influence of personal values are much in evidence in decision making. Consider these two examples:

—The president of National Duplicating Products Corporation, a small manufacturer of office duplicating equipment, ranked relatively high on the social value, giving particular attention to the security, welfare, and happiness of his employees. Second in order of relative importance in his scheme was the aesthetic value. The remaining four values were undifferentiable in importance on the basis of the available evidence.

When faced with increasing product and sales competition from other firms in the industry and with increasing opportunity from expanding markets, the president chose to stay with the company's traditional strategy. The key elements of this strategy were:

- Slow to moderate company growth.
- Emphasis on a single product.
- An independent-agent form of sales organization.
- Very high-quality products with aesthetic appeal.
- Refusal to compete on a price basis.

In addition, this strategy included a policy of refraining from setting time standards or other production-scheduling constraints on the factory workers for fear of "making a slave shop out of the place." Another critical policy set by the president was to spend considerable amounts of money on the maintenance of elaborate physical facilities for both himself and the employees of the company.

The president was aware of many of the economic risks and losses of opportunity entailed by this strategy. But the dominance of his social value over his other values was so great that he chose to take the economic risks and opportunity losses in order to maximize what in his view was the stability, security, welfare, and happiness of the employees of the company, and the aesthetic appeal of his company's offices, plant, and products.

Though not a major stockholder in the company, the president had voting control over a majority of the stock outstanding. This element of the situation helped to minimize the amount of pressure on him to pay greater attention to the satisfaction of economic values.

—Except for the vice president and treasurer, the top management team members of Acoustic Research, Inc., a manufacturer of high-fidelity loudspeaker systems, placed theoretical and social values over other values; the company's strategy reflected this orientation. The key elements of the company's strategy were:

- Scientific truth and integrity in advertising.
- Lower margins to dealers than competitors were paying.
- Maintenance of "truth and honesty" in relation to suppliers, dealers, and employees.
- High quality at the lowest possible price to the consumer (based on a vaguely defined concept of a minimum acceptable level of profitability).

These policies were maintained in the face of significant pressure from the optimistic claims and nonscientific appeals in the advertising of competitors; from dealers, many of whom refused actively to push the company's products;

and from economically oriented outsiders, who insisted that changes in company policies should be made in order to capitalize on the substantial opportunities for growth which existed in the rapidly growing high-fidelity phonograph market.

In both of the foregoing cases it was our judgment as close observers that the top managers involved had realistically assessed opportunities, risks, and resources of their firms. Just as the president of National Duplicating Products Corporation chose to forgo the opportunities for rapid growth and increased profitability in order to minimize the pressures of change and growth on himself and on his employees, so the executives of Acoustic Research chose to forgo the opportunity of greater sales through less "scientific" advertising and more dealer "push" in order to keep the price of their products low and to retain their scientific integrity.

Consistency and Conflict

At the same time that personal values serve as the basic ends or goals toward which an executive would like to see company activity directed, they also affect his decisions concerning implementing policies. If, for example, the dominant value of an individual executive is economic and he faces two new product alternatives promising to yield equal degrees of growth, he may choose one course over the other because it is more consistent with his other values. To illustrate:

- Hugh Hefner, president and founder of HMH Publishing Company, publisher of *Playboy,* worked for several magazines prior to striking out on his own. Having dominant economic and aesthetic values, he found the jobs with other magazines wanting in opportunity to achieve personal satisfaction. Accordingly, he started his own company to publish a magazine which represented his aesthetic point of view. Fortunately for him, his particular form of aesthetic value was shared by many others, and a market existed for *Playboy*. As a result, Hefner not only works each day on something consistent with his concept of what a magazine should be, but his labors also make him increasingly wealthy, bringing economic satisfaction as well.
- The executives and staff of *The New York Times,* according to all published sources of information, appear to have a highly dominant theoretical and social value orientation. Their product—yesterday's news reported intelligently, accurately, and without bias or sensationalism—is apparently valued more for its own sake than as a means to economic ends. This high level of personal commitment to the product has been a defense against increasing pressures to modify *The New York Times* in the interest of economy and expanded circulation. The present product and the pattern of operations supporting it yield at best only moderate growth and return on investment.

For a great many managements, of course, economic values are in fact dominant, and these may come into conflict with other values dominating in other groups in American society. For example:

Some of the pharmaceutical companies have found that their efforts to achieve economic growth and profits through manufacture, distribution, and sale of medicines have come into conflict with the social value of some powerful individuals to whom virtually any effort to relate economic growth and profits with sickness raises the image of unhealthy, unfortunate people being bilked for private gain.

Even publications about the extensive advances in pharmacology made possible by the industry's reinvestment of earnings in research and development have tended to be ineffective against this value perspective. The fact that many companies in this industry have experienced relatively high returns on investment in comparison with industry in general reinforces the negative judgments made of them, rather than serving as an indication of their relative competence as economic institutions.

Steps to Understanding

Businessmen are seldom self-conscious and articulate about their values, although they feel uncomfortable when these values are violated and at ease when they are fulfilled. Also, they often do not clearly perceive the strategy that underlies and guides their business and corporate actions.

The manager could benefit by paying more attention to the operation of his values. He may then be able to kill two birds with one stone; for if his strategy is not explicit and if his values play a role in its formation, then by making his values more clear he may also become more aware of the actual nature of the strategy itself. In addition, he may be better able to analyze the relationship and interdependence between values and strategy.

This is *not* to say that he should try to filter out the influence of his values on his concept of corporate strategy and alter it in order to make, for example, a "hard economic choice." On the contrary, if he understands more exactly the nature of what he is doing, he may be able to attain an even more satisfying match between personal values and corporate strategy. In other words, under conditions of clarity of assumptions, personal values may be allowed to influence the manager's concept of corporate strategy more than they would otherwise, not less.

Self-analysis. How does a manager go about making his values explicit to himself? One thing he can do is examine his behavior from time to time with the question in mind of what values he holds. Here, the approach of comparing and contrasting his behavior with the behavior of others facing similar situations and problems is very helpful. But care must be taken to distinguish variations due to the nature of the information available about the situation and problem from variations that result from different values. The latter is what we are interested in.

This approach has been very effective in helping students in management programs at the Harvard Business School to identify and clarify their personal values. The instructors separate, in the case material, the factual description of the situation from the analysis and corporate strategy choices made by the individual managers actually involved in the case. They then ask the students to make strategy recommendations based on their own analysis of the *situation,* being careful to ensure that the class has a common understanding of the facts. Then they present the students with descriptions of the strategic analyses and conclusions of the executives in the case. Through the process of comparison and contrast with their own analyses and recommendations, the students are often able to achieve some clarification of their personal values.

Another useful approach is for the manager to take time to analyze the situation when he feels that his values have been violated or when he is prompted to explain others' behavior in terms of such phrases as "They have different values." This is the time to note the nature of elusive standards and assumptions—when they are, so to speak, stirred to the surface.

A manager can also learn something about his values by taking one or more of the tests designed to identify the relative strength of an individual's values and by analyzing the results, preferably with the help of an appropriately trained person.

What matters most, however, is the attitude or frame of mind with which the manager approaches the problem of identifying the part his values play in his work. Two requirements are important for him to observe:

1. There must be personal acceptance of the fact that his personal values are related to his implicit or explicit strategy choices. This will in itself make him more sensitive to what they are and how they may operate. Yet this may be a hard first step to take. Some of us have a difficult time accepting our personal involvement in situations, often insisting that we are being completely objective and that anyone who does not agree with us as to the validity and desirability of a particular strategic choice is simply "letting his emotions run away with him." Personal values are always involved in arriving at concepts of and "feels for" corporate strategies, and objectivity consists exactly of taking them into account, as we do with other elements in our analysis.
2. There must be a willingness to focus on personal values as a possible explanation of differences among the concepts of corporate strategy held by various executives. Many of the same forces leading to the struggle for "objectiveness" in business practice lead to suppression of discussion of value differences among executives. The purpose of such discussion should not be to attempt to change anyone's values, a difficult task anyway, but rather to clarify the nature and source of differences and disagreements. It is often possible, through identification of similarities and differences in personal values, to cast up new strategy alternatives that will be more satisfying to all concerned than are those choices initially contributing to the conflict.

Appraisal of Others. Understanding and taking one's own values into explicit account unfortunately is not always enough to arrive at a viable strategy. Where management operates as a team, understanding the values of the other members becomes important if a strategy is to be developed that will gain the genuine support of all concerned. (An example of the successful solution of this problem was given at the beginning of this article.) Here articulate, explicit statements of strategies and their ramifications become especially important, for without them there is no good way for a member of the group to understand what the other members' values are and what they really have in mind.

And there must be a willingness to accept the idea that while other men's values may be different from our own, they are not necessarily better or worse. Such acceptance can result in improved interpersonal relations and effectiveness in a company's executive group. There is no standard or accepted method of proving that one value is better or worse than another, and so it is foolish to view the question in these terms. One may not feel attracted to a person with very different values, but one is not intellectually justified in condemning him for holding them.

People not infrequently misjudge other persons' values. This is borne out by a study of how research managers, scientists, and executives assess each other. The study is based on the questionnaire described earlier and covers nearly 1,000 men who filled out the questionnaire anonymously:

- 178 research managers, in charge of research personnel, who attended the Industrial Research Institute's R & D Management seminars at the Harvard Business School in 1961, 1962, or 1963.
- 157 scientists who have been in industry for at least seven years with no management responsibilities except supervision of research assistants.
- 653 businessmen who attended the Advanced Management Program at the Harvard Business School between 1960 and 1964.[5]

The mean values of the three groups are shown in Exhibit 2 *inside* the body of each "man" representing each set of people. Also shown, on the side of each man, are the values *attributed to him by the others,* as indicated by the arrows. The "attributed" data were obtained by asking each respondent to fill out the questionnaire as if he were a typical member of one of the other two groups.

It can be seen, for example, that the research managers attribute higher economic and political value scores to the executives than the executives actually indicate for themselves. At the same time, the research managers attribute to the scientists much higher theoretical scores than the scientists give themselves. Thus while the research managers correctly identify the high values of the other two groups, they also exaggerate them, and thus perceive the two groups —scientists and executives—as being more different than they really are.

In such cases, finding a strategy acceptable to the people involved is made more difficult by the exaggeration of value differences. The opposite difficulty —assuming similarity of values when not warranted—also is common in

[5] See Renato Tagiuri, op. cit.

Exhibit 2. Values of Scientists, Research Managers and Executives—Self-ratings Versus Ratings Expected from Others

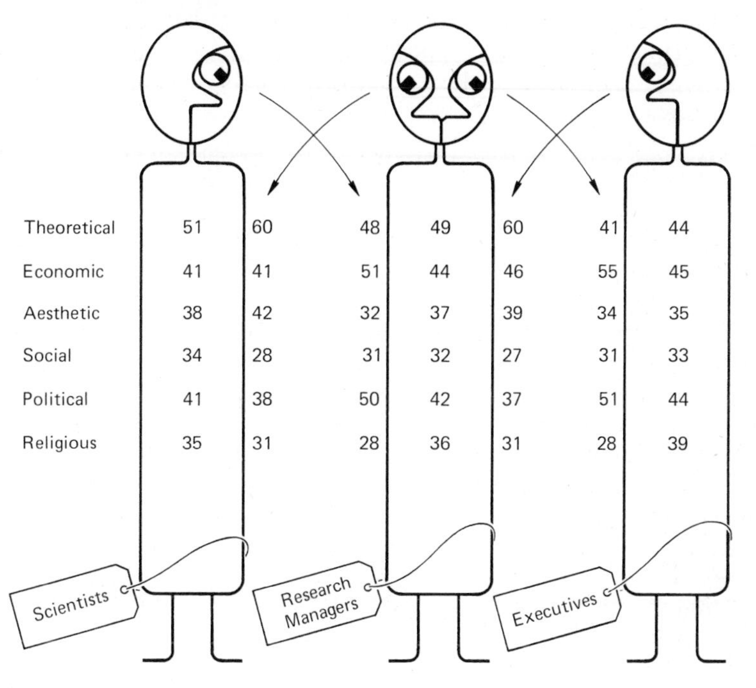

society. When this latter error occurs, a strategy is in danger of failing because it has less consensual support in the value systems of the members of the executive team than those concerned expect.

Conclusion

Personal values influence corporate strategy choices. It is useful for managers to understand this influence in the process of considering strategic alternatives. But what should be the role of values in such decisions? Should they ultimately determine the final choice? Should they be but one of the factors considered? Or should they always be disregarded in an effort to focus exclusively on maximizing the economic use of company resources?

The issues involved in these questions disappear in many situations in which the corporate managers are predominantly economically oriented. In such situations, choices dictated by personal values agree with choices dictated by the maximum economic opportunities which are identified.

In situations where the managers involved are not predominantly economically oriented, however, the issues are brought sharply into focus. We noted earlier that there were enormous variations in the relative importance which a group of high-level executives attached to the six values in the Spranger classification. A number of these executives (a minority) ranked the economic value very low. These executives probably have faced and are likely again to face conflicts in the strategy-formulation processes of their firms when choices dictated by their personal values clash with choices dictated by identification of maximum economic opportunity.

In facing such conflicts, the executives involved might ask themselves two questions:

1. Are there new strategic alternatives which might effect a closer match between economic opportunity for the company and the other-than-economic values which they or their associates possess?
2. How much of an economic sacrifice must be made by the company to serve the other-than-economic values?

If the executive can identify no better alternatives and perceives that the economic sacrifice associated with serving other-than-economic values is great, he may well choose the strategy which maximizes economic opportunity. He may continue his search for new alternatives, however, in the hope that ultimately he can identify a strategy which serves his dominant values well, while at the same time leading toward the maximization of economic return on the company's assets.

In dealing with conflicts between personal values and the maximization of economic opportunity, managers should keep in mind that corporate strategy must ultimately inspire personal commitment or else it will not be implemented. At the same time, of course, the corporation must remain viable as an economic institution.

9

Managerial Behavior and Interpersonal Competence

Abraham Zaleznik

The question of what, if anything, is competent interpersonal behavior and how such competence relates to the functioning of managers have been of long-standing concern to practicing managers, researchers, and educators. The strength of this concern is attested to by the ubiquity of human-relations training within and outside of universities. A central objective of these training efforts is to modify behavior, usually interpersonal, according to some set of norms that relate to organizational effectiveness or improved individual and group performance.

The purpose of this paper is to raise for inquiry the adequacy of existing notions of what interpersonal competence is, how it relates to the manager's

Reprinted from *Behavioral Science,* Vol. 9, No. 2, 1964, pp. 156–166, by permission of James G. Miller, M.D., Ph.D., editor, and the author.

job, and the best means for helping managers achieve this competence. By stating my purpose as *inquiry* rather than *advocacy* I mean to cast doubt on ideas that have been too readily accepted as firm conclusions rather than departures for exploration.

Classes of Executive Functions

Homeostatic Functions

Involvement in interpersonal processes is one dimension along which the managerial career is generally distinguished from other professional careers. This characteristic results from the interpersonal complexities of the organization milieu. Organizations are viewed as systems of relationships, bound together by purposes, ideologies, and expectations that set the organization off from its environment and that also serve to differentiate the many parts of the system. A manager, according to Barnard (1958), operates in two spheres simultaneously. He performs a set of functions that relate directly to the technical aspects of his job, such as deciding on a brand name for a new product, or preparing a capital expenditures budget for the firm. Barnard calls these functions nonexecutive, and they can be expected to vary in content from job to job and organization to organization. Another set of functions that Barnard calls the executive functions of the manager deal with the organization as a cooperative system in which interpersonal phenomena are a significant aspect. To quote Barnard:

> It is important to observe, however, that not all work done by persons who occupy executive positions is in connection with the executive functions, the coordination of activities of others. Some of the work of such persons, though *organization* work, is not executive. For example, if the president of a corporation goes out personally to sell products of his company or engages in some of the production work, these are not executive services. If the president of a university gives lectures to a class of students, this is not executive work. If the head of a government department spends time on complaints or disputes about services rendered by the department, this is not necessarily executive work. Executive work is not that *of* the organization, but the specialized work of *maintaining* the organization in operation. [1958, p. 215.]

Earlier, Barnard states:

> *Organization results from the modification of the action of the individual through control of or influence upon* . . . [(1) purposes, desires, impulses of the moment, and (2) the alternatives external to the individual recognized by him as available.] Deliberate conscious and specialized control of them is the executive function. [1958, p. 17.]

The juxtaposition of these two quotations serves to raise one fundamental issue in considering the nature of interpersonal competence as an aspect of the executive role. Barnard stresses as the core of the executive function the problems arising from personal and interpersonal attributes of organizations as systems of cooperation. With his emphasis on executive work as "the specialized work of *maintaining* the organization" he implicitly points to interpersonal behavior of the executive that is directed toward assuring the internal stability of the organization. This function may properly be related to the homeostatic processes discussed by Cannon (1915, 1945), whose concept of an organism suggests that certain automatic devices must operate within the system to maintain a steady state in the face of changing conditions in the environment.

Following this line of thought, one's attention is then directed toward an understanding of the interpersonal processes that are associated with *maintenance* of this organization. These processes we shall refer to as the interpersonal behavior directed toward the *homeostatic* functions of the executive.

Mediative Functions

The second part of the quotation from Barnard cited earlier produces a note different from maintenance. "Organization results from the modification of the action of the individual through control and influence." This statement suggests that the executive function proceeds through a kind of intervention, not directed necessarily toward maintaining a steady state, but directed instead toward altering behavior and attitudes with conscious intent. The way behavior is to be altered presumably is determined by the organization's problems of mutual adaptation with its environment. We can conceive of the environment as establishing a press on the organization, requiring some internal change. The executive function, then, is to influence individuals and groups within the organization to modify behavior and attitudes so that some different adaptation to the environment is established.

This second set of executive functions we shall call *mediative,* since it is concerned with internal change in response to environmental press. Now presumably mediative functions imply certain kinds of interpersonal processes that may or may not be different from the homeostatic. We shall return to this issue because, as it should be clear, we are attempting to analyze the different interpersonal processes with which managerial behavior is concerned, and to reexamine competence in terms of the *multiple* functions of the executive rather than a single function that dictates a rather limited kind of interpersonal activity.

There is still a third kind of executive function that is not too clearly delineated by Barnard or other students of organizations. If we were to seek for a set of continua along which to describe the executive functions, particularly those implying different modes of interpersonal behavior, one such continuum clearly implied in the discussion so far is the passive-active.

The homeostatic function is positioned toward the passive end of the scale, since it views the organization as a system tending toward a steady state. The way the steady state is maintained presumably depends on an interpersonal process where the executive intervenes least. He uses instead the existing forces within the system to permit the modest alterations necessary to return to the steady state. The problem is comparable to the healing process in medicine which adopts a conservative point of view concerning the role of the physician. This view was stated well by Cannon and is worth quoting:

> The fathers of medicine made use of the expression, 'the healing force of nature' . . . it indicates, of course, recognition of the fact that processes of repair after injury, and restoration of health after disease go on quite independent of any treatment which a physician may give. [1932, p. 240.]

Earlier, Cannon stated:

> The ability of living beings to maintain their own constancy has long impressed biologists. The idea that disease is cured by natural processes . . . an idea which was held by Hippocrates (460–377 B.C.) implies the existence of agencies which are ready to operate correctively when the normal state of the organism is upset. [1932, pp. 20–21.]

If only by analogy, we can visualize the homeostatic functions as requiring very modest activity on the part of the executive to set in motion forces already existing within the organization to reestablish the steady state.

While space does not permit detailed illustrations, it would be worthwhile to note the types of situations that involve homeostatic processes in organizations. A good instance would be one where an internal disruption such as vying for informal leadership takes place in the otherwise cooperative relations among a group of employees. Such a disruption can occur at any level in the organization and requires the introduction of a corrective procedure. This procedure often consists of listening to the complaints of involved persons and helping them to assess reality. Such executive behavior is homeostatic in character and calls for a relatively passive response.

The mediative functions are more active in character than the homeostatic functions. The primary difference arises from the source of the stimulus. Mediative processes occur under the impact of environmental press. A set of forces in the environment creates the need for internal adaptation. As indicated above, the homeostatic functions become necessary where internal disruptions act as stimuli.

Mediative functions require a more active mode of behavior, since they tap into functions that only managers can perform. Because of their location in the organization, managers stand closer to the environmental processes than do other employees, and the higher the manager's status, the more he becomes concerned with issues arising outside the boundaries of the firm.

In response to environmental press, the manager activates change. He formulates goals, and communicates them within the internal network of the organization. Comparing the mediative with the homeostatic functions, the mode of interpersonal behavior tends to be more aggressive and less permissive in the former. Nevertheless, the aggressive mode has certain limits in mediative functions. When it is possible, for example, to separate goals and objectives from means and procedures, managers may seek to limit aggressive responses to the formulation and communication of goals while withdrawing in favor of informal processes for establishing means and procedures. Something of this pattern occurs under conditions of decentralization in an organization.

Proactive Functions

We are now ready to examine the third class of executive functions underlying the various modes of interpersonal behavior. It would be grossly inadequate to leave executive behavior restricted to the homeostatic and mediative functions. Ordinary observation shows a type of executive function that actively seeks out environmental possibilities. Instead of being reactive to environmental press, the behavior is proactive and in a sense induces changes in the environment to conform to the creative use of resources available within the organization. We need not dwell too long on establishing the significance of proaction. The automobile, for example, did not emerge from environmental press, but rather from innovative behaviors of certain individuals who used a new level of scientific and technological sophistication. Let us for purposes of discussion call the third set of executive functions the proactive, although innovative would do just as well.

All too little is known about the psychology of proactive behavior, and this area of our understanding is at the frontier of knowledge. But what we do know suggests a conversion and release of aggressive energy directed toward altering the environment. It is anything but conservative, and typically becomes the type of managerial behavior that in its interpersonal frame tends to induce resistance, counter-aggression, and in some cases outright hostility. We should note also how sharply the proactive set differs from the more conservative homeostatic and mediative sets. In terms of the primacy of goals, the homeostatic function stresses maintaining the stability of the system as the fundamental goal, sometimes to the point where it becomes a substitute for activity in the environment. Proaction, on the other hand, disrupts internal relations in the service of changing the environment.

To recapitulate, we have implicit in the delineation of three sets of executive functions, homeostatic, mediative, and proactive, a series of dimensions that relate to modes of interpersonal behavior, cognition, and problem-solving. These dimensions include the passive-active, conservative-innovative, inward-oriented–outward-oriented (in relation to the environment), a narrow-wide effective scope of thought and relationships. (Lazarsfeld & Thielens, 1958, pp. 262–265), a short-range–long-range span of thought.

It should be quite evident from this discussion of executive functions that the differences in modes of behavior implied in each of the three types of functions is significantly different. Just how these differences become manifest in organizations and with what consequences requires far more research than has been done to date. But enough is available to underscore the basic differences. It should also begin to be clear that any consideration of interpersonal competence has to center on just what executive functions the competence is directed toward. I shall return to this issue later in the paper. In the meantime, I should like to shift the course of this discussion from the functions implied in an analysis of organizational requisites to the nature of personality development and character structure as these are pertinent for an understanding of the inner determinants of interpersonal behavior.

Personality Development and Interpersonal Behavior

The psychoanalytic study of personality and character provides, in my view, potentially the fullest and most challenging statement of the conditions in human development that determine the way executives pattern their role within the framework of the three types of functions discussed above.

The three sets of executive functions provide the nucleus of a description of an individual's adaptive mode. In establishing a career and in developing an organized way of working, the individual manifests the state of his ego organization. Reflected in this organization are the precipitates of the identifications with objects important in the individual's personal history. Successively, the mother, father, teachers, and later authority figures provide the building blocks out of which a unique ego may emerge. Coupled with the identifications, the ego also contains the residues of competencies that the individual has cultivated, learned, and expressed in the course of his life history. These competencies reflect his constitutional endowment and the way it enters into transactions with the environment. Did the individual activate talents, cultivate them, and express them in ways that resulted in rewards from his environment? If so, these successive experiences of producing and being rewarded help form a core sense of self-esteem and a basic knowledge about the talents one has and those one does not have. This sense of self-esteem yields a tendency to seek situations and experiences where one can make the greatest use of himself. I have preferred in other contexts to call this tendency "leading from strength" rather than weakness. It is paradoxical, yet borne out by observation, to note that the tendency to lead from strength is a developmental gain that assures continued growth. The reverse, leading from weakness, reflects a developmental failure where a stage in the person's history resulted in unsolved problems of significant proportions. The learning process failed, and in an effort to master the unsolved problems the individual seeks in his current reality to repeat the experiences of the past, but usually with the same negative outcome (S. Freud, 1922).

A third relevant aspect of the ego organization is the nature of the individual's defenses and the energy available for work and human relationships. Psychic energy, its biological derivations and the process by which it becomes converted into action, remains a mystery in psychology. Psychoanalytic theory assumes that a basic energy reservoir exists undifferentiated as an aspect of biological endowment (S. Freud, 1927). In the course of development, primitive drive energy becomes free of intrapsychic conflict, is neutralized and then is available to the ego for goal-directed activity and expressivity (Hartmann, 1958). A certain portion of the available energy becomes engaged in defensive processes to control anxiety that arises from dangers of intrapsychic conflicts (A. Freud, 1937). The ego defenses are a normal and necessary part of ego development, but when a disproportionate share of available energy is utilized in defending against anxiety, then presumably less is available for utilization in need satisfaction and work. Under these conditions, the individual functions with relatively severe construction of the ego, and has difficulty in career development as well as in human relationships.

The state of the ego as reflected in identity, self-esteem, and energy utilization is genetically determined. The genetic hypothesis in psychoanalytic theory views development as a function of a biologically determined timetable in which sexual development proceeds according to a pattern of shifting zones of excitation. Interacting with the changing zones or centers of instinctual excitation are the changing relevances of object relationships and the demands of society (Erikson, 1959; S. Freud, 1949). Each stage in development helps establish the conditions under which the successive life stages are experienced.

Now one of the most common sources of confusion in the minds of many people concerning Freud's theory of human development is the belief that Freud viewed development as effectively concluded and sealed off by the time the individual experiences the oedipal-phallic stage of development and enters the latency period (approximately age six). This erroneous belief probably exists because emphasis is in fact given to the three stages of infancy as major precursors of later development. Freud did not, however, suggest that developmental processes in later life stages are irrelevant. Rather, he established the crucial role of the formative years, and part of the unfinished business in developmental theory is to establish the connections among all the stages of the life cycle, including the career years.

Predispositional Sets

In considering the issues of interpersonal competence in the managerial role, we are faced immediately with problems of understanding development in the career years, as these relate both to earlier and later stages in the life cycle. By the time an individual joins an organization to embark on a managerial career, he has established internal sets that frame how he seeks to engage his environment. The sets represent essentially the direction of emotional energy outward, or the individual's energy cathexes. The objects toward which the cathexes are directed are of two main kinds: persons and ideas. In one internal set the individual may direct his emotional energy toward the tasks —technically, we speak of his cathecting the idea aspects of work. The personal and interpersonal aspects of work are not cathected to the same degree and may even, in fact, be defended against (Moment & Zaleznik, 1963).

A second internal set consists of a strong orientation toward persons—the cathexis is directed toward human relationships. Tasks may assume relatively little significance in the individual's inner need and value structure, and in fact the cognitive-technical aspects of work may be defended against. To indicate how these two predispositional sets relate to stimuli in the environment, let us examine a data specimen from my current research.

A population of professional personnel completed a series of imaginative stories written in response to ambiguous pictures, part of the series in Murray's Thematic Apperception Test (1938). Two of the pictures showed a single individual. Each of the two pictures was otherwise unpopulated. A simple analysis of the story content designed to measure the extent to which respondents populate their stories with persons showed a sharp division between two groups among our respondents: those whose manifest career goal is along a technical route, and those whose goal is along a managerial route. As you might expect, the managerial subgroup wrote stories involving interpersonal situations while those in a technical career route had few persons in the story plots. We would assume that the extent to which an individual's fantasy world incorporates other persons reflects his outward orientation toward other individuals.

A third predispositional set represents a fusion of cathexes. In this case, the individual in his inner world weighs both persons and ideas as important to him and blends them in his concerns with situations in the real world.

A fourth set exists which is real enough, but which for purposes of this paper had best be excluded from consideration. This set can be characterized as conflicted or ambivalent, in the sense that the cathexes are shifting and subject to immediate internal resistances and conflicts.

The three main predispositional sets we have presented in our discussion of individual development (cathexis of persons, ideas, and a fusion of persons and ideas) represent the center of outward concern of the ego. These concerns are a product of the ego processes discussed earlier (identification, self-esteem, and energy utilization) and emerge through the various precareer stages of the life cycle. We have some evidence suggesting how the ego processes are related to the formation of the predispositional sets and it would be useful to cite some of this evidence, although it must be viewed as highly tentative at this stage (Moment & Zaleznik, 1963).

Ego Processes and Predispositional Sets

In terms of identifications and identity formation, the person-oriented individual tends to have been influenced far more by the feminine figures in his life than by the masculine. His dominant identification trend is passive-feminine. Just how this trend occurs is subject to alternate explanations, ranging from excessive maternal dominance with relatively passive male influences in his development, to traumatic experiences in the infancy stages of development.

The identification patterns for the fusion types represent the results of parents who tended to minimize role differentiation. Both parents were capable of and showed affection and nurturance while exercising influence and dominance. In the case of the idea set, parental role differentiation appeared sharply drawn along classical lines. The mother appeared affectionate and nurturant, while the father appeared distant, cold, but also influential in the course of development. The distant father should not be confused with the laissez-faire father. The idea set suggests a strong identification with a cold father who himself probably cathected ideas against persons in the career setting.

In terms of self-esteem, the idea set appears to have a strong sense of competence and self-worth, although it may manifest itself later in life than in the case of the fusion set. In our culture, the idea man comes into his own relatively late simply because the earlier stages of latency and adolescence are rooted in interpersonal settings. The idea man tends to show a history of individual work, while his counterparts in the fusion sets excell in sports and group activity, but not necessarily to the exclusion of good school work. The self-esteem of the fusion types revolves around a sense of being with others in cooperative activity. Our data do not permit many statements regarding the self-esteem issues of the person-oriented set. While appearing congenial in interpersonal settings and valued as friends, they are less valued for leadership functions. We should also note the fact that a male who is strongly person-oriented may not fare too well in our culture, largely because his activity may be incongruent with the types of performances that receive the more tangible rewards. Furthermore, a male whose dominant identifications are passive-feminine may be subject to self-doubting and reduced self-esteem.

Self-esteem is built in part through intimate experience with the cycle of productivity and reward. An individual acts and produces; he is evaluated and rewarded. This simple 2-step cycle is important for building competence and self-esteem. We should not ignore the significance of environmental opportunities in this cycle because it is here that we see the effects of relative deprivations associated with membership in the lower social classes. Individuals with backgrounds in lower socioeconomic classes generally have less environmental opportunity and consequently less direct experience with a productivity-reward cycle that is free of anxiety.

With the introduction of the concept of anxiety, let us examine briefly the energy-utilization process in ego development as it relates to the three predispositional sets under consideration. We suggested earlier that energy available for work, interpersonal or otherwise, is derived from the sources of instinctual energy that is neutralized and freed of internal conflict. Available energy is also a function of the defensive requirements of the ego in its efforts to ward off anxiety. No individual can be free of anxiety and a system of defenses. Nevertheless, an excessive proportion of energy for defensive purposes results in a constriction of the ego (S. Freud, 1959).

We can speculate, based on various kinds of evidence, on the defenses characteristic of the person, fusion, and idea predispositional sets. The person set defends against conflict and aggression. The conscious attitudes are generally altruistic as against egoistic, with strong identification with the underdog. The idea set supports aggression but defends against feelings, particularly the more tender and ambiguous feelings frequently encountered in human interaction. The fusion set may in the net have less need for strong defenses than the other two types, but the system of defenses would be mobilized to assume responsibility and to internalize conflict, both of which are highly socialized mechanisms. Responsibility and internalization are defensive insofar as they counter instinctual wishes of a potentially regressive character. When these defenses become excessive, one observes in such individuals marked feelings of guilt and depression (Moment & Zaleznik, 1963, Ch. 8). This defensive aspect of responsibility is even more significant if it becomes tied to fear of loss of love and approval.

This brief and somewhat oversimplified discussion of ego processes in the predispositional sets will serve as a foundation for our later consideration of the development of interpersonal competence through educational procedure. Before we can consider this issue more directly, we have one further piece of work ahead of us.

We have indicated so far the existence of at least three classes of executive functions that are organizational requisites—the homeostatic, the mediative, and the proactive. These functions define the shifting emphasis of managerial behavior from concern with internal processes (homeostatic) to concern with changing the environment (proactive). On the side of the individual who assumes a managerial role, we have examined the developmental issues that affect the condition of the ego as it presents itself in the work career. Here, our intent was to differentiate three predispositional sets that determine the particular way the individual builds his career on the one hand, but *that* is, on the other hand, determined by the individual's history and experience. We called these predispositional sets person-oriented, fusion-oriented, and idea-oriented.

The questions we shall pose at this juncture are as follows: What are the interrelations between the executive functions and predispositional sets? Although we may need to speculate, can we foresee how the various predispositional sets will interact with the executive functions?

Interrelations Between Functions and Sets

Our approach to these questions follows from arranging the two variables in the form of a matrix, as presented in Figure 1.

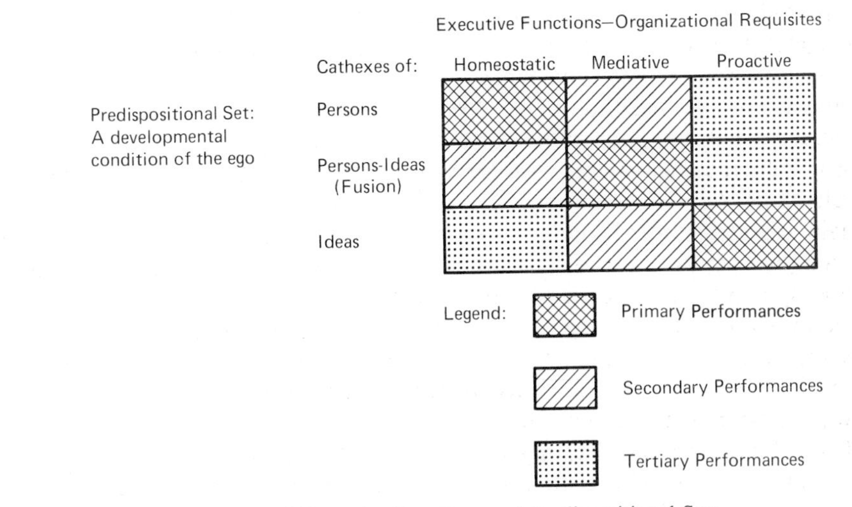

Figure 1. The Interaction of Executive Functions and Predispositional Sets

The matrix in Figure 1 permits us to ask several questions: (1) Would there be a tendency for an individual with a dominant set of one kind to select for specialization one of the three executive functions? (2) What types of interpersonal modalities are represented by the specializations implicit in each cell? (3) From the point of view of organizational effectiveness, does optimal managerial behavior imply the capacity for flexibility in interpersonal modalities, or is there a requirement that the functions be performed within a constellation of executive roles that exemplify mutuality and complementarity? (4) From the point of view of individual development through the career years, should emphasis be placed on flexibility in both functions performed and consequent modifications of the underlying predispositional sets? (5) Or does individual development proceed more fruitfully by optimization of performance within an existing predispositional set?

We can only speculate on the answers to these questions, since these serve to indicate new avenues for investigation, rather than as issues that can be decided on the basis of existing evidence.

It would seem that the predispositional sets are conducive for performance within specialized functions. This idea is expressed by the shadings within each cell. While every individual can probably shift interpersonal modes to conform to the various functional requisites, each set would appear to be selectively oriented toward a particular function. The person-oriented individual would perform most easily in the range of interpersonal behaviors associated with the homeostatic functions. We would assume that such an individual would, relatively speaking, avoid proactive functions. Under conditions where proaction was thrust upon him and avoidance became difficult, the defensive apparatus of the individual would be under stress.

The idea-oriented individual, on the other hand, would perform most easily in the proactive functions, utilizing aggression and dominance as major components of his interpersonal style. Presumably, the homeostatic functions are not well understood by a proactive individual and may be strongly avoided. To continue our speculations, organizational effectiveness would seem to require as a prerequisite some mix in the performance of executive functions to assure both the securing of purpose and the maintenance of the internal capacities of the organization. Parson and Bales (1955) express this most clearly in their view of a social system. The achievement of a purpose, or work, requires the release of energy, the engagement in aggressive-competitive activity directed toward solving problems. This activity results in buildup of tension that, beyond a certain level, must be discharged to assure the continuity of the system. Tension-release processes are closely related to the homeostatic functions discussed earlier. Activity in a social system, then, proceeds in cycles of tension buildup and tension release. Following this broad hypothesis, the absence of relevant executive functions can result in the reduction of organizational effectiveness.

There are two main competing views presented for understanding the structure and dynamics of executive performances. As a result of experimental work with small groups in problem-solving activity, Bales and his associates present the view that the effectiveness of a social system depends on a distribution of functions to appropriate specialists (Bales, 1953; Slater, 1955). The task specialist exercises leadership through task performances; the social specialist exercises leadership through his efforts to restore the equilibrium in the system by emotional expressivity and tension release. This view sees leadership as occurring in bipartite distribution of executive functions.

The bipartite model is prototypical insofar as it represents the condition in the nuclear family where the maternal figure is equivalent to the social specialist and the paternal figure to the task specialist. This model may well be oversimplified, yet it presents an excellent point of departure for the exploration and analysis of performances in social systems.

The alternate view, implied in a paper by Benne and Sheats (1948), views organizational effectiveness as the result of flexible performances by individuals who are capable of responding according to the demands of the situation. Benne and Sheats, like Bales, start with the assumption that functional requirements of a social system are of two kinds: task and maintenance. But, rather than establishing joint leadership according to the bipartite principle of specialization, they develop the view that both organizational effectiveness and individual development are enhanced under conditions of distributive leadership, where the social system is of a kind that permits all members to become flexible in their interpersonal performances and to meet the changing situational requirements.

This view is most closely associated with the group dynamics movement but is also an accepted premise of most workers in the human relations field, whether or not they are students of Kurt Lewin and his followers (Argyris, 1962; Bradford et al., 1953; Roethlisberger et al., 1954). These two positions lend themselves to many significant comparisons including the values implicit in each, their scientific validity, implications for a theory of interpersonal behavior in organizations, and implications for management education and development. It is to this last comparison that we shall now devote attention.

Education and Development

Role Specialization. Depending on which of the two views one adopts, the implications for managerial training and development differ. The theory of role specialization would not necessarily attempt to establish one ideal of role flexibility. It would view performances of the individual as an aspect of his ego development and character structure that is itself genetically determined. The dynamics of developmental experience become the main sources for understanding the type of functions an individual will assume in his managerial role. To a certain extent most individuals do perform within a range of the behavioral spectrum—extreme specialization occurs under conditions of severe restrictions in personal development. To broaden further the range of behavior may in and of itself require marked alterations in personality structure that are not feasible within the limits of educational processes, and are not necessarily desirable. Role specialization, then, is viewed as a condition *within which* education seeks to improve interpersonal performance. To attempt to achieve competence otherwise ignores the constraints of developmental history and may involve ill-advised direct attempts at shifting the defensive and adaptive balance the individual has achieved.

A further position in role specialization views alterations in interpersonal performances as guided by the individual's stage in the life cycle. The young man embarking on a managerial career will most likely be sensitive to social processes because of his own needs for security and membership. In his early thirties, a shift can begin in his performances where he stresses, relatively speaking, ideas and technical functions rather than social processes. Other shifts can also occur during other periods in his career development.

The alterations in performance are contained within the individual's dominant cathexes, but reflect individual concerns and situational pressures that are specific to particular phases of development. One would therefore conclude that a single overriding objective of increased flexibility in functions performed would be difficult to achieve, if not irrelevant for certain stages in the career period of the life cycle.

Role Flexibility. The second view, that of role flexibility as a normative principle in training for interpersonal competence, assumes in the first place that situational constraints are strategic in determining managerial performance. The kind of social system in which one performs will establish through the structure of behavioral norms permissible limits on behavior. By altering the norms, one achieves increased flexibility, especially as this is supported by appropriate training methods and experiences.

Educational procedures following this second set of assumptions seek to establish an ideal type of social system based on broad philosophical foundations of democracy and the scientific method (Bennis, 1962). With this ideal culture, individual growth, which includes flexible performances and distributive leadership, flourishes.

The proponents of this second view, while placing the strategic variable for interpersonal competence within the social system, tend to ignore the developmental determinants of individual behavior. Their view is in keeping with a liberal tradition of social reform, but the object of the reform is the organization rather than the individual. How organizations or societies can change apart from individual change is still an open question.

One further distinction between the individualistic-organizational frames of reference is important for our purposes, although it has been implied in the previous discussion. An individualistic frame of reference seeks to avoid the highly charged and abstract philosophical constraints characteristic of the organizational reform groups. Broad normative premises become molds to which individuals have to adapt and in this sense are inconsistent with a philosophy of education for individual growth.

Conclusions

Professional education for a managerial career rightfully concerns itself with issues of competence in the management of human affairs. It is here that the behavioral sciences may make a lasting contribution to business. A danger exists, however, when certain normative premises are accepted without critical scrutiny. One such set of premises seeks to establish criteria of interpersonal competence within a tradition of organizational and cultural reform, ignoring the significance of what has been learned of human development.

It is fallacious to describe the managerial role and interpersonal behavior underlying it in terms of one set of ideals, especially a set of ideals that are attributes of a culture. There are many different types of managerial role performances that present different configurations of interpersonal behaviors. The validity of a performance can be understood in terms of its relation to ego development, not in its degree of conformity to cultural ideologies. One set of behaviors that conforms to cultural norms may exist at the expense of a tenuous internal balance in ego functioning. Another set of behaviors may violate tenets of good human relations practice, but represent a developmental continuity that builds successively upon new ego strengths. This latter position, I believe, contains the greatest degree of validity and, in the final analysis, may result in a highly moral individual.

References

Argyris, C. *Interpersonal Competence and Organization Effectiveness.* Homewood, Illinois: Dorsey and Irwin, 1962.

Bales, R. F. "The Equilibrium Problem in Small Groups," edited by T. Parsons, R. F. Bales, & E. A. Shils, *Working Papers in the Theory of Action.* Glencoe, Illinois: Free Press, 1953, pp. 111–161.

Barnard, C. *The Functions of the Executive.* Cambridge, Mass.: Harvard University Press, 1958.

Benne, K. D., and Sheats, P. "Functional Roles of Group Members," *J. soc., Issues,* 1948, pp. 4, 2, 41–49.

Bennis, W. G. "Towards a 'Truly' Scientific Management: The Concept of Organization Health," *Industrial Management Review,* 1962, pp. 4, 1–27.

Bradford, L. P., et al. *Explorations in Human Relations Training.* Washington: National Training Laboratory in Group Development, 1953.

Cannon, W. B. *Bodily Changes in Pain, Hunger, Fear and Rage.* New York: Appleton-Century-Crofts. 1915.

Cannon, W. B. *The Wisdom of the Body.* New York: Norton, 1932.

Cannon, W. B. *The Way of an Investigator.* New York: Norton, 1945.

Erikson, E. H. "Identity and the Life Cycle," *Psychological Issues,* 1959, pp. 1, 18–49.

Freud, Anna. *The Ego and Mechanisms of Defense.* London: Hogarth, 1937.

Freud, S. *Beyond the Pleasure Principle.* London: International Psychoanalytical Press, 1922.

Freud, S. *The Ego and the Id.* London: Hogarth, 1927.

Freud, S. *Three Essays on the Theory of Sexuality.* London: Imago, 1949.

Freud, S. *Collected Papers,* Vol. 5. *Analysis Terminable and Interminable.* New York: Basic Books, 1959.
Hartmann, H. *Ego Psychology and the Problem of Adaptation.* New York: International Universities Press, 1958.
Lazarsfeld, P. F., and Thielens, W. *The Academic Mind.* Glencoe, Illinois: Free Press, 1958.
Moment, D., and Zaleznik, A. *Role Development and Interpersonal Competence.* Cambridge, Mass.: Division of Research, Harvard University, 1963.
Murray, H., et al. *Explorations in Personality.* New York: Oxford University Press, 1938.
Parsons, T., and Bales, R. F. *Family, Socialization and Interaction Process.* Glencoe, Illinois: Free Press, 1955.
Roethlisberger, F. J., et al. *Training for Human Relations.* Boston: Division of Research, Graduate School of Business Administration, Harvard University, 1954.
Slater, P. E. "Role Differentiations in Small Groups," edited by A. P. Hare, E. F. Borgatta, and R. F. Bales, *Small Groups.* New York: Knopf, 1955, pp. 498–515.

10

Corporate Behavior and Balance of Power

James M. Patterson

Concern over the ethical implications of business behavior is a recurring problem that remains stubbornly unresolved. Furthermore, the problem is not trivial. We live in what has frequently been called a business society, and the social role of the businessman is a dominant one, influencing the tone of our everyday life. Other reasons for this continuing interest in the ethical responsibilities of business are especially worth noting. One has to do with the phenomenal growth of the large corporation as the major economic institution. By whatever measures one chooses—earnings, sales, employment, assets, or value added—the large corporation looms large on the social landscape.

For example, General Motors had sales of $22.8 billion in 1968. This is more than the gross national product of all but about fifteen nations of the world. It is far in excess of the gross revenue of any state and is roughly 20 percent of that of the federal government. Furthermore, GM provides about one out of every fifty manufacturing jobs in the United States; it pays $1 of every $12 in dividends paid by manufacturers.[1] In 1967, the largest five industrial corporations had assets of roughly $50 billion. Approximately 130 manufacturing corporations account for one-half of the total U.S. output,

Reprinted from *Business Horizons,* June 1969, pp. 39–52.

[1] *The Wall Street Journal,* Feb. 10, 1969, p. 1.

and the 500 largest embrace nearly two-thirds of total nonagricultural economic activity.[2]

These huge modern corporations also have wide discretion in their decision making. The decline of competition as the ubiquitous regulator of corporate conduct, the separation of management from ownership, and the increasing judicial willingness to allow management wide latitude in exercising its legal obligations to ownership all add to this discretion.

Another reason for this continuing, if not increasing, concern with business ethics stems from the increasing dependence of the ordinary citizen on the large corporation for employment and general well-being. Fifty years ago, it was not a matter of critical concern that a firm chose to be opportunistic in its location policies, that it used hiring criteria that ultimately excluded culturally deprived persons, or that it raised its prices faster than its productivity. Taken separately, the number of jobs involved or the economic and social impact of such decisions was not that large—absolutely or even relatively. Not so today!

Furthermore, the ability to escape from corporate dominion—the "reign of corporate rules"—is now considerably diminished. Boulding has described this bureaucratization of economic life as an "Organizational Revolution."[3] Whatever it is called, the ethical content of business behavior is now too important to ignore.

Recent Approaches

Attempts to spell out the ethical responsibilities of business and to influence the character of business behavior have proceeded in a variety of ways. One common approach has been to apply various ethical concepts such as equity, fairness, justice, and honesty to business problems.[4] Specific practices or types of recurring problems are examined and judged by the commentator. Where the practice or policy is considered irresponsible or unethical, the commentator indicates what changes would in his opinion produce an ethical or responsible result. Such an approach can be described as ethical criticism.

Others have approached the problem of ethical responsibility in business in a slightly different way. Instead of trying to second-guess the executive, they have sought to help him decide what is ethical or responsible. Leys, for example, has developed a series of deliberative questions that offer ethical guidance when answered by the decision-maker.[5] These questions are distilled from major philosophical schools. Some examples are:

[2] *The Fortune Directory,* June 15, 1968.

[3] Kenneth E. Boulding, *The Organizational Revolution* (New York: Harper & Brothers, 1953).

[4] For recent examples, see Thomas M. Garrett, *Business Ethics* (New York: Appleton-Century-Crofts, 1966); Thomas A. Petit, *The Moral Crises in Management* (New York: McGraw-Hill Book Company, 1967).

[5] Wayne A. R. Leys, *Ethics for Policy Decisions* (Englewood Cliffs, N. J.: Prentice-Hall, Inc., 1952).

What are the probable consequences of alternative proposals?
Which policy will result in the greatest possible happiness for the greatest number?
Is the practice right? Is it just? Honest?
Does the policy put first things first?
Are you treating humanity as an end and not merely as a means?
What will relieve the conflicts and tensions of the situation?
Does the proposed solution anticipate consequences in the larger environment as well as the immediate situation?

Finally, some have argued that the problem of ethical responsibility in business is essentially contextual, and that the search for general answers is inappropriate.[6] They argue that each situation is in a sense unique, and that what is ethical or responsible is a function of the facts and circumstances of the specific situation.

The frustrations of ethical criticism need little elaboration. For example, take the rule, "Thou shalt not steal." Is accepting gifts or entertainment from a prospective supplier or taking "payola" for playing a new record on the air "stealing"? Furthermore, equally prominent ethical principles are often in conflict, leaving the decision maker to take his choice. For example, the the principle that all persons should be treated equally may conflict with the principle that all persons should be treated fairly. Eastman Kodak's recent battle with the militant Negro group FIGHT over whether Negroes should receive preferential or only equal employment opportunity is this type of situation.

The deliberative question approach escapes some of the problems of ethical criticism, since it focuses on problem solving instead of abstract speculation. When it is not possible to get wide agreement on an ethical course of action, one can at least use these questions to eliminate courses of action that most observers would agree to be clearly unethical. Still, this approach runs into trouble when the implications of a decision are complex and hard to trace, or when they involve a trade-off of one "good" for another.

The situational or contextual approach has gained a considerable following in recent years and is commonly used in business school courses dealing with the social problems of business. Typically, such courses ask the student to react to a complex case situation and, on the basis of open discussion, to make up his own mind about what represents the responsible or ethical course of action. Such an approach has also been used by executives in making marketing decisions in a going concern. This approach has considerable merit in sensitizing actual or potential executives to ethical problems. Unfortunately, since unanimity seldom results, situational evaluations are much better at highlighting the issues than they are at guiding action. Also, to the extent that the discussion is among persons who do not have a real stake in the situation,

[6] See, for example, Joseph Fletcher, *Moral Responsibility: Situation Ethics at Work* (Philadelphia: The Westminster Press, 1967).

the participants often underestimate the complex personal motives, loyalties, and commitments that characterize decisions in real life.

This overview of some of the main approaches for treating the ethical problems of business is not intended to be comprehensive; it seeks only to highlight the difficulty of delimiting ethical behavior in business. In a great many important areas of business activity, knowing the right thing to do is still far from clear, even for sincere men of good-will. And in those few cases where the right course of action is clear, pursuing it may be difficult or impossible, given the competitive or organizational setting in which it must be implemented.

Executive and Corporate Ethics

A key difficulty that has hampered analysis in business ethics results from a failure to distinguish between those areas of choice that are essentially personal, and which might be called "executive ethics," and those areas where choices are made in the name of the company, and which might be termed "corporate ethics." In the first category, the problem is not so much determining what rules are appropriate as it is applying accepted ethical rules to the specific issue at hand. For example, if we are talking about a possible conflict of interest, we would probably all agree that an executive should not—in his capacity as an officer of one firm—deal with another firm where his judgment about the interests he is charged to serve in his executive capacity is affected. This problem is reasonably well settled in law. If the personal interest in the transaction is large enough to cloud the executive's judgment or to make a difference in his decision, the transaction is unethical and perhaps illegal. The only problem is how large an interest must be to produce this cloudy judgment.

The problems in the area called corporate ethics are clearly different. It is not so easy to develop operational rules for deciding what is proper; a consensus is hard to come by. If a company is considering moving from its present location in order to realize certain tax and labor cost advantages in a new location, what rule is applicable? How is a company to decide whether the responsible decision is to stay where it is and put up with a militant union and high local taxes out of some sort of loyalty to the host community and to its employees, or whether it should take advantage of a tempting industrial development subsidy and nonunion work force in the new location out of loyalty to its shareholders and other constituents. Questions of pollution abatement or the hiring of disadvantaged but unqualified persons are other examples of corporate policy not easily resolved.

It would thus seem to be a mistake to treat executive and corporate ethics as though they were similar. In one case, the problem has to do with applying an agreed-upon rule to a specific personal action. In the second case, there is no agreed-upon rule for evaluating what is essentially a corporate action. It is this latter area which is the prime interest of this paper; it is frequently referred to as the social responsibility of business.

A Structural Approach

Another difficulty traditional approaches have had in dealing with the problem of ethics in business results from a failure to factor the ethical problem down into its essential elements. It would aid analysis considerably if we would define precisely the nature of the particular relationship about which an ethical issue centers. The classes of relationships in business about which we are ethically concerned are not all alike, and we are hampered when we implicitly treat them as though they were. The law has not been so naive. It is a well-established legal principle that the duty one owes another arises out of the specific nature of the relationship between the parties in question:

> The most valuable moral lesson the law can teach concerning loyalty (responsibility) is the lesson of relations. . . . The duty always remains a function of the relation. . . . By the same token, there can never arise in anyone's moral life an indefinite, unlimited duty of loyalty to any one creature or institution. Loyalty—however light or intense it may be—always has reference to a defined and specific relation. . . .[7]

If it is true that duty arises out of the nature of the relationship, it would appear to be helpful to examine some of the ways that relationships can vary. Relationships can be conflicting or cooperative; they can be satisfying or unpleasant; they can be continuous or intermittent; and so on. One especially relevant dimension of variation is along the power-dependence continuum. In fact, it might be argued that unless there are ties of mutual dependence —that is, unless the parties have an interest in influencing or controlling each other's conduct—there can be no ethical problem.

Power Dependency. When mutual dependency exists, as it does in most business relationships, the problem of power necessarily emerges and becomes a key element in defining the ethical requirements of the relationship. Obviously, this power dependency difference underlies the difference in legal liability referred to earlier. There is a greater dependence, and hence power, in a trust relationship than there is in a bailment. It follows that a trustee has a greater liability than an ordinary bailee.

By definition, power resides implicitly in dependency. It is as though they were the two sides of a coin. The dependence of one party provides the basis for the power of the other. Formally stated, the power of *A* over *B* is equal to the dependency of *B* on *A* and vice versa. There is, of course, no reason why the power of *A* should be equal to that of *B;* there can be and often is an imbalance of power. It is the analysis of this differential power between *A* and *B* both in terms of its scope and source that serves to define the respective duties of one to the other. In other words, the responsibility *A* owes to *B* is a function of this power differential and vice versa.

Consider the situation where the power of *A* over *B,* which is derived from the dependence of *B* on *A* is greater than the power of *B* over *A,* which is in

[7] Edmond Cahn, *The Moral Decision* (Bloomington, Ind.: Indiana University Press, 1955), pp. 151–52.

turn derived from the dependence of *A* on *B*. Such an imbalance could arise for several reasons. Ultimately, it is due to the fact that the desire *B* has for goals mediated by *A* is greater than the desire *A* has for goals mediated by *B*. Specifically, this difference may be the result of a number of different practical reasons. It may be because *B* has fewer alternatives for satisfying his goals than does *A*. It may be that *A*'s ability to absorb loss or to wait for goal satisfaction is greater than *B*'s. Or *A* may have better access to relevant information than *B* or may possess greater analytical skills or more experience. Each of these situations could create a dependency imbalance and hence a power imbalance.

The resultant inequality can be dealt with in two basically different ways. First, and most obvious, the extent of the power inequality can be determined and the specific derivative obligation can be defined. This is the most common approach. The second approach takes a different tack. Rather than accepting the power imbalance and then specifying the obligations, it seeks to eliminate the power imbalance, and hence the source of the need for defining obligations in the first place. This is a key strategy, for once the power imbalance is destroyed, the reciprocal duties can be determined by mutual bargaining between *A* and *B*.

This approach has special merit in those situations where the obligations that follow from the power imbalance are not obvious and are not easily inferred. The duties of a trustee may be inferred quite clearly from an analysis of the nature of the imbalance in the trust relationship; the duties of an advertiser or supplier may not be so easy to infer. In fact, in many corporate relationships, it is much easier to identify the power imbalance than it is to see clearly the nature of the obligations that this condition implies. In such cases the bargaining solution has great appeal; in fact, it may be the only workable strategy.

There are several ways of correcting a power imbalance. Balance can be established either by an increase in the dependence of *A* on *B* or by a decrease in the dependence of *B* on *A* in one of four ways:

Reduce the dependence of B on A

1. *B* can reduce his desire for goals mediated by *A*.
2. *B* can cultivate alternative sources for gratification of these goals.

Increase the dependence of A on B

3. *A*'s desire for goals mediated by *B* can be increased.
4. *A* can be cut off from sources other than *B* for achieving these goals.

Note that two of these ways of establishing balance (2 and 4) can be manipulated by outsiders as well as by *A* and *B*. The first and third are essentially personal, and can only be altered by *A* and *B* themselves. Note further that the fourth can be achieved by coalition formation—by *B* combining with *A*'s other alternatives, and by presenting a common front in order to increase their collective power relative to *A*. Unionization of the work force or a conspiracy among competitors to restrain trade represent familiar examples of this method of enhancing or balancing power in a relationship.

In sum, what is proposed is that we should assess the power dependence dimensions of the various relationships in corporate ethics and then, on the basis of this analysis, either specify the reciprocal duties when they are clearly implied, or introduce various structural changes to bring about a balance of power that reduces the need for definition of duties. Once balance is established, the reciprocal duties can be determined by bargaining between the parties concerned.

There is sound precedent for this balance of power approach in the political sphere where the control of power has long been a central concern. In fact, if there is a lesson to be learned from the historical evolution of the "rule of law," it is that the structural approaches for controlling power (for example, separation of powers, specific delegation of duties, the reservation of other powers, and other checks and balances) have been much more satisfactory in controlling power than the substantive limitations of the "Thou shalt not" variety.[8]

There are business precedents as well. Collective bargaining, the extensive disclosure requirements of the Securities Exchange Act, the Day in Court Act for automobile dealers, and the Truth in Lending Act are all structural devices for creating a workable balance of power in business. Instead of trying to specify the substance of the relationship, the strategy has been to try to create a balance of power by protecting the weaker party at the point of maximum vulnerability—for example, loss of job or franchise or inability to obtain relevant and reliable information—and then to let the parties work out the terms of the responsible relationship for themselves.

These and other devices demonstrate some of the strengths and weaknesses of this structural approach. They also provide a basis for evaluating the possibility of extending it into other areas where the question of responsible behavior has recently emerged.

Antitrust. The strategy of maintaining competition that underlies the antitrust movement represents the prototype of the structural approach for dealing with the problem of responsible business behavior. The classic explanation of how free market forces channel scarce resources into preferred uses and ultimately distribute them in ways that maximize consumer welfare is well known. When prices and other economic decisions are determined by the free interplay of market forces, there is no need to inquire whether they are just or ethical. No actor in the system has the power to behave arbitrarily with respect to any other actor. The structural constraints of the system completely eliminate power. And when power is absent, so is the need to consider whether a resultant decision is responsible. It is only when there are imperfections in market structure and economic power differentials emerge that the need arises to consider whether a price is just or a wage is fair. Consequently, the proponents of the antitrust approach argue that, to the extent market power

[8] Abram Chayes, "The Modern Corporation and the Rule of Law," in Edward S. Mason, ed., *The Corporation in Modern Society* (Cambridge, Mass.: Harvard University Press, 1959), p. 25ff.

can be reduced, the need to evaluate economic decisions is also reduced.

Stigler has long argued that steel and various other industries should voluntarily move in the direction of increasing competition. Otherwise, he argues, they are inviting public utility status, that is, detailed substantive government intervention into many economic decision areas.[9]

Labor Relations. Recent developments in labor relations in the United States further demonstrate this balance of power concept in operation and point up strengths and weaknesses of fostering coalitions among the weak so that they can present a united front against the strong. The National Labor Relations Act no longer allows the powerful employer to arbitrarily and unilaterally determine the terms and conditions of employment. Public policy, in effect, now says: "We do not think this unilateral determination is proper. Nor do we think this is an area where outside authority (courts or legislature) has a clear view of what specific terms and conditions are in fact proper. Rather, we think the better approach would be for equally powerful parties to jointly bargain over the terms which are to govern their own relationship."

To implement this approach, the law sanctions collective bargaining and requires the parties to bargain in "good faith" and to refrain from certain practices such as termination of employment for union activity. The approach sought primarily to specify the *structure* within which the relationship was to function. Except for minimal substantive provision, such as the requirement to bargain in good faith, the approach was silent on the terms of the relationship. Wages, hours, operating rules, grievance procedures, fringe benefits, and even the appropriate subject matter of collective bargaining were to be determined by collective bargaining, not by fiat of external authority.

Power Balancing Problems. While the Wagner Act exemplifies one aspect of the balance of power principle in operation and highlights its advantages, some of the problems that have emerged in labor relations since 1935 point up certain difficulties with this approach. A primary problem, which in the labor relations setting resulted in the Taft-Hartley Act, is to keep the power in balance. Furthermore, encouragement of the growth of power in order to deal with a problem in one set of relationships often may upset a balance that was working in another set and therefore create other problems. For example, the sanctioning of collective bargaining and the certification of an exclusive bargaining agent on the basis of a majority vote of the employees, along with acceptance of the union shop arrangement and the check-off, led to an imbalance of power between the union and the individual employee. Solving one problem sometimes merely creates another.

Third-Party Side Effects. Perhaps a more important disadvantage in the balance of power approach is the problem of third-party side effects, or what in some cases the economist might call externalities. One of the problems the Taft-Hartley Act sought to redress through its injunctive procedures and cooling-off periods was the harmful side effects to the public of a long strike

[9] George Stigler, "The Case Against Big Business," *Fortune* (May, 1952), p. 123ff.

in key industries, where continued operation is essential to public health and safety. It was clear that the public had a stake in the "bargain" that was reached and that a bilateral balance of power which resulted in a stalemate overlooked this interest. This problem is even greater in the case of public employees. The power to collectively withhold one's contribution is a key factor in bargaining. And yet, in certain cases, disagreement is intolerable if it cuts off a vital service to the public. The public's interest is not so much in the actual terms of the bargain but in assuring that the parties come to terms without interruption of service.

Cost-Push Inflation. A related problem is one that emerges in connection with cost-push inflation. Here, it is not the lack of labor-management agreement so much as it is the actual inflationary terms of agreement that cause a problem. In so-called administered price industries (industries where firms have some market power), management is free, in the short run at least, to pass on wage increases in the form of higher prices. Thus management may be more inclined to agree to higher wage demands than would be the case if the increase were coming out of profits. The result is that the terms of a bilateral bargain worked out between two equally powerful parties may have undesirable side effects on others.

When side effects are present, the answer may be not to abandon the bargaining approach, but rather to supplement it by enlarging the scope of negotiations and requiring that all relevant interests have a say in the bargaining process. This could be done by allowing certain third parties to have at least a veto power over the bargain. Other checks and balances such as public opinion can also be used creatively by having the bargain take place in the public limelight. There is need for imagination here.

Manufacturer-Dealer Relations. The manufacturer-dealer conflict illustrates another structural approach for dealing with the ethical problems of a significant business relationship. In the mid-1950's, tensions between the major automobile manufacturers and their dealers were given a public airing by two Congressional investigations. The hearings revealed a substantial power imbalance between the auto manufacturers and their dealers, and the possibility of unilateral and arbitrary behavior by the manufacturer. The terms of the franchise agreement that governed their relations were clearly stacked in favor of the manufacturer, and the dependence of any single dealer on his manufacturer-supplier was greater than the reverse. In such a situation, the relationship could be abusive. Hence, the behavior of the manufacturer with respect to his dealers raised a question of equity and fairness, that is, it posed an ethical problem.

Several solutions were possible. The power imbalance theoretically could be dissolved by fostering collective bargaining on the part of the franchised dealers, or by marshaling public opinion on the side of the dealers. However, this did not prove workable since the dealers, who typically saw themselves as independent businessmen, had traditionally resisted organizing effort.

Another solution might have been for the manufacturers to acknowledge an obligation to treat their dealers objectively and assure a kind of due process of law. This would require them to establish equitable objective rules to govern the relationship and to create an impartial means for their day-to-day administration. This approach also proved to be unacceptable, since there was no widespread agreement on what rules ought to govern the relationship. Certainly, there was no reason to give the dealers what they wanted. To do so would probably have resulted in higher prices, reduced competition, and a general decline in the efficiency of distribution. And yet there was considerable merit in the dealers' grievances. How is one to know when the relationship is equitable?

This ambiguity about appropriate rules is, you will remember, a characteristic of the substantive approach generally. The same defect is also present in the third possible solution: Congress could spell out the content and terms of the relationship. But since there was no agreement on what the proper relationship should look like, an imposed relationship would also be arbitrary.

The solution finally adopted showed considerable wisdom. In effect, Congress asked, "What is the basis of the manufacturer's power over the dealer?" The answer seemed to lie in the manufacturer's unilateral ability to terminate the one-year franchise on short notice or to refuse to renew it when it automatically expired. Instead of getting snarled up in trying to specify the substance of the relationship. Congress said, "Let's check this power and then let the parties work out the terms of their own relationship." This was a structural solution of a different sort than that used in the labor relations case, where the power of the weaker was increased. In the manufacturers dealer case, the power of the stronger was reduced.

Under the pressure of adverse public opinion and with the threat of governmental intervention looming in the background, Congress was able to get the manufacturers to extend the terms of the franchise from the previous one-year pattern. In addition, Congress enacted a law that allowed any terminated dealer to challenge the action in the federal courts if he felt he had been terminated in "bad faith" as that term is interpreted in the common law. This right of redress in the courts had previously been denied. The manufacturers also agreed to allow disputes to be arbitrated by an independent umpire. This was counter to the previous arrangement, when disagreements could only be appealed to divisional managers of the manufacturing firms without benefit of counsel or subsequent appeal.

Social vs. Private Costs. It would be naive to suppose that all problems of corporate ethics can be resolved by either increasing the power of the weaker party or reducing the power of the stronger. We have already encountered the third-party side effects problem. There is still another. It stems from the fact that social costs and economic costs are not always coextensive. In such cases, the market-determined outcome may be socially deficient. But, even in this case, structural arrangements other than power balancing can be developed to bring the two types of costs closer together and to make the market outcome responsible.

The straight market solution to the problem of pollution abatement, for example, is clearly defective since the social cost of dumping waste into the environment is not taken into account in the private economic calculation. On the other hand, clean air or pure water may represent completely unrealistic social objectives. The problem is therefore to determine what level of polution satisfies the public interest. The solution becomes one of balancing the benefits (both social and economic) of producing goods and services in a particular way against the costs (both economic and social, including environmental pollution) of that mode of production. This is a problem that lends itself ideally to structural, as opposed to substantive, solutions.

For example, it is entirely conceivable that the social costs of pollution for a particular airshed or watershed could be estimated for various levels, and that these costs could be imposed on the private economic calculation, perhaps via variable taxes. If society is still willing to pay more for the output than the total costs of producing that output, then presumably the public interest is satisfied even though some pollution remains. That level is the responsible level.

The Consumer Area

Although structural solutions to problems of business responsibility have been successfully applied in the past, it would, of course, be a mistake to assume that all problems of corporate ethics can be so resolved. It is perhaps inevitable that in some relationships an element of power must always remain, and in these cases, judgments about the wisdom and equity of decisions must be made. However, such cases are rarer than one might at first suppose. For example, the structural solution may have application even in the area of consumerism, which suffers from an inherent weakness; while other groups seem to combine naturally to further their interests, consumers seem to lack a community of interest and are difficult to organize. There has never been a vital consumer movement in the United States. Consequently, one would expect the consumer relationship to be one that would be difficult to treat structurally. It would be a useful test of the generality of the structural approach to see if it can be effectively applied in this relationship.

For a number of years now, especially since President Kennedy's 1962 message to Congress on protecting the consumer interest, there has been a heightened concern over the marketing practices of American business. Consumer credit practices, high-pressure selling techniques, bait merchandising, ghetto dweller exploitation, shoddy products, unsafe autos, marketing games and trading stamps, crass and excessive advertising over the airways and along highways, poor service, unsatisfactory warranty performance, and dozens of other practices have come into the public spotlight.

The response has been twofold. On the one hand, there are those who argue that "there ought to be a law." On the other hand, there are those who argue that business should assume the responsibility for putting its own house in order. True, this second response is often prefaced with the warning that if business doesn't act, government will, and that if government does act, business will not like the results. More often, the argument for self-reform is based not so much on the fear of government intervention as on a moral conviction that there are problems in the buyer-seller relationship and that they ought to be resolved. To some extent, both approaches have been followed. Business has in fact made a number of reforms, and various sharp practices have been voluntarily curbed when they have come under public scrutiny. Also, new legislation has been enacted—truth in lending, truth in packaging, and the auto safety law come quickly in mind. But any objective appraisal suggests that the sum product of these moves makes only a small dent in the problem. The nature and extent of business responsibility in the consumer area as well as the appropriateness of various forms of government intervention in the buyer-seller relationship are still hotly debated.

Rise of the Seller's Power. In large measure, the consumerism problem emerges because of the failure of competition to protect the buyer's interests automatically and satisfactorily. There has been a breakdown of a fundamental structural arrangement for resolving the questions of customer rights and seller's duties. And, despite thousands of public relations speeches to the contrary, there is clear and present evidence that this balance of power continues to shift in favor of the seller. In part, this unfavorable shift can be blamed on an antitrust policy that has yet to deal effectively with the issue of bigness, but it is primarily due to other causes—especially in the consumer goods area.

In large measure, this shift in power is due to the basic nature of an advanced and affluent economy. For competition to effectively balance buyer-seller power in the marketplace, the consumer must be informed. But in a market where the average supermarket carries 8,000 to 10,000 items and where even clothing is subject to technical change in fabrics and finishes, not to mention the mechanical and electronic complexity of most durables, the art of spending has truly become a backward art. The average buyer is bewildered, to say the least. In addition, merchandising strategies that stress brand image and reference group themes, and that play down potentially relevant information about operating characteristics and physical properties, have not helped. And yet, given its competitive setting, no single firm can act unilaterally to counter this trend without serious chance of loss. Ford's unsuccessful attempt to emphasize safety in design and advertising in its 1956 models is a case in point. The social-psychological forces that underlie purchase behavior cannot be ignored—nor should they be. But they do create a problem for the informed choice.

Further, the widespread disagreement over what operating features and physical properties are critical to an informed purchase of many of the complex products of modern technology compound the problem. Anyone in the least familiar with the problem that testing organizations such as Consumers Union face in deciding what factors ought to be rated knows how arbitrary this decision must frequently be.

In sum, we have a fundamental corporate relationship that is not only out of balance, but one which is perhaps even accelerating in its imbalance. Can this imbalance be checked by structural means, must the seller assume special duties, or must the government specify the substantive nature of the relationship? Lack of agreement on the specific nature of the rights and interests of the buyer and seller much beyond what is contained in the law of deceit argues for the use of the structural approach if at all possible. In any event, one point is clear—the maintenance of the status quo is no longer possible, and standing pat is not a viable option. Further, the problem with the relationship is not so much the accidental product of the Ralph Naders and the Rachel Carsons or even of the temptation to try to make political hay by dragging a bunch of corporate big shots over the congressional coals with full television coverage. The problem is due to a power imbalance, and any imbalance of power is always unstable and must sooner or later lead to reform.

Possibilities of Structural Reform. As a starting point in appraising the possibilities of structural as opposed to substantive reform in this area, it will be useful to distinguish between those relationships that involve the voluntary use of a product and those that involve involuntary use, as when one has no alternative but to drive one of a number of unsafe automobiles or consume pollutants and residues if he is to eat certain foods.[10] It is perhaps inevitable that the government must act substantively to prescribe tolerable levels of safety and proper standards of quality. This becomes doubly true when third-party side effects are present, as is the case with the unsafe automobile. Substantive intervention may also be necessary in those cases where markets such as housing or public accommodations are not open to all persons on equal terms. And substantive reform may even be necessary in the production and marketing of tobacco products and liquor, though it is less obvious that this is true. But for most situations where the purchase and use of the product or service is voluntary, and there are no third-party side effects, substantive measures should be avoided until the structural remedies have been exhausted.

The Information Gap. An obvious structural remedy for restoring some semblance of balance in the seller-buyer relationship would be to increase the quantity and quality of information readily available at the point of purchase. To the extent that the seller's power is derived from the buyer's ignorance, this is crucial. The recent truth-in-packaging and truth-in-lending legislation is in this vein and will help restore balance. For example, in a 1963 shopping experiment conducted by the California Office of Consumer Counsel, a panel of college-educated women failed in 34 out of 70 simple attempts to buy the most quantity for their money when purchasing fourteen categories of staple food items in a supermarket.[11] And this was just a test of their ability to evaluate

[10] I am indebted to Ralph Nader's excellent article, "The Great American Gyp," *New York Review of Books* (Nov. 21, 1968) for this point. This idea is also expressed in his interview in *Playboy* (October, 1968), p. 73ff.

[11] E. B. Weiss, "Marketers Fiddle While Consumers Burn," *Harvard Business Review* (July–August, 1968), p. 45ff.

price-quantity relationships; no effort was made to measure their ability to get the most value for their money. One of the results of this information gap has been that shoddy products tend to drive out the good ones, and competition forces firms to cut quality in order to compete with low-quality price cutters rather than to improve quality as a competitive strategy. The result is a sort of market version of Gresham's Law.

"Truth-in" legislation is supposed to counter this trend toward quality deterioration and is based on the theory that if companies know that products can be quickly and conveniently compared with others, they will be compelled to improve their offer. Unfortunately, the mere disclosure of a minimum set of facts such as weight, volume, and contents is a necessary but not a sufficient condition for making competition an effective regulator of quality. Only if the buyer has information about quality and performance, as well as quantity, and only if facts are somehow linked to satisfaction in use will competition serve to reward the producer of superior products and drive out the shoddy.

For example, if the buyer has no basis for deciding whether a hand-wired chassis is better than one using printed circuits, or if solid state is better than transistorized, how is he to choose rationally even if the "facts" are disclosed? Facts in a purchase situation don't speak for themselves any more than they do in other contexts. What is needed, if the buyer is not to be at the mercy of the marketer or advertising copywriter, is consumer-oriented information at the point of purchase. Only then will the checks and balances of the market work effectively to protect the buyer and to restore a balance of bargaining power in the buyer-seller relationship.

There are several ways of providing this information. Existing independent sources could be expanded, perhaps with public subsidy, and the results could be made readily accessible to all buyers in a form that would be relevant to their purchase decision. Or the government could itself undertake to generate this type of information. In fact, this may be the better approach. Sen. Philip Hart has proposed a National Consumer Service Foundation, which would use computers to assemble individual product information cheaply and quickly and transmit it to shopping centers and other decentralized locations close to the point of purchase. For example, a shopper who has narrowed her choice of an appliance down to three or four brands could request a print-out of relevant information, which she could then use as the basis for making her final selection.

No one, however, should underestimate the difficulties of such an undertaking, nor the associated problems of getting buyers to use the information—even when large-ticket items are involved. Theoretically though, there is no reason why it couldn't be made to work.

Opening Avenues of Redress. Another possible structural reform that would help restore a balance of power in the buyer-seller relationship would be to streamline and otherwise to open up the avenues of redress for buyers who have been deceived, defrauded, or in some way bilked. Given the small unit value of many items one purchases, or the small value of the loss one suffers in the malperformance of large-ticket purchases, the expense of litigation effectively precludes normal legal remedies. Many producers hide behind this knowledge. This is true even in the case of otherwise reputable companies as the recent congressional hearings on automobile warranties have disclosed.

However, if refunds had to be made in cash and if disputes involving less that $1,000 could be adjudicated by a local arbitrator, the automatic policing of the market would improve. The recent experiences of the Office of Economic Opportunity in providing ghetto neighborhood consumer and legal advisory services represent a workable pilot model which could be generalized easily, and would help restore a balance of power.

Reform in the law of garnishment and repossession and a general upgrading of the legal rights of debtors so that they are on a par with the rights of the creditors would help, as would a careful overhaul of the court system and its procedures. These would have special impact on those markets where slum merchants have been using the courts to exploit the poor and ill-informed. The proposed Uniform Consumer Credit Code represents a big step in this direction in that it prohibits wage assignments as security on loans and sales; exempts all wages from garnishment before judgment; exempts from garnishment after judgment wages of $96 a week for heads of families and up to $64 a week for single persons; limits the use of balloon payments on loans and sales; and restricts deficiency judgments in consumer credit sales where the cash price of the goods does not exceed $1,000.

The code also allows the buyer three days to cancel an agreement made with a seller who enters his home to make the sale, which checks the persuasive power of the high-pressure door-to-door salesman. Equally important is the provision allowing the buyer three months to file a claim under the terms of the contract of sale against a finance company who has purchased the installment contract from the selling firm, even though the purchase by the finance company was made "free of defenses against the selling firm." The theory is that the finance company is in a better position to assess the value of the product and the reputability of the selling firm than is the consumer, and this new liability will give them reason to do so. Thus, this new provision ought to make it much more difficult for fly-by-night dealers to get financing, and this in turn hopefully will serve to curb a major area of abuse in marketing.

Even with disclosure and special rules to offset recognized imbalances in bargaining power, certain types of customer, because of lack of education or for other reasons, still are not able to bargain effectively in a free market. In such cases, substantive reform may still be necessary as a structural supplement. In this connection, the recent move by the courts to hold certain contract provisions unconscionable and therefore, unenforceable, has been an important substantive breakthrough. It would perhaps speed this trend if some of the more common and flagrant unconscionable clauses were defined by statute so as to encourage uniformity in court rulings. Note, however, that within the limits of conscionability, the specific terms of the relationship are still structurally determined.

Reform in the common law of personal injury, or tort law as it is called, can also have an important structural impact on restoring the balance between the buyer and the seller. Recent cases that have expanded the concept of implied warranty, and which have allowed buyers who purchased a defective product from an independent reseller to sue the manufacturer directly even though technically no privity existed, represent a major new balance restoring development.

The emergence of the class suit is also a structural development that shows considerable promise for restoring buyer-seller balance in those situations where the small value of the purchase precluded resort to legal remedies in the past. In such a suit, the action is brought on behalf of all customers who have been mistreated in the same way. If the case is won, the attorney's fee can be quite high, and even though the individual damage any one person receives is quite small, in total the amount involved is quite large. Thus, enterprising lawyers can be counted on to police the market.

Setting Minimum Standards. The possibility of action from the National Commission on Product Safety also holds some promise of reducing the power imbalance. The significance of its role, however, will depend not only on the nature of the minimum safety standards for various household products and chemicals which it establishes, but also on how diligently it enforces these standards and on the imposition of penalties large enough to deter violation.

This latter point has represented one of the major weaknesses of the Federal Trade Commission's efforts to police the marketplace. By the time a cease-and-desist order is finally issued and a court injuction secured, the unscrupulous firm has already made a killing. Without the ability to impose criminal penalties or fines, or to assess damages, its enforcement powers are largely empty. For example, the Holland Furnace Company perpetrated a sales swindle for thirty years; even after a cease-and-desist order had been issued by the commission and ordered by the court, Holland continued its illegal practices for seven more years. The subsequent fine for violating the court order (not for the practices as such) amounted to only $100,000. This was a negligible deterrent; it has been estimated that Holland was bilking the public out of $30 million a year at the height of its business.

The large corporation is a key institution in modern society, and its conduct is a matter of considerable social concern. A large measure of freedom from the constraints of the market and supervision of ownership have given management a new degree of discretion. Given this freedom, the question arises, "For whose benefit should the modern corporation be run?" No one has yet had the temerity to propose that the corporation be run for the benefit of management, though some perhaps secretly believe it. In any event, a virtual chorus of voices answer that it should be run for the benefit of society.[12]

[12] A body of literature exists which asserts that the corporation should be run for the benefit of society. One of the earliest writers to make this proposal was Walter Rathenau in his *Von Kommenden Dingen* (Berlin, 1918) translated by E. and C. Paul (London: Allen & Unwin, 1921). Rathenau is quoted in A. A. Berle, Jr. and Gardiner C. Means, *The Modern Corporation and Private*

But what does this entail? It has been proposed that it involves the development and maintenance of an equitable working balance among the competing claims of the constituent groups who depend on the corporation—its employees, its customers, the host community, and so on.

The broad outlines of an equitable working balance begin to take shape in many cases, but in only a few does the specific nature of the power imbalance imply the substance of the responsible relationship. Here is where the structural approach comes in. Instead of trying to infer obligations where none appear obvious, much can be gained by trying to restructure the relationship so the substance of the responsible relationship can be worked out by the parties themselves.

The specifics of the buyer-seller relationship suggest the possibility of extensive structural reforms in this area. They attest to the viability of this structural strategy for dealing with the problem of corporate responsibility even in a relationship that many have held to be the most difficult relationship to treat in a balance of power sense.

Property (New York: The Macmillan Company, 1933), Book IV, p. 352. See also Morrell Heald, "Management Responsibility to Society: The Growth of an Idea," *The Business History Review*, XXXI (Winter, 1957), 375–84.

corporate strategy formulation

part two

Corporate strategy consists of a set of long-range decisions which establish objectives, policies, and plans to exploit opportunities or combat threats in response to environmental forces and developments. Those decisions are the result of a complex decision-making process designed to establish organizational goals and long-range plans for resource allocation and action. The readings in this part deal with aspects of the entire strategy formulation process.

The decision process for strategy formulation consists of identifying and assessing the opportunities and threats posed by the competitive situation, deciding organizational goals in light of that assessment, and formulating broad strategies and plans for total corporate action. Those decisions should be based upon an analysis of the total situation within which the organization operates. That analysis entails determining what variables are to be considered in defining or evaluating directions for the enterprise, obtaining relevant information, and assessing it in terms of organizational competence, associated risks, and values of the executives.

A major difficulty in the decision process is the problem of identifying and analyzing the factors bearing on the question. The issue is further complicated by the interdependence of the variables. At the risk of oversimplifying this complex decision area, the following diagram summarizes the major variables and their relationships.

Each of these activities may be considered separately for purposes of analysis and understanding, but the process is a highly dynamic and continuous one. It will go through many iterations, partial and complete, in the analysis, determination, and re-evaluation of strategy. The diagram employs the systems concept of the business firm wherein the firm is considered a subsystem of its industry and total environment. Consequently, strategic decision making requires close attention to the interactions of the systems. The remainder of this section deals with a description and discussion of the elements of the strategy formulation process and their interrelations.

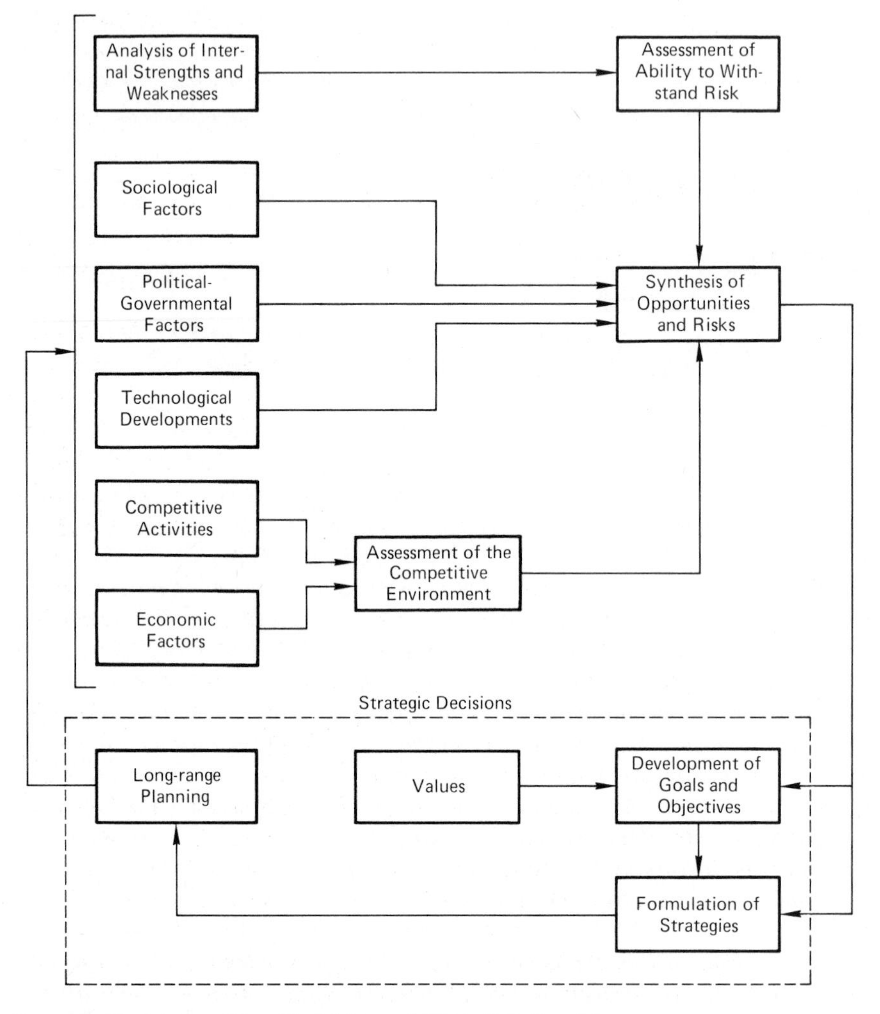

Strategic Decision-making Variables and Their Relationships

Situation analysis has two major components—environmental (or external) and internal. Environmental variables include, broadly, economic, technological, competitive, political, and social developments. These classifications are not mutually exclusive, and variables may contain characteristics of several categories. Not only will environmental developments vary in scope of influence, but their implications for the firm may also be immediate or long-range, direct or indirect.

Of the external factors, the nature of the competitive environment exerts the greatest influence on the business firm and consequently is of prime importance. Whether a firm adopts a policy of innovation or imitation, developments in relevant technologies must be monitored and evaluated for their impact on the firm. This process should be a formal one, not left to casual observation by unspecified individuals, if it is to receive proper weight at the policy-making level. Although the readings emphasize economic and technological forecasting, the effect of political and social factors must not be ignored. Some important aspects of those variables are highlighted in the selections of Sections 2 and 8.

The point of key importance for policy is that the executive be cognizant of the appropriate variables and project their probable effect on the organization in the form of opportunity and challenge, threat, or constraint. Conducting an analysis of environmental developments will permit the formulation of a range of general strategies available to the firm.

The internal aspect of situation analysis consists of assessing the firm's capability to pursue alternative opportunities in terms of its strengths and weaknesses, real or potential. Unless these factors are carefully analyzed in the decision process, the firm may be committed to a strategy having an excessively high risk. Although a business organization's principal capability is measured in terms of manufacturing and marketing an economic good or service, a more specific delineation of capabilities is necessary because of wide differences among firms in terms of functions they perform and competitive conditions. An organization's capabilities are determined by its total resources consisting of manpower, functional expertise, and tangible assets (or the familiar men, money, material, machines, methods). In addition, intangibles such as values and acknowledged social responsibilities may exert a qualitative influence on decisions.

The process of combining all the information obtained in the analysis of external and internal factors is a formidable one. The data are not usually well organized or complete. Decision makers must order, weight, rank, and assign probabilities so that they can cope with the task of establishing priorities and allocating resources.

In Section 3 the selections focus on the formulation of corporate goals and objectives, and long-range plans. William Newman discusses the concept of the firm's master strategy and guides for its development. Seymour Tilles attacks the issue of the role of corporate strategy in determining the future of a company by raising crucial questions and relating experiences of a number of companies. Walter Hill provides insights to goal formation by presenting foundations for a theory emphasizing the firm's external environment, the internal social system, motives of individuals in positions of power, and the coalition bargaining process through which objectives are determined. Myles Mace discusses effective and useful steps for corporate planning emphasizing the executive role. Of particular note is the appendix to his article in which the elements of a five-year plan are identified. Again on a theoretical note the John Friedmann article presents a conceptual model and hypotheses for planning processes in which he distinguishes four modes of planning: developmental and adaptive, allocative and innovative. We strongly urge the reader to consult the additional references, particularly those dealing with long-range planning, or additional depth.

In Section 4 the selections deal with some specific variables in situation analysis that are identified in the preceding section. Richard Vogt presents a general discussion of forecasting and its relation to strategic planning. Murray Weidenbaum provides a focus on economic forecasting. Raymond Isenson describes types, objectives, and methods of technological forecasting. Daniel Roman discusses the topic less technically but also highlights positive and negative aspects of technological forecasting as a management tool as well as organizational considerations. An environmental audit from a marketing research viewpoint is the focus of J. Thomas Cannon's article. He describes profiling the company's status in the market place and then presents a functional analysis of the firm in light of the market analysis. This article provides insight into the relationships among the variables discussed here, and it can be used as a framework for applications other than marketing strategies.

Part Two. References for Further Study

Section 3: Goals, Strategies, and Long-range Plans

Gilmore, Frank F., and Richard G. Brandenburg. "Anatomy of Corporate Planning." *Harvard Business Review,* **40,** 6 (November–December 1962), 61–69.
Presents a framework for corporate planning with emphasis on researching and understanding top-management planning problems. Flow charts illustrate key points and the integrative nature of the framework.

Kline, Charles H. "The Strategy of Product Policy." *Harvard Business Review,* **33,** 4 (July–August 1955), pp. 91–100.
Discusses the importance of and means for developing a long-range product strategy.

Mason, R. Hal. "Developing a Planning Organization." *Business Horizons,* **XII,** 4 (August 1969), 61–69.
Outlines five phases of development for a mature and effective planning organization.

O'Meara, John T., Jr. "Selecting Profitable Products." *Harvard Business Review,* **39,** 1 (January–February 1961), 87–93.
Suggests a comprehensive method for analysis of product alternatives.

Payne, Bruce. "Steps in Long-Range Planning." *Harvard Business Review,* **35,** 2 (March–April 1957), 95–106.
Covers a wide range of topics for comprehensive long-range planning including criteria for evaluating the plan.

Simon, Herbert A. "On the Concept of Organizational Goal." *Administrative Science Quarterly,* **9,** 1 (June 1964), 1–22.
Discusses the term "organizational goal" including sets of constraints (organizational, personal, and decisional) that must be satisfied to make it an operational concept.

Skinner, Wickham. "Manufacturing—Missing Link in Corporate Strategy." *Harvard Business Review,* **47,** 3 (May–June 1969), 136–145.
Describes a systematic approach to integrating manufacturing with corporate strategy. Emphasizes relationships between production operations and corporate strategy and top management use of manufacturing policy in corporate strategy.

Thune, Stanley S., and Robert J. House. "Where Long-Range Planning Pays off." *Business Horizons,* **XIII,** 4 (August 1970), 81–87.
Results of a study of the changes in economic performance associated with formal long-range planning. Comparison of formal planners with informal planners and an industry-by-industry analysis.

Section 4: Situation Assessment

Anderson, Theodore A. "Regional Industry Forecasting." *California Management Review,* **VIII,** 3 (Spring 1966), 51–56.
Describes, illustrates, and evaluates four methodologies for regional business forecasting.

Cassady, Ralph, Jr. "The Intelligence Function and Business Competition." *California Management Review,* **VI,** 3 (Spring 1964), 85–92.
Discusses and illustrates business intelligence about new products, new markets, and competitors' plans.

Gibson, R. E. "The Strategy of Corporate Research and Development." *California Management Review,* **IX,** 1 (Fall 1966), 33–42.
Describes basic definitions, variables, and their interrelationships for formulating research and development strategy.

Gross, Alfred. "Adapting to Competitive Change." *MSU Business Topics,* **18,** 1 (Winter 1970), 13–22.
Analyzes managerial adaptation to change and develops a program for improving a firm's capacity to resolve problems generated by reaction to severe competitive pressure.

McFarlane, Dale D., and Ira Horowitz. "Risk and the Business Decision." *Business Horizons,* **10,** 2 (Summer 1967), 81–90.
Discusses the quantitative approach to risk assessment and its contribution to managerial decision making.

Morton, Jack A. "A Systems Approach to the Innovation Process." *Business Horizons,* **10,** 2 (Summer 1967), 27–36.
Describes a total systems approach (utilized in the Bell System) to technological innovation. Shows linkages among the parent company, research laboratories, and manufacturing and operating companies.

Quinn, James Brian. "Long-Range Planning of Industrial Research." *Harvard Business Review,* **39,** 4 (July–August 1961), 88–102.
Discusses the role of top management in the research planning process. Covers a range of considerations from corporate strategy formulation, through long-range forecasting and planning, to operations.

Turner, Robert C. "An Economic Projection Designed for Businessmen." *Business Horizons,* **8,** 1 (Spring 1965), 4ff. (9 pages).
Identifies and illustrates basic inputs for a ten-year economic projection.

goals, strategies, and long-range plans

section **3**

11

Shaping the Master Strategy of Your Firm

William H. Newman

Every enterprise needs a central purpose expressed in terms of the services it will render to society. And it needs a basic concept of how it will create these services. Since it will be competing with other enterprises for resources, it must have some distinctive advantages—in its services or in its methods of creating them. Moreover, since it will inevitably cooperate with other firms, it must have the means for maintaining viable coalitions with them. In addition, there are the elements of change, growth, and adaptation. Master strategy is a company's basic plan for dealing with these factors.

One familiar way of delving into company strategy is to ask, "What business are we in or do we want to be in? Why should society tolerate our existence?" Answers are often difficult. A company producing only grass seed had very modest growth until it shifted its focus to "lawn care" and provided the suburban homeowner with a full line of fertilizers, pesticides, and related products. Less fortunate was a cooperage firm that defined its business in terms of wooden boxes and barrels and went bankrupt when paperboard containers took over the field.

 This article is adapted from a chapter in *The Process of Management*, second edition (Englewood Cliffs, N.J.: Prentice-Hall, Inc., 1967).

Product line is only part of the picture, however. An ability to supply services economically is also crucial. For example, most local bakeries have shut down, not for lack of demand for bread, but because they became technologically inefficient. Many a paper mill has exhausted its sources of pulpwood. The independent motel operator is having difficulty meeting competition from franchised chains. Yet in all these industries some firms have prospered—the ones that have had the foresight and adaptability (and probably some luck, too) to take advantage of their changing environment. These firms pursued a master strategy which enabled them to increase the services rendered and attract greater resources.

Most central managers recognize that master strategy is of cardinal importance. But they are less certain about how to formulate a strategy for their particular firm. This article seeks to help in the shaping of master strategies. It outlines key elements and an approach to defining these. Most of our illustrations will be business enterprises; nevertheless, the central concept is just as crucial for hospitals, universities, and other nonprofit ventures.

A practical way to develop a master strategy is to:

- Pick particular roles or niches that are appropriate in view of competition and the company's resources.
- Combine various facets of the company's efforts to obtain synergistic effects.
- Set up sequences and timing of changes that reflect company capabilities and external conditions.
- Provide for frequent reappraisal and adaptation to evolving opportunities.

New Market or Services

Picking Propitious Niches. Most companies fill more than one niche. Often they sell several lines of products; even when a single line is produced an enterprise may sell it to several distinct types of customers. Especially as a firm grows, it seeks expansion by tapping new markets or selling different services to its existing customers. In designing a company strategy we can avoid pitfalls by first examining each of these markets separately.

Basically, we are searching for customer needs—preferably growing ones—where adroit use of our unique resources will make our services distinctive and in that sense give us a competitive advantage. In these particular spots, we hope to give the customer an irresistible value and to do so at relatively low expense. A bank, for example, may devise a way of financing the purchase of an automobile that is particularly well-suited to farmers; it must then consider whether it is in a good position to serve such a market.

Identifying such propitious niches is not easy. Here is one approach that works well in various situations: Focus first on the industry—growth prospects, competition, key factors required for success—then on the strengths and weaknesses of the specific company as matched against these key success factors.

As we describe this approach more fully, keep in mind that we are interested in segments of markets as well as entire markets.

The sales volume and profits of an industry or one of its segments depend on the demand for its services, the supply of these services, and the competitive conditions. (We use "service" here to include both physical products and intangible values provided by an enterprise.) Predicting future demand, supply, and competition is an exciting endeavor. In the following paragraphs, we suggest a few of the important considerations that may vitally affect the strategy of a company.

Elements of Demand

Demand for Industry Services. The strength of the desire for a service affects its demand. For instance, we keenly want a small amount of salt, but care little for additional quantities. Our desire for more and better automobiles does not have this same sort of cut-off level, and our desires for pay-television (no commercials, select programs) or supersonic air travel are highly uncertain, falling in quite a different category from that of salt.

Possible *substitutes* to satisfy a given desire must be weighed—beef for lamb, motorboats for baseball, gas for coal, aureomycin for sulfa, weldments for castings, and so forth. The frequency of such substitution is affected, of course, by the relative prices.

Desire has to be backed up by *ability to pay*, and here business cycles enter in. Also, in some industries large amounts of capital are necessarily tied up in equipment. The relative efficiency, quality of work, and nature of machinery already in place influence the money that will be available for new equipment. Another consideration: If we hope to sell in foreign markets, foreign-exchange issues arise.

The *structure of markets* also requires analysis. Where, on what terms, and in response to what appeals do people buy jet planes, sulphuric acid, or dental floss? Does a manufacturer deal directly with consumers or are intermediaries such as retailers or brokers a more effective means of distribution?

Although an entire industry is often affected by such factors—desire, substitutes, ability to pay, structure of markets—a local variation in demand sometimes provides a unique opportunity for a particular firm. Thus, most drugstores carry cosmetics, candy, and a wide variety of items besides drugs, but a store located in a medical center might develop a highly profitable business by dealing exclusively with prescriptions and other medical supplies.

All these elements of demand are subject to change—some quite rapidly. Since the kind of strategic plans we are considering here usually extends over several years, we need both an identification of the key factors that will affect industry demand and an estimate of how they will change over a span of time.

Supply Situation

Supply Related to Demand. The attractiveness of any industry depends on more than potential growth arising from strong demand. In designing a company strategy we also must consider the probable supply of services and the conditions under which they will be offered.

The *capacity* of an industry to fill demand for its services clearly affects profit margins. The importance of over- or undercapacity, however, depends on the ease of entry and withdrawal from the industry. When capital costs are high, as in the hotel or cement business, adjustments to demand tend to lag. Thus, overcapacity may depress profits for a long period; even bankruptcies do not remove the capacity if plants are bought up—at bargain prices—and operated by new owners. On the other hand, low capital requirements—as in electronic assembly work—permit new firms to enter quickly, and shortages of supply tend to be short-lived. Of course, more than the physical plant is involved; an effective organization of competent people is also necessary. Here again, the case of expansion or contraction should be appraised.

Costs also need to be predicted—labor costs, material costs, and for some industries, transportation costs or excise taxes. If increases in operating costs affect all members of an industry alike and can be passed on to the consumer in the form of higher prices, this factor becomes less significant in company strategy. However, rarely do both conditions prevail. Sharp rises in labor costs in Hawaii, for example, place its sugar industry at a disadvantage on the world market.

A highly dynamic aspect of supply is *technology*. New methods for producing established products—for example, basic oxygen conversion of steel displacing open-hearth furnaces and mechanical cotton pickers displacing century-old hand-picking techniques—are part of the picture. Technology may change the availability and price of raw materials; witness the growth of synthetic rubber and industrial diamonds. Similarly, air cargo planes and other new forms of transportation are expanding the sources of supply that may serve a given market.

For an individual producer, anticipating these shifts in the industry supply situation may be a matter of prosperity or death.

Climate of Industry

Competitive Conditions in the Industry. The way the interplay between demand and supply works out depends partly on the nature of competition in the industry. *Size, strength, and attitude of companies* in one industry—the dress industry where entrance is easy and style is critical—may lead to very sharp competition. On the other hand, oligopolistic competition among the giants of the aluminum industry produces a more stable situation, at least in the short run. The resources and managerial talent needed to enter one industry differ greatly from what it takes to get ahead in the other.

A strong *trade association* often helps to create a favorable climate in its industry. The Independent Oil Producers' Association, to cite one case, has been unusually effective in restricting imports of crude oil into the United States. Other associations compile valuable industry statistics, help reduce unnecessary variations in size of products, run training conferences, hold trade shows, and aid members in a variety of other ways.

Government regulation also modifies competition. A few industries like banking and insurance are supervised by national or state bodies that place limits on prices, sales promotion, and the variety of services rendered. Airlines are both regulated as a utility and subsidized as an infant industry. Farm subsidies affect large segments of agriculture, and tariffs have long protected selected manufacturers. Our patent laws also bear directly on the nature of competition, as is evident in the heated discussion of how pharmaceutical patents may be used. Clearly, future government action is a significant factor in the outlook of many industries.

Crucial Factors

Key Factors for Success in the Industry. This brief review suggests the dynamic nature of business and uncertainties in the outlook for virtually all industries. A crucial task of every top management is to assess the forces at play in its industry and to identify those factors that will be crucial for future success. These we call "key success factors." Leadership in research and development may be very important in one industry, low costs in another, and adaptability to local need in a third; large financial resources may be a *sine qua non* for mining whereas creative imagination is the touchstone in advertising.

We stressed earlier the desirability of making such analyses for narrow segments as well as broad industry categories. The success factors for each segment are likely to differ in at least one or two respects from those for other segments. For example, General Foods Corporation discovered to its sorrow that the key success factors in gourmet foods differ significantly from those for coffee and Jello.

Moreover, the analysis of industry outlook should provide a forecast of the *growth potentials* and the *profit prospects* for the various industry segments. These conclusions, along with key success factors, are vital guideposts in setting up a company's master strategy.

The range of opportunities for distinctive service is wide. Naturally, in picking its particular niche out of this array a company favors those opportunities which will utilize its strength and bypass its limitations. This calls for a candid appraisal of the company itself.

Position in Market

Market Strengths of Company. A direct measure of *market position* is the percentage that company sales are of industry sales and of major competitors' sales. Such figures quickly indicate whether our company is so big that its activities are likely to bring prompt responses from other leading companies. Or our company may be small enough to enjoy independent maneuverability. Of course, to be most meaningful, these percentages should be computed separately for geographical areas, product lines, and types of customer—if suitable industry data are available.

More intangible but no less significant are the relative standing of *company products* and their *reputation* in major markets. Kodak products, for instance, are widely and favorably known; they enjoy a reputation for both high quality and dependability. Clearly, this reputation will be a factor in Eastman Kodak Company strategy. And any new, unknown firm must overcome this prestige if it seeks even a small share in one segment of the film market. Market reputation is tenacious. Especially when we try to "trade up," our previous low quality, service, and sharp dealing will be an obstacle. Any strategy we adopt must have enough persistence and consistency so that our firm is assigned a "role" in the minds of the customers we wish to reach.

The relationship between a company and the *distribution system* is another vital aspect of market position. The big United States automobile companies, for example, are strong partly because each has a set of dealers throughout the country. In contrast, foreign car manufacturers have difficulty selling here until they can arrange with dealers to provide dependable service. A similar problem confronted Whirlpool Corporation when it wanted to sell its trademarked appliances publicly. (For years its only customer had been Sears, Roebuck and Company.) Whirlpool made an unusual arrangement with Radio Corporation of America which led to the establishment of RCA-Whirlpool distributors and dealers. Considering the strong competition, Whirlpool could not have entered this new market without using marketing channels such as RCA's

All these aspects of market position—a relative share of the market, comparative quality of product, reputation with consumers, and ties with a distributive system—help define the strengths and limitations of a company.

Service Abilities

Supply Strengths of a Company. To pick propitious niches we also should appraise our company's relative strength in creating goods and services. Such ability to supply services fitted to consumer needs will be built largely on the firm's resources of labor and material, effective productive facilities, and perhaps pioneering research and development.

Labor in the United States is fairly mobile. Men tend to gravitate to good jobs. But the process takes time—a southern shoe plant needed ten years to build up an adequate number of skilled workers—and it may be expensive. Consequently, immediate availability of competent men at normal industry wages is a source of strength. In addition, the relationships between the company and its work force are important. All too often both custom and formal agreements freeze inefficient practices. The classic example is New England textiles; here, union-supported work habits give even mills high labor costs. Only recently have a few companies been able to match their more flourishing competitors in the South.

Access to *low-cost materials* is often a significant factor in a company's supply position. The development of the southern paper industry, for example, is keyed to the use of fast-growing forests which can be cut on a rotational basis to provide a continuing supply of pulpwood. Of course, if raw materials can be easily transported, such as iron ore and crude oil by enormous ships, plants need not be located at the original source.

Availability of materials involves more than physical handling. Ownership, or long-term contracts with those who do own, may assure a continuing source at low cost. Much of the strategy of companies producing basic metals—iron, copper, aluminum, or nickel—includes huge investments in ore properties. But all sorts of companies are concerned with the availability of materials. So whenever supplies are scarce a potential opportunity exists. Even in retailing. Sears, Roebuck and Company discovered in its Latin American expansion that a continuing flow of merchandise of standard quality was difficult to to assure, but once established, such sources became a great advantage.

Physical facilities—office buildings, plants, mines—often tie up a large portion of a company's assets. In the short run, at least, these facilities may be an advantage or a disadvantage. The character of many colleges, for instance, has been shaped by their location, whether in a plush suburb or in a degenerating urban area, and the cost of moving facilities is so great that adaptation to the existing neighborhood becomes necessary. A steel company, to cite another case, delayed modernizing its plant so long that it had to abandon its share of the basic steel market and seek volume in specialty products.

Established organizations of highly talented people to perform particular tasks also give a company a distinctive capability. Thus, a good research and development department may enable a company to expand in pharmaceuticals, whereas a processing firm without such a technical staff is barred from this profitable field.

Perhaps the company we are analyzing will enjoy other distinctive abilities to produce services. Our central concern at this point is to identify strengths and see how these compare with strengths of other firms.

Finances and Management

Other Company Resources. The propitious niche for a company also depends on its financial strength and the character of its management.

Some strategies will require large quantities of capital. Any oil company that seeks foreign sources of crude oil, for instance, must be prepared to invest millions of dollars. Five firms maintain cash reserves of this size, so financial capacity to enter this kind of business depends on: an ability to attract new capital—through borrowing or sale of stock—or a flow of profits (and depreciation allowances) from existing operations that can be allocated to the new venture. On the other hand, perhaps a strategy can be devised that calls for relatively small cash advances, and in these fields a company that has low financial strength will still be able to compete with the affluent firms.

A more subtle factor in company capacity is its *management.* The age and vitality of key executives, their willingness to risk profit and capital, their urge to gain personal prestige through company growth, their desire to insure stable employment for present workers—all affect the suitability of any proposed strategy. For example, the expansion of Hilton Hotels Corporation into a world-wide chain certainly reflects the personality of Conrad Hilton; with a different management at the helm, a modification in strategy is most appropriate because Conrad Hilton's successors do not have his particular set of drives and values.

Related to the capabilities of key executives is the organization structure of the company. A decentralized structure, for instance, facilitates movement into new fields of business, whereas a functional structure with fine specialization is better suited to expansion in closely related lines.

Picking a Niche

Matching Company Strengths with Key Success Factors. Armed with a careful analysis of the strengths and limitations of our company, we are prepared to pick desirable niches for company concentration. Naturally, we will look for fields where company strengths correspond with the key factors for success that have been developed in our industry analyses described in the preceding section. And in the process we will set aside possibilities in which company limitations create serious handicaps.

Potential growth and profits in each niche must, of course, be added to the synthesis. Clearly, a low potential will make a niche unattractive even though the company strengths and success factors fit neatly. And we may become keenly interested in a niche where the fit is only fair if the potential is great.

Typically, several intriguing possibilities emerge. These are all the niches—in terms of market lines, market segments, or combinations of production functions—that the company might pursue. Also typically, a series of positive actions is necessary in order for the company to move into each area. So we need to list not only each niche and its potential, but the limitations that will have to be overcome and other steps necessary for the company to succeed in each area. These are our propitious niches—nestled in anticipated business conditions and tailored to the strengths and limitations of our particular company.

An enterprise always pursues a variety of efforts to serve even a single niche, and, typically, it tries to fill several related niches. Considerable choice is possible, at least in the degree to which these many efforts are pushed. In other words, management decides how many markets to cover, to what degree to automate production, what stress to place on consumer engineering, and a host of other actions. One vital aspect of master strategy is fitting these numerous efforts together. In fact, our choice of niches will depend in part, on how well we can combine the total effort they require.

Synergy is a powerful ally for this purpose. Basically, synergy means that the combined effect of two or more cooperative acts is greater than the sum which would result if the actions were taken independently. A simple example in marketing is that widespread dealer stocks *combined with* advertising will produce much greater sales volume than widespread dealer stocks in, say, Virginia and advertising in Minnesota. Often the possibility of obtaining synergistic effects will shape the master strategy of the company—as the following examples will suggest.

Combination of Services

Total Service to Customer. A customer rarely buys merely a physical product. Other attributes of the transaction often include delivery, credit terms, return privileges, repair service, operating instructions, conspicuous consumption, psychological experience of purchasing, and the like. Many services involve no physical product at all. The crucial question is what combination of attributes will have high synergistic value for the customers we serve.

International Business Machines, for instance, has found a winning combination. Its products are well designed and of high quality. But so are the products of several of its competitors. In addition, IBM provides salesmen who understand the customer's problems and how IBM equipment can help solve them, and fast, dependable repair service. The synergistic effect of these three services is of high value to many customers.

Each niche calls for its own combination of services. For example, Chock Full o'Nuts expanded its restaurant chain on the basis of three attributes: good quality food, cleanliness, and fast service. This combination appealed to a particular group of customers. A very limited selection, crowded space, and lack of frills did not matter. However, if any one of the three characteristics slips at an outlet, the synergistic effect is lost.

Adding to Capabilities

Fuller Use of Existing Resources. Synergistic effects are possible in any phase of company operations. One possibility is that present activities include a "capability" that can be applied to additional uses. Thus, American watch companies have undertaken the manufacture of tiny gyroscopes and electronic components for spacecraft because they already possessed technical skill in the production of miniature precision products. They adopted this strategy on the premise that they could make both watches and components for spacecraft with less effort than could separate firms devoted to only one line of products.

The original concept of General Foods Corporation sought a similar synergistic effect in marketing. Here, the basic capability was marketing prepared foods. By having the same sales organization handle several product lines, a larger and more effective sales effort could be provided and/or the selling cost per product line could be reduced. Clearly, the combined sales activity was more powerful than separate sales efforts for each product line would have been.

Vertical Integration

Expansion to Obtain a Resource. Vertical integration may have synergistic effects. This occurred when the Apollo Printing Machine Company bought a foundry. Apollo was unsatisfied with the quality and tardy delivery of its castings and was looking for a new supplier. In its search, it learned that a nearby foundry could be purchased. The foundry was just breaking even, primarily because the volume of its work fluctuated widely. Following the purchase, Apollo gave the foundry a more steady backlog of work, and through close technical cooperation the quality of castings received by them was improved. The consolidated set-up was better for both enterprises than the previous independent operations.

The results of vertical integration are not always so good, however; problems of balance, flexibility, and managerial capacity must be carefully weighed. Nevertheless, control of a critical resource is often a significant part of company strategy.

Unique Services

Expansion to Enhance Market Position. Efforts to improve market position provide many examples of "the whole being better than the sum of its parts." The leading can companies, for example, moved from exclusive concentration on metal containers into glass, plastic, and paper containers. They expected their new divisions to be profitable by themselves, but an additional reason for the expansion lay in anticipated synergistic effects of being able to supply a customer's total container requirements. With the entire packaging field changing so rapidly, a company that can quickly shift from one type of container to another offers a distinctive service to its customers.

International Harvester, to cite another case, added a very large tractor to its line a few years ago. The prospects for profit on this line alone were far from certain. However, the new tractor was important to give dealers "a full line"; its availability removed the temptation for dealers to carry some products of competing manufacturers. So, when viewed in combination with other International Harvester products, the new tractor looked much more significant than it did as an isolated project.

Negative Synergy

Compatibility of Efforts. In considering additional niches for a company, we may be confronted with negative synergy—that is, the combined effort is worse than the sum of independent efforts. This occurred when a producer of high quality television and hi-fi sets introduced a small color television receiver. When first offered, the small unit was as good as most competing sets and probably had an attractive potential market. However, it was definitely inferior in performance to other products of the company and, consequently, undermined public confidence in the quality of the entire line. Moreover, customers had high expectations for the small set because of the general reputation of the company, and they became very critical when the new product did not live up to their expectations. Both the former products and the new product suffered.

Compatibility of operations within the company should also be considered. A large department store, for instance, ran into serious trouble when it tried to add a high-quality dress shop to its mass merchandising activities. The ordering and physical handling of merchandise, the approach to sales promotion, the sales compensation plan, and many other procedures which worked well for the established type of business were unsuited to the new shop. And friction arose each time the shop received special treatment. Clearly, the new shop created an excessive number of problems because it was incompatible with existing customs and attitudes.

Broad Company Goals

Summarizing briefly: We have seen that some combinations of efforts are strongly reinforcing. The combination accelerates the total effect or reduces the cost for the same effect or solidifies our supply or market position. On the other hand, we must watch for incompatible efforts which may have a disruptive effect in the same cumulative manner. So, when we select niches—as a part of our master strategy—one vital aspect is the possibility of such synergistic effects.

Master strategy sets broad company goals. One firm may decide to seek pre-eminence in a narrow specialty while another undertakes to be a leader in several niches or perhaps in all phases of its industry. We have recommended that this definition of "scope" be clear in terms of:

- Services offered to customers.
- Operations performed by the company.
- Relationships with suppliers of necessary resources.
- The desirability of defining this mission so as to obtain synergistic effects.

But master strategy involves more than defining our desired role in society. Many activities will be necessary to achieve this desired spot, and senior executives must decide what to do first, how many activities can be done concurrently, how fast to move, what risks to run, and what to postpone. These questions of sequence and timing must be resolved to make the strategy operational.

Strategy of Sequence

Choice of Sequence. Especially in technical areas, sequence of actions may be dictated by technology. Thus, process research must precede equipment designs, product specifications must precede cost estimation, and so forth. Other actions, such as the steps necessary to form a new corporation, likewise give management little choice in sequence. When this occurs, normal programming or possibly PERT analysis may be employed. Little room—or need—exists for strategy.

Preordained sequences, however, are exceptional in the master strategy area. A perennial issue when entering a new niche, for instance, is whether to develop markets before working on production economies, or vice versa. The production executive will probably say, "Let's be sure we can produce the product at a low cost before committing ourselves to customers," whereas the typical marketing man will advise, "Better be sure it will sell before tooling up for a big output."

A striking example of strategy involving sequence confronted the Boeing company when it first conceived of a large four-engine jet plane suitable for handling cargo or large passenger loads. Hindsight makes the issue appear simple, but at the time, Air Force officers saw little need for such a plane. The belief was that propeller-driven planes provided the most desirable means for carrying cargo. In other words, the company got no support for its prediction of future market requirements. Most companies would have stopped at this point. However, Boeing executives decided to invest several million dollars to develop the new plane. A significant portion of the company's liquid assets went into the project. Over two years later, Boeing was able to present evidence that caused the Air Force officials to change their minds—and the KC 135 was born. Only Boeing was prepared to produce the new type of craft which proved to be both faster and more economical than propeller-driven planes. Moreover, the company was able to convert the design into the Boeing 707 passenger plane which, within a few years, dominated the airline passenger business. Competing firms were left far behind, and Convair almost went bankrupt in its attempt to catch up. In this instance, a decision to let engineering and production run far ahead of marketing paid off handsomely.

No simple guide exists for selecting a strategic sequence. Nevertheless, the following comments do sharpen the issue:

- Resist the temptation to do first what is easiest simply because it requires the least initiative. Each of us typically has a bias for what he does well. A good sequence of activities, however, is more likely to emerge from an objective analysis.
- If a head start is especially valuable on one front, start early there. Sometimes, being the first in the market is particularly desirable (there may be room for only one company). In other cases, the strategic place to begin is the acquiring of key resources; at a later date limited raw materials may already be bought up or the best sites occupied by competitors. The importance of a

head start is usually hard to estimate, but probably more money is lost in trying to be first than in catching up with someone else.

- Move into uncertain areas promptly, preferably before making any major commitments. For instance, companies have been so entranced with a desired expansion that they committed substantial funds to new plants before uncertainties regarding the production processes were removed.
- If a particular uncertainty can be investigated quickly and inexpensively, get it out of the way promptly.
- Start early with processes involving long lead-times. For example, if a new synthetic food product must have government approval, the tedious process of testing and reviewing evidence may take a year or two longer than preparation for manufacturing and marketing.
- Delay revealing plans publicly if other companies can easily copy a novel idea. If substantial social readjustment is necessary, however, an early public announcement is often helpful.

In a particular case, these guides may actually conflict with each other, or other considerations may be dominant. And, as the Boeing 707 example suggests, the possible gains may be large enough to justify following a very risky sequence. Probably the greatest value of the above list is to stimulate careful thought about the sequence that is incorporated into a company's master strategy.

Resource Limitations

Straining Scarce Resources. A hard-driving executive does not like to admit that an objective cannot be achieved. He prefers to believe, "Where there's a will there's a way." Yet, an essential aspect of master strategy is deciding what can be done and how fast.

Every enterprise has limits—perhaps severe limits—on its resources. The amount of capital, the number and quality of key personnel, the physical production capacity, or the adaptability of its social structure—none of these is boundless. The tricky issue is how to use these limited resources to the best advantage. We must devise a strategy which is feasible within the inherent restraints.

A household-appliance manufacturer went bankrupt because he failed to adapt his rate of growth to his financial resources. This man had a first-rate product and a wise plan for moving with an "economy model" into an expanding market (following rural electrification). But, to achieve low production costs, he built an oversized plant and launched sales efforts in ten states. His contention was that the kind of company he conceived could not start out on a small scale. Possibly all of these judgments were correct, but they resulted in cash requirements that drained all of his resources before any momentum was achieved. Cost of the partially used plant and of widely scattered sales efforts was so high that no one was willing to bail out the financially strapped venture. His master strategy simply did not fit his resources.

The scarce resource affecting master strategy may be managerial personnel. A management consulting firm, for instance, reluctantly postponed entry into the international arena because only two of its partners had the combination of interest, capacity, and vitality to spend a large amount of time abroad, and these men were also needed to assure continuity of the United States practice. The firm felt that a later start would be better than weak action immediately—even though this probably meant the loss of several desirable clients.

The weight we should attach to scarce resources in the timing of master strategy often requires delicate judgment. Some strain may be endured. But, how much, how long? For example, in its switch from purchased to company-produced tires, a European rubber company fell behind on deliveries for six months, but, through heroic efforts and pleading with customers, the company weathered the squeeze. Now, company executives believe the timing was wise! If the delay had lasted a full year—and this was a real possibility—the consequence would have approached a catastrophe.

Forming Coalitions. A cooperative agreement with firms in related fields occasionally provides a way to overcome scarce resources. We have already referred to the RCA-Whirlpool arrangement for distributing Whirlpool products. Clearly, in this instance, the timing of Whirlpool's entrance into the market with its own brand depended on forming a coalition with RCA.

Examples of Coalitions

The early development of frozen foods provides us with two other examples of fruitful coalitions. A key element in Birdseye master strategy was to obtain the help of cold-storage warehouses; grocery wholesalers were not equipped to handle frozen foods, and before the demand was clearly established they were slow to move into the new activity. And the Birdseye division of General Foods lacked both managerial and financial resources to venture into national wholesaling.

Similarly, Birdseye had to get freezer cabinets into retail stores, but it lacked the capability to produce them. So, it entered into a coalition with a refrigerator manufacturer to make and sell (or lease) the cabinets to retail stores. This mutual agreement enabled Birdseye to move ahead with its marketing program much faster. With the tremendous growth of frozen foods, neither the cold-storage warehouse nor the cabinet manufacturer continued to be necessary, but without them in the early days widespread use of frozen foods would have been delayed three to five years.

Coalitions may be formed for reasons other than "buying time." Nevertheless, when we are trying to round out a workable master strategy, coalitions—or even mergers—may provide the quickest way to overcome a serious deficiency in vital resources.

The Right Time to Act

Receptive Environment. Conditions in a firm's environment affect the "right time" to make a change. Mr. Ralph Cordiner, for example, testifies that he launched his basic reorganization of General Electric Company only when he felt confident of three years of high business activity because, in his opinion, the company could not have absorbed all the internal readjustments during a period of declining volume and profits.

Judging the right time to act is difficult. Thus, one of the contributing factors to the multimillion-dollar Edsel car fiasco was poor timing. The same automobile launched a year or two earlier might have been favorably received. But buyer tastes changed between the time elaborate market research studies were made and the time when the new car finally appeared in dealer showrooms. By then, preference was swinging away from a big car that "had everything" toward compacts. This mistake in timing and associated errors in strategy cost the Ford Motor Company over a hundred million dollars.

A major move can be too early, as well as too late. We know, for instance, that a forerunner of the modern, self-service supermarket—the Piggly Wiggly—was born too soon. In its day, only a few housewives drove automobiles to shopping centers; and those that could afford cars usually shunned the do-it-yourself mode so prevalent today. In other words, the environment at that time simply was not receptive to what now performs so effectively. Other "pioneers" have also received cool receptions—prefabricated housing and local medical clinics are two.

No Simple Rules

The preceding discussions of sequence and timing provide no simple rules for these critical aspects of basic strategy. The factors we have mentioned for deciding which front(s) to push first (where is a head start valuable, early attention to major uncertainties, lead-times, significance of secrecy) and for deciding how fast to move (strain on scarce resources, possible coalition to provide resources, and receptivity of the environment) bear directly on many strategy decisions. They also highlight the fundamental nature of sequence and timing in the master strategy for a firm.

Master strategy involves deliberately relating a company's efforts to its particular future environment. We recognize, of course, that both the company's capabilities and its environment continually evolve; consequently, strategy should always be based, not on existing conditions, but on forecasts. Such forecasts, however, are never 100 per cent correct; instead, strategy often seeks to take advantage of uncertainty about future conditions.

This dynamic aspect of strategy should be underscored. The industry outlook will shift for any of numerous reasons. These forces may accelerate growth in some sectors and spell decline in others, may squeeze material supply, may make old sources obsolete, may open new possibilities and snuff out others. Meanwhile, the company itself is also changing—due to the success or failure of its own efforts and to actions of competitors and cooperating firms. And with all of these internal and external changes the combination of thrusts that will provide optimum synergistic effects undoubtedly will be altered. Timing of actions is the most volatile element of all. It should be adjusted to both the new external situation and the degrees of internal progress on various fronts.

Consequently, frequent reappraisal of master strategy is essential. We must build into the planning mechanisms sources of fresh data that will tell us how well we are doing and what new opportunities and obstacles are appearing on the horizon. The feedback features of control will provide some of these data. In addition, senior managers and others who have contact with various parts of the environment must be ever-sensitive to new developments that established screening devices might not detect.

Hopefully, such reappraisal will not call for sharp reversals in strategy. Typically, a master strategy requires several years to execute and some features may endure much longer. The kind of plan I am discussing here sets the direction for a whole host of company actions, and external reputations and relations often persist for many years. Quick reversals break momentum, require repeated relearning, and dissipate favorable cumulative effects. To be sure, occasionally a sharp break may be necessary. But, if my forecasts are reasonably sound, the adaptations to new opportunities will be more evolution than revolution. Once embarked on a course, we make our reappraisal from our new position—and this introduces an advantage in continuing in at least the same general direction. So, normally, the adaptation is more an unfolding than a completely new start.

Even though drastic modification of our master strategy may be unnecessary, frequent incremental changes will certainly be required to keep abreast of the times. Especially desirable are shifts that anticipate change before the pressures build up. And such farsighted adjustments are possible only if we periodically reappraise and adapt present strategy to new opportunities.

Master strategy is the pivotal planning instrument for large and small enterprises alike. The giant corporations provide us with examples on a grand scale, but the same kind of thinking is just as vital for small firms.

An Example

A terse sketch of the central strategy of one small firm will illustrate this point. The partners of an accounting firm in a city with a quarter-million population predicted faster growth in data processing than in their normal auditing and tax work, yet they knew that most of their clients were too small to use an electronic computer individually. So they foresaw the need for a single, cooperative computer center serving several companies. And they believed that their intimate knowledge of the procedures and the needs of several of these companies, plus the specialized ability of one partner in data processing, put them in a unique position to operate such a center. Competition was anticipated from two directions: New models of computers much smaller in size would eventually come on the market—but even if the clients could rent such equipment they would still need programmers and other specialized skills. Also, telephonic hook-ups with International Business Machines service centers appeared likely—but the accounting firm felt its local and more intimate knowledge of each company would give it an advantage over such competition. So, the cooperative computer center looked like a propitious niche.

The chief obstacle was developing a relatively stable volume of work that would carry the monthly rental on the proposed computer. A local insurance company was by far the best prospect for this purpose; it might use half the computer capacity, and then the work for other, smaller companies could be fitted into the remaining time. Consequently, the first major move was to make a deal—a coalition—with the insurance company. One partner was to devote almost his entire time working on details for such an arrangement; meanwhile, the other two partners supported him through their established accounting practice.

We see in this brief example:

- The picking of a propitious niche for expansion.
- The anticipated synergistic effect of combining auditing services with computing service.
- The sequence and timing of efforts to overcome the major limiting factor.

The project had not advanced far enough for much reappraisal, but the fact that two partners were supporting the third provided a built-in check on the question of "how are we doing."

References

Executives who wish to explore the meaning and method of shaping master strategies still further can consult the following materials:

1. E. W. Reilley, "Planning the Strategy of the Business," *Advanced Management,* XX (Dec. 1955), 8–12.
2. T. Levitt, "Marketing Myopia," *Harvard Business Review,* XXXVIII:4 (July–Aug. 1960), 45–66.
3. F. F. Gilmore and R. G. Brandenburg, "Anatomy of Corporate Planning," *Harvard Business Review,* XLI:6 (Nov.–Dec. 1962), 61–69.
4. H. W. Newman and T. L. Berg, "Managing External Relations," *California Management Review,* V:3 (Spring 1963), 81–86.

12

How to Evaluate Corporate Strategy

Seymour Tilles

No good military officer would undertake even a small-scale attack on a limited objective without a clear concept of his strategy. No seasoned politician would undertake a campaign for a major office without an equally clear concept of his strategy. In the field of business management, however, we frequently find men deploying resources on a large scale without any clear notion of what their strategy is. And yet a company's strategy is a vital ingredient in determining its future. A valid strategy will yield growth, profit, or whatever other objectives the managers have established. An inappropriate strategy not only will fail to yield benefits, but also may result in disaster.

In this article I will try to demonstrate the truth of these contentions by examining the experiences of a number of companies. I shall discuss what strategy is, how it can be evaluated, and how, by evaluating its strategy, a management can do much to assure the future of the enterprise.

Decisive Impact

The influence of strategy can be seen in every age and in every area of industry. Here are some examples:

- From the time it was started in 1911 as the Computing-Tabulating-Recording Co., International Business Machines Corporation has demonstrated the significance of a soundly conceived strategy. Seeing itself in the data-system business at a time when most manufacturers were still preoccupied with individual pieces of equipment, IBM developed a set of policies which resulted in its dominating the office equipment industry.
- By contrast, Packard in the 1930's was to the automobile industry everything that IBM is today to the office machine industry. In 1937, it sold over 109,000 cars, compared with about 11,000 for Cadillac. By 1954 it had disappeared as an independent producer.

Strategy is, of course, not the only factor determining a company's success or failure. The competence of its managerial leadership is significant as well. Luck can be a factor, too (although often what people call good luck is really the product of good strategy). But a valid strategy can gain extraordinary results for the company whose general level of competence is only average. And, conversely, the most inspiring leaders who are locked into an inappropriate strategy will have to exert their full competence and energy merely in order to keep from losing ground.

Reprinted from *Harvard Business Review*, Vol. 41, No. 4 (July–August 1963), pp. 111–121, by permission of the publisher.

When Hannibal inflicted the humiliating defeat on the Roman army at Cannac in 216 B.C., he led a ragged band against soldiers who were in possession of superior arms, better training, and competent "noncoms." His strategy, however, was so superior that all of those advantages proved to be relatively insignificant. Similarly, when Jacob Borowsky made Lestoil the hottest-selling detergent in New England some years ago, he was performing a similar feat—relying on strategy to battle competition with superior resources.

Strategy is important not only for aspiring Davids who need an offensive device to combat corporate Goliaths. It is significant also for the large organization faced with a wide range of choice in domestic and international operations. For instance, the following corporations are all in the midst of strategic changes, the implications of which are worldwide in scope:

- Massey-Ferguson, Ltd., with 26 factories located around the world, and vying for leadership in the farm-equipment industry.
- General Electric Company and Westinghouse Electric Corporation, the giant producers of electrical equipment, who are recasting their competitive policies.
- Singer Sewing Machine Company, trying to make its vast assets yield a greater return.

Dynamic Concept

A strategy is a set of goals and major policies. The definition is as simple as that. But while the notion of a strategy is extremely easy to grasp, working out an agreed-upon statement for a given company can be a fundamental contribution to the organization's future success.

In order to develop such a statement, managers must be able to identify precisely what is meant by a goal and what is meant by a major policy. Otherwise, the process of strategy determination may degenerate into what it so often becomes—the solemn recording of platitudes, useless for either the clarification of direction or the achievement of consensus.

Identifying Goals. Corporate goals are an indication of what the company as a whole is trying to *achieve* and to *become.* Both parts—the achieving and the becoming—are important for a full understanding of what a company hopes to attain. For example:

- Under the leadership of Alfred Sloan, General Motors achieved a considerable degree of external success; this was accomplished because Sloan worked out a pattern for the kind of company he wanted it to be internally.
- Similarly, the remarkable record of Du Pont in the twentieth century and the growth of Sears, Roebuck under Julius Rosenwald were as much a tribute to their modified structure as to their external strategy.[1]

[1] For an interesting discussion of this relationship, see A. D. Chandler, Jr., *Strategy and Structure* (Cambridge, Massachusetts Institute of Technology Press, 1962), pp. 1–17.

Achieving. In order to state what a company expects to achieve, it is important to state what it hopes to do with respect to its environment. For instance:

Ernest Breech, chairman of the board of the Ford Motor Company, said that the strategy formulated by his company in 1946 was based on a desire to "hold our own in what we foresaw would be a rich but hotly competitive market."[2] The view of the environment implicit in this statement is unmistakable: an expanding over-all demand, increasing competition, and emphasis on market share as a measure of performance against competitors.

Clearly, a statement of what a company hopes to achieve may be much more varied and complex than can be contained in a single sentence. This will be especially true for those managers who are sophisticated enough to perceive that a company operates in more external "systems" than the market. The firm is part not only of a market but also of an industry, the community, the economy, and other systems. In each case there are unique relationships to observe (e.g., with competitors, municipal leaders, Congress, and so on). A more complete discussion of this point is contained in a previous HBR article.[3]

Becoming. If you ask young men what they want to accomplish by the time they are 40, the answers you get fall into two distinct categories. There are those—the great majority—who will respond in terms of what they want to *have.* This is especially true of graduate students of business administration. There are some men, however, who will answer in terms of the kind of men they hope to *be.* These are the only ones who have a clear idea of where they are going.

The same is true of companies. For far too many companies, what little thinking goes on about the future is done primarily in money terms. There is nothing wrong with financial planning. Most companies should do more of it. But there is a basic fallacy in confusing a financial plan with thinking about the kind of company you want yours to become. It is like saying, "When I'm 40, I'm going to be *rich.*" It leaves too many basic questions unanswered. Rich in what way? Rich doing what?

The other major fallacy in stating what you want to become is to say it only in terms of a product. The number of companies who have got themselves into trouble by falling in love with a particular product is distressingly great.[4] Perhaps the saddest examples are those giants of American industry who defined their future in terms of continuing to be the major suppliers of steam locomotives to the nation's railroads. In fact, these companies were so wedded to this concept of their future that they formed a cartel in order to keep General Motors out of the steam locomotive business. When the diesel locomotive proved its superiority to steam, these companies all but disappeared.

[2] See Edward C. Bursk and Dan H. Fenn, Jr., *Planning the Future Strategy of Your Business* (New York: McGraw-Hill Book Company, Inc., 1956), p. 8.

[3] Seymour Tilles, "The Manager's Job—A Systems Approach," HBR January–February 1963, p. 73.

[4] See Theodore Levitt, "Marketing Myopia," HBR July–August 1960, p. 45.

The lesson of these experiences is that a key element of setting goals is the ability to see them in terms of more than a single dimension. Both money and product policy are part of a statement of objectives; but it is essential that these be viewed as the concrete expressions of a more abstract set of goals—the satisfaction of the needs of significant groups which cooperate to ensure the company's continued existence.

Who are these groups? There are many customers, managers, employees, stockholders, to mention just the major ones. The key to corporate success is the company's ability to identify the important needs of each of these groups, to establish some balance among them, and to work out a set of operating policies which permits their satisfaction. This set of policies, as a pattern, identifies what the company is trying to be.

The Growth Fad. Many managers have a view of their company's future which is strikingly analogous to the child's view of himself. When asked what they want their companies to become over the next few years, they reply, "bigger."

There are a great many rationalizations for this preoccupation with growth. Probably the one most frequently voiced is that which says, "You have to grow or die." What must be appreciated, however, is that "bigger" for a company has enormous implications for management. It involves a different way of life, and one which many managers may not be suited for—either in terms of temperament or skills.

Moreover, whether for a large company or a small one, "bigger," by itself, may not make economic sense. Companies which are highly profitable at their present size may grow into bankruptcy very easily; witness the case of Grayson-Robinson Stores, Inc., a chain of retail stores. Starting out as a small but profitable chain, it grew rapidly into receivership. Conversely, a company which is not now profitable may more successfully seek its survival in cost reduction than in sales growth. Chrysler is a striking example of this approach.

There is, in the United States, a business philosophy which reflects the frontier heritage of the country. It is one which places a high value on growth, in physical terms. The manager whose corporate sales are not increasing, the number of whose subordinates is not growing, whose plants are not expanding, feels that he is not successful. But there is a dangerous trap in this kind of thinking. More of the same is not necessarily progress. In addition, few managers are capable of running units several times larger than the ones they now head. The great danger of wholehearted consumer acceptance or an astute program of corporate acquisition is that it frequently propels managers into situations that are beyond their present competence. Such cases—and they are legion—emphasize that in stating corporate objectives, bigger is not always better. A dramatic example is that of the Ampex Corporation:

From 1950 to 1960, Ampex's annual sales went from less than $1,000,000 to more than $73,000,000. Its earnings went from $115,000 to nearly $4,000,000. The following year, the company reported a decline in sales to $70,000,000, and a net loss of $3,900,000. The *Wall Street Journal* reported: "As one source close to the company put it, Ampex's former management 'was intelligent and well-educated, but simply lacked the experience necessary to control' the company's rapid development."[5]

Role of Policy. A policy says something about *how* goals will be attained. It is what statisticians would call a "decision rule," and what systems engineers would call a "standing plan." It tells people what they should and should not do in order to contribute to achievement of corporate goals.

A policy should be more than just a platitude. It should be a helpful guide to making strategy explicit, and providing direction to subordinates. Consequently, the more definite it is, the more helpful it can be. "We will provide our stockholders with a fair return," is a policy no one could possibly disagree with—or be helped by. What *is* a fair return? This is the type of question that must be answered before the company's intentions become clear.

The job of management is not merely the preparation of valid policies for a standard set of activities; it is the much more challenging one of first deciding what activities are so strategically significant that explicit decision-rules in that area are mandatory. No standard set of policies can be considered major for all companies. Each company is a unique situation. It must decide for itself which aspects of corporate life are most relevant to its own aspirations and work out policy statements for them. For example, advertising may be insignificant to a company which provides research services to the Defense Department, but critical to a firm trying to mass-merchandise luxury goods.

It is difficult to generalize about which policies are major, even within a particular industry, because a number of extraordinary successful companies appear to violate all the rules. To illustrate:

- In the candy industry it would seem safe to generalize that advertising should be a major policy area. However, the Hershey Company, which is so successful that its name is practically the generic term for the product, has persistently followed a policy of no advertising.
- Similarly, in the field of high-fidelity components, one would expect that dealer relations would be a critical policy area. But Acoustics Research, Inc., has built an enviable record of sales growth and of profitability by relying entirely on consumer pull.

Need to Be Explicit. The first thing to be said about corporate strategy is that having one is a step forward. Any strategy, once made explicit, can quickly be evaluated and improved. But if no attempt is ever made to commit it to paper, there is always the danger that the strategy is either incomplete or misunderstood.

Many successful companies are not aware of the strategy that underlies their success. It is quite possible for a company to achieve initial success without

[5] "℞ for Ampex: Drastic Changes Help Solve Big Headache of Fast Corporate Growth," *Wall Street Journal*, September 17, 1962, p. 1.

real awareness of its causes. However, it is much more difficult to successfully *branch out into new ventures* without a precise appreciation of their strategic significance. This is why many established companies fail miserably when they attempt a program of corporate acquisition, product diversification, or market expansion. One illustration of this is cited by Myles L. Mace and George G. Montgomery in their recent study of corporate acquisitions:

> A basic resin company . . . bought a plastic boat manufacturer because this seemed to present a controlled market for a portion of the resin it produced. It soon found that the boat business was considerably different from the manufacture and sale of basic chemicals. After a short but unpleasant experience in manufacturing and trying to market what was essentially a consumer's item, the management concluded that its experience and abilities lay essentially in industrial rather than consumer-type products.[6]

Another reason for making strategy explicit is the assistance it provides for delegation and for coordination. To an ever-increasing extent, management is a team activity, whereby groups of executives contribute to corporate success. Making strategy explicit makes it far easier for each executive to appreciate what the over-all goals are, and what his own contribution to them must be.

Making an Evaluation

Is your strategy right for you? There are six criteria on which to base an answer. These are:

1. Internal consistency.
2. Consistency with the environment.
3. Appropriateness in the light of available resources.
4. Satisfactory degree of risk.
5. Appropriate time horizon.
6. Workability.

If all of these criteria are met, you have a strategy that is right for you. This is as much as can be asked. There is no such thing as a good strategy in any absolute, objective sense. In the remainder of this article I shall discuss the criteria in some detail.

1. *Is the Strategy Internally Consistent?* Internal consistency refers to the cumulative impact of individual policies on corporate goals. In a well-worked-out strategy, each policy fits into an integrated pattern. It should be judged not only in terms of itself, but also in terms of how it relates to other policies which the company has established and to the goals it is pursuing.

In a dynamic company consistency can never be taken for granted. For example:

[6] *Management Problems of Corporate Acquisitions* (Boston: Division of Research, Harvard Business School, 1962), p. 60.

Many family-owned organizations pursue a pair of policies which soon become inconsistent: rapid expansion and retention of exclusive family control of the firm. If they are successful in expanding, the need for additional financing soon raises major problems concerning the extent to which exclusive family control can be maintained.

While this pair of policies is especially prevalent among smaller firms, it is by no mean limited to them. The Ford Motor Company after World War II and the New York Times today are examples of quite large, family-controlled organizations that have had to reconcile the two conflicting aims.

The criterion of internal consistency is an especially important one for evaluating strategies because it identifies those areas where strategic choices will eventually have to be made. An inconsistent strategy does *not* necessarily mean that the company is currently in difficulty. But it does mean that unless management keeps its eye on a particular area of operation, it may well find itself forced to make a choice without enough time either to search for or to prepare attractive alternatives.

2. *Is the Strategy Consistent with the Environment?* A firm which has a certain product policy, price policy, or advertising policy is saying that it has chosen to relate itself to its customers—actual and potential—in a certain way. Similarly, its policies with respect to government contracts, collective bargaining, foreign investment, and so forth are expressions of relationship with other groups and forces. Hence an important test of strategy is whether the chosen policies are consistent with the environment—whether they really make sense with respect to what is going on outside.

Consistency with the environment has both a static and a dynamic aspect. In a static sense, it implies judging the efficacy of policies with respect to the environment as it exists *now*. In a dynamic sense, it means judging the efficacy of policies with respect to the environment *as it appears to be changing*. One purpose of a viable strategy is to ensure the long-run success of an organization. Since the environment of a company is constantly changing, ensuring success over the long run means that management must constantly be assessing the degree to which policies previously established are consistent with the environment as it exists now; and whether current policies take into account the environment as it will be in the future. In one sense, therefore, establishing a strategy is like aiming at a moving target: you have to be concerned not only with present position but also with the speed and direction of movement.

Failure to have a strategy consistent with the environment can be costly to the organization. Ford's sad experience with the Edsel is by now a textbook example of such failure. Certainly, had Ford pushed the Falcon at the time when it was pushing the Edsel, and with the same resources, it would have a far stronger position in the world automobile market today.

Illustrations of strategies that have not been consistent with the environment are easy to find by using hindsight. *But the reason that such examples are plentiful is not that foresight is difficult to apply.* It is because even today few companies are seriously engaged in analyzing environmental trends and using this intelligence as a basis for managing their own futures.

3. *Is the Strategy Appropriate in View of the Available Resources?* Resources are those things that a company *is* or *has* and that help it to achieve its corporate objectives. Included are money, competence, and facilities; but these by no means complete the list. In companies selling consumer goods, for example, the major resource may be the name of the product. In any case, there are two basic issues which management must decide in relating strategy and resources. These are:

- What are our critical resources?
- Is the proposed strategy appropriate for available resources?

Let us look now at what is meant by a "critical resource" and at how the criterion of resource utilization can be used as a basis for evaluating strategy.

Critical Resources. The essential strategic attribute of resources is that they represent action potential. Taken together, a company's resources represent its capacity to respond to threats and opportunities that may be perceived in the environment. In other words, resources are the bundle of chips that the company has to play with in the serious game of business.

From an action-potential point of view, a resource may be critical in two senses: (1) as the factor limiting the achievement of corporate goals; and (2) as that which the company will exploit as the basis for its strategy. Thus, critical resources are both what the company has most of and what it has least of.

The three resources most frequently identified as critical are money, competence, and physical facilities. Let us look at the strategic significance of each.

Money. Money is a particularly valuable resource because it provides the greatest flexibility of response to events as they arise. It may be considered the "safest" resource, in that safety may be equated with the freedom to choose from among the widest variety of future alternatives. Companies that wish to reduce their short-run risk will therefore attempt to accumulate the greatest reservoir of funds they can.

However, it is important to remember that while the accumulation of funds may offer short-run security, it may place the company at a serious competitive disadvantage with respect to other companies which are following a higher-risk course.

The classical illustration of this kind of outcome is the strategy pursued by Montgomery Ward under the late Sewell Avery. As reported in *Fortune:*

> While Sears confidently bet on a new and expanding America, Avery developed an *idée fixe* that postwar inflation would end in a crash no less serious than that of 1929. Following this idea, he opened no new stores but rather piled up cash to the ceiling in preparation for an economic debacle that never came. In these years, Ward's balance sheet gave a somewhat misleading picture of its prospects. Net earnings remained respectably high, and were generally higher than those of Sears as a percentage of sales. In 1946, earnings after taxes were $52 million. They rose to $74 million

in 1950, and then declined to $35 million in 1954. Meanwhile, however, sales remained static, and in Avery's administration profits and liquidity were maintained at the expense of growth. In 1954, Ward had $327 million in cash and securities, $147 in receivables, and $216 million in inventory, giving it a total current-asset position of $690 million and net worth of $639 million. It was liquid, all right, but it was also the shell of a once great company.[7]

Competence. Organizations survive because they are good at doing those things which are necessary to keep them alive. However, the degree of competence of a given organization is by no means uniform across the broad range of skills necessary to stay in business. Some companies are particularly good at marketing, others especially good at engineering, still others depend primarily on their financial sophistication. Philip Selznick refers to that which a company is particularly good at as its "distinctive competence."[8]

In determining a strategy, management must carefully appraise its own skill profile in order to determine where its strengths and weaknesses lie. It must then adopt a strategy which makes the greatest use of its strengths. To illustrate:

• The competence of *The New York Times* lies primarily in giving extensive and insightful coverage of events—the ability to report "all the news that's fit to print." It is neither highly profitable (earning only 1.5% of revenues in 1960—far less than, say, the *Wall Street Journal*), nor aggressively sold. Its decision to publish a West Coast and an international edition is a gamble that the strength of its "distinctive competence" will make it accepted even outside of New York.

• Because of a declining demand for soft coal, many producers of soft coal are diversifying into other fields. All of them, however, are remaining true to some central skill that they have developed over the years. For instance:

—Consolidation Coal is moving from simply the mining of soft coal to the mining *and transportation* of soft coal. It is planning with Texas Eastern Transmission Corporation to build a $100-million pipeline that would carry a mixture of powdered coal and water from West Virginia to the East Coast.

—North American Coal Company, on the other hand, is moving toward becoming a chemical company. It recently joined with Strategic Materials Corporation to perfect a process for extracting aluminum sulfate from the mine shale that North American produces in its coal-running operations.

James L. Hamilton, president of the Island Creek Coal Co., has summed up the concept of distinctive competence in a colorful way:

> We are a career company dedicated to coal, and we have some very definite ideas about growth and expansion within the industry. We're not thinking of buying a cotton mill and starting to make shirts.[9]

[7] "Montgomery Ward: Prosperity Is Still Around the Corner," *Fortune*, November 1960, p. 140.

[8] *Leadership in Administration* (Evanston, Illinois, Row, Peterson & Company, 1957), p. 42.

[9] *Wall Street Journal*, September 11, 1962, p. 30.

Physical Facilities. Physical facilities are the resource whose strategic influence is perhaps most frequently misunderstood. Managers seem to be divided among those, usually technical men, who are enamored of physical facilities as the tangible symbol of the corporate entity; and those, usually financial men, who view physical facilities as an undesirable but necessary freezing of part of the company's funds. The latter group is dominant. In many companies, return on investment has emerged as virtually the sole criterion for deciding whether or not a particular facility should be acquired.

Actually, this is putting the cart before the horse. Physical facilities have significance primarily in relationship to over-all corporate strategy. It is, therefore, only in relationship to *other* aspects of corporate strategy that the acquisition or disposition of physical facilities can be determined. The total investment required and the projected return on it have a place in this determination—but only as an indication of the financial implications of a particular strategic decision and not as an exclusive criterion for its own sake.

Any appraisal of a company's physical facilities as a strategic resource must consider the relationship of the company to its environment. Facilities have no intrinsic value for their own sake. Their value to the company is either in their location relative to markets, to sources of labor, or to materials; or in their efficiency relative to existing or impending competitive installations. Thus, the essential considerations in any decision regarding physical facilities are a projection of changes likely to occur in the environment and a prediction about what the company's responses to these are likely to be.

Here are two examples of the necessity for relating an evaluation of facilities to environmental changes:

- Following the end of World War II, all domestic producers of typewriters in the United States invested heavily in plant facilities in this country. They hypothesized a rapid increase of sales throughout the world. This indeed took place, but it was short-lived. The rise of vigorous overseas competitors, especially Olivetti and Olympia, went hand in hand with a booming overseas market. At home, IBM's electric typewriter took more and more of the domestic market. Squeezed between these two pressures, the rest of the U.S. typewriter industry found itself with a great deal of excess capacity following the Korean conflict. Excess capacity is today still a major problem in this field.
- The steady decline in the number of farms in the United States and the emergence of vigorous overseas competition have forced most domestic full-line manufacturers of farm equipment to sharply curtail total plant area. For example, in less than four years, International Harvester eliminated more than a third of its capacity (as measured in square feet of plant space) for the production of farm machinery.

The close relationship between physical facilities and environmental trends emphasizes one of the most significant attributes of fixed assets—their temporal utility. Accounting practice recognizes this in its treatment of depreciation allowances. But even when the tax laws permit generous write-offs, they should not be used as the sole basis for setting the time period over which the investment must be justified. Environmental considerations may reveal that a different time horizon is more relevant for strategy determination. To illustrate again:

As Armstong Cork Company moved away from natural cork to synthetic materials during the early 1950's, management considered buying facilities for the production of its raw materials—particularly polyvinyl chloride. However, before doing so, it surveyed the chemical industry and concluded that producers were overbuilding. It therefore decided not to invest in facilities for the manufacture of this material. The projections were valid; since 1956 polyvinyl chloride has dropped 50% in price.

A strategic approach to facilities may not only change the time horizon; it may also change the whole basis of asset valuation:

Recently a substantial portion of Loew's theaters was acquired by the Tisch brothers, owners and operators of a number of successful hotels, including the Americana in Florida.[10] As long as the assets of Loew's theaters were viewed only as places for the projection of films, its theaters, however conservatively valued, seemed to be not much of a bargain. But to a keen appraiser of hotel properties the theater sites, on rather expensive real estate in downtown city areas, had considerable appeal. Whether this appraisal will be borne out is as yet unknown. At any rate, the stock, which was originally purchased at $14 (with a book value of $22), was selling at $23 in October 1962.

Achieving the Right Balance. One of the most difficult issues in strategy determination is that of achieving a balance between strategic goals and available resources. This requires a set of necessarily empirical, but critical, estimates of the total resources required to achieve particular objectives, the rate at which they will have to be committed, and the likelihood that they will be available. The most common errors are either to fail to make these estimates at all or to be excessively optimistic about them.

One example of the unfortunate results of being wrong on these estimates is the case of Royal McBee and the computer market:

In January 1956 Royal McBee and the General Precision Equipment Corporation formed a jointly owned company—the Royal Precision Corporation—to enter the market for electronic data-processing equipment. This joint operation was a logical pooling of complementary talents. General Precision had a great deal of experience in developing and producing computers. Its Librascope Division had been selling them to the government for years. However, it lacked a commercial distribution system. Royal McBee, on the other hand, had a great deal of experience in marketing data-processing equipment, but lacked the technical competence to develop and produce a computer.

The joint venture was eminently successful, and within a short time the Royal

[10] See "The Tisches Eye Their Next $65 Million," *Fortune*, January 1960, p. 140.

Precision LPG-30 was the leader in the small-computer field. However, the very success of the computer venture caused Royal McBee some serious problems. The success of the Royal Precision subsidiary demanded that the partners put more and more money into it. This was no problem for General Precision, but it became an ever more serious problem for Royal McBee, which found itself in an increasingly critical cash bind. In March 1962 it sold its interest in Royal Precision to General Precision for $5 million—a price which represented a reported $6.9 million loss on the investment. Concluding that it simply did not sufficient resources to stay with the new venture, it decided to return to its traditional strengths: typewriters and simple data-processing systems.

Another place where optimistic estimates of resources frequently cause problems is in small businesses. Surveys of the causes of small-business failure reveal that a most frequent cause of bankruptcy is inadequate resources to weather either the early period of establishment or unforeseen downturns in business conditions.

It is apparent from the preceding discussion that a critical strategic decision involves deciding: (1) how much of the company's resources to commit to opportunities currently perceived, and (2) how much to keep uncommitted as a reserve against the appearance of unanticipated demands. This decision is closely related to two other criteria for the evaluation of strategy: risk and timing. I shall now discuss these.

4. *Does the Strategy Involve an Acceptable Degree of Risk?* Strategy and resources, taken together, determine the degree of risk which the company is undertaking. This is a critical managerial choice. For example, when the old Underwood Corporation decided to enter the computer field, it was making what might have been an extremely astute strategic choice. However, the fact that it ran out of money before it could accomplish anything in that field turned its pursuit of opportunity into the prelude to disaster. This is not to say that the strategy was "bad." However, the course of action pursued *was* a high-risk strategy. Had it been successful, the pay-off would have been lush. The fact that it was a stupendous failure instead does not mean that it was senseless to take the gamble.

Each company must decide for itself how much risk it wants to live with. In attempting to assess the degree of risk associated with a particular strategy, management may use a variety of techniques. For example, mathematicians have developed an elegant set of techniques for choosing among a variety of strategies where you are willing to estimate the payoffs and the probabilities associated with them. However, our concern here is not with these quantitative aspects but with the identification of some qualitative factors which may serve as a rough basis for evaluating the degree of risk inherent in a strategy. These factors are:

1. The amount of resources (on which the strategy is based) whose continued existence or value is not assured.
2. The length of the time periods to which resources are committed.
3. The proportion of resources committed to a single venture.

The greater these quantities, the greater the degree of risk that is involved.

Uncertain Terms of Existence. Since a strategy is based on resources, any resource which may disappear before the payoff has been obtained may constitute a danger to the organization. Resources may disappear for various reasons. For example, they may lose their value. This frequently happens to such resources as physical facilities and product features. Again, they may be accidentally destroyed. The most vulnerable resource here is competence. The possible crash of the company plane or the blip on the president's electrocardiogram are what make many organizations essentially speculative ventures. In fact, one of the critical attributes of highly centralized organizations is that the more centralized they are, the more speculative they are. The disappearance of the top executive or the disruption of communication with him, may wreak havoc at subordinate levels.

However, for many companies, the possibility that critical resources may lose their value stems not so much from internal developments as from shifts in the environment. Take specialized production know-how, for example. It has value only because of demand for the product by customers—and customers may change their minds. This is cause for acute concern among the increasing number of companies whose futures depend so heavily on their ability to participate in defense contracts. A familiar case is the plight of the airframe industry following World War II. Some of the companies succeeded in making the shift from aircraft to missiles, but this has only resulted in their being faced with the same problem on a larger scale.

Duration of Commitment. Financial analysts often look at the ratio of fixed assets to current assets in order to assess the extent to which resources are committed to long-term programs. This may or may not give a satisfactory answer. How important are the assets? When will they be paid for?

The reasons for the risk increasing as the time for payoff increases is, of course, the inherent uncertainty in any venture. Resources committed over long time spans make the company vulnerable to changes in the environment. Since the difficulty of predicting such changes increases as the time span increases, long-term projects are basically more risky than are short ones. This is especially true of companies whose environments are unstable. And today, either because of technological, political, or economic shifts, most companies are decidedly in the category of those that face major upheaval in their corporate environments. The company building its future around technological equipment, the company selling primarily to the government, the company investing in underdeveloped nations, the company selling to the Common Market, the company with a plant in the South—all these have this prospect in common.

The harsh dilemma of modern management is that the time span of decision is increasing at the same time as the corporate environment is becoming increasingly unstable. It is this dilemma which places such a premium on the manager's sensitivity to external trends today. Much has been written about his role as a commander and administrator. But it is no less important that he be a *strategist.*

Size of the Stakes. The more of its resources a company commits to a particular strategy, the more pronounced the consequences. If the strategy is successful, the payoff will be great—both to managers and investors. If the strategy fails, the consequences will be dire—both to managers and investors. Thus, a critical decision for the executive group is: What proportion of available resources should be committed to a particular course of action?

This decision may be handled in a variety of ways. For example, faced with a project that requires more of its resources than it is willing to commit, a company either may choose to refrain from undertaking the project or, alternatively, may seek to reduce the total resources required by undertaking a joint venture or by going the route of merger or acquisition in order to broaden the resource base.

The amount of resources management stands ready to commit is of particular significance where there is some likelihood that larger competitors, having greater resources, may choose to enter the company's field. Thus, those companies which entered the small-computer field in the past few years are now faced with the penetration into this area of the data-processing giants. (Both IBM and Remington Rand have recently introduced new small computers.)

I do not mean to imply that the "best" strategy is the one with the least risk. High payoffs are frequently associated with the high-risk strategies. Moreover, it is a frequent but dangerous assumption to think that inaction, or lack of change, is a low-risk strategy. Failure to exploit its resources to the fullest may well be the riskiest strategy of all that an organization may pursue, as Montgomery Ward and other companies have amply demonstrated.

5. *Does the Strategy Have an Appropriate Time Horizon?* A significant part of every strategy is the time horizon on which it is based. A viable strategy not only reveals what goals are to be accomplished; it says something about *when* the aims are to be achieved.

Goals, like resources, have time-based utility. A new product developed, a plant put on stream, a degree of market penetration, become significant strategic objectives only if accomplished by a certain time. Delay may deprive them of all strategic significance. A perfect example of this in the military sphere is the Sinai campaign of 1956. The strategic objective of the Israelis was not only to conquer the entire Sinai peninsula; it also was to do it in seven days. By contrast, the lethargic movement of the British troops made the operation a futile one for both England and France.

In choosing an apporpriate time horizon, we must pay careful attention to the goals being pursued, and to the particular organization involved. Goals must be established far enough in advance to allow the organization to adjust to them. Organizations, like ships, cannot be "spun on a dime." Consequently, the larger the organization, the further its strategic time horizon must extend, since its adjustment time is longer. It is no mere managerial whim that the major contributions to long-range planning have emerged from the larger organizations—especially those large organizations such as Lockheed, North American Aviation, and RCA that traditionally have had to deal with highly unstable environments.

The observation that large corporations plan far ahead while small ones can get away without doing so has frequently been made. However, the significance of planning for the small but growing company has frequently been overlooked. As a company gets bigger, it must not only change the way it operates; it must also steadily push ahead its time horizon—and this is a difficult thing to do. The manager who has built a successful enterprise by his skill at "putting out fires" or the wheeler-dealer whose firm has grown by a quick succession of financial coups is seldom able to make the transition to the long look ahead.

In many cases, even if the executive were inclined to take a longer range view of events, the formal reward system seriously militates against doing so. In most companies the system of management rewards is closely related to currently reported profits. Where this is the case, executives may understandably be so preoccupied with reporting a profit year by year that they fail to spend as much time as they should in managing the company's long-term future. But if we seriously accept the thesis that the essence of managerial responsibility is the extended time lapse between decision and result, currently reported profits are hardly a reasonable basis on which to compensate top executives. Such a basis simply serves to shorten the time horizon with which the executive is concerned.

The importance of an extended time horizon derives not only from the fact that an organization changes slowly and needs time to work through basic modifications in its strategy; it derives also from the fact that there is a considerable advantage in a certain consistency of strategy maintained over long periods of time. The great danger to companies which do not carefully formulate strategies well in advance is that they are prone to fling themselves toward chaos by drastic changes in policy—and in personnel—at frequent intervals. A parade of presidents is a clear indication of a board that has not really decided what its strategy should be. It is a common harbinger of serious corporate difficulty as well.

The time horizon is also important because of its impact on the selection of policies. The greater the time horizon, the greater the range in choice of tactics. If, for instance, the goals desired must be achieved in a relatively short time, steps like acquisition and merger may become virtually mandatory. An interesting illustration is the decision of National Cash Register to enter the market for electronic data-processing equipment. As reported in *Forbes:*

> One committed to EDP, NCR wasted no time. To buy talent and experience in 1953 it acquired Computer Research Corp. of Hawthorne, California . . . . For speed's sake, the manufacture of the 304's central units was turned over to GE . . . . NCR's research and development outlays also began curving steeply upwards.[11]

6. *Is the Strategy Workable?* At first glance, it would seem that the simplest way to evaluate a corporate strategy is the completely pragmatic one of asking:

[11] "NCR and the Computer Sweepstakes," *Forbes*, October 15, 1962, p. 21.

Does it work? However, further reflection should reveal that if we try to answer that question, we are immediately faced with a quest for criteria. What is the evidence of a strategy "working"?

Quantitative indices of performance are a good start, but they really measure the influence of two critical factors combined: the strategy selected and the skill with which it is being executed. Faced with the failure to achieve anticipated results, both of these influences must be critically examined. One interesting illustration of this is a recent survey of the Chrysler Corporation after it suffered a period of serious loss:

> In 1959, during one of the frequent reorganizations at Chrysler Corp., aimed at halting the company's slide, a management consultant concluded: "The only thing wrong with Chrysler is people. The corporation needs some good top executives."[12]

By contrast, when Olivetti acquired the Underwood Corporation, it was able to reduce the cost of producing typewriters by one-third. And it did it without changing any of the top people in the production group. However, it did introduce a drastically revised set of policies.

If a strategy cannot be evaluated by results alone, there are some other indications that may be used to assess its contribution to corporate progress:

- The degree of consensus which exists among executives concerning corporate goals and policies.
- The extent to which major areas of managerial choice are identified in advance, while there is still time to explore a variety of alternatives.
- The extent to which resource requirements are discovered well before the last minute, necessitating neither crash programs of cost reduction nor the elimination of planned programs. The widespread popularity of the meat-axe approach to cost reduction is a clear indication of the frequent failure of corporate strategic planning.

Conclusion

The modern organization must deploy expensive and complex resources in the pursuit of transitory opportunities. The time required to develop resources is so extended, and the time-scale of opportunities is so brief and fleeting, that a company which has not carefully delineated and appraised its strategy is adrift in white water.

In short, while a set of goals and major policies that meets the criteria listed above does not guarantee success, it can be of considerable value in giving management both the time and the room to maneuver.

[12] "How Chrysler Hopes to Rebound," *Business Week*, October 6, 1962, p. 45.

13

The Goal Formation Process in Complex Organizations

Walter Hill

Although some students in both economics and administration have recognized that organizational aims may vary in nature and importance not only among enterprises but also within a single establishment over time, no universally-accepted theory has evolved which explains the process of goal formation.[1]

The purpose of this paper is to suggest some foundations upon which such a theory can be constructed. This presentation will suggest that objectives are a function of the firm's external environment, its internal social system, the motives of individual participants who possess organizational power, and the bargaining process through which these people coalesce in order to marshal sufficient resources to determine objectives. Each of these variables will be explained then integrated into theoretical constructs.

Exogenous Variables. A complex organization does not possess unlimited goal-setting discretion; its choices are being increasingly influenced by external forces. Executive officers in all types of institutions must constantly be aware of each of their relevant environments and learn to define workable relationships with them in order to assure survival, much less success.

Successful adaptation to environmental pressures depends upon (1) the identification of relevant exogenous groups, (2) the determination of the form, focus, and intensity of their expectations, and (3) a measurement scheme to predict the impact of each of their requirements on organizational outputs and other identified outside claimants.

Identifying the Relevant Environment. A primary responsibility of executive officers is to identify those environmental forces which are capable of imposing constraints on goal-setting discretion. Although a precise definition of these groups will vary among organizations and within a single establishment over time due not only to a firm's own growth pattern and internal composition but also to the size, diversity, and instability of the exogenous influences, some general superordinate systems and their criteria have been identified for a business enterprise.

Many organizational members provide the chief administrator with salient information concerning environmental cognizance. Executives must synthesize this intelligence and identify those claimants whose demands must be recognized.

Reprinted with permission from *Journal of Management Studies*, Vol. 6, No. 2, May 1969, pp. 198–208.

[1] This paper uses the terms goals, objective, aims, and purposes interchangeably. This phenomenon is defined as the motives of executives which serve as value premises in the decision process.

Superordinate Systems	*Criteria*
Stockholders	Price appreciation of securities
	Dividend payout
Labor force (unions)	Wage levels
	Stability of employment
	Opportunity
The market: consumers	Value given
The market: competitors	Rate of growth
	Innovation
Suppliers	Rapidity of payment
Creditors	Adherence to contract terms
Community	Contribution to community development
Nation (government)	Public responsibility

Figure 1. Systems Criteria for Judging Company Performance

Source: Tilles, Seymour, "The Manager's Job: A Systems Approach," *Harvard Business Review,* Vol. 41 (January–February, 1963), p. 78.

The Form, Focus, and Intensity of Environmental Expectations. Environmental exchanges take the form of information transfers. On the one hand, organizational leaders can search out relevant outside groups and learn their criteria and reactions to policies and practices. Conversely, exogenous claimants can provide well prescribed or, more frequently, general cues concerning their expectations.

The acquired information may affect an enterprise's aim by: (1) prescribing or suggesting appropriate goals, (2) prohibiting some pursuits, (3) pointing out plausible means of achieving objectives, and (4) evaluating the extent to which adopted purposes have been attained. The impacts of exogenous claimants on organizational outputs (hence goals) can be shown in systemic constructs.

This illustration suggests that an organization has three major inputs; money, energy, and information. These enter a managerially determined conversion function which emits a set of outputs which are received and evaluated by the enterprise's superordinate systems which then feed back information to organizational leaders who analyze it, and if necessary, revise corporate intentions, policies, and procedures thus altering the original inputs and/or the conversion function.

Business leaders cannot neglect for long the demands (which can take the form of maximum or minimum constraints) imposed upon them by any of the systems which judge their performance. Two factors make the executive's task especially perplexing. First, every organization has a relatively fixed number of resources which can be allocated to satisfy claimants' demands. In the usual case these resources are insufficient to satisfy completely all demands therefore allocation priorities must be established. These are subject to controversy as well as modification.

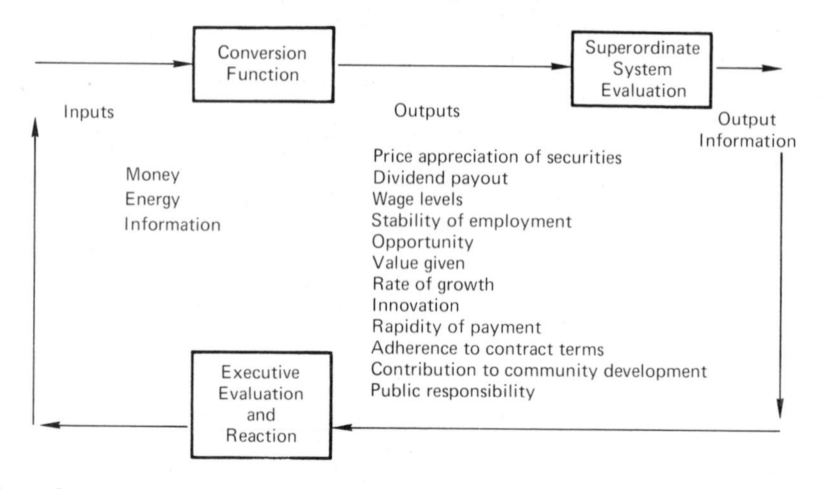

Figure 2. The Organization as a System

Second, a high degree of interdependency exists among the exogenous groups' demands. On the one hand, the demands of one system (e.g., unions' desires for higher wages) may conflict with those of other systems (e.g., stockholders' wishes for dividends and the nation's desire for price stability). On the other hand, individual participants may be members of several systems and thus seek satisfaction from many outputs. A customer, for example, may be a worker, a stockholder, and a member of the community. Thus even if an executive was not confronted with scarce resources, the conflicting nature of the demands of external forces would create administrative dilemmas.

The objectives adopted by administrative officials must be compatible with the expectations of each of the superordinate systems which can impose demands upon them. Although, at a particular moment in time, one claimant's requirements may acquire more organizational attention (e.g., union contract negotiations), the method of resolving these claims must not be disruptive to establish relationships with other groups. As Simon has stated: "The goal of an action is seldom unitary, but generally consists of a whole set of constraints the action must satisfy."[2]

One theoretically feasible method of resolving conflicting claims for scarce resources is to treat them in linear programming constructs.[3] This model assumes that (1) the satisfaction of each exogenous group can be defined in terms of the firm's outputs; (2) a variable number of organizational resources can be assigned to each output thus increasing or decreasing its magnitude;

[2] Simon, Herbert, "On the Concept of Organization Goal," *Administrative Science Quarterly* Vol. 9, June 1964, p. 1.

[3] For an example of a recent attempt to apply linear programming to the analysis of the impact of environmental variables see Buck E. Vernon. "A Model for Viewing an Organization as a System of Constraints," in Thompson, James D., (Ed.), *Approaches to Organizational Design* (Pittsburgh: The University of Pittsburgh Press, 1966), pp. 105–72.

Table 1. A linear programming approach to goal setting

Outputs/Claimants	*Stock holders*	*Labor force* (Unions)	*Consumers*	*Competitors*	*Suppliers*	*Creditors*	*Community*	*Nation*
Price appreciation	a11	a12	a13	a14	a15	a16	a17	a18
Dividends	a21	a22	a23	a24	a25	a26	a27	a28
Wages	a31	a32	a33	a34	a35	a36	a37	a38
Stable operations	a41	a42	a43	a44	a45	a46	a47	a48
Opportunity	a51	a52	a53	a54	a55	a56	a57	a58
Value given	a61	a62	a63	a64	a65	a66	a67	a68
Rate of growth	a71	a72	a73	a74	a75	a76	a77	a78
Innovation	a81	a82	a83	a84	a85	a86	a87	a88
Rapidity of payment	a91	a92	a93	a94	a95	a96	a97	a98
Adherence to contract terms	a101	a102	a103	a104	a105	a106	a107	a108
Contribution to community development	a111	a112	a113	a114	a115	a116	a117	a118
Public responsibility	a121	a122	a123	a124	a125	a126	a127	a128

and (3) organizational leaders can assign and alter priorities (utilities) for each of the outside claimants. Given these assumptions (admittedly they are *somewhat* heroic), the demands of exogenous groups will form a technical feasibility polygon which will define executive discretion in goal setting. Each of the boundaries of the polygon will represent the claims of an exogenous group. The enclosed region will indicate the area in which executives are free to pursue their own motives in establishing corporate aims. Naturally a corner solution will exist if the administrative officials choose to maximize the objective function.

The utilization of a linear programming approach would enable the goal-setters to ascertain the focus of each of their relevant outside claimants' demands as well as to predict the impact of a change in a constraint on existing objectives and the claims of other outside groups.

Predicting the Impact. The specific impact of each claimant's demands is a function of its power *vis-à-vis* that of the firm and other claimants. The precise measurement of the impact outputs is predicated on (1) the identification of a specific set of relevant exogenous groups, (2) the known requirements of each of these variables and each's power *vis-à-vis* the firm and other factors, and (3) the exact relationship of each of these factors to each of the outputs and to all other external forces. This information is seldom available.

An administrator deals with this enigma heuristically, i.e., through a process of trial and error. He subjectively speculates about many of the environmental demands and about the impact of changes in one variable on output and other exogenous factors. These factors are treated sequentially in order of importance. Goal choices then are made. Because of the uncertainty involved, these tend to be "satisfying" rather than maximizing in nature. This procedure is a learning process which can be improved by continuous, accurate feedback. Our knowledge of role theory is relevant here. Goal-setters define a role for the firm; environmental forces develop role expectations for the firm. Conflicts arise when role definitions and expectations are not congruent.

The process of adjusting to outside claimants influences the choices that can be made within the area of discretion as well as the size of the area itself. Thompson and McEwen suggest that administrative officials may adopt either a competitive, bargaining, co-optation, or coalition strategy in dealing with these forces. All these forms of accommodation subject the firm to some environmental control by "providing for 'outsiders' to enter into or limit the organization decision process."[4] The degree of control which a firm must relinquish varies with the strategy it selects where the choice of available strategies is a function of the company's power *vis-à-vis* that of the relevant exogenous group(s).

Although the simultaneous satisfaction of all these requirements is difficult, executives must establish tractable relationships with each external group.

[4] Thompson, James D. and McEwen, William J., "Organization Goals and Environment: Goal Setting as an Interaction Process," *American Sociological Review*, Vol. 23, February 1958, pp. 23–31.

The astute administrator can partially resolve this dilemma by (1) scheduling the sequence and frequency with which the demands of exogenous parties are processed; (2) making settlements with the various forces vague so that other groups do not become fully aware of their magnitude; and (3) stating objectives in broad, ambiguous terms so that all groups can perceive the plausibility of their demands being met. These practices provide a certain degree of stability within the technical feasibility polygon.

In summary, exogenous variables are important determinants of executive goal-setting discretion. These outside groups serve as evaluators of organizational outputs and their recognized requirements may be envisaged as forming a technical feasibility polygon within which objectives will be tractable. Administrative officials become aware of these demands either through self-initiated search or, more usually, through information feedback from these groups in the form of goal prescriptions, suggestions, and restrictions. This intelligence is analyzed, and if necessary, executives may alter system inputs and/or the conversion process to conform to environmental demands. The feasibility polygon is used to guide short and long run administrative goal choices, a process which Simon refers to as "alternative testing" when he states, "The goals (constraints) may be used to test the satisfactoriness of a proposed solution."[5] Since no theoretical models have been utilized to determine optimally the area within which objectives will be workable to all exogenous groups, they have evolved through a heuristic learning process predicated upon environmental feedback. The mode of accommodation to outside forces which the decision maker adopts influences the degree of discretion which he will have in reflecting his personal motives in the firm's ultimate purposes.

The Internal Social System. The internal social system is defined to include all organizational participants who, as individuals, do not control sufficient resources to influence significantly the goal-setting process.

The influence of the endogenous system is two-fold. First, individuals will remain in an organization only if they perceive that (1) their rewards will be equal to or greater than their contributions over some future time span; (2) this opportunity affords them a greater residual (rewards minus contributions) than others of which they are aware and capable of filling; and (3) enterprise purposes are either consistent with or neutral to their value premises.[6] The stability of the firm depends upon the designation of goals and rewards which are at least minimally acceptable to members of the internal social system. Second, the value premises of the enterprise's employees restrict the methods by which leaders may pursue their own motives. It should be remembered that lower participants only can attempt to influence the goal choice; they cannot make it. Executives can ignore these influences as the ultimate decision is theirs.

[5] Simon, Herbert, op. cit., p. 7.

[6] It is recognized that an important distinction can be drawn between an individual's motivation to affiliate with an organization and his motivation to produce within the enterprise. The former is our major interest. The latter is related to the efficiency with which an objective is pursued rather than its determination.

Individual's Possessing Power. It is well to recognize at this point that goals were defined to be a function of the reflection of the motives of the governing officials. Before an individual can insert his motives in the goals adopted by the organization, he must achieve power (usually, but not exclusively related to hierarchical position). Length of service, expertise, effort, interest, attractiveness, location and position are factors conducive to the acquisition and maintenance of power which is not inherent in the office itself. These factors plus the advantages associated with hierarchical position enable an individual to control organizational resources.

Personal Motives. Individuals possess diverse needs which may be altered over time as a function of whether or not their aspiration levels have been achieved. These motives may be manifested within the goal-feasibility polygon if the personnel control sufficient resources.

In general, individuals who possess organizational power seek satisfaction of esteem requirements. Esteem needs may be quite varied. Maslow has classified them into two categories: (1) those which can be satisfied by the person himself such as the desire for strength, achievement, confidence, independence, or freedom, and (2) those whose fulfillment depends upon others, e.g., reputation, prestige, recognition, attention, importance, or appreciation.[7] Since the specific form these needs may take differs with individuals, one can expect that the value premises which they set for organizational decisions may be dissimilar.

The specific direction which drives for esteem take also depends upon organizational traditions as well as the manager's learning process. Just as enterprise customs sanction some aims and reward others, the person's past experience, previous goals, and the experiences and intentions of his perceived reference group and the group to which he aspires to belong will influence the focus and degree of his drive.

An individual's ability to have his personal motives serve as enterprise aims depends upon the extent to which he controls the resources required for goal-setting. If a person attains sufficient power, his motives can be reflected as the organization's purposes. If he does not possess adequate control, he must combine with others to make sure that his motives are incorporated in the chosen goal constellation.

The Role of Coalitions. Before explicating the role coalitions play in the goal-setting process, some parameters must be established: (1) there are a few key individuals (those who possess organizational power) who can marshal sufficient resources to influence the direction of the firm; (2) these people may possess divergent motives; (3) a decision must be made; (4) no single alternative satisfies all participants; (5) a known number of resources must be controlled before one person or a group of individuals can determine the goal; and (6) any tractable decision must occur within the feasibility polygon estab-

[7] For a comprehensive explanation of the need hierarchy, see Maslow, Abraham H., "A Theory of Human Motivation," *Psychological Review*, Vol. 50, July 1943, pp. 370–96.

lished by the external system and must reflect motives acceptable to the internal social system.

The Coalition Formation Process. Given the above parameters, it is suggested that coalitions will form in the following manner.

> Any participant, A, estimates the payoff to himself from a prospective coalition as a product of the total payoff to that coalition and A's expected share of that total. The total payoff is known to A and the general hypothesis specifies the share which A will expect to give to others. Thus, A can assign to any prospective coalition a personal payoff value—his proportion of the resources in the coalition multiplied by the total payoff for that coalition.
>
> These values can be assigned to payoff classes of which A will prefer the highest. He does not recognize payoff differences between coalition strategies (prospective coalitions in the same payoff class). Within any class, he will pursue that coalition strategy whose members have the highest mean rank on his scale of non-utilitarian preferences.
>
> When a player must choose among alternative coalition strategies where the total payoff to a winning coalition is constant, he will maximize his payoff by maximizing his share. The theory states that he will do this by maximizing the ratio of his resources to the total resources of the coalition. Since his resources will be the same regardless of which coalition he joins, the lower the total resources, the greater will be his share. Thus, when the total payoff is held constant, he will favor the cheapest winning coalition.[8]

Table 2 depicts a situation involving three persons. The specific coalitions which will develop under varying resource distributions are illustrated.

Table 2. Predicted coalitions in triads of varying strength

Type number	*Distribution of Resources* — *Relative Strength*	*Absolute Strength**	*Predicted Coalition*
1	$A > (B + C), B = C$	$A = 60\%, B = C = 20\%$	None
2	$A > (B + C), B > C$	$A = 60\%, B = 30\%, C = 10\%$	None
3	$A = B = C$	$A = B = C = 33\frac{1}{3}\%$	Any
4	$A < (B + C), A > B, B = C$	$A = 40\%, B = C = 30\%$	*BC*
5	$A < (B + C), A > B > C$	$A = 40\%, B = 35\%, C = 25\%$	*BC*
6	$A < (B + C), A < B, B = C$	$A = 20\%, B = 40\%, C = 40\%$	*AB* or *AC*
7	$A < (B + C), A < B < C$	$A = 25\%, B = 35\%, C = 40\%$	*AB*
8	$A = (B + C), B > C$	$A = 50\%, B = 30\%, C = 20\%$	*AC*
9	$A = (B + C), B = C$	$A = 50\%, B = 25\%, C = 25\%$	*AB* or *AC*

Source: Gamson, William A., "A Theory of Coalition Formation," *American Sociological Review*, Vol. 26, June 1961, p. 377 (Modified).

* It is assumed that 51 per cent of the resources is sufficient to form a winning coalition.

[8] Gamson, William A., "A Theory of Coalition Formation," *American Sociological Review*, Vol. 26, June 1961, p. 374.

This table suggests that three general resource distribution patterns exist. First, one person may possess sufficient resources to determine organizational objectives unilaterally (Type 1 and 2). If he does, he will do so; no coalition will occur. Second, each individual has equal means, but none has sufficient power to decide goals (Type 3). A coalition is needed in this situation; any of the two members may combine. The winning alliance will consist of those two whose non-utilitarian preferences for each other are strongest. Third, varying degrees of strength exist among triad members, but no person has enough to make the choice. This case can be classified according to whether or not any individual has veto power; i.e., whether he must be included in the winning coalition. Coalition types 8 and 9 represent cases in which one member, A, must be part of any winning coalition. Since his membership is crucial to the alliance, he has a preferred bargaining position and may be able to procure more of the payoff than his resources dictate. Types 4–7 represent situations in which no person must be included in the winning alliance. These cases are decided by determining the cheapest winning coalition; i.e., that in which each member gets the largest possible share of the payoff. Thus, in Type 4, it is predicted that B and C will join together because both of their shares of the payoff will be larger than if either joined with A. (This same phenomenon holds for Types 5 and 7.) Type 6 illustrates the interesting case where the member with the smallest amount of resources actually is in a position to determine which alliance will form. This preferred bargaining advantage enables him to acquire a higher share of the payoff than his resources dictate by playing B off against C. Buck supports this approach when he suggests that "Organization goals are a function of the amount of agreement between resource controllers about what constitutes a desired end state. Since this is subject to individual change, organizational goals can change over time."[9]

Although the examples posed in Table 2 involve only three participants, the illustration can be expanded to include any number of individuals if one is willing to accept the premise that the determination of the winning coalition is a step-by-step procedure where members join two or more at a time.

The Goal Formation Process. The previous discussion suggests that goals are a function of the enterprise's external environment, its internal social system, the motives of individuals (usually executives) who control relevant resources, and the winning coalition formed through a bargaining process. These variables interact in the following manner. First, exogenous forces such as stockholders, suppliers, and the government establish a series of criteria which adopted purposes must satisfy. These forces assume the form of either minimum or maximum constraints, which can be envisaged as forming a feasibility polygon within which enterprise aims must lie if they are to be acceptable to outside forces. Since information sufficient to formulate a linear programming problem generally is not available, the process is heuristic.

Second, the internal social system acts as a constraint upon the motives organizational leaders are free to pursue. It can perform this function because

[9] Buck, Vernon, op. cit., p. 124.

participants will join and continue to affiliate with an organization only if its stated purposes are either congruent with or neutral to their values. This factor should not be considered a major deterrent to choice because those in a position to make such selections largely are influenced by the same cultural mores as members of the endogenous system. Hence, there is little likelihood that adopted administrative aims will be drastically different than those normally acceptable to society.

Third, individuals who can marshal sufficient resources are able to assert their preferences or objectives. These will tend to reflect their own need preferences. The goals which they seek to impose can be viewed as means to their own ends; i.e., they are intended to satisfy esteem needs.

Last, since the number of resources necessary to control the goal choice is large and since one administrative official normally does not possess sufficient power to make the selection by himself, coalitions must be formed to perform this function. The chosen objectives generally will be somewhat vague in order to reflect the fact that an integrating force (one which relates the overall aims to those of all members of the winning alliance) must be developed to elicit the support of enough resources to implement the decision.

14

The President and Corporate Planning

Myles L. Mace

Throughout the early 1960's, many top executives have been concerned about the need for more formalized corporate planning in their respective organizations. Some chief operating executives have searched for the "best system" and the "best methods" with the hope that the installation of another company's successful approach would achieve more effective results in their own corporate planning function. This situation is somewhat similar to that of the early 1950's, when many company executives were searching for the best system to provide for the growth and development of key personnel.[1]

As in the 1950's, preoccupation with the forms, procedures, and techniques of a best system produces lip service to an important management function, but accomplishes little toward achievement of real, honest-to-goodness plans for the future direction of corporations. To mechanically adopt the methods and procedures which appear to be useful in the ABC Corporation does not assure fulfillment of the planning function in the XYZ Corporation. Such

Reprinted from *Harvard Business Review,* Vol. 43, No. 1 (January–February, 1965), pp. 49–62, by permission of the publisher.

[1] See my book, *The Growth and Development of Executives* (Boston, Division of Research, Harvard Business School, 1950).

thinking is analogous to believing that the adoption of a "suggestion system" automatically builds employee morale.

Administrative Focus

Effective corporate planning does not consist simply of a system. Rather, it is an administrative process and a critically important job which should concern the management of every corporation. Forms and procedures may be employed as convenient and useful tools. But the success of corporate planning is not measured by the writing of procedures, the addition of a new box on the organization chart, or the production of an impressive-looking book entitled "Corporate Goals and Plans—1965–1970—Confidential."

Some executives have indicated that corporate planning is required only in large and diverse enterprises and that managements of small and medium sized companies need not be concerned. Planning as an essential business function is as important to the small company as it is to the large.[2] Indeed, individual planning is important for each person who has aspirations for success in a business organization.

In 1961 and 1962, George G. Montgomery, Jr., now a vice president of White Weld Company in New York, and I made a research study of the problems involved in the acquisition of one company by another.[3] A segment of that study was concerned with planning for growth through acquisition. With this background, which has been augmented by continued interest and experience, especially with regard to the planning function, I shall undertake to deal in this article with what seem to be some of the most important and practical steps involved in the attainment of effective and useful corporate planning.

President's Involvement. Probably the single most important problem in corporate planning derives from the belief of some chief operating executives that corporate planning is not a function with which they should be directly concerned. They regard planning as something to be delegated, which subordinates can do without responsible participation by chief executives. They think the end result of effective planning is the compilation of a "Plans" book. Such volumes get distributed to key executives, who scan the contents briefly, file them away, breathe a sigh of relief, and observe, "Thank goodness that is done—now let's get back to work."

George Montgomery and I found in the course of the acquisition research mentioned above that effective corporate planning is not possible without the personal involvement and leadership of the chief operating executive. Subsequent study confirmed this conclusion. Involvement and leadership mean spending the time and energy to manage the function—to see that something

[2] See Roger A. Golde, "Practical Planning for Small Business," HBR September–October 1964, p. 147.

[3] *Management Problems of Corporate Acquisitions* (Boston, Division of Research, Harvard Business School, 1962).

concrete is done. They mean personally putting into action what is too often abrogated by general words and phrases. In specific terms, there are two fundamental functions which absolutely demand the chief executive's active involvement:

1. *Leadership in the tough and laborious process of realistically evaluating existing product lines, markets, trends, and competitive positions in the future.*
2. *Leadership in the establishment of corporate objectives.*

After examining each of these critically important leadership functions, I shall discuss the basic elements of a planning program.

Realistic Evaluation

Among many corporate executives, the concept of planning is believed necessary only to find new areas of product opportunity. Planning programs organized to achieve this limited scope completely overlook the possibility of augmenting or strengthening existing product lines or product divisions.

Analysis of the history of sales, margins, and profits by product or product line discloses significant trends which are frequently unnoticed in the course of the day-to-day management of companies. For example:

A five-year history was compiled of the products which comprised 80% of a company's sales. It became clear that some product margins had steadily declined, others had remained stable, and the increase in total company sales and profits was attributable to a few high gross-margin items. The company's success had camouflaged what was happening to products which once had been substantial contributors to profits.

This relatively simple analysis led to further study of market prospects for the less profitable items. It was concluded that an inability to raise market prices or reduce costs required the addition of new, higher margin products if the sales and profits of the corporation were to be maintained or grow in the future.

Some chief operating executives find it difficult to recognize that product lines which have produced generous profits over many years are in jeopardy. Competitive facts of life encroach on markets, but a sentimental attachment to the past leads to a euphoric attitude about the future. Reluctance to face up to the situation is characterized by such statements as, "We have been through tough times before and we can do it again," or, "This business has been mighty good to us in the past and we are going to stick with it," or, "Sooner or later the competitor's prices have got to come back in line, and when that happens, we will be on our way again."

Admittedly it is painful to accept the unpleasant fact that uncontrollable outside competitive forces have depleted long-standing markets and margins. But a chief operating executive who procrastinates in adopting an action-planning program to adjust to changing conditions jeopardizes profits and, in some cases, the company's solvency. For example:

In a situation where competitors had moved in and taken over a certain company's once very profitable market, the chief operating executive of the company recognized the fact that the market was completely gone. However, sentimentally aware of the score of key people whose careers were identified only with that market, he refused to make the hard decision to reduce sharply or eliminate outright the jobs of the people working on the lost cause. The last several years have been characterized by increasing annual deficits, and the inevitable decision remains to be made.

When chief operating executives do not, as an integral part of their planning role, recognize realistically the status of their existing operations and fulfill the leadership role by adapting to changing conditions, they jeopardize current profits as well as the capacity of the organization to prosper in the future.

Corporate Objectives

In some companies a distinction is made between corporate objectives and corporate goals. Here I regard objectives and goals as synonymous, because corporate planning consists of creating the goals and defining in detail the corporate plans to achieve those goals.

I have found that the phrase "creation of corporate objectives" is regarded by some chief operating executives as rather meaningless, academic language—they think creating objectives is something professors talk about, and that such goals have little real value in the management of a business enterprise. Discounting the value of defining corporate objectives probably arises in part from the many published statements which describe the goals in broad general terms—such as increased sales, increased profits, a broader base of operations, a better environment for the growth of personnel, and so forth. Such expressions of objectives are, indeed, neither meaningful nor useful.

Direction Needed. In some companies I have found no explicit or implicit concepts of corporate goals. One consequence of this lack of direction is that product and division managers more often than not create their own goals, and the result is a hodgepodge of unrelated, unintegrated, and expensive internal research and product development programs. Consider this example:

In one company, the division managers were urged by the chief operating executive to "do something about increasing sales and broadening the base of operations." Each of four division managers embarked on independent and uncoordinated product development projects. Later, capital appropriations and operating budgets were approved by headquarters management, and after a four-year period and a loss of $3 million, the four division managers were engaged in liquidating their respective abortive ventures.

A product development program with carefully defined goals certainly is no guarantee that the product produced and marketed will be successful. But a product development program with goals certainly is financially more economical and less wasteful of management talent at the division level.

Discussions with chief executives about the concept of creating corporate goals indicate that many think there is something mysterious about the process. There is concern about the method or approach to be used in outlining corporate objectives. How does one go about deciding the mission of an organization? Do statements of goals spring full blown from the minds of presidents? Should we hire consultants to tell us what our objectives should be? Or perhaps hire an economist who can forecast the most promising markets of the future? How do we know what business conditions will be like two years or five years from now? How can we plan effectively when our business is so fast moving that the creation of long-range goals means anticipating what we will do next week?

Thinking Required. Some companies neglect corporate planning because the process intrinsically requires thinking about the future and the future is always uncertain. Anticipating all the factors which affect a company's sales and profits means dealing intellectually with mercurial and intangible elements. This is especially difficult for the action-minded, decision-oriented executive who enjoys and derives great satisfaction from "doing things." Also, and this is one of the most common reasons for deferring thinking about the future, day-to-day crises need decisions right now, and there are usually enough crises to occupy most or all of each business day.

One president stated that "the tyranny of the moment prevents me from paying attention to the important future of the company." Another president said:

> Thinking seems to have lost respectability in some companies. If a vice president is caught sitting at his desk without papers, people, or telephone calls and, in response to a query by the president as to what he is doing, says "thinking," the typical reaction of the president is likely to be, "Thinking! If you are going to think, think on your own time."

But despite the obstacles, real and imagined, to corporate planning, many chief executives regard the function as one of their principal duties and are actively engaged in planning the future paths of their organizations.

Simple Process. Yet the process of corporate planning is relatively simple and straightforward. Much of the mystery of planning comes from the many general admonitions provided by students of management who describe planning as a composite of abstract elements made up of strategy, tactics, purpose, specifications, alternatives, and so on. Chief executives who are doing effective planning jobs describe the process in more practical and meaningful terms. From conversations with them, I shall summarize and illustrate briefly the five basic elements of a planning program, including the creation of corporate goals.

Analyzing the Present

Planning for the future starts with an intimate and realistic understanding of existing products, divisions, markets, margins, profits, return on investment, cash flow, availability of capital, research and development abilities, and skills and capacities of personnel. These significant aspects of operations can be looked at in an orderly manner, and there is nothing mysterious about an analysis of the company's strength and weakness in each of these areas. Basic to consideration of a mission for the company in the future is a clear recognition of how well the organization is doing today.

Analysis of present operations can be done effectively by reviewing the past few years' performance as part of the evaluation of the current year's operating and capital budget forecasts. In some cases, top managements ask division or functional managers to submit the proposed annual budgets together with budgets for the next three to five years. The headquarters review of the short-term forecast is thus combined with the long-term forecast, which otherwise would be a separate, second step. This method of reviewing and evaluating both forecasts simultaneously has the apparent advantage of economy of management time and effort.

However, many top executives find that the discussion invariably focuses on the short-term prospect because of its imminence, and that the long-term problems are deferred or given only brief attention. Current operating problems should be distinguished from the longer-term goals and plans. The purposes of evaluating short-term forecasts and long-term projections—both extremely important—are so different that two separate presentations and evaluations need to be made. Short-term budgets require headquarters modification and approval for financial commitments, whereas long-term forecasts are not subject to authority to spend or commit.

Predicting the Future

Forecasts for each of the next three of five years, based on current operations and existing plans for improving operations, are an important element of a sound planning program. If the company continues to do what it is doing and planning to do today, what will be its future sales, profit, market position, and so on?

Many different approaches produce useful forecasts. These vary from elementary dollar results to more detailed and complex breakdowns of business functions. In one company, which is organized on the basis of decentralized, autonomous divisions for which profit and loss are measurable, each of the seven division managers is asked to submit five-year plans based on an eight-point outline. (A detailed breakdown of this type of outline is given in the Appendix for the reader who would like a more concrete picture of such a forecast.)

In another company, as an illustration, division managers are asked to supply the following information for a three-year forecast:

- Sales by product line.
- Gross profits by product line.
- Personnel requirements.
- Capital expenditure needs.

Normally, the data prepared by division or functional managers is submitted in writing two or three weeks in advance of a review date so that the president and other headquarters executives can thoroughly examine the forecasts prior to the meeting.

Reviewing the Forecasts

Here again, practices vary among the companies I have observed. In one, for example, eight divisional managers meet for two days at headquarters, and each manager is allowed two hours to make a presentation of his present operations and his plans for the future. The president and key headquarters executives listen to each presentation and typically ask general, unchallenging questions. It is an essentially meaningless exercise for all concerned.

In contrast, in a certain company where the president regards corporate planning as his most important job, full-day reviews are made of each division manager's report on his goals and his plans to achieve those goals for each of the next three years. Here the president and key headquarters executives study the written portions of the presentation prior to the meeting and are well armed with perceptive and challenging questions about the validity of their managers' forecasts. Several years' experience with this approach has resulted in increasingly effective, realistic forecasts by the division managers and complete recognition by executives in the company that, while the president is the leader in planning, all key personnel have a share in making the planning function real and meaningful.

Critical evaluation of forecasts prepared by division or functional managers is also required to prevent subordinates from regarding the process of preparing forecasts as an exercise and not an integral part of responsible planning. For example:

- In some companies managers supply financial forecasts by product line by mechanically projecting 5% increases in sales and profits for each year. Such an approach observes the amenities of corporate procedures but, if unchallenged by top executives, adds little effectiveness to statements of what can be expected in the future.
- In other companies managers purposely overstate their expectations with the hope of manifesting to headquarters executives what fine performances can be expected in the future.
- Still other managers employ the strategy of understating forecasts for the purpose of establishing financial goals relatively easy to achieve. Thus approbation will come from headquarters if the forecasts are subsequently exceeded. Hopefully, this will be expressed in higher salaries and bonuses.

Careful and thoughtful review, therefore, is required to validate the reasonableness of managers' forecasts and to provide a realistic composite picture of the future achievement of the entire enterprise.

Critical evaluation by top executives of division or functional managers' longer-range goals and plans has another important advantage. A discussion by able, experienced, and interested executives about the operations of a division inevitably results in the disclosure of some new opportunity not thought of previously. The interplay of active minds dedicated to greater growth and success stimulates new avenues of thought which can be enormously helpful to the division and to the company.

When all of the division or functional managers' goals and plans have been reviewed, a composite report representing the totals for the entire company should be prepared. Some companies accept the forecasts of divisions as presented, and the total becomes the program. In others, the chief executive and his key subordinates review again all the separate programs and adjust the division figures according to their previous experience with the respective division managers. History indicates that some managers are unreformed optimists and others are perpetual pessimists. If discussion during the review does not result in adjustment, the chief executive must make appropriate increases or decreases in order to arrive at a realistic overall forecast.

Evaluating the Program

When all managers' forecasts have been reviewed critically and adjusted to represent more appropriately the judgment of the company's top executives, the total program can be evaluated for the purpose of (1) accepting the forecasted performance as reasonable, or (2) deciding that the stated program does not comprise a suitable growth rate for the company.

Dominant Considerations. A significant and controlling determinant in arriving at a conclusion as to the adequacy of proposed division or functional plans is the attitude, personal desire, and aspiration of the chief operating executive. It is frequently assumed that every chief executive aspires to head a growing and increasingly profitable enterprise—that by taking into account the interests of stockholders, employees, customers, and the communities within which the company operates, he will make thoughtful decisions to grow, prosper, and fulfill social and public responsibilities. While this is generally true, some chief executives are motivated by other primary considerations which dominate many major policy decisions. For example:

In a western consumer products company the president and his key subordinates recognized that their major strengths were in the research, development, and manufacturing of potentially profitable new products, but the company's marketing organization had proved to be ineffective in establishing distribution to thousands of outlets in the United States. Several unsuccessful attempts were made to strengthen the marketing group.

Meanwhile, a competitor with a superb marketing staff continued to increase its share of the market. The president of the competing company, in planning the future growth of his enterprise, perceived that continued growth in sales and profits would be possible only with more effective product research, development, and manufacturing facilities. Dissatisfied with the time which would be required to build a stronger development and manufacturing group, he explored the alternative of acquiring another company with the necessary strengths to complement his organization.

A study of possible acquisitions resulted in the identification of the western company described above, and the two presidents initiated negotiations to merge the two companies. Continued discussions disclosed that the fit was even better than originally conceived—stock prices and dividend policies were substantially alike, terms of exchange were agreed on, antitrust laws were not an obstacle—and a plan for the integration of the two organizational structures was evolved which met the desires and aspirations of both groups.

The one snag was: Who would be the chief operating executive of the merged enterprises? It was clear that joining the two companies would substantially benefit the stockholders, the employees, and the communities where the companies had operations. Negotiations continued intensively for several weeks, but were terminated when it was apparent that both presidents wanted to be the chief operating executive of the merged companies. Neither was willing to take the second position, although many possible divisions of authority and responsibility were considered and rejected in turn. The personal desire of each president to retain the position as chief executive prevented the merger, and the two companies continued to operate competitively.

I have found similar examples of dominant personal considerations in other situations, but the real reasons for termination of merger discussions are rarely publicized. The usual explanation is that differences on price or differences on major policies have led both parties to conclude that each company should remain independent and autonomous.

Hidden Motives. In other cases, the chief operating executives disguise their personal desires and goals for their companies. They profess the conviction that their companies should adjust to changed conditions in their respective industries, that new areas of activity should be searched for and entered. But personal, and usually unexpressed, reasons control the decisions not to take the risks involved in moving into promising market opportunities.

At a research seminar conducted at the University of California, Los Angeles, to discuss long-range planning, one of the participants, Rex Land, described his experience with a company which tried to hide its basic objectives, but eventually was found out. Land said:

> I know of a company, very closely held, the executives of which (after a great deal of probing action) finally admitted they were primarily interested in maintaining the prestige of other members of the family. The top executive was not going to take certain risks that would jeopardize his income or that of four or five members of his family. His could have been a growing and healthy company if it had brought in and held executives, but he could not keep people for very long. It took people five years to realize what the real objectives of this company were.[4]

[4] Reported in *Managerial Long-Range Planning*, edited by George A. Steiner (New York, McGraw-Hill Book Company, 1963), p. 38.

In another company, the president made a review of a five-year forecast of sales and profits based on the continuation of status quo operations. It seemed possible with existing products, he reasoned, to maintain the same flat curve of sales and profits achieved over the last several years. He concluded, therefore, that the company's plan would be to maintain this level of performance and not to try to grow in size or profitability. In a lengthy discussion of his plan and planning process, he conceded that he felt personally comfortable heading the organization at its present size. "If I grow and take on more people, I am not too sure I could do it. And even if I could, I am not willing to pay the price of the extra effort required."

Personal Fears. Other chief operating executives, after reviewing forecasts of gradually declining sales and profits based on present operations and plans, resignedly accept the anticipated results because of personal fears of risking substantial sums of development or capital expenditure money. Consider this example:

The president of a large family corporation in the East regarded his role as that of a conservator. Several members of the family held corporate executive titles, and the value of the company constituted the principal of the family trust created for them by their deceased father, who had founded the company.

Technological changes in the industry resulted in a gradual erosion of the company's sales and profits which, for years, had enjoyed the dominant position in a segment of the industrial instruments business. None of the company's top executives could foresee anything except continued declines in sales, profit, and market position unless the company risked an estimated $3 million investment in product development.

The policy dilemma of whether to risk $3 million of what was regarded as the assets of the family trust or whether to accept the forecasted future of further declines was resolved by the president when he chose to "ride out this temporary decline trend." The company president has continued to reject the alternative risk, and the company sales and profits have continued to deteriorate.

While these foregoing examples illustrate the importance and influence of attitudes, personal desires, and aspirations of chief operating executives, indeed they are not at all typical of the majority of companies.

Typical Executives. Usually presidents are found to be searching for ways to increase the size and profitability of their respective corporations. And if the forecasted performance of existing operations fails to produce expectations of profitable growth, plans are initiated to build on the business of the present. In my studies the more common president is one who is rarely satisfied with nominal growth rates, who stretches the forecasts of divisional or functional managers, and who establishes new and challenging standards of performance for the organization to achieve. Such presidents regard lack of growth as stagnation, an attribute they abhor.

When chief operating executives review and evaluate the forecasted performance for three to five years and conclude that the financial figures are reasonable and plans for their realization feasible, the composite documents constitute the corporate plan for the stated period of years ahead. Sometimes these "working papers" are regarded as "company goals and plans." In other cases the significant elements of them are formalized into "corporate goals," and the various segments of the corporate plans for achievement are spelled out in great detail. The mission and the plan for achievement are thus clearly defined.

However, when the chief operating executives conclude that the anticipated results are not adequate, it becomes imperative to think through and construct a new or modified set of goals and a new plan to fulfill these desired objectives.

Creating the Goals

In my discussions with presidents who are concerned about the anticipated lack of growth in their companies, the query recurs, "Just how do I go about creating a new set of corporate goals?"

While I have found several successful approaches in the many companies studied, my major conclusions will be discouraging to those who are looking for a quick and easy method. There is no mechanical or expert "instant answer method." Rather, defining corporate goals—and modifying those goals as the future becomes the present—is a long, time-consuming, and continuous process. Each president in each company must regard the construction and adjustment of goals as an important, absolute, and—in a sense—unique requirement of his job.

There are, however, several ways of defining company goals that may suggest a modus operandi to those concerned with this requirement.

Reorganize Work Habits. With the background and essential information resulting from (1) a realistic analysis of existing operations, including opportunities for growth, (2) adjusted forecasts by division or functional managers of their anticipated performance, and (3) an evaluation of the three-, four-, and five-year forecasts, the chief operating executive can embark on the difficult process of creating a structure of corporate goals.

The process is particularly difficult for some chief executives because accepting corporate planning as an important function means not engaging in parts of the satisfying activities which have kept them completely occupied in the past. Planning takes time, and time becomes available for busy men largely through modification of their work habits. The president of a large eastern company stated recently, "The creation and manning of three new group vice presidential positions to cover nine domestic divisions and our international subsidiaries ought to enable me to give more attention to our corporate goals."

Another said, "In the past I did not take the time as skipper of this corporate ship to plot our course. The absence of direction created a vacuum into which rushed improvisation. The resulting chaos and hodgepodge forced me to recognize that I must take the time to think through where we want to go."

Enlist Key People. While the main responsibility for defining corporate goals rests on the chief executives, they can enlist the minds and imaginations of other key people in their organizations. To do this, some chief operating executives ask the top eight or ten executives to join them in a three- or four-day retreat to help them start thinking through together what the corporate goals should be. Preferably, such a meeting should be held away from "headquarters" to avoid the diversions of telephones, problems, and decisions. Such "think" or "skull" sessions are found to be most effective when tentative drafts of ideas are prepared prior to the meeting to serve as the focus of discussion. Such preliminary drafts can, but need not, delimit the considerations, since thoughtful and imaginative executives usually extrapolate quickly. One president observes that these sessions should also provide for a break of an hour or two in the afternoon for exercise; otherwise everyone gets to thinking in circles.

Some company presidents look for more from such skull sessions than can be reasonably expected. The thinking and planning process, as indicated earlier, is a long, continuing, and tough process. It is long because answers are not easily come by; continuing because the corporate goals are subject to change, adapting to new conditions; and tough because the process of thinking about the future means dealing with intangibles and assumptions. If an organization is formalizing its planning program for the first time, the most that can be expected from such a meeting is the beginning of an understanding of the magnitude of the problems and the start of the process of formulating possible elements of a statement of goals.

Some presidents assign the job of defining corporate goals to a task force made up of three or four key members of the organization. Others ask an experienced line or staff executive to study the problems and recommend a statement of mission for the company. But, irrespective of the approach used, I find that no real and meaningful goals are outlined without the direct involvement of the chief operating executive. Without his active leadership in the function, resulting concepts are usually interesting but irrelevant products of an academic exercise. With his leadership, it is possible to analyze, to think through alternatives, and to arrive at a practical, workable, and useful outline of the mission of the enterprise.

Hire Responsible Consultants. Other presidents employ management consultants to advise on what the goals of their corporation should be. Responsible consultants, unbiased and unprejudiced by the way things have been done, can bring to the task the benefit of outside objectivity. Most organizations include undisclosed sacred cows which executives of the company have learned not to molest. Sometimes the unmolested sacred cow is the reason for lack of interest in growth, and the consultant feels a responsibility to report his conclusions objectively. Many times suggestions by consultants on sacrosanct subjects have opened them up for re-examination and, sometimes, even change. New points of view injected by consultants often stimulate corporate top management to audit anew many policies, practices, and other matters which have continued unchallenged over the years. Here is an example:

In one company in the East, a substantial part of its sales and profits over the last 20-year period had been derived from one product line in the electronics industry. More recently, competitive Japanese products had entered the United States and pre-empted a large portion of the market. The eastern company sought protection through increased tariffs and intercountry agreements on the amounts to be imported, but neither approach stemmed the increasing market share taken over by the Japanese products. The company management was slow in recognizing the business facts of life and continued to maintain a large and expensive manufacturing facility and a high-salaried marketing group.

A consultant was employed to analyze the company's operations and to recommend a program of remedial action. A few months after he began his analysis of the company, he asked the president and the executive committee, "Why do you stay in that part of the electronics industry when you have been losing money steadily for three years and there are no prospects you can ever make profits there again?"

The directness of the question on a clearly vulnerable point jarred the executives into facing up to a decision not previously even discussed—liquidation of the unprofitable product line with no potential for improvement.

In addition to a hard-nosed look at sacrosanct subjects, the consultant (with wider experience in different companies and industries than corporate executives whose careers may have been limited to one company, one industry, or one geographical area) can often bring to the task new insights. In one company, the president and nine out of ten of the other top executives had devoted their entire careers to the same company. Their understanding of business was limited to a single industry with its small tangential and related activities. Here the consultant—knowing that the world of business is larger than the manufacture and sale of umbrellas, or file cabinets, or maple furniture—was able to suggest possibilities for a broadened base of operations.

No consultants are known, however, who have instantaneous, magic answers as to what goals a particular company might adopt. Surprisingly, some presidents think, "There must be someone, somewhere, who can tell us quickly what we ought to do." Here again, no such consulting sources can be found. The responsible consultant will take the time—and this does take time—to analyze objectively a company's existing operations before he is prepared to recommend programs of action and goals.

Adopt a Statement. The form and detail of the actual statements which define company goals vary from very simple to elaborate verbal descriptions. In one company, for example, the corporate goals are briefly stated:

1. To increase the return on investment from 4% to 6% by 1966.
2. To increase earnings from $3 per share in fiscal 1965 to $5 per share in 1967.

Another company's objectives are stated in a more detailed way:

1. To raise after-tax earnings from $12 million to $18 million by 1967 without diluting the equity.

2. To change the proportion of the company's military business from 65% to 40% in two years. (In another company a goal was expressed "to raise the percentage of military business from 40% to 65%.")

3. To liquidate in an orderly manner Division A and those parts of Division B which are unprofitable as soon as possible.

4. To search for and acquire one or more companies in the United States with sales of at least $10 million in the XYZ industry.

5. To establish in the Common Market at least three bases of operations, either by acquisition or by starting our own operations, by 1967.

Design a Plan. The creation of a statement of reasonable goals, in turn, leads to the need for a plan to realize those goals. Here, again, the plan may be a written description or exist only in the minds of top executives, and it may be relatively simple or exceedingly detailed and complex. Many companies of substantial size write descriptions of their goals and an over-all company plan to arrive at those goals, and support these with a marketing plan, a technical plan, a manufacturing plan, a personnel plan, and a financial plan which includes a cash-flow plan.

Planning Staff

The importance of involvement by the chief operating executive has been stressed throughout this article to underline my conviction of the need for his participation. But clearly much of the data collection, procedures for the collection of data, and analysis can and should be done by subordinates in the organization or by a corporate planning office. The need for a separate planning staff is determined largely by the capacities, interests, and time of line and staff executives available. Sometimes the vice president of finance is given the responsibility of heading the planning function because the number aspects constitute a common language of plans.

I find, however, that the most effective way of accomplishing corporate planning is to create a new staff group—reporting to the president—free from the diversion of day-to-day crises and charged with the responsibility of assisting the president. The assistance includes, among other things, helping the chief operating executive "to crystallize goals in the leadership and direction of the company."

Functions & Qualifications. The functions of a planning group vary, but the vital ones are included in the following statement adopted by a large western company:

1. To assure that divisions and subsidiaries prepare annual and five-year plans for growth.

2. To assist divisions and subsidiaries in the preparation of annual and five-year projections.

3. To identify areas of product opportunity for divisions and subsidiaries, and for corporate investment.

4. To perform market research as requested by divisions and subsidiaries.

5. To coordinate and monitor the preparation of a written, company-wide, five-year plan.

6. To analyze the economic future of existing operations and to recommend programs of growth or divestment.

7. To make analyses of business, economic, and political conditions bearing on existing or prospective areas of operations.

8. To be responsible for all negotiations with possible companies to be acquired.

During the past few years, many company managements have come to recognize the need for more formalized planning activities. This often leads to the creation of new units, ranging in size from one man to a dozen or more. Frequently, the personnel assigned to the function are transferred from existing line or staff activities. In some cases, these people perform admirable jobs. In a New York chemical company, for example, when the need for intensive planning was recognized, a statement was drafted of the ideal personal qualifications and experience for the job. Here are the important elements of that statement:

- Technical knowledge of organic and inorganic chemistry.
- Ability to manage people.
- Ability to inculcate division managers and headquarters staff officers with the importance of planning as an essential part of their jobs.
- Analytical capacity.
- Knowledge of financial data, including ability to analyze balance sheets, profit and loss statements, cash-flow forecasts, and operating and capital budgets.
- Imagination—ability to perceive new applications for corporate competence.

A review of personnel employed within the company disclosed that the manager of the research and development laboratory possessed most of the desired qualities, and he was moved to the new post, "Director of Product Development and Corporate Planning."

Job Requirements. Often, however, chief operating executives do not think through the job requirements of the important role to be performed by the head of planning. Consequently, they assign somebody who just happens to be available. In some companies, retired, about-to-retire, pseudo-retired, or quasi-retired executives are asked to take on this function during their remaining years with the company. The rationale is: "Joe has been with the company for 40 years, and he knows it inside and out. The planning responsibility will keep him busy for three or four years, and, besides, we need a younger man in his important operational job." When the planning group is regarded so lightly that it becomes a dumping ground for the aging or less competent, it is likely to achieve nothing of consequence. Planning today is a critically important function in management, and it requires the best talent, not the infirm of mind or body.

The need for additional personnel is dictated by the magnitude of the corporate tasks and the availability of staff help in the organization. For example:

• In one company, the director of budgets had had extensive experience in another company with financial operating forecasts and cash flows, and their analyses. He was able and interested in serving the needs of the director of plans, and it was not necessary to assign a financial analyst to the plans office.

• In another company, the market research department, part of the marketing group, regarded assignments from the plans department as an important part of its responsibilities and was equipped to handle them.

Many companies have assigned only a few personnel to the planning task initially and added others only when the job requirements indicated need for additional help.

Planners' Problems

Two critical problems which are sometimes encountered by the director of plans call for special attention and close monitoring by the chief executive to assure the success of the corporate planning function. Let's look at what can be done about each one.

Inculcating Awareness. One difficult problem of a director of plans is to inculcate line managers of divisions, subsidiaries, or other company operations with an awareness of the importance of planning as a vital part of *their* jobs. In some situations, long-range planning means nothing more to a division manager than going through the needless task of preparing an annual operating budget, getting it done, sending it to the vice president of finance, and forgetting about it until the next year.

In one eastern company with five years' experience with formalized corporate planning, the vice president for plans summarized his concepts of what remained to be done on this problem in future planning meetings:

1. *Create an awareness in division managers of the need for planning beyond the next 12 months into 1966, 1967, and beyond.* This can be done by directing the questions and discussion away from the current year whenever possible and talking about 1967 and 1968 objectives.

2. *Assess how well the divisions have integrated all the elements of planning in their programs (including timing) to make sure that programs have been thought through.* The use of a checklist in this connection may be helpful, of which the key elements should be:

- Analysis (e.g., product line breakdowns).
- Potentials—available skills, and available and needed resources.
- Problems—deficiencies evident.
- Establishment of best alternatives—suggested economic goals.
- Coordination-implementation-timing—the results expected, both financial and non-financial.

3. *Create a means of implementing* continued *planning so that the divisions will complete any unfinished plan or revise any inadequate parts of it during 1965.* As the discussion progresses, it is wise to examine areas in which planning is not complete and ask that a timetable and action plan be set up for putting together the missing elements after the meeting. Such a plan can be worked up between the division and the director of plans. In this instance, it is necessary to cover (a) the need for planning responsibility to be centered in a capable individual, and (b) the importance that management attaches to this function—which might require additional expenditure.

4. *Determine what standards for measurement, if any, the divisions have in setting goals.* For example, have the divisions set some over-all goal to strive for in sales, profits, investment, and return, as a measuring stick of their own performance? Do they feel that the goals are adequate? What restrictions are holding them back from enlarging these goals?

5. *Determine whether the divisions have compared the amount of technical effort (either at the division level or at the company's headquarters laboratory) on their long-range projects with the profit potential in these projects.* In addition, it is important to determine whether they have considered the degree to which they should be investing profits from existing business in technical effort for potential future rewards. (Similar consideration can be given to marketing's planning for future sales by strengthening or adding to the market organization.)

6. *Get across to the divisions that they should be striving to add more projects to their existing base than they or the corporation can absorb in terms of research and development and capital facilities, so that the most desirable projects can be selected from a wide list.*

7. *Assess the reasonableness of the goals, so as to come up with a consolidated, long-term corporate goal, adjusted to take into account undue optimism or pessimism in the divisions.* The plans should be weighed against past ability to get the job done, how tight a timetable is possible, and how capable the organization is, or can rapidly become, to accomplish the task.

8. *Determine the degree to which the headquarters staff, including marketing, planning, research laboratory, market research, manufacturing, can help implement the divisions' programs.*

9. *Make sure a program is established to see that the advice given by the headquarters staff is followed up.*

10. *Identify the ways in which the divisions can work together in projects requiring complementary skills.*

Unplanned Plans. Another critical—and frustrating—problem of directors of corporate planning evolves from the actions of the chief operating executive who accepts and approves a carefully worked out set of corporate goals and plans for achievement and then, by his arbitrary decisions, moves the company into activities neither related nor contemplated. Indeed, the most carefully thought-out corporate goals and plans must yield to the emergence of some new and previously unthought-of opportunity. Any planning program must be flexible. But, on fundamental plan principles, deviation from agreed-upon programs ought to be restudied before commitments are made. Consider:

In a company where a substantial part of its total investment was subject to the risks of operations abroad, the chief operating executive stated that the ratio of domestic to foreign investment should be increased and that no new money should be exposed to risks from abroad. Shortly after the corporation goals were discussed and adopted by the executive committee, the president learned of a possible acquisition in Italy. He flew to Rome and, within a relatively short time, negotiated and arranged for the purchase of a company. The foreign investment commitment increased by several million dollars, and the stated ratio goals became meaningless standards for the organization.

Concluding Note

Corporate planning is an inseparable part of the job of all chief operating executives; the futures of their companies depend upon the corporate courses prescribed by them. The only constant in the management of business organizations is change. The leadership in adapting corporate operations to the changing business world must come from the chief executives. Unless company presidents who have heretofore shunned the role give hard and fast attention to the future of their enterprises by personal involvement in planning, only the most fortuitous circumstances will enable their companies to avoid declines in sales, profits, and market positions.

Appendix: Outline of a Five-Year Forecast

I. *Product-line and Customer-class Planning*

A. Reports on major long-term, high-priority product-line or customer-class programs. Each such report should be a 15–30 minute summary giving the highlights of the technical marketing and production aspects of the program with a general timetable and financial projections. These reports should cover the two or three most important programs aimed at any one of these:

1. Markedly expanding the division's participation in present product lines.
2. Expanding present customer classes.
3. Entering a new product area.

B. A report on the compilation of information needed to do an effective job of long-range planning. Such information might include:

1. Lists of appropriate product lines in which the division is now making products and product lines which might be considered for the division in the future.
2. Lists of appropriate customer classes now being served by the division and new ones that might feasibly be served by it in the future.

3. Market data on:
   a. Size of market—past, present, future.
   b. Rate of growth of market.
   c. Our sales to the market, if any.
   d. Rate of growth of our sales, if any.
4. Financial data to cover these questions:
   a. In each product line and customer class in which we now participate, what is our *net* profit, investment, and return on investment?
   b. To the extent that it is possible to say, what are our competitors' profits in the same fields?
   c. In new areas, what level of profitability can be expected?
5. Analyses of:
   a. Resources (technical, marketing, production) available and required to expand our position.
   b. Competitive situation.

II. *Marketing Planning*

Obviously the previous section has included much of marketing planning, but more general subjects should be discussed under this heading. Possible examples are—

A. Marketing organization planning, including possible changes in:

1. Assignment of responsibilities by product line vs. customer class vs. geographical areas.

2. Greater use of product managers, market managers, or specialists.

B. Increase or decrease in the use of dealers or distributors to sell the division's products.

C. Possibility of distributing products manufactured by others.

D. Statement of pricing policy and pricing practices and discussion of possible changes.

E. Salesmen's compensation plan—evaluation, expense control, incentives.

III. *Technical Planning*

Insofar as possible give a breakdown of 1964 actual and 1965 estimated expenses of the division's technical program, both in division laboratories and at central research, by the classes of work listed below. Cite the principal projects now being worked on and being considered for the future.

A. Long-range offensive research—work requiring more than one year to complete that will be aimed at creating new or improved products for markets in which the division either does not participate or has such a small share as to be negligible.

B. Long-range defensive research—work requiring more than *one* year to complete that will be aimed at maintaining or expanding the division's business in its present markets.

C. Offensive development work—work requiring more than a few days, but usually less than a year, to complete that will be aimed at developing products for markets in which the division either does not participate or has a very small position.

D. Defensive development work.

E. Production service—short-range work aimed at troubleshooting in plant, routine formulation changes, routine process improvements, and the like.

F. Customer service—work required to help the customer use the division's products.

G. Quality control—inspection of incoming raw materials, in-process materials, and finished goods.

IV. *Production Planning*

A. What major new facilities are being considered?

B. What, if any, possibilities are there for major improvements in processing efficiency, and what plans are being made to investigate them?

C. Report on status of program to obtain data on the capacity of each plant, preferably by major departments, covering:

1. What percent of capacity is now being utilized.
2. What further capacity will be required.
3. What steps must be taken to provide more capacity where needed or to utilize excess capacity where available.

V. *Export Planning*

A. Summary of past export sales by product line.

B. Plans, if any, for expanding these sales or adding new product lines.

VI. *Acquisition Suggestions*

A. In which geographical areas, product lines, and/or customer classes does the division think that acquisition of allied businesses should be considered as a route toward future growth?

B. What specific companies, if any, might be desirable acquisitions?

VII. *Manpower Planning*

A. Projection of manpower requirements in 1965, 1966, and 1967 for:

1. Key salaried employees.
2. Other salaried employees.
3. Production (manufacturing) labor.

B. In forecasting manpower requirements consider the present number in the group modified by:

1. Turnover (including anticipated requirements).
2. Needs anticipated for future growth of organization.

[An expanded outline must be prepared to assist the divisions in estimating manpower requirements, and mailed to division heads in advance.]

C. Brief summary of recruiting and training program.

VIII. *Financial Statements*

A. 1963 and 1964 actual; 1965, 1966, 1967 projected.

B. Sales by product line.

C. Gross profit by product line.

D. Sales, administrative, and general expense.

E. Profit.

F. Investment—working and fixed.

G. Return on investment.

[Sample forms must be provided for these items.]

15

A Conceptual Model for the Analysis of Planning Behavior

John Friedmann

Until a few years ago, discussions of planning were restricted to consideration of an abstract model of perfect rationality in social decision making.[1] In use, however, this model turned out to be unsatisfactory. As a theoretical model, it failed to lead to fruitful hypotheses and, because of its logical rigidity, it was incapable of substantial modification. As a normative model it failed because rationality in real life is always "bounded," so that the recipes for planning that could be drawn from the model were frequently inapplicable.[2]

With the recent upsurge of interest in national planning, however, social scientists have begun to study the actual workings of the planning process.

Reprinted with permission from *Administrative Science Quarterly*, September 1967, pp. 215–252.

[1] A concise description of this model will be found in Edward Banfield's "Note on Conceptual Scheme" in Martin Meyerson and Edward C. Banfield (eds.), *Politics, Planning and the Public Interest: The Case of Public Housing in Chicago* (Glencoe, Ill.: The Free Press, 1955), pp. 303–330. In a more sophisticated version, this model also underlies much of Jan Tinbergen's influential work, *Economic Policy: Principles and Design* (Amsterdam: North Holland, 1964). For a critique of classical decision theory, see Charles Lindblom, *The Intelligence of Democracy* (New York: The Free Press, 1965).

[2] On the concept of "bounded rationality," see James G. March and Herbert A. Simon, *Organizations* (New York: John Wiley, 1958), pp. 203–210.

Some students are focusing on the substantive contents of national plans and on the propriety of the strategies adopted; others are doing research on the administrative machinery evolved; still others are curious about how planning got started in particular societies and how the first plans came to be made.[3] But where the earlier theorists erred in ignoring planning practice, the new empiricists are leaning too much in the other direction: they simply look at activities called planning and describe what they see. Although this is leading to the collection of much information, it is also giving rise to unwitting distortions when basic preconceptions have not been made explicit. Simple descriptions of something as ephemeral as national planning is scarcely even of historical value, and certainly does not add significantly to *verifiable* knowledge, which alone is capable of serving as a sound foundation for a theory of planning.[4] The importance of these studies lies primarily in their fresh approach, which has brought the study of planning within the scope of empirical social research.

The present paper is an attempt to create that minimum of conceptual order which is necessary for a scientifically more disciplined study of planning.[5] There are various ways of defining planning.[6] Here planning will be considered as the *guidance of change within a social system.*[7] Specifically, this means a process of self-guidance that may involve *promoting differential growth* of subsystem components (sectors), *activating the transformation of system structures* (political, economic, social), and *maintaining system boundaries* during the course of change.[8] Accordingly, the idea of planning involves a confrontation of expected with intended performance, the application of controls to accomplish the intention when expectations are not met, the ob-

[3] Recent examples include Everett E. Hagen, *Planning Economic Development* (Homewood, Ill.: Richard D. Irwin, 1963); John and Anne-Marie Hackett, *Economic Planning in France* (Cambridge, Mass.: Harvard University, 1963); chapters on the Netherlands, France and Japan in Bert G. Hickman (ed.), *Quantitative Planning of Economic Policy* (Washington: Brookings Institution, 1965); Albert Waterston, *Development Planning: Lessons of Experience* (Baltimore: Johns Hopkins University, 1965); and the several volumes in the National Planning Series published by Syracuse University Press under the general editorship of Bertram M. Gross.

[4] Planning theory was formerly little more than an exercise in the logic of rational decision making; its reformulation on an empirical basis will involve extensive work in the description and explanation of planning phenomena and in generalizations derived from these data.

[5] A study complementary to the present one and fundamental for any serious research into planning is Bertram M. Gross, "The Managers of National Economic Change," in Roscoe C. Martin (ed.), *Public Administration and Democracy: Essays in Honor of Paul H. Appleby* (Syracuse: Syracuse University, 1965).

[6] For some frequently used definitions of planning, see Yehezkel Dror, The Planning Process: a Facet Design, *International Review of Administrative Sciences,* 24 (1963), 1–13.

[7] This definition is in line with, if somewhat more general than, Bertram M. Gross' definition of planning as the "processes whereby national governments try to carry out responsibilities for the guidance of significant economic change." See his National Planning: Findings and Fallacies, *Public Administration Review,* 24 (1965), 264.

[8] The distinction between self-guidance systems and those in which guidance is imposed by agents external to the system is of theoretical and practical importance, but will not be pursued further in this paper.

servation of possible variances from the prescribed path of change, and the repetition of this cycle each time significant variations are perceived.[9]

To this view of planning as a self-guidance system, a still more general conception may be added that will lead directly into the structure of the model. Planning may be simply regarded as reason acting on a network of ongoing activities through the intervention of certain decision structures and processes. The emphasis here is on intervention and, hence, on *planning for change.* This intervention is made on the basis of an intellectual effort or, more simply, of thought. "Introducing" planning, then, means specifically the introduction of ways and means for using technical intelligence to bring about changes that otherwise would not occur.

This is fundamental in my view. Society is a going concern. The ongoing stream of life does not wait for planners to give it direction. Planners must act upon social and economic processes with the fragile instrument of their minds (amplified by whatever practical means they may command) to guide society towards desired objectives. A comprehensive model of planning must, therefore, include forms of thought as an important category for analysis.

The Model

The model proposed here for the analysis of planning behavior has three general characteristics (see Figure 1): First, it is valid only for what is here called planning for change. Other forms of planning may be identified, such as operations research, but these are not included. Second, it is an attempt to distinguish among different forms of planning for change and to show the relationships among them. Third, the model is intended as an aid to empirical research. On the basis of the actual findings, it will almost certainly need to be refined, modified, and expanded. Specifically absent from the model are the institutional forms of planning and explicit recognition of the time dimension in which planning processes occur.

Forms of Planning. A convenient way for entering the model is to consider the two major forms of planning for change. The criterion for distinguishing between them is the relative autonomy of planning units in the making of decisions. Under *developmental planning,* there is a high degree of autonomy with respect to the setting of ends and the choice of means; under *adaptive planning,* most decisions are heavily contingent on the actions of others external to the planning system. In practice, of course, most planning decisions are made along the continuum between complete autonomy and complete dependency, and the behavior of planning systems will differ according to the distribution of decision functions between the two extremes. For instance, planning for urban development at the level of the city will usually be more adaptive than developmental: to a great extent, it will need to respond or adapt

[9] This description of the logic of planning coincides with Neil W. Chamberlain's model as developed in his *Private and Public Planning* (New York: McGraw-Hill, 1965), especially ch. 7.

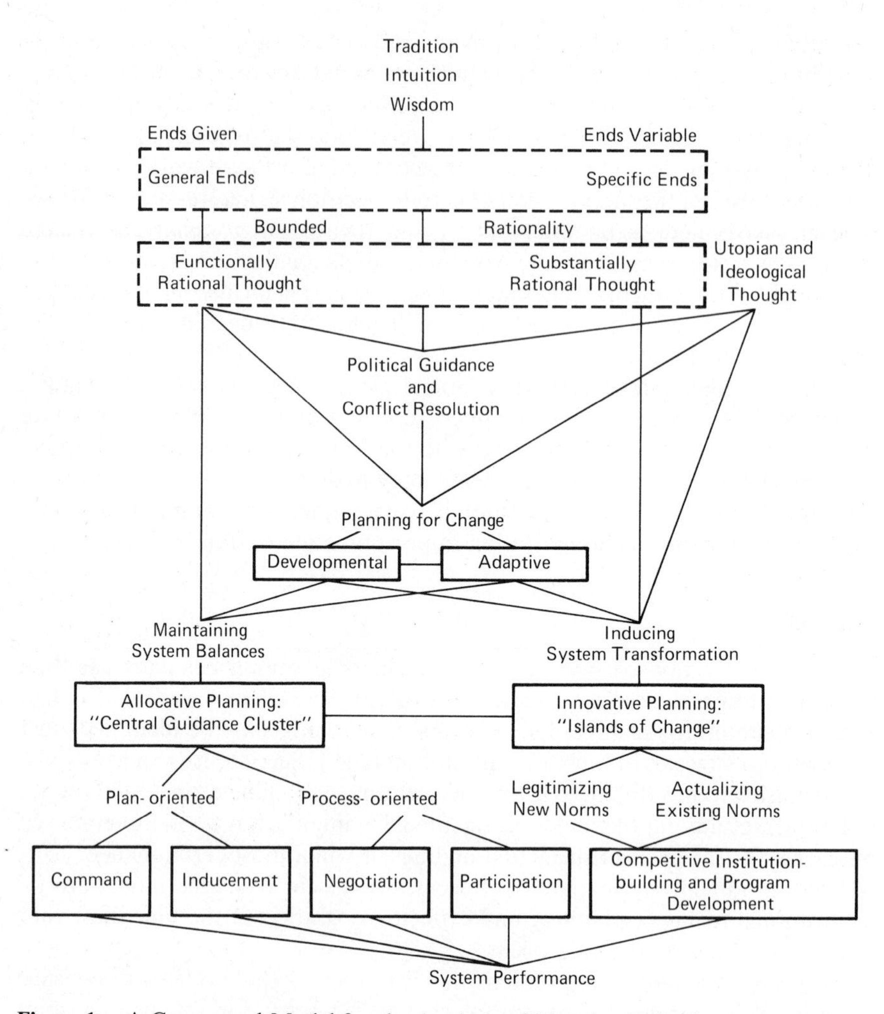

Figure 1. A Conceptual Model for the Analysis of Planning Behavior

to external forces, such as shifts in the locational preferences of national industries, which the municipality cannot significantly influence through its own actions. In planning for national development, on the other hand, the public authorities are able to control a larger number of the variables relevant to its own objectives, so that the nation is much more independent than any of its municipalities. Even among nations, however, there may be differences in the degree of dependency on external forces; and a small, weak nation such as Haiti has to plan more adaptively with respect to international conditions—if it is planning at all—than the city of São Paulo with respect to Brazil.

What are the main differences in the expected behavior between developmental and adaptive planning?

Adaptive Planning. In adaptive planning, there will be a tendency, to push decisions upward to centers of developmental planning where the parameters for choice at lower levels may be changed. In attempting this, lower-level planning systems will generally rely on political manipulation to achieve their ends. So that negotiations with the central authorities may be conducted with equal technical competence, however, counterplanning may be added to political action. Since, on the government's side, any bargaining in a complex advanced economic system is usually done by qualified technical experts, the contending parties must enter negotiations at least as well prepared.[10]

At the same time, the gradual recognition of interdependence within the system may lead the separate, partisan interests—each engaged in a measure of adaptive planning—to discover a common or public interest. Such an interest, as the work of the Bureau of Economic Research, the Brookings Institution, the Committee for Economic Development, and the National Planning Association in the United States clearly demonstrates, will lead partisan interests gradually in the direction of quasi-governmental policy planning, although the interests they nominally represent are private. Thus, on the technical side at least, adaptive planning may become fused with developmental planning, that is, subsystem with system planning.

Finally, adaptive planning is typically opportunistic. For instance, one reason for the frequently noted instability of long-term capital improvement programs for municipalities in the United States is that cities cannot afford to lose the federal or state financial aid that frequently plays a decisive part in municipal public works. Since funds from external sources often become available only upon short notice, are tied to specific performance criteria, and normally require matching contributions, significant modifications in the program are frequently made to accommodate the emergence of sudden opportunities for external financing.[11] Similarly, so-called national planning is often related to the availability of funds and the requirements of international sources, as for example, the sudden creation of national planning agencies in Latin America in response to a call for national plans as a basis for Alliance for Progress assistance. These plans closely reflect what each country believes will, at a given time, be the most persuasive program for obtaining funds from the Alliance; they are not necessarily related to the priorities of domestic needs.

[10] A typical example of counterplanning is the large number of national planning agencies that were set up in Latin America when it became known that the Alliance for Progress would make financial aid contingent on the preparation of national plans. In order to deal with the international agencies in Washington, a country had to send economists who could negotiate for aid on the basis of a logical program for development. This program was then compared to the Alliance's own planning for Latin America, whether by the Committee of Nine, the Agency for International Development, or the Interamerican Development Bank. In many Latin American countries today, national planning is primarily a means of obtaining international assistance rather than a means of guiding the use of resources within the country.

[11] W. H. Brown and C. E. Gilbert, *Planning Municipal Investment. A Case Study of Philadelphia* (Philadelphia: University of Pennsylvania, 1961), ch. 8.

Different degrees of autonomy and dependency in decision making tend to be mirrored in a hierarchy of planning authorities which stand in more or less systematic technical and political relation to one another, each level having its appropriate function and decision power. Since each higher level is capable of changing some of the relevant conditions for decisions at all lower levels, and since every change of this sort represents some change of policy, policy planning tends to be emphasized at higher decision levels and programming—the detailed specification of investments in volume, time, and place—at lower levels. Or, put in another way, developmental planning tends to shade off into policy making, adaptive planning into programming. In fact, however, the two become mixed in varying proportion, according to the point on the autonomy-dependency continuum where planning occurs.

Developmental Planning. In developmental planning, the role of political institutions for guidance and conflict resolution becomes obviously crucial; for it is here that the basic policy decisions are made and that the clashing interests of adaptive planners must be resolved. Developmental planning is not only a technical, but also, and to a large degree, a political function. The relationship between planning and politics is therefore a crucial one.[12]

First, an effective decision process almost always involves both experts and politicians (or policy makers) simultaneously in close interdependency. No politician who values the services of an expert can afford consistently to disregard his judgment, nor will any expert desiring influence, systematically oppose the wishes of his employer. Therefore every decision will be influenced by political interests in varying degrees and, at the same time, it must satisfy some technical criteria. Once a decision is made, it becomes exceedingly difficult to separate the contributions made by each group, for it represents a synthesis of political and expert judgment. Failure to achieve this synthesis will mean that the plans are not carried out or, that policies adopted, being exclusively political, will be inadequate or inappropriate.[13]

Second, successful planning in its more technical aspects must meet certain needs internal to the political process itself. Although these uses of planning are not usually made explicit, they are nevertheless real. They may include: (1) symbolic representation of progress, modernity, and so on; (2) mobilization of external resources; (3) redistribution of the relative influence or weight of participants in a diffused power structure (for example, strengthening the role of the Presidency, of technicians, of the industrial sector, and so forth); (4) helping to build a national consensus on fundamental values; (5) stimulating

[12] For excellent discussions of the relation of planning to politics, see Alan Altschuler, *The City Planning Process: A Political Analysis* (Ithaca: Cornell University, 1966). At the national level, one of the best accounts will be found in the forthcoming study by Robert T. Daland, *Brazilian Planning: A Study of Development Politics and Administration* (Chapel Hill: University of North Carolina, February 1966, mimeographed).

[13] Józef Pajestka, Dialogue Between Planning Experts and Policy Makers in the Process of Plan Formulation, paper presented to the International Group for Studies in National Planning, November 15–22, 1966, Caracas, Venezuela.

an acceptance of development; and (6) encouraging counterplanning.[14]

For example, in his recent study on planning in Tanzania, Anthony Rweyemamu writes:

> In a new nation like Tanzania, a national plan is a major, albeit incomplete, substitute for the goods which were promised explicitly or implicitly during the struggle for independence. Insofar as it is indicative of a future of abundance, a national plan serves as a unifying agent of an otherwise loose and fragile society . . . . Therefore, even if the economic and social goals are not completely realized, a plan is successful to the extent to which it serves to mobilize the people's energies, bring about national integration and a measure of political consensus.[15]

These varied uses of planning are frequently not only more important than the explicit purposes for which planning is undertaken (more rapid growth, greater efficiency, better coordination) but also inconsistent with these purposes. It is evident that they will also define the respective roles of experts and politicians and help to shape the institutional framework of planning.

In any system, there are large areas of indifference where political behavior is possible without planned intervention. The relative influence of a technical planning function in guiding social and economic change will depend chiefly on five variables: (1) the clarity of system objectives, (2) the extent of consensus about them, (3) the relative importance that politicians attach to them, (4) the degree of variance relative to objectives expected in the performance of the system, and (5) the extent to which a technical (as contrasted with a purely political) approach is believed capable of making system performance conform to these objectives. Technical planning, therefore, moves temporarily into the foreground whenever goals are clear, widely held, and deemed to be important; whenever in such a situation system performance is believed to depart significantly from the norm; and whenever, given all of these conditions, expert judgment coupled with a variety of control mechanisms is held to be more effective than political manipulation. Where these conditions do not occur, planning is likely to be reduced to a vestigial function only.

Relation of Kinds of Thinking to Planning. All political and planning activities are in varying degree influenced by different kinds of thinking that may be classified as rational or extra-rational. Rational thought can be further considered as bounded or nonbounded. And bounded rationality may be considered as functionally or substantially rational. Far from being superfluous categories for the analysis of planning, these kinds of thinking are decisive in influencing both the prevailing styles of planning and the actual behavior of planners.

Bounded Rationality. This refers to the fact that thought and consequent

[14] These and other functions are discussed in J. Friedmann, *Venezuela: From Doctrine to Dialogue* (Syracuse: Syracuse University, 1965). For corroborative evidence, see Robert T. Daland, op. cit., ch. 6.

[15] Quoted in Bertram M. Gross' preface to Fred G. Burke, *Tanganyika: Preplanning* (Syracuse: Syracuse University, 1965), pp. 19, 20.

action intended to be rational are contingent on environmental conditions—the social context of planning—which represent the medium in and through which planning decisions are made.[16] This environment for decision is often discussed in terms of so-called obstacles to planning, but it seems preferable to speak of it simply as the specific set of structural conditions under which planning must occur.[17] In discussing planning in Italy, Joseph LaPalombara underlines the critical importance of the decision environment. He writes:

> No one with even the most cursory knowledge of the Italian bureaucracy could seriously hold that, within its present structure, it is able to support state intervention in the economic sphere, much less to direct and to coordinate economic planning on a national scale.[18]

But, in fact, the limitations of bureaucracy are only one aspect of the decision environment, which is more adequately described in categories such as the following:

1. The number and diversity of organized interest groups and their power to influence decisions.
2. The degree to which political opposition is tolerated or accepted, and the role assigned to it.
3. The dependence of the economic system on private enterprise, and the characteristics of enterprise (size, monopoly, and others) and of entrepreneurial behavior.
4. The efficiency of the relevant information systems: their capacity, load, reliability, promptness, secrecy, etc.
5. The structure of bureaucratic institutions and their performance.
6. The educational level of the population and size of the university-educated elite.
7. The availability of relevant information and its reliability.
8. The predictability of change within the system and of external changes that will affect its performance.

In short, to be "bounded" means that a decision can be no more rational than the conditions under which it is made; the most that planners can hope for is the most rational decision *under the circumstances*. "Until administrative improvements are clearly foreseeable," writes Albert Waterston, "planners must prepare plans which take account of administrative capacity. This

[16] Reference to "adaptive" rationality is made in J. Friedmann, "The Institutional Context," in Bertram M. Gross (ed.), *Action Under Planning* (New York: McGraw-Hill, 1966), ch. 2. The equivalent concept of *bounded* rationality was introduced into the literature by Herbert Simon (see footnote 2). The importance of "context" for planning has also been stressed by Fred W. Riggs, *The Ecology of Development*. Comparative Administration Group, American Society for Public Administration, *Occasional Papers*. (Bloomington, Indiana: 1964).

[17] Albert Waterston, op. cit., ch. 8.

[18] Joseph LaPalombara, *Italy: The Politics of Planning* (Syracuse: Syracuse University, 1966), p. 106.

means, among other things, that complex forms of planning must be avoided when a country's administration is not ready for them."[19] The author might have broadened this statement to include all conditions that provide the social context for decisions and action.

The concept of bounded rationality suggests the possibility of identifying a number of discrete planning styles which result from the adaptation of the institutional forms and procedures of planning to relatively stable characteristics of their institutional environment. These environments and the forms of planning adapted to them can both be reduced to a few general types. The study of planning styles would therefore be helpful in formulating hypotheses for the comparative study of planning behavior.

It is useful to distinguish two basic forms of bounded rationality. *Functionally rational thought* is rational with respect to the means only; the ends are assumed by the planner to be given and may be more or less rational or even, according to certain criteria, irrational.[20] The ends must remain fairly stable, however, because the decision must appear rational not only before but also *after* implementation. As a rule, the more general the objective, the more stable it will tend to be. It may therefore be concluded that functional rationality in planning is found chiefly in connection with stable, general ends that are applicable to the system as a whole or at least to major portions of it. For example, the general ends of national economic development usually include such values as growth, more equitable income distribution, and full employment. These ends undergo relatively little change through time; but at the same time, they point only in a general direction. Functionally rational thought will try to guide the evolution of the system in this direction.

Substantially rational thought is rational with respect to both the ends and means of action. But this clearly implies the possibility of altering the ends during the action as a result of changing circumstances or new information. One would, therefore, expect to meet with frequent modifications of the ends. Since only specific ends are capable of being modified in this way, it is permissible to posit a strong correlation between substantial rationality and variable ends.

In any planning system, both forms of rationality will usually occur: functional rationality with respect to system ends and substantial rationality with respect to more specific, subsystem ends; that is, one would expect to find stability in the general direction of the planning effort and adaptability in detailed planning. For example, lengthy conferences operate on what might be called "daily blueprints," that is, frequent revisions of the detailed schedule to accommodate unforeseen events, yet the main purposes of the conference will usually remain the same, although the course towards them may be tortuous and seemingly anarchic.

[19] Albert Waterston, op. cit., p. 292.

[20] This is Karl Mannheim's terminology for describing the two forms of rationality, in *Man and Society in an Age of Reconstruction* (New York: Harcourt, Brace, 1949) pp. 51–60.

Nonbounded Rationality. The nonbounded form of reason, free from temporal constraints may be called *utopian and ideological thought.* In such thinking there is a picture of an ideal social order, often in considerable detail, and almost always as a final state existing in a perfect equilibrium outside of historical time. The images of perfect communism and perfect capitalism are such utopias, as are the corporate state, national socialism and participant democracy.

Utopian and ideological thought may be considered rational in two senses. Its constructions are not only logical and coherent; they are also concrete representations of abstract social values such as equality, freedom, and social justice, and it is primarily these qualities that make this kind of thinking so often persuasive.[21] Forms of planning are often historical precipitates of utopian and ideological thought. Agricultural planning in the United States, for instance, can be illuminated by analyzing it against a background of Jeffersonian democratic thought; national planning in Spanish-speaking Latin America needs to be viewed in the light of the philosophy of the corporate state; and Indian planning still reflects the influence of Gandhi's social philosophy. What is still more significant is that many of the internal conflicts that rage about specific planning proposals turn precisely on philosophical issues such as these rather than on more pragmatic problems. The outcomes of these conflicts are usually decisive in setting the direction of development for an entire sector or even the whole nation.[22]

Extra-rational Thought. The category of extra-rational thought includes what may be loosely called *tradition, intuition,* and *wisdom.* These forms of thought are not derived from coherent, logical structures, nor based on specific technical expertise. They are, however, the source of most political decisions and, therefore, play an exceptionally large part in planning processes. It must be admitted, however, that recently there has been a steady diminution of the role of extra-rational thought in public decision making. Measurement and calculation are driving intuition and wisdom into more and more exclusive spheres, whereas the rapidity of change renders tradition meaningless as a source of decisions oriented towards the future. The result appears to be a weakening of the political elements in planning accompanied by a strengthening of the role of the technician. How this trend should be assessed is not yet clear.

Allocative Planning. Allocative planning is the assigning of resource increments among competing uses. Typically, this is the task of national planning institutions and, for many people, it is the only task with which planning should be properly concerned. Four characteristics of allocative planning help to define it.

[21] Martin Meyerson, Utopian Traditions and the Planning of Cities, *Daedalus* (Winter 1961), 180–193. The influence of utopian thought on economic planning has barely been recognized, however, and merits a full study.

[22] John H. Kautsky (ed.), *Political Change in Underdeveloped Countries: Nationalism and Communism* (New York: John Wiley, 1962). See also J. Friedmann, Intellectuals in Developing Societies, *Kyklos,* 13 (1960), 513–544.

1. Comprehensiveness. Allocative planning must be comprehensive with respect to at least the following: (a) the interdependence among all of the explicitly stated objectives of the system (or subsystem), (b) the interdependence in the use of all available resources of the system (or subsystem), and (c) the influence of all external variables on the setting of intermediate targets.[23]

Comprehensiveness has become a preoccupation with allocative planners. They believe that their special contribution to social decision making derives mainly from their ability to manipulate a comprehensive set of variables and objectives and to acquire, as a result, a point of view that necessarily coincides with the interests of the system (or subsystem) as a whole, that is, with the public interest. Their close association with executive power reinforces this conception of themselves. Thus, far from being mere experts, neutral with respect to values, allocative planners will often defend a set of value propositions as essential to the survival and well-being of the system (or subsystem). Since the concept of a public interest is difficult to maintain, however, especially in pluralistic or in nonintegrated societies, the powers of allocative planning are often resented by groups whose partial concerns are threatened by an insistence on public values arrived at independently of any political process.

2. System-wide Balances. The optimality criterion, the basic norm for allocative planning, requires a balance among the variable components of the planning system. The model with which allocative planners customarily work is necessarily in equilibrium. Thus, planned investment must not exceed the capacity to invest; total imports must not exceed projected exports; employment gains must not be less than the increase of the labor force; electric energy production must meet projected power consumption. It is a question of determining the right magnitudes as the targets of the economic system. Accompanying a set of carefully worked out quantitative targets, is usually a text suggesting changes in existing policies that are thought necessary for their achievement.

3. Synthesis. Neither comprehensiveness nor systematic balance can be obtained without the aid of one or more synthetic models of the economy. These models allow study of the functioning of the system under quasi-experimental conditions as different conditions are considered and their implications are observed. The most common models include national economic accounts, input-output matrices, simulation models, and econometric policy models.[24] These models are abstracted from the institutional and legal framework of the economic system and from the persons through whom the system works.

4. Functional Rationality. Allocative planning is an attempt to be functionally rational in that the objectives of the system are supposed to be determined externally through a political process that does not significantly involve

[23] Jan Tinberger, op. cit., passim.

[24] See Bert G. Hickmann, op. cit., for a discussion of the current planning models.

the planners themselves. Planning, therefore, appears as only a working out of the implications for public policy of norms established independently. As a well-known economist has recently explained it:

> The tendency now is to abandon the effort to determine through economic analysis, what is the best form of economic organization or the "best" set of economic policies, and to accept goals established through the political process and stated by governments—full employment, price stability, more rapid economic growth, elimination of pockets of poverty or distressed areas, and the like. For the most part, such goals seem reasonable to economists, but by starting their analysis at the point where government policy is already determined, they avoid value judgments of their own. They may point out inconsistencies among goals, or worry about such new dilemmas as rising cost of living and increasing unemployment side by side, but choice between goals is left to the government, as is the establishment of priorities. Usually some set of measures for achieving goals—once priorities are established—can be suggested, even if there remains doubt as to whether they constitute the best possible set of measures.[25]

The impossibility of remaining uninfluenced by values has already been pointed out. Nevertheless, by shifting the major burden of choice among values to the political process, allocative planning can appear as an activity intended in large measure to be functionally rational and thus, presumably, objective.

Implementation. The institutions charged with implementation of the plans must remain constantly aware of the need to carry out the policies and advance towards the targets of the models. Implementation, however, is not an independent step taken subsequent to plan making; *the kind of implementing mechanism adopted will itself influence the character of the plan and the way it is formulated.* The formulation and implementation of plans are closely interdependent processes, so that the choice of one will in large measure also determine the second. For this reason, allocative planning will be either *plan-oriented* or *process-oriented.*[26]

In Italy, where central planning has not yet advanced very far, the question of the appropriate mechanisms for plan implementation, and consequently for the whole structure of the planning system, is basic to the present controversy there. According to LaPalombara,

> The question of control is a critical one. Is planning to be by "inducement" or "indication," as some Italians claim, or is it to have "compulsive" dimensions? If the latter, will compulsion apply only to the public sector or will it be extended to the private sector as well? If planning is to be compulsory or obligatory for the public sector, what instruments will the government utilize to enforce private-sector ad-

[25] Benjamin Higgins, "An Economist's View," in H. M. Phillips (ed.), *Social Aspects of Economic Development in Latin America* (UNESCO, 1963), p. 247.

[26] The best current discussion of problems of planning implementation is that of Bertram M. Gross, "Activating National Plans," in his *Action Under Planning,* op. cit. The terminology adopted in the present paper, however, differs from that of Gross.

herence to the plan? Will the plan encompass the whole economy or will it be limited to only particularly important sectors? These are merely a few of the questions. Although the 1965 plan provides some tentative answers, many of them remain unclear.[27]

The production of a blueprint and adherence to its basic structure of goals may be viewed so essential by the political leadership of a country that maximum use will be made of the available powers of command and inducement in the endeavor to carry out the plan. In *command planning*, sanctions are applied to compel adherence to clearly formulated objectives and targets. The plan itself may have legal force or may be promulgated in a series of executive decrees in order to obtain specific results.[28] For Jean Maynaud, for instance,

> A plan is not a plan unless it is central and global, involving specific objectives, and directly inserted in the existing socio-economic context even if it anticipates some social change . . . . Public authorities must make a strong effort to assure that the results of planning will be close to what is predicted. This suggests that some compulsion is essential, even in places like Italy, where it appears that the forces of the free market have created rapid economic expansion.[29]

Inducement is a weaker form of activation in that its effects are not, as a rule, experienced as coercion. It arranges the decision environment of others in such a way that one kind of decision will tend to be preferred over possible alternative decisions. Typical instruments of inducement are special lines of credit, interest manipulation, subsidies, exchange-rate policies, tax exemptions, and preferential import tariffs.

Both command and inducement are clearly plan-oriented in that the plan will tend to be regarded as a serious long-term commitment in which changes can be made, but not made easily. However, where the performance of subsystems is important for the attainment of system-wide goals (where the carrying out of the plan depends, for instance, on the actions of the private sector), and the imposition of sanctions or indirect controls is impracticable, allocative planners will tend to stress *process* over plan. In this case, the participation of all the principal interests will be enlisted in the formulation of the plan itself. This has come to be known, following the recent French experience, as indicative planning.[30] And, according to LaPalombara, "The very fact that planning procedures will include pluralistic participation undercuts the idea of compulsion."[31]

[27] Joseph LaPalombara, op. cit., p. 103.

[28] The concept of command planning has been suggested by Peter Wiles in his brilliant analysis of *The Political Economy of Communism* (Cambridge, Mass.: Harvard University, 1962). See also his "Economic Activation, Economic Planning, and the Social Order," in the aforementioned volume edited by Bertram M. Gross, as well as Zygmunt Bauman, "The Limitations of 'Perfect Planning' " in the same volume.

[29] Joseph LaPalombara, op. cit., p. 104.

[30] John and Anne-Marie Hackett, op. cit., for a comprehensive account of French planning.

[31] Joseph LaPalombara, op. cit., p. 104.

Both strong and weak forms of process-oriented planning are encountered. The strong form makes extensive use of bargaining; planning appears, therefore, as a process of continuous *negotiation*, with central government agencies among the list of main protagonists. According to Neil W. Chamberlain,

> There are few policies which are so "technical," so independent of people's reactions, that they can be instituted without question. Most matters of any consequence involve discussion and compromise. The views of those on whom the functioning of the system depends cannot be wholly ignored unless the system is prepared to part with their services—in which case it must come to terms with their replacements.
>
> A system of bargains among people must be contrived, and it presumably can be contrived more or less efficiently from the viewpoint of achieving the objectives of the system—that is, with varying degrees of sacrifice of system objectives to subsystem (individual) goals.[32]

The weaker form of process-oriented planning depends for its implementation on nothing more persuasive than the participation of key actors in the planning process, those who will be charged with implementation. There is but a minimum of negotiation, and the plan document itself will come to be regarded as less important than the possible benefits resulting from a joint consideration of targets, policies, and instruments. These benefits include establishing a dialogue among contending sectors, creating a wider awareness of national problems, providing the main economic actors with a common information base, encouraging socially more responsible decision making, reducing uncertainty in the calculation of sectoral investment programs, and so on.

In the pure case, process-oriented planning would probably not need to have a plan at all except as an informal discussion document which would register the temporary consensus of all the parties involved. But the pure case of process-oriented planning is rare; usually it will be found strongly mixed with a command and inducement, so that a formally adopted plan may have some substance, after all.

Hagen and White in their appreciation of French experience, write:

> On approval of the plan, comprehensive and vigorous intervention by the government began to see that the targets were attained. Or rather, the intervention under the preceding plans continued. French planning, M. Pierre Massé, the present director of the *Commissariat au Plan* has said, is "more than indicative and less than imperative." The phrases are correct, but how much more than indicative, even though also much less than imperative, is the actual process! In M. Massé's delicate Gallic phraseology in another place, "the heart of the matter is that French planning is active; it . . . regulates the stimuli and aids at the disposal of the public departments in such a manner that the objectives assigned to the private sector are achieved."[33]

[32] Neil W. Chamberlain, op. cit., pp. 7 and 8.

[33] Everett E. Hagen and Stephanie F. T. White, *Great Britain: Quiet Revolution in Planning* (Syracuse: Syracuse University, 1966), p. 105.

Choice of Kind of Planning. Which kind of planning predominates will depend on the nature of the decision environment and the urgency of the problems to be solved. Allocative planning can occur under either developmental or adaptive planning. In adaptive planning, planners will be chiefly concerned with predicting the behavior of external variables and with adjusting the available policy instruments in order to maintain the system in some sort of equilibrium under the impact of changes which may impinge upon the subsystem (for example, national economic plans are not yet drawn up so as to optimize development potentials concurrently at national and local levels; the local impact of national plans is, therefore, determined largely by chance). The actual scope for allocative planning under these conditions is quite limited, since adaptations are made to external conditions, special opportunities are seized, and decisions are made about what are probably matters of only secondary importance to the community and, hence, are politically more vulnerable.[34]

Under developmental planning, allocative planners perform a quite different role, although they continue to build models or set targets. Their functions in this case can be best understood with reference to innovative planning.

Innovative Planning. This appears as a form of social action intended to produce major changes in an existing social system. According to Neil W. Chamberlain, it creates "wholly new categories of activity, usually large in scale, so that they cannot be reached by increments of present activity, but only by initiating a new line of activity which eventually leads to the conceived result."[35] Unlike allocative planning, it is not *preliminary* to action but, a fusion or synthesis of plan-making and plan-implementing activities within an organizational frame. Four characteristics help to distinguish innovative from allocative planning.[36]

1. Innovative planning seeks to introduce and *legitimize new social objectives.* Its central attention is, therefore, on the main points of leverage that will accomplish this task. By concentrating on only a few variables, innovative planners inevitably ignore large parts of the total value spectrum of the society into which the innovation is to be introduced. At the same time, only the most general consequences are considered, with attention to those which relate to expected structural changes in the system. The emphasis, therefore, is on the guidance of change through a selective repatterning of the influences on social action rather than on the multiple consequences of alternative allocations.

2. Innovative planning is also concerned with *translating general value propositions into new institutional arrangements and concrete action programs.* This difficult task usually falls upon a creative minority, which is basically dissatisfied with the existing situation. The organization of these groups, their

[34] W. H. Brown, Jr. and C. E. Gilbert, op. cit.

[35] Neil W. Chamberlain, op. cit., p. 175.

[36] This form of planning is discussed more fully in J. Friedmann, Planning for Innovation: the Chilean Case, *Journal of the American Institute of Planners*, 32 (June 1966), 194–203.

self-articulation, and their functioning—until they themselves become subject to inevitable routinization—may all be thought of as part of the process of innovative planning.

For example, Bertram Gross referring to what he calls an "institutionalized capacity to build other institutions," writes in his introduction to Robert Shafer's treatment of Mexican planning:

> A new institutional infrastructure was needed. To build it in small pieces, however disconnected, seemed infinitely superior to the piling up of a vast hierarchical bureaucracy in a small number of ministries. It provided more upward career channels for people with ability and ambition. By placing scarce eggs in many baskets, there was more room for trial and error, more protection against failure. Promotion of new institutions took precedence over their coordination.
>
> This kind of institution building has a pulse rate of its own. The more successful it is in getting things done, the more problems the new institutions create. This leads to increasing pressure to pull things together a little more tightly . . . . But then the effort to get important things done leads once again to new spurts of decentralized institution building. Central promotion of decentralized institutions once again races ahead of central coordination.[37]

3. From this it follows that innovative planners are public entrepreneurs who are likely to have more interest in *mobilizing resources* than in their optimal allocation among competing uses. They will seek to redirect financial and human resources to those areas which promise to lead to significant changes in the system. In contrast to allocative planners who strive for equal marginal returns, innovative planners seek to obtain the largest amount of resources for their projects, even if this should mean weakening the purposes of competing organizations. Innovative planners are only peripherally concerned with these other purposes; by weakening other parts of the system, they may even gain a temporary advantage for themselves and facilitate the process of transformation.

4. Innovative planners propose to guide the process of change and the consequent adjustments within the system through the feedback of information regarding the actual consequences of innovation, in contrast to allocative planners, whose main endeavor is accurately to predict the chain of consequences resulting from incremental policies and then to adapt these policies to the prospective changes. To state the difference more succinctly: innovative planners are not, as a rule, interested in gradually modifying existing policies to conform to expected results. Innovative planners are more limited in focusing mainly on the immediate and narrowly defined results of the proposed innovation, and more ambitious in advancing a major project and laboring diligently to introduce it into society. Modifications of this project will tend to occur only as a result of political compromise in the course of getting it

[37] Bertram M. Gross, "The Dynamics of Competitive Planning," preface to Robert J. Shafer, *Mexico: Mutual Adjustment Planning* (National Planning Series No. 4, Syracuse: Syracuse University, 1966), p. xix.

accepted and the actual consequences of the policy in operation that suggest the desirability of change in its original form. In place of experiments *in vitro* (through the manipulation of econometric models), innovative planners prefer the device of pilot schemes, where the utility of an idea can be observed in action.

Innovative planning is especially prevalent in rapidly changing social systems. It is, in fact, a method for coping with problems that arise under conditions of rapid change, and it will tend to disrupt existing balances. There is much still to be learned about the different ways that major changes are introduced into an established society or how new social systems emerge. But it is certain that equal progress cannot be made on all fronts simultaneously. Rather, the image that comes to mind is that of successive waves and wavelets of innovation spreading outwards from a number of unrelated focal points, or innovating institutions, from Clarence Thurber's "islands of development."[38] Since it is difficult to sustain innovation at any of these points over prolonged periods, there may be frequent shifts of emphasis in innovation, one wave succeeding another, but in a different direction. It is even more difficult to succeed in establishing effective organizational linkages among institutions engaged in innovative planning, although clearly where a massive effort for change is intended, this is a necessary condition for the successful transformation of the system.

The strategic problem is to identify the critical points for system transformation and to activate innovative planning at these points. But if a system is already undergoing rapid change, the importance of this strategic problem decreases sharply; for the system generates change automatically. It is engaged in what Akzin and Dror call "high pressure" planning. Speaking of Israeli experience, they write:

> The high rate of unpredicted change and the central social roles of government activities impose a fast pace of operation upon the civil service. Although nearly all ministries are overloaded with pressing day-to-day problems, energetic senior civil servants continue to launch relatively large numbers of new projects and activities. The constant pressure of issues necessarily lessens systematic long-range thinking and encourages a problem-by-problem manner of decision-making.[39]

But this pragmatic approach, they say, "is frequently the optimal master strategy. For many problems in the economic, social, political, and technological fields, no applicable knowledge is available. Rather than be misled by theories and recommendations based on quite different circumstances, it is wiser to proceed pragmatically."[40]

[38] Clarence E. Thurber, "Islands of Development: A Political and Social Approach to Development Administration in Latin America," paper presented to the National Conference of the Comparative Administration Group, April 17, 1966.

[39] Benjamin Akzin and Yehezkel Dror, *Israel: High Pressure Planning* (Syracuse: Syracuse University, 1966), p. 17.

[40] *Ibid.*, pp. 16–17.

Under high-pressure planning, detailed target achievement is not possible. The general ends will remain fairly stable and give rise to efforts of allocative planners to keep the system in balance and generally moving in the desired direction. But specific ends may be frequently revised in the light of changing conditions and a constant reevaluation of the action. Innovative planning thus appears as a concrete form of substantial rationality.

Innovative planning is typically uncoordinated and competitive, and this is yet another reason why target achievement is, in any functional sense, unattainable. The top leaders of the Israeli government, writes Bertram Gross,

> have deliberately nourished the institution-building, empire-constructing, resource-grabbing expansionism of organizations in all sectors of society, including science and education as well as the trade union movement, political parties, and private business. This has meant the promotion of sectoral (or facet) planning. The result has been more and more high-pressure planning and implementation by competitive institutions. Under such circumstances clear-cut coordination by command of central authorities has been neither feasible, essential, nor desirable.[41]

Role of Allocative Planners in Innovative Planning. But not all systems find themselves already engulfed in a process of rapid internal transformation. Allocative planning is sometimes advanced as a means of generating more rapid changes, especially in the economic field. Dissident young engineers and economists, eager to transform traditional stagnation into dynamic industrial systems, regard the creation of central planning agencies as in itself a major act of innovative planning. For them a central planning agency represents a "permanent institutionalized symbol of the Government's sustained commitment" to the goal of rapid economic growth.[42]

But in their enthusiasm, they may forget that their comprehensive econometric models accommodate discontinuous change only with difficulty. The more allocative planning relies on such models, the more conservative is it likely to be. Detailed awareness of interrelations tends to make experts cautious and hesitant to prescribe radical solutions. Allocative planners, then, confront essentially two choices: either to remain satisfied with the *symbol* they have created and to move gradually towards the bureaucratization of the planning function—but, at the same time, to forfeit ambitious goals, or to risk the seeming anarchy of rapid change, consciously using allocative planning for compelling and inducing maximum efforts in key areas and for endeavoring to maintain only a reduced number of strategic balances throughout the system. In the second case, allocative planners will not only resort increasingly to command as a form of implementation, but will encourage large-scale innovative planning to carry out major elements of the plan or to respond to new problems that are generated by rapid change.

In this vitally important interrelationship between allocative and innovative

[41] In the preface to Akzin and Dror, op. cit., pp. 26–27.

[42] Bertram M. Gross in his preface to Robert J. Shafer, op. cit., p. 13.

planning, the role of allocative planners is to develop new kinds of leadership, to channel resources to priority areas or points of change, to facilitate communication among the highly competitive innovative organizations, to search for areas of agreement, to help resolve interinstitutional conflicts especially with regard to the use of limited resources, and to encourage organizational links among the many "islands of development." Over time, and as the pace of change slows down, allocative planning tends to replace innovation in the management not only of organizations but also in the social system as a whole.

In general, then, we may conclude, first, that innovative planning is needed to accomplish a major—as compared to only a marginal—reallocation of resources. New institutions and new programs are needed if money is to be spent in radically different ways. The second conclusion concerns the process of translating abstract values into specific projects and programmed activities (goal reduction). Contrary to the belief of some theorists, this is not inherently a logical process but one that requires institutional innovation.

Conclusion

The model suggested furnishes a skeleton for the analysis of planning. But why carry out such an analysis in the first place? What may be gained from an analysis of planning behavior?

First, *empirical findings may be incorporated into a positive theory of guided system change.* Many of the elements of such a theory already exist; what has been lacking up to now is a preliminary theoretical framework for ordering the available data and for supplementing them with studies that will ask theoretically relevant questions and begin to test promising hypotheses. In this paper, some of the hypotheses suggested are:

1. Under adaptive planning, there will be a tendency to push decisions upward towards centers of developmental decision making where the conditions for choice at lower levels may be changed.
2. The formulation and implementation of plans are closely interdependent processes, so that the choice of one will in large measure also determine the second.
3. General, system-wide objectives are modified less frequently than more specific subsystem objectives.
4. Innovative planning is typically uncoordinated and competitive.

Second, *empirical findings will permit a systematic analysis of planning pathologies.* What leads to the breakdown of guided system change? Under what conditions and for what reasons does planning cease to be effective? The reasons may include such variables as the failure of planning to adapt itself optimally to its decision environment, the resilience of this environment to change, conflicting relations between experts and policy makers, failure to achieve an optimal distribution of planning functions according to their position on the dependency-autonomy continuum, neglect of either innovative or allocative planning functions, rigidity in planners' attitudes and procedures, and inappropriate mix between plan-oriented and process-oriented forms of implementation.

Third, *empirical findings may serve as a basis for formulating a prescriptive planning theory*. In the light of positive theory and a systematic knowledge of planning pathologies, a normative theory of planning may be formulated that should be superior to existing formulations. Such a theory will have to be expressed as a function of the decision environment of planning.

On the basis of these several purposes, the model raises important questions that can serve as a useful starting point for any research into planning behavior:

1. What is the role of political institutions in goal formulation policy making, and conflict resolution under different planning systems? (The analysis will have to specify not only the social context of planning but also whether planning is developmental or adaptive, and the relations between allocative and innovative planning.)
2. What is the relation of planning institutions and processes to their social context? Can typical planning styles be identified, especially in relation to the mix of implementation procedures? What is the relative importance of allocative and innovative planning under different environmental conditions?
3. What are the political uses served by planning under different systems and how do these uses influence planning behavior?
4. What is the influence of utopian and ideological thought on the formulation, implementation, and substance of planning decisions?
5. What are the dynamic relations between developmental and adaptive planning under different environmental conditions? Under what circumstances does counterplanning appear, and how are the resulting conflicts resolved? Does something like a public or common interest arise from a system in which counterplanning is prevalent? How are planning functions distributed along a centralization-decentralization continuum, and what are their relations horizontally at each level as well as vertically among a hierarchy of ordered centers?
6. What is the relation of policy makers (or politicians) to experts (or technicians) under different planning systems? How does this relationship influence the effectiveness of planning? Does planning lead inevitably to a "depolitization" of major developmental issues?
7. What is the relation of allocative to innovative planning? What are the roles of either type of planning in guiding system change?
8. What are the relations of competitive innovative planning units to each other? What conditions are conducive to greater coordination among them, and which may be claimed to represent "obstacles to change"?
9. What are the self-images of planners in contrast to the images of planners held by others, and how do these images affect behavior?

Perhaps a philosophical postscript will be permitted. If planning is accepted as the attempted intervention of reason in history, then it is clear that such intervention cannot be immediate and direct, but must be filtered through a series of complex structures and processes to be effective. A definitely anti-heroic picture of reason emerges. It is not the great mind that intervenes, but a multitude of individual actors, each playing his role in a collective process that he does not fully comprehend because he is involved in it himself and lacks perspective. Reason, therefore, to the extent that it operates on society, is a "collective representation" in Durkheim's sense, whose functioning is contingent on structures and forces which are independent of itself.

section 4

situation assessment

16

Forecasting As a Management Tool

Richard J. Vogt

Time will tell how closely future events follow their expected course in shaping the business environment of the 1970s. The important thing at this juncture is not how the forecasts work out. The significant thing today is that businessmen in advanced nations throughout the world, as well as right here at home, are planning the future to a greater degree than ever before possible. Implicit in the process of planning is improved control, from which there is reasonable assurance of improved performance. A judgmental discussion of the subject develops useful ideas and perspective.

Era of New Techniques

These years of our times have been identified variously, but perhaps most significantly, as the Cybernetic Age, the age of the computer. The computer has given Man a new tool with which to extend his own intellect and decision-making capability almost beyond conception.

These new capabilities on a broad front of science, of education, of business and economics, and even of ethics, have wrought many changes in the business

Reprinted by permission from the January 1970 issue of the *Michigan Business Review*, pp. 20–24, published by the Graduate School of Business Administration, The University of Michigan.

environment and in the art of management. They have greatly accelerated the rate of change of environmental factors influencing business and the economy. They have greatly increased the complexities of business and, through new techniques of planning and control, they have advanced the art of business management into a science, the practice of which has become one of the outstanding economic forces of this era.

Stated more simply in the focus of my subject, new analytical capabilities and new techniques are providing better tools for forecasting, for business planning, for performance evaluation, and for control, than businessmen ever have had. A major challenge of the 1970s is making effective use of these tools to attain programmed objectives in the expected environment. As businessmen our performance in competitive marketplaces of the 1970 decade may largely be determined by how well we understand and make use of forecasting as a management tool.

Planning vs. Forecasting

Planning and forecasting go so much hand in hand that many businessmen confuse the two. Forecasting is predicting, projecting, estimating some future event or condition of the organization's environment; matters mostly outside of management control. Planning, on the other hand, is concerned with setting objectives and goals and with developing alternative courses of action to reach them; matters generally within management control.

As Peter Drucker, in his writings on the subject has pointed out so well, forecasting is an attempt to see probable events in the future and to evaluate probable conditions; while the entrepreneurial—the planning—problem is to innovate and to find the unique strategy with which to control in a desired manner the impact of the expected environment.

A forecast of company sales obviously is not a plan. There must be goals, strategy for attaining them, alternative courses of action, and a realistic fit with other environmental factors. Thus, while forecasting is not planning, forecasting is an indispensible, even an automatic, part of planning; a vital planning input, a management tool for deciding now what a business must do to realize in the future its profit and other goals.

Predictive Accuracy Ranges Widely

It is unfortunate that some businessmen believe that because the future cannot be predicted with certainty nor influenced in a significant way, forecasts are of questionable value, particularly in a period of rapid environmental change. This view reveals a misconception about the purpose of forecasting.

We have discovered that the degree of predictive accuracy can be relatively small and the results of forecasting still useful to management. The very process of forecasting is useful because of critical relationships which are uncovered and alternative actions that are suggested. While the ability to forecast accurately, though greatly enhanced by new techniques, remains limited, it is far better to work with reasoned estimates than with extrapolations of past trends as often done or, what is worse, with an implied extension of the present.

There is a syllogism which runs like this: Economic forecasts are needed in order to do effective planning. Planning is necessary because there are uncertainties about the future. Uncertainties are so wide spread and unpredictable that useful forecasts cannot be made. The syllogism, of course, is in error, for two reasons: first, because society and the economy do behave in a nonrandom purposeful fashion; and second because there are different kinds of uncertainties, some of which are more important to the usefulness of a forecast than to its accuracy. There are what one observer has called "big uncertainties" and "small uncertainties." Big uncertainties are either wholly random or totally unpredictable as well as important. Big uncertainties, for example, relate to such things as military conflicts, political change, domestic upheavals, new technology, or even whether the world's fertility rate will out-pace the food and space supply. Purposeful business forecasting should treat big uncertainties by assumption. Little uncertainties in this context relate to calculating imprecisions and to reaction responses. These are relatively controllable and predictable within a range of usefulness which sometimes requires only a correctness of direction.

Using Forecasts

The real issue is how to use forecasts rather than how to make forecasts. The rules here relate to management and the planning process. Obviously, plans should not be immutable; they should be constantly monitored against events; control mechanisms and feedbacks should be part of the planning; and irreversible decisions not hastily made.

Even when management cannot evaluate the degree of probability or accuracy in a forecast, the same rules can be applied and several techniques effectively employed. One of course, is to develop a set of alternatives for executing a corporate reaction to an uncertain forecast to which the business is sensitive. Another is to provide alternatives in the projections themselves, using different policy assumptions, but not too many, as the purpose will be defeated. The National Planning Association projections provide only two alternative techniques: a Target Projection and a Judgment Projection. To this I would add a third, sometimes called a Horizon Projection.

An example of a Target Projection is an economic forecast that reflects the best relationship among the economic performance objectives of full employment, rapid growth in output, and price stability. Another example, applicable to banking, might be objectives of deposit growth with minimal requirement for new capital. A Judgment Projection would take into account probable failures in diagnosis, the possibility of wrong advice, intrusion of external influences, failure to take necessary measures, and the like. A Horizon

Projection is one which describes a balanced set of conditions at some selected future time, for a particular market or industry or for the economy. This is a situation forecast without regard to the expected progress toward it. It is a valid and useful method.

Sensitivity tests which no user of forecasts can avoid, are sometimes purely judgmental, other times intricate, and always useful in developing alternative strategies. Often forecasts use key variables to reflect what might be expected under "worst," "most likely," and "best" conditions. Forecasts made this way encourage the very desirable objective of developing plans designed to cope with alternative future conditions.

Great advances have been accomplished in the ability to deal with complex variables that go into a forecast; such as in modeling and simulation techniques, input-output computations, and measures of subjective probability. This progress is continuing.

An executive must use a prediction system in order to determine what it is to which he has to react in business planning. He may use a programming system to determine how to react. The prediction system can be incorporated in the programming system which is a child of the Cybernetic Age.

The Programming System

What the programming system provides is a quantitative understanding of the indirect as well as direct consequences of specific actions; for example, what the productivity response will be to a capital investment program, or how demand for a product or service will react to income or price changes. By these simulations a planner can identify what will happen as a result of some assumed action, even though he does not know whether the action will occur. To provide guidance for his behavior, the user can then ask the programming system to be responsive to various kinds of questions; for example, he can ask how some action taken by others would influence the characteristics of the economy or the market in which he is particularly interested. Based on whatever criteria he chooses, he can then evaluate the results as favorable or unfavorable; and if the latter and if he thinks the action can be influenced, perhaps develop a plan to prevent or modify the action. If on the other hand he is convinced the action will occur and cannot be influenced, this factor would become a prediction in his programming system. Additionally, the user might ask how some action he would take would filter through important sections of the market or of the economy and return to influence those markets or characteristics in which he is most interested. Again assuming he has the criteria by which to judge, he can then determine how to select among alternative possible actions. Finally, the user of a programming system might have some particular goal in mind and use the system to determine whether the objective is feasible or which set of actions would best promote its achievement.

Within the business sector one must look hard for successful applications of the sophisticated kinds of simulating and programmed analyses just described. Its more general and effective use may well be a development of the challenging 1970 decade.

Strategic Planning

The use of forecasting as a management tool is worthy of further discussion in a more immediate and practical sense. The National Planning Association has set forth a conceptual framework for organized formal business planning, specifically the "Strategic" plan in a framework that also includes a "Corporate Development" plan and an "Operations" plan.

Essentially, strategic planning formulates the purpose of the organization, determines its strategy and translates these two into specific attainable goals. It gives direction to today's Operations Planning and to tomorrow's Development Planning, but embraces a longer time span than either. It reaches into the future far enough to allow time for making and executing development plans that reflect all predictable factors and alternatives appropriately relating to the forecasts.

Because in this conceptual framework the Strategic Plan is most directly related to forecasting, it is appropriate to dwell upon this a little more and briefly review three components of the strategic planning process: corporate purpose, corporate strategy and corporate goals.

Purpose is the basic long-range objective of an organization; its reason for existing and what management wishes it to become. Determination of corporate purpose involves a merging of several major sources of influence. The first influence arises from the expectations of all persons who have a stake in the company and its performance, that is, employees, stockholders, creditors, lenders, suppliers, and so on. The second influence on corporate purpose derives from the competence of the organization itself; its tangible and human resources, its momentum, its flexibility and the effectiveness of its present operations. The third influence is environment, present and future. Typical environmental factors that must be analyzed and forecasted include the supply-demand needs of customers, the impact of government regulation, technological opportunities and threats, the general state of the economy, the availability of capital and properly trained manpower.

Strategy, as a component of the strategic planning process, is the calculated means by which the organization will deploy its resources—men, equipment and capital—to accomplish its purpose under the most advantageous circumstances forecasted. There is usually more than one satisfactory way of making this calculation. In the process of selecting a strategy among alternatives, forecasts of environmental probabilities are required, the development of information, evaluation of alternative actions, and the making of management choices.

Corporate Goals

Corporate goals are mutual to a degree with corporate purpose; generally, however, quantified and time-related. A corporate purpose may be to gain a larger share of a particular competitive market. The strategy could be a combination of many things, as intensified promotion, new design, price changes. The corporate goal in this matter could be in terms of a given volume of sales to be developed within a specified period of time.

The relative emphasis given to the types of information needed by management for planning decisions of course depends on the present status of the organization and the magnitude of the planning effort contemplated. In some instances the information may be acquired by simple observation, by examination of records and discussions with key personnel. When these methods prove inadequate, more detailed, intensive and organized methods must be undertaken. Throughout the process a primary requirement is to relate the strategic plan with the expectations of stockholders and with the thrust of current trends. To do so, management must have sound forecasts and appraisals of the environmental factors that will impede or aid each of the possible courses of strategy the organization may choose.

Concluding

In conclusion, there are two developments which greatly enhance the potential of forecasting as the valuable management tool we know it to be. The first is greater understanding among businessmen of how forecasting can be used for effective management. The second is increasingly accurate, timely, and useful forecasts.

Successful forecasting, combined with the art of corporate planning, is making business management a new science, the effectiveness of which I predict will explode in the decade ahead.

17

The Role of Economics in Business Planning

Murray L. Weidenbaum

An economist may make a number of contributions to business planning, particularly in relating the external economic environment to company operations. This article briefly describes the business planning process and

Murray L. Weidenbaum, "The Role of Economics in Business Planning," pp. 46–55, *MSU Business Topics*, Summer 1962. Reprinted by permission of the publisher, Division of Research, Graduate School of Business Administration, Michigan State University.

then discusses some of the more important contributions that economics and economists can make to that process. It is a synthesis of available information on industrial economics and is not limited to the experience of any single company.

The literature on business planning is sufficiently voluminous without adding to the available descriptions of techniques to be used in preparing planning documents or in organizing the planning operation. However, the repetition of a few fundamentals of planning may be beneficial both to those who participate in the process and those outside of it who wish to understand it.

Fundamentally, business planning is not, or at least should not be, merely a collection of estimates of future sales, profits, manpower, or other statistical forecasts. To cite the obvious, Webster's *New International Dictionary* informs us that to plan is "to devise or project as a method or course of action." Here we have the essence of business planning: it is a process which is designed to provide a *course of action* for a business enterprise. The statistical data merely furnish a basis for decisions. The present article is primarily concerned with the overall planning of a diversified business enterprise rather than the planning performed by an individual division or department. Much of the approach and methodology is equally pertinent.

Economics and business planning certainly are not synonymous, although many people may take them to be so or would like them to be so. Business planning properly is a multidisciplinary field, utilizing economics, accounting, engineering, marketing, and many other specialties.

It should be acknowledged, perhaps with some pride, that a goodly number of directors of business planning are economists. By rough count, approximately a dozen members of the National Association of Business Economists are planning directors. Their titles range from the simple Director of Planning to Economist and Director of Planning and Coordination.

In many other instances, the planning directors have come up through the financial or marketing routes. In any event, the planning organization must contain or draw upon men with all of these capabilities as well as others.

The following are some of the major phases of the business planning process, especially those to which economists may contribute. Each phase will be discussed in turn.

- Setting forth the external environment in which the business enterprise will be operating during the planning period.
- Establishing goals and objectives for the enterprise.
- Analyzing the capability and resource availability of the enterprise.
- Developing the specific programs to be undertaken.
- Evaluating the projected performance of the enterprise.

Forecasting the External Environment

Most business plans, particularly those of a long-range nature, begin with or are prepared on the basis of an evaluation of the external environment in which the company will be operating. This is the area in which business economists may make their most important contribution. All available surveys of the role of company economists indicate that forecasting is the predominant activity which they have in common.

A survey of economic staffs of American industry conducted by the National Industrial Conference Board revealed that "periodic forecasting is reported by respondents to be the most important single activity of staff economists."[1] A similar survey conducted by the Socony Mobil Oil Company concluded,

> If there is a single activity common to all the company economists surveyed . . . it is forecasting long- and short-term trends in the national economy and relating them to sales and profits.[2]

It was reported that such forecasts are of value to management in preparing sales objectives and planning inventories, procurement, production, and capital expenditures for periods from five to twenty years in the future.

Types of Forecasting. Company planning may utilize different types of economic forecasting. These vary from sophisticated models of the gross national product (and other items in the national income and product accounts) to a naive assumption à la Sewell Avery that the storm cellar is the most likely symbol of the economic outlook.

Almost all of the long-term economic forecasts used by business firms which have come to the attention of the writer in recent years are based, with varying degrees of sophistication, on the following simple formula:

$$G = E \times H \times P$$

G stands for the gross national product; E is the average number of persons employed during the period; H is the average hours worked per employee; and P represents the output per man-hour or productivity. This, of course, is the projection of potential supply of gross national product.

Employment Estimates. The employment estimates are generally based on Census Bureau and Labor Department projections of population and labor force. Given the population forecast—and the Census Bureau obligingly provides several alternatives, based primarily on different assumed fertility rates—the estimate of the labor force primarily is a question of determining participation rates among the groups of working age. For forecasts up to about fifteen years in the future, the relevant population distributions involve little guesswork, except for in- and out-migration and mortality rates, which are factors of lesser order of magnitude than fertility.

Assumptions are then necessary as to the portions of the labor force not involved in civilian employment: the members of the armed forces and the

[1] "Sources of Economic Intelligence," *Conference Board Business Record,* September 1960, p. 28.

[2] C. S. Teitsworth, "Growing Role of the Company Economist," *Harvard Business Review,* January–February 1959, p. 100.

unemployed. A 4 percent unemployment ratio seems to be the most popular assumption. The estimate of hours is generally based on the historical experience of a declining secular trend in the average work week—usually a reduction of less than 1 percent a year.

Productivity. Productivity is estimated to increase as the result of expanded research and development, new business investment, and increasing application of new technologies such as those spawned by the entire field of electronics. The differences in assumed rates of productivity can be crucial to the GNP figures finally obtained. A rise in the annual increase in productivity from $2\frac{1}{2}$ to 3 percent, assuming the same employment and hours, may raise the GNP in 1970 by $50 billion.

Table 1. Projections of gross national product in 1970 (in billions of 1959 dollars)

Source of Projections	*Amounts*
National Planning Association (judgment model)	803
American-Marietta Company	750
Stanford Research Institute	725
McCann-Erickson, Inc.	700
B. F. Goodrich (conservative)	675

Note: Some of the projections were originally made on the basis of "1957" or "1958" dollars and were converted to 1959 dollars by the author, using the implicit deflators of GNP contained in the January 1961 issue of *Economic Indicators.*

As would be expected, the various estimates of GNP obtained by different forecasters cover a broad range, although there is virtual unanimity that the trend of GNP is upward sloping. Table 1 contains some representative forecasts of GNP in 1970 which have been used by business firms.[3] The range is striking—from $675 billion to $803 billion, in terms of 1959 dollars.

Models of the Economy. Many long-term forecasters cross-check these projections of supply of GNP against a more complete model of the economy. Such a model may show, on the one hand, the demand for output by consumers and others, and, on the other hand, the cost of producing the output (national income, by component, plus the adjustment factors between national income and GNP). Table 2 shows an example of this type of approach, based on the actual data for 1959. Such a model provides a useful cross-check of the internal consistency of the estimates used.

[3] National Planning Association, *Long-Range Projections for Economic Growth,* Planning Pamphlet No. 107, October 1959; American-Marietta Company, *The Years Ahead: 1960 to 1975,* 1960; Stanford Research Institute, *Indications of Tomorrow,* November 1958; McCann-Erickson, Inc., *A Marketing Profile of "The Big Sixties"*; J. W. Keener, President, B. F. Goodrich Company, "Marketing's Job in the 1960's" (Keynote address to the 42nd National Conference of the American Marketing Association, June 17, 1959).

Table 2. National income and product account, 1959
(in billions of dollars)

Compensation of employees	277.8	Personal consumption expenditures	313.8
Proprietor's income	46.5	Gross private domestic investment	72.0
Rental income of persons	12.4	Net exports of goods and services	–1.0
Corporate profits	46.6	Government purchases of goods and services	97.1
Net interest	16.4		
National Income	399.6		
Business transfer payments	1.8		
Indirect business tax liability	42.6		
Current surplus of government enterprises less subsidies	–.6		
Capital consumption allowances	40.5		
Statistical discrepancy	–1.8		
Gross National Product	482.1	Gross National Product	482.1

Source: *Survey of Current Business*, July 1960, p. 12.
Note: Details may not add to totals shown due to rounding.

In many cases, much detailed analysis of economic history and a very considerable amount of judgment and insight goes into the preparation of these forecasts. Also, the spelling out of the basic assumptions underlying the forecast serves as a description of much of the external environment in which the enterprise will be operating. Typical assumptions include the following:

- The current state of international tensions—the cold war—will continue. No major war will occur during the forecast period, nor will a workable disarmament program be adopted.
- Scientific and technological advances will continue at the current rate or higher.
- The federal government will take necessary action to avoid major depressions or runaway inflations.
- Prices will rise at the average rate experienced during the 1950's (or, alternatively, all estimates are prepared in "constant" dollars).

Projections of the overall performance of the economy are in the nature of a starting point and need to be related to specific industries and geographical areas. For military producers, for example, the forecast of GNP is used in projecting the military budget, which is the basic market research task for that industry and central to long-range planning.

Methodology. A widely used methodology for military market forecasts is based on a three-fold process.[4]

[4] Murray L. Weidenbaum, "The Military Market in the 1960's," *Business Horizons*, Spring 1961.

1. A long-term projection of GNP.
2. A projection of the military budget on the basis of the economic forecast.
3. A statistical analysis of the composition of the military budget.

Figure 1 shows the relationship between steps (1) and (2). The simplest method is to take military expenditures as a constant percentage of GNP. A slightly more sophisticated approach, somewhat in line with recent experience, is to estimate the military expenditure level as a declining percentage of GNP.

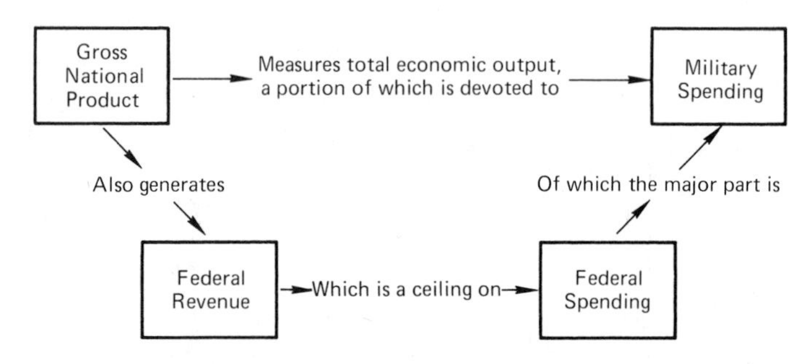

Figure 1. The Relationship Between GNP and Military Spending

However, as Figure 1 illustrates, the situation is more complex than that. In the post-World War II period, military expenditures have been a major part, but only a part, of the federal budget and certainly a much smaller proportion of GNP. Within the constraint of a budget which is approximately in balance over the cycle, the GNP, and its growth, is far more of a limitation on federal revenues than on military spending directly. A model of the federal

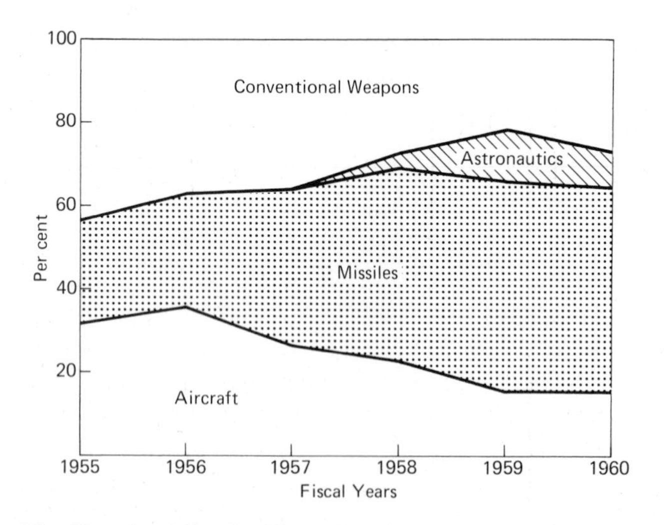

Figure 2. The Changing Mix of Military R and D

budget is needed, which is built up from both the revenue side and the expenditure side, which encompasses the various non-defense programs as well as defense programs, and possibly, tax and debt reductions over the period.

The economist's contribution to projecting the future composition of defense spending is two-fold: Through even the simplest of statistical analyses of historical data, he may bring to light emerging trends in military procurement and research and development which may have escaped others in the planning process who are less familiar with economic statistics. Figure 2 is an example of such an analysis of shifts in the product mix of military R&D. Incidentally, we have here a "lead" indicator, for the shifts in R&D from aircraft to missiles, for example, herald future shifts in the same direction in the larger category of procurement. Figure 2 shows an emerging shift to astronautics. Significantly, expenditures for military space programs have not yet shown up in the procurement statistics.

Goals and Objectives

The second phase of the business planning process mentioned earlier is related to goals and objectives. It is problematical whether, in this area, economic theory may necessarily make a practical or acceptable contribution. Economists have generally been nurtured on the doctrine of profit maximization as the rational mode of conduct for entrepreneurs. The transition is almost instinctive from the belief that profit maximization should be the desired goal to the certainty that it must "obviously" be the accepted goal of entrepreneurs. Profit maximization may be the dominant goal of a business enterprise, but that is not necessarily the situation. A large business organization may have a diversification of goals.

Professor William Baumol is the rare example of an outstanding economic theorist with a substantial amount of business consulting experience. He has concluded:

> . . . most oligopolistic firms aim to maximize not profits, but sales volume (measured in money terms; sales are what the economist in his jargon calls "total revenue"). So long as profits remain at a satisfactory rate, management will devote further effort to increasing its sales rather than its profits.[5]

In practice, there are many forms which the goals and objectives of an enterprise may take. Management may wish to maintain—or increase—the historical growth in sales or earnings. It may wish to attain a given percentage rate of return on investment. A certain diversification of the product line or market served may be desired. Some or all of these objectives may be aimed at. In fact, they may be interrelated and many of them may be derivatives of an

[5] William Baumol, "Price Behavior, Stability, and Growth," *The Relationship of Prices to Economic Stability and Growth,* Compendium of Papers Submitted by Panelists Appearing Before The Joint Economic Committee (Washington: Government Printing Office, 1958), pp. 54–55.

explicit or implicit profit maximization goal. The economist may aid both in selecting the type of goal to be followed and in providing statistical measuring sticks for gauging attainment.

Sales Goals. In the case of sales goals, the economist can point out the historical and projected rates of growth in the economy as a whole, in the industry or industries in which the company is operating, and for other companies of comparable size or market position. Similar data can be obtained for profit rates.

Sales objectives can be set in the form of maintaining or improving market shares. Here, knowledge of the historical trend of the pertinent industries and markets, as well as usable economic forecasts can play an important role. In some cases, the identification and measurement of the market or industry may be no simple task. The electronics "industry," to cite an important example, still has not come into its own in the Standard Industrial Classification which underlies the data of the Census Bureau and many other governmental agencies. Bits and pieces of electronics production are contained in a dozen or more SIC codes. The case of missile production would be even more difficult, were it not for the fact that the customer is in position to make comprehensive reports available.

Resources and Capabilities

The economist can make a contribution to the analysis of an enterprise's resources and capabilities during the planning period by stressing the element of futurity. For example, financial and engineering personnel may be in the best position to estimate the basic costs of future programs. Yet, they may or may not need to be reminded that price levels may change, and possibly at different rates than those that obtained in the recent past. Some simple analyses of overall supply and demand factors for the commodities involved may prove to be quite helpful. This is illustrative of a general function of the industrial economist, to relate the activities of his individual company to broader trends in the national, and increasingly the international, economy.

Statistical Data. Personnel management may perform the basic projections of manpower requirements. Yet, they may or may not need to be advised concerning future trends in national or regional labor force availability. In this connection, the U.S. Department of Labor's studies of the future composition of national employment can be extremely useful.[6] Figure 3 is an example of the kind of economic statistical data that can be helpful to management in relating the problems that a company may consider peculiar to its operations to fundamental developments in the national economy. The anticipated shift from relatively unskilled workers to professional and technical personnel is striking.

[6] U.S. Department of Labor, *Manpower—Challenge of The 1960's* (Washington: Government Printing Office, 1960).

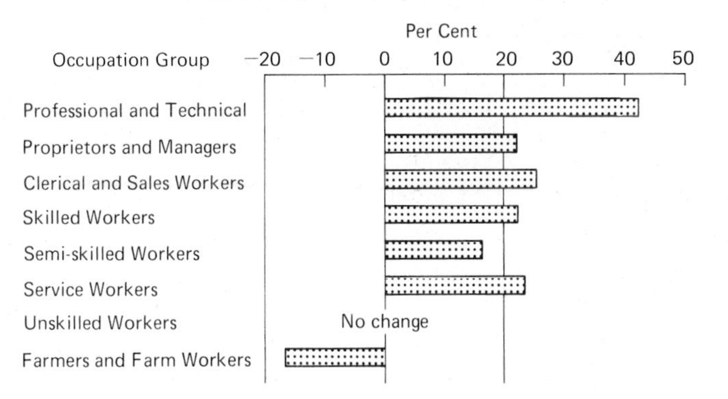

Figure 3. Projected Shifts in National Employment Requirements

In the short run, the analyses of the external business environment may be required by treasury officials concerned with estimating the cost and availability of corporate funds and the preferences among stock issues, bonded indebtedness, and bank debt.

In some cases, the proposed capital asset portion of the business plan may usefully be related to the outlook for business investment generally and to sales-investment ratios for specific industries. Types of economic data and guidance required in developing the resource aspects of business planning vary with the individual firm.

Development of Programs

The development of specific programs to utilize the enterprise's resources in meeting established goals is generally a function of line or divisional management. Here, too, the role of the economist is essentially that of advice or review.

The most apparent utilization of economic analysis is in connection with sales forecasting. Forecasts of the sales of specific products need to be checked against appraisals of the market potential. Hopefully, the sales estimates were prepared on the basis of a comprehensive market research job in the first place, which included use of the analyses and forecasts of the national economy and of the specific industries in which the firm is operating.

In a more fundamental way, continuing analysis of the various segments of the national economy may yield selected "growth" markets which the enterprise might wish to penetrate with new products or adaptations of existing products. Conversely, information on differential growth and profit rates can be useful in selecting, among the various possibilities, products to be developed and marketed.

Evaluating Performance

A critical aspect of business planning is the evaluation of the adequacy of the individual divisional and departmental plans as well as that of the company total. The evaluation itself is a proper function of management. The economist and other staff specialists mainly provide the materials for making the evaluation, such as the quantifications of the performance of the larger group of which the enterprise is a part: the industry or the economy as a whole. The goals and objectives described earlier can play a crucial role in evaluating performance.

Here we close the loop. The reasonableness of the goals and targets set earlier are checked against the likely accomplishments of the enterprise in view of its resources and capabilities in the expected environment. Necessary modifications may then be made in the goals and targets as well as in the programs to accomplish them.

Conclusions

In planning, as in the other phases of business operations, the economist must be guided by the special problems being faced by the company, its particular history and outlook, and the stated needs of its management for staff work. The role of the economist, or of any staff specialist, is not to identify the most intellectually stimulating problems to work on or necessarily to use the most advanced and sophisticated techniques. His function is to make, on the basis of his special training and capability, the most useful contribution to his management. This contribution certainly is not to talk down to management or to put some intellectual window dressing on the most fashionable current opinion.

This contribution consists of bringing to bear on business problems the tools of economic analysis, the results of economic research, the findings from economic statistics and, in a generalized way, the value of professional objectivity. The role of the business economist might be considered to be the furnishing of a window through which the firm can see aspects of the outer world it may otherwise ignore or not fully comprehend. Sir Dennis Robertson, in an address to the Royal Economic Society entitled, "On Sticking to One's Last," stated,

> I do not want the economist to mount the pulpit or expect him to fit himself to handle the keys of Heaven and Hell . . . I want him to be rather humble . . . I like to think of him as a sort of Good Dog Tray. . . .

18

Technological Forecasting—A Management Tool

Raymond S. Isenson

Technological forecasting may be defined in two ways. The first can be thought of as an attempt to predict a technological application, such as stating: "In 1972, the United States will fly the prototype of the supersonic transport." The second attempts to forecast some potential, such as: "In the year 2000, physicists will have the knowledge and techniques to harness the fusion of hydrogen." In either case, the purpose of technological forecasting is to provide a tool for management, an input to the planning process of a corporate or governmental decision maker. To be truly useful, the forecast should be stated in terms of probabilities and at a rather high confidence level, for management tools should be explicit rather than general.

As an explicit, formally recognized management tool, technological forecasting began to receive attention in the United States at about the end of World War II. However, compared with the current level of interest, activities in this area prior to 1960 may almost be discounted as random happenings. Since 1960, management interest in explicit technological forecasting has grown at an astonishing rate. Technological forecasting is now being used or considered for use on the domestic and international scenes, and at corporate and government levels.

During 1966 the industrial sector of the United States spent approximately $5 million on formal technological forecasting services, about the same amount for contracted consultative studies, and an additional $50 million on formally established in-house technological forecasting functions. But the growth, while considerable, has been somewhat restricted, interest tending to concentrate within some 500 medium-sized and larger corporations.

Expenditures by the U.S. government are considerably more difficult to estimate because the forecasting functions have generally been performed by individuals in addition to other primary responsibilities. The military services, which were probably the first government users of technological forecasting in any significant amount, appear to have spent about $1–$2 million in 1966. Other federal agencies apparently are investing considerably less in continuing forecasting activities but have displayed an interest in special single topic studies. For example, the Department of Transportation is currently supporting a study that is concerned with the future of private ground transportation vehicles.

In addition, the federal government's interest in technological forecasting may be inferred from the report to the President's Committee on Manpower and to the National Commission on Technology, Automation, and Economic

Reprinted from *Business Horizons*, Summer 1967, pp. 37–46. Copyright, 1967 by the Foundation for the School of Business, at Indiana University. Reprinted by permission.

Progress.[1] This report was prepared in January of 1966 by a task group from the Department of Commerce and the Department of Health, Education, and Welfare. At the state level, probably the best known examples are four studies commissioned by the state of California in an attempt to assess the future potentials of transportation, crime prevention, waste management, and information handling.

Purposes and Objectives

The increasing appeal of technological forecasting to management is apparently based on its promise to satisfy several of management's needs. A principal objective is to minimize risk in planning by being able to array before the decision maker those potential eventualities which might constitute a major threat to the organization. This risk minimization is clearly important both to military services and to industrial corporations. Each seeks to avoid being technologically surprised by the "competition"; hopefully, an array of potential eventualities will help avoid such a surprise. For the military, this array refers to the potential capabilities of the weapons or systems that a future enemy might field. Industry is more concerned with either possible improvements in a competitor's products or the introduction of different products that could satisfy the same market needs and thus become competition—for example, the replacement of the glass bottle by the tin can and now, perhaps, by the aluminum can.

A second significant reason for technological forecasting is to facilitate the planning of the scientific and technical research activities to be undertaken for corporate or national goals. The purpose of this type of forecast is to identify those areas offering the greatest potential return on investment in scientific and technical investigations.

A third purpose, differing from the second only in that the user is more likely to be an exploiter than a producer of technology, is to develop lists of technical opportunities that might be profitably exploited by the corporation or the nation. Undoubtedly, other reasons for undertaking a technological forecast can be suggested. In my experience, however, they are likely to be variations or combinations of the above three needs of management.

Despite its recent rapid growth, technological forecasting is still far more an art than a science. A few analytical models have been suggested, some of which will be discussed. However, these models generally cannot be applied simply. That forecasting is still an art can also be inferred from the facts that subscription forecasting services have been successfully offered by so few organizations—primarily Arthur D. Little, Inc., The Diebold Group, Inc.,

[1] *The Role of Federal Government in Technological Forecasting*, Report to the President's Committee on Manpower and to the National Commission on Technology, Automation, and Economic Progress (Interagency Task Group on Technological Forecasting in the Federal Government; Washington: U.S. Gov't Printing Office, 1966).

Quantum Science, and the Stanford Research Institute—and that only a few management consulting services have made strong overtures in the area. Finally, if one concedes, as I do, that technological growth is primarily a function of social behavior, technological forecasting will remain an art at least until the time when laws describing social behavior can be identified and defined.

In the introductory paragraph, the point was made that the objective of the forecast might be either future technology application or future technological potential. The difference between these alternatives is significant. Currently, each definition finds strong proponents among practitioners, so it is important to highlight the differences.

One measure of the difference between these two types of forecasts is found in the number of factors to be evaluated by the forecaster. If he is trying to predict a future technological application, he must consider not only the technical "state of the art" but also future political, social, and economic forces that may influence the probability of converting technical potential into a marketable item. On the other hand, if the product of the forecaster is the assessment of technical potential, his task, although not necessarily simple, is considerably less complex.

The economist, the demographer, and the city planner would prefer that the focus of the technological forecast be on future application. To satisfy their requirements, such conclusive statements as, "In 1980 transoceanic aircraft will be flying at Mach 5" are most useful. But the primary interest of the industrial or military planner is in avoiding a technological threat or discovering the potential for exploiting a technological advance, rather than assessing the impact of an advanced technology on society. For these planners, the comparable statement might be, "By 1980 the engineering community will have the technical knowledge necessary to build a Mach 5 transport aircraft." There are a number of valid arguments for either type of forecast.

If it is recognized that the technological forecast is accomplished solely as an input to the planner, and that the planner frequently must also have political, economic, and sociological forecast inputs, then a system approach—merging all four—appears to be quite reasonable. Consequently, the product should be a forecast of application. Conversely, however, social and political factors may be of relatively little interest to the industrialist; economic factors may be of relatively lesser interest to the military planner. Here the detailed technological input is the only common factor; therefore, a forecast of potential is more appropriate.

Next, and perhaps more important for the time being, technological forecasting is still an art. Complicating its practice by insisting upon the immediate inclusion of what may well be exogenous factors could serve primarily to inhibit the development of forecasting skills.

Finally, although social, political, and economic factors may well influence the growth of a technology as well as its application, such is not necessarily the case. For example, social pressures appear to have blocked the exploitation of chemical warfare weapons since World War I. These pressures have not, however, as markedly inhibited the growth of the relevant technologies.

On balance, at the present time, the more limited definition of technological forecasting appears to be more acceptable. This does not mean that the influence of social, political, and economic pressures on the growth of technology should be ignored. It does mean that we cannot focus too heavily on the application aspect.

Procedural Approaches

Just as there are the two significantly different definitions of technological forecasting, so are there two distinct approaches to forecast procedure. These approaches are fundamentally different, one being opportunity oriented, and the other goal or objective oriented. Unlike the two definitions, each approach serves a different purpose. Thus it is unlikely that either will or should become dominant.

The opportunity-oriented approach is most useful to the industrial corporation that has essentially selected its product line and is concerned with maintaining a competitive position within that line. It is also the approach that is most likely to be of use to the military planner. In essence, this approach looks at a particular functional capability, such as private transportation in the commercial sector or strategic warhead delivery in the military sector. It estimates the growth of the technologies relevant to the accomplishment of that function and examines the likely impact of future technological potentials. Management decisions are based on the assessment of the significance of the impact.

As an example of opportunity-oriented technological forecasting, consider the following situation. Corporation X is a major manufacturer of fluorescent lamps and is considering the construction of a new plant for an expanded production capability. This question should be asked early in the planning process: "Is there a reasonable possibility that fluorescent lamps will become obsolete for industrial lighting purposes before the new plant will repay the investment?"

For the industrial sector, an important factor is cost of illumination in which cost of electricity is dominant. Therefore, the efficiency of conversion of power to light is a useful parameter to examine. Extrapolating the trend shown in Figure 1 suggests that before too long there might be severe competition for the fluorescent lamp. Realizing that the power conversion efficiency of the gas flourescent lamp is limited at about 75 lumens per watt, Corporation X planners would be well advised to defer new plant construction until after a diligent search for an improved lighting technique. This search most likely would consist of a survey of all advanced device concepts which are reasonably possible, and analyzing the growth potential of each.

The other primary approach, the goal or objective-oriented technological forecast, starts with the decision to accomplish some end and then seeks to identify those technological potentials that will permit realizing this goal. This approach is most useful to the nonmilitary federal planner or to the corporate planner seeking diversification. A historical example of a major objective-oriented forecast was the exercise that the National Aeronautics and Space Administration undertook prior to the announcement by the late President Kennedy that the United States would put a man on the moon before the end of this decade. Technological requirements such as propulsion, on-board power supplies, central timing control units, environmental control, life support systems, communications systems, and so forth were beyond the state of the art. A quantitative statement of the minimum acceptable level of capability for each of these requirements had to be developed, and then projected technological growth curves examined to determine when certain key pacing items might be available.

Again, as in the example of the opportunity-oriented forecast, surveys of the most promising technical approaches for accomplishing a function had to be undertaken. For just one function, propulsion, the forecaster undoubtedly examined solid propellants, hybrid (combined liquid and solid) propellants, hypergolic liquids, and cryogenic liquids, magnetohydrodynamic concepts, ion drives, and many others. Thus, neither goal-oriented nor opportunity-oriented forecasting is significantly easier. The choice of approach is simply a matter of the interests of the planner and how they may be best satisfied.

Forecasting Techniques

A recent study of the growth of weapon system technology concluded that three factors pace the growth of utilized technology: the recognition of a problem to be solved, resources, and a pool of technical talent—typically, scientists and engineers.[2] Considering the nation or the world as a whole, the supply of problems and of resources is inexhaustible—for all practical purposes and in the short term. Thus, the real pacing factor for technological growth appears to be the availability of scientific and engineering talent. Limiting factors are the upper bounds imposed by natural law, political or social constraints, the contemporary level of scientific and technical understanding, and the ability of the scientific and technical communities to communicate their new findings.

In another article, I have shown that the rate of growth of knowledge can be expressed as an equation embodying most of these limiting factors.[3]

[2] G. Raisbeck and others, *Management Factors Affecting Research and Exploratory Development* (DDC No. AD 618321; New York: Arthur D. Little, Inc., 1965), pp. 1–13.

[3] R. S. Isenson, "Technological Forecasting in Perspective," *Management Science* (October, 1966), pp. B70–83.

The equation is:

$$dK/dt = p(t) \cdot Q \cdot N_i(t)\,[1 + N_i(t)]$$

where:

$p(t)$ is the probability that a given scientist will make a contribution during an increment of time, t, and is a function of the state of the art relative to limits imposed by natural law; $p(t)$ may use-

The influence of social, political, and economic pressures manifests itself primarily through the control it exerts on the number of individuals who are willing to work in a field and who may gain financial support for such work. National and industrial security measures will tend to reduce the communication factor below an otherwise possible level. Thus, although these factors are not explicitly considered within the footnoted equation, they are not ignored.

Historians of technology have noted that almost every functional capability grows at an exponential rate over a long time period. Such a trend is plotted in Figure 1. To account for this rate of growth of knowledge, the equation requires that there should have been an exponential increase in the number of scientists available over the years. In fact, Price has shown this to be the case.[4] There is no reason to believe that this rate of growth in either technology or number of scientists will be continued into the *indefinite* future. But, fortunately, such an assumption is not essential for the technological forecaster. Most current practitioners of explicit analytical forecasting apparently have been satisfied to observe the exponential nature of the growth rate and have assumed that it will continue through the *immediate* future.

This assumption probably is valid for the near term. The current decrease in the rate of growth in the number of people seeking degrees in the technical

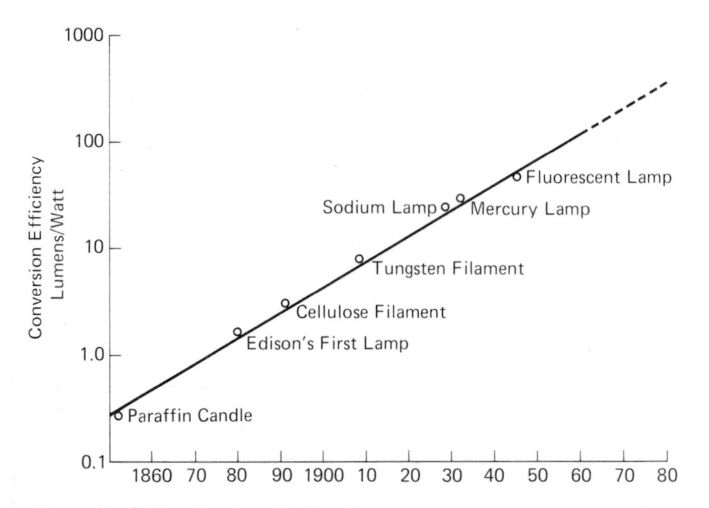

Figure 1. Growth of Illumination Technology

fully be thought of as a function of $(1\text{-}K(t) / K^*)$, with $K(t)$ representing the current state of the relevant art and K^* representing some natural limit, as "the speed of light," for example.

Q is a measure of the mean productivity factor per scientist or engineer.

$N_i(t)$ is the number of scientists and engineers actively engaged in the ith and related fields.

b is the communication factor, a measure of the ability of each scientist to keep up with all else that is going on in his field, and takes a value between 0 and $\frac{1}{2}$.

[4] D. J. deSolla Price, "A Calculus of Science," *International Science and Technology* (March, 1963), pp. 41 ff.

fields in U.S. universities may be a precursor to a reduced rate of technological growth at some point in the future, or it may be only a temporary situation. At any rate, an exponential growth of technology, or some slight modification of this growth, remains the popular assumption. This assumption is the basis for certain interesting new techniques, models, or methods in technological forecasting that should be mentioned briefly.

Analytical Modeling. Lenz has found the exponential growth curve analogous to a biological population growth under constraint.[5] He refers to Pearl's model, based on observation of the rate of increase of fruit flies in a bottle, yeast cells in a controlled environment, and so on. This analogy is particularly appealing because it includes a self-limiting factor and results in an S-shaped growth curve as shown in Figure 2. This curve appears to be typical of the specific technical area. There is an early period of growth when relatively little advance is being made, followed by a very sharp increase, and then a flattening out as some limiting natural law or other inhibiting factor is approached.

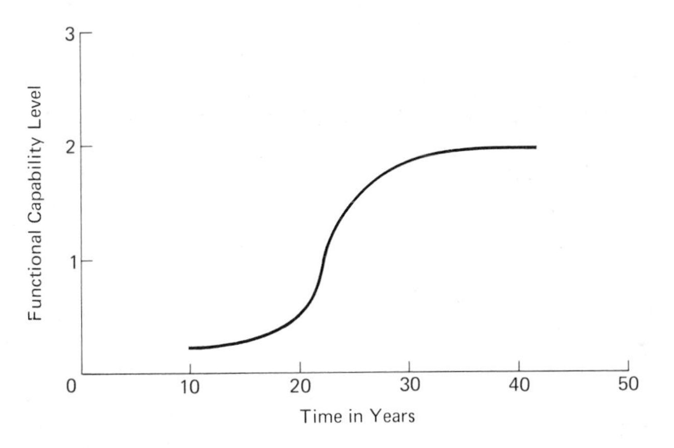

Figure 2. Technological Growth Curve

The two examples shown in Figure 3 faithfully follow the suggested curve. The lower one describes the historical growth of the efficiency of the incandescent lamp, and the upper one, the fluorescent lamp. Each of these is an enlargement of a small section of the curve shown in Figure 1, plotted on a time scale that emphasizes the S-curve.

Hartman has found a useful analogy in chain nuclear reaction and suggests that a model for the technological forecast can be derived directly from the Boltzman equation.[6] His model is particularly useful because it explicitly

[5] R. C. Lenz, Jr., *Technological Forecasting* (ASD, AFSC, Report No. ASD TDR-62-414; Dayton, Ohio: Wright-Patterson Air Force Base, 1962).

[6] L. M. Hartman, *The Prospect of Forecasting Technology* (New York: The Macmillan Company, 1966), pp. 237 ff.

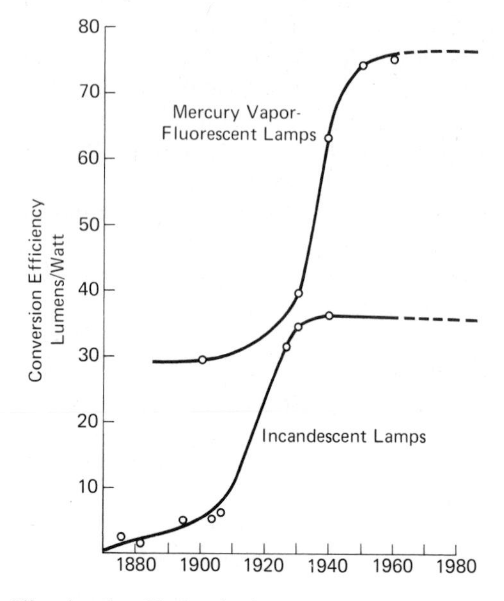

Figure 3. Specific Illumination Technologies

introduces the factors described as being direct contributors to technological growth. He pictures scientists and engineers immersed in an ocean of information, recognizing that this information is a necessary input for the creation of new information. Occasionally, a bit of information collides with a scientist or engineer, sometimes triggering a new idea or sometimes not. Because it is impossible to predict what piece of information will collide with which scientist and whether a particular collision will be "elastic" or "inelastic," the process is only statistically definable—a situation that is quite acceptable for the purposes of technological forecasting.

Informed Judgment. Gordon and Helmer of The RAND Corporation have introduced the Delphi technique to technological forecasting.[7] Because they present primarily the consensus and distributions of many "informed judgments" as to when some technological capability will most likely be achieved, the techniques employed by their individual sources in generating individual opinions are obscured. Their general approach warrants mention, however, because the intuition of the best-informed individuals may, in the last resort, turn out to be the most useful source of technological forecasts.

Precursive Analysis. One technique suggested by Lenz appears to be particularly amenable to "single point" predictions—that is, forecasts like "Such and such will occur in the year so and so."[8] He describes this technique

[7] T. J. Gordon and O. Helmer, *Report on a Long-Range Forecasting Study* (Report P2982; Santa Monica, Calif.: The RAND Corporation, 1964).

[8] *Report on a Long-Range Forecasting Study.*

as "forecasting by analysis of precursive events." The forecaster using this method must first determine which relationships are appropriate and highly significant. Lenz describes, as an example, the relationship between the performance of combat aircraft and commercial transport aircraft. By comparing historical trends in the maximum speeds of these two classes of aircraft, he notes that the speed attained by combat aircraft in 1930 was not attained by commercial transports until 1940. The speed lag has since been gradually increasing. The speed of combat aircraft has doubled about every ten years, and that of the transport about every twelve years. With this information and information based on the performance of the U.S. Air Force's RB-70 bomber, a forecast would suggest that a Mach 3 commercial transport is about eight to ten years away, depending upon what is accepted as the date the RB-70 first attained that speed.

Trend Analysis. In an unpublished document that was prepared as a possible guide for technological forecasters within the U.S. Army, Rafferty recognized the historical existence of sequences of increasingly better techniques for accomplishing certain functions, for example, transportation.[9] He noted that when the S-curves of a family of techniques used for accomplishing a common function were plotted on the same chart, an upper "envelope" could be fitted to these curves, providing a base line for extrapolating long-range trends for that function. The potential for such an envelope can be seen in Figures 1 and 2. A line connecting the upper half of the S-curves for incandescent and for fluorescent lamps would be a segment of an envelope such as Rafferty describes. Figure 1 approximates the entire envelope.

Dr. Paul Siple, the Arctic explorer, takes another but not significantly different approach to defining a trend curve. He surveys the history of a functional capability, considers the contemporary capability of each technique for accomplishing that capability, and plots the "pace setter" for each year. For example, in one of his earlier exercises he considered the speed with which man could sensibly travel. The exercise was qualified with "sensibly" because, allegedly, an ancient Chinese emperor strapped a number of rockets to his throne and took a ride. He undoubtedly moved much faster than his contemporaries but, again according to the story, when he stopped, he stayed stopped! Siple used speed records for his information rather than manufacturer's specifications on production items. Thus he was able to eliminate the consequence of artificial constraints such as legal speed limits or railroad schedules.

It is not obvious that Siple or Rafferty would achieve significantly different trend lines as a consequence of the somewhat different techniques. Either approach appears to be adequate; the difficulties appear to be comparable.

Forecasting Accuracy. An obvious question to be asked of technological forecasting is, "How accurate have forecasts been?" The paucity of serious

[9] James A. Rafferty, "Guide to Technology Forecasting," unpublished, Executive Research Council, Inc., Alexandria, Va., 1960.

forecast attempts in the past forces one to consider the imaginative efforts of writers such as Jules Verne or H. G. Wells. Clearly, many of their fanciful projections have been realized. However, in the sense of the analytical, purposeful technological forecast, it is difficult to find examples from much before 1960. Figure 4 is taken from a forecast made by the Aerospace Industries Association of America in 1962, assuming an exponential growth.[10] I have added small triangles to indicate the approximate state of the art in 1967. The forecasters appear to have been reasonably accurate in their predictions —at least over the five years.

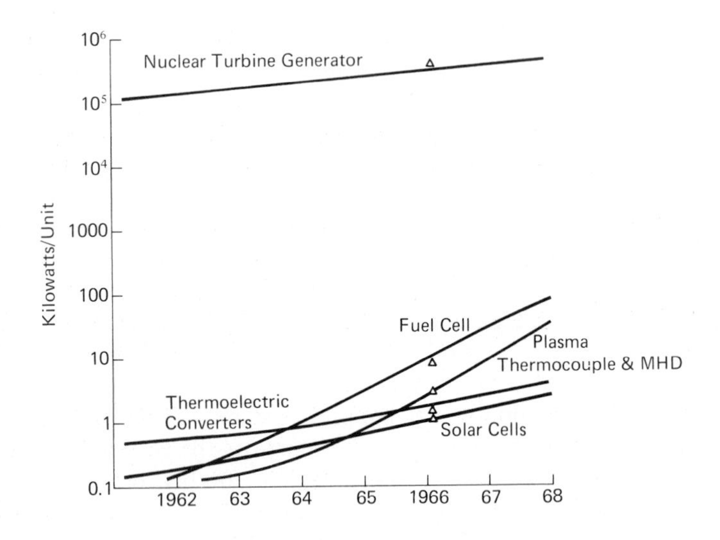

Figure 4. New Energy Source Growth (Forecast Accuracy)

There are two fundamentally different approaches to technological forecasting—different in terms of the needs satisfied. These are opportunity-oriented forecasts and goal- or objective-oriented forecasts. Within the opportunity-oriented class, analytical modeling, informed judgment, precursive analysis, and trend analysis offer useful techniques for the forecaster. Within the objective-oriented forecast, each of these techniques is equally valid.

The forces and factors that appear to directly control technological growth can be identified and measured; consequently, it is not necessary to forecast on the naïve assumption that historical growth assures future growth. An increasingly important role for technological forecasting is assured as long as international political instability forces the continuing development of ever more potent weapons and as long as a free market exists where an entrepreneur can introduce an article that threatens the continued success of older product lines.

[10] *Aerospace Technical Forecast 1962–1972* (Washington: Aerospace Industries Association of America, Inc., 1962), p. 102.

19

Technological Forecasting in the Decision Process

Daniel D. Roman

Introduction

The New Technology. Companies in the United States are spending billions of dollars each year to research and develop new products. Technological expansion has vital economic, sociological and political implications.

The economic impact of technology is so great that some industries derive most of their current business from products which did not exist 20 years ago.[1] A study of 11 industries indicated that somewhere from 46 to 100 percent of anticipated short-term corporate growth could be attributed to new products.[2] It is now commonplace for major companies to derive 50 percent or more of current sales from products developed and introduced in the past 10 years.[3]

In a dynamic technology there must be recognition of potential human and capital obsolescence. Productive utilization of new knowledge will affect the demand and supply of present skills and new occupations not yet identifiable will emerge. Additionally, it is reasonably safe to assume that technological pressures will encourage increased interdisciplinary communication.

It is difficult to isolate the economic, sociological and political consequences of technology. It is obvious that economic and sociological factors could not be disassociated from political factors. It is also difficult to do justice to the full range of economic, sociological and political possibilities in a paper of this nature. However, recognition of the extent and direction of technological expansion can help provide the means to minimize disruption, lead to an orderly transition and assist in maximizing the positive aspects of technology.

The impact of technical developments such as lasers, jet aircraft, atomic energy and communication devices, to name a few, has been significant. On the horizon are such developments as new rapid transit systems, mechanical devices to replace human organs,[4] undersea farming and mining, economically useful desalinization of sea water, new synthetic materials for ultra-light construction, automatic language translators, and reliable weather fore-

Reprinted from *Academy of Management Journal*, Vol. 13, No. 2 (June 1970), pp. 127–138 by permission of the publisher and author.

[1] *Investing in Scientific Progress, 1961–1970*, Report NSF 61–27 (Washington, D.C.: National Science Foundation, 1961), p. 7.

[2] *Management of New Products, 4th ed.*, (New York: Booz, Allen and Hamilton, Inc., 1964), p.6.

[3] Ibid., p. 2 and *Report of the Joint Economic Committee*, U.S. Congress, 88th Congress, 2nd session (1964), p. 56.

[4] In the November 1969 issue of *Industrial Research* there is an interesting discussion of the potential use of glassy materials in product design, specifically glass that won't clot blood which could be used for producing artificial organs.

casts. Other major technological breakthroughs are not so remote as to preclude planning for integration of these developments.[5]

As we move into a "post industrial society" phase, science and technology will be a compelling force for change.[6] In some environments managers must be alert and plan to compensate for change; in other situations a prime managerial function is to instigate technological change.[7]

In either case the manager must be aware of technological impact and be sensitive to the need for more precise planning for the future. Technological forecasting has been a response to this need.

Technological Forecasting

Technological Forecasting—A Distinction. Technological forecasting, as distinct from general forecasting activity, has been described as "the probabilistic assessment, on a relatively high confidence level, of future technology transfer."[8] According to Jantsch, technology transfer is usually a complex process taking place at different technology transfer levels. These levels can be segregated into development and impact levels and are composed of vertical and horizontal technology transfer components. Vertical transfer of technology progresses through a discovery phase, a creative phase, a substantiate phase, a development phase and an engineering phase. The engineering phase leads to a functional, technological system that could involve a hardware product, a process, or an intellectual concept. Jantsch feels that the extension of the vertical transfer by substantial subsequent horizontal technology transfer represents technological innovation.[9]

Cetron essentially supports Jantsch's definition. He cautions that a technological forecast is not a picture of what the future will bring; it is a prediction, based on confidence, that certain technical developments can occur

[5] Olaf Helmer, *Social Technology* (New York–London: Basic Books, Incorporated, 1966), pp. 56–57, and "New Products—Setting a Time Table," *Business Week* (May 27, 1967), pp. 52–61. Bright identifies seven technological trends: (1) increasing capability in transportation, (2) increased mastery of energy, (3) increased ability to control the life of animate and inanimate things, (4) increased ability to alter the characteristics of materials, (5) extension of man's sensory capabilities, (6) growing mechanization of physical activities, and (7) increasing mechanization of intellectual processes. James R. Bright, "Directions of Technological Change and Some Business Consequences," appearing in *Automation and Technological Change,* Report of the Assembly Jointly Sponsored by Battelle Memorial Institute and the American Assembly (May 9–11, 1963), pp. 9–22. Also P. Michael Sinclair, "10 years Ahead," *Industrial Research* (January 1969), pp. 68–72. Also, William O. Craig, "The Technology of Space—Earth," *Transportation & Distribution Management* (October 1969), pp. 22–26.

[6] Editorial, "Managing Technology," *Science and Technology* (January 1969), pp. 72–73.

[7] Marvin J. Cetron and Alan L. Weiser, "Technological Change, Technological Forecasting and Planning R&D—A View From the R&D Manager's Desk," *The George Washington Law Review,* Vol. 36, No. 5, (July 1968), p. 1079.

[8] E. Jantsch, *Technological Forecasting in Perspective,* (Paris: Organization for Economic Cooperation and Development, 1967), p. 15.

[9] Ibid.

within a specified time period with a given level of resource allocation. According to Cetron, "the foundation underlying technological forecasting is the level that individual R&D events are susceptible to influence." The periods where these events occur, if they are possible, can be significantly affected by the diversion of resources. Another fundamental of technological forecasting is that many futures can be achieved and the route to these occurrences can be determined.[10]

Exploratory and Normative Forecasting. It is important to recognize the two fundamental types of technological forecasts—exploratory and normative. The exploratory technological forecast starts from the existing base of knowledge and proceeds to the future on the assumption of logical technological progress. Exploratory technological forecasting is passive and primarily an analysis and reporting of anticipations. As a simple illustration, technological development in electronics can be cited. Starting with the post World War II period, transistors have evolved from an expensive and qualitatively unpredictable commodity to a modestly priced, reliable component. If exploratory forecasting were used in the 1940's to target in on this phase of technology, it would have been possible to predict increasing availability, lower price and more extensive use of transistors. The anticipations suggested would have been miniaturization of electronic systems and the potential for a vast number of new products resulting from application, such as portable radios, home appliances, etc.

It would seem that most industrial firms could effectively use exploratory forecasting. Reasonable identification of emerging technology and analysis of technological implications could provide clues for the firm as to competition, possible expansion of existing product lines, related product lines—which the firm should ease into, and new product areas where a foothold could provide a competitive edge. In short, a look into the future would enable better planning, more effective use of resources and considerable avoidance of human and capital obsolescence.

Normative forecasting represents a different approach; it is mission- or goal-oriented. As distinct from exploratory forecasting, normative forecasting is an active or action-directed process.

In the normative method, future objectives are identified exclusive of the fact that technological gaps may currently exist that might act as constraints to attainment of these technological objectives. Normative technological forecasting can provide incentive to technological progress by focusing on the problems to be surmounted and solved. Perhaps the supersonic transport (SST) can be used to demonstrate normative forecasting. At a given time the state of the art for aircraft technology can be determined. It is decided that a

[10] M. Cetron, "Prescription for the Military R&D Manager: Learn the Three Rx's," unpublished paper presented to The NATO Defense Research Group Seminar on Technological Forecasting and its Application to Defense Research (Teddington, Middlesex, England: (November 12, 1968), p. 2.

need will exist five years from the base period for an aircraft incorporating the SST specifications. On a logical technological progression using exploratory forecasting some technical advancements can be predicted. However, technical gaps appear which indicate that the SST will not be an evolutionary development by the time the need or market will require the product. There are many problems beyond the technical expertise of this author which must be surmounted but some examples could be the development of materials necessary to make flying at supersonic speeds economical, safe and technically feasible.[11] Also, ways must be found to cope with sonic booms so the SST can be used over land routes.

In normative forecasting situations, the analyst works backward from the planned mission operational date and determines the technical obstacles. Normative forecasting could act as a directional force to channel effort and resources. In the example used, these resources would be diverted to solving such problems as the sonic boom or developing new materials. Since resources are limited, normative forecasting could be used in deciding priorities and decisions could be made in conjunction with cost effectiveness studies to determine whether the mission requirements are as critical as presented, are possible within the stipulated time and if the ultimate accomplishment of the mission is worth the resource expenditure.

Normative forecasting has been used primarily by the military, but industrial organizations could possibly use it. With the normative approach, the firm could examine the market potential, explore the technical feasibility, look at its expertise in the area, estimate the cost to accomplish product development and then decide whether the project should be undertaken.

Jantsch contends that presently the most difficult technological forecasting problem is establishing the correct time-frame in normative forecasting. In exploratory forecasting difficulty exists in conceiving an end-effect in the future due to the time covered, but it is relatively simple to prognosticate compared to the normative forecast difficulties. In the normative method the forecast is predicated on objectives, requirements, and sociological factors; the problem is the assumption that present requirements or anticipations are representative of the future.[12]

Methodologies of Technological Forecasting. Technological forecasting methods range from naive intuitive approaches to ultra-sophisticated procedures.[13] Most of the methods are academic with limited practical adoption. Essentially, the methods can be refined to intuitive, extrapolative and correlative, and logical sequence or network type techniques.

[11] One such material emerging as a possibility is boron filament which has remarkable strength for its weight. See "Tough Featherweight Plays Hard to Get," *Business Week* (November 15, 1969), p. 38.

[12] Jantsch, op. cit. pp. 29–32.

[13] Extensive treatment of technological forecasting methodologies can be found in: M. J. Cetron, *Technological Forecasting* (New York: Gordon and Breach, 1969), Jantsch, op. cit., and J. R. Bright (Ed.), *Technological Forecasting for Industry and Government* (Englewood Cliffs, N.J.: Prentice-Hall, Inc., 1968).

Intuitive forecasting, the most common method employed, can be done individually by genius forecasting or by consensus. Generally this method represents an "educated guess" approach. It can vary from a very naive approach in a localized situation to a broad sampling and consensus of authoritative opinion. Delphi, the best known method under this classification, was developed by Olaf Helmer of the Rand Corporation.

A plethora of methods exist which are essentially variations of PERT. Relevance trees, graphic models, Planning-Programming-Budgeting Systems (PPBS), Mission networks, Decision Trees and Systems Analysis all use network construction to derive technological forecasts.

If numbers are any criteria it would seem that after some variation of Delphi, the network technique is the most popular avenue to technological forecasting. Networks help in identifying and establishing a logical pattern from an existing point to an anticipated goal. An intuitive method, regardless of individual technological perception, might ignore or minimize a significant obstacle to technological attainment. On the other hand, the network system is vulnerable in that all critical events might not be recognized, parallel technology might be ignored or unknown, information may be inaccurate, fragmentary, or misinterpreted (leading to wrong conclusions) and, finally, optimism or pessimism might permeate the forecast.

After examining the multitude of techniques available for technological forecasting, the author is of the opinion that while some methods appear quite scientific on the surface, minute examination almost invariably shows reliance on non-quantifiable and subjective factors before reaching conclusions. Additionally, the rationale of seemingly more sophisticated methods is often difficult to follow and the cost compared to ultimate value of the forecast could also be questioned, all of which might explain the popularity of the Delphi method or its derivatives.

Technological Forecasting As a Management Tool

Some General Observations. Technological forecasting as an organized management concept is relatively new. The model depicted in Figure 1 shows how technological forecasting might be integrated into the management process. Objectives which represent the initial *raison d'être* generally become fluid as the organization moves through its operational life cycle. The degree of modification of objectives and the extent of operational flexibility can be dictated by external and internal factors.

In the model, technological forecasting is shown as a prelude to operational activity. Technological forecasting, depending on the nature of the operation, can encompass the universe or it can be used to focus on a relatively small segment of the universe. It can be used by management in probing the general environment and then be refined to help in determining the implications for the industry and the specific organization. As each technological phase is explored, objectives should be reviewed and modified for compatibility with potential accomplishment. From this, procedure strategy can be derived

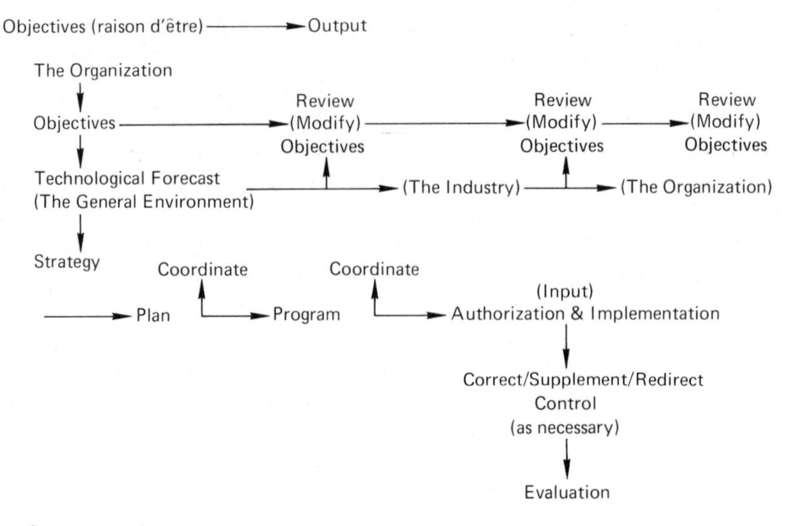

Figure 1.

to guide planning, programming, authorization, implementation, control and evaluation.

Advantages and Application. The incorporation of technological forecasting into the process of management is an extension of existing methodology. In the past it would appear that management has often intuitively drifted in this direction. Evidence can be advanced to support this contention from the information in Table 1 which shows a condensation of the time gap from innovation to application.

Table 1.*

Innovation	*Year of Discovery*	*Year of Application*
Electric motor	1821	1886
Vacuum tube	1882	1915
Radio broadcasting	1887	1922
X-ray tubes	1895	1913
Nuclear reactor	1932	1942
Radar	1935	1940
Atomic bomb	1938	1945
Transistor	1948	1951
Solar battery	1953	1955
Stereospecific rubbers & plastics	1955	1958

* Seymour L. Wolfbein. "The Pace of Technological Change and the Factors Affecting it," *Manpower Implications of Automation*, Papers presented by U.S. Department of Labor at the O.E.C.D. North American Regional Conference on Manpower Implications of Automation (Washington, D.C.: December 8–10, 1964), p. 19.

To be useful, technological forecasting does not have to be precise. If an innovation can be identified, and if the innovation can be translated into constructive action within a reasonable and discernible time frame, it can substantially contribute to the decision-making process.

Often, long-term commitments are undertaken on the basis of short-term technology. In many cases inability to anticipate technology leads to built-in obsolescence. Attendant to obsolescence are high modification costs to update facilities and operations, difficulty in selling change to entrenched interests and failure to exploit market potential.

An illustration of potential benefit from technological forecasting would be in product development. The technological forecasters have not yet developed the precise refinement of being able to localize specific innovations within a technological continuum. However, most technologies follow an "S" shaped curve and evaluation of existing and anticipated status of the technology can be meaningful in the decision to undergo or forego investment in product development. The technical scope, cost and time to develop a new product may be attractive or unattractive after technological forecasting information is assembled.

Generally, technological forecasting can assist management in several ways. It can represent an organized approach to a selective search for information. It can provoke thought by expanding horizons. It can help provide perspective and facilitate interdisciplinary communication. It can encourage operational sensitivity. It can assist management in determining the magnitude of anticipated change and provide a basis for estimating costs and requirements for people, facilities, equipment, etc. It can aid in giving direction to product development and market penetration. It can assist in recognizing competition and other possible restraints such as natural resources or technological limitations. It can be used to help determine sociological and economic trends.

Limitations. Several limitations to technological forecasting should be apparent to the discerning reader. The fact that limitations exist in technological forecasting just as there are limitations in other techniques should not discourage management; awareness should lead to more critical and productive application.

Information may be the greatest limitation to contributive technological forecasting. The information problem is extensive. For instance: What information is needed? How much information is required? Is the information accurate? Have related and unrelated disciplines been explored for possible information transfer or possible technological fallout?

Information interpretation is a vital ingredient in technological forecasting. No mechanical process presently exists which will evaluate the information in terms of available technical solutions, cost and value, product applicability and market potential. Human judgment is a factor in interpreting information and interpretation can be colored by optimism or pessimism and courage or conservatism. Information analysis can also differ due to the competence of the analyst and his functional orientation. Augmenting the difficulties cited is the fact that often pertinent information may not be available due to security restrictions and trade secrets. The unavailability of essential information may negate the entire process by establishing the technological forecast on incomplete or erroneous premises.

Forecasting is far from an exact science, so much so that standard methods and procedures have not been generally established. Although the literature abounds with methodology, in practice, it appears that variations of the Delphi technique and network construction are most commonly used. More exact and understandable techniques must be developed which are practical and provide management with reasonable confidence in their accuracy. However, a standard method may not be feasible since each organization based on its size and mission must develop forecasting techniques to suit its own operational environment.

Another limitation is that unanticipated discovery can lead to demand for a family of products which were previously inconceivable. Good examples are the transistor and the laser. A major discovery can instigate derived demand for related and supporting products and technology and give rise to satellite industries.[14]

Quinn points out that the interaction of many technological breakthroughs could lead to unforeseen prospects which would have a negating effect on all forecasts. He says,

> Similarly, one cannot at present anticipate specifically how biological studies of cellular and molecular coding will interact with extremely high-polymer investigations which are beginning to produce synthetic molecules with many of the characteristics of living organisms. In such advanced areas one can only recognize that there is a strong probability of potential interactions which will increase the importance of both fields, and therefore do more extensive research or monitor such activities more closely.[15]

Organizing for Technical Forecasting

Many functions survive in organizations because of defensive management attitudes. Most managements desire a progressive image and as a consequence may install publicized new techniques without really embracing the concept. Utilization failures can often be attributed to management's unwillingness to get involved with things about which they are not familiar, and subsequently have misgivings about. Contributing to this attitude are the practitioners who lose themselves in technique and take little or no pains to translate their work into understandable terms and useful concepts which management would be willing to implement. This represents a very real threat to expanded management acceptance of technological forecasting.

[14] J. B. Quinn, "Technological Forecasting," *Harvard Business Review* (March–April 1967), pp. 101–103.

[15] Ibid., p. 102.

A review of the literature leaves the impression of enamorment with technique. This can be disastrous if substance is sacrificed for method.

Some Organizational Considerations. There are several factors management must consider before commiting itself to technological forecasting. It must look at the type of operation in which it is involved. Is the organization in a technologically sensitive environment? Is the organization a leader or follower in its operational environment? Are operations large and diverse enough to justify commitment to a technological forecasting activity? How extensive a commitment should be made in terms of people, facilities and budget? Would management want sporadic technological forecasts on an informal basis or would there be formal reviews at set intervals? The answer to the last question could dictate the extent of commitment management is willing to make and the type of people it will have to train or recruit. In line with the aforementioned, management will have to select people with compatible skills to achieve technological forecasting objectives. Does management want a group of specialists in a range of technical areas? Does management want a group composed of multi-viewed individuals with broad perspective and minimal functional allegiance? Or is a combination of generalists and specialists more desirable? The range of possibilities is not exhausted because management can use in-house functional specialists in concert with management types to act as a technological forecasting advisory board. Finally, management may not want any internal commitment and may prefer to use outside specialists or consulting organizations to bring in fresh views to reconcile against internal prognostications.

Organizational Location. Technological forecasting can be a function or an activity within a function. Several organizational affiliations appear logical such as placement in long-range planning, marketing, materials management or in the research and development group. Technological forecasting can also be elevated to functional status with independent identity.

There are no clear cut answers or universal solutions to organizational location of technological forecasting. Strong arguments can be advanced for affiliation with each of the functions indicated or for independent status. The ultimate answer of placement might be dictated by factors such as functional utilization of the technological forecast or management's orientation. Functional affiliation may lead to high utilization but it can also mean that the technological forecasting activity is functionally captive and narrow in its perspective. A danger in this situation is that technological forecasting may be slanted to support the functional parent rather than provide general direction more compatible with the objectives of the total organization.

There are some compelling advantages to having technological forecasting as an independent operation and functional entity if the size and scope of the organization warrants technological forecasting. As a noncaptive operation it can be used by management for organizational checks and balances and as a directional force in assessing the validity of long-range planning and objectives. It can help in determining what emphasis to place in research and development and to give management insight into the reality of marketing goals. What must be guarded against if technological forecasting has functional independence is excessive cost generated by operational practice inconsistent with the organization's need and capacity.

Conclusions

Several significant theories and techniques have been incorporated into management practice in the past quarter of a century. Often these ideas have been accepted without critical examination. Adoption without adequate evaluation has, in many instances, initially led to disillusionment and obscured the true value. Uncritical acceptance and over commitment frequently can be attributed to the disciples of innovations who oversell a concept. The fact that all tools are not applicable in all situations, or, where applicable, have differing degrees of utility should not minimize the potential contribution. Management must recognize that no single panacea exists and must judiciously exploit ideas with consideration of the operational environment.

Technological forecasting as a formal concept can be traced back to the mid-1940's. Its present structure and direction took shape around 1960.[16] To date the greatest application and methodology development has been military-oriented. The military services have had encouraging success and indications are for intensification of effort in this area.

The idea of technological forecasting is relatively unknown in business circles. Professor Bright has probably been the most active disciple in promoting technological forecasting to industry. Indications are that inroads are being made. There has generally been enthusiastic reception from those industrial executives exposed to technological forecasting.

Technological forecasting in proper context should seriously be considered as an addition to the management process. As Jantsch so aptly stated,

> Technological forecasting is not yet a science but an art, and is characterized today by attitudes, not tools; human judgment is enhanced, not substituted by it. The development of auxiliary techniques, gradually attaining higher degrees of sophistication (and complexity) since 1960, is oriented towards ultimate integration with evolving information technology.[17]

[16] Jantsch, p. 17.
[17] Jantsch, p. 17.

20

Auditing the Competitive Environment

J. Thomas Cannon

The typical marketing research requirement for evaluating markets and competition is almost limitless. The data which can be accumulated is never-ending, in view of continuous changes in the marketplace. It therefore requires a results-oriented discipline to establish cut-off points for both data and time and to assure the pertinence of the findings. Both the audit approach and the end product must be kept simple to encourage their use by management and to avoid discouraging or hampering updating in real-time whenever external or internal changes require it. The audit should be dynamic and frequent.

One of the simplest ways to accomplish these things is to rely primarily on a "share-of-market" approach. This technique is highly pertinent for most businesses, but is much too limited to be the major support for strategic planning. It is certainly one of the key *what* measurements, but often leaves implicit the *"why"* of market performance. Consequently, a minimum audit program ought to include a basic set of market-oriented questions that management periodically asks itself.

One of the best approaches starts from the viewpoint of outsiders, particularly the customers and prospects who comprise the company's market. Some of the tough questions to be answered as objectively as possible are these:

- What is my market standing with my established customers? What is my share of market? What is my pattern of repeat business? Am I expanding customers' product use? What is my *trend* in market standing?
- What benefits are my customers deriving? What are they getting in economics, displaceable cost, and better performance?
- What uses are some making of my product which I could promote more widely to broaden sales?
- What deficiencies do I have in servicing or assisting customers in using the product? What is my record in responding to and remedying customer complaints?
- For what reasons may customers be turning to other sources of help in using my products?
- What competitive product advantages are causing me to lose sales and customers? What sales policy deficiencies do I have?
- What potential customers or customer sets am I missing? How successful have my attempts been to win new customers for present uses and products? What new uses could I promote to add customers?
- What are my marketing and distribution expenses in maintaining and

servicing present customers? Are any present customer sets uneconomical to keep? Can I reduce services in areas where customers are becoming more self-sufficient in using my product?

• What is my over-all reputation with the market? Am I innovative or merely responsive? Do they believe I am interested in bringing them better products and services? Do they think first of bringing their usage problems and needs to me or to my competitors?

• What emerging or developing resources do I have (technical, marketing, product development, etc.) which could expand or open new markets for me? Do I have "squeal-of-the-pig" opportunities?

This type of profiling of the company's status in the marketplace is results-oriented in contrast with the traditional inventorying of functional activities. Tough-minded grappling with product-market questions such as these raises the additional question "Why?" in every case of deficiency. This sharpens the functional analysis of the company by pinpointing the specific organization and management-practices problems to be examined. Conceivably, a host of weaknesses will be brought to light which might not be identified by other approaches. For example, it may suggest:

• The need to more formally define customer requirements as a basis for product development.
• Overhauling of the company's service policies and organization.
• The desirability of using additional or alternative channels of distribution.
• Closer involvement of top management in the basic product-market strategies.
• Revamping of the over-all approach to goal setting, including the types of quantitive and qualitative targets to be established.
• Improved measurements of market standing, including use of objective appraisals such as the A. C. Nielson survey or periodic use of market surveys to audit company standing.

For some companies, the preceding line of questions should suffice to get at the essentials of competitive position and requirements. In other instances an evaluation of the competitive environment and the company's role in that environment might involve four or five distinct steps, the actual number depending, of course, on the complexities of the product line, the competition, and the customer categories involved. After going through the process the first time, these steps can be performed and kept current with a very reasonable expenditure of time and money.

Step 1. Establish a clear definition of the company's markets, including the requirements for success in each of them. Then be prepared to revise the definition whenever necessary. This provides a limiting framework, which will aid in the fact-finding and analysis required in the succeeding steps.

Step 2. Determine the performance differentials of each significant factor in the industry. Concentrate on clarifying the significant differences in results accomplished by each competitor. Restrict fact-finding primarily to differentials related to key requirements of the market. This is the real time-saver in marketing research.

Step 3. Determine what variations in competitive programs and policies, or their execution, account for each key differential in performance.

Step 4. Profile competitive strageties.

Step 5. Define the most suitable market structure for the company's strategic planning efforts. Based upon the performance differentials, the programs which explain them, and the competitive strategy profiles, decide the most advantageous dimension or dimensions by which your markets should be segmented to assign strategic planning responsibilities.

Several suggestions for undertaking each of these steps and some useful concepts for approaching them are discussed below.

Step One: Define the Market

An enlightened approach to the definition of the company's market or markets, should include consideration of such elements as:

- Definition or purpose statement, in terms of user benefits.
- Product scope.
- Applications.
- Size, growth rate, maturity stage, need for primary versus selective strategies.
- Requirements for success.

In the process of initial definition of requirements, the above elements should be carefully identified and evaluated. Doing so will provide clues as to the adequacy of a company's own definition in terms of scope and emphasis. It is safe to assume that there is always an opportunity to refine and strengthen the definition.

One way is to *go broader*. Chrysler did this for its basic automotive business, conceptualizing it as "transportation-creation" and "selling satisfactory transportation service for an extended period of time." Then it looked at the boat business as a leisure-time transportation-recreation market and further defined it in terms of a broader scope represented by boats, motors, boat trailers, campers, and cars. Chrysler was viewing this market in the context of a full recreation system.

Another redefinition approach is to *go deeper*. The Clark Equipment Company has become eminently successful by specializing deeply in the materials-handling business and by building its product lines around in-depth engineering expertise with a single product: the axle.[1] For its first 37 years, Clark specialized almost entirely in axles and transmissions for trucks, buses, and tractors.

[1] "Clark Equipment," *Forbes*, September 1, 1966, p. 29.

In subsequent years it has still remained a highly profitable capital goods producer, serving some of the most cyclical segments of industry (construction in particular). The line is broader than originally, with forty-one percent of sales in fork-lift trucks, twenty-three percent in construction machinery, eleven percent in truck trailers, and seven percent in refrigerated food displays.

The bulk of these lines are supported by a relatively limited area of manufacturing know-how where Clark excels. It has established a deep understanding of the drive mechanism, axles, power-shift transmissions, and torque converters and their performance requirements under an almost endless range of applications. The materials-handling area is an explosive growth industry with many different markets that smooth out cyclical sales valleys. This has made it possible for Clark to maintain a healthy payoff from its outstanding, but quite narrow, engineering specialization.

Still a third redefinition approach is to *go process,* i.e., define one's market in terms of applications. The Carborundum Company expanded its abrasives market definition along these lines when it moved from grinding wheels to total systems for metal removal. This substantially broadened Carborundum's market.[2]

Whether breadth, depth, process, or even status quo is the dimension used, it should be standard practice to go through this market concept exercise at least annually. More often than not the effort will stretch the sights of management and alert it to new competitive factors or to threats of market erosion or obsolescence. Assuming the company has a good base of marketing research, the technique involves only a few simple questions, although the answers to these can have a profound effect on the business.

- What market do we think we are in? How big is it? What is its expected rate of growth?
- What competitors (and customers) appear to disagree with our definition? What and how big do *they* say the market is and why?
- What scope or dimensions of the market might everyone be missing?
- What are the requirements for success from each of these views? Which set of requirements favors our position most?
- What market shall we go after?

All of these questions are key, but the fourth in particular gets to the heart of the problem. If the question of requirements is addressed tough-mindedly, the decision on how to define the market itself is almost made. One company which went through the rigors of a redefinition of its markets and their requirements with considerable success was the Automatic Canteen Company of America.[3] This company had been involved in an aggressive diversification program in many directions when a new president took over to reverse some

[2] See p. 127 [of *Business Strategy and Policy*] for a full discussion of Carborundum's application-integrated product strategy in this area.

[3] "Where Profits Are Really Food and Drink," *Business Week,* July 3, 1965, p. 88.

unfavorable trends. One of his first moves was to question what markets the company was pursuing. He then initiated research to determine where it should be going.

The market was redefined more sharply as "supplying food and drink —mechanically and manually—to the leisure-time captive market and to the institutional and industrial captive markets." Some of the unprofitable or unrelated ventures were disposed of, such as factoring companies and cup manufacturing. This put the business principally in vending, manual feeding, and vending-machine manufacturing. A strenuous budgeting and cost control system was installed as a prime requirement for Automatic Canteen's service types of business.

The president moved aggressively to "go where the crowds are," securing the concessions for food and drinks at such entertainment centers as Yankee Stadium, the old and new Metropolitan Opera houses, and the Los Angeles Angels' baseball park. To build the volume and profit of these services he researched the attitude of the crowds to find what they wanted and needed most. As a consequence, he spent considerable sums upgrading facilities, products, and services. For example, at Yankee Stadium he installed carving stations for beef and ham sandwiches, made area assignments so hawkers would cover the crowds evenly, and set up separate stands to cater to ethnic tastes for shrimp rolls on Fridays, pizza pies, and kosher hot dogs. Per capita consumption at the various events rose dramatically.

Similar moves were initiated in the vending and catering markets in hospitals, schools, and ocean liners (using packaged frozen-food menus for the latter). Each step was characterized by careful researching of long-term growth trends and the market requirements unique to the new situation. This gave the company confidence to meet these needs with modernization investments built into its bids. Most competitors were unwilling to make such commitments.

Step Two: Determine Performance Differentials

One of the difficulties in coming up with useful marketing research is that the analysis of *what* is being accomplished by different companies in the market gets confused with *why* and *how* they are approaching the market differently. It is elementary but useful to break marketplace performance down into two parts. Hence, step two stresses only *what* the differentials are in marketplace competition. Step three separately identifies and evaluates the variations in competitive plans, programs and policies which explain *why* and *how* differences were accomplished.

Meticulous observance of this distinction has two advantages. Since individual performance factors are seldom the result of a single program element, attention is more properly focused on the competitors' marketing mix. Also, a company avoids looking into alternative methods too soon. This reduces the temptation to copy competitors before it can thoughtfully be decided whether such a course of action is, ultimately, desirable. Sometimes it is not.

What, then, are the principal characteristics of the marketplace which require auditing of performance differentials? Obviously, they will be different for Automatic Canteen, which seeks long contracts for captive markets, than for Carborundum's repetitive abrasives sales pattern, or the Chrysler boating group's need to stimulate both primary and trade-user demand for larger and more expensive boats, while settling for infrequent purchase by any one type of consumer.

For convenience and a sense of perspective, it is useful to examine market performance in three cuts. The first is an over-all assessment of competitive companies and the aggregate industry performance. The second is a deeper look at differences in products, applications, and geography. The third is to relate all of these factors to differences by customer set.

Company and Industry Performance. Some of the pertinent company and industry factors to be considered in the first phase are shown in Figure 1. While the use of a number of these factors is as old as competition itself, several points should be mentioned which are sometimes overlooked. One is the value of attempting to describe the image of each key competitor from the viewpoint of the consumer ("Is Company X known as an innovator?"). Does its strength derive from deep specialization, full-line capabilities or a combination approach? And how important are these things to the consumer?

Another suggestion of the figure is to supplement the traditional profit comparisons with a special look at the profits; or rather, clues as to the profits companies may be deriving from selectivity or squeal-of-the-pig strategies. Such approaches can give a competitor added flexibility which could leave one's own strategies vulnerable in spots.

Differentials in Products, Applications, Geography, and Distribution Channels. After the companies' over-all performances have been structured as suggested above, a deeper cut is then informative. Scaling down the detail and effort required can be done selectively only for the leading companies and for those newcomers who are on the move in industry. Some of the considerations to be probed are suggested in Figure 2.

Differentials by Customer Set. Where meaningful differences exist by customer category (e.g., industry, size, channels of distribution), it is pertinent to evaluate competitive standings for the kinds of factors shown in Figure 3. Even in a market where it would be pointless to differentiate by customer category, the right-hand column of factors should be applied to each significant competitor.

The task of structuring the market by customer categories is least complicated for single-product companies. This is shown in the matrix on page 257, which outlines the minimum essential information to be obtained and evaluated. The example used is an industry classification. The ABC company is concerned mainly with users in three industries (1, 2, and 4), whereas three competitors have found active markets in two additional industries (3 and 5). Moreover, some market development activity is underway in three more industry categories.

Element	*Prime Characteristics to Be Evaluated*	*Key Differentials to Be Considered*
Companies	Total product/market scope of each company Scope in the prime market or markets under study Definition of the market Company images	Relative importance of the market to each competitor Market orientation versus lab orientation Innovative or responsive Specialist, rifle-shot or full-line Squeal-of-pig approaches Latent, new resources as potential competitive threats
Industry performance	Volume: $ and units Company shares, percentage ranks Profit: ROI, net profit percent of sales, turnover Major expense ratios	Significant trends and ranking changes Differences in key profit and expense ratios, including unique factors for the industry concerned Profit implications of selectivity strategies Profit advantages from squeal-of-pig diversification

Figure 1. Selected Company and Industry Performance Differentials

The actual documentation may include various types of supplementary information such as indications about the relative importance of different industries or variations in product price ranges. The identification of potential industries is perhaps the most important part of the entire structuring process. This will come from a number of sources including market research, instances of competitive test activity reported by salesmen, and prospect inquiries. A major reason for this structuring is to stress continuously the search for ways of expanding the market's parameters.

Element	*Prime Characteristics to Be Evaluated*	*Key Differentials to Be Considered*
Products	Types and share Components of line: product, policies, services Chronology of introduction Obsolescence factors Developmental and potential products	Innovations Comparative advantages and user benefits Leapfrogging successes and opportunities Hitchhiking, bandwagon approaches Product customization flexibility Product service responsiveness Variations in market position by product
Applications	Uses by product type User benefits Chronology of introduction Use assistance, customer education Potential uses, expanded, latent, and new	Innovation leadership Practicality of applications Responsiveness on customer education and assistance Variations in market position by application
Geography	Scope of market Intensity of coverage Location of key market concentrations	Coverage gaps Differences in saturation intensity Differences in placement of plant and field resources Variations in market position by area
Channels of Distribution	Types and share Intensity of use by territory Market categories covered Caliber and effectiveness of classes and individual middlemen Types of services performed for manufacturers	Variations in sales importance, total and by class and market category Differences in use policies (intensive, selective, exclusive) Variations in caliber of performance Variations in stocking, parts and repair, and other services

Figure 2. Selected Product, Application, Geographic, and Distribution-Channel Performance Differentials

Prime Characteristics to Be Evaluated	*Key Differentials to Be Considered*
1. Customer sets by: Industries Size categories Key accounts Distribution channels	a. Sales-mix differences by customer set by company b. Expansion and addition of sets c. Differences in productivity, uneconomical customer sets
2. Variations in customer sets by: Company Product Application Geography Degree of penetration Sales potential	d. Over-dependence on key accounts e. Cross-industry usage opportunities f. Customer turnover g. Expense of adding customers by set h. Different requirements for success by customer set
3. Customer loyalties, repeat business, turnover	
4. Rate of customer additions: number, new types, new sets	

Figure 3. Performance Differentials by Customer Set

Market classification by industry customer sets

Industry Segments	*Relative Volume (% of present base)*	*Manufacturers*				
		ABC	*W*	*X*	*Y*	*Z*
Present Industries:						
# 1	40	x		x	x	
# 2	30	x	x	x	x	x
# 3	15			x		x
# 4	10	x	x	x		
# 5	5		x	x		
Potential Industries:						
# 6	30	x		x		
# 7	10			x		
# 8	Unknown			x		

Table 1. Market structure outline for fiberglass products of ABC Company

Applications	Current Sales Percent	5th Year Potential Sales	Product								
			Chopped Strand Mat	Glass Cloth	Roving	Woven Roving	Surfacing Mat	Veiling	Filter Media	Yarn	Insulation
Present Industries:											
1. Structural pipe and panels	10	11	xxx			xx	x				
2. Transportation equipment	29	31	xxx	xxx	xx	x	x	x			
3. Containers, trays and tanks	10	12	xxx	x	xx	x	x	x			
4. Electrical sheeting	3	2	x	xx							
5. Dies and fixtures	5	5	x	xx	x	x					
6. Pipe-line wrap	12	9					xx				
7. Filter media	13	11					xx		xxx		
8. Roofing material	2	3	x				xx				
9. Misc. industries (7)	16	16	xx	xx	xx	x	x				
	100%	100%									
Potential Industries:											
A. Adhesive sheeting	Small	5%		x			x				
B. Swimming pools	1	5	x	x		x					
C. Plastic poles	Small	5				x					
D. Misc. potential uses	Small	10					x				
Principal Manufacturers:											
ABC	2						x	x	x		
V	74		xxx	xxx	xx	xx	x		xx	xx	xxx
W	6				x	x			x	x	x
X	8						x				x
Y	1						x				
Z	7								xx		
Others	2						x		x		
	100%										

xxx = most important   xx = of moderate importance   x = least important

It is even more important to document a market structure matrix for the multi-industry, multi-product company. Here strategic planning is complicated geometrically because rarely do any two companies have completely matching product lines or customer sets. Complete documentation of each competitor's total market structure provides invaluable clues relative to opportunities for broadening product lines, new industries to cover, shifts in methods of distribution, and guidelines for development effort. Such a matrix adds the product dimension as shown in Table 1.

This table portrays the market structure and competitive interests for a very small manufacturer of fiberglass products. The industry was dominated by one very large concern, Owens-Corning Fiberglas Corporation, yet the market was expected to expand by at least 50 percent over the next five years, and technological change also afforded growth opportunities for the specialized manufacturer.

The ABC Company was a relative newcomer, with only 2 percent of industry sales and a limited product line (as shown by the small entry on the table). It had a unique production process for its fiberglass surfacing mat, which had applications and a small degree of market acceptance in a number of the major industry segments. However, a different company's well-established product, chopped strand mat, dominated the surfacing-mat market. There was also significant competition from a few other specialty producers in ABC's principal applications. For these reasons its strategic plans were extremely critical to its future growth.

The first formalized step in ABC's planning was a comprehensive market research study that structured the company's markets and competition, as outlined in Table 1. The supporting documentation revealed in depth the specific applications, market sizes, and potentials and the standings, strengths and weaknesses of each product and competitor for almost twenty-five industry segments.

This complicated market pattern illustrates the type of strategic planning problem found in such businesses as basic chemicals, steel, copper, other metals industries, and construction materials. It clearly shows the problems of selecting goals and strategies from among a wide variety (and many combinations) of market opportunities. It further illustrates the problems of competing with both broad-line and highly-specialized one- or two-product companies.

Step Three: Determine Differences in Competitive Programs

A solid, continuing audit of performance differences along the general lines of the second step above establishes the foundation for determining the *"whys"* of marketplace performance. This brings the audit to the stage of identifying and evaluating the *what* and *how* strategies of various competitors. The framework and the content of these aspects (market development, product development, distribution channels, etc.), will be dealt with comprehensively in Parts Two and Four [*of Business Strategy and Policy*]. They need not be gone into in great length here. However, it is pertinent at this point to illustrate some of the advantages of a fresh look at competitors' functional strategies.

In Chapter Two some of the newer strategies of the Howard Johnson Company were outlined, including its entry into the soft-drink business. Faced with formidable competition from the franchised bottlers of Coca Cola, Pepsi Cola, and Seven-Up, the company discovered a fundamentally different approach to distribution.[4] Howard Johnson concluded that the existing franchise system had two weaknesses. First, many franchises did not want to give up returnable bottles because of the substantial investment they represented, even though consumers prefer throw-aways. Second, traditional economics and distribution techniques limited a franchisee to a certain geographical area. Yet the chains whose supermarkets cut across several bottlers' boundaries preferred to have advertising support originate from a single source.

Howard Johnson's departure from the traditional practice was to produce concentrates at its own plant and deliver them to contract bottlers who would re-constitute and package the drinks in disposable containers and deliver them to the chain warehouses. No franchised bottlers or territories would be involved and Howard Johnson would use food brokers to sell. The success of this approach is yet to be proven, but its logic is persuasive. It suggests what can be done by applying fresh views to this type of market analysis.

A number of methods are applicable to both the second and third steps of the audit. Industry has gained considerable experience and has developed many effective techniques for the measurement of market position, determination of customers' buying attitudes and preferences, and identification of competitors' strategies. Among the techniques which are extremely well known and widely available to the individual business are:

- Trend analyses of sales, as broken down into the customer, product, market, and distribution channel categories.
- Special bellwether or key account sales reports.
- Regular systems, based on salesmen's reports which feed back information gleaned from calls and other trade contacts.
- Logging and analysis of customer complaints and returns and the circumstances of service calls and repair work.
- Use of warranty cards to classify the kinds of customers who are buying.
- Periodic dealer and distributor field surveys.
- Sophisticated sampling techniques for customer interviews and mail questionnaires.
- Consumer panels.
- Executive field calls.
- Monthly activity and competition reports by field sales management.
- Regular reporting of sales by category to the industry's trade association for summary and reporting back to each association member.

[4] *Business Week*. op. cit., p. 45.

- A wide range of advertising agency services on customers' brand acceptance and merchandising effectiveness.
- Independent brand sales measurement services by such companies as the A. C. Nielsen Company.
- Newspaper brand surveys.
- Motivation and other market potential studies by independent consultants and research organizations.

In the face of numerous, well-developed techniques and approaches, it is surprising how much progress is yet to be made in many companies' measurement and evaluation of their market standings. The most significant opportunities for improvement exist, not so much in what information is obtained or how it is gathered but more often in how the measurement system is structured and what use is made of it once it has been obtained. Four problems stand out as most pertinent.

First, there may be gaps in the definition and concept of the market structure itself as discussed in the preceding section. The nature of these gaps or inconsistencies gives a basis for the needed information, and establishes what kinds of data should be sought. It is axiomatic that the analysis of position will be no better than the blueprint established by the structure definition.

Second, the various types of input are not well unified into a total position profile. Because of the range of intelligence sources and the different line and staff groups that are receiving information, it is often difficult to bring total findings of the various sources to one common evaluation point. For example, there is often a tendency for line management to consider its field managers' reports as confidential and proprietary, and they may never reach the market research group.

Third, insufficient attention is given to obtaining and determining the *"whys"* of the market position, as contrasted with *what* it is. This is a critical gap, since the *"whys"* are the link between past performance and the necessary future plans and strategies.

Fourth, under day-to-day pressures of competition and crisis, key management decisions are too often made without taking into account all inputs pertinent to the problem at hand. Thus, inputs already inside the company are wasted.

These kinds of market analysis problems can be avoided by specifying completely the performance factors to be evaluated. The specific aspects will often vary somewhat for each market being structured. This point in itself underscores the advantage of separating the second and third steps of the audit process, at least for the initial go-around.

Step Four: Profile the Strategies of Competitors

The purpose of the whole environmental audit is to put management into a posture where it can be more influential in "managing" its environment with superior strategies. Except for the very first company in an entirely new market, the challenge is a matter of relative competitive effectiveness. In planning its next major moves, a company needs the clearest possible indication of significant competitive strategies, both individually and in terms of their aggregate impact on the market. This profiling is the best possible test of whether the audit efforts have been pertinent and comprehensive. It is also a convenient way of disciplining the research and keeping it from getting out of hand.

Step Five: Determine the Strategic Planning Structure

In the small company, the total strategic planning may be a one- or two-man job. In this event, it is usually academic which dimensions of the market are used as the framework for strategy development. Depending on the nature of the business, prime emphasis might be placed on products or applications, or customer sets, or geography. Where a company is large enough to justify specialized marketing staff work, the structure chosen for strategic planning can be significant. There is an opportunity to achieve deeper marketing power from product managers, industry managers, or other marketing supervisors.

The key question is, What subdivisions of the company's total market deserve to be approached in significantly different ways? Some companies take the cellular approach shown schematically in Figure 4. In addition to, or instead of, any of the three dimensions shown on the cube, size, applications, or channels of distribution might be specified. The dimension chosen to be "prime" should be the one which affords the greatest opportunities for specialized strategies and programs, and at the same time is separately measurable. Thus, a manufacturer of household appliances might use product managers, whose priority of planning and measurement might be:

Product.
  Channels of distribution.
    Size of customer.
      Geography.

A computer maker might establish industry managers whose efforts might be sequenced by:

Industry.
  Application.
    Product.
      Geography.

Or a basic chemicals producer might set up application managers with strategic planning by:

Application.
  Product.
    Geography.

The use of planning cells on some such consistent basis as these increases

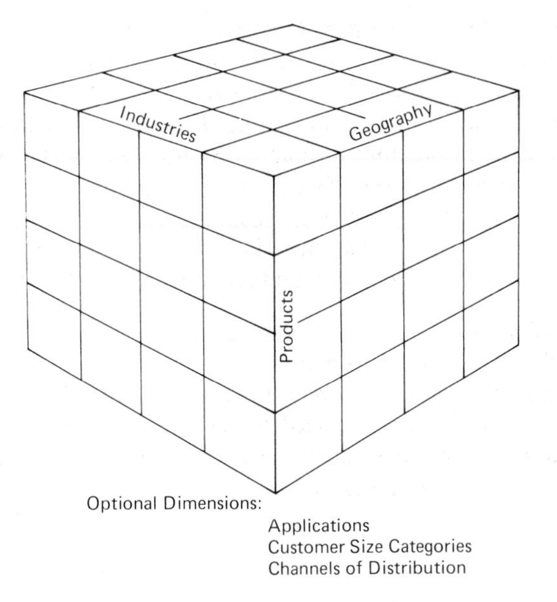

Figure 4. Structure of the Market by Planning Cells

the precision of determining potential, measuring market penetration and share, selling, product planning, development, and a variety of marketing support efforts. The rationale for the approach is that management can break down a total market into more manageable proportions for more astute strategic planning which relates the market cells to potentials and results, and then in turn to the organizational units responsible for success or failure.

Broader Environmental Influences

This chapter has purposely concentrated on direct competition, which is only one of the basic dimensions of the company's total strategic environment, in order to stress two key points. One is the advantage of streamlining competitive analysis by focusing on differentials in marketplace performance and competitive programs in order to avoid being deluged by an endless flow of non-essential information. The second is the value of structuring the analysis through such devices as market re-definition and specialized strategic planning assignments. However, as crucial as the analysis and "management" of the competitive dimension may be, they run the risk of becoming dwarfed by other forces within the company's total area of operation. Some of the most significant of these forces (several of which are discussed in detail in subsequent chapters) deserve mention at this point:

- Increased governmental regulation and influence in many sectors, such as wage-price formulas for labor contract settlements.

- Intensified anti-trust investigations by the Department of Justice relative to mergers and acquisitions and the Congressional interest in legislation restricting vertical integration by companies.
- Proposed simplification and loosening of patent protection.
- Social-interest implications of companies involved in the production and marketing of such products as drugs, tobacco, automobiles, and those with health, welfare, and safety considerations.
- Increased sensitivity to such basic issues as de-segregation, involvement in Vietnam-type wars and conflicts, and trade with Communist countries.

Full consideration of the altruistic, economic, moral, and ethical implications of such forces on a company's purposes and strategies is a study in itself. It is pertinent at this point only to call attention to these complicating dimensions and to point out the need for evaluating them fully in any well-rounded audit of the total strategic environment. Their specific impact is considered further in later chapters.

Summary

The strategy of a business is pertinent only in relation to the total competitive environment in which it chooses to, or must, operate.

This chapter has presented a dynamic approach to understanding all aspects of that elusive environment. The objective has been to convert the all-too-frequently used academic market research approach to an action-oriented basis for more effective strategic decision making by management. The result should be an improvement in initiative as an influencing force in the company's environment, to the extent such a result can be achieved in a free enterprise economy.

In discussing the interrelated aspects of the environment with which the business must cope, the following central points have established themselves:

1. Almost without exception, any business has the opportunity to maximize its profits by increasing its effectiveness as concerns managing its total environment.
2. Improvement efforts are complicated, but by no means made insurmountable, by the environmental characteristics of imperfect information, choice of action, chance, and interdependence on the actions of others.
3. Ability to cope with these complications is enhanced in direct proportion to the comprehensiveness and pertinence of a planned corporate strategy.
4. Development of such a strategy requires five preparatory activities in auditing the company's environment. These are summarized in Figure 5.
5. The competitive audit must be continuously augmented by assessment of the broader governmental, social, economic, ideological, and other forces which will influence the company's character, purposes, and strategies over the longer term.

		Key Elements
Step one:	Define the market	Develop: 1. Statement of purpose in terms of user benefits 2. Product scope 3. Size, growth rate, maturity stage, need for primary versus selective strategies 4. Requirements for success 5. Divergent definitions of the above by competitors 6. Definition to be used by the company
Step two:	Determine performance differentials	1. Evaluate industry performance and company differences 2. Determine differences in products, applications, geography, and distribution channels 3. Determine differences by customer set
Step three:	Determine differences in competitive programs	Identify and evaluate individual companies for their: 1. Market development strategies 2. Product development strategies 3. Financing and administrative strategies and support
Step four:	Profile the strategies of competitors	1. Profile each significant competitor and/or distinct type of composite strategy 2. Compare own and competitive strategies
Step five:	Determine strategic planning structure	When size and complexity are adequate: 1. Establish planning units or cells and designate prime and subordinate dimensions 2. Make organizational assignments to product managers, industry managers, and others

Figure 5. Steps in Auditing the Competitive Environment

It is unimportant whether a company shortcuts these steps or uses a full-blown auditing approach. There is clearly an opportunity for the individual company to exert a more effective influence on its market. It can do this by broadening the way it defines that market and by periodically profiling and comparing the strategies of its major competitors with its own. These efforts are the prelude to the strategic decision-making process. . . . Added understanding of how strategic planning can be made more effective is first gained by probing more deeply into what types of strategy alternatives are available to the company. A number of the *what* strategies of product, market, geography, and channels of distribution are surveyed comprehensively in Part Two [of *Business Strategy and Policy*].

strategy implementation

The preceding sections have dealt with activities of top management in policy formulation. Specific attention has also been directed to the environment within which managerial activities and decision making take place. The results are goals, objectives, major policies, and broad plans for the total enterprise. If management has carried out its activities well, the organization is armed with strategies and plans to attack the competitive environment.

The realization of those plans and the successful utilization of those opportunities depend upon the skill with which the over-all strategies are implemented and the degree to which those at the corporate policy level modify strategies to meet the challenges of a dynamic environment. Managers at all levels and in all functional components (e.g., finance, marketing, production, R&D, and personnel) are involved in strategy implementation.

The managerial tasks of implementation are administrative in nature and focus on bringing all organizational resources to bear on activities which will contribute to the achievement of the corporate strategies. The entire field of administrative theory is pertinent in understanding how resources must be combined and managed to achieve goals. Because a background is assumed in this area, the readings in this part focus on those activities which contribute most to concepts of integrating activities and interdepartmental relationships.

Although the emphasis is on administrative processes rather than on the functional operations of the firm, knowledge of functional operations is important. The functional areas provide much of the information upon which formulation and implementation decisions are based. The ability of the functional areas to perform determines to a large extent the conditions of strength or weakness which must be assessed in determining strategy, as discussed in Part Two. Operations of functional areas will influence implementation alternatives. For example, the details of technologies and procedures in functional departments may affect the choice of coordination and control techniques for strategy implementation.

The readings in this part are in two sections. Those in Section 5 deal with selected administrative functions having a broad applicability to implementation problems. The selections cover planning and controlling, organization, coordination, and communication. Section 6 deals with issues related to implementation of strategies of growth, diversification, and realignment of corporate resources. Those activities involve special questions of interdivisional and intercompany relationships which are quite different from the operation of a single-plant or single-industry firm.

Plans, Programs, and Control

Strategic plans must be translated into specific, short-range operational plans. Theodore Andersen analyzes major problems of achieving efficient interrelationships between the two and suggests approaches to the problems created by the differences. David Novick discusses planning-programming-budgeting (PPB) and describes the interrelationships among long-range plans, budgets, and operational planning. William Souder reviews and criticizes some of the budgetary practices in R&D and proposes improvements. This article not only deals with a significant problem of functional planning and control, but also can serve to guide the reader to extend the application of the methods described to other budgeting activities. The article by Edward Roberts deals with management control systems and related managerial problems. His discussion includes the integration of control systems with planning.

Organization

The range of strategies available for organizing components of a firm is extensive. The optimum configuration is dependent upon many variables. In addition to principally structural issues, the interpersonal aspects of organization are extensive. The readings in this section focus on issues concerning establishing and maintaining effective organizational relationships in order to implement the corporate strategies.

Robert Golembiewski discusses a range of approaches to a variety of organizational issues. Although he writes in a personnel context, it will be easy for the reader to draw general applications from the ideas described. Zenon Zannetos attacks, on a conceptual basis, the issue of centralization vs. decentralization. He discusses research bearing on the topic, suggests a definitional decision framework, and analyzes some factors that favor centralization and decentralization. In addition, he highlights pertinent issues to operational problems of management.

Project organization is a powerful concept and is one which can be applied to many activities in a dynamic organization. John Stewart describes the concept, difficulties involved, and guidelines for operations. David Wilemon and John

Cicero direct attention to the problems project managers face—human relationships, balance between technical and managerial project functions, coping with associated risks, and surviving organizational constraints placed upon the project manager.

Coordination and Communication

Coordination is a frequently mentioned managerial activity. Literally all activities within the firm need to be coordinated for effective operations. Despite this, little mention is made of types of coordination and means for achieving it. The article by Franklin Huddle provides a categorization of coordination tools and techniques. George Berkwitt discusses understanding the problems of integrating the operations of diverse disciplines (i.e., functions and organizational units). Paul Lawrence and Jay Lorsch explore the techniques of integration employed by managers facing the task.

As with coordination, communication is a pervasive managerial activity of crucial importance. Arlyn Melcher and Ronald Beller explore communication channel selection and communications media for effective operations.

Expansion and Contraction

The principal dimensions of corporate expansion and contraction are identified and discussed in this section. Donald Thain develops the concept of corporate stages of growth as a means to assist in identifying and analyzing problems of growth and diversification as they relate to general management problems of formulating and implementing corporate strategy. Willard Bright discusses reasons for diversification, why such strategies might be employed, and limitations on the firm's ability to diversify. Robert Attiyeh deals with environmental and internal constraints operating on conglomerates and the challenge of managing corporate assets. He then discusses divestment as an alternative to coping with some of the problems. The article by David Judelson deals with the nature of and outlook for conglomerates. He discusses characteristics and reasons for growth of conglomerates as well as issues having major corporate strategy implications.

Part Three. References for Further Study

Section 5: Administrative Functions

A. Plans, Programs, and Control

Arrow, Kenneth J. "Control in Large Organizations." *Management Sciences,* **10,** 3 (April 1964), 397–408.
Outlines the problems of control in modern organizations, states essentials of the control problem and examines the use of price systems as a solution to the problem of control.

Dearden, John. "Appraising Profit Center Managers." *Harvard Business Review,* **46,** 3 (May–June 1968), 80–87.

Advocates replacement of profit budget systems with a technique of formal, periodic analyses of past performance in a wide range of areas.

Ridgeway, Valentine F. "Dysfunctional Consequences of Performance Measurements." *Administrative Science Quarterly,* **1,** 2 (September 1956), 240–247.

Analyzes the impact of single, multiple, and composite criteria upon job performance from a motivational and behavioral point of view.

Schaffer, Robert H. "Putting Action Into Planning." *Harvard Business Review,* **45,** 6 (November–December 1967), 158–166.

Identifies reasons why planning often fails to achieve its purposes and proposes strategies for implementing a successful planning program.

Warren, K. Kirby. "Where Long-Range Planning Goes Wrong." *Management Review,* **51,** 5 (May 1962), 4–15.

Analyzes the elements of long-range planning (forecasting, budgeting, goal-setting, and direction of planning activities) and identifies ways in which planners err.

B. Organization

Hodgetts, Richard M. "Leadership Techniques in the Project Organization." *Academy of Management Journal,* **11,** 2 (June 1968), 211–220.

Reports on techniques used by project managers to bridge the authority gap inherent in project organization, including negotiation, persuasion, competence, and reciprocity.

Hunt, Raymond G. "Technology and Organization." *Academy of Management Journal,* **13,** 3 (September 1970), 235–252.

Reviews means of classifying organizations and discusses the relevance of technology to organization structure. Distinguishes between performance and problem-solving models of organization.

Litschert, Robert J. "Some Characteristics of Organization for Long-Range Planning." *Academy of Management Journal,* **10,** 3 (September 1967), 247–256.

Examines the strategies for organizing a specific corporate activity, and identifies the characteristics that are environment-dependent and environment-independent.

Logan, Hall H. "Line and Staff: An Obsolete Concept?" *Personnel,* **43,** 1 (January–February 1966), 26–33.

Discusses the responsibility and authority elements of various tasks as major determinants of working relationships.

Walker, Arthur W., and J. W. Lorsch. "Organizational Choice: Product versus Function." *Harvard Business Review,* **46,** 6 (November–December 1968), 129–138.

Evaluates criteria used in deciding on structure and suggests a procedure for organizational style based on the nature of the task, together with examples of some mixed strategies.

C. Coordination and Communication

Bedford, Norton N., and Mohamed Onsi. "Measuring the Value of Information: An Information Theory Approach." *Management Services,* **3,** 1 (January–February 1966), 15–22.

Suggests the use of information theory as a means of locating the point at which the cost of data collection outweighs the value of information gained.

McMurry, Robert N. "Clear Communications for Chief Executives." *Harvard Business Review*, **43,** 2 (March–April 1965), 131–147.

Examines the barriers to the chief executive's knowledge of what's going on and the sources of error that hinder his ability to communicate with subordinates. Suggests major remedies and reorganization steps.

Wickesburg, A. K. "Communications Network in the Business Organization Structure." *Academy of Management Journal*, **11,** 3 (September 1968), 253–262.

Reports the results of studies on the actual dimensions and characteristics of individual communications networks within the firm.

Wren, Daniel A. "Interface and Interorganizational Coordination." *Academy of Management Journal*, **10,** 1 (March 1967), 69–81.

Analyzes interface relationships between organizations as a means of understanding systems theory. Has relevance for coordination of divisions as well as multicompany activities.

Ziller, R. C., B. J. Stark, and H. O. Pruden. "Marginality and Integrative Management Positions." *Academy of Management Journal*, **12,** 4 (December 1964), 487–495.

Suggests that the marginality component of personality, with its attribute of open-mindedness, is an appropriate personality orientation for those men in integrative management positions.

Section 6: Expansion and Contraction

Berg, Norman A. "What's Different About Conglomerate Management." *Harvard Business Review*, **47,** 6 (November–December 1969), 112–120.

Compares management practices between conglomerates and large corporations with regard to staff size, autonomy, decentralization, planning, information systems, motivation, and financial resources.

Bettauer, Arthur. "Strategy for Divestments." *Harvard Business Review*, **45,** 2 (March–April 1967), 116–124.

Outlines alternative approaches to divestment together with detailed procedures and activities for effecting the plan.

Boulden, James B. "Merger Negotiations: A Decision Model." *Business Horizons*, **XII,** 1 (February 1969), 21–28.

Develops an analytic model which takes into account the emotional and economic dimensions of merger negotiations. Computer program allows evaluation of alternatives.

Gilmore, John S., and Dean C. Coddington. "Diversification Guides for Defense Firms." *Harvard Business Review*, **44,** 3 (May–June 1966), 144–159.

Discusses the consideration of distinctive competencies in developing strategies for diversification and the problems in implementing the program.

Hanan, Mack. "Corporate Growth Through Venture Management," *Harvard Business Review*, **47,** 1 (January–February 1969), 43–61.

Describes the venture concept (an attempt to make innovation more predictable) and outlines a critical path plan for implementing venture management.

Leighton, Charles M., and G. Robert Tod. "After the Acquisition: Continuing Challenge." *Harvard Business Review*, **47,** 2 (March–April 1969), 90–102.

Analyzes the steps necessary in planning and managing an acquisition based on carefully developed acquisition strategy and objectives.

Lippitt, Gordon L., and Warren H. Schmidt. "Crises in a Developing Organization." *Harvard Business Review,* **45,** 6 (November–December 1967), 102–112.
Identifies critical concerns, key issues, required actions, and consequences attendant to stages of corporate development.

"The Multicompanies: Conglomerate, Agglomerate and In-Between." *Forbes,* **103,** 1 (Jan. 1, 1969), 77–86.
Discusses the strategies underlying the formation of multicompanies together with problems of administration and performance. Distinguishes between types of multicompanies.

administrative functions

section **5**

A. Plans, Programs, and Control

21

Coordinating Strategic and Operational Planning

Theodore A. Andersen

Business managers who must cope with the many dynamic forces at work influencing their market and profit prospects are giving more attention to strategic planning. Looking ahead, the business planner sees major technological advances, a relatively short life for many of his firm's products, numerous opportunities for new and modified products, and major changes in the production and management processes involving greater use of automation and EDP. To further complicate the problem of strategic planning, the growth rate of the economy showed a 30 per cent expansion in the first half of this decade. Prospects are favorable for continuation of this trend, leading to a GNP of over $1 trillion in less than ten years.

Strategic planning involves decisions about the breadth and structure of the technological base the firm intends to develop, the managerial skills that are to be strengthened, and the planned rate and processes of growth. This type of planning needs to be performed in close relationship with operational (sometimes referred to as functional) planning. Traditionally, operational

Reprinted from *Business Horizons,* Summer 1965, pp. 49–55. Copyright, 1965 by the Foundation for the School of Business, at Indiana University. Reprinted by permission.

planning has received considerable attention and has been conducted somewhat independently of other types of planning.[1] As a result of major advances in the role of strategic planning made particularly since the Korean conflict, it is natural that the interrelationships between the two should grow in importance.[2] Writers have analyzed problems of strategic planning in some detail and have noted the need to blend short- and long-range planning, but relatively little has been written about the various specific problems often involved in coordinating the two types of planning.

This article proposes to analyze some of the major problems involved in achieving efficient interrelationships between strategic and operational planning. Accordingly, the following sequential analysis will be observed:

Review of the basic aspects of strategic and operational planning and their importance differences

Analysis of the major problems of coordinated management planning created by these differences

Suggestion of approaches for achieving effective working relationships between the two planning activities.

Aspects and Differences

No precise separation exists between strategic and operational planning, but some broad differences ought to be clearly understood in order that sound interrelationships be established between the two.[3] In general, strategic planning deals with the following areas of decision making:

Planned growth rate in sales, by product lines, and for the firm on an over-all basis; consideration of how much growth is to be achieved by internal development as opposed to mergers and acquisitions

Planned diversification by technologies, types of products, customers, and geographical areas

Product research and development policies

Planned levels of aggregate profits, profit to invested capital ratios, earnings per share, and price-earnings ratios

Comparably important planning activities in the areas of organization, staff, and finance that affect all major functions.

[1] Melville C. Branch, "A View of Corporate Planning Today," *California Management Review* (Winter, 1964), pp. 89–91; R. G. Murdock, "The Long Range Planning Matrix," *California Management Review* (Winter, 1964), pp. 35, 3–40.

[2] The seminar in managerial long-range planning held at UCLA in May, 1963 indicated that formal comprehensive strategic planning is relatively new in the firms that now provide for this type of activity. Major emphasis in planning has been on functional or operational planning. See George A. Steiner, ed., *Managerial Long Range Planning* (New York: McGraw-Hill Book Company, Inc., 1963), pp. 312–26.

[3] Professor George Steiner has developed an excellent and comprehensive description of the differences between strategic and tactical planning. See George A. Steiner, "Multinational Corporate Planning," *Economie Appliquée* (1964, II–III), pp. 13–16.

Strategic planning deals primarily with long-term prospects but may also influence relatively short periods. For example, a decision to cut prices to strengthen the firm's competitive position may be put into effect fairly quickly. Results may also be produced quickly, and price adjustments may have to be made periodically. These actions may have strategic consequences but may be made on a short-term basis.

Operational planning, in contrast to strategic, is concerned primarily with the following activities:

Adjusting the production, marketing, and financial capacity of the firm to the expected level of operations, in both the short and long run.

Increasing the efficiency of operating activities through analyzing past performance, budgeting future costs, developing and administering controls over costs and efficiency, and planning and implementing capital investment project.

Programming in comprehensive and specific detail future short-term operations.

Turning now to the important differences between the two types of planning, the following generalizations can be made. Strategic planning guides the choice among the broad directions in which the company seeks to move and concerns the general planned allocations of the firm's managerial, financial, and physical resources over future specified periods of time. Operational planning, on the other hand, focuses on the ways and means by which each of the individual functions may be programmed so that optimum progress may be made toward the attainment of strategic objectives.

Strategic planning should precede operational planning since the latter is primarily an implementation of the former. It usually is concerned with the five-, ten-, and twenty-year company trends, whereas operational planning is heavily concerned with the short-run programs implementing step-by-step progress toward basic goals. The functional capacities of a firm are generally restricted because of limited managerial skills, organizational depth, and financial resources. These restrictions on the firm's potential accomplishment are more prevalent in a short term than over a longer term; therefore, strategic planning must recognize the limits of what operational planning can realistically be undertaken in given time periods. Thus strategic planning is restricted by the practical limitations under which operational planning operates.

Unlike operational planning, strategic planning is usually conducted by top management and its immediate staff. It may be the responsibility of a director, aided by several staff assistants, who reports to the president, division manager, or another executive at the top level of management. Operational planning, however, may be spread over a wide range within the organizational structure and is generally performed by operating people, including salesmen, foremen, and even production workers.

These two types of planning focus generally on different environments—one outside the company, the other inside. Strategic planners concern themselves primarily with growth problems while operational planners emphasize improving efficiency. Some basic incompatibility does exist between these objectives since the two planning groups are usually widely separated within the organizational structure. It is not surprising, therefore, that in practice serious problems of integrating the two types of plans are often encountered.

Many examples may be cited to illustrate problems of coordinated planning. For example, the growth prospects of an individual firm may best be served by broadening or shifting its technological base into areas where development prospects are greater. Such shifts, however, are likely to decrease efficiency as new products with which the firm has had little or no experience are scheduled to be developed and manufactured. Similarly, the manager of sales may be reluctant to take on the problems involved in shifting the marketing effort from traditional to newer products. Problems of salesman training and recruiting, and customer education for new products may be discouraging, and it may seem preferable to concentrate on marketing present products. The *status quo,* therefore, as far as product lines are concerned, may be a more attractive company policy to functional managers. While open resistance to significant product change may not develop, functional managers often find subtle reasons for supporting more static policies.

Alfred Sloan, in his book *My Years With General Motors,* described a good example of the reluctance of functional managers to follow the policy guidelines developed by strategic planners.[4] Sloan, who had become a GM vice-president in 1918, concluded in 1921 that the company lacked an adequate concept of the industry and, as a result, had no sound product policy or marketing strategy. As evidence, he pointed out that they had no car in the $500 to $800 price field although this price was above the Ford line and, hence, would involve limited direct competition with it. At the same time, however, they had Chevrolet, Oakland, Olds, Scripps-Booth, Sheridan, and Buick engaged in considerable direct competition with each other in the $800 to $2,000 price field.

This array, Sloan asserted, was the result of lack of strategic planning and the independence of the operating divisions in carrying out programs. The strategy that Sloan and the advisory staff developed to cope with these problems was to reduce to six the number of cars in price fields ranging from $450 to $3,500. They wished to provide competition in each price field with a minimum of overlap within the company. Quality of design, and efficiency in production and volume were to be the keys to the financial success which the company had lacked up to that time.

As Sloan set out in 1921 to achieve some integration of strategic and functional planning, he found the operating executives in the various manufacturing divisions more concerned with their own problems and interests than with those of the corporation as a whole. This condition was natural, but

[4] Alfred P. Sloan, Jr., *My Years with General Motors* (New York: Doubleday & Company, Inc., 1964), pp. 58–70, 99–114, 121–40.

harmful in certain major respects; in such matters as capital budgeting, inventory policy, and hoarding of cash, the operating practices were counter to corporate policy. To achieve the integration he believed necessary, Sloan vigorously educated and persuaded his top management of the importance of continuous strategic planning to help ensure that the company's product line and prices were systematically developed and kept in balance with the continuously changing structure of the demand for cars.

Moreover, he stressed that effective communication had to be maintained between strategic and other staff planning groups and operational managers in order that company policies be properly understood and implemented. A two-way process of communication was maintained in General Motors that encouraged and required the flow of ideas, information, proposals, and plans from the bottom of the organization to the top. In addition, information on policy decisions and approved programs and budgets flowed from the top to the bottom of the management structure. Considerable use of committees was made to provide for the exchange of information and communication of policy decisions. Operating decisions, authority, and responsibility remained concentrated in the hands of division and line managers.

Because of Sloan's remarkable leadership qualities and administrative skills, he was able to achieve coordination of strategic and operational planning in relatively few years. A major change in company management resulted; the importance of this advance can hardly be exaggerated as the company went on to be the greatest producer of profits in the history of U.S. business enterprise.

An inherent conflict between the strategic planning staff and the financial manager is a common problem. Financial managers may be unenthusiastic about the findings of the strategic planners because of the greater financial risks that would be incurred if implementation of certain strategic plans were undertaken. Mergers may dilute price-earnings ratios and book values. Moreover, attempts to speed company growth rates often have a short-run adverse effect on profit margins. In sum, costs and investments go up before additional profits are realized in most instances of accelerated growth.

Strategic planners analyze a broad environment, including all technologies, domestic and world markets, and future developments. Operational planners, on the other hand, focus on their present personnel and facilities, have major day-to-day operating responsibilities, and are often under pressure to immediately accomplish a higher level of activity at lower cost. Thus, there is some tendency for the former group to be "on Cloud 9" while the latter "have their feet in the mud." Furthermore, if there is a tendency for each of the two groups of planners to exaggerate its own importance and underestimate the importance of the other, the difficulties of blending the two types of planning are all the more compounded.

Strategic planning is likely to proceed at a more leisurely pace than operational planning, yet the latter is in many cases dependent on the former. In the resulting conflict of time schedules, operational planners may undertake strategic decisions on their own and proceed accordingly. Production managers may allocate unused factory space for their own purposes without regard to basic company strategy for the eventual utilization of this space. Or sales managers may send salesmen into new territories without waiting for a top management strategic decision as to where new efforts should be concentrated. Thus, the timing of strategic planning decisions and operational decisions may be in conflict, with the latter preceding the former to the detriment of the company concerned.

Professor Steiner has pointed out that more and more companies are dividing responsibility for long- and short-range planning. In such cases the work of the two groups must be in phase timewise, so that it is possible for short-range planners to give adequate consideration to the targets established in the long-range plans.

Another problem in blending strategic and operational planning lies in the partial overlap of the two. For example, product planning may be undertaken by the sales department because of its close relationship with customers; strategic planners, or long-range planning staff as they are often called, will also be concerned with product planning because of their analysis of the prospective comparative growth rate of the various technologies, industries, and product lines. The production, engineering, and R&D staffs are also usually involved to a greater or lesser degree in product planning. Thus, the pervasive interest in product planning among both staff and operating managers necessitates some coordination of these efforts while allowing for some overlap of efforts.

Strategic and operational planners may also become jointly involved in pricing. The sales manager has an important contribution to make because of his knowledge of customers and competition; strategic planners, on the other hand, may have a broader knowledge of sales potentials in marketing areas as yet undeveloped and dependent in part on price. For example, in 1954 when the list price to be established for the Ford Thunderbird was under study, the sales department of the Ford Division was considering a price comparable to that of the Chevrolet Corvette, which had come on the market the previous year. The list price on the Corvette at that time was approximately $4,000, and sales were generally made only to buyers in the higher-priced field. Based on studies of the high price elasticity of demand for that type of product, the division's strategic planning staff concluded that the Thunderbird should be priced to appeal to car buyers in the medium-priced field, at a list price close to $3,000. In approaching this particular pricing problem, significantly different results were found when competition from the most comparable product was used as a basis for pricing and when the staff used a broad analysis of the distribution of consumer income and price elasticity of demand for luxury products. Consequently, the strategic planners argued for a significantly lower price than the operational planners.

Methods of Coordination

Despite the numerous points of potential conflict between strategic and operational planning, much can be done to resolve differences previously discussed. For example, a senior officer might be appointed to work for the coordination, where necessary, of the two types of planning effort. This officer would be knowledgeable in some detail regarding the planning efforts of the two groups.[5] Periodic joint meetings of strategic and operational planners might be held to review the role of each group and the specific projected programs of each. Particular emphasis may be placed on those aspects of planning where significant interrelationship and interdependence are involved. Some representatives of operational planning groups might, on particular matters, participate in meetings of the strategic planners, and vice versa. This would provide more continuous contact between the two groups, beginning with the early stages of planning major projects and activities.

Efforts might be made to educate the various planning groups about the importance of each, the need for eventual integration of certain planning activities, and above all, the need for constructive cooperative attitudes among various specialists. Professor Ansoff noted that after moving from strategic planning to a position of general manager he would have handled his earlier responsibility differently had he had more line experience.[6]

A minimum requisite for achieving adequate coordination of the two types of planning is recognition that an important problem may exist and need attention. The detailed solution for a given situation will, of course, depend on the nature of the individual problem and the personalities involved. Considerable close communication between the two types of planners certainly would be basic to any method for dealing with this problem.

As planning grows with the complexity and dynamic nature of the business enterprise and its environment, it is to be expected that specialization of these efforts will also increase. These trends toward specialization in planning add to the problem of blending the efforts of the expanding and proliferating planning units. In turn, more time and effort must be spent to coordinate these planning groups and to solve the problems they generate. If the generally accepted methods for improving communication among specialized units within management structure are employed, the competition and conflicts between strategic and functional planning groups can be more easily held to minimal levels.

[5] Townsend Hoopes suggests that the director of corporate planning, where one exists, coordinate the plans prepared by the functional planners. See Townsend Hoopes, "The Corporate Planner (New Edition)," *Business Horizons,* V (Winter, 1962).

[6] *Managerial Long Range Planning,* p. 66.

22

Long-range Planning Through Program Budgeting

David Novick

A plan for an organization, whether a government agency or a business firm, prescribes actions to be taken and activities to be carried on to advance the organization's perceived objectives. Plans vary widely in substance and form according to the nature of the organization, the scope of the plan, and the time-frame to which it applies. However, one element is universal in the planning of any organization that produces goods or services: at some point, the plan must deal with the question, "How shall the organization make use of its available resources?" This—the resource allocation question—is fundamental, because in every sphere of the organization's activity the amount of resources sets limits to what can be accomplished.

The strategic and most comprehensive form of planning is long-range planning of the organization's total program. In business, such planning may embrace the full set of product lines and productive functions of a diversified corporation. In government, it may encompass the programs of an entire department or ministry or, perhaps, the development of a "five-year plan" for an entire jurisdiction. This article deals with a system for organizing the long-range planning function and for helping managers to reach the key resource allocation decisions that confront them in this context.

For more than twenty-five years I have been developing a management tool—program budgeting—which is designed to strengthen an organization's capability to do long-range planning and to provide a systematic method for resolving major resource allocation issues.[1] Program budgeting—or the planning-programming-budgeting systems abbreviated to PPB—focuses on the basic function of management, which is to use the organization's available resources in the way that will be most effective in meeting its goals. Basically, the PPB system contributes to the planning process in two ways.

First, it establishes and makes explicit the relationships or linkages among the organization's objectives, its programs and activities, the resource implications of those activities, and their financial expression in a budget. In so doing, it provides much of the information needed for rational planning in an easily usable form. *Second,* PPB contributes directly to management decision making by providing analyses of the consequences, in terms of estimated costs and expected benefits, of possible program decisions.

This may sound like a broad charter, but it should be borne in mind that PPB does not do a number of important things. As it is discussed here, PPB is an instrument for over-all planning that utilizes existing systems for directing

Reprinted from *Business Horizons,* February 1969, pp. 59–65.

[1] "Introduction," in David Novick, ed., *Program Budgeting: Program Analysis and the Federal Budget* (2nd ed.; Cambridge, Mass.: Harvard University Press, 1967).

and controlling operations and therefore does not necessitate change in either the existing organization or methods of administration. In addition, PPB is specifically designed for long-range planning and budgeting; it is not primarily a tool for conducting the annual budgeting-accounting cycle, although next year's budget must be included in its purview, and accounting supplies part of the reports. Last, although PPB stresses the use of quantitative analytical methods and, in some cases, a rather extensive use of modern computer technology, it does not attempt to quantify every part of the problem or to computerize the decision-making process.[2]

PPB has been in operation for seven years in the U.S. Department of Defense, and, since 1965, efforts have been under way to extend the system to other departments and agencies. Many state and local governments have applied PPB methods to their own planning problems, and similar methods are in use in major business firms. Nevertheless, in some organizations, the adoption of PPB has caused apprehension and insecurity, largely as the result of a misunderstanding of what PPB is and does. People assume program budgeting is revolutionary and complex. When in operation and understood, the real content comes through; it is revolutionary but simple and based on common sense.

The Program Budget Concept

The PPB system is constructed on a few basic concepts related to objectives, programs, resources, cost, effectiveness, and benefits.

Objectives are the organization's aims or purposes, which, collectively, define its raison d'etre. They may be stated initially in broad and relatively abstract terms, as, for example, when we say that the objective of a defense program is to provide national security or the objectives of education are to provide good citizens and productive participants in the economy. However, objectives at this level are too remote from the organization's specific activities to be useful for formulating or evaluating programs to be operational; they must be translated into lower-level objectives that can be stated in concrete terms.

Programs are the sets of activities undertaken to accomplish objectives.[3] A program generally has an identifiable end product. (Some programs may be undertaken in support of others; if so, they have identifiable intermediate products.) Several programs may be associated with an objective, in which case they may be identified with distinct subobjectives or with complementary, but distinguishable, means for accomplishing the objective.

Resources are the goods and services consumed by program activities.

[2] David Novick, *The Role of Quantitative Analysis and the Computer in Program Budgeting*. The RAND Corporation, P-3716. October, 1967.

[3] M. Anshen, D. Novick, and W. C. Truppner, *Wartime Production Controls* (New York: Columbia University Press, 1949), pp. 109–11.

They may be thought of as the inputs required to produce each program's end product. Program cost is the monetary value of resources identified with a program.

Effectiveness is a measure of the degree to which programs accomplish their objectives. It is related to benefit, which is a measure of the utility to be derived from each program.

Program budgeting for an organization begins with an effort to identify and define objectives, and group the organization's activities into programs that can be related to each objective. This is the revolutionary aspect, since it requires grouping by end product rather than by administrative organization or by function. This method allows us to look at *what* we produce—output—in addition to *how* we produce or what inputs we consume. The program budget itself presents resources and costs categorized according to the program or end product to which they apply. This contrasts with traditional budgets found in most organizations that assemble costs by type of resource input (line item) and by organizational or functional categories. The point of this restructuring of budget information is that it aids planning by focusing attention on competition for resources among programs and on the effectiveness of resource use within programs. The entire process by which objectives are identified, programs are defined and quantitatively described, and the budget is recast into a program budget format is called the structural phase of planning-programming-budgeting.

Often, both in government and in business, responsibility for the work required to accomplish a coherent set of objectives is divided among a number of organizations. In the government, for example, programs with objectives for health and education are each fragmented among a dozen bureaus and independent agencies. The activities of each one are sometimes complementary, sometimes contradictory, or in conflict with those of the others. As a result, there is no over-all coordination of the resource allocation decisions relevant to program objectives. One of the strengths of program budgeting is that it cuts across organizational boundaries, drawing together the information needed by decision makers without regard to divisions in operating authority among jurisdictions. The advantage for planning is obvious: a program can be examined as a whole, contradictions are more likely to be recognized, and a context is supplied for consideration of changes that would alter or cut across existing agency lines.

One product of the structural phase is a conversion matrix or "crosswalk" from the budget in program terms to the traditional or functional budget, which treats of organizations like departments and sections in categories such as wages and salaries, supplies, equipment, and the like. Through the crosswalk we are able to translate ongoing methods of recordkeeping and reporting into data for program planning; we are also able to translate program decisions into existing methods for directing, authorizing, controlling, recording, and reporting operations. If existing management methods in any of these areas are inadequate or unsatisfactory, they should be upgraded and improved whether or not the organization has a PPB system. In any case, the program budget must derive information and relationships from existing management records and practices, and must rely on them for the implementation of the programs.

The long-range planner encounters problems of choice at several levels. At the highest level, the different programs and objectives compete for their shares of the organization's total resources or total budget. For example, in a government Transportation Ministry, programs for international transportation, domestic intercity transportation, and local transportation compete with each other. In a business firm, competition for investment funds may involve different product lines, different research and development projects, and so forth. At a lower level, the problem of choice focuses on decisions among alternative ways of carrying out a program. For instance, in connection with the Transportation Ministry's program of domestic intercity transportation, choices have to be made among alternative transport modes—railway, automobile, and air transport—or among alternative combinations of modes.

In program budgeting, the approach to this problem is to apply analysis wherever it is possible, so that decision makers will be able to make the final judgments with as much objective information as can be assembled. Thus, a planning-programming-budgeting system subsumes a systems analysis capability with which the resource and cost implications of program alternatives and their expected "outputs" or accomplishments may be estimated, examined, and compared. (When a systems analysis capability does not exist or is inadequate, it should be created or upgraded since analysis is perhaps the most important part of PPB.) A wide range of techniques is employed in these program analyses, including statistical analysis: modeling, gaming, and simulation: operations analysis; and econometric techniques. Systems analysis examines both the resource/cost side and the benefit/effectiveness side of program consequences.

An important aspect of systems analysis in connection with program planning is that it often goes far beyond the decision problem as initially given. Program analysis is not confined to examination of predetermined alternatives; development of new and better alternatives is part of the process. It is likely that analysis of possibilities A, B, and C will lead to the invention of alternatives D and E, which may be preferable (more cost/effective) to the original candidates. Therefore, the analytical aspect of PPB cannot be viewed merely as the application of a collection of well-defined analytical techniques to a problem. The process is much more flexible and subtle, and calls for creativity by the analyst and interaction between the analyst and the decision maker during the decision process.

Other Important Features

Some other features of the PPB system will convey a fuller impression of the context in which these principles are applied. First, since program decisions that we make today often have implications that extend far into the future, and since program costs may be incurred and benefits enjoyed many years after a decision is made, meaningful planning requires a *long-time horizon.* Generally, the program budget itself and the associated program analyses cover at least a five-year period and, where appropriate, should extend ten, fifteen, or more years into the future.

Planning, not forecasting, is the purpose of the PPB system. Our aim is to examine the cost and benefit implications for the future of relevant alternative courses of action. The program budget, which conveys a projection of existing programs and a display of decisions already made, provides a base line and serves as a frame of reference for specification and analysis of alternatives. It should not be thought of as a static extrapolation of a program.

Comparability rather than accuracy is the main consideration in our analysis of program cost and benefits. Because of intrinsic uncertainties in long-range planning, absolute accuracy is not attainable. The relevant criterion for analyses is consistency in treatment of different alternatives; this must be accompanied by explicit treatment of uncertainties, including tests of the sensitivity of analytical results to variations in circumstances. Excessive concentration on absolute accuracy is likely to be self-defeating since it would tend to overwhelm the work with detail and make this kind of planning impracticable. In addition, aggregate, not detailed, data must generally be used in cost and benefit estimation. Examination of many alternatives is costly or impossible, so we must focus on variables that have important impacts on program consequences.

Several points may be made about the cost concepts that enter into program analysis. *Full costing* of programs and program alternatives is required if we are to achieve consistency in our estimates. Programs often have indirect cost implications that are difficult to trace; important interdependencies may exist between "direct" and "support" programs or among direct programs themselves (for example, joint cost situations). In order to sort out the full cost implications of alternatives, it is often necessary to have a cost model or its equivalent that is capable of translating the total program of the organization into resource and cost implications. The cost figures that will actually be compared with benefit estimates are incremental costs associated with specific program decisions, but these must be derived by comparing the full costs of either another program alternative or a base case.

Resources and costs are generally divided into three categories, corresponding to differences in the time pattern by which they are incurred and in the duration of their contribution to benefits. Research and development costs are the one-time outlays to create new capability, for example, studies of new products, services, or technologies, or of new methods for accomplishing programs. Investment costs are the nonrecurring outlays required to install new capability, for example, construction of plants or facilities, purchase of equipment, or training of personnel for participation in new programs. Annual operating costs are the recurring costs required either to operate new capability to be installed or existing capability to be maintained. Each of these elements of cost enters into the full cost of a program. All three are projected on a year-by-year basis and summed for each program and for the total program of the organization. Capital and operating cost implications of programs are looked at together, not separately as is the traditional practice.

A planning-programming-budgeting system provides for communication between analysts and decision makers and between analysts, operating organizations, and decision makers at different organizational levels. Some specific documentary forms have been developed to facilitate this exchange of information. For example, *program memoranda* provide the communication between the analysts within a program area and the analytical staff that services the decision-making group. In these paper studies the program group lays out the issues it identifies in the program area, the alternatives it recommends, and the pros and cons for its recommendations, as well as the data, analysis, and arguments for the possibilities it has rejected.

The top-side analytical group reanalyzes the program memorandum and writes its memorandum in response. The reply may accept the recommendations for the same, different, or modified reasons; determine issues that have not been raised; suggest alternative program packages that have not been considered; or modify alternatives that were examined. After as much study, analysis, and reanalysis as time permits, the top staff with concurrence or objection from the program manager, drafts the final program memorandum covering all issues and all alternatives for consideration by the decision maker.

Special studies require more time and/or study resources than are available during the program memorandum period as scheduled. These areas are assigned for completion in the near future in order of importance and will frequently (not always) cut across areas handled by two or more program managers. For reasons of time or specialized knowledge, parts or all of these studies may be contracted out.

Program change is another administrative step calling for analysis and study. Program budgeting aims at a continuing, fluid management process. This means setting up a "base case" or set of decisions taken now, which are revised and updated as required. When change is or appears to be in order, the proposed change is considered in a total resource, over-all time context, just as though it was a program memorandum in the original deliberations. Ideally, this would mean only one over-all program budget exercise. Changes would be made as required and the revised total plan would become the new base case, which would be used for the crosswalk from the program budget into the immediate changes in the budget as well as next year's organizational and functional operating budgets.

Introducing PPB

Two possible courses of action are open for the introduction of program budgeting. One is to set up a study group to examine the government's or company's objectives, develop a program structure tailored to those objectives, recommend alternative organization and administration schemes, examine the organization's analytical capabilities, and recommend education, training, and hiring policies to be followed in developing the analysis capacity required for program budgeting. (Reassignment, upgrading, and so on would obviously be included.) This approach would aim at an operation to start eighteen months to two years in the future.

The other course of action starts with the assumption that program budgeting is the thing to do and to get on with it. This would mean taking some great leaps to put it in use in a current planning and budget cycle, and to learn in the process the answers the study group would otherwise have provided. This procedure is described in the following steps.

1. Set up a program structure that uses major activities or lines of business as final product programs, taking major government agency-wide or company-wide activities like electronic data processing (EDP), and calling them major support programs and putting everything else, like research, planning, and executives, into a general support program category. This may or may not be the right program basis. Probably, it is not. However, it will fit existing practice and is a satisfactory starting point for developing improvements.
2. Have several final product programs and major support programs made the subject of program memoranda to be completed in six to eight weeks. Use the existing analytic capability. The development of program memoranda and the other communication materials of the program budget relies heavily on analysis. Therefore, if the analytic organization is either understaffed or inadequate, immediate steps should be taken to expand and upgrade.
3. Designate the individual or individuals to complete the program structure in order to accommodate all activities to the three major areas identified in step 1 above. These studies should be completed in eight to ten weeks.
4. Designate the individual or individuals to develop a first-cut study on alternatives available for organization and administration of program budgeting in the government unit or the business organization.
5. Agree on program identification, possible program manager, organization and administration, schedule of steps to be taken, and dates.
6. Get executive approval and move on.

One of the major advantages of this approach is that from the outset we get the required interaction between the operating, analytical, and decision-making parts of the organization; this interaction is essential to the development of an effective program budgeting system. Time is saved and more intimate knowledge of the content of the administrative procedure is developed by both analytical and operating personnel.

Relationship Described

The relationship between program and budget and planning, programming, and budgeting merits more complete description. It is rather commonplace in the literature on budgeting for business to say, "The budget is the financial expression of a plan." Many people apply the same definition for government. Nonetheless, we are all familiar with the budget that was developed without a plan (particularly a long-range plan). In fact, it is probably fair to say that in most budgets any planning is a projection of the status quo with increments added on the basis of the most current experience. A statement made by Roswell Gilpatric, when he was Deputy Secretary of Defense in 1961, typifies one of these situations: "In the past, the Defense Department has often developed its force structure by starting with a budget and sending it off in search of a program."[4] On the other hand there are elaborate plans made by either government or business that never get beyond top level approval—that is, are never budgeted.

Planning is the production of a range of meaningful potential courses of action through a systematic consideration of alternatives. In the short range, it deals with a limited number of alternatives because past actions have already locked in the available paths. However, for the long range (the major emphasis of program budgeting) the planning activity attempts to examine as many alternative courses of action as appear to be feasible and to project the future course of the organization against these in cost-benefit terms. Since the objective is not to make specific decisions but rather to turn up likely possibilities, the work is done in a general and highly aggregative form.

Programming is the more detailed determination of the manpower, equipment, and facilities necessary for accomplishing a program-feasibility testing in terms of specific resources and time. The program and its elements used in the planning process in highly aggregative terms are moved down the scale to more detailed terms (as detailed as is appropriate) required for determining the feasibility of the possibilities. Even here, for most cost elements, we are at a level of aggregation above that required for the detailed determinations involved in next year's budget. That budget is the translation of program cost elements into the specific funding and time requirements identified in traditional terms such as object class, function, and organization.

How do we distinguish the program budget from the traditional next-year's budget? PPB is the development and preparation of a budget in a planning context, that is, with information about what is in store for the future. The planning context puts it in contrast to the short-range fiscal management and expenditure control objectives that categorize the traditional approach. This new method allows for major shifts among purposes for which resources are to be used, ranging from changes in funding levels to the introduction of completely new activities.

[4] Roswell L. Gilpatric, "Defense—How Much Will It Cost?" *California Management Review*, V (Fall, 1962), p. 53.

Under the program budget, annual allotments to administrative organizations allow them to take the next step along a path thoughtfully set by policy makers at all levels. Probably more important, the direction of the path and the distance to be covered in the next year will have been established after considering a number of possible futures.

23

Budgeting for R&D

William E. Souder

Today, research and development is truly "big business." And it becomes even bigger business with each passing year. In 1950, total domestic R&D expenditures amounted to $4.2 billion; ten years later, this figure had tripled to $12.8 billion, and by 1965 the figure was $18.2 billion.

R&D exerts considerable influence on our lives through the variety of new products produced, and has a vital role in our economy in supplying new employment opportunities. In addition, this effort often determines the success of an enterprise; how much a firm spends on what kind of R&D in today's world can determine whether it is a proprietary giant or a struggling commodity dwarf in tomorrow's world. R&D budgetary decisions are therefore vital to both the individual company and the total economy. Yet few industrial firms appear to give the R&D budgeting decision adequate attention. This article reviews and criticizes some of the budgetary practices in R&D today, and proposes some improvements.

R&D Budgetary Functions

Figure 1 distinguishes two basic types of budgetary functions in R&D. Policy functions involve the nature, scope, and direction of the total effort. Operational functions involve the optimal planning and control of the project efforts over their life cycles.

As the figure indicates, effective policy planning for R&D begins as a long-range corporate planning function. Deciding where the company wants to go and how it will get there must be done in the corporate planning function, because this is the only point in the organization that completely overlooks both the performance and the financial aspects of the R&D program. An effective program requires considerable financial support in the form of both the initial cash outlays and continuing "patient money" or "venture money." Frequently,

Reprinted from *Business Horizons*, June 1970, pp. 31–38.

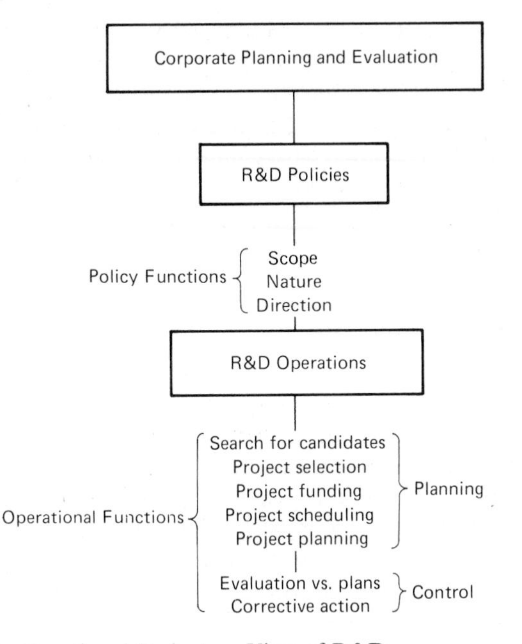

Figure 1. The Functional Budgetary View of R&D

a diversified combination of R&D investments is developed in the hope of generating the proper flows of profits to achieve both long- and short-range corporate goals. In this way, a well-planned R&D program can ultimately be self-financing; profits from shorter-range successes can cover the costs of longer-range efforts.

Closely related to the policy functions are the operational functions of planning the R&D efforts, as shown in Figure 1. Specific projects must be tailored around the policies. To do this, some companies have set up special departments to search for, evaluate, and select proposals on a continuing basis. The objective is a storehouse of suitable projects that can be quickly phased in as soon as other efforts are terminated. Once a set of projects is selected, funds must be allocated to them in such a way that the effectiveness per dollar spent is maximized. This problem of how much to spend on which individual projects is often a critical one. A misallocation of funds at this stage of the planning process can result in overemphasis on some projects and too little emphasis on others.

Scheduling, the problem of deciding when to pursue which project, can be equally critical. This is especially true with certain consumer products where the first company to introduce a new product often captures the largest market share. Finally, the quality of the project planning and the amount of coordination of interdepartmental efforts on the project is often a critical factor in determining the timely success of an R&D project.

Control is another important operational budgetary function. R&D efforts frequently tend to diverge from the planned efforts more often than non-research activities. Researchers continually discover side problems that are temporarily more academically interesting than the central problem of the project; to investigate them, however, would delay obtainment of the primary goal. In addition, R&D efforts must be replanned frequently to reflect rapidly changing technologies or competitive situations. Timely and effective re-planning depends on the existence of close control and good feedbacks from the market place.

Performing Budgetary Functions

Few R&D managers would argue that the policy and operational functions that have been described are not necessary. However, they are likely to disagree on the methods for performing them. In some organizations, R&D tends to be highly exploratory and long range; in others it tends to be short range or current market oriented. In some organizations, it is regarded as just so much "fat," trimmed when profits are low and increased when profits are high. In some organizations, the function is closely controlled and performance is closely monitored. Other organizations permit many R&D personnel to work on their own ideas.

These differences reflect the fact that there are few generally accepted principles of R&D management. Thus, the budgetary functions tend to be carried out in the fashion the executives feel are best. Personal philosophies are used in place of guiding principles or hypotheses that can be statistically supported or discredited. Without a framework to guide the conduct of the policy and operational functions, they tend to be performed through dynamic interplays of conflicts, negotiations, and compromises within the framework of informal organizational groups and power structures.

The process of deciding on the scope and nature of the R&D program is likely to be one of conflict and negotiation among competing departments. Pure bargaining is often the means for setting satisfactory corporate budgets. At the department level, conflicts may arise over vested interests on various projects, over the funding levels, or over budgetary allocations. But even when satisfactory policies are established, the policies may not be feasible at the operational level, and new policies may be sought at the corporate level. This cycle of trying out various policies may repeat until an over-all satisfactory policy and its operational plan are found.

Four unique forces within the R&D process and its interaction with the organizational environment naturally operate against the optimal performance of the planning and control functions. *First,* top organizational R&D decisions are seldom self-contained. Few top corporate executives feel exclusively competent to formulate policies in this area; they rely on feedbacks from the lower levels. This subjects top policy decisions to bias and distortion from power groups or cliques, and to biases from the lower levels. *Second,* there are always competing alternative uses for R&D funds, such as advertising or plant improvements. The inherent difficulties of accurately forecasting the costs and returns from R&D projects make many executives reluctant to accept an R&D proposal when competing alternatives seem more certain to pay off. *Third,* experience has shown that most R&D programs eventually require vastly more funds than are originally budgeted. *Finally,* management has erroneously attempted to apply traditional planning and control techniques to an area that requires more powerful approaches. The whole R&D area is a dynamic one; plans and estimates that are made today are usually outdated by tomorrow. Data flows in the area are extremely complex and subjective, and budgetary estimates are tentative and often include considerable error.

Because of the operation of these four forces, handicraft methods must give way to newer management science techniques. More sophisticated budgetary techniques must be used in the planning and control functions—techniques that can combine and digest more data, collate estimates from various organizational levels, and simultaneously evaluate multiple and competing alternatives. These are necessary for optimal budgeting.

Many formal techniques for R&D budgeting have been developed. Mathematical methods and quantitative approaches have been devised for selecting projects, allocating funds among projects, scheduling, planning project efforts, and controlling ongoing efforts. The various classes of techniques that have been developed to date will be reviewed and evaluated. The evaluation is based on a review of more than one hundred articles from the current literature.[1]

Project Selection Techniques

Several types of techniques have been proposed for R&D project selection. They are: capital budgeting formulas, cost prediction formulas, scoring and ranking methods, and resource allocation methods.

Capital Budgeting Formulas. The capital budgeting approaches that have been used are modifications of the standard return on investment and discounted rate of return methods. The major modification is the inclusion of risk parameters such as the probability of commercial and technical success. In general, for each project a "value" is computed, which is some variation of the ratio of anticipated profits to the project's estimated cost. This value is then discounted for the risk of the project, usually by multiplying the value figure by the probability of success of that project. The projects are then ranked on the basis of the resulting value, with the higher rank going to the project with the higher value. Projects are then selected from the top of the ranked list down until the budget is exhausted. Considerable use of this approach has been reported for the chemical industry. An example of such a capital budgeting formula is equation (1) in Figure 2.

[1] A list of the references surveyed and some supplementary material will be supplied without charge to interested users. The author asks that these persons provide reimbursement for postage.

$$(1)\quad \text{Value} = \frac{\text{Anticipated profit}}{\text{Anticipated costs}} \times \text{Probability of success}$$

$$(2)\quad \text{Cost} = \text{Predicted cost} \times \text{Certainty factor}$$
$$(\text{Predicted cost} = \text{Ratio} \times \text{Anticipated sales})$$

$$(3)\quad \text{Score} = \frac{\text{Patent rating} + \text{Sales rating} + \text{Technology rating}}{\text{Expected project cost}}$$

Figure 2. Planning Models

The deficiencies of the capital budgeting formulas lie in their often incorrect assumptions that the same rate of return exists over the life of the project, that the earnings can be reinvested at this same rate, and that the same level of risk exists throughout the life of the investment. These defects become critical for R&D projects. A project is an ever-changing bundle of information and technology; its chances for failure and its rate of return are constantly changing throughout its life cycle. Furthermore, because competitive R&D activities are often unknown and rapidly changing markets may quickly make new products obsolete, one never knows if earnings can be reinvested in the project at acceptable rates. Therefore, capital budgeting methods should *not* be used for R&D project selection, despite the fact that such approaches appear to have won much favor among many R&D managers, particularly within the chemical industry.

Cost Prediction Formulas. In general, these formulas estimate the amount of investment necessary to complete specific R&D projects, given certain related parameters such as the expected sales. An example is shown as equation (2) in Figure 2. The "certainty factor" is the probability that the cost estimate is correct. The "ratio" is the historical ratio of project costs to sales for prior successful projects.

Underlying such cost estimating approaches is the premise that historical relations exist between the cost of an R&D project and the total sales from the product of the effort. Since the variable "sales" is often easier to estimate reliably than R&D costs, it is logical to try to predict those costs from estimates of sales. However, to make accurate sales estimates, one needs to know the performance of the product from R&D, and this information is seldom known until the project is completed. Thus, there is often little basis for estimating R&D costs from sales estimates.

Scoring and Ranking Techniques. Scoring and ranking criteria are the most numerous of all of the single classes of project selection methods in the literature. In general, these methods consist of simply ranking projects according to some list of criteria, and then selecting projects from the top to the bottom of the list until some cutoff point is reached. The approach is similar to some of the capital budgeting methods in that the objective is to obtain a ranking of projects. However, the capital budgeting and the scoring methods differ in the criteria used to rank projects and the methods used to determine cutoff points in selecting projects from the ranked list. A scoring model is illustrated as equation (3) in Figure 2.

Uses and applications of scoring and ranking methods at several large companies are reported in the literature. The types of criteria used in developing scores were product (life, patentability, and so on), market (price, competition, and so on), and financial criteria (cost, personnel, and so on), with market considerations often predominantly influencing the scores and rating numbers developed. Some companies treated different types of R&D differently, with basic R&D being weighted more heavily in the product aspects in determining scores.

The scoring and ranking methods have been even more popular than capital budgeting formulas for R&D. On the whole, managers have preferred the scoring methods to capital budgeting techniques because of the greater uncertainty in accurately estimating the necessary data for the latter. However, like the capital budgeting formulas, these approaches are pseudo-funding methods; they do not take into account the fact that there are alternative funding levels on every project. A project does not have to be, say, "100 percent selected" this year; it can be 50 percent selected both this year and next. Thus, ranking methods are not necessarily optimal. They treat only part of the R&D budgeting problem—the "what to work on" question.

Because ranking and scoring models treat only part of the over-all R&D planning problem, they are suboptimal. Suboptimization is like starting your automobile and letting it idle in the driveway! This author is of the opinion that ranking and scoring techniques should not be used because they do not treat the entire problem. Rather, resource allocation techniques should be used.

Resource Allocation Techniques. Resource allocation techniques address themselves to the problem of "how much to spend for what projects." Only a few such models have been developed. Similarly, few applications of resource allocation models to actual R&D budgeting problems exist. However, work is known to be progressing at this time on such models at Monsanto,[2] American Cyanamid, and North American Rockwell.

In general, resource allocation models hold the best current hope for methods that can collate masses of data and analyze multiple and competing candidate projects. Alert R&D executives would do well to keep abreast of the literature on resource allocation model applications to their problems. Resource allocation techniques may well represent present-day prototypes of future techniques which smart managers will routinely use to effectively combat the organizational dynamics forces discussed above. Resource allocation techniques are flexible and dynamic, and can be used to merge feedback data at all levels of the organization.

[2] William E. Souder, "Planning R&D Expenditures with the Aid of a Computer," *Budgeting,* XIV (March, 1966), pp. 25–32.

Project Scheduling Techniques

Scheduling treats the "when do we do it" question in R&D budgeting. The whole area of scheduling has been largely dominated by one basic technique: PERT/Critical Path. A recent bibliography cited 205 references on PERT/Critical Path techniques.

PERT/Critical Path techniques have been combined with decision tree methods, sensitivity analyses, and with minimax computations, and have been successfully applied to problems ranging from opening a Broadway play to building the St. Louis Gateway Arch visitor's center. When one basic approach can do so much, there is little reason to develop other methods.

Project Control Techniques

When one looks hard at the literature on project control, one gets the impression that here indeed is a situation where everyone talks about it but no one does anything about it. The control methods in use today for R&D appear to center largely around the "periodic confessional" and the "pressure" approaches. In the former, R&D management asks the project personnel from time to time to "tell us where you are." Such a treatment may lead to a destruction of creativity and to distorted reporting, as the personnel cover up undesirable results. The other approach is a sort of "beat the horse to get him to go faster" approach. Both methods are straight out of the Dark Ages! The alternative seems to be a free rein, where there is little control and little constructive communication. Perhaps this is a method straight out of modern permissiveness!

An effective R&D project control model may be defined as one which informs the manager of any achievement/cost/time deviations from the plan, indicates the corrective actions needed by management, and communicates these to the project manager. Effective techniques are simply largely nonexistent at this time. However, one can see the forerunners of effective project control techniques in the monitoring methods used by NASA, defense contractors, and other industry sectors.[3]

Where Do We Stand?

The general picture that emerges is that management has been, on the whole, reluctant to adopt many of the emerging management science methods for budgeting R&D. In planning expenditures, the favored methods appear to be a combination of judgment and subjective opinion, tying the investment to the sales dollar (next year's R&D as a percentage of last year's sales), or spending whatever the competition spends. In controlling R&D, budgetary cost performance has been overemphasized, integrated cost/progress methods

[3] William E. Souder, "Cost/Progress—a Pattern for Operational Budgeting," *Managerial Planning*, XVII (Jan.–Feb., 1969), pp. 1–9.

have not been considered, and insidious personal involvement of the manager is more often the rule rather than the exception.

Why are we not using more formal techniques and budgetary procedures? To a degree, the fault lies with those who are in the business of developing formal R&D budgeting techniques: the operations research specialists and the management scientists. Frequently, they have preferred to talk to themselves rather than to their practical-oriented management counterparts. The communications link between management and management scientists has traditionally been weak. One consequence of this is an absence of good techniques where they are perhaps needed most—in the performance of all the policy R&D budgeting functions and in the performance of the operational functions of searching for candidates and controlling ongoing projects. Surely the reader has noticed an absence of these kinds of techniques from our list.

It simply is not reasonable to believe that these areas are impregnable to attack by the management scientist or operations researcher. The fault probably lies with a simple lack of understanding between managers and management scientists. Management scientists cannot maintain an ivory tower attitude if their profession is ever to advance. They must become aware of and build their models to reflect the realism of the R&D environment, including the above organizational dynamics aspects. But managers also have a professional responsibility to maintain a patient attitude and train themselves to understand the quantitative approach. Management science techniques *are* complex. But so are managerial problems! Complex techniques are just simply necessary for complex problems.

We all must also understand that organizational dynamics naturally operates against the use of rigorous budgeting procedures. Anything that dilutes the power of the various informal cliques and factions will automatically be resisted. By substituting objectivity for subjectivity in many cases, budgeting techniques remove the informal group's authority. Anything that improves the ability of the organization to assume more risk, as formal techniques may do, will be resisted. The fear of failure is great in every one of us. And there are many small empires in every organization that fear the disruption in their comfortable existence that might result from taking a larger risk and failing to succeed. (Of course, there is also a natural resistance to success; success may result in promotions that destroy the clique.) Finally, anything that tends to cut off negotiation, conjecture, and conflict, or anything that lubricates decision making will be resisted because this is not the normal way of operating.

R&D management involves many budgetary functions: policy planning of the scope and nature of the program; investment planning of the types of projects; scheduling that will maintain the proper balance between cash flows into new projects and cash flows out of successful projects; planning and controlling projects over their life cycles; and integrating R&D into the entire company budget. Budgetary planning is the essence of good R&D management.

The timing, amount, and sources of funds needed will depend upon the timing and amount of flows from R&D, the degree of long-range orientation of the R&D, and its probability of success.

However, several peculiarities of R&D make the performance of the budgetary functions difficult, and their integration into the firm's over-all financial functions even more difficult. First, a prima donna complex may surround R&D, which makes it difficult to measure results and obtain good estimates of future trends. Sometimes industry feels that R&D cannot be planned in detail. Second, R&D is highly technical and the budgetary functions are therefore often not easy to divorce from the technical aspects. Whether or not a proposal is worth financing may hinge directly on its technical probability of success, and few budgetary decisions are made without the advice of scientists and technical specialists. Furthermore, top management often promotes competent scientists into managerial positions, so that the budgetary functions are performed largely by technically trained people with little knowledge and appreciation for budgeting. Finally, the R&D budgetary functions are particularly susceptible to the perverse effects of organizational dynamics.

A number of techniques and methods have been proposed by management scientists to help management perform the operational R&D finance functions of planning and control. Beyond certain simple capital budgeting formulas, certain project scoring methods, and PERT/Critical Path scheduling techniques, it appears that few of the proposed models have actually been used or even tried.

There is a definite need for R&D managers to study these techniques and use them. How else will management scientists be able to provide more powerful, improved second- and third-generation techniques? Companies that are foremost in using and improving such approaches will also be foremost in profits.

24

Industrial Dynamics and the Design of Management Control Systems*

Edward B. Roberts

The Organization As a Control System

Every organization is a control system. Each has direction and objectives, whether explicit or implied. Each has beliefs as to its current status. Each has

From *Management Controls: New Directions in Basic Research* by Bonini, Jaedicke & Wagner, pp. 102–126.

* This article is based on studies supported by grants of the Ford Foundation and the National Aeronautics and Space Administration. The computer simulations were carried out at the M.I.T.

policies and procedures whereby it reaches decisions and takes actions to attain its goals more closely. Every organization actually contains a myriad of smaller control systems, each characterized by the same goal-striving, but not necessarily goal-attaining, behavior.

The organization as a whole or any one of its component subsystems can be represented by the feedback process shown in Figure 1. Four characteristics of this diagram are noteworthy. First, the transformation of decisions into results takes place through a complex process which includes a basic structure of organizational, human, and market relationships; this structure is sometimes not apparent because of its numerous sources of noise or random behavior and due to its often lengthy time delays between cause and effect.

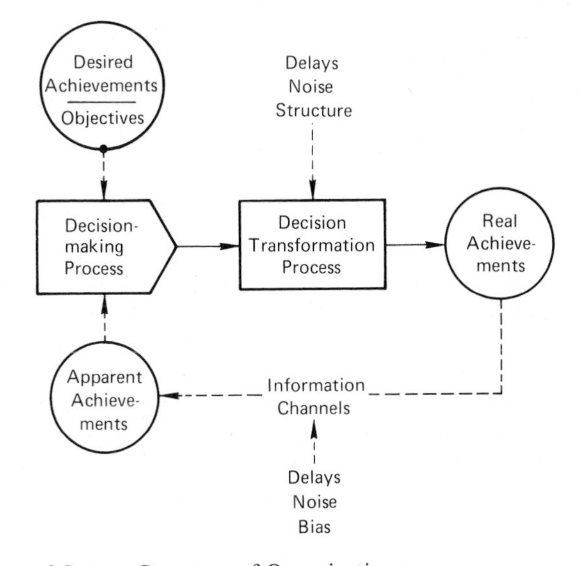

Figure 1. Control System Structure of Organization

The second aspect to be noted is the distinction between the achievements that are apparent in the organization and those which are real. The real situation is translated into the apparent through information and communication channels which contain delays, noise, and bias. These sources of error may be the inadvertent features of an organization's communication system, or they may result from the chosen characteristics of a data-processing system which sacrifices accuracy for compactness. In any event, however, the bases of actual decisions in an organization may be assumptions which bear but little relation to fact.

The third feature of the diagram is that the decision-making process is viewed as a response to the gap between objectives of the organization and

---

Computation Center. The paper was presented at the Stanford University Seminar on Basic Research in Management Controls, February 20, 1963. The writer is grateful to Professors Donald C. Carroll, Jay W. Forrester, and Donald G. Marquis for their many helpful comments.

its apparent progress toward those objectives. Although both the objectives and achievements may be difficult to define precisely and measure accurately, such a goal-seeking behavior is nonetheless present in all organizations and in every subsystem of the organizations. At any level of an organization, many similar decisions are being made. The real problem of the management control system designer is to recognize these multiple decision loops and their interrelationships, and to develop policies and an organizational structure that will tie these activities into progress toward total organization objectives.

The fourth characteristic of Figure 1 is the continuous feedback path of decision-results-measurement-evaluation-decision. It is vital to effective system design that each element of this feedback path be properly treated and that its continuous nature be recognized. Whether the decision in the system is made by the irrational actions or logical deductions of a manager or by the programmed response of a computer, the system consequences will eventually have further effects on the decision itself.

Industrial Dynamics—Philosophy and Methodology for Control System Design

Industrial Dynamics is a philosophy which asserts that organizations are most effectively viewed (and managed) from this control system perspective. It is also a methodology for designing organizational policy. This two-pronged approach is the result of a research program that was initiated and directed at the M.I.T. School of Industrial Management by Professor Jay W. Forrester. The results of the first five years of this program are described in Professor Forrester's book, *Industrial Dynamics,* which also discusses a variety of potential applications to key management problems.[1]

Industrial Dynamics recognizes a common systems base in the flow structure of all social-economic-industrial-political organizations. This perspective ties the segmented functional aspects of formal organizations into an integrated structure of varying rates of flow and responsively changing levels of accumulation. The flow paths involve all facets of organizational resources —men, money, materials, orders, and capital equipment—and the information and decision-making network that links the other flows.

Industrial Dynamics views decisions as the controllers of these organization flows. Such decisions regulate the rate of change of levels from which the flows originate and to which they are sent. In the flow diagrams drawn as part of an Industrial Dynamics study, decisions are even represented by the traditional control valve symbol of the engineer. Figure 2 shows such a decision, based in part on information about the contents of the source level, controlling the rate of flow to the destination level.

The system structures and behavioral phenomena that are studied by the

[1] Jay W. Forrester, *Industrial Dynamics* (Cambridge: The M.I.T. Press, 1961).

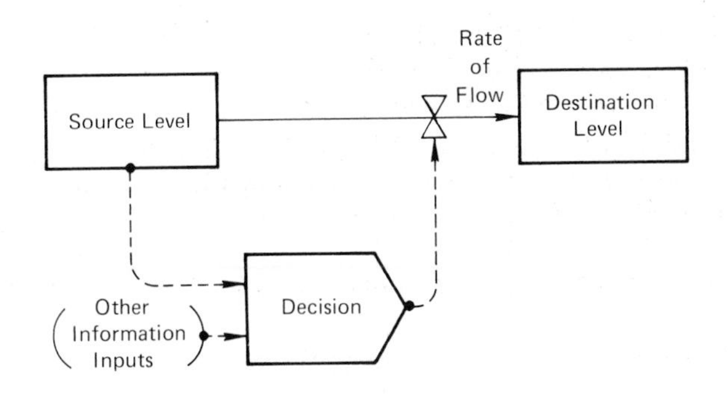

Figure 2. The Decision As a Controller

Industrial Dynamics methodology are present at all levels of the corporation. The top management of the firm is involved in a system that can be studied and aided in the same manner as the middle management of the organization, and again in the same fashion as the physical operating system of the plant. The potential payoff from changes derived from system studies increases greatly, however, as the study is focused higher up in the organization. For all studies the pattern of forming a dynamic verbal theory, developing mathematical equations, computer simulation of the model, and derivation of improved policies is followed. The problems encountered in these phases do not significantly change as we move from the bottom to the top of an organization. Only during the final stage of implementation of system change does the problem complexity get significantly greater the higher the level of organization involved. But the impact of improved corporate-level policy on company growth, stability, and profitability can readily justify this added effort to renovate top management policy making.

Problems of Management Control Systems

The preceding discussion has focused on the nature of organizational problems as management control system problems, and on the intended applicability of Industrial Dynamics to these problems. Observation of several different types of management control systems and a survey of the literature in this field lead to a belief that a new attack on control system design is needed. The traditional approaches to management control systems have mushroomed in number and sophistication of applications as operations research and electronic data processing have developed during the post-war era. Although these systems have made significant and successful inroads, many fail to cure the problems for which they were designed; other management control systems even amplify the initial difficulties or create more significant new problems. All this is taking place even as we derive enhanced but misplaced confidence in the systems.

Several examples will help to illustrate these problems and lead us to some findings about the design of management control systems.

Systems Inadequate for Their Problems

Sometimes the management control system is inadequately designed for the problem situation. In such a case the control system may improve performance in the trouble area, but be far short of the potential gains. At times the limited effectiveness may transform a potentially major benefit to the company into but a marginal application.

The Control of Research and Development Projects

One example of an area in which the traditional approach to control system design has proved inadequate is the management of research and development projects. The intangibility, lack of precise measurements, and uncertain character of R and D results are partly responsible for this failure. But a more basic lack of system understanding has implications of even greater significance. All systems of schedule and/or budget controls that have been tried till now have failed to achieve success in R and D usage. These techniques have included Gantt charts, milestone schedules, and computerized systems of budgetary and manpower control.

The latest approaches to control of research and development projects are based on PERT (Program Evaluation Review Technique) or PERT/COST. The management control systems implied by the methods used can be represented by the diagram of Figure 3. As shown here, the basis of the current sophisticated methods is a single-loop system in which the difference between desired completion date and forecast completion date causes decisions to change the magnitude or allocation of project resources (manpower, facilities, equipment, priorities). As these resources are employed, they are assumed to produce the progress that is reported during the project. These reports are processed through a PERT-type evaluation and forecasting system to create the forecast completion time.

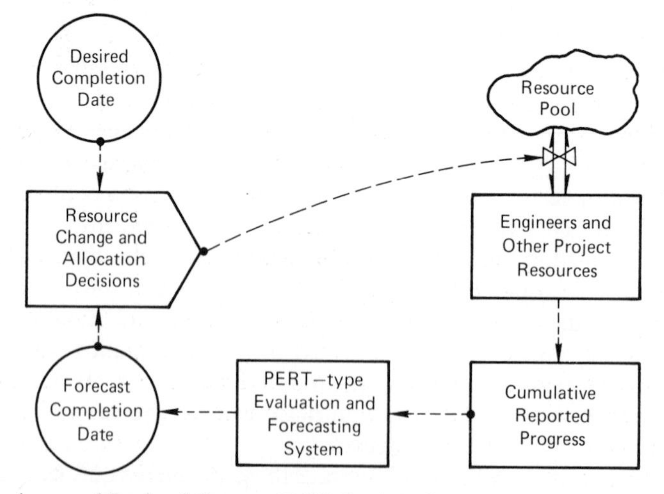

Figure 3. Assumed Basis of Current R&D Project Controls

But the design of a management control system based on such a set of assumptions is doomed to failure, since some of the most vital aspects of the real system have been excluded from the underlying analysis. For example, the lack of tangible, precise measurement sources is entirely ignored. Yet these factors contribute much of the error between the *real* situation in the project (its true scope and actual progress to date) and that which is *apparent* to those doing the engineering work.

Another part of the real system which appears to be ignored by current R and D control system designers is the human element in the project actions and decisions. The attitudes and motivations of the engineers and managers, their knowledge of the schedules and current estimates in the project, the believed penalty-reward structure of the organization—all affect the progress and problems that are reported upward in the organization. Furthermore, these same factors even affect the rate of real progress toward project objectives. All systems of measurement and evaluation (in R and D, manufacturing, government, universities, or what-have-you) create incentives and pressures for certain actions. These interact with the goals and character of individuals and institutions to produce decisions, actions, and their results. For example, a system which compares "actual to budgeted expenditures" creates an incentive to increase budgets, regardless of progress; one which checks "proportion of budget spent" creates pressures on the manager or engineer to be sure he spends the money, whether or not on something useful. The presence of such factors in research and development ought to be recognized in the design of systems for R and D control.

Adding these two additional sources of system behavior to the earlier diagram produces the more complete representation of a research and development system that is pictured in Figure 4. But even this is an incomplete representation of the complex system which interrelates the characteristics of the product, the customer, and the R and D organization. A proper characterization of research and development projects must take into account the continuous dynamic system of activities that creates project life cycles. Such a system will include not just the schedule and accumulated effort, costs, and accomplishments. Rather, it will encompass the full range of policies and parameters that carry a research and development project from initial perception of potential need for the product to final completion of the development program. The fundamental R and D project system is shown in Figure 5, from which we have developed an Industrial Dynamics model of research and development project dynamics.

Some of the results of simulation studies of this model are of particular interest to designers of management control systems. They demonstrate the importance of taking cognizance of the complete system structure in attempting to create and implement methods of system control. For example, one series of simulations of the general project model was conducted in which only the scheduled project duration was changed in the various runs. Within the model the effort allocation process *attempts* to complete the project during

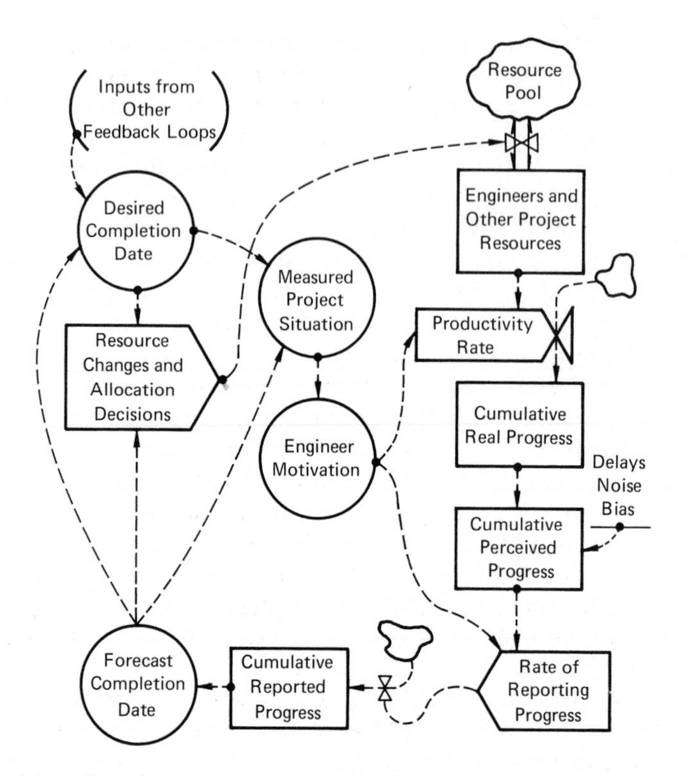

Figure 4. More Complete Representation of R&D System

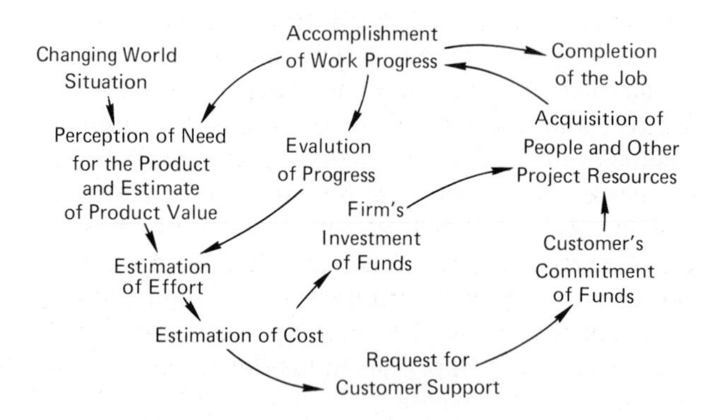

Figure 5. Dynamic System Underlying R&D Projects

this scheduled period. However, the actual completion dates of the projects seem only remotely responsive to the changes in desired completion time.

Figure 6 demonstrates the nature of this response, using the outputs of four model simulations. The horizontal axis is an index of the scheduled project duration as a percentage of the maximum schedule used; the vertical

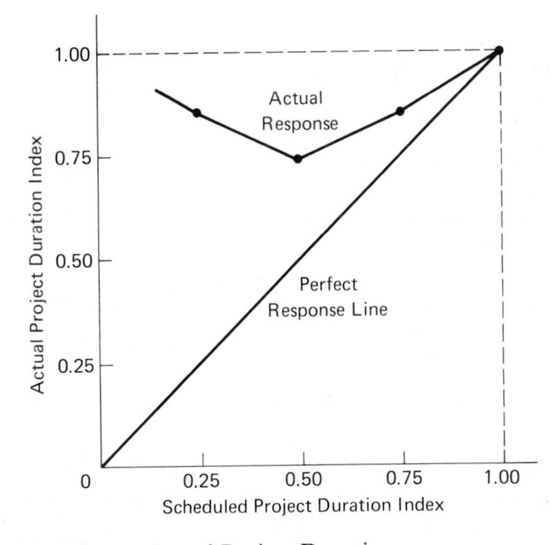

Figure 6. Scheduled Versus Actual Project Duration

axis shows actual completion time in a similar percentile manner. If changes in schedule produced corresponding changes in actual completion dates, the curve of results would have followed the diagonal "perfect response" line; that is, a 50 percent reduction in scheduled duration should produce a 50 percent reduction in actual duration, if control is *perfect.* But the actual response is far from perfect; a 50 percent schedule change effects only a 25 percent actual change. And at the extreme, the actual change is even in the opposite direction, taking longer to complete the urgent crash project because of the resulting organizational confusion and inefficiencies. Of course, this response curve does not present the simulation data on the manpower instability, total project cost, and customer satisfaction changes that also accompany shifts in the project schedule.

Some of the implications of Figure 6 are more clearly presented in the next curve. Here the slippage in project schedule is plotted as a function of the scheduled duration, the points on the curve coming from the project model simulations. A completion time slippage of 242 percent of schedule was incurred in the crash project, with a rapid decrease in this percentage completion date overrun as the schedule is dragged out. When the project is slowed too much, the slippage increases again as lack of enthusiasm induces further stretch-out during the project life.

The principal point made by these two illustrations is that many factors other than desired schedule determine the resultant actual schedule of research and development projects. *Control systems for R and D which resort to schedule and effort rate control without full understanding of the system structure of projects are bound to be ineffective.* The current PERT-based project control systems seem guilty of this error in design philosophy. In

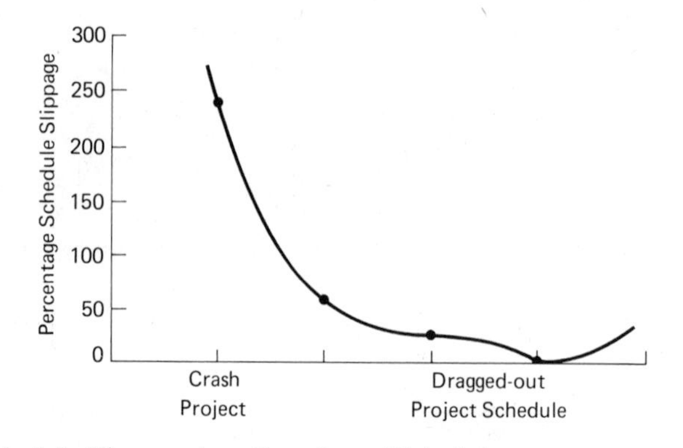

Figure 7. Schedule Slippage As a Function of Schedule

fact, many aspects of our government contracting program suffer similar faults of inadequate system understanding, producing ill-conceived policies with attendant poor results. For example, increased risk-taking (i.e., greater willingness to invest company funds prior to contract receipt) and higher bidding integrity by R and D companies would act in the best interest of the government customer of research and development. However, our simulation studies show that neither policy is in the short-term best interests of the R and D companies, under existing government regulations and practices. Thus the contracting policies, a government control system for R and D procurement, act to the detriment of national objectives by inducing company behavior which produces unsatisfactory project outcomes.[2]

The proper design of research and development control systems, for both company and customer, should take into account three things: (1) the source of internal action, information, and control in a project is the individual engineer; measurement and evaluation schemes and the internal penalty-reward structure must be designed with him in mind; (2) the total results of research and development projects are created by a complex dynamic system of activities, which interrelates the characteristics of the product, the customer, and the R and D firm; control systems which ignore vital aspects of these flows cannot succeed; (3) institutional objectives of R and D companies (profits, growth, stability) can be aligned with the objectives of government customers; procurement policies constitute the system of control which can effect or destroy this alignment.

A Production-Inventory-Employment Control System

As another example, let us take the case of an industrial components manufacturer who initially has no formal production-inventory-employment control

[2] A general theory of research and development project behavior, a model of the theory, and extensive simulation studies of parameters and policies influencing R and D outcomes are reported in the author's book, *The Dynamics of Research and Development* (New York: Harper and Row, 1964).

systems. Such a firm operates by its response to current problems. It follows the example of the firemen trying to use a leaky hose—as soon as one hole is patched up, another leak occurs elsewhere. A company operating in this manner does not keep sufficiently close tabs on changes in sales, inventories, backlogs, delivery delays, etc. Rather, when customer complaints build up on company delivery performance, people will be hired to increase production rate and repair the inventory position. Similarly, when a periodic financial report (or the warehouse manager's difficulties) shows a great excess in inventory, workers will be laid off to reduce the inventory position. Despite the obvious faults, the majority of our manufacturing firms have these problems. The dynamic behavior of such a firm (as here illustrated by simulation results of an Industrial Dynamics model) has the appearance of Figure 8, with wide swings in sales, inventories, employment, order backlog, and correspondingly in profitability. The potential for a well-designed management control system in such a firm is enormous.

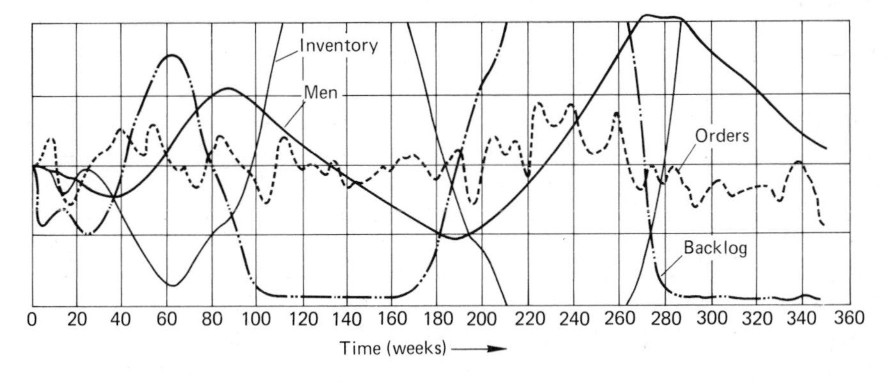

Figure 8. Management by Crisis

The traditional approach (some may prefer calling it the "modern approach") to the design of a control system for such an organization will recognize that: (1) better information on sales is necessary; (2) such information should properly be smoothed to eliminate possibilities of factory response to chance order-rate variations; (3) inventories should be periodically (perhaps even continuously) checked, and reorders generated when needed to bring stocks into line with target inventories; (4) order backlogs should not be allowed to drift too far from the normal levels; and (5) work force should be adjusted to meet the desired production rate that stems from consideration of current sales volume and the manufacturing backlog situation. Using our earlier company model, we can readily build into the model a management control system that incorporates all these features. The modeled company would then be a leader in its use of management control techniques. And, as Figure 9 illustrates, the company would have benefited by this approach. With the new control systems installed, fluctuations in the business

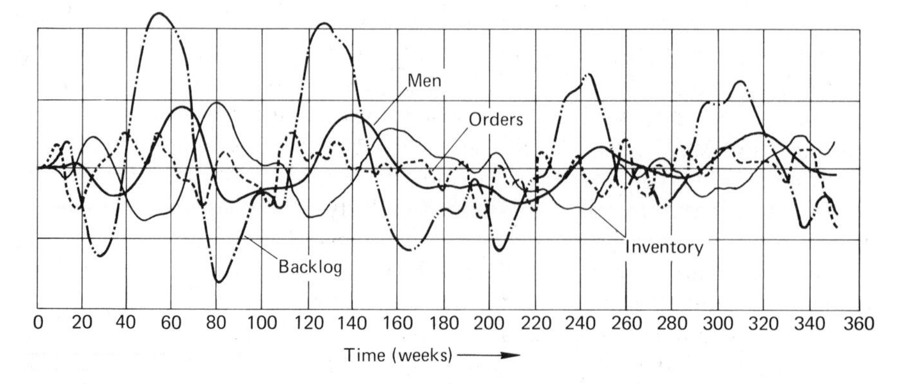

Figure 9. Effects of Management Control Systems

have in general been reduced in magnitude as well as periodicity. Yet the basic dynamic pattern observed in the earlier diagram is still present—periodic fluctuations in sales, larger ones in inventories, and corresponding variations in production rate and work force. The latter situation is similar in character to that which we encountered at the Sprague Electric Company, at the beginning of our Industrial Dynamics study program with them several years ago.

Let us briefly review their case. The Sprague Electric Company is a major producer of electrical components, with an annual sales volume of approximately 75 million dollars. The particular product line which was selected for Industrial Dynamics research is a relatively mature industrial component, developed by Sprague several years ago and now past its market introduction and major growth phases. The principal customers of the product are manufacturers of military and high-grade consumer electronic systems. The industry competition is not price-based, but is rather dependent on product reliability and delivery time.

The work structure of the company, including its inventory and manufacturing control aspects, is diagrammed in Figure 10. Orders arrive from the customers, and a determination is made as to whether or not they can be filled from existing inventories. Orders for those catalogue items not ordinarily stocked, or for those which are currently out of stock, enter into the backlog of manufacturing orders. The customer orders for which inventory is in stock are processed and shipped from inventory.

The inventory control system of the company attempts to maintain a proper inventory position for the product line. Target inventories are adjusted to take into account average sales, and inventory reorders are generated to reflect the shipping rate from inventory and the desired inventory corrections. The orders for inventory replacements enter into the manufacturing backlog.

Production rate in the company is determined by the level of employment, with manufacturing output being sent to the customers or to inventory in reflection of the relative production order backlogs. Control of both backlog

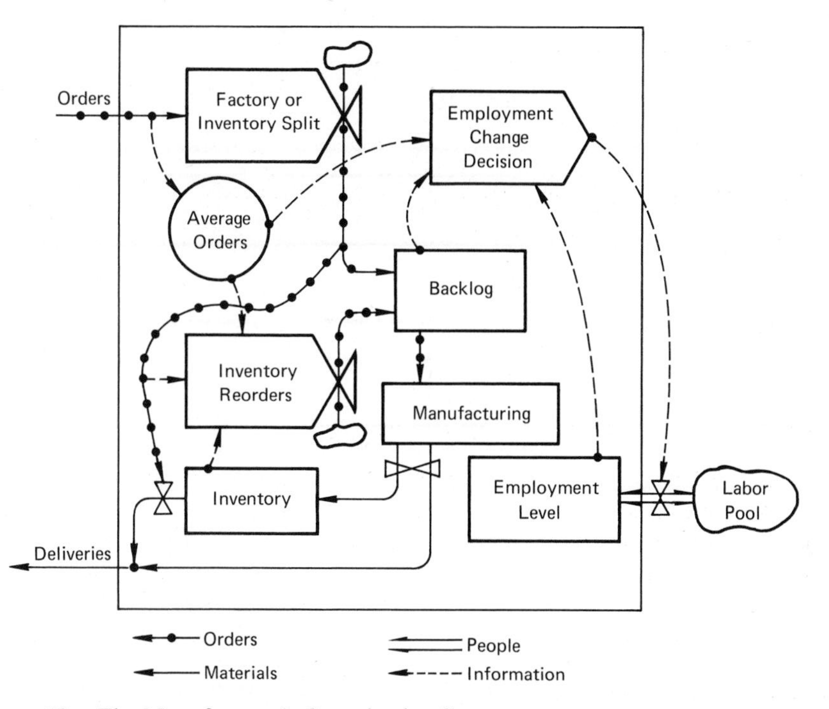

Figure 10. The Manufacturer's Organization Structure

size and employment level is attempted by means of the employment change decision of the company.

As the curves of Figure 9 demonstrated, inventory, backlog, and employment all had sizable fluctuations, despite the existing controls in these areas. They seem to reflect, with some amplification, the variability in incoming orders. Given this situation of fluctuating sales, the traditional management control designer would either express satisfaction with the system performance or perhaps seek additional improvement by parameter adjustment. Neither approach would get at the source of the difficulties, and this source is not the fluctuations in incoming customer orders.

To determine the real system problem, let us examine our next diagram (Figure 11). Here we have duplicated the manufacturer's organization of Figure 10 and added a representation of the customer sector of the industry. The customers receive orders for military and commercial electronic systems. These are processed through the engineering departments, resulting in requirements for components. Customer orders for components are prepared and released as demanded by the delivery lead time of the component manufacturers. Delivered components enter into the system manufacturers' component inventories and are used up during production of the systems.

Having added this sector to our diagram, we now discover the presence of another feedback loop in the total company-customer system: changes

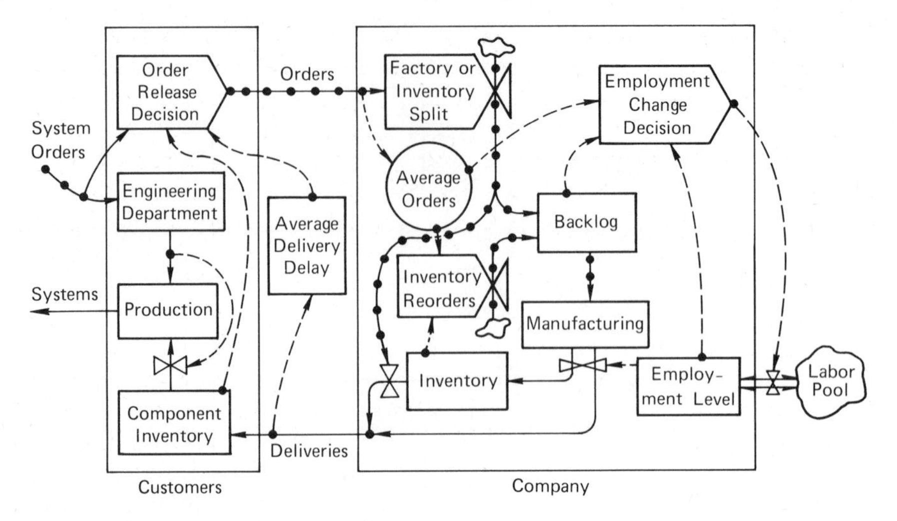

Figure 11. Company-Customers Systems

in the company delivery delay will affect the customer release rate of new orders, which in turn will influence the company delivery delay. This loop amplifies the system problems of the company, being able to transform slight variations in system orders into sustained oscillations in company order rate, producing related fluctuations in company inventories, backlog, employment, and profits.

Let us follow through a possible dynamic sequence that will illustrate the full system interactions. If, for any reason, system orders received by the customers temporarily increase, the customers will soon pass this along to the component supplier as an order increase. Since, even under ordinary circumstances, weekly fluctuations in order rate to the component manufacturer are sizable, some time will elapse before this order rate change is noticed. In the meantime, the component manufacturer's inventory will be somewhat reduced, and the order backlog will be increased. Both of these changes tend to increase the delivery delay. The smaller inventory allows fewer incoming orders to be filled immediately; the larger backlog causes a longer delay for the now increased fraction of orders that must await manufacture. As the customers become aware of the longer lead time, they begin to order further ahead, thus maintaining a higher order rate and accentuating the previous trend in sales.

Eventually, the component manufacturer notes the higher sales, larger backlog, and lower inventory, and begins hiring to increase his factory employment. The employment level is set higher than that needed to handle the current customer order rate, so that backlog and inventory can be brought into line. As the increased work force has its gradual effect on inventory and backlog, the changes tend to reduce the delivery time. The information is gradually fed back to the customers, lowering the order rate even below the initial value. This set of system interactions can produce order rate fluctuations unrelated to the basic demand pattern for the customer products.

To dampen the fluctuations in customer order rate, the component manufacturer must control not inventory or backlog or employment, but rather he must stabilize the factory lead time for deliveries. This can readily be accomplished once the nature of the need is recognized. System behavior can also be improved to a great extent when the component manufacturer becomes aware that his inventory control system does not really control inventory, but it does contribute to production overshoots of any change in orders received.

The details of the Sprague case, the model for its study, and the new policies now being implemented at Sprague are discussed fully in Chapters 17 and 18 of *Industrial Dynamics*. It is sufficient for our purposes to show the effects of the new policies applied to the same situation shown earlier in Figure 9. The curves shown on the next graph (Figure 12) demonstrate a higher degree of stability achieved in all variables except inventory, which is now being used to absorb random changes in sales. In particular, the employment swings have been dampened significantly. The simulation results forecast significant benefits to the company deriving from the application of this new approach to management policy design. Our experiences during the past year of system usage at Sprague seem to support the initial hypotheses, and the product line is currently benefiting from higher productivity, improved employment stability, higher and smoother sales, and lower inventories.

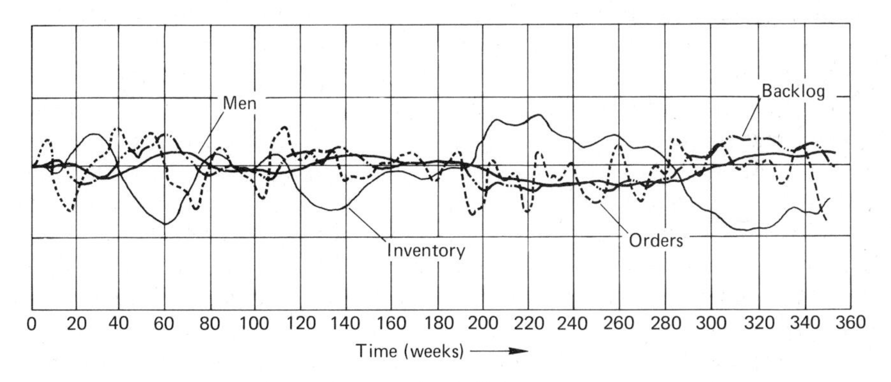

Figure 12. Effects of Industrial Dynamics Policies

Systems Creating New Management Problems

The two control system areas discussed above were intended to demonstrate that many management control systems are designed in a manner that makes them inadequate to cope with the underlying problems. In each example, however, certain aspects of the systems were described which actually aggravated the existing problems. Our discussion of research and development project control indicated that government contracting policies often create resulting behavior that is contrary to the government's own interests. In the Sprague case, the inventory control system amplified sales changes to create wider swings in production and employment than actually existed in orders received from the customers. Other examples can be presented which have similar effects: the attempt to achieve management control leads to situations in which initial difficulties are amplified or significant new problems are created.

Problems of Logistics Control

One apparent instance of this type occurs in the Air Force Hi-Value Logistic System. This inventory control system was developed over a long period of time at great government expense by some of the nation's most sophisticated control system designers. The Hi-Value System is intended to provide conservative initial procurement and meticulous individual item management during the complete logistic cycle of all high-cost Air Force material. Yet an Industrial Dynamics study of this system by a member of the M.I.T. Executive Development Program concluded that the system behavior can result in periodic overstatement of requirements, excess procurement and/or unnecessary repair of material, followed by reactions at the opposite extreme.[3] These fluctuations produce undesirable oscillations in the repair and procurement work loads and in the required manpower at Air Force installations, supply and repair depots. The study recommended changes in policy and information usage that tend to stabilize the procurement system behavior.

Quality Control Systems

A commonly utilized management control system has as its purpose the control of manufacturing output quality. The feedback system apparent to the designers of such quality control systems is pictured in Figure 13. Component parts are produced by a process that has a certain expected quality or reliability characteristic. The parts are inspected for flaws and rejects discarded or reworked. Statistically designed control charts determine when the production process is out of control, and reports are fed back to production to correct the problem sources.

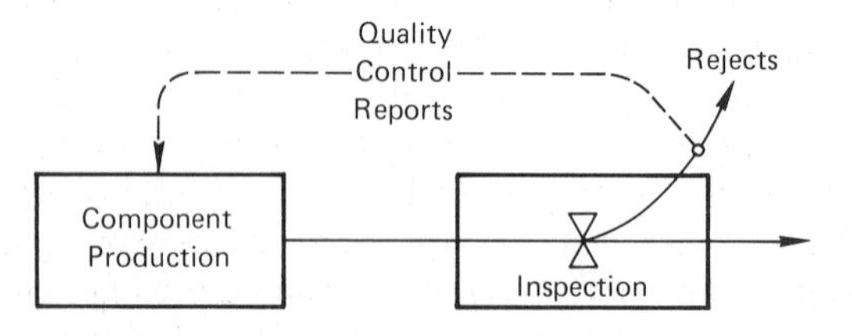

Figure 13. Theoretical Quality Control System

[3] Max K. Kennedy, "An Analysis of the Air Force Hi-Value Logistic System; An Industrial Dynamics Study" (unpublished S.M. thesis, M.I.T. School of Industrial Management, 1962).

The effectiveness of such quality control systems becomes questionable when we view the performance curves generated by a typical system. Figure 14 plots component production rate and inspection reject rate over a period of two years. Wide periodic swings in reject rate produce violations of the control system tolerance limits which cause machine adjustments in production and temporarily lower production rates. But what causes the oscillations in the reject rate? Its periodic nature suggests seasonal fluctuations in production quality, often strangely encountered in many manufacturing plants. The manager has almost no way of checking the validity of such an assumption. Therefore, since the explanation seems reasonable, it would probably be accepted under most circumstances.

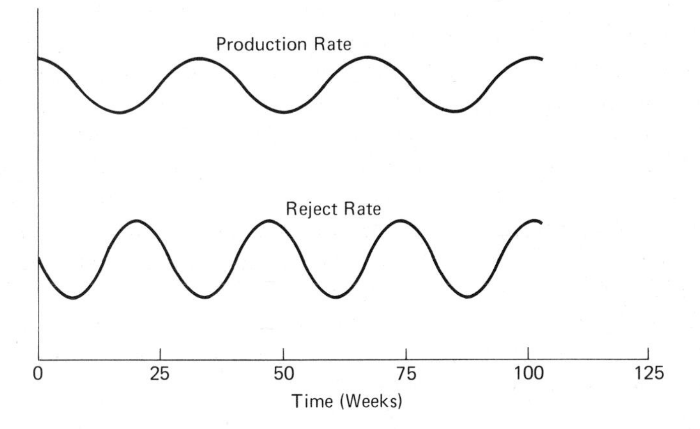

Figure 14. Quality Control System Performance

This situation illustrates one of the key problems in quality control—the lack of an objective confirming source of information. We are in a more favorable position to understand the phenomenon, however, since the results were produced by a computer simulation. The surprising fact is that the actual production quality was held constant, without even random variations, throughout the two years of the run. This means that the oscillations of reject rate and production shown in Figure 14 are not responses to outside changes, but rather are internally created by the behavioral system.

Let us examine a more complete picture of the total factory system, as shown in the next diagram. Components are produced, then inspected, rejects being discarded. The accepted components are forwarded to an assembly operation, where they enter into the manufacture of complete units. In an electronics plant, for example, the component production and inspection might correspond to a grid manufacturing operation, with the assembly operation putting together complete electronic tubes. When the tube is put through a life test, tube failure and the source of failure are far more obvious than are the grid imperfections during the component inspection. Should too many imperfections get through component inspection, eventual tube failure rate will produce complaints by the assembly manager to the quality control manager. As these complaints continue to build, the quality control manager puts pressure on his inspectors to be more careful and detect more of the poor grids. In response to this pressure, the inspectors reject far more grids. Without an objective measure of grid quality, the reject rate tends to be a function of subjective standards and inspection care. Under pressure from the manager, the inspectors will reject any grid which seems at all dubious, including many which are actually of acceptable quality. As the rejects rise, fewer poor grids enter the assembly process, thus causing fewer tube failures in test. The assembly manager's complaints drop off and, in fact, soon switch to a concern for getting more grids for his assembly operation. Without pressure from the quality control manager and with counterpressure to get more grids to the assembly operation, the grid inspectors tend to slacken gradually their care and their reject standards. Eventually, the number of rejectable grids getting into the tube assembly creates the problem of tube failures again, and the cycle repeats. Given normal delays in such a process, the entire cycle takes on a seasonal appearance. Thus, a system intended to assure control of the product quality actually creates serious fluctuations of rejects, component production, and tube failures, all attributed to unknown factors "out of our control."

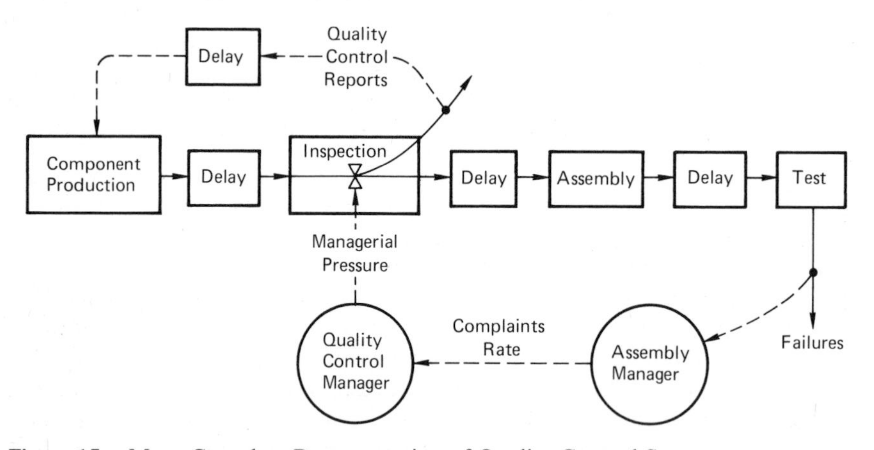

Figure 15. More Complete Representation of Quality Control System

The consequences of such a situation are even more serious when the inspection output is distributed to eventual customers through the normal multi-stage distribution system. In this case the customer complaints and store returns also affect sales. These influences combine after a long delay to produce significant top management pressure on the quality control manager in reflection of a situation which existed many months before. In both Figures 15 and 16, the quality control manager's response is a key to system behavior. Here the manager of the formal quality control system is himself the most important aspect of the total system of quality and production control.

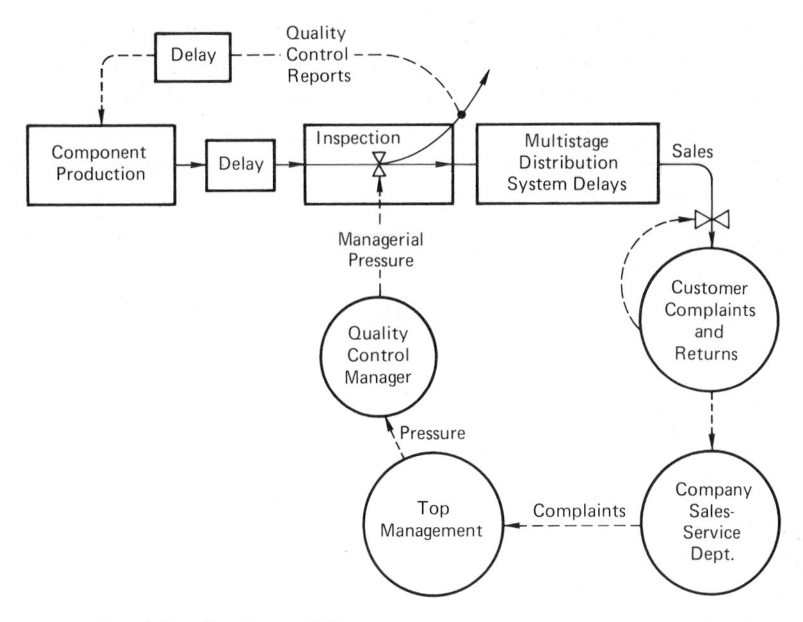

Figure 16. Total Quality Control System

Some Principles of Management Control System Design

The examples discussed represent a wide range of management control systems. Study of these applications produces some general principles of management control system design.

A. The key to effective control often lies outside the boundaries of *conventional* operational control systems; in fact, it is sometimes outside the *formal* boundaries of the company organization.

Too many organizations give up altogether too soon the battle for mastering a management problem caused by factors apparently "out of our control." Government changes in project funding of research and development, the cyclic swings in customer orders in the production-inventory case, seasonal variations of product reject rate in the quality control problem are all examples of such factors. Yet in each case successful control system management rests within the access of company policy.

Project success in R and D is strongly influenced by company integrity and risk-taking. Yet the customer can affect these results by redesigning his own policies to achieve more desirable company behavior. Again, in the Sprague case the system requiring control included the ordering decisions of the customer, certainly not part of Sprague's formal organization. But the basis for system control exists in the stabilization of the input to the customer decision, the component delivery delay. And the key to quality control involves recognition of the total system of product flow to assembly (or to customers) and the resulting feedback of complaints and pressures.

The boundaries of a management control system design study must not be drawn to conform with organizational structure merely because of that structure. System boundaries cannot ignore vital feedback channels for information and action if the system is to be effective.

B. The proper design of management control systems often requires inclusion of the effects of intangibles; in particular, the role of decision makers who are part of the total system of control must be treated carefully.

Control system designers who are working with computers often have as their end product a computer model for calculating (or searching for) an optimal control decision. Yet while being willing to model a decision for a machine, they seem unwilling to include in their studies any models of man—of human decision making within the control loops. Our initial example emphasized that a properly designed R and D control system should be based on models of engineer and manager decision making in both the company and customer organizations. In the production-inventory control case, the modeling of aggregate customer decision makers is a vital part of the system. Finally, we observed that the decision making and responses of both managers and inspectors are crucial aspects of the quality control case.

These illustrations emphasize the usual failure to recognize and cope with the nature of human response in organizations. The decision makers, single or aggregated—their motivations, attitudes, pressures, and models of response—must be included in management control system design. *The man (and manager) is part of the system of control, and management control system design must be viewed as a form of man-machine system design.*

C. A true understanding of total system basis and system behavior can permit effective design of both operational control systems and top management policy, without differences in philosophy or methodology of approach. In fact, most significant control system applications inherently require suprafunctional or multi-departmental organization.

In the Sprague case, for example, successful control involved consideration of such aspects as customer service (marketing), inventory and production rate (manufacturing), and employment policies (personnel). Thus what often gets treated as a middle-management problem becomes resolvable only at the top policy-making level of the firm. The important elements in research and development tend not to be middle-management concerns for schedules, but rather top management policy affecting investment planning, customer relations, and company-wide attitudes. Management control systems can therefore seek to achieve the major goals of the organization as a whole, and not just the sub-optimizing aims of individual segments. A great present hazard, in fact, is the common planning and programming of control systems at the wrong level of the company, by people who lack total system perspectives and the authority to achieve broad system integration.

The Industrial Dynamics program has demonstrated the possibilities of examining and treating system problems of great variety and scope of complexity. We have dealt with many situations in which stabilization was needed and more recently with other cases in which balanced growth was the objective of the policy design efforts. The potential advantages to companies who pioneer in this work are significant and may become the basis of our future industrial competition. In this regard, it seems fitting to close with the implied advice of the Japanese scholar who said: "When your opponent is at the point of striking you, let your mind be fixed on his sword and you are no longer free to master your own movements, for you are then controlled by him."[4]

[4] Takawan, as quoted by Charles H. Townes, "Useful Knowledge," *Technology Review*, January, 1963, p. 36.

B. Organization

25

Organization Patterns of the Future

Robert T. Golembiewski

Charting future organization patterns involves questions of what the administrative world is and how it should be. Two alternative sets of ideas may be distinguished. The first and dominant view amounts to a kind of managerial push-theory. In it, the employee scrambles and innovates and burns the midnight oil to avoid possible and perhaps inevitable harsh outcomes. In one version of this view, men work hard because it is morally bad to do otherwise. The properties of this view are like those of McGregor's Theory X or 9, 1 on the Grid.

Whyte's *The Organization Man* illustrates the managerial push-theory, and laments its demise. Gone are the old stimuli to heroic effort such as survival-of-the-fittest "training programs" that tested a man's desire and skills, or broke him. In their place, Whyte saw manifold nicely-nicelies such as longish training programs that effectively closed the school of hard-knocks. In Whyte's view, organization men were whistling their way through the dark, hand-in-hand, neglecting harsh realities for which they were less and less prepared. Given the push-theory, no harshness, no progress.

In the managerial pull-theory, the focus is more on what you are reaching toward than on what you are seeking to avoid. In it, the employee also scrambles and innovates and burns the midnight oil. However, work is so need satisfying that it elicits massive employee efforts. The goal is dual: doing the job better,

Reprinted from the November–December 1969 issue of *Personnel Administration*, pp. 9–24.

and doing it in ways that permit unprecedented personal freedom in organizations. Indeed, this view almost says that *it is only through greater personal freedom* that a better job can be accomplished. Organization life is demanding in this view, but it does promise fulfillment at work. Warren Bennis articulates both emphases clearly:[1]

> I think that the future I describe is not necessarily a "happy" one. Coping with rapid change, living in temporary work systems—all augur social strains and psychological tensions. . . .
>
> In these new organizations of the future, participants will be called upon to use their minds more than at any other time in history. Fantasy, imagination, and creativity will be legitimate in ways that today seem strange. Social structures will no longer be instruments of psychic repression but will increasingly promote play and freedom on behalf of curiosity and thought.

The managerial pull-theory seeks to integrate personal needs and organizational demands.[2] In essence, the underlying rationale proposes that:

1. Many individuals find little satisfaction in their work, and this is a major deprivation for them personally and for their organization.
2. Many or all individuals will be more productive as they exercise greater control over their work, and as work permits satisfaction of a broadening range of needs.
3. Organizations increasingly need superior output from more and more of their employees; technological and skill requirements are such that these contributions must be elicited more than forced. Expenditures to redesign jobs and work relations, and to change managerial styles or techniques are reasonable; indeed, in the longer run they are probably necessary.

Concern with Managerial World-Views

It seems clear that personnel administration will have to be consciously concerned with both managerial theories. Thus, the pull-theory becomes increasingly appropriate as organizations move in the directions suggested in Table 1, and such movement seems very probable.

The reader can supply the full rationale for the relevance of the pull-theory under the conditions in the right column. To illustrate, you can order someone to obey when work or decisions are programmed. Ordering someone to be creative is quite another matter.

Personnel administration probably will also give significant attention to structure and policies consistent with the push-theory. Briefly, technological requirements influence which structure and managerial techniques are likely to be successful, and not all organizations will or even can move sharply

[1] Warren G. Bennis, "Beyond Bureaucracy," *Trans-Action*, Vol. 2 (July–August, 1965), p. 35.

[2] See especially Chris Argyris, *Integrating the Individual and the Organization* (New York: Wiley, 1964).

Table 1

From Basic Emphasis upon:	*To Growing Emphasis upon:*
Regularity in operations →	creativity in concept; adaptability in execution
Programmed decisions →	novel decisions
Stable and simple competencies, technologies, and market →	volatile and complex competencies, technologies, and markets
Stop-and-go processing →	continuous processing
Stable product lines, programs →	volatile product lines, programs
Monolithic product lines, programs →	variegated product lines, programs
Demands of hierarchy →	demands of task, technology, profession
Departmental orientation →	system orientation
Expanding volume at central site →	developing national and international field units

rightward on the dimensions above. Certainly, at least different technologies and markets will move rightward at different times and paces. Thus today's plastics industry reflects the characteristics in the right column, but the cardboard industry does not. As compelling new evidence suggests, opposite managerial styles are effective in these two industries.[3] Roughly, the push-theory is more appropriate to the technology and market of the cardboard carton industry than to the plastics industry. To the degree that technologies and markets like the carton industry will continue to exist, then, so also will personnel administration have to give attention to structure and policies consistent with the push-theory.

The Managerial Pull-Theory

Since the managerial pull-theory seems congenial to the technology of the future, our focus narrows. We live in a transitional period, and the following analysis extends what is already happening into a reasonably coherent view of what the future implies for personnel administration.

Probable changes in organizational patterns consistent with the pull-theory can be described in terms of four polarities. Different times and technologies give different emphases to each. The four polarities are:

1. Differentiation/integration.
2. Repression/wriggle room (freedom to act).
3. Stability/newness.
4. Function/flow of work.

[3] Paul R. Lawrence and Jay W. Lorsch, *Organization and Environment* (Boston: Harvard Graduate School of Business Administration, 1967).

Short of anarchy, there is no real choice of structure or no structure. The emphases placed on these four polarities, however, significantly influence the kind of structure that does develop in organizations. A wide range of alternative organization patterns are possible.

First, any organizing pattern reflects relative emphases on differentiation/integration. Following Lawrence and Lorsch, "differentiation" can be defined in terms of the development among the several units of an organization of "different formal reporting relationships, different criteria for rewards, and different control procedures." In sum, differentiation is defined in terms of "the difference in cognitive and emotional orientation among managers in different functional departments." Integration refers to "the quality of the state of collaboration that exists among departments that are required to achieve unity of effort by the demands of the environment."[4]

Organization patterns of the near-future will no doubt emphasize integration. Early organizational experience tended to reflect integration, as in the crafts. Over the first half of this century, however, the emphasis shifted to the differentiation of functions and skills. Thus "bureaucracy" dominated this phase of organization history, and that concept is rooted in differentiation. Bureaucracy includes:

1. A well-defined chain of command that vertically channels formal interaction.
2. A system of procedures and rules for dealing with all contingencies at work, which reinforces the reporting insularity of each bureau.
3. A division of labor based upon specialization by major function or process that vertically fragments a flow of work.
4. Promotion and selection based on technical competence defined consistently with 1–3 above.
5. Impersonality in relations between organization members and between them and their clients.

More recently, integration has received increasing emphasis. The "system approach" and the computer are the major contemporary technical expressions of this integrative thrust. Behaviorally, integration implies meeting both human needs and technical demands at work.

Second, a basic foundation of any pattern for organizing deals with the relative emphasis on repression and "wriggle room." No technical definitions seem necessary here; and "surplus repression" is commonly seen as a major product of bureaucracy. Increasingly, an emerging integrative emphasis seeks an organizational climate having the minimal constraints consistent with quality performance. This is the essence of the contemporary stress on "management by objectives." Similarly, the popularity of sensitivity training reflects massive concern about such costs of repression as withheld effort or information.

[4] Lawrence and Lorsch, op. cit., pp. 10–11.

There is no mistaking the root-cause of such de-emphasis on repression. Today's organizations reflect a growing need for an organic and evolving integration, as opposed to a mechanical structuring. Adherence to a mechanical system can be enforced; but commitment to an organic integration can only be elicited and encouraged. Put another way, the integrity of a stable and simple technology may be safeguarded by culling deviants. But changing and complex technologies require the careful husbanding of selected kinds of innovation or adaptability in a widening range of employees. Hence the growing importance of wriggle room, or freedom to act.

The change in emphasis on repression/wriggle room may be characterized broadly, and with essential accuracy. The bureaucratic spirit is oriented toward developing a system to guard against man at his worst, to preclude error or venality. Hence flows of work are differentiated as functions or positions or motions, and surplus repression is the glue used to pull them together. The integrative spirit, on the other hand, is oriented toward creating an environment in which man can approach his productive best. Hence the emphasis on wriggle room, on learning how and when individuals can more often meet their own needs while contributing more effectively to a total flow of work with which they identify their interests.

Third, the relative emphasis on stability/newness also constitutes a major decision underlying any organizing pattern. The acceleration of newness has been described in many places, even if one cannot feel it in his bones. Hence the bare notice here that all-but-overwhelming newness is a trademark of our times, and that it is poorly served by bureaucratic properties.

Fourth, different emphases on the three polarities above imply different organization structures built around functions and flows of work, respectively. Take an easy case, to begin, the organization of three activities A, B, and C which when combined yield some product or service.[5] Figure 1 presents the skeletal structure consistent with these three emphases: differentiation, repression, and stability.

This characterization is easy to support. For example, Figure 1 essentially puts the same or similar activities together in its basic units of organization. That is, the model builds on departments *differentiated* by kinds of activities, usually called "functions" at high levels of organization and "processes" at lower levels. Relatedly, the narrow span of control is well designed to facilitate surplus *repression* in the details of operation. That is, the structure encourages centralization of decision-making at the level of MABC, who alone can make reasonable decisions about the flow of work A + B + C. Hence he alone controls a "managerial unit." Finally, the model presumes a *stable* state. The underlying model is that of a mechanical meshing of parts rather than of a dynamic flow of work.

[5] For a comparison of these models, see Robert T. Golembiewski, *Men, Management, and Morality* (New York: McGraw-Hill, 1965).

Underlying Properties

1. Authority is a vertical, or hierarchical, relation.
2. Departments are organized around the same or similar activities, called "functions" at high levels of organization and "processes" at low levels; that is, "like" activities are put together.
3. Only a relatively small number of people should report directly to any superior.

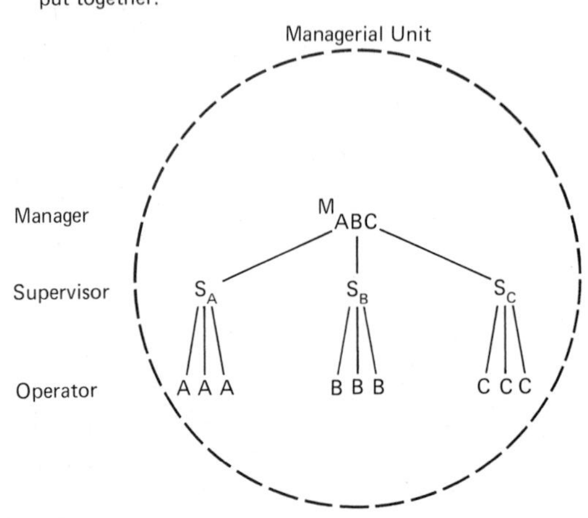

Figure 1. A Structure Consistent with the Values of Bureaucracy: Emphasis on Differentiation, Repression, Stability, and Function.

Figure 2 presents an alternative structure that is consistent with the principal adaptive arrangements to the on-going organizational revolution. These adaptive arrangements include: decentralization; project management; matrix overlays; independent profit centers; management by objectives; autonomous teams; and numerous other variations on a theme. In common, as the Figure 2 model suggests, these adaptations stress integration, wriggle room, change, and flow of work.

Thus, the unorthodox model organizes around *integrative* departments, that is, it groups together activities that are related in a total flow of work. This integrative thrust can be extended to the operators, as through job rotation and job enlargement. In addition, the model seeks the *minimum control* that is consistent with end-item quality and quantity. The multiple opportunities for self-discipline and self-control built in the model, for example, reduce the need for external repression in tying individual needs to organizational goals. The key factors are teams which control a flow of work whose performance is easily and meaningfully comparable.

Moreover, Figure 2 variously facilitates adapting to *change* and *growth*. For example, Figure 1 structures tend to grow "tall" very quickly, with consequent increases in reaction time, in communication costs, and so on. The limited span of control is the major culprit. Figure 2 structures are much less

Underlying Properties

1. Authoritative relations occur up, down, and across the organization, and all these vectors should be directed to similar goals by an effective structure.
2. Departmentation reflects the "flow of work"; that is, related activities are put together whether they are "like" or "unlike."
3. A relatively large number of people may report to any superior, given a structure that facilitates measuring performance.

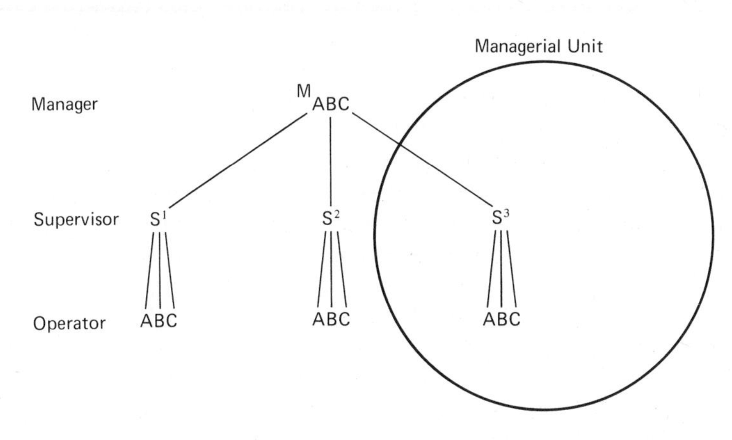

Figure 2. An Alternative Structure: Emphasis on Integration, Wriggle Room, Change, and Flow of Work

growth-sensitive and can remain relatively "flat" even with manifold increases in size.

Finally, Figure 2 structures departmentalize around *flows of work* as opposed to functions. Each S now controls a managerial unit.

The two structures are ideal types in that they are analytical extremes. In practice, they can be approached only in degree, often in complex mixtures. But approaches to one ideal model or the other will tend to generate significantly different consequences.

The Managerial Pull-Theory

1. *Differentiation/Integration.* At least three major challenges for personnel administration are involved in shifting emphasis from differentiation toward integration. As used here, "personnel administration" usually refers to both the staff personnel job as well as to those personnel aspects for which a line manager is responsible. Basically, the interest here is in "what" needs to be done rather than "who" will do it. "Who" questions do get some attention, however.

First, new strategies must be developed for motivating individuals and groups while facilitating interpersonal and intergroup collaboration. Inducing win-lose competition between individuals and groups has been the stand-by strategy, and it does have its attractions. Thus starting rivalry or conflict is easy. Keeping it within bounds often is the difficult part. Moreover, the competitive strategy can engage substantial energies. In addition, much line and staff experience has been accumulated about "cattle prod" activities useful for inducing rivalry or win-lose competition.

The disadvantages of win-lose competition loom increasingly significant,[6] and particularly in organizations with structures like that in Figure 1. Overall, technological demands require growing collaboration between functions or processes, but great potential for conflict and rivalry is built into Figure 1 structure.

For example, the work of departments in a Figure 1 structure is not directly comparable, which often precludes reliable and non-arbitrary measures of performance. Each department provides only a partial contribution to a variety of flows of work, which implies major problems in factoring-out departmental successes and failures. Because of this complexity, one department may "win" only as another department "loses," e.g., in a cost-accounting allocation.

Structures like that in Figure 2 require that S perform a managerially-integrative role, in contrast. The S takes a generalist role in fact as well as intent, in that he can make reasonable decisions about a total flow of work. These integrative features of Figure 2 structures have numerous advantages. Because the basic units of organization below MABC are autonomous and control an entire flow of work, for example, reliable and non-arbitrary measurement of performance is relatively simple. In addition, the basic unit of organization includes the full sequence of operations. Effort and performance are more likely to be congruent, as a consequence. Moreover, the "wins" of one department do not preclude "wins" by others. Even the competition in Figure 2 structures has integrative tendencies.

Since a Figure 2 structure may not exist, or cannot always be approached, the development of strategies for motivation that facilitate interpersonal and intergroup collaboration deserve high priority. For example, inter-departmental conflicts and rivalries encouraged by Figure 1 structures may be ameliorated by improving the processes of interpersonal and group interaction. Consider the chief executive of an organization patterned after Figure 1 who spotlighted the divisive forces induced by the traditional structure in these words:[7]

> The trouble with ABC is that nobody aside from me ever gives one damn about the overall goals of this place. They're all seeing the world through the lenses of their departmental biases. What we need around here are people who wear the ABC hat, not the engineering hat or the sales hat or the production hat.

[6] To extend the argument, win-lose competition also is less useful at an inter-firm or inter-nation level. The magnitude of many projects requires exquisite coordination between "competing" firms, for example. And I have heard a major aerospace official say that, whatever the political issues between us, acute practical considerations require advanced cooperation on the SST between American firms and the French.

[7] Warren G. Bennis, "Organizations of the Future," *Personnel Administration,* Vol. 30 (September, 1967), p. 16.

This complaint inspired the development of the ABC Hats, a group representing several functions and hierarchical levels that filled the integrative gaps resulting from a Figure 1 structure. Organizational applications of sensitivity training seek similar integration via improved interpersonal and group relations.[8]

Improving interpersonal and intergroup relations in a Figure 1 structure implies an uphill struggle all the way. Whatever improvement in communication processes results from sensitivity training or from a team-building experience, that is, the structure will tend to keep on generating conflict and rivalry. Consequently, "booster shots" are necessary. Indeed, some organizations have evolved a "change-agent" role to provide just such a stimulus to effective interaction between individuals and groups. Providing change-agent services, and particularly organizing for them, will generate major problems for personnel administration.

Second, personnel administration must give massive attention to developing a viable integrative function. Consider two possible approaches: some integrative role may be grafted to the basic functional structure, in Figure 1; or integrative teams may become the basic units of departmentation, as in Figure 2. Both cases present problems. The second case is more attractive in concept, but for most organizations it would mean a major and difficult organization development effort.

Consequently, integrative roles in organizations tend to be superimposed on a Figure 1 structure, as by establishing an interdepartmental coordinating committee or a "project manager." Both are integrative overlays designed to counteract the fragmenting tendencies of the traditional structure of departments organized by functions or processes. To illustrate, the project manager develops a temporary integrative team to do some specific job, making requests for personnel as necessary from the functional departments. Team members then respond to two authoritative sources: to their more-or-less temporary project manager; and to the head of the functional department to which they will return when the project is complete. The resulting multiple lines of authority are sometimes called a "matrix overlay."

Integrative arrangements superimposed on a traditional structure can help reduce the conflict and rivalry characteristic of a Figure 1 structure, but they are tricky.[9] Thus questions of multiple authority may vex personnel administration. Or power may remain in the permanent functional departments, and this can make life difficult for integrative agents such as project managers or interdepartmental coordinating committees. In both cases, in addition, what is to be done with a project manager when his project is terminated? The experience in the aero-space industry does not suggest

[8] For an analog of sensitivity training that shows promise, see Robert T. Golembiewski and Arthur Blumberg, "Confrontation as a Training Design in Complex Organizations," *Journal of Applied Behavioral Science,* Vol. 3 (December, 1967), pp. 525–47.

[9] Richard M. Hodgetts, "Leadership Techniques in the Project Organization," *Academy of Management Journal,* Vol. II (June, 1968), pp. 211–20.

any easy ways out. Making conscious arrangements for an integrative role, then, implies serious problems for personnel administration.

Third, shared-values that encourage organizational unity must be developed and broadly accepted. Otherwise, a significant shift of emphasis toward integration is unlikely. Prevailing organizational values—the "values of bureaucracy"—are hierarchy-serving in that they reinforce superior-subordinate relations, but they do so only at the expense of inhibiting the development of socio-emotional ties that can integrate individuals or groups performing different functions in different departments in a Figure 1 structure. Since today's organizations increasingly must be integrative, and since they increasingly must stress dynamic knowledge-gathering because they are truth-requiring, the values of bureaucracy will increasingly generate troublesome consequences.

The alternative to the values of bureaucracy is not yet clear. However, the following "climate of beliefs" seems adaptive to the knowledge-gathering and truth-requiring demands of today's technology:[10]

1. Full and free communication, regardless of rank or power.
2. Reliance on consensual processes in dealing with conflict, as opposed to coercion or compromise.
3. Basing influence on technical competence and knowledge, as opposed to personal whim or hierarchical status.
4. An atmosphere that easily admits emotional expression as well as task-oriented behavior.
5. Acceptance of conflict between the individual and the organization, which conflict is to be coped with openly.

Getting acceptance of such values in principle and practice should constitute a major near-future challenge for personnel administration.

2. *Repression/Wriggle Room.* Two issues involved in the shift of emphasis toward wriggle room deserve special attention because they pose major problems for personnel administration. One issue involves tailoring both organization structure and interaction processes so as to meet human needs at work. The second issue deals with values and representational vehicles capable of supporting such changes in structure and interaction processes.

One major approach toward emphasizing wriggle room involves shaping organizations to fit people in the design of tasks and structure. Historically, people were fitted to the organization. Many observers have argued the merits of tailoring tasks to man,[11] as through job enlargement, so we note only two major derivative demands on personnel administration. In the federal government, "classification experts" still far outnumber "specialists in job design." A traditional personnel specialty, especially in the federal

[10] Warren G. Bennis, *Changing Organizations* (New York: McGraw-Hill, 1966), pp. 15–16.

[11] David S. Brown, "Shaping the Organization to Fit People," *Management of Personnel Quarterly,* Vol. 5 (Summer, 1966), pp. 12–16.

government, needs to be reoriented if more wriggle room is the goal. Moreover, job enlargement is easiest in a Figure 2 structure. Since a Figure 1 structure is what most organizations have, the implied challenge to public personnel administration is the development of a potent OD, or organization development, specialty. Experience in the federal government suggests the road will be arduous and long.

Relatedly, interaction processes can also usefully be tailored to man. Argyris has posited needs of man that are seen as typically frustrated in large organizations, and especially in organizations patterned after Figure 1.[12] Building satisfying interaction processes into organizations is a gargantuan task, and only scarcely begun. Thus some change-agents attempt to build sensitivity training groups directly into organizations, which raises major issues with traditional ways of organizing and managing. Others argue that building need-satisfying interaction into organizations is hopelessly utopian. Many variations exist between those anchor-positions.

However matters evolve, the face of personnel administration is certain to change substantially. That much is clear from these broad values of sensitivity training that imply what is often seen as lacking in organizations:[13]

1. An attitude of inquiry, reflecting a "hypothetical spirit" and an emphasis on experimentation.
2. An expanded awareness on the part of organization members, with a corresponding sense of a broader choice of alternatives for action.
3. An undergirding system of norms that stress collaboration and a problem-solving orientation to conflict.
4. An emphasis on the helping relationship as a major way to concretely express man's interdependence with man.

Changes in tasks and interaction processes must be supported by appropriate values and representational vehicles. As an example, greater managerial concern for due process and sharing of influence seems necessary. Either the pull-theory or the push-theory can guide how the two are approached—since due process and influence-sharing will receive major attention, for good or ill—and the choice is a matter of real consequence. That is, influence-sharing or due process can be granted with top management support in sensitive dialog with employees whose needs and capabilities are diversely evolving; or at a polar extreme, they can be wrested away by employees after heated battle with a boulwareian management. The pull-theory recommends the former, of course.

No doubt much of the near-future resolution of issues involving due process and influence-sharing will be in familiar terms: employee unionization, more or less grudging management assent, and more or less successful efforts

[12] Chris Argyris, *Personality and Organization* (New York: Harper, 1957), especially pp. 49–53.

[13] Edgar H. Schein and Warren G. Bennis, editors, *Personal and Organizational Change Through Group Methods* (New York: Wiley, 1965), pp. 30–35.

at rapproachement. Increasingly, however, the resolution will involve the breaking of new and uncertain ground. At least at managerial levels in many organizations, for example, determined efforts are underway to develop new and enhanced representational vehicles, encompassing "tell all" dinners, management councils, and God knows what. Only the brave fool would try to guess the product of this maelstrom, or even whether we can avoid a kind of organizational totalitarianism borne of ineptness or unwillingness in developing appropriate values and vehicles. That personnel administration vitally depends on the outcome of the search for viable approaches to power-sharing and to organizational due-process seems undeniable.

3. *Stability/Newness.* Any shift in emphasis toward newness implies at least two major issues.

First, the "change function" must be given greater priority, with such attendant challenges as better equipping people to tolerate ambiguity. We have only clues as to how to cope successfully with such an increased priority, both as to mechanics and organization.

As for mechanics, an increased priority for change implies an appropriate reward system. Existing reward systems usually are keyed to how much one produces, however, or how long one has been a producer. Neither bias facilitates change; both biases are at best irrelevant to change, if they are not inimical to it. Likely reinforcers of change imply a host of problems. I have in mind one labor agreement that rewards employees for their willingness to be continually retrained, as opposed to rewarding them for their productivity or for their seniority. Such arrangements imply very significant labor-management issues, with which we have precious little experience. One thing is clear, however. Much of the heart of traditional personnel administration—as in the classification and pay plans at the federal level—poorly suits arrangements designed to facilitate change. Nothing better could be expected of these products of our bureaucratic phase.

Organizationally, increased emphasis on change also poses real problems for personnel administration. The issues are most sharply joined in the evolving role of the "change-agent" which is devoted to facilitating change and inducing appropriate interpersonal and intergroup climates for change. Where is the change-agent to be located? Who is to be the change-agent?

Working answers to such questions have tended to be unsatisfactory. Relying on "external change-agents" such as consultants has some real advantages, but this places the change-agent outside the organization's authority-and-reward structure and may compromise his effectiveness. Relying on internal change agents ties them into the system, but this cuts both ways. If things got rough for them, change-agents might be motivated to become a kind of non-directive and even gentle but nonetheless efficient gestapo in the pursuit of their own interests.[14]

[14] The temptation is great where such change-agents use sensitivity training sessions, for example, during which much data about individuals and groups may be divulged. A similar problem faces such professionals as psychiatrists employed by organizations.

If the line manager becomes the change-agent, you avoid many ticklish authority problems but you run the risk of placing reliance for change in an individual who may be overbusy with day-to-day problems. Moreover, there is no guarantee that line officials will have the appropriate skills or training, or even the interest. Embody the change-agent role in a staff man or unit, and that implies all of the problems that have plagued line-staff relations. Managing the change-agent role, in sum, implies one grand job for personnel administration, conceived in its broad sense as an amalgam of line and staff responsibilities.

Second, the shifting emphasis to newness implies a growing need to quickly develop and disband both large and small work-units. The point clearly applies to the teams formed in project management, for example. Moreover, the need to revitalize today's organizations so as to prepare them for adapting to tomorrow's markets or programs also raises questions about managing temporary social systems.

Managing temporary social systems presents a formidable task in at least two major ways. Such management requires that people develop a kind of instant but still intense commitment. This is difficult, but seemingly unavoidable. Complex systems often permit no alternative to the technical and social compatibility of team members. In addition, organization members will need to learn how to experience the loss of one temporary social system in ways that do not inhibit their commitment to future systems.

We are gaining some experience with effective management of temporary social systems, as via "team-building." The approach uses learning analogs derived from the laboratory approach, whose purest form is the sensitivity-training group. For example, such team-building has proved useful in one multi-plant firm using periodic rotation of management teams.[15] Plant technology is based on continuous processing and delicate integration of activities, and rotation typically caused a variety of dislocation that registered as decreases in productivity and employee satisfaction. Roughly, the typical relearning dip in several plants of this firm approximated six months. Moreover, as the plant technology became more integrated, that break-in period seemed to lengthen. Now, three or four day team-building experiences are provided early in the life of each new team. The re-learning dip has been halved.

Less is known about disbanding a temporary social system in ways that do not inhibit the commitment of its members to future systems. Work with sensitivity training suggests that such "separation anxiety" can be effectively managed. However, socio-emotional de-briefing is still uncommon.

Experience with both creating and terminating temporary social systems seems worth developing. Consider aerospace firms, which typify what many organizations are increasingly becoming. One prominent feature of aero-

[15] "Team-building" has also been utilized on a mass scale, by such firms as Alcan and TRW. See Alexander Winn, "The Laboratory Approach to Organization Development: A Tentative Model of Planned Change." Paper read at the Annual Conference, British Psychological Conference, Oxford, September 1968.

space experience is the socio-emotional turmoil associated with developing, and more particularly with terminating, project teams. Members of teams gear themselves up to unflinching commitment, working long and hard. When the project is concluded, depression often sets in, marital difficulties seem unusually common and severe, and so on. Both research and popular magazines have painted an alarming picture of this new problem, which we can expect to become increasingly common.[16]

Managing temporary social systems also implies two major technical issues. One of these concerns structural arrangements that encourage quick group identification and that also permit reinforcement by reward systems keyed to meaningful measures of performance. These dual goals are within reach. That is, both identification and the measurement of performance will be facilitated as organizations move toward Figure 2 structures. The point is of crucial significance. Indeed, Figure 2 offers a way out of nagging organizational problems. Thus managing the change-agent role might be handled effectively through team effort by members of a small integrative managerial unit. A line manager and a staff personnel man could be assigned to each managerial unit, and be jointly responsible for the change-agent role. Team effort also could provide a basis for redefining line-staff relations, as is urged below. Consequently, such structural change must occupy much of the effort of personnel administrators over the near future.

Figure 2 structures also permit convenient changes in incentive systems and philosophy. In one Figure 1 structure, for example, a very complex system of different wage rates for specific jobs required an elaborate supervisory and clerical apparatus for wage administration. Under a Figure 2 structure, a simpler system was possible. Management negotiated a base-price tied to output with a producing team that controlled the entire flow of work, and the unit handled the internal distribution of its income.[17] That is, group incentives in a Figure 2 structure can help integrate a total flow of work and reinforce the allegiances encouraged by that structure. Supervision is consequently simplified. Compensation systems in Figure 1 structures, in contrast, tend to fragment flows of work and to complicate supervision.

A second major technical issue in managing temporary social systems concerns position classification. Figure 2 structures, and the temporary teams within them, encourage classification plans that place rank in the man rather than the job. On this score, the federal public service can expect special problems in managing temporary social systems. Although recent policies permit some recognition of the impact of the man on the job, the federal approach to classification emphasizes rank-in-position.

4. *Function/Flow of Work.* Basic structural change that shifts emphasis from particularistic to integrative departmentation, from functions to the

[16] Warren G. Bennis and Philip E. Slater, *The Temporary Society* (New York: Harper and Row, 1968).

[17] P. G. Herbst, *Autonomous Group Functioning* (London: Tavistock Publications, 1962).

flow of work, will make it easier to respond effectively to the challenges facing personnel administration; but that change will be difficult. The root-need is the development of a solid core of organization development (OD) specialists who can maintain real momentum in long-run programs of change. Ideally, perhaps, every manager should be his own OD specialist. Practically, the OD function often will become a staff personnel specialty.

Redefined line-staff relations are necessary if personnel officials are to operate effectively in an OD role, it is particularly important to note. Redefinition is necessary because OD means change, change in basic attitudes and values and ways of organizing work. Hence, the inappropriateness of the traditional concept of staff as outside the chain of command, as advisory, and as organizationally inferior to the line.

Structural arrangements for a suitable redefinition of line-staff relations also seem clear, in general. A Figure 2 structure, for example, could provide a common organizational home for both a line manager and a staff personnel man. Their shared responsibility for the success of a total managerial unit would encourage a team effort, rather than line vs. staff tension. The approach gets much support, both from experience[18] and from theoretical analysis.[19] In contrast, Figure 1 structures are organized around separate functions or processes. This encourages fragmentation of line from staff, and differentiation between line and staff.

Realistically, and especially in the public service, such a core of OD specialists can anticipate a formidable task. The difficulty is multidimensional. Unlike OD specialists in many business organizations, for example, such specialists in public agencies must not only convince their top management, but they must also reach powerful legislators or standing committees as well as multiple interest groups. This gives agency bureaus or groups such as Foreign Service Officers an opportunity to develop a resistance to top agency management (Note Figure 3).

On this score, OD specialists will have their work cut out for them. In

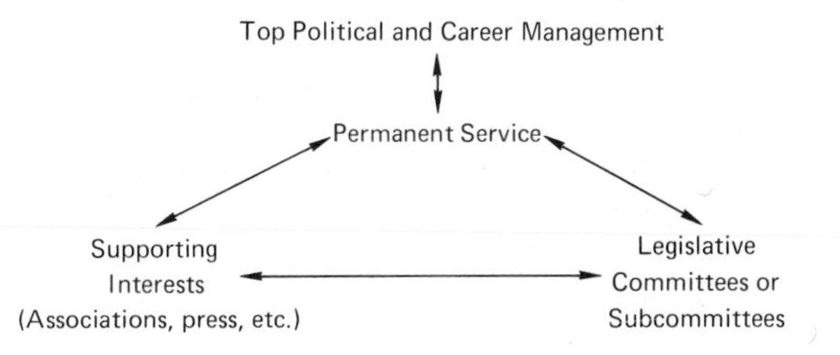

Figure 3.

[18] Blake, Robert R. and Jane Snygley Mouton, *Corporate Excellence Through Grid Organization Development* (Houston: Gulf Publishing, 1968), Appendix II.

[19] Robert T. Golembiewski, *Organizing Men and Power: Patterns of Behavior and Line-Staff Models* (Chicago: Rand McNally, 1967).

addition, the brief average tenure of political appointees adds to the problem. Finally, any protectionism induced by the civil service concept as it has evolved can serve to complicate any process of change. Perhaps the clearest reflections of the point are the complex "bumping arrangements" that apply to reductions-in-force.

Assuming the development of a core of OD specialists, three specific re-orientations in outlook also seem necessary. They will only be sketched.

First, an emphasis on flow of work as opposed to functions will require a "bottom, up" approach to organizing work and to locating services. The first point need not be emphasized, but the location of services has been given less attention. Given a "top, down" approach, services tend to drift upward in the typical hierarchy. For example, staff probably would report to MABC in Figure 1, even though many of their inputs might be made at the level of SA or below.

A "bottom, up" approach would generate a different pattern. The point may be illustrated briefly. Typically, an overhead staff unit would both design and monitor patterns of work motions. In one large electronics firm, however, "time and methods" has been handled differently. Employees are themselves instructed in the basics of motion analysis by overhead staff. These employees then design and monitor their own work-motion patterns.

Such "bottom-up" approaches as the example above imply multiple problems for personnel administration. Thus they may raise troublesome status questions for both MABC and the men who report to him. Moreover, suitable work environments for such approaches must have one or both of two characteristics: employee efforts must be measurable, easily and validly; or the employees must be motivated to apply the principles of motion analysis. These are major problems, but they are less troublesome than the problems of enforcement and evasion likely under a "top-down" approach to motion analysis. For example, Figure 2 structure can help significantly to reduce both mensural and motivational problems.[20]

Second, shifting emphasis to the flow of work requires a new "line-staff" concept. I have dealt with the matter at length elsewhere at the analytic level, and fragmentary research has proved very encouraging.[21] Note here only the multiple mischief of conceiving staff as a glorified prosthetic device, as a kind of enlargement of the senses of MABC in Figure 1. Such a notion does encourage centralized identification and location of staff. And such identification and location always will be necessary for some staff, at least some of the time. Often too much is made of a good thing, however, with obvious costs in increased managerial complexity, heightened line-staff conflict, long communication chains, and a general rigidifying of relations at work.

[20] Golembiewski, *Organizing Men and Power,* pp. 90–110 and 154–73.

[21] Robert T. Golembiewski, "Personality and Organization Structure: Staff Models and Behavioral Patterns," *Journal of the Academy of Management,* Vol. 9 (September, 1966), pp. 211–30.

Third, greater emphasis on the flow of work will require basic value reorientations in wide segments of the population. This socialization of adults will require both defusing and infusing of values, as it were. As some intriguing research demonstrates, at least "middle-class" children seem to be acquainted with the essentials of a Figure 1 structure as early in life as the third or fourth grade.[22] This suggests the extent of the value-defusing that will be required, and implies a major training burden that extends far beyond the workplace into the value-generating processes of the socialization of children.

There seems a solid base on which to infuse values more appropriate for Figure 2 structures, however. Thus many observers explain the fascination with McGregor's Theory X/Theory Y formulation in terms of a broad managerial desire to increase the congruence between their personal values and the presently-legitimate organization values. The former values tend toward Theory Y; but the latter are Theory X-ish, decidedly. In addition, some evidence shows that managers in larger and technologically sophisticated firms are more likely to reflect Theory Y attitudes.[23] This suggests that contemporary technological demands will supply push/pull forces that will help change values such as those underlying a Figure 1 structure.

Summary

Three generalizations may be drawn regarding the challenges facing the staff personnel man:

1. To the degree that the developmental trends sketched above do in fact become reality, so will personnel administration experience profound challenges.
2. To the extent that specialists in personnel respond to those challenges, so will these specialists be able to ride the tiger of our ongoing organizational revolution.
3. If personnel specialists do not make the required adaptations, someone else will try.

Five major themes will characterize successful approaches by specialists in personnel, none of which will come easy.

First, and most broadly, reorienting the basic concept of personnel administration is in order. Crudely, the reorientation must emphasize training and organization development more than orthodox approaches to position classification, compensation and incentives. Roughly, the reorientation is away from a punitive approach and toward a participative and hopefully a

[22] Herbert G. Wilcox has accumulated evidence of this socialization-effect with an interesting research design. "The Culture Trait of Hierarchy in Middle Class Children," *Public Administration Review,* Vol. 28 (May, 1968), pp. 222–35.

[23] Mason Haire, E. E. Ghiselli, and Lyman W. Porter, "Cultural Patterns in the Role of the Manager," *Industrial Relations,* Vol. 2 (February, 1963), pp. 95–118.

rewarding approach. Such a reorientation is fortunately underway in many areas, albeit in wildly diverse degrees.

Second, specialists in personnel administration must transcend the limitations of the traditional staff role as an appendage for human needs tacked on to an immutable technical structure for work, of staff conceived of as outside the lines of command. A basic redefinition of line-staff relations is in order. Basically, a training or OD role for personnel implies broad involvement in the go-go of the organization. A Figure 2 structure aids in developing line-staff relations necessary to permit such involvement.

Third, specialists in personnel administration must gain support for their new effort, but in an interdependent mode. That is, personnel specialists must avoid the temptation of forcing OD programs down the line, after having gained top-level backing by subtly or grossly playing the informant's role. Such things do happen,[24] and they are the death of OD programs. This more or less standard staff strategy illustrates a dependent mode of promoting an OD program, much more consistent with the push-theory than the pull-theory.

Fourth, the processes within personnel departments will have to be analogs of the processes desired in the broader organization. If integrative teams are seen as the answer to the organization's ills, for example, personnel specialists must demonstrate their willingness and ability to develop such integrative teams and participate in them. At the very least, this means that other members of such teams will have trust, backed by experience, that their openness will not return to haunt them in the form of tales carried upward in the organization.

Fifth, personnel specialists will need fine skills in managing dependence-hostility as they broaden their role. It is a mature relation, indeed, in which "help" is given and accepted, period. When the issue is the change of long-standing patterns of behavior, both dependence on the "helper" and hostility toward him will become more prevalent. Both dependence and hostility will have to be confronted willingly and openly, which only means that everyone must be more heroic and emotionally healthy than sometimes is the case.

[24] See Melville Dalton, *Men at Work* (New York: Wiley, 1959), esp. pp. 18–109.

26

On the Theory of Divisional Structures: Some Aspects of Centralization and Decentralization of Control and Decision Making

Zenon S. Zannetos

I. Introduction

As the size of firms increases managers become increasingly preoccupied with problems of organization. More recently this preoccupation has been accentuated by the advent of computers and the realization that a new era in management practices may be dawning. To some, this new era foretells "recentralization" of business organizations.

While there is no argument that we are in the midst of an evolutionary process, with or without the computer, the direction we are heading, as far as organization structures are concerned, is not so clear cut in the general case, and cannot be described simply in one word. Besides, a lot of confusion exists on what we mean when we use the terms "centralization" and "decentralization."

The purpose of this paper is threefold. It will first of all present a short historical review of the centralization-decentralization research, then suggest a definitional framework and finally analyze the factors that favor centralization and decentralization. Hopefully, businessmen and students of organizations, by applying the framework and tools of analysis that we will provide, will be able to determine the impact on particular organization structures of any changes that may occur in the environment within which their firms operate. In any event there is a real need for an integration of the diverse views on the subject of centralization and decentralization, and the development of a theory which can help us derive operationally meaningful propositions. It is toward these ends that this paper is aimed.

II. Historical Review

Over the years many professional disciplines dealt with problems of organization. Up until recently, however, most of these investigations were only descriptive and often in terms of the vague notions of "unity of command," "span of control," "responsibility" and "authority." Today we find that this type of approach is not satisfactory, because it does not provide operationally meaningful propositions and tools for analysis.

The earliest attempts toward an "analytical" approach to the design of organization structures were made by accountants. The objective of their efforts, however, was limited to the control of behavior for fraud detection

Reprinted with permission from *Management Science,* December 1965, pp. B49–B68.

and hopefully fraud prevention. In order to prevent duplicity and make the assessment of responsibility possible, the accountant of the early days designed a structure of non-overlapping subentities, and an ingenious system of checks and balances that compartmentalized authority. Under such a system, if not circumvented of course, fraud could be perpetrated only by means of a conspiracy by two or more people.

The accounting approach in its pure form is not satisfactory either, because it presupposes a deterministic world of inviolable pre-established interrelationships among the various factors of production, the parts of an organization, and the organizational goals. Consequently, the traditional accounting approach is incompatible with notions that in certain cases we consider vital for successful business operations, such as participative goal setting, group decision making and the exercise of initiative, and so it tends to discourage innovation. Without wishing to underestimate the influence of personal managerial philosophy, business characteristics, and in general environmental and even irrational determinants of organization structures, one could say that even today a significant number of business organizations reflect for the most part requirements of accountability. It is for this reason that we often hear the adage that "authority must accompany responsibility."

Following, in terms of chronology, the accounting stage of organizational development, psychologists, sociologists and human relations experts, excited by the results of the research conducted at the Hawthorne Works of the Western Electric Company, began investigating the many aspects of motivation in an industrial setting and the relationships between organizational structures and employee morale and behavior. In particular, among the topics studied by the aforementioned researchers were the adaptation of group members to the various facets of pressure, the resolution of conflict, the emergence of leadership and organization, the communicational patterns among group members and the relationships between task characteristics, information flow, group structure and performance.

The results of the research that we have just mentioned, are often very interesting and also provide useful insights. They cannot, however, be applied to issues of centralization and decentralization of total business entities, because:

(a) The investigations often focus primarily on special subactivities of the firm.[1]

(b) The inferences drawn from the results obtained are not usually tested for statistical significance. Consequently, the conclusions are mostly in the realm of hypothesis and are not readily amenable to generalizations.

(c) A great number of these experiments are of problem-solving nature.

[1] One of the most favorite subjects for study of social psychologists and sociologists is the scientific research laboratory. Here we have a situation where the overall objective may exist in the substantive terms but it is often undefinable in terms of prior operational plans and subplans, thus allowing task independence.

Often the problem-solving situations studied do not require that the group members undergo extensive learning experience, which in the process will undoubtedly create a hierarchy of knowledge and influence the design of organization structures.

In business practice, the simplicity of the microcosm of *independent* problem-solving activities is usually absent. For the accomplishment of complex objectives there is often a necessity for mutual interaction of subactivities, each of which in turn realizes extensive economies of scale through specialization. Consequently, by concentrating on relatively simple and often programmable tasks, one cannot claim that the results so obtained can be automatically extended to complex tasks.

Research in organizational matters of general applicability has not been completely neglected. Some of the most distinguished researchers in the area of human relations have studied these issues and made significant contributions to the literature. The results of their studies, which are mostly based on extensive personal experience and philosophy, are usually characterized by suggestions for "more decentralized and participative decision making," and for substitution of inner control and motivation for "punitive accounting control" [1], [7], [12, pp. 33–49].

In addition to providing a new general frame of reference, the research in human relations has pointed out some dynamic interrelationships between aspirations, motivation, initiative, individual satisfaction and productivity, which had been completely neglected before. Effectively it has shifted the focus from a theory of antagonism and incompatibility of interest between management and workers, to one of cooperative behavior and mutual benefit, and thus opened horizons for research that are literally inexhaustible. But the problems involved in designing efficient business organizations are for the most part still with us, and the human relations approach does not offer us much help. For in the aggregate it neglects many *economic* aspects of total structure design and it is not analytical, while at the micro level it focuses too much on individual welfare. No one can honestly claim that the firm should be a "charitable" organization nor that it should be expected to shoulder responsibility for all the problems of the society. Yet one is often left with this feeling when reading the literature in the field of human relations.[2]

Traditionally, theoretical economists have not concerned themselves with issues relating to the organizational structure of the firm. By viewing the size of the firm as small enough to be directed by the entrepreneur, and within a purely competitive setting at least as far as the input factors of production are concerned, they found no need for delving in issues of organizational structures and internal controls. The behavior of the factors of production within such setting is optimal, because it is governed by impersonal market

[2] The role of the business sector in a free enterprise economy will receive increasing attention in the future as new ways of exploiting economies of size become available.

interactions. Little by little, however, economists have been moving away from the entrepreneurial model of the firm with unidirectional and uniform goals and have begun dealing with organizational problems [4], [5], [14].

It must be noted that once we abandon the entrepreneurial notion of the firm and relax the assumptions regarding the existence of free market information for optimizing behavior, we are faced with a vast array of issues that demand resolution. We must analyze the factors that favor centralization and decentralization, find substitutes for market prices whenever the latter are absent, find ways to set goals and guarantee goal consistency within an organization, determine the economics of information that is necessary for motivating efficient behavior, and analyze the patterns of interaction—human as well as knowledge—within a group. Some of these issues have attracted considerable attention lately [2], [10], [11], [19, Ch. 4], [20, Ch. II, IV, VI], but unfortunately most efforts focused on isolated problems which were not viewed within the context of the total organization. As a result, little progress has been made toward a cohesive theory of divisionalization.

One notable exception to the above criticism is the work of Herbert A. Simon [9], [17] which following the pattern set by Barnard [3] gave impetus toward a more analytical approach to the relationships between organization structures and the decision-making process in its totality. Even in this case, however, rather undue emphasis is given to the behavioral determinants of organizations at the expense of the economic.

III. Definitional Framework

The notion of centralization and decentralization can be classified among the terms whose meaning on the surface appears to be self-evident and common knowledge, yet very few of the users ever attempt to precisely define. The reasons for this imprecision are not necessarily related to carelessness, but rather to the difficulty and complexity of the issues involved.

Most writers on subjects related to organizational structures, accept Simon's definition of centralization and decentralization. In his study of the "Controllers' Department," Simon stated that:

> An administrative organization is centralized to the extent that decisions are made at relatively high levels in the organization; decentralized to the extent that discretion and authority to make important decisions are delegated by top management to lower levels of executive authority [18, p. 1].

This is admittedly a neat statement which is not likely to draw any strong objections but it is not as simple as it may appear to be. Indeed, the notion of centralization and decentralization is quite complex and if put to a test it will not stand the rigor of clarity either. One has to define first of all what is "high" and what is "low" level of "authority" in organizations composed of multiple tiers, and also explain what determines the number of tiers. These questions are important for definitional as well as comparative purposes.

Furthermore, to the extent that decisions are continuously made at all levels within organizations, one must introduce a scale for distinguishing between the various types of decisions.

It appears to us, that in order to impart a meaningful empirical content to the notion of centralization and decentralization, one has to interpret these terms relatively to the overall objectives of the firm. In effect this is the approach taken by the students of functionalization and the so-called "federal decentralization," although often only implicitly and in very general and vague terms [6, Ch. 11, 17], [15, pp. 680–682], [17, pp. 190–192]. Once such an approach is followed, it soon becomes clear that the unqualified use of these terms for the description of empirical findings is rather meaningless.

We will say that *a unit is decentralized absolutely, always of course within the overall objectives of the total organization,*[3] *if and only if its index of overall objectives is qualitatively identical to those of its parent.* Furthermore, if more than one such unit exists within an organization, the latter must not realize any economies or diseconomies of scale in the intensity of pursuit of these objectives. The latter qualification is necessary because otherwise the decentralized subunits, if more than one exists, will not be absolutely independent of each other in their efforts to maximize the overall objective of the firm. In our case absolute decentralization and absolute independence are synonymous within the organizational context. If we denote with $V = v(\sum_{i=1}^{n} C_i f_i(\alpha_i))$ the value that the firm derives from the successful pursuit of its n objectives, then given k subentities our arguments imply that:

$$V = v(\sum_{j=1}^{k} \sum_{n=1}^{n} C_{ij} f_i(\alpha_i)) = \sum_{j=1}^{k} v_j(\sum_{i=1}^{k} C_{ij} f_i(\alpha_i))$$

Qualifications such as the one mentioned above, however, are not serious or in any way limiting in empirical research, because absolutely decentralized sub-units within an organization are non-existent. It is only for a frame of reference and a point of departure that we need the definition. If we look at functioning organizations, we will notice that these appear to have one or more "independent" objectives. The latter are assigned to one or more sub-entities before they are translated and reassigned. Such an arrangement is partial decentralization, because the freedom of each subactivity is limited in its choice of objectives and often in the degree of pursuit of such objectives.

At this point it may be necessary to digress for a moment and make a few comments concerning our use of the notion of independence of multiple objectives. It is necessary for our purpose to deal with multiple objectives, because of the various translations of objectives that take place at the various levels in the organizational structure of the firm. Whether there is such a thing as an array of

[3] Given that no organization in the whole world is absolutely independent and autonomous, we must define first of all the context within which a unit is viewed. In business structures, the highest context that we will consider is the firm as an administrative entity.

purely independent overall substantive objectives of the firm is very debatable. However, by means of translations (mappings) one can develop for subentities multi-dimensional objective vectors, whose components appear, *at that particular organizational level*, to be absolutely independent. The process of translation results in the gradual reduction of the amount of value judgment a subunit is allowed to exercise, and also gives rise to hierarchical structures and *external* subunit interdependencies.

In general a *hierarchy* is an ordinal ranking on the basis of some rules of supremacy. Although the number of tiers from top to a particular subentity within an organization may serve as a measure of cardinality, the latter cannot help us in deciding how centralized or decentralized a subunit is.

From our discussion so far three definitional conclusions emerge.

1. That the notions of centralization and decentralization are relative and not universal. Consequently we cannot make unqualified general statements as to whether a company or a subunit is decentralized or centralized. Only in comparative (relative) terms can we express an opinion, after applying as a criterion of measurement the number of translations and the dimension of such translations of the overall substantive objectives. For example, given any two organizational structures with at least two hierarchical tiers, which are governed by the same task and human characteristics, then the greater the number of hierarchical levels the greater will be the *diffusion of authority* within the organization. *Nothing can be said, however, about the degree of centralization or decentralization at any level unless an analysis is made of the relationship between overall objectives and subunit subobjectives.*

2. That hierarchical structures although related to the general issue of centralization and decentralization do not necessarily prejudice its nature or form.[4] Any organization which is short of the utopian absolute decentralization must be hierarchical because it necessitates a translation of the overall objectives into subobjectives.[5] In fact, if we were to view the process toward relatively more and more decentralization as occurring in a semblance of a continuum, but with only rational graduations of objective coefficients, the organizational structure may be looked upon as becoming more and more hierarchical up to the point it is composed of an infinity (denumerable) of hierarchical layers, only to collapse to one layer upon reaching absolute de-

[4] Simon in his *The New Science of Management Decision,* op. cit., p. 44, states that: "Hierarchy always implies intrinsically some measure of decentralization." While the latter statement is true, so is its complement and opposite, that hierarchy implies *some* measure of centralization. As we have previously mentioned *centralization and decentralization are relative terms, and not absolutes.*

[5] Later we will show that entities which are absolutely decentralized and are also paper thin, are only *decentralized in their external relations. Internally,* these organizations are *highly centralized in their totality.* That is *one* reason why we made the statement that hierarchical structures do not necessarily prejudice the nature or form of centralization and decentralization. Under conditions of *partial decentralization,* hierarchies are necessary. However, let us stress again, that there is no connection here between the necessary condition and the final form or degree of partial decentralization.

centralization. Such a collapse occurs because then the objectives of the various layers become indistinguishable and the superstructure appears to be unnecessary as we approach the absolute limit.[6]

We must stress here that the preceding paragraph refers to the external structural relationships between subunits. In other words we are viewing the unit, however defined, as an entity and study its position vis-a-vis other units in the hierarchy, especially the units in higher tiers. The units of lower tiers may be viewed for convenience as embedded in or internal to the subunit.

3. That another dimension of relativity must be introduced to distinguish relationships that emanate "from within" versus "from without" a unit. To the extent that we are dealing with embedded structures that are quite complex even in their smallest subdivision, we must make the proposed classification in order to distinguish between inter- and intra-subunit organizational problems. For example, if a subunit is part of a hierarchy, this does not perforce imply that it should be also hierarchically organized internally.

The above discussion of inter- versus intra-subunit relationships brings us to the definition of *equalitarian* or *mutual interaction* structures. *The latter terms are applicable purely within an organizational subentity and to the whole array of subunit objectives and tasks.* An equalitarian structure is defined as one where superior-subordinate roles are absent, and where decisions are made through the mutual and equal interaction of all the members within the unit. Such a structure is by definition nonhierarchical.[7]

A question may now arise, however, as to whether an equalitarian structure is centralized or decentralized. "From without," that is to say looking at the relationship between the equalitarian unit and any other (higher) units in the organization, one has to examine the relationship between the substantive objectives of these units and apply the definition as we previously explained. Internally, however, to the extent that there is no further translation of objectives and no hierarchical or lateral diffusion of decision making, the equalitarian unit must be considered as highly centralized. As in the case of hierarchical

[6] As the reader may remember, we specified that in order to establish the degree of relative decentralization of any two subunits within a firm, we must compare their index of objectives to that of the firm. The unit whose objectives are a closer representation (image) of those of the firm, is then judged to be relatively more decentralized. Given that for absolute decentralization we require linearity, then we have a system by means of which we can introduce between any subunit and the top as many hierarchical layers as we wish, with each one becoming a better and better image of the firm. Or alternatively we can view each subunit, through changes of objectives, becoming more and more decentralized by going through the denumerable number of steps that we have already mentioned. In the end all subunits will be separated by infinitesimal differences not worthy of the superstructure. This process is similar to the one we follow in order to count all the rational numbers between any two of them.

[7] This does not necessarily imply that the knowledge of the members of an equalitarian unit cannot be specialized and ranked in a hierarchical fashion given a specific task. It only implies that the task cannot be accomplished unless all members of a subunit mutually interact on an equal basis. The hierarchy of knowledge usually is temporary, and shifting depending on the characteristics of the particular task on hand.

structures and their relation to the decentralization issue we have here what may appear to be a paradox.[8] In the extreme absolute decentralization results in independent unicellular structures that are non-hierarchical, completely decentralized "from without," and highly centralized "from within," although the power within the structure is horizontally and equally shared. There is no contradiction, of course, in this, because *the centralization of power "from within" rests with the totality* in a democratic manner.

Finally a few words on the difference between centralization and decentralization of control versus decision making. Although control and decision making are not mutually exclusive and often interdependent, these two processes and activities are not identical. Control refers to the function by means of which observations are collected and the resultant information is transmitted for adapting or changing behavior and instigating remedial action. Decision making on the other hand goes beyond control in that it includes also future planning and the assessment of the future consequences of present decisions. In this sense, control is grounded in present or past operations, and it is a combination of communication and of those aspects of decision making that refer to adaptive behavior. Whether the decision-making aspects of this feedback-control process are performed automatically by the system, through man–machine interaction or through purely human initiation, is rather immaterial. What is important is the fact that some type of decision making follows the information communicated by the control system.

The definition of control, as given above, is concerned with the allocation of resources within a given activity vector, and presupposes the existence of an objective or objectives. As a result, the type of information that is transmitted and the criteria which determine the desirability of behavior changes and remedial actions, are a function of the goals and tasks of the activity. The decisions that are generated by the control process are thus limited in scope, nature and durability, by *policy decisions that are more often determining than determined by the characteristics of the control system.* Furthermore, while the decisions motivated by control processes have their origins in the past, a major classification of decision making, as we have already pointed out, refers to future planning, control-system design, and determination of objectives and activity vectors.

We can now summarize the preceding discussion by saying that other things equal, mere control decentralization ranks lower in terms of significance than decision-making decentralization, and is included in the latter (but of course not the other way around).[9] The objective vector of a decision-decentralized unit is

[8] In stating our definitional conclusion No. 2 we pointed out that as we proceed toward more and more decentralization the hierarchical levels approach denumerable infinity, only to disappear when we reach absolute decentralization. Now we see that in the end this process results in structures that are self-sufficient in their simplest form but *highly centralized from within in their totality*.

[9] To illustrate this difference, a foreman on an assembly line has control responsibilities in administering decisions taken by higher levels in the organization. The decisions that the foreman can make (which are control-information motivated) are also part of the original decision setting up the control procedures.

usually in substantive terms, thus leaving room for the exercise of a great degree of value judgment in the process of its *translation* into operational objectives, *a process that often affects the fringes of subunit interdependence.* In contrast control-decentralization delegates to a subunit the function of ascertaining that a *given* activity vector is realized.

IV. Determinants and Characteristics of Divisionalization

We have thus far developed the expositional setting for analyzing the factors affecting centralization and decentralization of control and decision making. In the process, we have reviewed the literature, commented on the results of previous organizational research in terms of contributions, validity, and shortcomings, and then embarked on establishing the analytical definitional foundation on which we will now build.

In discussing the determinants of organizational structures, we will be viewing the various factors as affecting the internal structure of—"from within"—the particular unit. Since structures are embedded, this approach will somewhat facilitate and simplify the conceptual part of our discussion. As we have already stressed the terms centralization and decentralization are relative and not universal, and this qualification will be implied but not stated every time these notions are used.

Some Determinants of Centralized Structures

Among the factors that favor centralized structures we have:[10]

A. The Existence of Unified Overall Objectives. In our previous discussion we stressed that theoretically we cannot very well justify within an organization the existence of multiple *overall* objectives which are absolutely independent of each other, and that as a result we cannot find absolutely decentralized structures. For partial decentralization, one can assign to subentities parts of the overall objective or objectives with or without translation. This latter process requires that the objectives are in various degrees separable; consequently the translation becomes more difficult the fewer the components of the objective to be assigned. If the objective or objectives, therefore, cannot be broken into subobjectives and factored without introducing excessive interdependencies then other things equal the tendencies will be toward centralization. The difficulty, for example, in breaking the profit objective successively into many profit subobjectives, encourages cost control "decentralization" (cost centers) rather than creation of profit centers within business entities.

B. Complementarity of Resources and Operations for Accomplishing Unified Objectives. Under *A* above, we referred to the impact of objectives on organizational structures. The same type of impact will be caused by the characteristics of operations that are necessary for implementing the objectives. It can be stated, of course, that the more unified the objectives are, the more

[10] These factors are not necessarily mutually exclusive or independent but are listed separately in order to underscore certain distinct points.

complementary are usually the operations, other things equal. There is another dimension of complementarity, however, that emanates from the technological as well as technical characteristics of operations and resource utilization, which is also reflected in the design of organizational structures.

The type of complementarity that we have in mind here, implies that there exist differences in the quality of resources and that the latter are highly specialized and indivisible. If no learning processes are necessary for such specialization, or else if the benefits of specialization are smaller than the cost of independent planning, then the structure that will result in the most efficient utilization of such resources will be one of mutual interaction (non-hierarchical), which as we have previously argued is highly centralized from within in its totality. Group planning and decision making are consequences of such complementarities. But as everyone who is familiar with group activities will attest, the amount of information that is necessary for group action is often quite formidable.

C. Interdependence of the Production Functions of Suboperations. This last reason is closely related to *B* above. It simply states that, if we have extensive externalities or "super-additivities" such that for any $X_1, X_2, \cdots, X_n$ sub-operations the value generated by all together $V(X_1, X_2, \cdots, X_n)$ is always greater than the sum of the individual values $\sum_{i=1}^{n} V(X_i)$ if pursued independently, then relative centralization should be favored. The particular type of centralization that is implied here applies more to decision making than control. In other words under the conditions as described here, the most efficient structure may be characterized by centralized decision making, so as to take advantage of the complementarities, but decentralized control, given the operational objectives, in order that the organization bring intimate operational knowledge to the remedial action process. Illustrating this point is the centralized planning that is characteristic of blast furnace and ingot producing activities of steel companies.

Some Determinants of Decentralized Structures

To the extent that centralization and decentralization are complements, the absence or opposite of the factors favoring centralization will favor decentralization and vice versa. There are several other important factors favoring relative decentralization, however, which merit individual attention. These factors, which again are neither mutually exclusive nor independent, include:

A. Economies of Scale Through Specialization of Homogeneous Functions and Entities, and the Existence of a Continuous Technological Learning Process. If resources were somehow *a priori* highly complex and specialized and did not have to be channeled in certain directions at the exclusion of others, then there would be no need for decentralization and independence for "learning" purposes. We know from experience, however, that there is a lot to be learned and that there are extensive economies of scale to be realized in the learning process itself. Furthermore we often observe discontinuities in the learning function that must be overcome through persistent effort. Consequently unless resources and processes, especially human, are allowed to concentrate on their task uninterrupted for a certain period of time,[11] the economies of specialization will not be realized, progress will be stymied, and stagnation will ensue. The organization will then be composed of a library card file, which will readily be available for retrieval of information at any moment of time, with the only problem that it will not be up to date.

Once knowledge is acquired, there will be a necessity for a centralized structure to spread the benefits of such knowledge. Mass education and production require central planning and standard procedures. One must leave room, however, so that the next breakthrough, which will destroy the existing standard procedures, can develop. All this implies that a viable and progressive organization must go through continuous cycles alternating between centralization and decentralization. Alternatively, it must separate the innovating from the mass producing activities leaving the former decentralized and the latter centralized.

B. The Cost of the Channels of Communication That Are Necessary if Control and Decision Making Is to Be Centralized Within the Unit. It was pointed out previously that for non-hierarchical (equalitarian or mutual interaction) structures, "the total amount of information that has to be transmitted in the organization will grow at least proportionately with the square of its size" [16, pp. 41–42].

The reasons behind the above observations are as follows:

If we have n members in a group and decide to couple two members of the group at a time, the total number of possible pairs is given by the binomial coefficient:

$$\binom{n}{2} = n(n-1)/2 \tag{1}$$

Let us now assume that the members of the group are increased by a factor $c > 1$. Then we have

$$\binom{cn}{2} = cn(cn-1)/2. \tag{2}$$

Dividing (1) into (2) we get

$$\binom{cn}{2} \Big/ \binom{n}{2} = c^2(n^2 - n/c)/n^2 - n, \tag{3}$$

but

$$n/c < n, \qquad \text{since } c > 1. \tag{4}$$

[11] The length of the time period of independence is a function of the conflicting advantages of mutual interaction and the economies of specialization.

and as a result:

$$(n^2 - n/c)/(n^2 - n) > 1 \tag{5}$$

Hence:

$$\binom{cn}{2} \Big/ \binom{n}{2} > c^2 \tag{6}$$

So by increasing the size of the group by a factor of c we caused an increase of at least c^2 in the channels of communication. At the other extreme the channels may increase by much faster than the index of the size of the group for each new number added. As we have previously pointed out, although a structure may be equalitarian, this does not necessarily preclude a hierarchical ranking of knowledge depending on the particular task on hand. Under these conditions we may need to provide channels of communication for all subsets of the group, in addition to coupling each new member with everyone else. That is why hierarchical structures require less information for performing their tasks.

The consequences of the increase in channels of communication are many.[12] First of all we have the cost of maintaining such an information network. Then we have the cost of the time delays, red tape, and possible distortion of information, that may be introduced by the various (inevitable) "filtering devices" that normally follow communication networks. Going now to the cause of the increase in channels of communication, the mutual interaction structure, we find that the latter has a tendency to produce chaos and inaction especially as its size increases. The chaos is not unlike what happens if the members of a group try to call one another on the telephone at the same time. The probability is quite large that a lot of callers will get busy signals, that is to say a lot of noise but no message. Given that an equalitarian structure is geared toward mutual interaction, for decision making, any congestion of the channels of communication will be catastrophic since it will lead to inaction and possibly complete paralysis.

Even if the messages succeed in going through, one has to worry lest the abundance of the channels of communication leads to inaction, due to the tendency of people to "get all the information available" whenever solving problems under uncertainty. Such an eventuality reinforces the arguments presented, under *A* above, on the conflict between mutual interaction structures and learning processes, and points out—on the negative side only of course—the destructive aspects of equalitarian organizations.

[12] Our arguments here apply to all types of information systems and both formal as well as informal channels of communication. Often the informal channels of communication are more costly, especially if they are "clandestine." The often advanced claim that the informal channels of communication are more efficient, appears to us to be relative and not universal, because the comparisons are always made between informal and inefficient formal systems. After all if the information systems are efficient there will be no need for "clandestine" surrogates.

C. Uncertainty, Instabilities and the Risks of Partial Failure. Organizational structures that are equalitarian (highly centralized "from within" and non-hierarchical), often create a multifold infinity of instabilities. The latter are caused by the extensive uncertainty that has its origin in the necessity of instantaneous mutual interaction of interdependent entities. The result may be oscillations in performance that widen with time rather than dampen out and reach a desirable or at least acceptable equilibrium.

One aspect of the uncertainty that we have just mentioned is reflected in the variance of the sum of dependent random variables. Given n random variables $X_1, X_2, \cdots, X_n$ then:

$$\text{Var} \sum_{i=1}^{n} X_i = \sum_{i=1}^{n} \text{Var } X_i + 2 \sum_{i<j}^{n} \text{Cov}\,(X_i X_j)$$

or the variance of the sum of n random variables is equal to the sum of the variances plus twice the sum of the covariances of the variables taken two at a time. But the covariance:

$$\text{Cov}\,(X_i, X_j) = \rho(X_i, X_j)$$

where $\rho\,(X_i, X_j)$ stands for the correlation coefficient of the random variables X_i, X_j, and $\sigma x_i, \sigma x_j$ for their respective standard deviations. If the random variables are independent then their covariance is zero.

As a result of the above, we notice that by definition the sign of the correlation coefficient and that of the covariance of two random variables is the same. Consequently whenever the correlation coefficient is positive then the variance of the sum of interdependent activities is greater than the sum of their variances taken separately, and for $\rho < 0$ the opposite is true. If the random variables are uncorrelated, then the variance of the sum equals the sum of the variances of the random variables.

To summarize then, only in the case where the random variables are independent or uncorrelated[13] do we have an equality between the variance of a sum and the sum of the variances of random variables. Consequently if our aim is to reduce any unnecessary variance of the overall results from expected objectives,[14] then by studying the covariance matrix we can determine which operations are crucial,[15] in a possible reorganization and assignment of

[13] If the Cov $(X_i, X_j) = 0$ it does not necessarily imply that the random variables X_i and X_j are independent. In the special case of the bivariate normal distribution, zero covariance implies independence. However, in general the only statement that we can make whenever Cov $(X_i, X_j) = 0$ is that the random variables are uncorrelated since $\rho = 0$.

[14] This assumes that even in the case where the deviations of the results of operations from established goals are positive, such occurrences are not particularly desirable in the case of interdependent subactivities. Such an assumption does not appear to be unreasonable for levels below the very top, whenever extensive complementarities exist.

[15] The diagonal of this matrix represents the variance of the random variables, and the other entries are symmetric with respect to the diagonal. As a result one need only concentrate on one of the two off-diagonal sections of the matrix.

objectives and operations. This approach has been applied in one industrial situation with great success, revealing interrelationships that no one suspected.[16]

In mutual interaction structures the covariances are expected to be positive. Only in cases where a lot of flexibility with no depth is required for the common task we may find negative covariances, but then of course, we revert to the case that we cited previously where the members of such a structure perform library card-file functions. Consequently if the uncertainty, as manifested in the magnitude of the variance, is more damaging to the objectives of a group than the elimination of mutual interaction and the cost of achieving it, then operations are "decoupled" to be made "independent" or uncorrelated.[17]

One way of reducing uncertainty, is to increase the channels of communication so as to keep all operatives informed on the factors that affect their mutual progress. To a certain extent this may produce desirable results. As we have explained under *B* above, however, there exists a point beyond which the benefits of mutual interaction, in the accomplishment of common objectives, are more than negated by the cost of maintaining the instantaneous communications network that is necessary for transmitting to the operatives continuous information on the moves of each other. Furthermore, we noted certain disadvantages of interference, inaction, and mutual destructiveness that one can attribute to the abundance of channels of communication. If information is received at a high rate then the attempts toward adjustment of behavior will result in erratic patterns of performance, and also the advantages of specialization through learning that we discussed under *A* will not be realized. All these consequences of an increase in the channels of communication and the rate of information flow have been observed by the author in industrial situations.

Another avenue toward the reduction of the amount of uncertainty surrounding the accomplishment of the overall objectives of an organization, is the creation of artificial barriers or substabilities to guarantee short-run independence. In this lies one of the most important theoretical justifications of divisional—horizontal as well as vertical—structures. Intuitively we can see that if the instantaneous mutual interaction of all the operatives is necessary for the accomplishment of each and all tasks leading toward unified overall objectives, then the failure of any one operation to contribute its expected share will cause the collapse of the whole structure. Consequently, for complex organisms, partial independence through divisionalization is necessary in order to create substabilities that will guarantee the survival of parts even though the total may not be accomplished. Our body is composed of an infinite number of such substabilities. The creation of buffer inventories

[16] This experiment is still being pursued and evaluated. The results and their implications on the accounting system will be the subject of a forthcoming paper.

[17] We must stress that these are also relative terms, and that this process of study suggested here should be also used in reverse. If for example the covariance of "decentralized" operations is found to be negative then one should examine the possibility of merging the operations together.

in process, the necessity for a waiting line efficiency coefficient of less than unity, the allowance for slack time in scheduling, the habit that we have of writing down the digits that we carry forward in long-hand additions, the myriad of industrial subassemblies, the shock absorbers of cars, are just a few illustrations of substabilities for the reduction of uncertainty, and also point out the cost that is associated with their presence.

In addition to the reduction of uncertainty through partial independence, substabilities often create flexibility by enabling multiple use of the results of such substabilities, especially subassemblies. Of course this may be considered as another aspect of uncertainty elimination.

Given our arguments concerning the economies of scale through specialization under *A*, and the economies of channels of communication under *B*, we can readily infer from our discussion under *C*—"Uncertainty, instabilities and the risks of partial failure"—that the planning horizon of a firm must be divided into two parts.

1. A period of artificial independence that is necessary for learning and specialization.
2. A period of duration longer than that of artificial independence over which the subunits need reassurance and guidance on the state of the external (to themselves) environment before these can effectively plan.

Any information and control system, as a result, must be aimed at satisfying these two basic planning needs of each particular subunit. It must, first of all, shield each subunit during the time it needs for learning and specialization from any extraneous information, and concentrate on providing "continuous" internally generated data. Secondly, it must provide periodic[18] information on all the "external" factors that affect the subunit's goal orientation and performance, in order to enable the subunit to plan for its subsequent period of isolation.

We must stress here two points that should be more or less obvious:

1. that the terms "internal" and "external" information are relative to the unit. What governs the appropriateness of information are the interrelationships that affect the subunit's objectives. As we go higher up in the organizational structure of the firm, we will find that part of the "external" information that is required is even external to the firm itself. And
2. that the system should have in it appropriate diagnostic properties and provisions for "two-way emergency interruption" procedures.

To summarize then, we have noticed that for the reduction of uncertainty an organization may divisionalize its structure and create substabilities (partial independence). The process by means of which decisions are made concerning the type of substability—how much, how far—is one of trial and error, due to the infinity of practical alternatives. In theory, however, we can say that,

[18] The length of the period is determined by the duration of artificial independence.

other things remaining equal, a marginal divisionalization (for elimination of uncertainty) is justified if:

(a) The expected value of overall goal accomplishment as generated by the various subunits into which the organization is to be divided, less the expected cost of:
  (i) the buffers or neutral zones that will be necessary for creating the artificial short-run independence and substability
  (ii) the information system that will provide "continuous" internal feedback and
  (iii) the periodic channels of communication that will serve for conditioning the expectations of the various subunits on the state of nature of the overall organization during the periods of assumed independence,

is greater than:

(b) The existing value of goal accomplishment less the channels of communication necessitated under conditions of relative mutual interdependence.

Finally, we must point out that the expected value of goal accomplishment under (a) and (b) may differ not only because the applicable probabilistic distributions are different, but also because the values of the variables are different. The difference in the values of the variables (goal accomplishment) may have its origin in at least two major sources:

1. The fact that any subdivision of a unitary objective involves sub-optimizations which will be also manifested in the additivity of the expected values of goal accomplishment as generated by the subunits. Under such circumstances, the summed value of the parts *expressed in terms of particular subunit criteria of efficiency* will be greater than the value of the end result to the overall organization.
2. The assumption of independence between the activities of the various subunits over the period of isolation.

D. Psychological Reasons of Motivation. Although the area of psychology of motivation is a vast field of esoteric issues to which we cannot do justice by a purely cursory exposition, we feel that we must say a few words on those aspects of this subject that relate to our main topic of discussion.

It has been claimed by many researchers in the field of human relations–social psychology, that equalitarian structures offer more satisfaction to the members of an organization than authoritarian structures [7], [8, Ch. 12, 18], [13]. Implicitly they criticize and attribute to "authority, controls and hierarchical structures" negative attitudes on the part of the workers and low productivity. While cases can be cited which substantiate these contentions,[19] yet as we have pointed out here and elsewhere [21], control systems and hier-

[19] Actually it is the wrong application and not the existence of controls that is causing trouble.

archical structures are necessary for economic reasons. But even on purely psychological grounds there is no theoretical justification for general condemnation of controls, nor is there any basis for expecting all people to be average members of average groups and purely externally (group) motivated. As long as the tasks are not homogeneous and there are differences among individuals, especially in terms of capacity to work with non-programmable tasks and uncertainty, there will be hierarchical stratifications. Furthermore, we have previously shown that equalitarian structures, although democratic and externally decentralized, are paradoxically centralized from within in their totality. Consequently, if we accept that recognition for outstanding accomplishments is a major factor in motivation and performance, non-equalitarian and relative decentralized structures will prove to be more efficient, because only then can the individual associate "end results" with his own efforts.

Although, certain aspects of decision making—especially those that refer to remedial action—cannot be divorced from control, there are others that are concerned more with future planning rather than with the study of the past.[20] The determinants of decentralized structures that we have so far analyzed apply more to the process of control, given objectives, than to decision making. Now we will turn to two issues that are concerned relatively more with decision making and with what we have previously termed the fringes of subunit and interperiod interdependence.

E. Time Sensitivity of Decisions. In determining where the locus of decision making should rest, one has to examine among other things the time sensitivity of the particular decisions. If the decision is made by the subunit, as we have already pointed out, it is in certain aspects suboptimal. However, the reaction time is faster, by the amount of time it takes for the following necessary steps to be performed.

1. The information system must first recognize the necessity for a decision, and transmit a signal indicating the necessity for remedial action, to a decision-making locus outside the subunit.
2. The outside locus must then analyze the information, digest it, recognize the existence and nature of the problem, associate it with other similar occurrences if any, determine the consequence of alternative courses of action, structure a decision and translate it into operational instructions, and finally

[20] This is not to deny that all decision making carries the advantages of study of the past. Nor can we claim that future planning is completely divorced of the output of control processes. The mere cognizance of the need for future planning is nothing more than the result of a more general feedback control system, that is partly external to existing operations. So for the total organization *as well as for each subunit,* there are hierarchies of information and control systems, with the more complicated referring to the longest feasible long-run decision making on top of the ladder, and the less sophisticated concerned with the short-run decision-feedback control of day-to-day operations at the bottom. And this let us repeat applies to the subunit as much as it does to the whole firm. Implicit here, of course, is the assumption that the impact of decisions on the overall objectives of the firm is lessened as one moves down in the hierarchy.

3. The information system must return the instructions to the point of action.

Consequently, if the expected cost of adverse effect during any period of a subunit's inaction (while waiting for instructions) plus the cost of the centralized information system are greater than the expected loss due to a relatively suboptimal decision at a low level, then decentralization of decision making is justified.

A major assumption behind the necessity for transmission of the information upward for instructions, is that higher levels in a hierarchical structure can make more optimal decisions although removed from the point of action (but see item *F* below). This is so mainly because at those levels people observe more and different interrelationships, and can recognize patterns that others at lower levels cannot recognize because they are preoccupied with limited details.[21] As we have argued previously, any translation of unified objectives to many subobjectives is per se suboptimal. Furthermore, in order to establish false independence and eliminate uncertainty, organizations buffer their subunits and thus hide existing interrelationships at the subunit level. That is mainly why the scope of subunits is limited.

F. Task Characteristics. Another factor that affects decentralization of decision making is inherent in the task characteristics. The latter are reflected, as we have already pointed out, in the degree of separability of operational objectives and activities, and the degree of interdependence introduced at the point of translation. The relevant question that has to be answered here, now is as follows: Is on-the-spot knowledge more vital for planning than the external subunit interrelationships? If the answer is yes, then other things being equal decentralization of decision making is advisable. If, on the other hand, the accomplishment of the objectives of a potential subunit is more dependent upon forces that originate outside the subunit than upon the knowledge generated from within, then the decision-making locus is placed outside the subunit.

From the short discussion on the time sensitivity of decisions and task characteristics, it appears, that if an organizational subentity is decentralized from without because of the specialized knowledge of the immediate operatives, then internally the subunit will probably operate in an equalitarian fashion. In contrast, if the external decentralization was dictated by the time sensitivity of decisions, then internally the subunit will probably be hierarchical and relatively decentralized.

In our previous arguments concerning centralization and decentralization of control and decision making, we concerned ourselves mostly with the qualitative characteristics of the various theoretical aspects of divisionaliza-

[21] Of course this can work both ways and may result in suboptimal centralized decisions. Also we must not forget the arguments that we presented when discussing the impact of the channels of communication. People at higher levels may be fed with so much information (often colored), that they may be unable to digest it and in the end make a poorer decision on a centralized basis.

tion, and thus had a single system of classification. It has been pointed out often in practice, a *general* category of decisions and controls may be vested with a subunit, provided that the quantitative level of a particular decision is not "catastrophic" for the subunit.[22] And this, not because the subunit "cannot be trusted" or because of excessive interunit interdependence, but possibly because of somehow general-inherent characteristics and capacities of people at the various levels in the hierarchy to think and behave in quantitative terms relative to the scope of their existing operations.[23]

A partial explanation of the above-mentioned observation can be found in our previous discussion concerning the risk of failure and its impact on the long-run existence of the subentity. In order to increase the probability of survival of the subunit as well as the total organization, management should impose quantitative constraints at the various levels of the hierarchy. Also, the limited exposure of the subunits to single large problems—of a magnitude that necessitates marshalling resources that are quite large relative to those in use—will undoubtedly affect the probability of subunit success adversely. Consequently it is not unreasonable to use an explicit quantitative constraint in addition to what we have suggested, in approaching problems of divisionalization.

Finally a comment on the implications of our discussion on personnel placement. We have argued that hierarchical structures, among other things, eliminate value judgments as one goes down the hierarchical ladder. Such an elimination of value judgment implies that the uncertainty surrounding the particular task environment is also reduced. Consequently, one of the critical factors that will determine the success or failure of the people who head the various subunits will be their capacity to adjust and effectively cope with the conditions of uncertainty that characterize their particular operations. As this capacity to live with uncertainty grows, the scope of their responsibilities should be also extended. Those who do not pass this test and cannot stand the pressures that decision making under uncertainty brings about, should be placed in positions where they will be dealing with programmable tasks and thus be led rather than lead.

References

1. Argyris, C., *The Impact of Budgets on People,* Cornell University, School of Business and Public Administration, New York, 1952.
2. Arrow, Kenneth J., "Optimization, Decentralization and Internal Pricing in Business Firms" in *Contributions to Scientific Research in Management,* Western Data Processing Center, University of California, Los Angeles, 1959, pp. 9–18.

[22] The author wishes to thank Frank H. Tyaack of Westinghouse for suggesting this dichotomy, and for providing empirical evidence attesting its significance.

[23] Capital budgeting procedures among other business practices seem to be based on such assumptions. Of course we must not exclude the possibility that such a behavior may be the result of successful managerial constraints rather than emanate from basic human characteristics.

3. Barnard, Chester I., *The Functions of the Executive,* Harvard University Press, Cambridge, 1938.
4. Cooper, W. W., "A Proposal for Extending the Theory of the Firm," *Quarterly Journal of Economics,* Vol. LXV, No. 1, February 1951, pp. 87–109.
5. ——, "The Theory of the Firm: Some Suggestions for Revision," *American Economic Review,* Vol. XXXIX, No. 6, December 1959, pp. 1204–1222.
6. Drucker, Peter, *The Practice of Management,* Harper and Brothers, New York, 1954.
7. Haire, Mason, "Philosophy of Organization," *Management Organization and Planning,* D. M. Bowman and F. M. Fillerup, Eds., McGraw-Hill Book Company, Inc., New York, 1963, pp. 1–16.
8. Leavitt, Harold J., *Managerial Psychology,* The University of Chicago Press, Chicago, Illinois, 1959.
9. March, James G. and Simon, Herbert A., *Organizations,* John Wiley & Sons, Inc., New York, 1958.
10. Marschak, Jacob, "Elements of a Theory of Teams," *Management Science,* January 1955, Vol. 1, No. 2, pp. 127–137.
11. ——, "Toward an Economic Theory of Organization and Information," *Decision Processes,* Thrall et al., Eds., New York, 1954, Ch. XIV.
12. McGregor, Douglas, *The Human Side of Enterprise,* McGraw-Hill Book Company, Inc., New York, 1960.
13. Myers, Charles A., "Lessons from Abroad for American Management," *The Journal of Business,* January, 1960, Vol. 33, No. 1, reprinted in Madenheim, Mazze and Stein, *Readings in Organization and Management,* Holt, Rinehart and Winston, New York, 1963, pp. 465–475.
14. Papendreou, Andreas G., "Some Problems in the Theory of the Firm," *A Survey of Contemporary Economics,* Vol. II, Haley Eds., Richard D. Irwin, Inc., Homewood, Illinois, 1952, pp. 183–219.
15. Shillinglaw, Gordon, *Cost Accounting: Analysis and Control,* Richard D. Irwin, Inc., Homewood, Illinois, 1961.
16. Simon, Herbert A., *The New Science of Management Decision,* Harper & Row, New York and Evanston, 1960.
17. ——, *Administrative Behavior,* The Macmillan Company, New York, 1957, (Second Edition).
18. ——, *Centralization and Decentralization in Organizing the Controllers' Department,* Graduate School of Industrial Administration, Carnegie Institute of Technology, 1954.
19. Wagner, Harvey M., *Statistical Management of Inventory Systems,* John Wiley and Sons, New York, 1962.
20. Whinston, A. *Price Co-ordination in Decentralized Systems,* O. N. R. Research Memorandum No. 99, Carnegie Institute of Technology, June 1962.
21. Zannetos, Zenon S., "Some Thoughts on Internal Control Systems of the Firm," *The Accounting Review,* Vol. XXXIX, No. 4, October 1964, pp. 860–869.

27

Making Project Management Work

John M. Stewart

Late last year, with a good deal of local fanfare, a leading food producer opened a new plant in a small midwestern town. For the community it was a festive day. For top management, however, the celebration was somewhat dampened by the fact that the plant had missed its original target date by six months and had overrun estimated costs by a cool $5 million.

A material-handling equipment maker's latest automatic lift truck was an immediate market success. But a few more successes of the same kind would spell disaster for the company. An actual introduction cost of $2.6 million, compared to planned expenses of $1.2 million, cut the company's profits by fully 10 percent last year.

A new high-speed, four-color press installed by a leading eastern printing concern has enabled a major consumer magazine to sharply increase its color pages and offer advertisers unprecedented schedule convenience. The printer will not be making money on the press for years, however. Developing and installing it took twice as long and cost nearly three times as much as management had expected.

Fiascos such as these are as old as business itself—as old, indeed, as organized human effort. The unfortunate Egyptian overseer who was obliged, 5,000 years ago, to report to King Cheops that construction work on the Great Pyramid at Giza had fallen a year behind schedule had much in common with the vice-president who recoils in dismay as he and the chief executive discover that their new plant will be months late in delivering the production on which a major customer's contract depends. The common thread: poor management of a large, complex, one-time "project" undertaking.

But unlike the Egyptian overseer, today's businessman has available to him a set of new and powerful management tools with the demonstrated capacity to avert time and cost overruns on massive, complex projects. These tools, developed only recently, are not yet in common use outside the construction and aerospace industries, where such projects are a way of life. But there is already solid evidence that they can be successfully applied to a host of important, nonroutine business undertakings where conventional planning and control techniques fail—undertakings ranging from a new-product introduction or the launching of a national advertising campaign to the installation of an EDP system or a merger of two major corporations (Figures 1 and 2).

Reprinted from *Business Horizons,* Fall 1965, pp. 54–68.

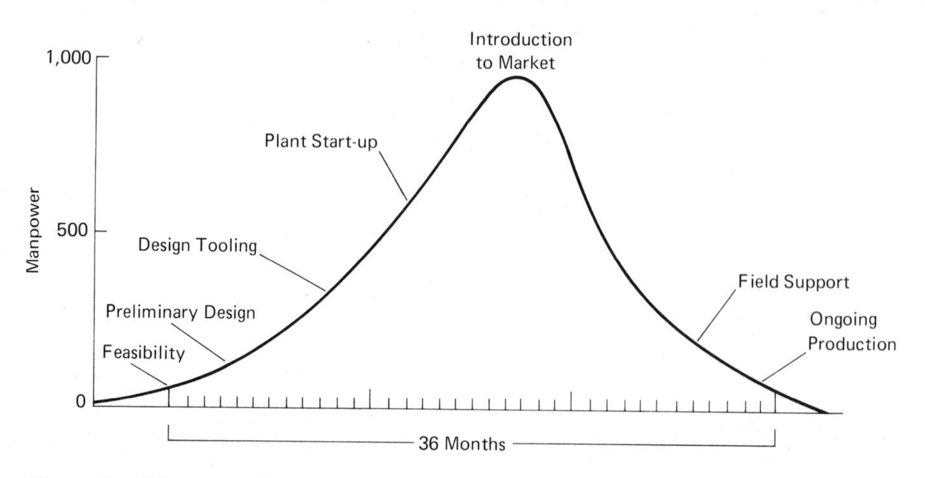

Figure 1. Manpower Commitment to a New-product Introduction Project

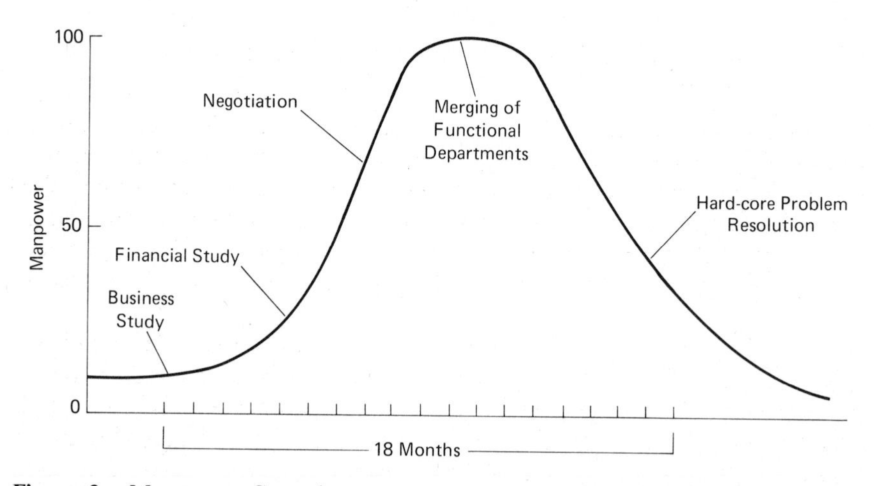

Figure 2. Manpower Commitment to a Merger Project

Project Management Organization

Commercial project management is usually a compromise between two forms of organization—pure project management and the more standard functional alignment. In the aerospace and construction companies (Figure 3), complete responsibility for the task, as well as all the resources needed for its accomplishment, is usually assigned to one project manager. In very large projects, the organization he heads, which will be dissolved at the conclusion of the project, resembles a regular division, relatively independent of any other division or staff group. Outside the aerospace and construction

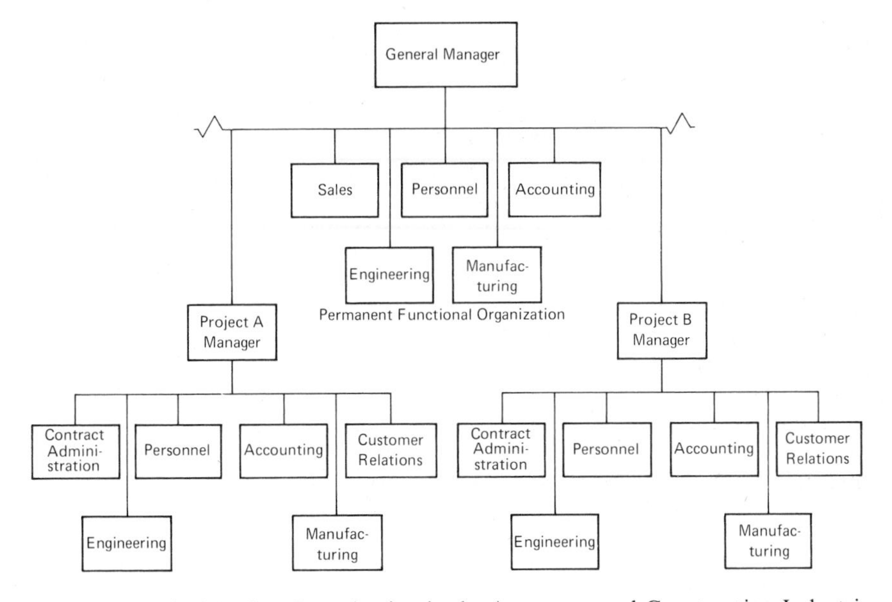

Figure 3. Typical Project Organization in the Aerospace and Construction Industries

industries, however, the project manager is usually not assigned complete responsibility for resources (Figure 4). Instead, he shares them with the rest of the organization. He may have a project organization consisting of a handful of men on temporary assignment from the regular functional organization. The functional managers, however, retain their direct line authority, monitor their staffs' contributions to the project, and continue to make all major personnel decisions.

Reluctance to adopt new tools is typical in any industry; thus, one should not expect the tools of project management to gain instant acceptance. Outside the aerospace industry, few business executives appreciate their value and versatility. Fewer still are able to recognize the need for project management in specific situations, nor do they know how to use the powerful control techniques it offers. Meanwhile, the few companies that have grasped the significance of the new management concepts and learned to apply them enjoy an extraordinary, if temporary, advantage. They are bringing new products to market faster than their competitors, completing major expansions on schedule, and meeting crucial commitments more reliably than ever before.

Project management, however, is far from being a cure-all for the embarrassments, expenses, and delays that plague even the best-managed companies. First, project management requires temporary shifts of responsibilities and reporting relationships that may disturb the smooth functioning of the regular organization. Second it requires unusually disciplined executive effort.

Basic to successful management is the ability to recognize where it is needed and where it is not. When, in short, is a project a project? Where, in the broad

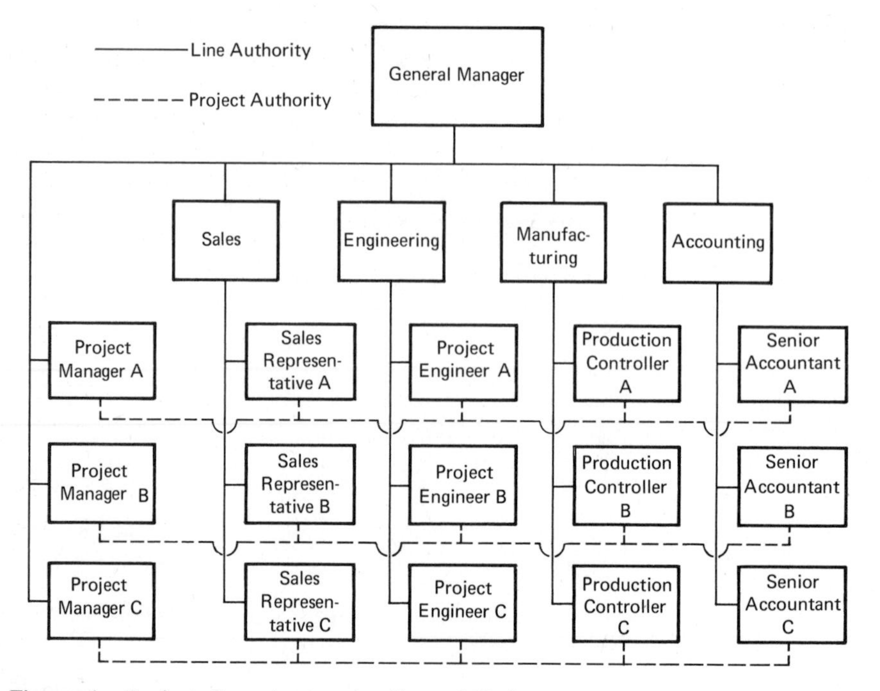

Figure 4. Project Organization in General Industry

spectrum of undertakings between a minor procedural modification and a major organizational upheaval, should the line be drawn? At what point do a multitude of minor departures from routine add up to the "critical mass" that makes project management operationally and economically desirable? Senior executives must have methods to identify those undertakings, corporate or divisional, that cannot be successfully managed by the regular functional organization working with routine planning and control methods. Although there are no simple rules of thumb, management can determine whether a given undertaking possesses this critical mass by applying four yardsticks: scope, unfamiliarity, complexity, and stake.

Scope

Project management can be profitably applied, as a rule, to a one-time undertaking that is (1) definable in terms of a single, specific end result, and (2) bigger than the organization has previously undertaken successfully. A project must, by definition, end at an objective point in time: the date the new plant achieves full production, the date the parent company takes over operating management of the new acquisition, or the date the new product goes on sale in supermarkets across the nation, to name a few.

The question of size is less easily pinned down. But where substantially more people, more dollars, more organizational units, and more time will be involved than on any other infrequent undertaking in the organization's experience, the test result is clearly positive. Such an undertaking, even though its component parts may be familiar, can easily overwhelm a divisional or corporate management. Project management forces a logical approach to the project, speeds decision making, and cuts management's job to a reasonable level. For example, a large service company, with years of experience in district offices, established a project organization to renovate its 400 district offices over a two-year period. Even though each task was relatively simple, the total undertaking would have swamped the administrative organization had it been managed routinely.

In terms of the number of people and the organizational effort it involves, a project could typically be charted over time as a wave-like curve, rising gradually to a crest and dropping off abruptly with the accomplishment of the end result. Consider, for example, the introduction of a new consumer product. The project begins with a few people studying the desirability of adding a product to the line. After some early decisions to proceed, perhaps a few dozen engineers are employed to design the product. Their work passes to scores of process planners, tool makers, and other manufacturing engineers, and finally involves entire manufacturing plants or divisions as the first month's production gains momentum. This momentum carries into the field as salesmen increase their efforts to introduce the product successfully. Finally, the project effort ebbs as the new product is integrated into routine production and marketing operation.

Again, a merger typically shows a similar "growth and decay" project pattern. Initially, a few senior executives from each company may be involved in discussing the merger possibility. As interest grows, financial and legal advisors are engaged by both sides. Key inside executives are added to the task force to assist in planning. Then, as the deal moves toward completion, widening circles of executives, technical people, and analysts become involved in identifying the changes required after merger. Once the merger has been approved by the directors and stockholders of the two companies, the process of meshing the philosophies, structures, policies, and procedures of the two organizations must begin, possibly requiring the active participation of hundreds or even thousands of people. Eventually, as most of the changes are accomplished, employees return to their normal duties, and the corporation resumes its orderly march toward the end of the fiscal year. The merger project is at an end.

Unfamiliarity

An undertaking is not a project, in our sense of the term, unless it is a unique, or infrequent, effort by the existing management group. Lack of familiarity or lack of precedent usually leads to disagreement or uncertainty as to how the undertaking should be managed. In such a situation, people at the lower management levels need to be told more precisely what they are to do, while senior executives are justifiably troubled by a greater than usual sense of uncertainty about the realism of initial cost estimates, time commitments, or both.

Thus, though a single engineering change to one part of a product would not qualify for project management by this criterion, the complete redesign of a product line that had been basically unchanged for a decade would in most cases call for project management treatment. Individual managers could accomplish the first change easily, drawing on their own past experience, but each would have to feel his way by trial and error through the second.

Complexity

Frequently the decisive criterion of a project is the degree of interdependence among tasks. If a given task depends on the completion of other assignments in other functional areas, and if it will, in turn, affect the cost or timing of subsequent tasks, project management is probably called for. Consider the introduction of a hypothetical new product. Sales promotion plans cannot be completed until introduction dates are known; introduction dates depend upon product availability; and availability depends on tooling, which depends in turn on the outcome of a disagreement between engineering and product planning over performance specifications. There are many comparable interdependencies among marketing, engineering, manufacturing, and finance. If, as seems likely in this situation, no one person can produce a properly detailed plan on which all those concerned can agree; if estimates repeatedly fail to withstand scrutiny; or if plans submitted by different departments prove difficult to reconcile or coordinate, the critical mass of a project has probably been reached.

Stake

A final criterion that may tip the scales in favor of project management is the company's stake in the outcome of the undertaking. Would failure to complete the job on schedule or within the budget entail serious penalties for the company? If so, the case for project management is strong.

The corporate stake in the outcome of a project is commonly financial; that is, the failure of a $50,000 engineering project might jeopardize $12 million in annual sales. But it may also involve costs of a different kind. As more than one World's Fair exhibitor can attest, failure to meet a well-publicized project schedule can sometimes do real harm to a company's reputation. Again, failure to meet time and cost objectives may seriously disrupt corporate plans, as in the case of an equipment manufacturer who was obliged to abandon a promising new product line when a poorly-managed merger soaked up earnings that had been earmarked for R&D on the new line. In all such cases, the powerful controls of project management offer a much firmer prospect of meeting the time, cost, and quality objectives of the major one-time undertaking.

The specific advantages of project management for ventures that meet the criteria just discussed are easily summarized. Project management provides the concentrated management attention that a complex and unfamiliar undertaking is likely to demand. It greatly improves, at very small cost, the chances of on-time, on-budget completion. And it permits the rest of the organization to proceed normally with routine business while the project is under way. But these benefits are available only if top management clearly understands the unique features of project management, the problems it entails, and the steps required to make it work.

The Nature of Project Management

With respect to organization, project management calls for the appointment of one man, the project manager, who has responsibility for the detailed planning, coordination, and ultimate outcome of the project. Usually appointed from the middle management ranks, the project manager is supplied with a team, often numbering no more than half a dozen men for a $10 million project.

Team members, drawn from the various functional departments involved in the project, report directly to the project manager. For the duration of the project, he has the authority to insist on thorough planning, the freedom to challenge functional departments' assumptions and targets, and the responsibility to monitor every effort bearing on the successful completion of the project.

Within the limits of the project, the project manager's responsibility and authority are functional, like that of top management for the company as a whole. Despite this similarity, however, his function cannot safely be superimposed on a top executive's normal workload. Every company I know that has tried giving operating responsibility for the management of a complex project to a division manager has found that he is soon swamped in a tidal wave of detail. Most projects call for more and faster decisions than does routine work, and clear precedents are usually lacking. Thus, a general manager who tries to run one of his own projects seldom has any guidelines for making reliable cost and time estimates, establishing cost control at commitment points, or setting adequately detailed targets for each department. Lacking precedents, he is obliged to invent them. This procedure may drain off far more of his time than the division can afford, without really providing the project with the concentrated attention it needs. He may well find that he is spending better than half his working time trying to manage a project representing less than a tenth of his division's annual budget, while divisional performance as a whole is slipping alarmingly. For these reasons, few projects are ever successfully managed on a part-time basis.

The essence of project management is that it cuts across, and in a sense conflicts with, the normal organization structure. Throughout the project, personnel at various levels in many functions of the business contribute to it. Because a project usually requires decisions and actions from a number of functional areas at once, the main interdependencies and the main flow of information in a project are not vertical but lateral. Up-and-down information flow is relatively light in a well-run project; indeed, any attempt to consistently send needed information from one functional area up to a common authority and down to another area through conventional channels is apt to cripple the project and wreck the time schedule.

Projects are also characterized by exceptionally strong lateral working relationships, requiring closely related activity and decisions by many individuals in different functional departments. During a major product development, for example, a design engineer will work more closely with the process engineer manager and the product manager from marketing than with the senior members of his own department. He will need common sense and tolerance to succeed in the scramble for available resources, such as test-cell time or the help of metallurgical specialists, without hurting relationships of considerable importance to his future career.

Necessarily though, a project possesses a vertical as well as a horizontal dimension, since those who are involved in it at various stages, particularly those who make the technical decisions that determine costs, must often go to their superiors for guidance. Moreover, frequent project changes underline the necessity of keeping senior executives informed of the project's current status.

Special Sources of Trouble

Understandably, project managers face some unusual problems in trying to direct and harmonize the diverse forces at work in the project situation. Their main difficulties, observation suggests, arise from three sources: organizational uncertainties, unusual decision pressures, and vulnerability to top-management mistakes.

Organizational Uncertainties

Many newly appointed project managers find that their working relationships with functional department heads have not been clearly defined by management. Who assigns work to the financial analyst? Who decides when to order critical material before the product design is firm? Who decides to delay design release to reduce unit cost? Who determines the quantity and priority of spares? All these decisions vitally concern the project manager, and he must often forge his own guidelines for dealing with them. Unless he does so skillfully, the questions are apt to be resolved in the interest of individual departments, at the expense of the project as a whole.

Because of the number of decisions or approvals that may arise in the course of a large project, and the number of departments that have an interest in each, innumerable possibilities always exist for interdepartmental conflicts. Besides coping with these conflicts, the project manager must juggle the internal schedules of each department with the project schedule, avoid political problems that could create bottlenecks, expedite one department to compensate for another's failure to meet its schedule, and hold the project within a predetermined cost. Moreover, he must do all this single-handed, with little or none of the experienced top-management guidance that the line manager enjoys.

Unusual Decision Pressures

The severe penalties of delay often compel the project manager to base his decisions on relatively few data, analyzed in haste. On a large project where a day's delay may cost $10,000 in salaries alone, he can hardly hold everything up for a week to perform an analysis that could save the company $5,000. He must move fast, even if it means an intuitive decision that might expose him to charges of rashness and irresponsibility from functional executives. Decisions to sacrifice time for cost, cost for quality, or quality for time, are common in most projects, and the project manager must be able to make them without panicking. Clearly, therefore, he has a special need for intelligent support from higher management.

Vulnerability to Top-Management Mistakes

Though senior executives can seldom give the project manager as much guidance and support as his line counterpart enjoys, they can easily jeopardize the project's success by lack of awareness, ill-advised intervention, or personal whim. The damage that a senior executive's ignorance of a project situation can create is well illustrated by the following example. A project manager, battling to meet a schedule that had been rendered nearly impossible by the general manager's initial delay in approving the proposal, found functional cooperation more and more difficult to obtain. The functional heads, he discovered, had become convinced—rightly, as it turned out—that he lacked the general manager's full confidence. Unknown to the project manager, two department heads whom he had pressured to expedite their departments had complained to the general manager, who had readily sympathized. The project manager, meanwhile, had been too busy getting the job done to protect himself with top management. As a result, project performance was seriously hampered.

Executive Action Required

Because of the great diversity of projects and the lack of common terminology for the relatively new techniques of project management, useful specific rules for project management are virtually impossible to formulate. From the experience of the aerospace and construction industries and of a handful of companies in other industries, however, it is possible to distill some general guidelines.

Guideline 1: Define the Objective

Performing unfamiliar activities at a rapid pace, those involved in the project can easily get off the right track or fall short of meeting their commitments, with the result that many steps of the project may have to be retraced. To minimize this risk, management must clarify the objective of the project well in advance by (1) defining management's intent in undertaking the project, (2) outlining the scope of the project, that is, identifying the departments, companies, functions, and staffs involved, and the approximate degree of their involvement, and (3) describing the end results of the project and its permanent effects, if any, on the company or division.

Defining Management's Intent. What are the business reasons for the project? What is top management's motive in undertaking it?

A clear common understanding of the answers to these questions is desirable for three reasons. *First,* it enables the project manager to capitalize on opportunities to improve the outcome of the project. By knowing top management's rationale for building the new plant, for example, he will be be able to weigh the one-time cost of plant startup against the continuing advantage of lower production costs, or the competitive edge that might be gained by an earlier product introduction. *Second,* a clear definition of intent helps avert damaging oversights that would otherwise appear unimportant to lower-level managers and might not be obvious to the senior executive. One company failed to get any repeat orders for a unique product because the project team, unaware of the president's intent, saw their job only in terms of meeting their schedule and cost commitments and neglected to cultivate the market. *Third,* a definition of the intent of the project helps to avoid imbalance of effort at the middle-management level, such as pushing desperately to meet a schedule but missing cost-reduction opportunities on the way.

Outlining the Scope of the Project. Which organizational units of the company will be involved in the project, and to what degree? Which sensitive customer relationship, private or governmental, should the project manager cautiously skirt? By crystallizing the answers and communicating them to the organization, the responsible senior executive will make it far easier for the project manager to work with the functional departments and to get the information he needs.

Describing the End Results. Top managers who have spent hours discussing a proposed project can easily overlook the fact that middle managers charged with its execution lack their perspective on the project. An explicit description of how a new plant will operate when it is in full production, how a sales reorganization will actually change customer relationships, or how major staff activities will be coordinated after a merger, gives middle managers a much clearer view of what the project will involve and what is expected of them.

Guideline 2: Establish a Project Organization

For a functionally organized company, successful project management means establishing, for the duration of the project, a workable compromise between two quite different organizational concepts. The basic ingredients of such a compromise are (1) appointment of one experienced manager to run the project full-time, (2) organization of the project management function in terms of responsibilities, (3) assignment of a limited number of men to the project team, and (4) maintenance of a balance of power between the functional heads and the project manager. In taking these steps, some generally accepted management rules may have to be broken, and some organizational friction will almost inevitably occur. But the results in terms of successful project completion should far outweigh these drawbacks and difficulties.

Assigning an Experienced Manager. Though the project manager's previous experience is apt to have been confined to a single functional area of the business, he must be able to function on the project as a kind of general manager in miniature. He must not only keep track of what is happening but also play the crucial role of advocate for the project. Even for a seasoned manager, this task is not likely to be easy. Hence, it is important to assign an individual whose administrative abilities and skill in personal relations have been convincingly demonstrated under fire.

Organizing the Project Manager's Responsibilities. While some organizational change is essential, management should try to preserve, wherever possible, the established relationships that facilitate rapid progress under pressure. Experience indicates that it is desirable for senior management to delegate to the project manager some of its responsibilities for planning the project, for resolving arguments among functional departments, for providing problem-solving assistance to functional heads, and for monitoring progress. A full-time project manager can better handle these responsibilities; moreover, the fact that they are normally part of the executive job helps to establish his stature. A general manager, however, should not delegate certain responsibilities, such as monitoring milestone accomplishments, resolving project-related disputes between senior managers, or evaluating the project performance of functional department managers. The last responsibility strikes too close to the careers of the individuals concerned to be delegated to one of their peers.

For the duration of the project, the project manager should also hold some responsibilities normally borne by functional department heads. These include responsibility for reviewing progress against schedule; organizing for, formulating, and approving a project plan; monitoring project cost performance; and, in place of the department heads normally involved, trading off time and cost. Also, the senior executive must encourage the project manager to direct the day-to-day activities of all functional personnel who are involved full-time in the project. Functional department heads, however, should retain responsibility for the quality of their subordinates' technical performance, as well as for matters affecting their careers.

Limiting the Project Team. Functional department heads may view the project manager as a potential competitor. By limiting the number of men on the project team, this problem is alleviated and the project manager's involvement in intrafunctional matters is reduced. Moreover, men transferred out of their own functional departments are apt to lose their inside sources of information and find it increasingly difficult to get things done rapidly and informally.

Maintaining the Balance of Power. Because the project manager is concerned with change, while the department head must efficiently manage routine procedures, the two are often in active conflict. Though they should be encouraged to resolve these disputes without constant appeal to higher authority, their common superior must occasionally act as mediator. Otherwise, resentments and frustrations will impair the project's progress and leave a long-lasting legacy of bitterness. Short-term conflicts can often be resolved in favor of the project manager and long-term conflicts in favor of the functional managers. This compromise helps to reduce friction, to get the job accomplished, and to prepare for the eventual phasing out of the project.

Guideline 3: Install Project Controls

Though they use the same raw data as routine reports, special project controls over time, cost, and quality are very different in their accuracy, timing, and use. They are normally superimposed upon the existing report structure for the duration of the project and then discontinued. The crucial relationship between project time control and cost control is shown graphically in Figure 5.

The project in question had to be completed in twenty months instead of the twenty and a half months scheduled by a preliminary network calculation. The project manager, who was under strict initial manpower limitations, calculated the cost of the two weeks' acceleration at various stages of the project. Confronted by the evidence of the costs it could save, top management approved the project manager's request for early acceleration. The project

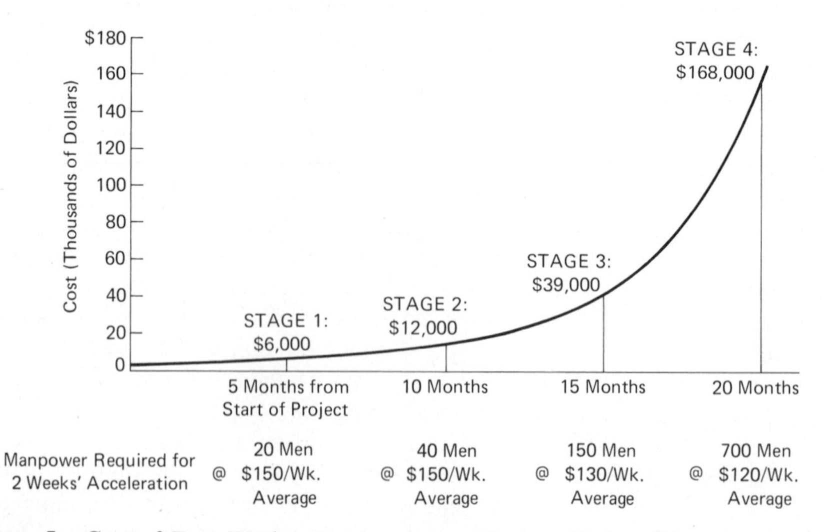

Figure 5. Cost of Two Weeks' Acceleration at Various Project Stages

was completed two working days before its twenty-month deadline, at a cost only $6,000 over the original estimate. Without controls that clearly relate time to cost, companies too often crash the project in its final stages, at enormous and entirely unnecessary cost.

Time Control. Almost invariably, some form of network scheduling provides the best time control of a project. A means of graphically planning a complex undertaking so that it can be scheduled for analysis and control, network scheduling begins with the construction of a diagram that reflects the interdependencies and time requirements of the individual tasks that go to make up a project. It calls for work plans prepared in advance of the project in painstaking detail, scheduling each element of the plan, and using controls to ensure that commitments are met.

At the outset, each department manager involved in the project should draw up a list of all the tasks required of his department to accomplish the project. Then the project manager should discuss each of these lists in detail with the respective departmental supervisors in order to establish the sequence in the project in relation to other departments. Next, each manager and supervisor should list the information he will need from other departments, indicating which data, if any, are habitually late. This listing gives the project manager not only a clue to the thoroughness of planning in the other departments but also a means of uncovering and forestalling most of the inconsistencies, missed activities, or inadequate planning that would otherwise occur.

Next, having planned its own role in the project, each department should be asked to commit itself to an estimate of the time required for each of its project activities, assuming the required information is supplied on time. After this, the complete network is constructed, adjusted where necessary with the agreement of the department heads concerned, and reviewed for logic.

Once the overall schedule is established, weekly or fortnightly review meetings should be held to check progress against schedule. Control must be rigorous, especially at the start, when the tone of the entire project is invariably set. Thus, the very first few missed commitments call for immediate corrective action.

In critical path scheduling, one of the major network techniques, the diagram is similar in principle to that of Figure 6 for a very simple hypothetical project.

In the diagram, each arrow represents a defined task, with a clear begin-

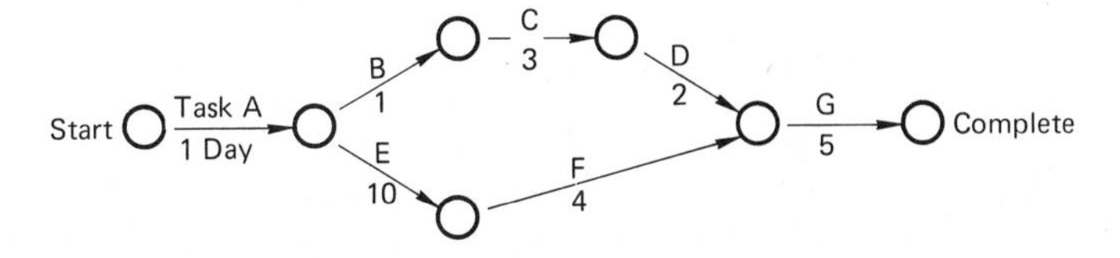

Figure 6. A Simple Critical Path Network

ning, end, and time requirement, that can be delegated to a single manager or supervisor. Each circle, or node (except the "start" node), represents the completion of a task. Task A, for example, might be "Define the technical objectives of the project." The numeral 1 indicates that the allotted time for its completion is one day.

The arrangement of the arrows is significant. As drawn here, B depends upon A; that is, it may not start until A *is* complete. Similarly, C may not start until B is complete. Also, while B and E may start at different times, neither may start until A is complete. Further along, G may not start until both D and F are complete. This diagram, then, is one of *sequence* and *dependency*.

The time required for the project corresponds to the longest part through the network from Start to Complete in terms of the time requirement associated with each task. In the diagram above, A-E-F-G is the critical path. To meet the overall schedule, each of these tasks must begin as soon as its predecessor is completed and must end within its allotted time. To shorten the schedule, one or more of the tasks on the critical part must be accelerated.

There are other more complex varieties of network scheduling. Critical path method calculates both normal and crash schedules (and costs) for a project. Program evaluation and review technique (PERT) allows the use of multiple time estimates for each activity. PERT/Cost adds cost estimates, as the name implies. RAMPS (resource allocation and multiproject scheduling) adds the further refinement of a tool for allocating limited resources to competing activities in one or more projects. All, however, rest on the basic network concept outlined above.

Cost Control. Project cost control techniques, though not yet formalized to the same degree as time controls, are no harder to install if these steps are followed: (1) break the comprehensive cost summary into work packages, (2) devise commitment reports for "technical" decision makers, (3) act on early, approximate report data, and (4) concentrate talent on major problems and opportunities.

Managing a fast-moving $15 million project can be difficult for even the most experienced top manager. For a first-line supervisor the job of running a $500,000 project can be equally difficult. Neither manager can make sound decisions unless cost dimensions of the job are broken down into pieces of comprehensible size. Figure 7, which gives an example of such a breakdown, shows how major costs can be logically reduced to understandable and controllable work packages (usually worth $15,000 to $25,000 apiece on a major project), each of which can reasonably be assigned to a first-line manager.

Cost commitments on a project are made when engineering, manufacturing, marketing, or other functional personnel make technical decisions to take some kind of action. In new-product development, for example, costs are committed or created in many ways—when marketing decides to add a product feature to its product; when engineering decides to insert a new part; when a process engineer adds an extra operation to a routing; when physical distribution managers choose to increase inventory, and so on. Conventional

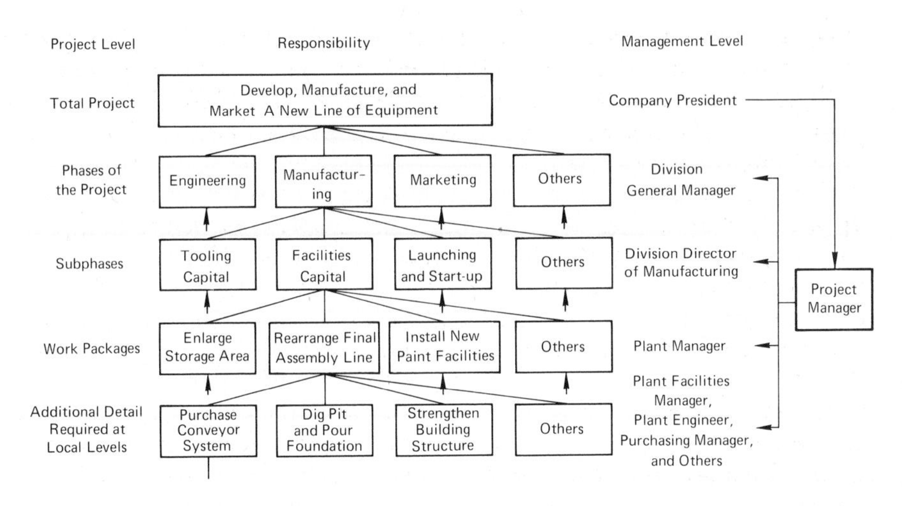

Figure 7. Breakdown of Project Cost Responsibility by Management Level

accounting reports, however, do not show the cost effects of these decisions until it is too late to reconsider. To enable the project manager to judge when costs are getting out of control and to decisively take the needed corrective action, he must be able to assess the approximate cost effect of each technical decision. In other words, he must have cost commitment reports at each decision stage.

Almost without exception, experience shows, 20 percent of the project effort accounts for at least 80 percent of the cost to which the company is committed. With the aid of a detailed cost breakdown and current information on cost commitment, the project manager is able, even after the project is under way, to take people off less important activities in order to concentrate more effort where it will do the most good in reducing costs. One company cut its product introduction costs by over $1 million in this way between the dates when the first print was released and the first machine assembled.

Quality Control. Experience with a wide variety of projects—new-product introductions, mergers, plant constructions, introduction of organizational changes, to name a few—indicates that effective quality control of results is a crucial dimension of project success. Quality control comprises three elements: defining performance criteria, expressing the project objective in terms of quality standards, and monitoring progress toward these standards.

The need to define performance criteria, though universally acknowledged, is generally ignored in practice. Such quality criteria can, however, be defined rather easily, that is simply in terms of senior executives' expectations with respect to average sales per salesman, market penetration of a product line, ratio of accountants to production workers, processing time for customer inquiries, and the like. If possible, these expectations should be expressed quantitatively. For example, the senior executive might expect the project to reduce emergency transportation costs from 15 percent to 5 percent of total shipping costs. Or he might expect a 30 percent reduction in inventory costs following installation of a mechanized control system.

Since achievement of these quality goals is a gradual process, the project manager should review progress toward them with the general manager monthly or quarterly, depending upon the length of the project. Sometimes there will be little noticeable change; in other cases major departures from expectation will be apparent. Here, as in the case of time and cost controls, the importance of prompt action to assure that the objectives will be met cannot be overemphasized.

Managing the Human Equation

The typical manager in a commercial business who is handed his first project management assignment finds adjustment to his anomalous new role painful, confusing, and even demoralizing. Lacking real line authority, he must constantly lead, persuade, or coerce his peers through a trying period of change.

Too often, in these difficult early weeks, he receives little support from senior management. Instead, he is criticized for not moving faster and producing more visible results. He may be blamed for flaws in a plan that, through the fault of top management, had to be rushed to completion mere days before the project began. Senior managers need to recognize that naming and needling the project manager is not enough. By giving him needed support at the start, by bringing a broad business perspective to bear on the overall project plan, and by giving the project manager freedom in the details of the doing, the senior executive can greatly enhance his prospects of success.

Another critical point comes at the conclusion of the project, when its results are turned over to the regular organization and the project manager and his team must be returned to their permanent assignments. By virtue of the interfunctional experience gained under pressure, the project manager often matures in the course of a project, becoming a more valuable manager. But he may have trouble slowing down to a normal organizational pace. His routine job is likely to seem less attractive in terms of scope, authority, and opportunity to contribute to the business. Even the best project manager, moreover, can hardly accomplish his project objectives without antagonizing some members of management, quite possibly the very executives who will decide his future. In one instance, a project manager who had brought a major project from the brink of chaos to unqualified success was let go at the end of the project because, in accomplishing the feat, he had been unable to avoid antagonizing one division manager. Such difficulties and dissatisfactions often lead a retired project manager to look for a better job at this time, in or out of the company.

To retain and profit by the superior management material developed on the fertile training ground of the project, senior executives need to be aware of these human problems. By recognizing the growth of the project manager, helping him readjust to the slower pace of the normal organization, and finding ways to put his added experience and his matured judgment to good use, the company can reap a significant side benefit from every successfully managed project.

28

The Project Manager—Anomalies and Ambiguities

David L. Wilemon and John P. Cicero

Organizational structures are being transformed into configurations of new and dynamic management models. These models are frequently established to accomplish complex technological tasks through manpower and resource integration. One of these new management models currently fixing itself in research and development is project management. In the last decade, project management has received increasing attention among organization researchers especially in terms of organizational design implications. However, not enough attention has been given to the role of the project manager and the problems he faces as a critical participant in complex organizations. This article examines project management from the viewpoint of the project manager.[1]

The Boundary Position of the Project Manager

A fundamental characteristic of project management differentiating it from traditional theory is the structuring of the role relationships within the project organization. A project, for example, is not generally bound by the constraints of a vertical chain of command, functional separation, distinct line and staff activities, and span of control.[2] Instead, a project organization tends to revolve around the fluid interaction of highly skilled personnel at various organizational levels.[3]

Reprinted from *Academy of Management Journal,* Vol. 13, No. 3 (September 1970), pp. 269–282, by permission of the publisher and authors.

[1] Research for this article was supported by a NASA research grant number NGL33-022-090 to Syracuse University to investigate the "Role of Apollo Project Management."

[2] See: Frank J. Jasinski, "Adapting Organization to New Technology," *Havard Business Review*, January–February 1959, pp. 79–86; Paul O. Gaddis, "The Project Manager," *Harvard Business Review*, May–June 1959, pp. 89–97; John F. Mee, "Project Management," *Business Horizons*, Fall 1963, pp. 53–55; Gerald H. Fisch, "Line-Staff Is Obsolete," *Harvard Business Review* September–October 1961, pp. 67–69; Robert E. Thompson, "Span of Control, Conceptions, and Misconception," *Business Horizons,* Summer 1964, pp. 49–58; and James E. Webb, Space Age Management: The Large Scale Approach (New York: McGraw-Hill Book Company, 1969), p. 136.

[3] See David I. Cleland, "Understanding Project Management," *Manage,* Vol. 19, No. 9, 1967.

The horizontal and diagonal relationships required in managing complex projects are preliminary indicators of a project manager's boundary position. If a boundary position is defined as "one for which some members of the role set are located in a different system—either another unit within the same organization or another organization entirely," the project manager's position, by definition of his organizational relationships, tends to generate potential boundary roles.[4]

The boundary role of the project manager also may be viewed in terms of his project functions and/or assignments. His responsibilities for coordinating, mobilizing, and allocating diverse project resource requirements within the organization and external to it represent the core of his task.[5]

The Overlay Organization and Boundary Relevance. Although the project organization is a specialized, task-oriented entity, it seldom, if ever, exists apart from the traditional structure of the organization.[6] The project structure is, so to speak, superimposed upon the functional organization, creating two operating systems, each with its own constraints. Add to this structure a contracting agent entirely outside of the organization, and the project manager may have to cross another boundary, that of the contractor's organization. The amount of interboundary contact and its importance to project success often places project managers in positions with a high degree of "boundary relevance."[7]

The high boundary relevance of the project manager's position combined with some of the differentiating characteristics of the project organization (e.g., the horizontal work flow, the cyclic nature of a finite project, and the stringent budget, schedule, and performance constraints) produce somewhat unique problems for the project manager. To inquire into some of these problems, we will examine these aspects of the project manager's role:

1. Managing human interrelationships in the project organization.
2. Maintaining the balance between technical and managerial project functions.
3. Coping with the risk associated with project management.
4. Surviving organizational restraints.

The problems discussed also draw on research in other related areas, such as research and development management, and on interview data collected

[4] Robert L. Kahn, et. al., *Organizational Stress,* (New York: John Wiley & Sons, Inc., 1964), p. 101.

[5] See Gaddis, op. cit.; and John M. Stewart, "Making Project Management Work," *Business Horizons,* Fall 1965, pp. 54–68.

[6] Allen R. Janger, "Anatomy of the Project Organization," *Business Management Record,* November 1963, pp. 12–18.

[7] Kahn, op. cit. Kahn states that positions vary with respect to boundary relevance. He distinguishes two dimensions: the amount of time a person spends in business contacts outside his work unit, and the importance of those contacts in terms of job performance.

by the authors from Apollo project managers and their support personnel within NASA.[8]

Two field trips were employed to gather data. The first trip was taken in the summer of 1968 to orient us to the complexities of the NASA/Apollo project management organization. Unstructured interviews were used to develop preliminary insights into the broad types of the problems that project managers faced. By using the information collected during this first field trip as a base, a semistructured interview procedure was then developed for the second sequence of interviews during the Spring of 1969. Over 40 interviews with project managers, subsystem managers, supporting research and development personnel, and various functional managers were conducted in both field trips. The more structured interview procedure allowed for the development of the behavior patterns and case studies reported in this study. Propositions have been advanced for each problem area to suggest avenues for future research. These propositions are derived from our data and from other related research, such as, research and development administration.[9]

Human Interrelationships in the Project Organization

Project organization often requires the services of diverse professional personnel. The motivations and goals of these professionals may be in conflict with such immediate project objectives and/or constraints as matters relating to budget, schedule, and performance. Our interview data suggest that the Apollo project manager is often faced with the problem of reconciling project and professional objectives; moreover, he may be operating across system boundaries in his dealings with professional personnel.[10] For example, the project manager may accept a reliability index of "x" for a hardware component while the research and development project participants, who support the project manager but who are outside of his immediate work unit, may insist on a higher reliability. The project manager is faced with the problem of maintaining his cost and schedule objectives while trying not to compromise the performance objectives advocated by his supporting research and development personnel. If the project manager is to maintain a smooth interface with his technical experts, his strategy for handling this type of situation may require

[8] Basic interview data are not footnoted to assure the anonymity of the project managers and project team members interviewed. All data were collected at NASA locations during 1968 and 1969 by the authors and fellow participants on the Syracuse University/NASA research team.

[9] For an excellent treatment of the methodological approaches to the study of formal organizations, see P. M. Blau and W. R. Scott, *Formal Organizations* (San Francisco: Chandler Publishing Company, 1962), pp. 8-26.

[10] For insights concerning a wide range of human problems in project management organizations, see: Clayton Reeser, "Some Potential Problems of the Project Form of Organization," *Academy of Management Journal*, December 1969, pp. 459–467; and T. R. LaPorte, "Conditions of Strain and Accommodation in Industrial Research Organizations," *Administrative Science Quarterly*, June 1965, pp. 21–38.

acute human relations skills including empathy for the professional positions of the diverse project participants. One manager, for example, noted the following:

> You have to understand who you are dealing with. An engineer in the laboratory may feel that we should settle for nothing less than zero leakage on a certain seal. He has a certain background, a certain psychological makeup that you have to understand, appreciate, and not violate. You can't tell a guy like that, go to hell, that he doesn't understand the problem. This guy can be a Ph.D. and can darn well know exactly what he's talking about. So, you've got to find within your own means the mechanisms for communicating with him . . . and then again you've got to realize that he's communicating with us.

Interviews with the supporting project personnel in the research and development laboratories indicate that they believe that sometimes they had to "compromise" their professional values so that the project could meet its overall of cost, scheduling, and technical performance objectives.

LaPorte has addressed in a broader context the "professional orientation" of scientists and has noted the following:

> For the scientist, a professional orientation means that he seeks . . . sufficient freedom to explore his particular specialty. . . . He has spent much time gaining the necessary knowledge and learning the tools of his discipline to learn to insure technical expertise, and he places a high value on conducting research with devotion and vigor.[11]

Moreover, LaPorte noted that "this professional orientation may also be a source of his (the scientist's) difficulties in industry, for the organization often requires him to take action and make decisions that run counter to his professional values."[12] In other words, the problem is not necessarily limited to the project environment, but is frequently a general problem in research and development organizations.

Minimizing Professional Conflict. Judging from interview data, one strategy which appeared to be widely employed by project managers to aid in minimizing professional conflict was to communicate explicitly, but tactfully, their position on various project issues such as the budget and schedule status. Through constant communication of project objectives to team members, the project managers, in effect, place some stated parameters on the activities of the project team before they can proceed too far in the "wrong" direction. As one project manager stated, "communicating your objectives to the team is vital in keeping everyone on target."

The effectiveness of the Apollo project manager's strategies in terms of resolving conflicts and motivating team personnel, as suggested, depends to a large extent on the methods used in dealing with project participants. His influence across boundaries may depend on how he handles recommendations for engineering changes made by either research and development or

[11] LaPorte, op. cit., p. 23.

[12] Ibid. LaPorte also notes in his study that "the restrictiveness of administrative procedures" was an important source of strain between scientists and managers.

other project participants. The project manager must know the conditions under which hardware change proposals should be accepted or rejected. Constant rejection of change recommendations may, for example, lower the motivation of supporting project participants. While constant rejection of change proposals may be detrimental to the project manager's position, the process of accepting recommendations for change must also insure the professional position of all participants. As one manager put it:

> I think it takes a person with a good technical background and good management qualities. He should be the type who can accept other people's work without a whole lot of picking; he should be the kind of person who can accept things done a little differently than he would do them. . . .

Thus, the project manager's strategy is more than one of mere rejection or acceptance; he must be aware of the conditions under which he accepts or rejects recommendations in terms of the potential payoff to his supporting personnel.

Reward and Conflicting Boundaries. The project manager's influence over the motivations of his team members, again, appears critical to maintaining project direction and control.[13] This leads to another conflict generated by the project manager's boundary position, rewarding project participants. The supporting project personnel in the laboratories, as suggested, are often motivated by problem-solving situations resulting in recommendations to the project manager. However, to meet the objectives of a project, scientists and engineers must often work on well-defined problems. In their studies on the motivations of engineers and scientists, for example, Pelz and Andrews found that enhancing the motivational levels of scientific personnel, while desirable, moves almost directly against the reward structure established in most organizational systems.[14]

While self-reliance and independence are important motivations for the project's support people, because of the structuring of project objectives, the support personnel are not only frequently directed to solve specific and often narrowly defined problems, but the project manager may not be in a position to directly reward their performance in terms of promotions, salaries, or merit increases. Although individuals are assigned as support personnel to a project and spend most of their time on a specific project, they may be evaluated by their section or department chief within their immediate organizational boundary.

In effect, the project manager must balance, to some degree, the objectives of the project with the things that motivate others connected with it. In retro-

[13] LaPorte, op. cit., p. 29, notes that in highly complex organizations "some accommodation of scientific and managerial orientation must be made" to satisfy the objectives of both groups. He notes, "there is a relationship of mutual dependence between managers and scientists." In the complex organization, "each group needing the support of the other to satisfy its goals."

[14] D. C. Pelz and F. M. Andrews, *Scientists in Organizations* (New York: John Wiley & Sons, 1966), p. 108.

spect, the problem resolves to how the project manager can establish an influence base strong enough to overcome two primary conflicts in the project organization—professionalism and motivation—without providing commensurate external rewards.

While the project manager, as pointed out, has little or no direct influence on promotions and salaries of his interfacing team members, he does have considerable latitude in providing challenging and personally rewarding work assignments for his project team. It should be recognized that the project manager, if not aware of this internal reward structure, is in a position to create increased conflicts within his project team. Consider, for example, the following comment by a project team member on rewarding project participants by offering them a challenging work environment:

> In managing a project, you're going to be working with people. You're going to be telling them to do things, placing requirements on them, and expecting some feedback. . . . You've got to understand how people are going to react, how's the best way to give them that direction so that they'll go away motivated and not resentful. . . . I think it's especially critical where you're getting work out of people which you have no control over. . . . If a guy within an engineering group looks up and sees him (a project manager) coming, he'd say, you know, here comes this guy, he's got a good program for me and I can't wait for him to tell me what it is. Rather than, here comes that guy again, I wish the hell he wouldn't come to see me today, you can never satisfy him. . . .

As the above comment indicates, the offering of internal rewards appears to be an effective method for the project manager to build an influence base strong enough to resolve the problem of motivating without commensurate external rewards.

Propositions on Human Interrelationships in Project Organizations. Although our data base will not support the testing of the following propositions, we believe that they are significant and should be considered in further research aimed at understanding the behavioral interactions of project managers with their supporting project personnel.

1. The degree to which engineering and scientific personnel associated with project teams are motivated to contribute to the specific objectives of the project varies with the project manager's ability to satisfy their professional goals within the project context.
2. The greater the necessity of utilizing scientific and specialized engineering personnel in project problem-solving, the more likely the tenets of the bureaucratic model of the organization will be violated.[15]
3. Internal rewards in terms of motivation and ego-involvement for the project manager's support personnel are related in a positive sense to the project manager's ability to encourage autonomous problem-solving when feasible for his support personnel.
4. The greater the diversity of problem-solving situations, the greater the

[15] See LaPorte, op. cit., p. 37.

propensity for high motivation levels among the project's technical support personnel.

5. The lower the degree of formal authority, the greater the necessity for a project manager to build an influence base in the project environment.

Maintaining a Balance Between the Technical and Managerial Project Functions

In managing complex tasks, a project manager is frequently forced to maintain some type of a "balance" between the technical and the managerial requirements of his task. When the Apollo project manager, for example, is confronted with a technical problem which may disrupt the established objectives of his project, he must usually make both a technical decision and a managerial decision before the problem can be resolved. If, for example, an interfacing research and development team member informs him that a critical project component has only a reliability factor of "X," the project manager most likely would weigh the technical decision of whether or not to accept the recommended reliability quotient against his budget and schedule objectives. When a problem occurs, however, that has a high risk quotient, in terms of safety, for example, a technical decision might normally outweigh the importance of a "management decision." A potential problem for the project manager lies in the possibility of over-stressing either the technical or the management aspect of a problem. To do so may be detrimental to the objectives of the project. The resolution of this problem appears to be in the project manager's understanding of his role and how he uses the project team to achieve technical performance objectives.[16] Most project teams are composed of highly trained technical specialists who are chosen for project work because of their technical expertise. While the management considerations of project cost and schedule are clearly the responsibility of the project manager, he also has final "formal" responsibility for the technical performance of his hardware system.

Through analysis of interview data, the most successful strategy appeared to be to keep abreast of the technical aspects of the problem while usually leaving their more detailed resolution to other technical specialists on the project team.[17] Such a strategy appears to allow the project manager to

[16] For an informative study on the qualifications of project managers, see I. M. Rubin and W. Seelig, "Experience as a Factor in the Selection and Performance of Project Managers," *IEEE Transactions on Engineering Management,* September 1967, pp. 131–135. Also see J. P. Cicero, "The Professional and Technical Qualifications of Apollo Project Managers," Syracuse/NASA Research Program, No. 6223-WP-25, August 1969. .

[17] For a discussion on the mutual dependency of managers and scientists in a complex organization, see LaPorte, op. cit., pp. 21–38. Also see, Ivars Avots, "Why Does Project Management Fail?" *California Management Review,* Fall 1969, p. 79. He notes that "While it is usually agreed that the manager must be a good technician and thoroughly familiar with the field to which the project belongs, his emphasis must be on the overall view and not of technical detail. In fact, his preoccupation with any single aspect of the project may contribute to a failure."

retain broad control of the project while also allowing for full participation by the project team. A statement by a project team member emphasizes this latter point.

> I've had experiences where I felt that the project manager was trying to exert too much influence in the technical areas in an attempt to make the decisions himself. . . that's what his project team is for. . . .

As indicated, if the project manager overstresses his technical function, it may have the effect of usurping the supporting research and development commitments and concomitantly creating a technical imbalance.[18]

Propositions on Balancing Technical and Managerial Project Functions. Propositions on balancing technical and managerial project functions are:

1. The greater the project manager's technical expertise, the higher the propensity that he will overly involve himself in the technical details of his project.
2. The greater the project manager's difficulty in delegating technical task responsibilities, the more likely it is that he will overinvolve himself in the technical details of the project (depending upon his expertise to do so).
3. The greater the project manager's interest in the technical details of a project, the more likely it is that he will defend the project manager's role as one of a technical specialist.
4. The lower the project manager's technical expertise, the more likely it is that he will overstress the nontechnical project functions (administrative functions).

Coping with the Risk Associated with Project Management

There are two categories of "risk" which appear to predominate for project managers. This risk categories are *project risk* and *professional risk*. Project risk involves the failure to do an adequate job as a project manager, which may result in project failure either in terms of task technical performance or in terms of severe budget or schedule deviations. Professional risk centers around the possibility of professional obsolescence as the result of long-term project affiliation.[19]

Project risk may be identified with the project manager's final responsibility for meeting and maintaining the technical performance, schedule, and budgetary objectives of the project. His success and the recognition of his ability

[18] A somewhat similar analogy existing between administrators and scientists has been noted by D. W. Conrath in his article on "The Role of the Informal Organization in Decision-Making on Research and Development," in *IEEE Transactions on Engineering Management,* September 1968, p. 111.

[19] For a recent study offering insights into the problem of professional risk, see Clayton Reeser, op. cit., p. 464. Reeser noted that in his interviews with project managers they exhibited "feelings of insecurity when they emphasized the potential of career retardation that appears to be inherent in project organizations."

as a manager primarily depends upon his achievements in these areas. In effect, the project manager is the focal point in a constantly exposed organizational responsibility system.

Complicating his primary project responsibilities are the necessary interfaces with other organizational participants. In a complex advanced technological undertaking, like the Apollo Program, project managers are required to maintain interfaces with research and development laboratories and with the project managers of other interfacing projects. In such cases, project managers not only have the responsibility for their projects, but share in an implied sense the responsibility for other project managers' hardware—especially in terms of interface compatibility.

In terms of project risk, two wide-ranging perceptions were found to exist among the Apollo project managers. The disparity in the perception of project risk may be illustrated by responses from two project managers.

1. If my hardware didn't work and it failed . . . it would be a catastrophic occurrence. I would completely expect to be replaced. . . . Put it that way.
2. If you don't want to accept the responsibility of the project, you don't have to, you just buck it up to the next manager and if he doesn't want to make the decision he can go to the program manager.

In the first instance, the project manager perceives his responsibility as final and complete with the risk of project failure resting entirely on his shoulders. In the second case, the project manager is left with an option of whether or not to accept complete responsibility in critical areas. The first case is relatively unambiguous; however, the second leaves assumption of project risk up to the individual manager. Further research may provide a workable hypothesis for understanding the conditions and behavioral variables that would determine the amount of risk a particular project manager is willing to assume. Our purpose here is to point out that different project managers perceive project risk differently.

Apart from project risk, the project manager may also be confronted with *professional risk* in terms of engineering or technical obsolescence. In effect, advancement of the state of the art may bypass the project manager if he is unable to keep up with the rapid changing practices in his engineering field.[20] This is especially relevant in complex organizations where major projects may have a life cycle of several years. One project manager who had been in a project manager position for a number of years stated the implications of professional risk this way: "I'm an obsolete engineer, I'm an untrained manager, and I'm too old to go back to school."

Closely tied with professional risk is the problem of what the project manager will do once his project is phased out. Uncertainty about the future seems most prevalent when the project is phasing down and the project manager sees other new exciting projects phasing in. To be placed in charge of one of the

[20] All the project managers interviewed had technical academic training.

new projects often appeared to be a function of the availability of a manager and not necessarily his prior effectiveness as a manager. In one sense, many project managers become "locked in" on a project and are not available for other projects as they develop. One Apollo project manager expressed his concern this way when asked about his future as a project manager:

> I have faith that another project will come along that needs me. . . . Of course, as far as job security is concerned, I don't have anything to worry about. However, I'm not sure whether my next job will really be anything more than working the bureaucracy . . . and I'm not sure I'm really interested in just working the bureaucracy.

Most of the project managers interviewed expressed the desire to continue working in the area of project management. Several also expressed that they would have difficulty in being placed back within the engineering laboratories since they had been removed from pure technical work for a long period of time.

Propositions on Risks in Project Management. Three propositions on risk involved in project management are:

1. The project manager's anxiety over *project risk* varies in relation with his willingness to accept "final" responsibility for the technical success of his project. Some project managers may be willing to accept full responsibility for the success or failure of their projects. Others, by contrast, may be more willing to share responsibility and risk with their superiors.
2. The greater the length of stay in project management, the greater the tendency for project managers to remain in administrative positions within an organization.
3. The degree of anxiety over professional obsolescence varies with the length of time the project manager spends in project management positions.

Surviving Organizational Restraints

While the concept of project management is often defined by the practitioner in terms of its flexibility and adaptive qualities (the antithesis of the bureaucratic model of organization) many Apollo project managers indicated that certain environmental parameters and restraints do develop over time which often diminish the effectiveness of the project organization. It was suggested by some of the project managers that project organizations certainly are not immune to "Parkinson's Law." As projects mature over their life cycle, various management systems, reporting mechanisms, and staff offices become affixed to the project organization which produce restraints and rigidities. For example, over the life of several projects we found that various "staff offices" had gradually placed some rather stringent demands on project organizations in terms of project reporting systems, project audits, and various management control mechanisms. One project manager explained this problem as follows:

> First you start out with a small organization and call it Apollo. . . . As you expand that organization you have more and more staff people and you have more people thinking up reasons why there's a need for a report. So, pretty soon you get hit with directives, some from top management and some from every level. Many of these directives require comprehensive reporting. We've got a lot of people who think it would be real nice to have this report or that report. . . .

As the above quote indicates, project managers must cope with increasing amounts of paperwork and "systems management" while maintaining their effectiveness in normal project responsibilities. Most indicate that a significant problem for the project manager is learning how to cope with the data reporting systems which, over time, become attached to the project.

While all of the reporting systems and the work in "maintaining" them may have obvious negative connotations, project participants have also expressed their positive aspects in terms of maintaining project control and as a method of self protection. In a complex program, however, the extensive documentation on actual or proposed engineering changes, while laborious, has the effect of clearly stating a project participant's position with regard to controversial performance areas in the hardware. If future technical or management problems develop, a manager or a supporting team member may rely on his own documentation as a means of self protection, especially if he was opposed to making the engineering change. This can be conceptualized as one of the "informal roles" of the engineering change documentation procedure. Informally, some project managers refer to these procedures as "protective documentation" or "maintaining your Pearl Harbor files."

Aside from documenting the system, another restraint that appeared to be a problem for the project manager was the Civil Service regulations and requirements operating within NASA. These regulations, because of their rigidities, often become problems for the project manager in selecting and molding a viable team.[21] The competition for talent between suborganizations may also cause problems for the project manager in building his team. For example, if a project manager desires a project participant, he must first be released from his present organizational position by his superiors. One project manager alluded to the problems of building the project team this way:

> Say, for example, that I need a good strong project engineer. Even if the center is in trouble and a man is around who isn't doing very much, if the person who is supervising his area feels strong about him and won't let him go, then you almost can't get him, no matter how badly you need him . . . and that's kind of bad.

The problem of assigning manpower to build the most effective project team

[21] We found that the project manager in private industry often has greater freedom in selecting and terminating project team members than does the Apollo Project Manager. A problem frequently develops in both cases, however, when several project managers are competing for the same potential project team members. A number of steps currently are being undertaken to alleviate the problems in personnel transfers, etc., within NASA.

also appears in the reverse situation. If a team member's performance is below an acceptable level, the project manager may also have problems in "spinning-off" project team members because of the employment regulations. One project manager concerned about the effectiveness of some members of his team made this comment.

> I've got three people I could do completely without. But if I asked for their release from this project, I would most likely have to give up my three best men, so, I just sit here and don't say anything.

The examples here relate some of the problems project managers experience in coping with various organizational restraints and regulations. If the project manager is evaluated in terms of how he meets his task responsibilities, any mechanism constraining optimum efficiency and flexibility is, in a real sense, a threat to the manager's capability of accomplishing the established objectives of the project.

Propositions on Surviving Organizational Restraints. Propositions concerning surviving organizational restraints are:

1. The autonomy of a project manager decreases over the life of a project as top management's desire to bureaucratize projects increases for the purpose of centralized project control.

2. The higher the degree of bureaucratization in terms of reporting systems, rules, and regulations, the more highly developed the informal communication channels of the project manager become.

Summary

The interview data reveal several problem areas that Apollo project managers face in their everyday management of complex tasks. Project managers occupy boundary positions within organizations, and their role as a boundary initiator and participant presents a number of challenging research opportunities. The complexities of the project manager's role are dependent upon both the organizational and technological demands required of him to accomplish task objectives. To meet his objectives, he must generate and maintain intensive interactions with highly skilled personnel at various levels of the organization. He must also be able to cope with the ambiguities of dealing with project contributors over whom he has no direct control. Frequently, he finds that the support he needs must come from project participants who have value systems which may conflict with the immediacy of the project's objectives. His abilities in managing the varied interrelationships in the project environment are thus critical to him in terms of his effectiveness as a manager.

The project manager also potentially faces the more personal problems in terms of potential project failure and the possibility of professional obsolescence. Because of his organization's dependence upon the success of his project, he normally receives considerable visibility as an organizational participant, but he also is constantly exposed by that same visibility. Contributing to his visibility are the sophisticated project management reporting systems which monitor the progress of his project. Finally, the project manager is faced with delineating his role properly in terms of his technical and management responsibilities. Knowing how to maintain such a balance is critical to him and his project team.

As additional research is undertaken on project management, management theorists may eventually construct a "general theory of project management." At this point, however, they must continue to analyze the research which is being advanced and view it in terms of building blocks for a broader theoretical construct.

C. Coordination and Communication

29

Coordination

Franklin Pierce Huddle

The late Harold Schlosberg, chairman of Brown University's Psychology Department, once complained that "our human sciences are about where physics was before Galileo." Indeed, the science of how and why people act as they do has been so splintered, so loaded with untested folklore and tradition, so infused with emotion, so dominated by academic priesthoods, and so contaminated by profit-minded intellectual gadgeteers, that no clear lines of analysis are available. The science of management languishes in a dark age. What, for example, is the meaning of the word that titles this article?

"Your People, Sir," said Alexander Hamilton arrogantly, "is a Great Beast." Today's management consultant will often respond that "all of us are smarter than any of us." Is it fair to suggest that *coordination* is the function that reconciles the seemingly contradictory characterizations of "man-in-the-multiple"?

A behavioristic view of coordination is that it is a means of rendering coherent a multiplicity of processes, either concurrently or sequentially. Thus, there are four stages in any human enterprise:

- *Planning*. Application of the associative faculties to the orderly sequencing or scheduling of the application of resources to the conduct of the enterprise.
- *Organizing*. Mobilization of physical and human resources in conformity with the planned sequence.

• *Executing.* Interaction of physical and human resources to produce the result.

• *Rewarding.* Distribution of rewards to gratify ("reinforce") the intelligence that has planned, organized, and executed the enterprise, and to reward what Barnard calls "the cooperators."

This sequence commonly applies in human endeavors, large and small. It may be a universal principle. If so, one can produce a model of any enterprise out of ultimate units that are always "go-no-go" bits of communicated information. Plus, of course, such inanimate resources as are required.

Any enterprise is, broadly speaking, a system of communications. An order or sequence of communication bits is an "operation," and the functional relating of several operations is cooperation or coordination. As human enterprises are assembled into larger and larger totalities, they comprise larger and larger numbers of individual operations. As Barnard perceived, the communication function of management appeared more and more to be the total function. Crude and primitive ideas of human psychology that have formed the theoretical basis of management are today increasingly inadequate to enable progress in large endeavors. Vast numbers of empirical approaches have been tried, with varying degrees of success. But no taxonomy of coordination has been developed, and no broadly accepted theory of human communication or coordination has appeared.

Many Meanings

No word is more used in management and administration than *coordination.* It is a cure-all. A universal panacea. Yet every management engineer has his own idea of what the word means. Or none. The Bureau of the Budget Library has no entry in its subject-index file for *coordination.* Neither does the Army Library, the *Encyclopaedia Britannica,* the *Columbia Encyclopaedia,* or the *Encyclopaedia of the Social Sciences.*

There should have been a quantity of elegantly discriminated subdefinitions of *coordinate* and *coordination* as used in organization and management—surely as much as are used by the mathematicians. That there are none suggests a lack of rigorous analysis in the discipline. This lack, in turn, suggests the lack of an accepted general theory of management. If we must be that empirical, every man is his own expert. It is meaningless to cite the "best authorities" because there are none. If we do not know *why* an approach works, we may be stimulated to adopt it in inappropriate circumstances and for the wrong reasons.

Skinner's Theories

The writings of B. F. Skinner, the Harvard psychologist, give some promise of leading us toward a coherent theory of behavior. For *behavior,* we may read *management.* And, if we are to believe Senator Flanders, for *management* we may equally read *coordination.*[1] He told a group of graduate students at Stanford University that the maintenance of the free enterprise system:

> . . . seems to depend on a precarious balance, skillfully maintained, between the interests of all the groups with which management is concerned. The problem seems complicated. It would seem to require the utmost skill to maintain this balance. It must be of a sort which brings advantage to all the parties concerned. Precarious though this balance seems, skillful though the moves taken to maintain it must be, the precariousness is not so great nor the skill so rare but that intelligent human beings are well able to carry out these difficult responsibilities. . . .

Skinner's provocative studies offer a succession of ideas that seem capable of being assembled into a system comprehending human organization and susceptible of scientific test. The rigorousness of Skinner's approach is manifested in his *Schedules of Reinforcement.*[2] In this text, he presents painstakingly the results of many different combinations or schedules of action and reward to assess, among other things, the strength of the conditioning thus imparted. He concludes:

> The experimental analysis of schedules now permits the experimenter to achieve a degree of control over the organism which is of an entirely new order. High levels of activity may be generated for long periods of time. Intermediate and low levels of of activity may also be generated. Changes in level which have hitherto seemed capricious may be more readily understood. Through an application of scheduling, extremely complicated examples of behavior can be set up, and behavior can be brought under subtle and complex stimulus control. . . . Other applications to the problem of the control of human behavior, as in law and penology, religion, industry, and commerce, offer considerable promise.

While Skinner began with rats and graduated to pigeons, it was evident to him, even in his earliest graduate work, that there were forces here that could be meaningfully characterized in human terms: "The only differences I expect to see revealed between the behavior of rat and man (aside from enormous differences of complexity) lie in the field of verbal behavior."[3] Unfortunately, when, in 1957, Skinner turned to the analysis of verbal behavior (which field he "did not find . . . unoccupied") he cast about without conspicuous success for behavioral clues and finally ground to a halt, still contending that "So far as a science of behavior is concerned, man thinking is simply man behaving."[4]

[1] Ralph E. Flanders, *The Function of Management in American Life,* pamphlet, Graduate School of Business, Stanford University, July, 1948, p. 10.

[2] Burrhus F. Skinner and C. B. Ferster, *Schedules of Reinforcement* (New York: Appleton-Century-Crofts, Inc., 1957), esp. pp. 3–4.

[3] Burrhus F. Skinner, *The Behavior of Organisms* (New York: Appleton-Century, 1938), p. 442.

[4] Skinner, *Verbal Behavior* (New York: Appleton-Century-Crofts, Inc., 1957), p. 452.

Conditioning Tools

From our point of view, Skinner's most fruitful study is his *Science and Human Behavior*[5] in which he summarizes his evaluation of some of the powerful conditioning tools the behaviorists have been able to identify. In this study, also, he departs from his discipline to consider (a course of behavior that Hume had earlier denounced as impossibly illogical) the translation of *can* into *should* and *is* into *ought*. On the powerful nature of the tools, Skinner reports that he conditioned a pigeon by intermittent reinforcement (i.e., rewarded the subject for the specific action on a random schedule), and the bird thereafter repeated the action 10,000 times without being rewarded, before the conditioning was totally erased.[6]

The ethical content of Skinner's discourse implies an extreme view of the potentialities of the behavioral science, as seen by a leading proponent. The conservative reader, with Winston Churchill, is likely to reply to the suggestion that science will ultimately be able to control man's thoughts with precision: "I shall be very content if my task in this world is done before that happens."[7] However, here is Skinner on the subject:

> We find ourselves members of a culture in which science has flourished and in which the methods of science have come to be applied to human behavior. If, as seems to be the case, the culture derives strength from this fact, it is a reasonable prediction that a science of behavior will continue to flourish and that our culture will make a substantial contribution to the social environment of the future. . . .
>
> When we turn to what science has to offer, however, we do not find very comforting support for the traditional Western point of view. The hypothesis that man is not free is essential to the application of scientific method to the study of human behavior. The free inner man who is held responsible for the behavior of the external biological organism is only a prescientific substitute for the kinds of causes which are discovered in the course of a scientific analysis. All these alternative causes lie *outside* the individual. . . . The environment determines the individual even when he alters the environment. . . .
>
> We may therefore find it necessary to change from a philosophy which emphasizes the individual to one which emphasizes the culture or the group. But cultures also change and perish, and we must not forget that they are created by individual action and survive only through the behavior of individuals.
>
> Science does not set the group or the state above the individual or vice versa. . . . We are not justified in assigning to anyone or anything the role of prime mover. . . .
>
> Even so, the conception of the individual which emerges from a scientific analysis is distasteful to most of those who have been strongly affected by democratic philosophies. . . . It has always been the unfortunate task of science to dispossess cherished beliefs regarding the place of man in the universe. . . . If science does not confirm the assumptions of freedom, initiative, and responsibility in the behavior of the individual, these assumptions will not ultimately be effective either as motiva-

[5] Skinner, *Science and Human Behavior* (New York: Macmillan Company, 1953).
[6] Ibid., p. 70.
[7] Ibid., p. 438.

> ting devices or as goals in the design of culture. . . . We may console ourselves with the reflection that science is, after all, a cumulative progress in knowledge which is due to man alone, and that the highest human dignity may be to accept the facts of human behavior regardless of their momentary inplications.[8]

Those who wish to pursue Skinner to the bitter end will find him at bay in his postwar novel, *Walden Two*.[9] It is a tentative work in which he attempts to apply his theories to systematize a culture. Here he was hampered by an unfamiliarity with other disciplines such as economics, and bedevilled by that ancient vice of utopians—gadgetry. More to the point, he was never able quite to decide whether his *deus ex machina* was a re-creation of Jesus Christ or Henry Ford. (One finds this reminiscent of Aldous Huxley's *Brave New World*.)

Understanding Reactions

If management equals coordination, and if both they and generalized human endeavors are concerned with communication, then language should logically have originated out of joint (or coordinated) human endeavor at a primitive level. Anthropology and historical speculation have produced little of value here. It would be asking too much to find a magnetic tape encased in the limestone walls of the cave of Font-de-Gaume. Still, one of our less popularly accepted theories of the origin of language does derive it from the need to coordinate the efforts of men working together on a task too large for one to perform alone. Here is what Mario Pei has to offer:

> The "pooh-pooh" theory is to the effect that language at first consisted of ejaculations of surprise, fear, pleasure, pain, etc. It is often paired with the "yo-he-ho" theory to the effect that language arose from grunts of physical exertion. . . .[10]

Without going whole hog, acquaintance with Skinner is persuasive that "we ain't farmin' as good as we know how already." Some extent of behavioral coordination is definitely feasible. Understanding of human reactions to reinforcement involves a straightforward extrapolation of the behavior of Skinner's pigeons under the schedules of reinforcement described in his book on the subject. This is a powerful general tool. Almost all of the successful efforts at management coordination, painfully acquired or intuitively arrived at by successful managers, can be described in Skinneresque terms.

A Continuing Process

Most remarkable, in this context, is the writing of Mary Parker Follett, who came too early on the scene to have benefited from Skinner's writings.

[8] Ibid., pp. 446–449.

[9] Skinner, *Walden Two* (New York: Macmillan Company, 1948).

[10] Mario Pei, *The Story of Language* (New York: Mentor Books, New American Library, 1960), p. 15.

Documentation can be found in her collected essays on *Freedom and Coordination.*[11] Here, and particularly in her essay on "Coordination," Miss Follett appears to anticipate many of the essential ideas more rigorously derived by Skinner from behavioral research in the laboratory. Doubtless he would agree with her statement that "Every organization has a form, a structure, and . . . what that organism does, its unified activity depends . . . on how these constituents are related to one another." Also, "A field of control is not a mere aggregation of specific controls."[12] To Miss Follett, coordination is a process, and out of it comes control: "Legitimate authority flows from coordination, not coordination from authority."[13]

Her process of coordination is a continuing process, toward unifying but never achieving unity. A genuine coordination or integration (a favorite word of hers) gives management control, and "that is why coordination is the most important point in organization."[14] The process of coordination rests on scientific knowledge—it is controllable by further and further developments.[15] To her, coordination is a form of decision making: it is mutual participation in decision making, but decision making takes place at all levels in an organization.

Miss Follett gives great emphasis to four aspects of coordination: *factual, human, initial, and continuous.* These are somewhat analogous to the mechanistic view of coordination outlined early in this study. (That is, in the suggested generalized description of any process of human endeavor.) As she puts them, the four fundamental principles of organization are:

1. Coordination as the reciprocal relating to all the factors in a situation.
2. Coordination by direct contact of the responsible people concerned.
3. Coordination in the early stages.
4. Coordination as a continuing process.

Unsolved Problem

Both Miss Follett and Skinner, at the last, retreat into a mystique insofar as the fate of individualism is concerned. Skinner has already been quoted. Miss Follett is less quotable. But, if I read correctly her message in a paper on "Individualism in a Planned Society,"[16] by 1932 she was prepared to apply her "integration" through "coordination" with a John Deweyish democratic planning continuum on a cosmic scale. In this brave new era, the indi-

[11] Mary Parker Follet, *Lectures in Business Organization* (London: Management Publications Trust, Ltd., 1949).

[12] Ibid., p. 12.

[13] Ibid.

[14] Ibid.

[15] Ibid., p. 13. See also p. 5.

[16] Henry C. Metcalf and L. Urwick, eds., *Dynamic Administration,* the collected papers of Mary Parker Follett (New York: Harper and Brothers Publishers, 1940), pp. 295–314.

vidual would participate in the process without sacrifice of his individuality, but would strive to reconcile it with all the other points of view relevant to the situation.

The rest of this paper is taken up with two sets of lists. The first is a list of twelve types of coordination, within the broad limits of the term as defined in the foregoing discussion. The second is a list of ten illustrative forms of coordinating actions. To each of these catalogs are added specific illustrations of the item—either documented or drawn from personal experience. These are used to build a bridge between the foregoing theory and the following specifics.

Kinds of Coordination

The twelve types of cordination are: First, *planning*. This might also be termed *system development coordination*. It is the preliminary blueprint of a complex operation.

Second, *mobilization*. This form of coordination takes place principally as an organization or a multi-agency function is getting under way. It consists in bringing together persons having related individual responsibilities to share knowledge and skills and to pave the way for future congenial and constructive relationships. During the Korean War, for example, Howard C. Coonley was "conservation coordinator" in the Executive Office of the President. He carried on this function largely by searching out persons in all government agencies remotely related to conservation. Once a month, he brought them all together at the Army-Navy Country Club for a luncheon at which various leaders would be introduced, programs proposed, ideas kicked around in open discussion, and people would meet people. Later on, he set up a more formal organization, but a good deal of spadework was done before it got started. This process can, of course, be intra-agency as well as inter-agency.

Third, *articulation*. Even within a single program, it is necessary that all operational elements are kept in balance. In his book, *Crusade in Europe*, General Eisenhower gives an example of this:

> Our Mediterranean experiences had reaffirmed the truth that unity, coordination, and cooperation are the keys to successful operations. War is waged in three elements but there is no separate land, air, or naval war. Unless all assets in all elements are efficiently combined and coordinated against a properly selected, common objective, their maximum potential power cannot be realized. Physical targets may be separated by the breadth of a continent or an ocean, but their destruction must contribute in maximum degree to the furtherance of the combined plan of operation. That is what coordination means.[17]

Fourth, *vertical*. Despite Mary Parker Follett, it is doubtful that our traditional concept of a hierarchical organizational structure will be readily

[17] Dwight D. Eisenhower, *Crusade in Europe* (New York: Doubleday & Co., Inc., 1948), p. 210.

displaced. Coordination must indeed occur—including the very basic function of decision making—at all levels. But there is a deep-seated tendency for decisions of greater consequence to rise toward the top of the organization. At the lower levels, it then becomes the job to prepare the question to make it suitable for decision at the next level above. This is reflected in "Washington Commonplace" that "nobody writes what he signs and nobody signs what he writes." The relationships described by Chester Barnard of "cooperators" in a hierarchical relationship are also of this type.

Fifth, *congruence*. This is the achieving of a necessary or convenient uniformity of conduct, procedure, forms, and the like to enable mechanical interaction. On this subject, Benjamin Melnitsky has some useful observations: "Standards touching on the sensitive, often-elusive human element (variously called *managerial standards, administrative standards, performance standards, standard practices, standard practice instructions,* and many more) have three main purposes":

- They serve to coordinate the efforts of separate groups working on different phases of the same problem.
- They promote consistency in the handling of repeated functions.
- They serve to convert solved problems into routine procedures, thereby making the solution a matter of record and a future guide for all concerned.[18]

Whether this is a form or a tool of coordination doesn't seem to matter very much. It is interesting that neither this form of coordination nor the related *modular coordination* of the building construction industry is given recognition by Merriam-Webster.

Sixth, *stimulation*. This word can be used to signify the function of management in attempting to achieve improvement in all substandard (or not) phases of an activity. Work simplification concepts generally aim to achieve this sort of coordination.

Seventh, *intersection*. This is the necessary cooperation of two persons each responsible for or concerned with programs having an interface. As people become immersed in their own programs and come to regard them as of overriding importance, the intersection can be a torrid clime. Sometimes it is necessary for the principal officers in each program to meet face to face, as if to negotiate a treaty. It is better, though, to have resolution and harmony generate at less elevated levels of officialdom. Thus, the decision as to whether to put a high dam or a low dam on the Potomac above Great Falls could be negotiated by the Chief of Engineers and the Secretary of the Interior. But it would be preferable for several civilian engineers in the office of the Director of Civil Works, Office of Civil Engineers, to meet with people of comparable rank in the Park Service in order to search—without deep commitment—for possible avenues of compromise.

[18] Benjamin Melnitsky, *Profiting from Industrial Standardization* (New York: Conover-Mast Publications, Inc., 1953), p. 357.

Eighth, *informational.* This highly important form of coordination entails communicating useful intelligence about a program to persons not directly concerned, but who might later be affected by the program. The author once strained every nerve to get a tungsten conservation program going during the Korean War only to have a change take place in the Army Ordnance use of tungsten that made his program completely inappropriate. It would have been helpful to know that this technological change was nearing the point of decision.

Ninth, *external.* This is a form of coordination in which a person undertakes to obtain action from persons over whom he has no jurisdiction. For example, it may be desired that private industry institute programs of industrial safety —so one arranges for the associated insurance companies to give prizes in different categories of the plant for excellence in safety record. Or, one might generate private industrial interest in materials conservation by persuading various trade associations to form "conservation committees" among their members.

Tenth, *intersovereign.* This is a form of coordination in which one nominally equal sovereignty extends a degree of leadership over other sovereignties by request or previous arrangement. Examples are the relationship of the Tennessee Valley Authority with the seven valley states and the participation of the United States in the Central Treaty Organization, involving Turkey, Iran, and Pakistan. (The principal United States official active in this relationship is the United States Economic Coordinator for Central Treaty Organization Affairs. His objectives are: "The stimulation of regional growth through regional cooperation and the promotion and exchange of technical skills between the countries of the region; and the encouragement, through joint planning and execution, of those projects which benefit individual nations, but can best be carried out through regional programs."[19])

Eleventh, *combined operations.* In this form of coordination, several sovereign powers, of more or less equal stature, seek to combine forces for a mutually desired objective toward which they are each prepared to contribute. Examples of this are the United States-Canadian joint defense system and the various Common Market arrangements evolving in Western Europe, as well as the various agencies under the aegis of the United Nations.

Twelfth, *conflict coordination.* This is one of the most interesting and currently absorbing forms of coordinate relationship. It entails the coordinated action by two hostile forces, within agreed limits, so that, as they punish each other, they avoid intolerable or unnecessary punishment. For example, the United States and the Soviet Union have continued for several decades in a conflict situation. Yet, they have tacitly agreed not to spoof each other's early warning systems, not to flood each other's country with counterfeit currency, not to send their submarines too close to each other's shoreline,

[19] *Progress Report of the Office of the United States Economic Coordinator for Cento Affairs,* March 1959 to November 1960, pamphlet (Beirut, Lebanon: Catholic Press, undated), p. 4.

not to attempt assassination of each other's leaders, not to do a number of other things that would signal conduct that might be termed provocative by the observing antagonist.

Coordination Tools

Unlike the twelve forms of coordination listed immediately above, the ten coordination tools listed below are related more specifically to government and are drawn from personal experience.

First, *command decision*. This is the most arbitrary form of coordination or decision making. It involves a situation in which a chain of command exists, in which each echelon responds to the one above, under military discipline. An order that overrides all advice and contrary recommendations by subordinates in staff or line and that relies on naked authority with disobedience punishable by court martial is known as a "command decision." The usual consequence of its excessive exercise is demoralization and relief of command. It is seldom employed. However, it has a nonmilitary counterpart that is sometimes used by green administrators. Unless they learn better practice, they fall from the tree, still green.

Second, *legal*. This is a tool of coordination established by law in the form of a set of alternatives, such that the less onerous is the one that the authority desires to be adopted. This is the form most usually employed by the Congress in shaping a grant-in-aid program.

Third, *agency*. This form consists in offering a reward of substance commensurate with the effort involved in performing a desired action or course of action. In its simplest form, it is exemplified by a procurement or personal service contract. A related form might be called a "hunting license." For example, a publication is widely circulated, indicating the possible opportunities or advantages to those who do what is desired. This approach proved effective in stimulating industrial mobilization planning by private industry, in encouraging private industry to set up conservation programs, in promoting nongovernmental research and development in materials, and in generating an interest in arms control research.

Fourth, *personal*. This consists in the bathing of the subject in a warm suffusion of friendly persuasion and cordial relationships—the sort of thing that President Lyndon Johnson calls "the laying on of hands."

Fifth, *military staff*. This form of coordination, in the pure genus, consists of a marshalling of all the arguments and reasons in support of a desired course of conduct, appended to a recommendation that the course be adopted. It implies a calm, rational, and dispassionate relationship. However, there is also an adulterated form in which a decision has already been made—usually for undisclosable reasons—and the staff paper is the window dressing to provide a disclosable justification for taking the action. Both forms are in wide use.

Sixth, *priesthood*. This is a real but hard-to-define form of pressure in which an instruction to act is accompanied by the threat of uncertain but undesirable consequences of failure to act. Examples of this form are the gangster's "or else . . ." and the bill collector's "or we shall have to resort to other measures possibly less convenient for you." In the federal government, it sometimes appears as: "I am afraid that I shall have to include an account of this situation in my report"—unless, of course, corrective action takes place forthwith. The word "priesthood" in this context signifies an assumed authority relying for its support upon unspecified and preferably mysterious authority capable of wielding undefined but presumably potent power. As Mark Twain said: "Both brothers were imaginary."

Seventh, *indirect*. This form involves the use of a chain of incentives. It is one of the handiest of tools for administrators, as it is for parents. The Tennessee Valley Authority used it in superb fashion when they devised a small, inexpensive trailer-thresher and arranged for its manufacture. A long chain of circumstances flowed from this one invention—encouragement of farmers to plant small grains, to harvest orchard grass seed and clover seed, and to plant more winter wheat; increased availability of seed for these purposes; decreased need for row crops for seed cash; reduction in area of earth exposed to winter rain and sleet erosion; and others.

Eighth, *indirect negative*. This is a technique of requiring the subject to take a legitimate action whose secondary consequence is a desired prohibition that is administratively out of reach. For example, assume that the metal perfidium is needed for some secret program and there isn't much available. You can't prohibit its use in established applications because, despite the fact that it is sometimes used unnecessarily, it is sometimes imperatively needed. To try to specify where it should be used is an impossibly complicated administrative task and quite unpoliceable. So you prepare a bland, innocuous order instructing all users, if they want any more perfidium, to keep track of every last half-ounce of it, make regular monthly reports of perfidium transactions, salvage every scrapped part containing perfidium, and so on—thus, you make the possession and use of perfidium such a complete headache that only those who must have it go to the pain of filling out all those forms. Presto! The situation is saved and nobody is denied his valid needs. (No wonder they hate bureaucrats.)

Ninth, *mirage*. This is a special form of indirect control in which the person being persuaded thinks he sees a motive that isn't really there—either by intent or in complete and naive innocence on the part of the controller. Any public announcement of technological progress in the use of a scarce mineral triggers off a tremendous effort by grubstake prospectors hoping to be first on the scene in a repetition of the great uranium hunt. This is not to intimate that federal administrators are an unscrupulous and cynical lot, but to suggest the degree of responsiveness of the general public where a possible profit is involved.

Tenth, *political control*. This is a form of "band wagon" approach. There is a great force in mass public opinion, even among technical people. A consensus among administrators can move a program along most powerfully. If enough well-informed people agree that a course is desirable, the person asked to take the course will be almost certain to accept the consensus. To be sure, there is an adulterated form of political control in which—observable at most Parent-Teacher Association meetings—a few friends of the speaker's, by muttering approval of his proposals at strategic points, convey an impression of unanimity. Votes taken under such auspices are often strictly *pro forma*.

This entire discussion has skirted the misty edges that separate the known from the unknown. "An astronomer," said Freud, "can without censure admit that there is a boundary to his vision, beyond which he cannot now penetrate. But we who deal in the problems of man and his nervous system are denied this retreat."

I started out by defining a mechanistic system of communications and suggesting the possibility that it could be generalized to describe all human endeavors. Then, I presented a few results of leading behavioral scientists who achieved high precision in affective communications. A close similarity was observed between the laboratory findings of these behaviorists and the empirical (or intuitive) observations of a leading writer in the field of human management.

Finally, I presented a short catalog of types and tools of coordination. Without dwelling too long on the point, I think that most, if not all, of these case histories simultaneously demonstrate Skinner's concept of reinforcement and Follett's concept of integration. If this is so, the consequences are far-reaching.

30

Collision at the Interface

George J. Berkwitt

William T. Bess Jr., Union Camp Corp. group vice president, heaved a sigh of relief when his company officially announced the opening of an 84,000-square-foot corrugated-box plant in Richmond, Virginia last July. Normally, opening a plant of this size would have caused hardly a ripple in the Union Camp executive suite. But this plant had given Bess a few special headaches. Solving one in particular made the opening especially satisfying.

At the planning stage, every rule of sound economics told Bess that there should be some attempt to consolidate the new plant with the company's 430,000-square-foot bag plant, also located in Richmond. Obviously, there

Reprinted with permission from *Dun's Review*, March 1969, pp. 64–67. Copyright 1969 by *Dun's Review*.

were great advantages in combining offices, maintenance and other operations. But a careful analysis uncovered one problem large enough to overshadow all the advantages: the labor force in the immediate area of the old plant was simply not large enough to support a consolidated plant. Two separate plants, even though separated by only eight miles, would make the difference.

A few years ago, most companies faced with such a problem would probably have put hard-and-fast economics first and consolidated without a second thought. Not so today. Increasingly, management is coming around to the systems-oriented view that a problem of any consequence in any given area of operations can cause a chain reaction across the entire company. Organization, at least in theory, is now regarded as a series of interdependent disciplines. A problem affecting one discipline, therefore, affects all others in varying degrees.

But theory is not enough. The problem in systems management is that a vast gap still exists between management's ability to understand the interdisciplinary nature of a problem and the more difficult job of translating this knowledge into action. Take Boeing Co.'s multimillion-dollar error that forced it to convert the SST from a swept-wing craft to a fixed-wing configuration. All the work of dozens of government agencies plus Boeing's own vast design facilities somehow failed to connect and come up with a workable swept-wing design for the mammoth plane.

In any large-scale project, from the building of a skyscraper to the construction of a spaceship, a huge input of men, materials and equipment must be precisely synchronized to be available in the right place at the right time. Such tasks, of course, have been helped immensely by the new network techniques such as CPM and PERT, which apply math, logic and usually the computer to the problem.

But as any top executive knows, even with the most advanced computerized planning technique, hardly ever is a project of any appreciable size completed according to plan or without its share of emergencies. Materials are delivered late or are way off specifications. Extra manpower is not available when needed. Equipment breaks down.

It is at these disaster points that so much of today's systems management falls short. Skilled mostly as an overseer who manipulates many strings at a a time, the systems manager perches high over the entire project, too far away in many cases to see the danger points. Beneath him are the specialists, totally involved in their own segments of the system and unable to see beyond their own narrow points of view.

The Missing Link

What is missing is management focus on the so-called interfaces: those points where the segments of the project come together. For it is at the interface that most of the breakdowns in plans occur.

These trouble spots can be found in every area of the company. In marketing an interface occurs, for example, where a separately prepared promotion campaign is introduced into an overall marketing plan; in finance, where bank and company officers meet to negotiate a loan. In building a factory, they appear at all the many different places where men, materials and equipment converge during the course of the project; in production, where assemblies converge for joining or where materials come into or leave the line. In plant management, they are evident where men from different departments face each other across the table to plan joint operating strategies or to solve common problems.

To coordinate operations at these and many other danger points, a new manager is emerging in the corporate hierarchy. Called variously the program integrator, project manager or program coordinator, he is the man whose job is to control the interface. Unlike the general manager or other managers with top-to-bottom line authority, the interface manager's area of control goes no further than the two opposing walls of the interface problem. Yet while he is usually trained in a specific operating discipline—engineering, finance, and the like—he must have enough general management skills to understand and coordinate all the elements in a project.

The need for such a combination of talents at the interface is being felt across industry. As Henry M. Boettinger, assistant comptroller at AT&T, puts it: "While we have been successful in developing line managers and scientific specialists of the highest caliber, we do feel some shortage of specialists in such areas as econometrics [statistics applied to economics], market research and operations research who have not only the highest professional qualifications but a grasp of corporate problems."

One management specialist compares interface management to air-traffic control in a large airport. "The controller doesn't tell the professional pilot how to fly his plane," he says, "but he sure enough tells him how and when to put it down. Interface managers are rare birds," the specialist adds, "because they are probably the only people in an organization who can coordinate—let alone identify—so many different factors."

"You begin to see the extent of this man's skill," adds Lawrence E. Stewart, director of program management for North American Rockwell's Aerospace & Systems Group, "when you look at the Apollo space program for which we are developing command and service modules. The command module alone," he points out, "has nearly 2 million separate parts as compared, for example, to an automobile, which has only 2,500. At its peak, which was in 1966, the program was using more than 20,000 subcontractors and provided work for some 350,000 people."

At North American, interface management is a fact of life, says Stewart. "Program management is a team effort with the program manager as captain. The team consists of key personnel in all of the supporting functions. The interface coordination is carried out at every organizational level by these program-oriented team members."

The only remaining gap for North American, concludes Stewart, "is the need for management information systems that will give us the necessary interface visibility and control and, of course, for interface managers capable of using these advanced management information systems effectively."

A Management Art

At Kaiser Industries' Kaiser Engineers division, which designs and builds shipyards, steel plants, mine facilities, nuclear power stations, manufacturing plants, dams, transportation systems and other major facilities, interface management is treated as a management art. The manager in charge of interface control (the project planner) is positioned high on the organization chart and operates as staff coordinator for the project manager, who, in turn, reports directly to the company vice president.

A case in point: Kaiser's use of interface management on design and construction of Armco Steel Corp.'s $175-million hot-rolling mill complex at Middletown, Ohio. The project manager was the top Kaiser official on the job. His responsibility was total, ranging from original planning right up to the point that the key to the plant was handed over to Armco.

Because of the complexity of the Armco project, made even more so by the the special nature of rolling-system equipment that is largely custom-built, Kaiser considered it essential to put an engineer in charge of interface control. The man chosen was Sabih Ustel, one of the company's principal engineers.

But where Ustel's duties as an engineer stopped, his duties as a people manager began. "Cooperation above and below was absolutely necessary to the project's smooth operation," he says. "To get it, you need a diplomat and a man respected in his own company. Above all, he's got to be a good communicator. We used to try to relay information to others just as we got it from computer printouts or some of our complicated diagrams. But how many people really understand them, let alone resist using them? You've got to know what kind of communications tools to use on the different kinds of people you're trying to reach. Understanding is the first rule of interface management."

As coordinator, of course, Ustel's job was to prevent trouble when elements of the project converged at the interface. During the ten-month start-up begun last fall, Ustel and his crew prepared questions for the Westinghouse engineers who were in charge of the major part of the start-up tests. The answers, arranged by Ustel in proper sequence, became the parameters for the test plan, including the target dates for start-up and final acceptance of the individual sections of the line.

As in most industrial projects involving massive machines and complicated systems, the start-up tests uncovered defects in certain vital components. But with control of the interfaces during the tests, even these defects, some of which required equipment to be pulled out of the system and sent back to the factory for repair, could not stop the plant from opening close to schedule.

Unlike other forms of management, interface management suffers rather than gains from line authority. As Ustel points out, rapport and cooperation —rather than the prerogatives of authority—are what make his job work.

Another company that has discovered this is Honeywell. At its Micro Switch division in Freeport, Illinois, Honeywell is manufacturing a trouble-free, solid-state electronic keyboard for computer input. The product coordinator for the new unit is Fred Brunka, a thirty-year veteran with the company. To Brunka, his job is one of interface manager. "It will be a bit difficult to play the role of *paterfamilias* and ferret," he says, "but that's basically what I'll have to do. I'm a good listener and I am thankful for a background [quality control] that will help me anticipate problems only vaguely suspected at the moment."

Technically, says Brunka, his job will involve personal interface with a multitude of disciplines. It will include "making sense out of the geometrically expanding problems of the keyboard program and reducing the hours lost waiting for essential decisions."

The ultimate responsibilities of the program belong to the line managers, explains Brunka. He sees his function as one of assisting in problem-solving by "consistent, orderly and prompt liaison." The toughest part, he adds, is maintaining a focus on the significant elements of all the problems he is bound to uncover.

Brunka has set up a system of status reports from each of the line managers. He, in turn, submits regular and special reports to top management. "This," he adds hopefully, "will relieve top management of many routine decisions, but will bring important issues to their attention more quickly."

At this early stage of development in interface management, men like Ustel and Brunka are borrowed from specific disciplines. But as more and more companies are finding out from experience, the major qualifications that an interface manager brings to bear on his job are his management skills. Except perhaps in highly technical projects, he need not be trained in a specific field any more than, say, the president of the company. Gerry E. Morse, vice president of Honeywell, puts it this way: "The type of training isn't everything in management. It's important for the man to be conditioned to *handle* the discipline. We'd hire an anthropologist to get a person with a disciplined mind and a logical way of approaching the job."

31

New Management Job: The Integrator

Paul R. Lawrence and Jay W. Lorsch

What will be new and unique about organizational structures and management practices of business enterprises that are their industries' competitive leaders a decade from now? Because of the rapid rate of market and technological change, with the accompanying strains and stresses on existing organizational forms, managers are becoming increasingly concerned with the difficulty of reconciling the need for specialization with the need for integration of effort.

Consequently, the purpose here is to explore this problem and to suggest that one of the critical organizational innovations will be the establishment of management positions, and even formal departments, charged with the task of achieving integration. Moreover, the integrative function will be on a par with such traditional functions as production, sales, research, and others.

That may seem to be a startling statement, particularly since we know of no organization which has yet established a department—even a small one—formally labeled "integration."

However, before we can evaluate our prediction, we first need to define what we mean by the term *integration.* As used in this article, integration is the achievement of unity of effort among the major functional specialists in a business. The integrator's role involves handling the nonroutine, unprogrammed problems that arise among the traditional functions as each strives to do its own job. It involves resolving interdepartmental conflicts and facilitating decisions, including not only such major decisions as large capital investment but also the thousands of smaller ones regarding product features, quality standards, output, cost targets, schedules, and so on. Our definition reads much like the customary job description of any company general manager or divisional manager who has "line" authority over all the major functional departments.

Although the need for organizational integration is not new, the traditional method of using the "shared boss" as the integrator is rapidly breaking down, and a radically new approach is becoming necessary. The increasingly dynamic nature of many organizational environments is making the integrating job so important and so complex that it cannot be handled by a single general manager, no matter how capable he may be.

Substance can be added to our definition of integration by identifying some of the diverse titles under which this activity is currently being performed. In recent years there has been a rapid proliferation of such roles as product

Reprinted from *Harvard Business Review,* Vol. 43, No. 5 (September–October, 1965), pp. 123–132 by permission of the publisher.

manager, brand manager, program coordinator, project leader, business manager, planning director, systems designer, task force chairman, and so forth. The fine print in the descriptions of these various management positions almost invariably describes the core function as that of integration, as we define it.

These new integrative assignments are joining some older ones, such as those carried on by production control people in resolving schedule conflicts between production and sales, and by budget officers in addressing inter-departmental conflicts around the allocation of capital and operating funds.

The emergence of these integrating jobs in considerable numbers now makes it practical to turn the spotlight of systematic research on them to learn how to manage them effectively. This article largely reports on the findings from our recent study, which answer four key questions about the management of the integrating function:

1. How should integrators be oriented and motivated?
2. What patterns of conflict resolution and influence should they employ?
3. What authority should they have, and how do they get it?
4. Who are the most qualified people for these positions?

To find answers to these questions, we have identified the characteristics of both the organizations and the people who are performing the integration task more effectively than others.[1] But before turning directly to these questions, we first want to shed more light on the reasons for the present emergence of the integrative function.

Emerging Need

When modern large-scale corporations appeared in considerable numbers in the first two decades of this century, they developed around such basic production technologies as oil-refining, iron-steel conversion, and automobile assembly. At first, engineers and other production specialists played a dominant role. Since the very productivity of these firms generated a need for a predictable and controllable distribution system, in the 1920's and 1930's marketing experts came to the fore. Channels of distribution were built up in each industry, and the entire mix of product design, promotion, advertising, pricing, and so on, was elaborated. The boundaries between industries were still relatively clear, and the markets were reasonably predictable.

However, once the effects of the depression abated, the very success of the marketers helped provide consumers with an abundance of standard products that led to a demand for product differentiation. This demand, combined with the stimulus of the post-World War II period, force-fed the widespread emergence in the late 1940's and 1950's of research and development as a major industrial function.

[1] For a complete report of our study, see *Organization and Environment* (Division of Research, Harvard Business School, 1967).

Crucial Activity

Industrial R&D technology has already broken down the existing boundaries between industries. Once-stable markets and distribution channels are now in a state of flux. Product differentiation has parlayed into a welter of choices at every stage of the sequence from basic raw materials to ultimate consumer items. The industrial environment is turbulent and increasingly difficult to predict. Many complex facts about markets, production methods and costs, and scientific potentials for product and process improvement are relevant to investment decisions about these myriad product varieties.

All of these factors have combined to produce a king-size managerial headache: there are just too many crucial decisions to have them all processed and resolved through the regular line hierarchy at the top of the organization; they must be integrated in some other way.

The current importance of R&D groups in modern organizations is making the integrator's role crucial for another reason. Research has introduced into the corporation an entirely new set of people—namely, the scientists—who have their own unique way of being productive. They are specialists who work by a different clock and in a different style from hard-nosed production managers or outward-oriented sales managers. Management has learned, by and large, that these differences are necessary if each type of specialist is to do his job well. But, as these specialists diverge in their working styles, it becomes increasingly difficult to achieve the necessary integration. New roles have to be introduced to get the integration job done. Company after company is committing more and more managerial manpower, under any guise or rubric, to achieve collaboration between highly specialized people spread throughout all organizational functions and levels.

Survey Findings

To this point in the discussion, we have demonstrated that integrative roles are needed and are being developed in many companies. In fact, our study of ten organizations in three distinctly different industries—plastics, consumer foods, and containers—provides dramatic evidence of the importance of effective integration in any industry. This is because our research reveals a close correlation between the effectiveness of integration among functional departments and company growth and profits. However, separate integrating roles or departments are not the solution for all organizations. While formal integrative roles are highly important in R&D-intensive industries, such as plastics and consumer food products, in a comparatively stable industry, such as containers, integration can often be achieved through the management hierarchy.

The important point is that in the future more organizations will be operating in rapidly changing environments, and the problem for managers will be to make certain that this integrative function is effectively carried out. In order to do this, they will need to learn how to select, train, organize, supervise, and control these new integrators.

Organization Structure

Two questions arise when we think of designing the structure of the organization to facilitate the work of integrators:

1. Is it better to establish a formal integration department, or simply to set up integrating positions independent of one another?
2. If individual integrating positions are set up, how should they be related to the larger structure?

In considering these issues it should first be pointed out that if an organization needs integrators at all, it is preferable to legitimize these roles by formal titles and missions rather than to leave them in an informal status. We derive the primary evidence on this point from an intensive study of an electronics company, where the limitations of using informal integrators are clearly revealed.[2] This research demonstrates that the effectiveness of the informal integrators is severely circumscribed when it comes to dealing with difficult interdepartmental relationships. Consider:

- In this organization the boundaries between the production and engineering departments were not well established, and there was intense competition and conflict between these two groups. The informal integrators were unable to achieve effective collaboration, at least in part because their roles were not clearly defined. Therefore, their integrative attempts were often seen as inappropriate infringements on the domains of other departments.

For example, an engineering supervisor, whose own inclinations and interests led him to play a coordinating role between the two departments, was frequently rebuffed by the production personnel because he was seen as intruding into their activities. Without a clearly defined role, his integration efforts were limited to exchanging information across the interface of the two departments.

These data indicate that the more intense the problem of interdepartmental collaboration is, the more need there is for the integrative roles to be formally identified so that such activities are seen as legitimate.

The question of whether to establish independent integrative roles or to create a formal department is illuminated to a considerable extent by our data. Consider:

- In the plastics industry, which has the fastest rate of technical change of the three industries we studied, the basic departments (production, sales, and research) are the most highly specialized and differentiated. Five of the six plastics companies studied, including the one with the best integration record, have what could be called "full-scale integrating departments," although they are not formally labeled as such. (See *Exhibit I* for suggested structural solutions to the integration problem.)..
- In the consumer foods industry, which has both a medium rate of tech-

[2] Unpublished study conducted by John Seiler and Robert Katz for the Division of Research, Harvard Business School.

Stable and homogeneous environment

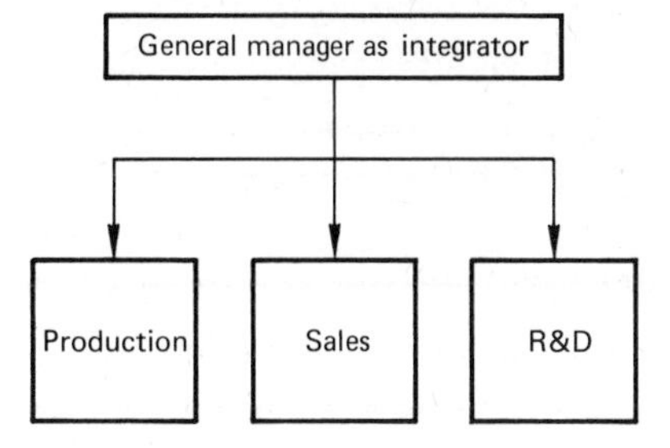

Semidynamic and heterogeneous environment

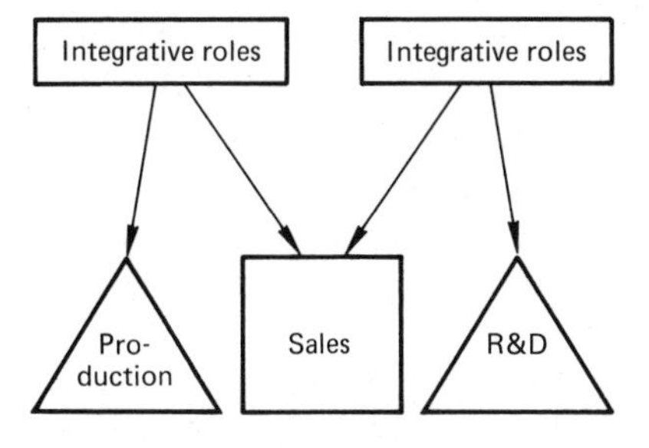

Highly dynamic and heterogeneous environment

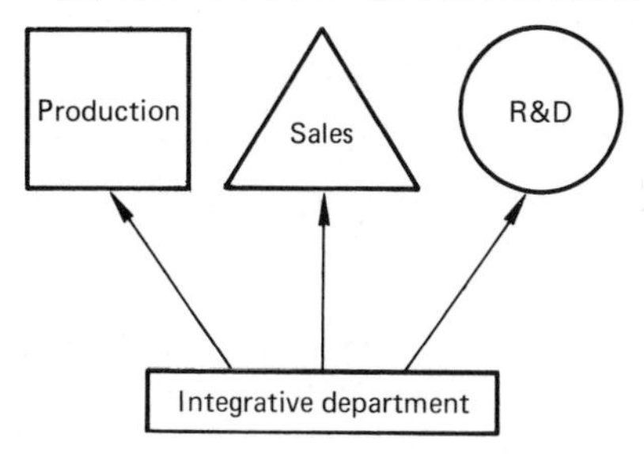

Exhibit 1. Structural Solutions to the Organizational Integration Problem

nical change and a medium degree of difference between basic departments, one of the two companies studied uses a full-scale "integrating department"; the other—with the better integration record—simply utilizes a set of scattered integration roles.

• The container industry has the most stable technology, and thus only slight differences are perceptible between basic departments. In this industry the company with the best integration record has no formal integrators of any kind; it relies entirely on its regular line organization to do the coordinating. By contrast, a second container company, employing a full-fledged integrating department, has experienced considerable integrating difficulties. This suggests not only that the department is redundant, but that it actually impedes the coordination process.

All of this evidence indicates that the elaborateness of the integrating function should vary both with the complexity of the problems and with the size of the gap that specialization creates between the basic departments. Moreover, management should keep in mind that it is possible to get too many integrators into the act as well as too few.

Behavior Characteristics

Our research enables us to identify four important characteristics about the behavior of effective integrators, as well as the organizational practices that contribute to their effectiveness:

1. Integrators need to be seen as contributing to important decisions on the basis of their competence and knowledge, rather than on their positional authority.
2. Integrators must have balanced orientations and behavior patterns.
3. Integrators need to feel they are being rewarded for their total product responsibility, not solely on the basis of their performance as individuals.
4. Integrators must have a capacity for resolving interdepartmental conflicts and disputes.

Since these findings offer some important prescriptions about the behavior of effective integrators, let us examine each of these characteristics more closely.

Decision Contribution

One of the major and most frequently expressed dilemmas facing managers in integrating positions is whether they are able to contribute to important decisions. An integrator interviewed in our study expressed this common concern:

"My key frustration is that I do not have the authority over the people I must deal with. I cannot yell at the research guy. I have to try to influence him by being persuasive. My major tool is strictly my personality."

Although this integrator, like many of his colleagues, complains that he does not have formal authority over the other groups with whom he works, our measures of actual influence on decisions in the organizations studied indicate that all integrators, except for those in the less well-integrated container company, have a larger voice in interdepartmental decisions than their peers in functional departments. And their influence is essential in industries requiring highly specialized and well-integrated organizations, where the integrator must often initiate activities for managers in other departments.

Personal Competence. There is another important factor related to influence that distinguishes the integrators in effective organizations from those in less effective ones. In the more effective, the integrators are influential because of their knowledge and expertise, while in less effective organizations they are influential only because of the formal authority of their positions.

In the well-integrated organizations, the functional managers described the influence of the integrators (although, again, they did not always call them integrators) in comments such as these:

"He [the integrator] has a powerful job if he can get the people to work for him. A good man in that job has everybody's ear open to him. A good coordinator has to be thoroughly oriented to his market or to his process. Whichever area he is working in, he has to be able to make good value judgments."

"They [the integrators] are the kingpins. They have a good feel for our [research] ability, and they know the needs of the market. They will work back and forth with us and the others."

"They [the integrators] are on the border of research, so we work closely together. They are just a step away from the customer, so when I make a change in a material, I let them know, because they may have a customer who can use it. The good thing about our situation is that they are close enough to sales to know what they are doing and close enough to research to know what we are doing."

These and similar comments indicate that the managers in effectively integrated organizations view the integrators as persons who have knowledge of and expertise in solving organizational problems. This personal competence appears to be the foundation on which their large voice in interdepartmental decisions rests.

Positional Power. In the organizations that were having difficulty in achieving integration, the tone of the functional managers' commentaries on the influence of the integrators was quite different:

"We [in research] have to go by what they [the integrators] say. They have the upper hand. And if we can't get their approval, we have to shut up."

"Nobody wants to pull the wool over his [the integrator's] eyes, since he reports to the general manager. That would be disastrous . . . I don't think anybody could be in that role and have many friends. You have to be too aggressive."

"He [the integrator] is supposed to know the field, and he may think our product isn't any good. This is fine if you have confidence in him, but we have had bad experiences with some of them. As the knowledge of chemistry grows, his [the integrator's] knowledge of the market must grow. I guess I would appraise the situation this way: just because they [the integrators] have had twenty years' experience doesn't mean they have twenty years of knowledge."

Comments like these suggest that the integrators in organizations having integration problems were influential only because of the formal authority given to them by the top management and because of their proximity to top management. Other responses stressed that generally the integrators in these companies were considered less knowledgeable about industry conditions. Moreover, the specialist managers frequently volunteered disparaging remarks about the integrators' abilities and knowledge.

Other Factors. In planning for these integrating positions, attention must be given to placing them at levels in the organization where the incumbents will have ready access to the knowledge and information relevant to decisions. In the well-integrated organizations we studied, for example, this level was usually at the middle of the management hierarchy. Since these organizations were in dynamic, rapidly changing industries where knowledge was complex and uncertain, only those middle managers with specific problem experience had been able to master the required knowledge.

If the integrator selected has had prior work experience in two or more of the several functional departments, the specialist managers will regard him as competent because of the knowledge that his experience has provided. While persons with these ideal qualifications may be extremely scarce, it is important to recognize the necessity of finding integrators with broad knowledge to fill these crucial positions. One common failing of the less well-integrated organizations is their tendency to assign young managers lacking sufficient experience in all facets of the business to these positions. Although this may provide a useful learning experience for the young managers, our evidence suggests that it really does not lead to effective integration.

Balanced Orientation

The second important characteristic of effective integrators is that their orientations and ways of thinking strike a good balance between the extremes of the members of the specialized departments whose efforts they are integrating. For instance, our study shows that:

- Research scientists think about long-term projects and issues and about solutions to scientific and technical problems.
- Production managers and engineers, on the other hand, are concerned with shorter term problems, especially those that relate to an efficient and timely plant operation.
- Sales personnel are also concerned with shorter term issues, but for them the important problems are those that deal with the market—that is, how to meet sales objectives, what to do about competitors' product changes, what characteristics a new product must have to meet the needs of customers, and so forth.

These differences in ways of thinking are, of course, part of what makes it difficult for these groups to collaborate effectively.

The fact that the effective integrators have balanced orientations means that they share more ways of thinking and more behavior patterns with the functional managers than those managers normally do with each other. In a sense, effective integrators speak the language of each of the specialist groups, and thus they are able to work at resolving interdepartmental conflicts. When integrators do not have balanced orientations, their ability to facilitate joint decision making between functional managers suffers. For example:

In several of the organizations studied the integrators did not have a balanced time orientation. Typically, because they were overly concerned with immediate, short-term problems, it was difficult for them to work effectively with the more long-term-oriented scientists. Several comments from the scientists illustrate this difficulty:

"I am no coordinator, but I can see that one of our troubles is that the [integrative] people are so tied up in day-to-day matters they can't look to the future. They are still concerned with 1967 materials when they should be concerned with 1968 markets."

"We get lots of reports from them [the integrators] and we talk to them frequently. The trouble is that all they present to us [in research] are the short-term needs. These aren't the long-range things we are interested in."

"They [the integrators] only find out about problems when they learn that somebody has quit buying our material and is buying somebody else's, and this keeps you on the defense. A lot of our work is catch-up. We would like more future-oriented work from them."

Similarly, there were complaints from production and research personnel when the integrators were so preoccupied with marketing problems that they did not seem to understand technical or production issues:

"Our relations with them [integrators] are good, but not as good as with research. They are not as cost conscious as the laboratory men. They are concerned with the customer."

"He [the integrator] is under a lot of pressure to work with the salesmen on existing products. What he should be, and often tries to act like, is a liaison person, but in reality he is not. He is too concerned with sales problems."

Our research also reveals that effective integrators tend to use an interpersonal style of behavior that falls between the two characteristic behavior orientations of specialized departments. At one extreme, sales personnel are most concerned with maintaining sound personal relationships with their colleagues in other departments. At the other extreme, production managers (and research scientists to a lesser extent) are primarily concerned with getting on with the job, even if this causes the disruption of some established relationships. Our evidence indicates that, to be effective, an integrator needs to think and act in ways which evenly balance the highly social and the highly task-oriented behavior patterns of the units he is attempting to link.

Our research further reveals that entire integrating departments are much more effective when they are intermediate in their degree of structure in relation to the specialized departments they are linking. To analyze the formalization of structure, we examined the degree to which formal rules are utilized, the average span of control, the frequency and specificity of both departmental and individual performance reviews, and the number of levels in the hierarchy.

We found, for example, that most of the formally integrated companies were in an industry where specialized departments had to develop distinctly different organizational practices to perform their respective tasks. Thus, at one extreme, the production units needed highly formalized organizational practices to perform their more routinized tasks. At the other extreme, researchers with problem-solving tasks were more effective in units that had less formalized structures. Between these extremes, the sales personnel operated most effectively with intermediate organizational practices.

When the integrators worked within an intermediate structure, they developed behavior patterns not too unlike those of the different specialists they were linking, and thus they were able to work effectively with all of them.

While our data on the need for intermediate orientations and structures are drawn from a study of integrators attempting to link research, sales, and production units, the same conclusions would seem to hold for integrators linking other functional units.

Performance Recognition

The third important characteristic of effective integrators is the basis on which they see themselves being evaluated and rewarded. For example, in organizations where the integrators were highly effective, they reported that the most important basis for their superior's evaluation was the overall performance of the products on which they were working. Where the integrators were less effective, the superior's evaluation was more on the basis of their individual performance.

This indicates that if integrators are to perform effectively in coordinating the many facets of complex decisions, they need to feel they are being evaluated and rewarded for the total results of their efforts. When they feel they are judged only on the basis of their performance as individuals, they may become so concerned with making decisions to please their superiors or to avoid rocking the boat that they will easily overlook what is desirable from the point of view of their total product responsibility.

Conflict Resolution

The final characteristic of effective integrators is the mode of behavior they utilize to resolve interdepartmental conflict. It seems inevitable that such conflicts will arise in any complex organization from time to time. So, rather than being concerned with the essentially impossible goal of preventing conflict, we are more interested in finding ways for integrators and their colleagues to handle it. Our analysis identifies three modes of behavior for resolving conflict.

Confrontation Technique. The first method, *confrontation,* involves placing all relevant facts before the disputants and then discussing the basis of disagreement until some alternative is found that provides the best solution for the total organization. Confrontation often involves extended discussion. Consider this typical comment from a manager who utilizes this technique:

"Our problems get thrashed out in our committee, at our level. We work them over until everybody agrees this is the best effort we can make. We may decide this isn't good enough. Then we may decide to ask for more plant, more people, or something else. We all have to be realistic and take a modification sometimes, and say this is the best we can do."

Smoothing Approach. The second technique for dealing with conflict, *smoothing*, essentially emphasizes the maintenance of friendly relations and avoids conflict as a danger that could disrupt these relations. Managers using this approach are, in effect, indicating anxiety about facing the consequences of their conflicting points of view. Such action, they feel, might not only threaten their continuing friendly relations, but even their jobs. So they smooth over their differences, perhaps by using superficial banter and kidding, and thus sidestep conflict. One manager described this method as follows:

"I said what I thought in the meeting, but it didn't bother anybody. Perhaps I should have been harsher. I could have said, 'I won't do it unless you do it my way.' If I had said this, they couldn't have backed off. I guess I didn't have the guts to push it that far because our relations are wonderful. We are friendly and happy as larks. We kid one another and go about our business. I've never run into more cooperative people. I think they think I am cooperative too, but nothing happens."

Forcing Method. The final approach, *forcing,* entails the straightforward use of power in resolving conflict. The disputing parties bring to bear whatever power or influence they have to achieve a resolution favoring their own point of view. This mode of behavior often results in a "win-lose" struggle. Unfortunately, it is often the objectives of the total organization that suffer the greatest loss. One manager described how he and his colleagues sometimes force the decisions they desire:

"We have lots of meetings that consist of only two members of our four-man team. They get together and discuss things because they think the other two members won't agree. Then, they try to force their decision on the others. Well, this obviously isn't acting as a team. It's our weak spot."

Our data indicate that there is a close relationship between the effectiveness of integration in an organization and the reliance of its members on confrontation as a way to resolve interdepartmental conflict.

While confrontation showed up as a common mode of resolving conflict in all of the ten organizations we studied, the integrators and functional managers in the six most effectively integrated organizations did significantly more confronting of conflict than their counterparts in the four less well-integrated organizations. Similarly, the managers and integrators in the two organizations that had achieved a medium degree of integration were confronting conflict more often than the managers in the least effectively integrated organizations.

There is one other point worth considering: in the highly integrated organizations, we also found that the functional managers were using more forcing, and/or less smoothing, behavior than their counterparts in the less effective organizations. This suggests that, while confrontation of conflict must be the primary basis for resolving interdepartmental issues, it is also important to have a backup mode of some forcing behavior to ensure that the issue will at least be addressed and discussed, and not avoided.

Personality Traits

The foregoing findings offer some significant clues about the behavior of effective integrators, but they leave unanswered one important question: What type of person makes an effective integrator? It is important, as we suggested earlier, that effective integrators have a combination of broad work experience and education. But it is also important that they have certain personality traits.

Underlying Motives

To learn about these predispositions, an exploratory study was made of nearly 20 integrators in one company, half of whom were highly effective in the judgment of their superiors and half of whom were less so.[3] Specifically, we were interested in measuring their underlying motives and preferred behavioral styles.

Affiliation need: Looking first at underlying motives, we find that the only significant difference between the highly effective integrators and their less effective colleagues is in the *need for affiliation.* The effective integrators are higher in this need than their less effective associates—that is, they pay more attention to others and to their feelings; they try harder to establish friendly relationships in meetings; and they take on more assignments that offer opportunities for interaction.

Achievement Need. There is no statistically significant difference between effective integrators and functional managers, in the *need for achievement* motive. However, there is a tendency for effective integrators to be slightly lower in this motive than less effective integrators. This is worth pointing out, even though the difference is not large, because it seems to run counter to the findings of several managerial studies, which report that managers with a higher need for achievement generally tend to be more successful.[4]

Our exploratory research suggests that to be effective, integrators must have achievement needs that are near the norm of managers in general, but are not especially high. On the one hand, integrators should set high personal goals, do well in competitive situations, have an entrepreneurial view of work, and seek managerial positions of high responsibility. But, on the other hand, they should not be any higher in their need for achievement than the average manager in the organization. In fact, if integrators are too high in this motive, it may reduce their effectiveness in achieving collaboration and resolving conflict, perhaps because they will see interdepartmental conflict as a competitive rather than a collaborative challenge.

Power Need. Both effective and less effective integrators are very similar in their *need for power* and are also close to the norm of managers in general.

[3] The data were collected and analyzed in collaboration with Professor George Litwin of the Harvard Business School.

[4] David McClelland, *The Achieving Society* (Princeton, D. Van Nostrand, 1961), Chapters 6 and 7; "Business Drive and National Achievement," HBR July–August 1962, p. 99; and "Achievement Motivation Can Be Developed" (Thinking Ahead), HBR November–December 1965, p. 6.

While we cannot distinguish between the two sets of integrators on this dimension, we can at least conclude that effective integrators *should* try to influence others by persuasive arguments or by taking leadership roles in group activities. In addition, they *should* aspire to managerial positions that allow exercise of power, influence, and control.

Preferred Styles

In addition to measuring the integrator's motives, their preferred behavioral styles were investigated, with certain interesting results:

- Effective integrators prefer to take significantly more initiative and leadership; they are aggressive, confident, persuasive, and verbally fluent. In contrast, less effective integrators are retiring, inhibited, and silent, and they avoid situations that involve tension and decisions.
- Effective integrators seek status to a greater extent; they are ambitious, active, forceful, effective in communication, and have personal scope and breadth of interests. Less effective integrators are restricted in outlook and interests, and are uneasy and awkward in new or unfamiliar social situations.
- Effective integrators have significantly more social poise; they are more clever, enthusiastic, imaginative, spontaneous, and talkative. Less effective integrators are more deliberate, moderate, and patient.
- Effective integrators prefer more flexible ways of acting; they are adventurous, humorous, and assertive. Less effective integrators are more industrious, guarded, methodical, and rigid.

We should stress one point about these personality traits of effective integrators compared with managers in general. In other managerial studies, as indicated earlier, high need for achievement has been associated with success. Furthermore, this drive for achievement has led to the behavioral styles of initiative leadership, capacity for status, and social poise. But while effective integrators prefer these same styles, their underlying drive is only a moderately high achievement need and—most importantly—a high affiliation need. If these motives in turn lead to relatively high initiative, capacity for status, social poise, and flexibility, then the integrators can be effective in meeting the requirements and demands of their jobs.

The reader probably has already recognized the connection between these personality traits and the behavior characteristics described earlier. Since effective integrators are predisposed to take the initiative, it is not surprising that they have high influence in their organizations. Similarly, it is to be expected that these individuals who prefer to take the initiative, who have social poise, and who are relatively flexible, are effective in helping to resolve conflicts.

This description of the effective integrator's behavior and personality perhaps dispels one widespread management myth—namely, that the word "integrator" is somehow associated with a passive, unassertive role, rather than with the role of an active "leader."

Conclusion

While American industry still needs many types of organizations, as the trend continues for more and more industries to be characterized by rapid rates of technological and market change, more organizations will be like R&D-intensive firms described here. These firms will require both high differentiation between specialist managers in functional units and tight integration among these units. Although differentiation and integration are essentially antagonistic, effective integrators can help organizations obtain both and thus contribute to economic success. This article has described the characteristics of effective integrators—how they should be rewarded, and where they should be placed in the organization. Organizations in dynamic industries that want to achieve a competitive advantage will have to give careful attention to the planning of their integrating jobs and to the selection and development of the people who fill them.

32

Toward a Theory of Organization Communication: Consideration in Channel Selection[1]

Arlyn J. Melcher and Ronald Beller

Introduction

The existence of the formal and informal aspects of organizations is widely known. Even so, there has been little progress in integrating the two in a theory of administration. Others have recognized the problem and called for a solution.

> Where formal organization theory stresses the deliberate planning of structural arrangements and correlation of the work to be done, informal organization takes account of the ways employees actually behave insofar as they deviate from the formal plan. . . . Until it has been corrected by what informal organization theory has to offer, formal organization theory is likely to be inaccurate and incomplete. The obvious challenge to the present generation is to work out a single theory of organization where heretofore there have been two.[2]

Reprinted from *Academy of Management Journal,* Vol. 10, No. 1 (March 1967), pp. 39–52, by permission of the publisher and authors.

[1] The suggestions of Prof. Rance Hill, Department of Sociology, Kent State University, and Dr. James Thompson, Graduate School of Business Administration, Indiana University, on a previous draft are gratefully acknowledged.

[2] Marshall E. Dimock, Gladys O. Dimock, and Lewis W. Koenig, *Public Administration,* rev. ed. (New York: Holt, Rinehart, and Winston, 1961), p. 132.

In part, the difficulty of working out a single theory of organization is the complexity of the problem. There are a number of dimensions to formal organization. These include formal channels of communication, formal policies, procedures, and rules, formal authority and duties assigned to each office, and Gesellschaft norms that the officeholder is expected to observe.[3]

The concept of "informal organization" is used so broadly that it may cover any deviation from the formally prescribed patterns. Progress in developing an understanding of the relationships between formal and informal aspects of organization probably requires that the problem be broken into parts.

This paper focuses upon the communications aspect of organization—a limited but important part of this area. Specifically, the questions posed are where the use of formal or informal communication channels or some combination would contribute to the effectiveness of the administrator and when verbal, written, or some combination of these methods would facilitate an administrator's effectiveness when using the formal or informal networks.

Some suggestions are made in this article for the substantive aspects of a theory of channel selection. The primary purpose of this paper, however, is to present a more systematic approach to the development of theory than presently exists.

The Problem of Channel Selection

Where there is broad acceptance that unofficial channels are and must be used extensively, there is still the question of *when* it would be more effective to use the formal channels and when the informal channels. Little of the extensive literature on the subject of communication is relevant to the problem of channel selection. A good part of the published material deals with effective speaking and writing, leadership of conferences and committees, and similar personal skills.[4] Most of the other books and articles discuss the design of the formal communication systems. Some authors focus upon special networks such as suggestion plans[5] and grievance procedures;[6] others deal with general problems of information flow associated with utilization of

[3] The Gemeinschaft-Gesellschaft continuum summarized and refined by Loomis clarifies the norms with which an officeholder is expected to conform. See Charles P. Loomis, *Social Systems* (New York: D. Van Nostrand, 1960), pp. 57–128.

[4] Illustrative examples are Charles E. Redfield, *Communication in Management* (Chicago: University of Chicago, 1958); Elizabeth Marting, Robert Finley, and Ann Ward (eds.), *Effective Communication on the Job* (New York: American Management Association, 1963); J. Harold Jones (ed.), *Business Communication Reader* (New York, 1958).

[5] Stanley G. Seimer, *Suggestion Plans in American Industry* (New York: Syracuse University Press, 1959); Herman W. Seinwerth, *Getting Results from Suggested Plans* (New York: McGraw-Hill, 1948); *Suggestions from Employees* (New York: National Industrial Conference Board, 1936).

[6] Neil W. Chamberlain, *Collective Bargaining* (New York: McGraw-Hill, 1951), pp. 96–119. Also Wilson Randle, *Collective Bargaining: Principles and Practices* (New York: Houghton Mifflin Co., 1951), pp. 466–492.

computers,[7] or the specification of hierarchical relationships that define the route for formal communication. The writers who deal with informal communication networks typically approach the topic on a descriptive level. Attention is primarily directed toward relating the ways in which deviations from the formal structure occur.[8]

A few investigators have offered clues to the functions alternative channels may serve.[9] Still, there is no framework that directs attention to the consequences of using official and unofficial channels. Since there is no systematic way of dealing with the problem, there is a nearly complete absence of theory.

Alternative Channels and Methods of Using Channels

The manager has a number of alternatives facing him in communicating. He can follow official channels,[10] proceed in the more nebulous area of using

[7] Robert H. Gregory and Richard Van Horn, *Business Data Processing and Programming* (Belmont, California: Wadsworth Publishing Co., 1963); Joseph Becker and Robert M. Hayes, *Information Storage and Retrieval: Tools, Elements, Theories* (New York: John Wiley and Sons, 1963); John Peter McNerney, *Installing and Using an Automatic Data Processing System* (Boston: Graduate School of Business Administration, Harvard University).

[8] For a summary of some of the literature see Delbert C. Miller and William H. Form, *Industrial Sociology* (New York: Harper and Brothers, 1951), pp. 272–307; Leonard Sayles, *Managerial Behavior* (New York: McGraw-Hill, 1964); Keith Davis, *Human Relations at Work* (New York: McGraw-Hill, 1962), pp. 235–260; Joseph A. Litterer (ed.), *Organizations: Structure and Behavior* (New York: Wiley and Sons, 1961), pp. 138–204; Peter M. Blau and W. Richard Scott, *Formal Organizations; A Comparative Approach* (San Francisco: Chandler Publishing Co., 1962), pp. 87–192 and 222–263; Henry Albers, *Organized Executive Action* (New York: John Wiley and Sons, 1961), pp. 339–342; Keith Davis, "The Organization That's Not on the Chart," *Supervisory Management* (July, 1961), pp. 2–7.

[9] Lyndall Urwick, "The Manager's Span of Control." *Harvard Review*, XXXIV, No. 3 (May-June, 1956), pp. 39–47; also "Fitting in the Specialist Without Antagonizing the Line," *Advanced Management*, XVII (January, 1952), pp. 13–16; Chester Barnard, *Functions of the Executive* (Boston: Harvard University Press, 1938), pp. 122–123.

[10] A number of terms will be used interchangeably in this paper. Official, organizational, and formal are used synonymously. Unofficial, nonorganizational, and informal are also used interchangeably. The official channels are defined as those that coincide with the formal chain of command. Messages follow the hierarchical pattern and cannot bypass any organization member on any level. For example, in the diagram below, a message from 31 to 34 would go to 21, then to 1, on to 22, and finally to 34.

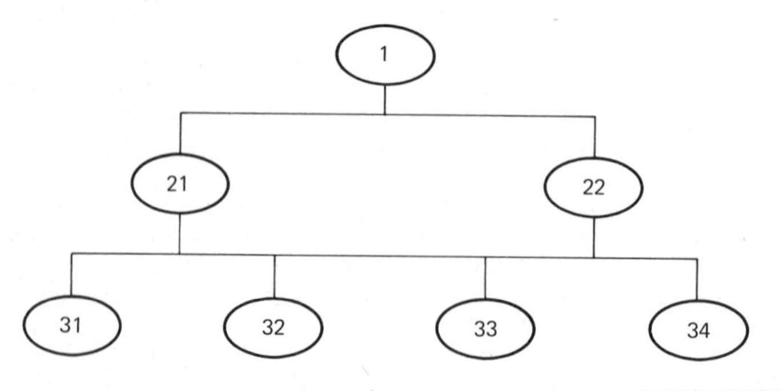

Table 1. Combinations of channels and methods of using channels in communicating channels[11]

Media	*Official*	*Unofficial*	*Official, then Unofficial*	*Unofficial, then Official*
Written	1	2	3	4
Verbal	5	6	7	8
Written, then Verbal	9	10	11	12
Verbal, then Written	13	14	15	16

unofficial channels, or combine the two. While using these channels, the manager may contact others by written media, by voice (either face-to-face, or through other less direct means such as the telephone), or with some combination. There is a fairly complex set of alternatives to choose from in communicating. Table 1 represents 16 combinations of using channels and methods.

Formal communication theory largely deals with combinations 1, 5, 9, and 13, with the emphasis on 1.[12] Writers emphasizing the importance of informal channels largely describe combinations 2, 6, 10, and 14 with emphasis on 6. Lydall Urwick has stressed the importance of combination 16 where communication occurs verbally on the informal level, then is formalized after consensus is reached or action taken.[13] There are a number of factors that should be considered systematically in deciding which of the combinations to use. These include (a) the nature of the communication, (b) the personal characteristics of those involved, (c) the character of the social system, and (d) the communicational attributes of the channels. The elements and their relationships are represented in Figure 1.

Where the nature of the communication is given, factors B, C, and D determine which of the 16 combinations of channels and methods in Table 1 would be most appropriate to use. Each of these factors is discussed in the following sections.

A. Nature of the Communication. Communication can be classified in a number of ways as indicated in Figure 2.

Unofficial channels are all communication routes which do not coincide with the formal structure. A message from 31 to 34 might go directly to 34 or indirectly through any number of intermediaries, some of whom may form a segment of the formal channel—e.g., 31 to 22 to 34; the path is a segment of the formal channel.

[11] The administrator operating according to combination 11 would send a written message through the official channel, supplementing this with a verbal contact using an unofficial channel. The remaining combinations of media and channels are similarly interpreted.

[12] For example, see W. V. Merrihue, *Managing by Communication* (New York: McGraw-Hill, 1960), pp. 174–179.

[13] Urwick, op. cit.

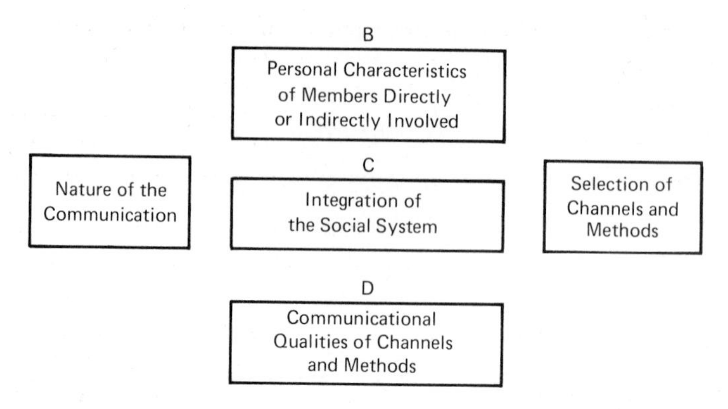

Figure 1. Factors to Consider in Selecting Channels and Methods[14]

1. The type of communication (a) giving an order, (b) giving or requesting information, (c) arriving at a consensus on problems or decisions.
2. The legitimacy / illegitimacy and the public / confidential nature of the message.
3. The extent resources in time, money, or material are involved in implementing the orders, obtaining the information, or achieving consensus.

Figure 2. Element A: Nature of the Communication

1. Type of Communication. The communication may involve giving or requesting information or striving for consensus on problems or decisions. Normally, the simplest communication acts are giving or requesting information or giving orders. Even in the case where the message involves detailed logical arguments, charts, tables, mathematical formulae to effectively convey the message, the communication is relatively simple.

A more complex communication problem is achieving consensus on a subject. There may be various combinations of agreement and disagreement in regard to what goals to pursue or the methods to follow in attaining these goals. These variations are partly summarized in Table 2. Situations B, C, and D are increasingly complex communication acts.

The problem facing an administrator is how to operate the most effectively within the given formal structure. He normally cannot modify the structure

[14] The use of the model should limit the search for a solution, thereby satisfying Deutsch's requirement that a model serve a heuristic function. See Kark W. Deutsch, "On Communication Models in the Social Sciences," *The Public Opinion Quarterly,* XVI (1952), pp. 360–362. The organizing, predictive, heuristic, and measuring capabilities of a model are a function of model content and sequence.

Table 2. Extent of consensus on goals and means of attaining goals[15]

Consensus on the Means of Attaining the Goals	*Consensus on Goals*	
	Agreement	*Disagreement*
Agreement	A	C
Disagreement	B	D

along more appropriate lines. Where there is disagreement on goals or means of achieving goals, for example, it is desirable to explore areas of possible common interest or conduct informal bargaining on the informal level. Once a consensus is reached at least among key individuals, the formal channels may then be used to legitimize the agreement. Policies such as those of RCA support informal combinations of this nature:

> The organization structure and the organization chart define the lines of responsibility and authority, but do not indicate channels of contact. The RCA organization permits and requires the exercise of common sense and good judgment, at all organization levels, in determining the best channels of contact necessary for the expeditious handling of the work. Contact between units of the organization should be carried out in the most direct way. In making such contacts, however, it is the duty of each member of the organization to keep his senior informed.[16]

Policies which encourage "oral" processing of grievances would have the same effect.[17] Much of the criticism of participation in decision making, or lack of it, in organizations may be based upon a misunderstanding of the interacting but separate functions that formal and informal action play. Contrary to the critics, low attendance and nominal participation in general meetings or committees where important decisions are made in unions, universities, government, hospitals, and other organizations may reflect a highly viable organization. For instance, when decisions are made with little more than pro forma participation and little discussion, it may indicate an appropriate use of the informal level before the agreement is formalized. Controversial proposals may be screened out or modified in informal negotiations so as to be made generally acceptable.

On the other hand, active participation in meetings may indicate an unstable organization or a misuse of the formal channels. The administrator may be attempting to achieve consensus on the formal level rather than legitimatizing

[15] Adapted from James D. Thompson and Arthur Tuden, "Strategies, Structures, and Processes of Organizational Decision," in James D. Thompson et. al. (ed.), *Comparative Studies in Administration* (Pittsburgh: University of Pittsburgh, 1959), pp. 195–216.

[16] *The Four Basic Organizational Concepts of the Radio Corporation of America* (New York: Radio Corporation of America, April, 1954), pp. 4–5.

[17] Robert B. McKersie and W. W. Shropeshire, Jr., "Avoiding Written Grievances: A Successful Program," *The Journal of Business,* XXXV (April, 1962), pp. 135–152.

decisions informally achieved. If, for example, the formal channels are initially used when disagreement exists either on goals or methods, it is likely to bring about a formal confrontation between contending groups or individuals. These open conflicts may contribute toward inflexible attitudes and positions that so stymie the administrative process that action cannot ever be taken even on noncontroversial issues. A formal decision under conflict conditions may result in loss of status and generate ill feelings that might poison relationships for many years. Effective administrators probably carefully choose the occasions when they are willing to have formal confrontations. Many others are probably ineffective largely because these formal conflicts occur often enough to disrupt the social fabric essential to cooperation in an organization.

2. Legitimacy of the Communication. A second aspect of the message is its legitimacy. The communication may not be legitimate in the sense of being within the authorized scope of the office or what would normally be approved if brought to the attention of higher level managers or outside auditors. For instance, requests may be made for information that is classified or confidential; informal orders may be given to ignore company policy, or to take some unauthorized shortcut. Arriving at consensus on means or ends may involve accommodations to individuals and groups that would hardly win approval of higher level supervisors or outside auditors. Case studies such as those by Dalton and Kuhn provide extensive examples of the way in which unsanctioned behavior may contribute to the viability of an organization.[18]

3. Resources Used in Communicating. Communication of either a legitimate or illegitimate nature may require the use of substantial resources of time, money or material. The combinations of these two sets of variables are presented in Table 3.

Table 3. Characteristics of information and resources required to obtain it

	Legitimate			*Non-Legitimate*		
Resources Required to Obtain Information	*Orders*	*Requesting or Giving Information*	*Arriving at Consensus on Goals and/or Methods*	*Orders*	*Requesting or Giving Information*	*Arriving at Consensus on Goals and/or Methods*
Requires resources of time, money or material	1	3	5	7	9	11
Requires little or no resources	2	4	6	8	10	12

[18] Melville Dalton, *Men Who Manage* (New York: John Wiley and Sons, 1959); James W. Kuhn, *Bargaining in Grievance Settlement* (New York: Columbia University Press, 1961).

Most writers implicitly assume communications are characterized by the combinations 1 through 6. However, a manager's effectiveness may often rest upon actions that might not be approved by higher management, auditors, or outside observers. In some cases, the activities may adversely affect the firm even if they are in the interest of the individual. More characteristically, though, the actions may be a way of adjusting to an obsolete structure, unrealistic rules or policies, incompetent superiors, or problems that are interdepartmental and require continuous contact among individuals in several formal units.

The willingness of a manager to deviate from formal prescriptions is likely to be closely related to the extent to which he can be held accountable for expenditures and the legitimacy of the action he is being asked to take. When organization resources would be utilized in following an order, or honoring a request for information, or if some question exists about the legitimacy, the receiver may ask that the message be transmitted along formal channels and be written so that he is protected if a question ever arises.

This type of request emphasizes a crucial trait of many nonorganizational dealings. There is an element of risk which must be assumed by each participant to permit meaningful cooperation. In these instances, a request for definition of accountability indicates a reluctance to accept this risk and may force adherence to formal channels and written messages. These factors suggest that the receiver, who strives to minimize risks, would require the sender to use the formal channels and written messages (combination 1 or 13 in Table 1). If the receiver is more flexible, he may be willing to use combinations 4 or 16 in Table 1.

B. Characteristics of the Channel Members. The characteristics of the message sender, receiver, intermediaries, and higher level supervisors are important variables in channel selection.[19] An outline of the relevant personality variables is given in Figure 3.

1. The goal vs. means orientation of those who are directly or indirectly involved in communication.
2. The reliability of those involved to interpret and relay the communication.
3. The language capabilities of the recipient and intermediaries.

Figure 3. Element B: Characteristics of the Channel Members

It is necessary to evaluate the communication potential of those who might be directly or indirectly involved in communicating. The term "potential"

[19] The message sender, receiver, and intermediaries in the respective channels will be referred to as channel members.

is used to represent their capabilities and restraints on the exercise of their abilities.

1. Goal vs. Means Orientation. The degree of commitment of the sending, receiving, and reviewing agents to follow the formal prescriptions of rules, procedure, and authority is a key consideration in selecting methods and channels. As others have observed, some individuals regard the formal prescription as ends. The policies, rules, and other restrictions are adhered to, even though it is impossible to carry out the assigned responsibilities by doing so.[20] Others are goal-oriented and observe the formal prescriptions when they support their efforts, but freely deviate from them when they impede achievement of goals. The latter attitude is well expressed by a Chinese general, 2000 years ago, who was questioned by his officers about a proposal that would violate government policy, but would counter a threatened annihilation of his unit:

> ... His officers asked how he was to take this initiative without first obtaining permission from the Chinese civil commissioner who was accompanying the army; an objection which exasperated Pan Ch'ao.
>
> "Our life and death is to be decided today; what do we care for the opinions of a common civil servant? If we inform him of our plan, he will surely take fright and our projects will be divulged."[21]

Where those involved are committed to attaining ends rather than following procedures, greater reliance can be placed on nonorganization channels and verbal exchanges.

2. Communication Reinforcement. A second determinant of channel selection is the "potential" to contribute to the communication that is to be relayed to others. The recipient and intermediaries can frequently aid the overall effort by adding useful information, by arriving at subsolutions to problems faced by the next member, and by checking the reliability and accuracy of the information transmitted. On the other hand, if the message will be misinterpreted readily or confused by intermediaries, it may be necessary to eliminate some individuals from the channel and require combinations of written and verbal amplification.

Certain individuals may be particularly useful in the communication process. The person could be the "funnel," referred to by Dalton,[22] who is apt to "talk out of turn and carry secrets to the right people," assuring almost predictable communication. The individual might be the leader of one of the informal groups to which the potential receiver belongs. It would also be helpful to identify those who might deal in nonorganizational channels for some personal reward.

[20] Robert K. Merton, "Bureaucratic Structure and Personality," *Social Forces*, XVII (1940), pp. 560–568; Dalton, op. cit., pp. 241–261.

[21] René Grousset, *The Rise and Splendor of the Chinese Empire* (Berkeley: University of California Press, 1964), p. 72.

[22] Dalton, op. cit., pp. 232–234.

3. Language Capabilities. The language capabilities of those potentially involved in communication may restrict or eliminate some from the channel. Modification can be made in the way the communication is expressed and supplementary information provided if it is needed for understanding or to establish the pertinence of the communication to the immediate administrative problem.[23] In practice, some individuals would be excluded and revision would be made in the content and method of communicating in order to adjust to the language capabilities of others.

C. *Integration of the Social System.* Critical factors in the selection of channels of communication are the two closely related items of interpersonal relationships and interaction patterns. Figure 4 outlines two sets of polar interaction and relationship characteristics.

These elements may characterize relationships among individuals in a group or express the relationships among groups. The groups may form along organizational or nonorganizational lines. Table 4 indicates the polar combinations of integration and disintegration that may exist in intragroup and intergroup relationships.

Table 4. Combinations of integration and disintegration within and among groups

	Relationships Among Groups	
Relationships Within Groups	*Integration*	*Disintegration*
Integration	A	C
Disintegration	B	D

The more that intragroup and intergroup relationships develop integrative qualities (combination A), the more it would be possible, and to a large extent necessary, to deal on an informal verbal basis. The use of the formal channels would normally be regarded as aloofness or falling back upon the effective neutral relationships of the formal organization.[24]

Where disintegrative relationships exist both within and among groups (D), communication would probably have to be limited to formal channels.

[23] See Albers, pp. 329–332; Lester Tarnpol, "Attitudes Block Communication," *Personnel Journal,* XXXVII (February, 1959), pp. 325–328.

[24] An alternative to the dichotomy represented in Figure 4 is the Gemeinschaft-Gesellschaft continuum as summarized and refined by Loomis. (See Loomis, op. cit.) To the extent that intra- and intergroup relationships are Gesellschaft in character, it probably would require adherence to written communications following formal channels. In terms of the categories developed by another specialist, Jack Gibb, individuals would approach each other with a supportive rather than a defensive orientation where intra- and inter group integration have developed. See Jack Gibb, "Defensive Communication," *Journal of Communication,* XV, No. 3 (September, 1961), pp. 141–148.

"I" Characteristics: Integration	*"D" Characteristics: Disintegration*
Part I: Action Relationships: Interaction, Communication, & Cooperation	
High Interaction. Interaction at work and off the job. Members may get together before or after lunch or in various recreational activities during evenings, weekends, and vacations.	*Low Interaction.* Little interaction except as required by patterns defined by formal organization or by instructions from a supervisor. Little or no talking or meeting together off the job.
Intensive and extensive communication. Ready flow of communication among members, particularly on informal basis; communication flow is extensive in that it may take place at all times interaction occurs, at work, lunch, before and after work, or at recreation. Little use of formal channels except to record communication when required by others.	*Little Communication.* Restricted flow of communication; careful screening and blockage when feasible; reliance upon formal channels with few informal exchanges.
High Cooperativeness. Spontaneous and ready assistance given without being asked; unhesitant response when requested.	*Low Cooperativeness.* Little assistance given without requests or direction; reluctant or negative responses to requests not formally and regularly part of the position.
Part II: Effective (Emotional) Relationships	
High Cohesiveness. Sense of unity and of being a part of a team; identification with others; "our group" and "we" feeling; sense of belonging; reluctance to leaving group or breaking up existing relationships.	*Low Cohesiveness.* Sense of isolation or in the extreme anomaly; associates regarded as "they" or "the others"; readiness to move into new relationships by leaving or breaking up the group.
High Loyalty and Commitment. Emotional attachment associated with being a group member.	*Low Loyalty and Commitment.* Effective neutral relationship, little emotional commitment to the group.

Figure 4. Polar Relationships That May Exist Among Individuals in Groups and Among Groups

More typical of relationship in organizations is probably the development of integrative elements within groups and disintegrative qualities among groups (C). In this case, the ability to communicate along informal lines among groups may be closely related to membership in various groups or personal contacts with individuals who are members of these various groups. One example of this type of relationship is the "symbolic clique" conceptualized by Dalton.[25] The manager develops contacts with others at various levels in the organization who keep him informed as well as acting as his spokesmen. Without these relationships, one has little choice but to rely on the formal network.

D. Channel Characteristics. Each communication channel and method of using the network has specific characteristics which are relevant to communication. Six key elements are speed, feedback, selectivity, acceptance, monetary cost, and establishing accountability.

1. Speed. Where the written or verbal approach is given, unofficial channels generally are more direct and faster than official networks. Where the channel is given, verbal contacts usually are speedier than written. The combination of unofficial channels with verbal communication normally is the fastest. However, any combination of verbal followed up by written forms is as fast when the written message is used for recording rather than immediate communication purposes.

2. Feedback. The more complex the message, the greater the need for two-way interaction between the sender and receiver. This helps the sender to determine the understanding by the receiver and the effectiveness of the channel selected (i.e., whether the channel performed as the sender anticipated in terms of speed, accuracy). Feedback is automatic in face-to-face contact where both can get what Thayer[26] calls "instructions" in interpreting words, gestures, facial expressions, inflection, tone, emphasis, etc. Thus, verbal communication provides greater and quicker feedback compared to written messages since it provides a complete circuit while written media typically provides a one-way transmission.[27] Even when feedback is actively sought by the sender of written messages, the inherent delay in such a process can lead to erroneous actions.

3. Selectivity. Those sending messages frequently wish to exercise control over circulation of the message in the organization. The legitimacy of the communication is an important factor determining the need for control. In other cases, there may be a plan for gradual dissemination of information where only a small group is initially informed of developments. Unofficial channels may permit a greater degree of control than formal channels since the sender can be more selective in determining who will be initially included. Those suspected of leaking secrets to unauthorized personnel would be excluded.

4. Acceptance. One vital skill is the ability to persuade others to take desired actions. Persuasive efforts normally require a large amount of personal interaction between the participants. The channel selected for message trans-

[25] Dalton, op. cit., pp. 57–59.

[26] Lee Thayer, *Administrative Communication* (Homewood, Illinois: Richard D. Irwin, 1961), p. 70.

[27] Redfield, op. cit., p. 74; Blau and Scott, op. cit., p. 118.

mission is crucial to the effort to enlarge the receiver's "area of acceptance."[28] Where persuasion or arriving at consensus is involved, it is essential to operate on the informal verbal level as positions can be changed without loss of official status. When agreement is achieved, the decision should then be formally processed and written. The latter is necessary since those that were not involved in making the decision are more likely to accept it when the decision is an official act of the authorized office. Barnard observed that the formal organization structure performs a valuable function in defining communication authoritativeness and authenticity.[29] This means that the hierarchical status differentiation is accepted as *prima facie* evidence of these qualities essential to message acceptance. Thus, requests for and giving of information upward in the hierarchy, and communicating decisions or information downward, are likely to receive greater acceptance when official channels are followed.

5. Cost. The monetary cost of using the various channels may be important in selecting a channel. For example, in a geographically dispersed organization, this factor could become important since it is expensive to travel from one location to another in order to meet face-to-face. Long-distance calls, closed circuit television, and other methods that enable verbal person-to-person exchanges may be substituted on economic grounds. Written communication may need to be used where many are competing for the recipient's time. It is considerably cheaper to queue written messages than it is verbal. A great deal of time can be wasted getting in to see the boss.

6. Accountability. Performance measurement and control depend on a clear establishment of accountability in carrying out assigned responsibilities. There must be accountability for (1) making past, present, and future decisions, (2) giving orders and requesting or giving information, (3) initiating communication contacts, and (4) utilizing organization resources in gathering information, or in carrying out orders. Written communications following formal channels are the most effective way of establishing accountability. The communication could initially take place on an informal level to speed up the process, but the communication would have to be officially recorded (written and sent along formal channels) if accountability is to be clearly established.

Conclusion

A practicing manager is faced with a choice of methods and channels when he is (1) establishing a program for a previously nonprogrammed activity, (2) reviewing an existing program for possible improvement, (3) working in an organizational context that is changing (new problems, personnel changes, increased cost and time pressures), or (4) orienting himself in a new job. At

[28] Barnard, *Functions of the Executive,* pp. 167–171.
[29] Barnard, "Functions of Status Systems," loc. cit.

these times, a judgment must be made on the value of the alternative official or unofficial channels and written or verbal communication. The specification of channels and the methods of using the channels clarify the alternatives available to the manager. Administrative effectiveness probably is critically affected by how quickly a manager familiarizes himself with the orientation of his superiors, subordinates, and members in other departments, the extent to which he integrates himself into the social system, and his awareness of the functional aspects of the alternative channels. He is then in a position to use the channels and media that would best fit the nature of the communication. It is unlikely managers have complete information on all these variables to arrive at rational judgments. The important point, though, is that they must make intuitive or explicit judgments about each of these items. Their general effectiveness is likely to turn upon whether they consider all the dimensions of communications that are involved.

While the theory offered in this article is of a tentative nature, it provides some hypotheses that can be further explored. Further, the framework provides a basis for systematically observing in research studies the behavior of effective administrators. As projects along these lines are pursued, we will be in a position to take a big step forward in developing a theory of organizational communication and to move toward a single theory of administration.

section **6**

expansion and contraction

33

Stages of Corporate Development

Donald H. Thain

With increasing pressures for growth and diversification, top managers, long-range planners, and consultants are confronted with many problems in regard to corporate and organizational development. Attempts to solve these key problems, integrally related to the formulation and implementation of corporate strategy, confront top managers with many basic issues:

Is growth and/or diversification desirable?
How do companies grow?
What are the basic stages of evolution in corporate development?
How can one tell what stage of development a company is in?
What are the particular problems and opportunities, strengths and vulnerabilities of each stage?
What are the key factors that management should emphasize at the different stages of development?
How can management plan the transition from one stage to the next?
Is growth to a conglomerate structure via internal product development, mergers and/or acquisitions desirable?

One of the most practical and powerful tools to assist in answering such questions and in identifying and analyzing problems of corporate growth and diversification is the concept of stages of corporate development.[1]

Several teachers of General Management and others have found this concept to be helpful in understanding and dealing with problems of corporate growth and organizational change in teaching, research and consulting. It also provides an overview that enables practitioners and students to integrate many other related ideas from fields such as human relations, organizational behaviour, marketing, control, and finance into a framework relevant to the general management problems of planning and executing corporate strategy.

The Stages of Corporate Development Concept

The stages of corporate development concept can be briefly described as follows:

As companies that are relatively successful grow larger in size and scope, they experience a number of fairly obvious changes:

—Sales, expenditures, gross profits and investments increase.
—The numbers of employees increase.
—Resources increase.
—Activities and functions increase in size, scope and number.
—Operating and management problems increase in size, complexity and risk.
—Operating and managerial specialization increases.
—Product lines increase either vertically (diversification in the same industry) or horizontally (diversification into different industries).
—The number and specialization of organizational sub-units increase.

This evolution of companies from small and simple to large and complex tends to be marked by three main stages of development as follows (see also Exhibit 1):

Small and Simple		Large and Complex
Stage I	Stage II	Stage III
One Unit "One-man show"	One Unit Functionally specialized group	Multi-unit General office and decentralized divisions

One unit means an internally independent, unified product-market business operation. This "nondiversified," "single" product or service unit buys,

[1] While the idea of stages or chapters in the development of industrial enterprises has been used by others (see, for example, Alfred D. Chandler, *Strategy and Structure,* Cambridge, Mass. M.I.T. Press, 1962), this particular version of the concept of organizational development was, to the best of my knowledge, first used explicitly in teaching Business Policy by Professors Christensen and Scott of Harvard Business School. I wish to acknowledge their innovation and leadership in bringing the concept to bear on the course.

sells and operates on its own; it constitutes a single profit centre; its operating results are logically represented by one profit and loss statement and its financial condition by one balance sheet.

Although all companies can be classified on this spectrum as to their stage of corporate development, not all are "pure" examples of any one of the stages: i.e., many are in a phase of transition from stage I to II or from II to III.

In the rest of this article we shall explain this concept in greater detail and describe and comment on some of the problems that it raises not only for top management but also for industry and government planners.

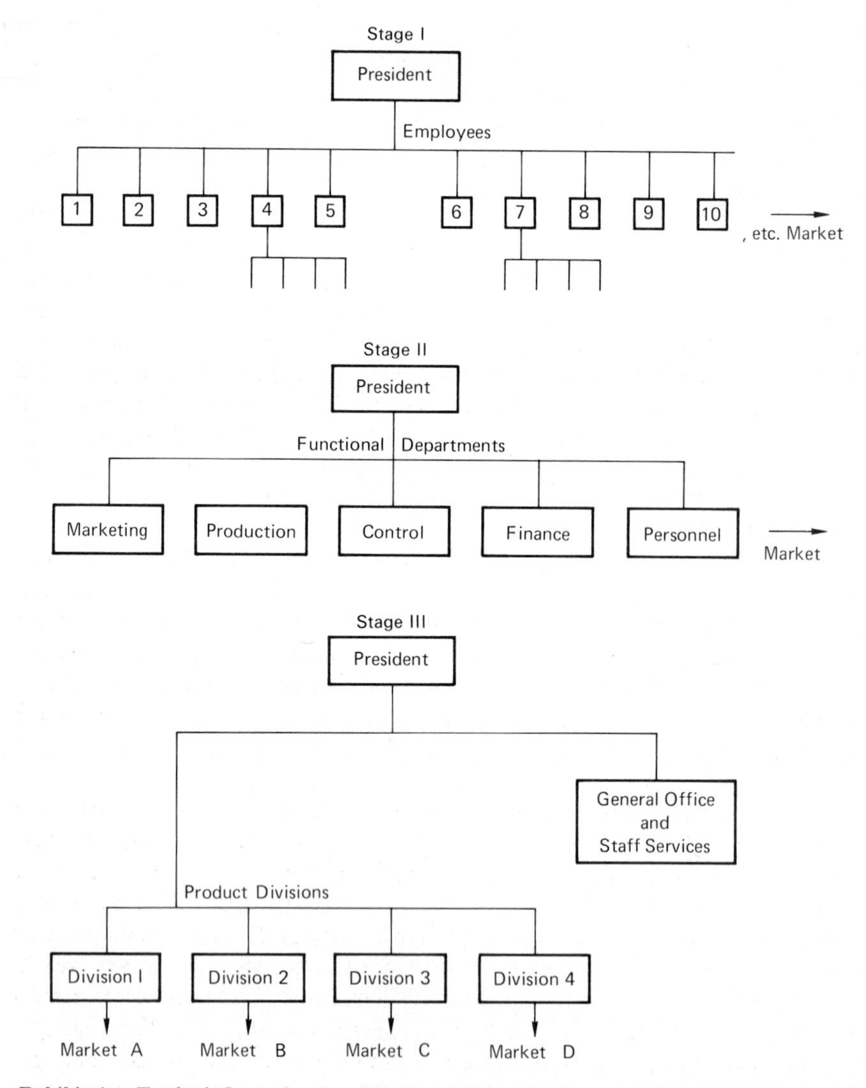

Exhibit 1. Typical Organization Charts of Stage I, II, and III Companies

Stage I

Except for the few that were founded "ready made" with substantial resources and a top management team, all companies began in Stage I. Many of the great names from the business hall of fame—Henry Ford, John D. Rockefeller, Timothy Eaton, Andrew Carnegie, and the Krupps—were, for a period at least, Stage I company managers.

The major characteristic of the Stage I company is that it is primarily a "one man show." With the exception of perhaps a few shares doled out to directors, relatives or long-time, key employees, he maintains absolute ownership and control. The company's strengths, vulnerabilities and resources are closely correlated with his personality, ability, style of management, and personal financial situation. He makes all the important decisions, relying on sales, production and office supervisors only to the extent necessary to see that his unilateral decisions are carried out. The organization chart is usually very simple—most employees report directly to the owner-manager with the exception of those whose work is supervised more or less by others with more seniority or experience.

Because of its tightly limited resources, the Stage I company must rely heavily on support from outside factors such as suppliers, sales agents, bankers, accountants and lawyers. The Stage I owner-manager tends to be a notoriously authoritarian, short-term operator. Because he can't afford back-up managers and staff, he is the proverbial "jack of all trades" and must spend most of his time tending to daily operations and constantly recurring crises, many of which could bring his venture to a sudden, sad ending. It is no accident that nearly all bankruptcies occur in Stage I companies. Although his flexibility for decision-making and organizational change may be great, the constraints resulting from lack of resources and narrow vistas impose severe limitations on his scope for action.

In the functional areas of the Stage I company, the major emphasis must be on operating. In marketing the push is on sales, in production on turning out products to meet shipping schedules, in control on keeping information for a simple accounting system frequently run by an outside accountant, in finance on liquidity and working with a banker as necessary, in personnel on hiring people, usually on short notice to fill holes in the staff. As one Stage I manager defined it, "Management here is just attending to one darn problem after another."

Although many Stage I managers are happy with their lot as "independent businessmen," when the attraction of "being my own boss" wears off, their many problems and vulnerabilities become apparent. His company is never more than a heartbeat away from crisis and perhaps disaster. I have been involved in at least two substantial Stage I businesses with a net worth of $200,000 to $400,000 that, except for a few hard assets, were practically worthless overnight as a result of the deaths of their owners. Decisions, frequently dictated by lack of resources, are highly vulnerable to uncontrollable changes by customers and outside suppliers. Unfortunately, the Stage I owner-manager is frequently his own worst enemy. Compelled to work long hours, constantly burdened by the total responsibility of a vulnerable enterprise, unable to manage, plan and organize, he succumbs to a Stage I managerial style—short-term thinking, operating orientation, swamped by detail, inability to delegate, playing his cards close to his chest and unwilling, perhaps for good reason, to place his confidence in others. This Stage I operating syndrome, as much as anything else, may lead to his undoing.

In spite of all the problems and risks, if all goes well, the Stage I company may prosper to the point where sales, profits and resources increase and a reasonable degree of stability is gained. Obviously, some Stage I managers are highly successful in terms of income, capital gains, independence, local status and the rewards related to self-actualization. I have known several Stage I owner-managers who, for good reason, would not exchange positions with anyone.

If the Stage I company owner can sell and earn enough to support the extra overhead costs, can promote or hire other managers and can adjust his personal style to work "with" others, he may build a management team that enables him to reach the point of corporate development that marks the transition to Stage II.

Stage II

The distinguishing characteristic of Stage II is that it is a one unit enterprise run by a team of managers with functionally specialized responsibilities. In other words, when the subtle transition has been made from management by one man to management by a group, the company has made it to Stage II! Although we tend to think of marketing, production, control, finance and personnel as being the major functions of the business (see Exhibit 1), this breakdown may vary widely depending on the size and scope of the company. In a small, simple, newly developed Stage II company the functional team might be limited—perhaps only the president, a sales manager and a production manager. In a large, highly developed, complex Stage II company the group might include marketing, production, engineering, control, finance, personnel, labor relations, long-range planning and public relations. In addition each of these functional units might be further subdivided: e.g., marketing might include departments for sales, advertising, brand management and marketing research. In other firms such as banks or steel companies, the traditional functional groupings might be sub-units that more effectively relate to the particular operating problems of the business. In a large integrated oil company, for example, the functional specialization might be exploration, drilling, pipelines, transportation, refining and marketing. The hallmark of the Stage II organization is that in spite of the variety of functional sub-units and the sometimes laboured and artificial attempts[2] to make them into performance or

[2] It is interesting to note two particular organizational developments that have been tried by many companies to break down large Stage II organizations, e.g., oil, steel or soap companies, into meaningful performance centres. The first was to divide such large companies into separate units that perform major operating tasks. When such operating units are required to rely on each other as suppliers or customers without the possibility of substantial outside buying and/or selling,

profit centres, they really stand or fall together in that they are built around one business, e.g., banking or aluminum, and must combine to sell primarily to one end market, e.g., petroleum or steel.

The size, scope and resources of Stage II companies vary widely—some of the largest companies in the world in industries such as steel, oil and agricultural implements are basically Stage II. Ownership is usually public but may be private or personal. The great strength of a Stage II company lies in its concentration and specialization in one field. Its great vulnerability is that all its eggs are in one basket. Stage II companies tend to be strong in solving functional and product problems and weak in coping with basic market changes and the general management problems related to strategic change.

Nearly all Stage II companies are much less reliant on external factors than Stage I companies. They are also much less vulnerable to failure or bankruptcy. Stage II companies usually have some "managers" (as contrasted with Stage I operators) and enough depth in resources that they can afford some planning.

Some Stage II companies, for good reasons, remain concentrated in one field which fully challenges their resources and abilities. They grow by expansion of present marketing and production activities and diversification through backward or forward integration into closely related products or services. However, many Stage II companies, seeking growth, profitability and security and realizing that they are vulnerable to the life cycle of one product as the Stage I company is to the life cycle of one man, attempt to diversify. If diversification via internal product development, merger or acquisition works out, additional product sub-units will emerge and, if these are successful in developing into independent units, the company can make the transition to Stage III.

Stage III

The hallmark of the Stage III company is a general office with ultimate control over multiple operating divisions, each similar to a Stage II company. Although the general offices may vary widely in size, organization, power and operating control, their central functions are investment trusteeship, supervision, control and evaluation of division managers and operations, staff advice and further diversification. As investment trustees, managing a "portfolio" of enterprises, they carry out the process of capital budgeting for the corporation as a whole. The cash flows from the divisions are remitted to the general office for reinvestment in the most necessary or highest payoff projects

they really constitute one overall integrated unit. Thus, even though a steel company might call its mining, transportation, blast furnace, converting, and marketing operations separate divisions, they tend to stand or fall together and would thus constitute sub-units of a Stage II company.

The brand management type organization is a second attempt to divide large Stage II companies into meaningful sub-units for management purposes. However, the brand management or related product breakdown has been unsatisfactory in several respects because of the difficulty of dividing overlapping functions and defining authority and responsibility in a way that makes performance measurement accurate and meaningful.

to be found across the company or outside. If a division cannot produce a profit above the required minimum rate of return, it is sold, liquidated, or otherwise disposed of.

Supervision of division operations is carried out primarily by reviewing plans and forecasts, evaluating results and working with the division managers and their staffs to insure their development and performance especially as measured by sales, profits and return on investment.

Staff advice or management consulting is "made available" to operating divisions sometimes by a large, highly qualified group that also provides a talent pool of potential line managers.

Since the emphasis is on finding and developing profit opportunities, most Stage III companies are also staffed and organized to pursue further diversification aggressively and systematically both internally via research and development and product development and externally via mergers and acquisitions.

The successful Stage III company has many strengths that can make it a formidable international economic unit. Its ownership is almost always public and its resources are tremendous—for practical purposes, almost unlimited. Companies such as General Motors have power and resources that dwarf even those of many small countries. In large Stage III companies resources seldom, if ever, limit decisions; it is strategic decisions and concepts of scope and control that limit resources. It can be relatively independent of outside resources. Large cash flows, management depth, functional specialization and market diversification make its vulnerability to bankruptcy practically zero. It has great powers to regroup and survive even in the event of such a serious crisis as the complete failure of an entire product division.

Perhaps the most significant weakness of the gigantic Stage III company is that its organization is so large and complex that it tends to become relatively inflexible. Organizational restraints are necessarily great, defense of the "status quo" becomes built in, and a time-consuming, bureaucratic approach complete with formal and informal administration by "due process" becomes institutionalized. So many checks and balances become operative that significant change may be beyond the power or control of any one man or small group. As one large Stage III company division manager put it to me: "This company has so many boards and committees that it would take us six months to get approval to buy ten dollar bills at a buck a piece." Some of these problems of organizational inflexibility, the "dinosaur factor," are, of course, a function of size and apply equally, if not more, to very large Stage II companies.

At this point the reader may be wondering: What is the difference between a Stage III company and a conglomerate? Although there is no strict definition of a conglomerate, the term usually implies a divisionalized company that has grown rapidly and diversified widely especially by acquisitions and mergers as well as by internal growth. If so, then all conglomerates are Stage III companies but a Stage III company is not necessarily a conglomerate, i.e., a Stage

III company may develop slowly and without mergers and acquisitions.

One frequent problem in analyzing Stage III or conglomerate type companies is confusion as to the approach and tactics of management. As I see it there are at least four different product-expansion approaches or philosophies expounded by the top managers in such companies. Some Stage III companies such as DuPont adopt what might be termed a *conservative* approach in regard to expansion and addition of new products—they favor diversification and the addition of new divisions but seldom, if ever, seek opportunities that do not evolve directly from present operations. Another group follows an *open-minded* approach as practised at Westinghouse. Top management does not rule out new and very different product-market opportunities if they make good sense and appear to be related. Other conglomerates, e.g. Litton Industries, pursuing an aggressive approach single out acquisition possibilities and attempt to acquire them, apparently backing off if there is considerable overt resistance from incumbent management. Finally, what I could call the *aggressive-attacking* approach is practised by conglomerates such as Hunt Foods and Industries Inc., headed by Norton Simon, who will bite at almost any attractive company where management looks slack or vulnerable. Their specialty is financial wheeling and dealing, shaking things up, getting rid of dead wood and redeploying assets presumably for the benefit of the shareholders.

Depending on one's point of view, the aggressive or aggressive-attacker type thinking may be a "breath of fresh air" or a lot of "dangerous thinking that should be investigated."

A great danger of conglomerates, already recognized by governments and financiers, is that they can provide great power to men whose tactics, motives and sense of responsibility may leave a lot to be desired (this is also true of large Stage I or II companies as well). There is also in some Stage III companies the tendency to push performance so hard that managers are forced to "play the numbers game," i.e., manipulate return on investment and other performance indicators to show continuous improvement.

Although moral judgments can and should be made of any manager's behavior, it is important that the student of corporate development does not confuse the philosophy of motives of management with the realities, strengths and weaknesses of the basic organization structure.

Since the Stage III corporate organization structure can probably be expanded indefinitely, it is interesting parenthetically to pose the question: What, if anything, lies beyond Stage III? Observation of current trends in regard to national economic planning in Canada and other countries suggests that a possible Stage IV may be the informal but systematic liaising of major companies and industries with government in an organization and communication framework for the formulation and implementation of national economic strategy. In fact it may be argued that the lack of an adequate Stage IV organization structure and concept of development is a major current problem in

Canada and many other countries. Needless to say, the problems and managerial challenges involved will be tremendous.

DuPont: A Classic Example of the Stages of Corporate Development. It is interesting and worthwhile to use the stages of corporate development concept in analyzing actual companies to understand their strategic problems and to learn how and why they develop. One of the clearest examples of corporate development through the three stages is found in the DuPont Company.[3] The fortunes of the DuPont Company came to a low ebb in the crisis of 1902 caused by the sudden death by pneumonia of president Eugene DuPont. "At the time of Eugene DuPont's death, the company and the [gun-powder] industry were being managed just as they had been for more than a generation. The DuPont Company itself administered only a few black powder plants and a smokeless powder works . . . until 1902 it remained a family enterprise. As one DuPont noted: "the business was entirely managed by the senior partner . . . the head of the firm was *ex officio* head of the family." This method of operation was anything but effective and efficient. As President, Eugene DuPont and his predecessors "may have controlled their properties but hardly administered them. . . . " "The lack of administrative control is suggested by the fact that Henry DuPont [Eugene's predecessor] carried on single-handedly from a one room office . . . most of the business of his company. He wrote nearly all of the business correspondence himself in long hand."

In the confusion following Eugene DuPont's death the remaining partners concluded that there was no qualified successor and decided to sell the company to an "ancient and friendly competitor."

Young and energetic Alfred DuPont, who refused to accept this possibility, joined with two cousins, Coleman and Pierre, to buy the company from the elder DuPonts. Their first move was to reorganize the company into a functionally specialized group of top managers who "embarked on the strategy of consolidation and centralization." This reorganization, of course, marked the transition of DuPont to Stage II.

Under the central control of a basic Stage II organization, consolidation of gunpowder operations, professional management, capital budgeting, and planning were all emphasized. Perhaps the key turning point in the history of DuPont came as a result of the tremendous expansion to supply the 1914–18 demand for gunpowder. Output, sales, assets, plants, employment and profits all mushroomed suddenly and unexpectedly. This mushrooming growth was also accompanied by backward, forward and horizontal integration. Toward the end of the war the pressures of excess plant capacity in post war reconversion intensified the modest efforts at diversification begun as early as 1903. Diversification policy, firmed up in 1917 and implemented soon after, rapidly changed the nature of the DuPont business. The mounting management

[3] All quotes in this section from Alfred D. Chandler, *Strategy and Structure*, M.I.T. Press 1962, Ch. 2.

problems, resulting from substantial diversification, so overwhelmed the centralized functional organized top management group that they lost effective control. After several attempts to strengthen the central office, some managers realized that they needed a new and different pattern of organization. Although the company was still experiencing many operating difficulties, the proposal to reorganize around product divisions suggested by a group of younger managers was repeatedly rejected by top management who thought the solution lay in making the old Stage II organization work better. Finally with the crisis and losses of 1921, perhaps the worst year in DuPont's history, the multidivisional, Stage III structure was finally accepted. Implemented in 1921, and improved in operation over the next few years, the Stage III organization is still in existence in DuPont and has served ever since as a model for the multidivisional or conglomerate organization introduced in many other large companies. Thus we have a clear record, almost to the exact day, of how and why DuPont made the transition from Stage I to II and then from II to III.

Key Management Problems of Stages I, II and III. One of the highest payoff uses of the stages concept is to red flag some of the basic strategic problems common to companies at different stages of development. Research and consulting in a wide variety of companies has convinced me that there are six key factors in the process of general management:

1. Sizing up the company—environment situation and defining problems and opportunities.
2. Setting objectives.
3. Formulating strategy.
4. Organizing.
5. Measuring and controlling performance.
6. Designing and implementing a reward-punishment system to influence motivation and performance.

Studying these factors in companies in different stages of development, we note major differences in the process (see Exhibit 2):

There are also major differences in the management of the basic functions—marketing, production, control, finance and personnel—as the company evolves. These tendencies are indicated in some detail in Exhibit 3.

Comparative analysis clearly indicates that the major challenges both in regard to the functions and the process to management are different in each stage of development. The key skills necessary to be an outstanding general manager also differ in each stage, shifting from short-term operating ability in Stage I to product-functional emphasis in Stage II and broad management abilities in investment trusteeship, diversification and management supervision and development in Stage III. It is not surprising that many top managers who are relatively successful in one stage may find their style and approach uncomfortable, if not inappropriate, in another stage.

Problems of Transition. Many interesting examples of a wide variety of

Functions of General Management

	I	II	III
1. Size-up 2. Objectives 3. Strategy 4. Organization 5. Measurement and control 6. Reward—punishment system	Emphasis is on the personal approach to each management function. Major problems are lack of functional expertise and broad management experience and necessary concentration on "fire fighting" operations necessary for survival.	Emphasis is on the functional approach and a one product, service, market or technology approach. Major weakness is attachment to one product life cycle and lack of strategic product-market options for investment and resource utilization.	Management problems and opportunities related to diversification and multi subunits. Great strength and resources but many problems in regard to planning, control, and integration.

Exhibit 2. Key Factors in Top Management Process in Stage I, II and III Companies

Key Factors in Management Process	*Stage I*	*Stage II*	*Stage III*
1. Size up: Major problems	Survival and growth, dealing with short-term operating problems	Growth, rationalization and expansion of resources, providing for adequate attention to product problems	Trusteeship in management and investment and control of large, increasing, and diversified resources. Also, important to diagnose and take action on problems at division level
2. Objectives	Personal and subjective	Profits and meeting functionally oriented budgets and performance targets	ROI, profits, earnings per share

3. Strategy	Implicit and personal; exploitation of immediate opportunities seen by owner-manger	Functionally oriented moves restricted to "one product" scope; exploitation of one basic product or service field	Growth and product diversification; exploitation of general business opportunities
4. Organization: Major characteristic of structure	One unit "one man show"	One unit functionally specialized group	Multi-unit general staff office and decentralized operating divisions
5. (a) Measurement and control	Personal, subjective, control based on simple accounting system and daily communication and observation	Control grows beyond one man, assessment of functional operations necessary, structured control systems evolve	Complex formal system geared to comparative assessment of performance measures, indicating problems and opportunities and assessing management ability of division managers
5. (b) Key performance indicators	Personal criteria, relationships with owner, operating efficiency, ability to solve operating problems	Functional and internal criteria such as sales, performance compared to budget, size of empire, status in group, personal relationships, etc.	More impersonal application of comparisons such as profits, ROI, P/E ratio, sales, market share, productivity, product leadership, personnel development, employee attitudes, public responsibility
6. Reward-punishment system	Informal, personal, subjective, used to maintain control and divide small pool of resources to provide personal incentives for key performers	More structured, usually based to a greater extent on agreed policies as opposed to personal opinion and relationships	Allotment by "due process" of a wide variety of different rewards and punishments on a formal and systematic basis. Company wide policies usually apply to many different classes of managers and workers with few major exceptions for individual cases

Exhibit 3. General Emphases in Business Functions in Stage I, II and III Companies

Function	*Stage I*	*Stage II*	*Stage III*
Major Emphasis	Usually an operating orientation as opposed to product or functional emphasis	Functional orientation	Investment trusteeship, orientation in president's office, functional orientation in staff and product orientation in line
Marketing	Major marketing problem is generating sales, usually only one or small number of employees involved	Specialization develops in advertising, sales promotion, marketing research etc.	Marketing functions become well developed with specialization in a wide variety of marketing functions by product or product line and geographical area
Production	Usually a simple, efficient factory operation geared to turn out maximum production with minimum investment	Production operations become more specialized, production management improves with attendent increases in overhead	Complex production function and product specialization usually accompanied by extensive engineering, research and development studies and careful consideration of vertical integration and make or buy problems

Measurement and control	Simple accounting system usually supervised by outside accountant	Accounting system becomes more complex with emphasis on cost accounting and simple statistical techniques, control system is adapted to functional decisions and problems	Complex accounting, control and mathematical decision-making tools supervised by functional specialists and emphasizing product profitability and capital investment decisions
Finance	Almost non-existent except to work with banker as necessary	More sophisticated forecasting and cash budgeting techniques used for purpose of planning capital needs and reducing cost of capital	Complex problems of portfolio management aimed at increasing return on invested capital in all divisions and overall
Personnel	Handled on a personal basis by owner-manager	Additional functional specialization and evolution of formal policies for hiring, firing, training and promoting	Development of considerable sophistication both in special head office staff department and in division line operating departments in regard to hiring and training personnel necessary to perpetuate the company complex "manpower planning" approach often utilized

problems in managing corporate development through the transition between stages could be cited. While organizational change may be the most obvious symptom of transition, market opportunity and corporate strategy should always take precedence. For top management, especially the president or operating executive, the transition requires basic changes in approach and behaviour. As a company evolves, his primary role must change from that of a one-man show, entrepreneur (Stage I) to product specialist, an "oil man" or a "steel man" (Stage II) to an investment trustee. "I'm here to use resources to make money for our shareholders" (Stage III). The president's management style, relationships, skills, and approach must change fundamentally to cope with the new roles necessarily arising from transition to a new stage.

Some companies have failed or stagnated because top management could not evolve from Stage I to II or from II to III. Others, such as the Singer Manufacturing Company, forced by foreign competition and stagnation to diversify, have struggled to make the transition apparently without a clear concept of what exactly they were trying to do. General Motors, one of the first and largest Stage III companies, was formed by the visionary William C. Durant who followed a strategy of consolidation and integration. The financial crisis of 1920 revealed that General Motors was really a noncoordinated string of Stage I companies whose collective lack of control, planning and organization had brought them to the brink of disaster. The company was rescued by DuPont capital and management and the great abilities of Alfred P. Sloan who, among other moves, installed the basic Stage II type functional controls necessary to keep inventories, accounts receivable, and production in line with sales.

Another example of a very different type of problem is that of the Solartron Electric Group Limited. In the late 1950's Solartron made the transition from Stage II to III only to have to reverse itself and reorganize back to Stage II because it could not generate the business and scope necessary to support an expensive, cumbersome and ineffective Stage III organization.

Another interesting problem of managing corporate development is found in the case of the Ford Motor Company. Henry Ford will be recorded in business history as the innovative president and owner of one of the largest Stage I type companies. His personal inability to advance beyond a Stage I managerial style constituted a severe handicap to Ford in the competitive race with General Motors.

The Drive for Corporate Development. The drive for corporate growth and development is almost continuous and universal because it is fueled by some very high powered motivators common to managers around the world.

To any observer, with even a passing involvement in corporate development, it is fairly obvious that companies grow and diversify, acquire and merge with other companies primarily because managers want to. Why? As I see it, for several reasons.

One of the most obvious reasons why managers push for development is that it makes them look smart and they gain in income, capital gains, approval and status because their company is larger, more profitable, more widely known and this is duly noted by the board of directors, shareholders and the investment community.

There is little doubt that as Galbraith and others have alleged,[4] nearly all managers have a basic drive for security—to survive and to reduce their fear of the unknown. One of the obvious routes to increased security is to sell more customers, add new products, develop new markets, acquire more and better production facilities, build a stronger financial base, have a larger, deeper and more skilled organization, and so on.

Another basic reason that top men have for developing the corporation is to gain power, the ability to influence behaviour in one's favour. Most managers seem to understand—either implicitly and instinctively or explicitly in a frankly Machiavellian sense—that the bigger and more secure their base of operations, the greater the resources at their command, the greater their power.

Another common and important reason for corporate development is fear of decline and failure of present operations. In my experience the most frequently encountered motivator for development to Stage III is poor and declining profit prospects in a Stage II company's operations. Management is really fighting a rear guard action against the threatened decline or failure of a major part of the company.

The need for challenge and emotional involvement in exciting activity and playing "the performance game" is another basic motivator that drives many other managers to plan and implement corporate development. While there are many other internal and external reasons for development from Stage I to II and from II to III, these appear to be the main fundamental drives. Obviously, these come from deep inside the manager. It is very doubtful that they could ever be stopped.

The Blocks to Corporate Development. If it is true that there is all this fundamental drive for corporate development, why is corporate development limited to the extent that it is? The operative forces for and against development represent a synthesis of the interaction of motivation and blocks and forces of attraction and forces of resistance. In a free enterprise society these countervailing forces form a very complex and subtle equilibrium subject to change from a variety of pressures such as changes in personal taxes, monetary and fiscal policy, business laws and regulations, national economic planning, and so on. Some of the major internal and external blocks to development may be briefly summarized as follows:

[4] J.K. Galbraith, *The New Industrial State,* Houghton Mifflin Company, Boston, 1967, p. 167.

(a) Internal Blocks to Development.

Stage I to II	*Stage II to III*
Lack of ambition and drive. Personal reasons of owner-manager for avoiding change in status quo. Lack of operating efficiency. Lack of quantity and quality of operating personnel. Lack of resources such as borrowing power, plant and equipment, salesmen, etc. Product problems and weaknesses. Lack of planning and organizational ability.	Unwillingness to take the risks involved. Management resistance to change for a variety of reasons including old age, aversion to risk taking, desire to protect personal empires, etc. Personal reasons among managers for defending the status quo. Lack of control system related to appraisal of investment of decentralized operations. Lack of budgetary control ability. Organizational inflexibility. Lack of management vision to see opportunities for expansion. Lack of management development, i.e. not enough managers to handle expansion. Management turnover and loss of promising young managers. Lack of ability to formulate and implement strategy that makes company relevant to changing conditions. Refusal to delegate power and authority for diversification.

(b) External Blocks to Development.

Stage I to II	*Stage II to III*
Unfavorable economic conditions. Lack of market growth. Tight money or lack of an underwriter who will assist the company "to go public." Labor shortages in quality and quantity. Technological obsolescence of product.	Unfavorable economic, political, technological and social conditions and/or trends. Lack of access to financial or management resources. Overly conservative accountants, lawyers, investment bankers, etc. Lack of domestic markets necessary to support large diversified corporation. "The conservative mentality," e.g., cultural contentment with the status quo and lack of desire to grow and develop.

Strategies for Development. The most straightforward strategic problems in regard to corporate development are those of the Stage I manager. His strategy (timed sequence of conditional moves) must be simply to put his head down and drive straight forward to increase sales and generate enough cash flow to carry the overhead cost of supporting a management team—maybe only two, three or four members—but still risky and expensive relative to his profit and loss statement and balance sheet. He must then switch from the role of player to coach, delegating operating responsibility and developing, challenging, encouraging, measuring and rewarding and punishing his top management group. Then, as growth permits he can add needed management specialists to the team and rationalize the operation around a sensible equilibrium relating market potential, sales force size, product line, economic lot size production facilities, extent of integration and financial structure and resources.

Corporate development for the Stage II company can in general take one or both of two routes: (a) expansion through the present product line or (b) diversification by adding new product divisions. Therefore, depending on prospects for the company's basic product-market niche, resources, distinctive competences, management ability and motivation and perceived market opportunities, the Stage II president can plan moves: (a) to increase growth and penetration in present product markets or (b) to enter new businesses. Strategy (a) is based on moves to compete more effectively so that the company can increase present shares in static or declining markets or hold present shares in growing markets and/or move to integrate backward or forward into closely related products and activities.

Strategy (b) requires that the company exercise the make or buy option and get into new, non-related products via the internal route—research and development, new product development and marketing—or the external route—acquisition of product-market niches that can be more favorably purchased than developed.

The options for growth in a Stage III company are to expand through present product divisions or to develop and/or acquire new product divisions. In most respects such decisions are similar to those confronting the Stage II company except that the Stage III company should be much more experienced and skilled in approaching and solving the many problems involved.

The Problems of Development. Acceptance and use of the stages of organizational development concept does not imply that corporate development must necessarily occur or that transition through the stages is any royal route to a Stage III corporate utopia. I have observed many problems related to corporate development that give one cause to stop and think before recommending it generally. One of the most interesting ways of analysing problems of development is to classify them as to whether they are related to moving from Stage I to II or II to III too soon or too late. A brief summary of the most frequently observed problems classified in this way follows:

Problems When Transition Is Premature

Stage I to II	*Stage II to III*
Loss of control by owner-manager. Overhead and fixed costs too high to be supported by sales volume. Overextension of resources, especially working capital, plant and management. Bankruptcy or failure.	Excessive conflict between functional and product-oriented managers. Unmanageable complexity. Unreasonably high overhead costs. Major functional weaknesses in product divisions. Lack of control over divisions. Inability to compete because resources have been spread too thin. Competitive vulnerability to companies with strong functional or product excellence. Lack of functional specialization. Diversification beyond resource and management capability. Excessive and uncontrolled risks. Loss of confidence in top management.

Problems When Transition Is Too Late

Stage I to II	*Stage II to III*
"Static psychology" and management. Permanent loss of opportunities for expansion. Management frustration. Loss of promising employees. Vulnerability in regard to survival and growth.	Lack of needed diversification and growth. Management turnover due to disillusion and inability to match development opportunities in company with personal expectations of managers. Loss of management development opportunities. Frustration of top and middle managers. Unmanageably complex product management problems, e.g., lack of attention to promising products or problem products. Excessive power appropriated by "empire building" functional managers.

Most of the above noted problems can be serious to say the least. The key to avoiding them is to plan logically the evolution of corporate and organization development with great emphasis on proper timing of any transition from Stage I to II or II to III.

Conclusions

There are three basic stages of corporate and organizational development—Stages I, II and III as described above.

Powerful, fundamental drives motivate most managers to develop their companies. This development requires the evolutionary growth and development of the entire internal system of the company.

In evolving from small and simple to large and complex, companies usually make two major transitions in stage of corporate and organizational development—from Stage I to II and from II to III.

The major problems of Stage I and II companies are their reliance on one man and one main product-market niche respectively.

The major advantages of the Stage III company are its built-in mobility of capital, management and technology, and, in most cases, its international outlook and flexibility to pursue profit opportunities in whatever businesses they may be found around the world.

In general corporate development is poorly planned and managers encounter many problems in making the transition between stages. Many of these difficulties result from not adequately understanding the different problems and functions of management that are particularly related to each of the three stages of development and making the transition too early or too late.

While there is no evidence of any limit to the size of corporations, there are many basic limits to the rate of growth, evolution and transition between stages of development.

One of the most useful methods for integrating many of the functional and strategic problems of corporate planning—both long and short range—is to relate them to the key factors and questions implied by a stage of development oriented analysis of problems and opportunities.

34

Alternative Strategies for Diversification

Willard M. Bright

When a company diversifies, its managers are faced with making choices between possible plans and directions for providing the desired variety in the business. Why such diversification should be undertaken, how, and the factors that can affect the program are what I propose to discuss in the following remarks.

The first step toward a larger, more responsive business, one that will have the strength and energy to remain competitive and grow, is for the corporate

 This article was given at the National Industrial Conference Board Mid-West Marketing Conference held March 27, 1968, in Chicago, Illinois.

purposes to be clearly defined. This means that the managers must outline the direction in which they want to move, the rate at which they want to travel, and the risks that they are able and willing to accept during the course of their actions. Without these objectives firmly established, the diversification program may be just a Pavlovian response to the latest thing in business fads. With established objectives, a strategy for diversification becomes pertinent.

Strategy is a concept that we in business have borrowed from its military origins and from the historians who utilize it so diligently. Strategy is generalship and planning, and combining and employing the means of war; all directed toward gaining more wealth and power for the state and its leadership. I think we have borrowed a good word and that history can lend further aid in our better understanding of its use in the diversification programs of modern corporations.

Consider for a moment the period between 400 and 100 B.C. when Ancient Athens, the Roman Empire, and the Macedonia of Alexander the Great became powerful states. In these historical examples, the governing leaders—management—chose a strategy which suited their needs and their resources. Just so, I think the management of a modern corporation which has the responsibility of building the strength and profitability of their company will use the methods that best suit the needs and resources of the organization. But there is no single method which ensures great success for all empires or all companies.

Just as empires grow from a single, small nation, most businesses start out with a simple idea. Someone recognizes or finds an unsatisfied need or desire in a group of consumers, and then gratifies this with a product or service that can be made and sold at a profit. Around this core, growth can occur as more consumers are found and sold, but many acts both inside and outside the business will take place, causing modifications in the simple original concept. Changes in selling and manufacturing skills, in markets and technology, in government actions and competitive pressure, are forces which make it imperative to introduce flexibility into the growing business. Variety in product or service is required to maintain the health and growth of the organization—and diversification must be undertaken.

Two Alternatives Available

Diversification can only come by one of two paths; either by the internal development of people, of organization and innovations; or by the acquisition of another business to provide the men, knowledge and facilities needed. Of course, in a mature and well-developed diversification program a company may need to follow both routes. They are the alternatives that are available. The factors are those implicit in any "build or buy" situation. As we all recognize, the most important factor involved is time. But it must be remembered that to gain time by the purchase of an organization, a technology, a product, a man, or a facility is never inexpensive. The seller can demand compensation for the risks he has faced, and payment of a premium for the time and effort which he has put into constructing the knowledge and experience, the product, the market or resource you want or must have in order to attain a goal more quickly.

By whichever route diversification goes, certain factors establish the need to undertake such a program in the first place. The aggressive reason is to make the company larger, more successful and more profitable. On the other hand, defensive reasons may motivate the action: For instance, the need to protect a market share, to diminish or avoid government or stockholder pressure, or to make more efficient use of available resources. Let us examine now some specific motivations for diversification with examples of company actions that have occurred.

1. *A Desire for More Growth Than the Present Line Yields.* When a management recognizes that its existing business is built on products that have marketing limitations, a broadened product line may be needed.

Introducing new products is a venturesome, risk-taking business. Having a competent group of managers who *want* to make the new items successful is an absolute necessity. The management must recognize that, *if these products are going to new users,* to new industries or through new distribution channels, some different ways of doing business may be necessary. Without recognition of these factors, and a *willingness to act*, ventures into new product introduction are likely to fail.

Sometimes the need for new products arises when old ones are successfully challenged by a competitor and the rules of the game are quickly changed. For example, Vincent Ziegler, Chairman of the Gillette Company, who experienced the stainless steel razor blade challenge, recently remarked that "we should not take our dominance (of the razor blade market) for granted, and that we should not be so narrow in products that we could be vulnerable again." With such a guide line established, Gillette has gone into one new market after another with a broadened product line.

Its aerosol shaving preparation is No. 1 in its field; Right Guard has moved to leadership of the deodorants; fragrances for women have been introduced; and, recently, a German small appliance maker has been acquired. With 70 to 75 per cent of the razor blade market in the United States in its control, this company has diversified into new products to broaden its growth opportunities.

2. *The Need to React to External Pressure.* External pressure on a company can come from many sources. For example, it may result from competitors, stockholders, or government action, and diversification may be needed to counter the threat. The pressures on the tobacco industry illustrate what can happen.

In recent years, the smoking and health controversy has decreased the consumption of cigarettes, and this crusade, coupled with higher taxation rates at both state and local levels, has led to a static market condition. There is no indication that these pressures will lessen, and, in such circumstances, prudent businessmen must take steps to broaden their base of operations by diversifying into other fields.

3. *A Desire for Better Use of Resources and Facilities.* A company with an excess availability of productive capacity, management skills, or financial resources will want to employ them to strengthen the company's total effort. Again, we can use the tobacco companies as our example. The opportunity for greater utilization of certain financial resources has existed for some time in the industry. Over the years, our Company has possessed more borrowing power than it has used—as did our competitors. Let me explain this. Each of the tobacco companies has a low long-term debt ratio, plus acres of warehouses which contain hogsheads filled with tobacco strips in storage lasting from two to four years while the tobacco "cures." These hogsheads of tobacco are as good as money in the bank—several hundred millions of dollars of it. Diversification into other industries can offer a more productive use for this resource of tobacco leaf dollars than allowing them to sit in a warehouse, as well as provide some relief from that pressure that I just mentioned.

4. *A Desire to Avoid Concentration in a Government Regulated Area of Business.* The moves of Tennessee Gas Transmission Company into banking, insurance, chemicals, packaging, farm machinery, land and petroleum products changed a regulated utility into Tenneco, Inc.—a diversified company, with minimal dependence on its regulated business.

5. *The Need to Produce the Services and Skills of One or More Key People.* More than one company has acquired another to gain a general manager or sales executive of proven and needed ability. Some thirty years ago, Monsanto Chemical Company acquired Thomas and Hochwalt Laboratories of Dayton, Ohio. This diversification brought a consulting organization into the fold, provided a research and development department, and, at least, two senior officers to the acquirer.

6. *A Desire to Use Profitably New Technology Developed in the Company.* Accepting the opportunity offered by a new material or a new process often requires diversification away from old markets. Let's say you're a manufacturer of chemicals, and your R and D people discover an economical new material to replace silver salts in photographic film. Of course, you can decide to be supplier of this new chemical to the film manufacturers along with your regular product line. But just before making this decision, you happen to pick up the *Wall Street Journal* and discover that silver has reached a new high for the third time in a week, photographic film prices have increased again, and you remember that a small film manufacturer with some production know-how and a good marketing team is alleged to be in financial trouble. Maybe you can use your new technology to produce a higher return by diversifying into a new business with the acquisition of this company. Or maybe the new material seems attractive enough for you to go into the film manufacturing business by setting up your own new business venture.

There are, of course, many other reasons for diversification. For example, the desire to use more fully the skills of a strong marketing team; or the wish to use more extensively available productive facilities; or the opportunity to capitalize on extra management capacity. You can recognize them and probably think of instances in which each played a dominant role in deciding a company's course of action.

Several Factors Can Limit Plans

In spite of all of these reasons to diversify, there exist real limitations that affect a company's possibilities of doing so. Let us examine some of these:

1. *Do Adequate Financial Resources Exist?* I know of one extremely large company where the application of a new "Space Age" technology plus their existing facilities would enable them to become a supplier of a new and exciting basic need to our society. But that new technology demands a heavy financial commitment now, in the advance of any cash influx from the investment. The company already has strained its financial resources; therefore, it would take a double diversification to make it go. A merger or acquisition combination could provide the necessary cash source and then the market diversification could follow.
2. *Does Management Have Enough Time to Do the Job?* Diversification of a market, or of the whole business entity, does not happen without a heavy demand on the time of the organization's top people. Sometimes, the president and his most important associates are unable to devote the required attention and energy to a new venture because the existing business occupies them fully.
3. *Is Specialization Best for the Company?* This is a fundamental anti-diversification motive buried deep in the minds of many company owners and managers. The example that leaps to mind fastest is Henry Ford, who made Model T cars and wouldn't even hear of diversifying from black ones. But sometimes this may be the best plan to maintain strength and profitability, as the Coca-Cola Company did for many, many years.
4. *Does an Adequate Marketing Capability Exist?* In some cases it does not, and is apparently unavailable. Failure to provide necessary marketing skill (I think), made Henry Kaiser's entrance into the automobile business after World War II a near disaster. Acquisition of Willys rescued the operation, enabling Kaiser to continue in a satisfactory, although specialized portion of the automotive field.
5. *The Risks of Diversification Can Be Too Great.* Now, all business has risks—some, one must accept; some, one can accept. And there are some we cannot afford—diversification in a particular direction may entail one of these. If the risk is too great, failure could cripple or destroy the basic business.
6. *Are There Anti-trust or Other Legal Limitations in the Way?* Consideration of any diversification by acquisition must be conditioned on a careful evaluation of its possibility of attack under some interpretation of the Sherman and Clayton Acts, as they emanate from the Justice Department, the Federal Trade Commission, and the Supreme Court. Logical economic reasons for merging and enhancing competition in a market are often suspect in the eyes of the

anti-trust enforcement agencies. Some writers have argued that decisions in recent years do more to protect competitors than to protect competition. In any case, good legal advice is necessary, since the anti-trust laws do pose real limitations on the means and directions to be used in diversification.

7. *Some Other Limiting Factors Will Occur to Each of You.* Perhaps, there are too few profitable opportunities in the fields which are chosen; or past failures in diversification have made your board of directors wary of a similar experience; or, the necessary people aren't available or can't be moved to the locations and jobs where they are needed to make the diversification a success; or, diversification depends on a merger and we have a problem with the price/earnings ratio for your stock versus mine. All of these factors work to limit the diversification actions.

These are the factors which affect a company's needs for diversification and those which can limit its possibilities for taking action. I have tried to weave into the fabric of the discussions threads that provide insight into the ways that management philosophy, corporate resources, and external and internal pressures influence the patterns of diversification.

Diversification Follows Three Forms

To me, three patterns are readily discernible in corporate diversification activities. I have chosen to describe these structures by the terms, concentric, contiguous, and conglomerate.

Where concentric diversification takes place, the corporate management focuses on the products and markets it wishes to supply, while providing whatever diversity of knowledge and skills needed to serve them. The Lockheed Aircraft Corporation is a good example of this strategy of diversification, having a related group of products encircling the needs of a particular market. The market is the U.S. Government, specifically the Department of Defense, while the product line includes airframes, missiles, electronics, defense research and development, ship-building and rocket engines. The knowledge needed to provide these products is broad, but the needs served are centered in one customer.

A contiguous diversification can be constructed in two ways. First, when a series of dissimilar products, services or technologies is aimed at related markets or alternatively, related products, services and technologies are directed at dissimilar markets. The R. J. Reynolds Tobacco Company is an example of the first of these contiguous structures. Hawaiian Punch, cigarettes, frozen Chinese foods, polyvinyl film for meat wrapping are all aimed at the supermarket customer. The technologies are quite different, but the primary customer, the retail stores, and the ultimate consumers are closely related, and thus provide the strategic basis for the diversification.

A conglomerate, according to the dictionary, is anything composed of heterogeneous materials or elements, collected together. As a diversified enterprise, this would include dissimilar products aimed at unrelated markets. Such a diversification is based on the strategy that dissimilar markets, products and knowledge bases can be merged and operated by financial and general management skills. Certainly, Textron, Litton Industries, and Gulf and Western, to mention three such conglomerates, suggest that such strategy can work, and may provide the most rapid route to growth. Critics have questioned this pattern and maintain that it will encounter difficulties in times of adversity. Lammot duPont Copeland has said, "Running a conglomerate is a job for management geniuses, not for ordinary mortals like us at duPont." Certainly, some conglomerate managers have had problems in the recent past, as well as spectacular growth.

No matter which of these structural forms diversification follows, there are two separate paths to accomplish it. Internal diversification and acquisition diversification are always alternatives, but they are also supplements. The choice between the two methods, or the weight of each in a combined diversification program, is controlled by the corporate goals and the rate desired to achieve them.

[To summarize, the alternative strategies for diversification will be composed of a plan for the form of organization—concentric, contiguous or conglomerate, in combination with the method, i.e., internal development, acquisition, or combination of the two. Whether diversification succeeds or fails depends upon two factors. The soundness of the strategic plan and the tactics employed to implement it.[1] . . .]

[1] This last paragraph appeared in the author's address, but it was not included in the journal article.

35

Where Next for Conglomerates?

Robert S. Attiyeh

As the 1960's draw to a close, the environment for conglomerates is rapidly changing. Following a decade of acquisition growth and historically unparalleled diversification, signs suggest that growth-oriented companies may well be forced to turn their attention to the effective use of assets already accumulated. This change is likely to come about for two reasons. First, external barriers to the conglomerate movement are being erected. Second, as conglomerates grow, their increasing size itself makes continued significant acquisition growth less feasible. This article will briefly consider these forces of

Reprinted from *Business Horizons,* December 1969, pp. 39–44.

change, and then examine in more detail how they will shape the management task for growth-minded companies in the 1970's.

External Constraints

Three main external forces are now at work to restrain further acquisition growth by conglomerates. These are governmental regulations, industry resistance to acquisitions, and declining stock prices.

The growing inclination of the federal government to restrain conglomerates has been apparent for some time. It is taking the form of administrative hindrances as well as possible legislative action. The new FTC requirement that companies file notice of major acquisition intentions with the commission before taking action can be put in the hindrance category. However, the Justice Department suit under the Clayton Act against the LTV/Jones & Laughlin merger could, if unsuccessful, prompt new regulatory antitrust legislation. The current investigation of conglomerates by the Antitrust Subcommittee of the House Judiciary Committee may have a similar outcome.

The reasons for this government action range from concern over the increased concentration of industry, and possible related restraint of trade, to a desire to respond to the calls for help from private companies resisting tender offers. Another factor is the impact on stock values of the financing games played by acquirers who favor the use of convertible preferred stock and debentures plus warrants for acquisitions. In some quarters, concern is great that inflated stock market prices resulting from such practices may be weakening our economy. The net effect of this range of concerns is bound to be increased regulation and restraints on acquisition practices and a consequent reduction in new mergers and acquisitions.

Industry resistance is a second external restraining force. Unwelcome suitors have rarely met such sophisticated resistance as conglomerates are experiencing lately from some of their acquisition targets. Opposition to tender offers has filled the courts with actions and counteractions. Often competitive merger offers from a series of suitors have been encouraged by acquisition targets. Many wary companies have reached mutual assistance understandings with other single friendly companies to help ward off future attacks upon their independence.

In addition to resistance by individual companies, other industry barriers are rising to inhibit future conglomerate growth. One of these is a form of management provincialism, seen in a company's desire to merge with someone from its home town rather than with an outsider. Examples are numerous: two are Cleveland-based Clevite's attempt to join locally headquartered TRW rather than succumb to U.S. Smelting, and the initial attempt of Blaw-Knox to join with a Pittsburgh-based company rather than be acquired by outsider White Consolidated Industries. In a slightly different way, the resistance of the steel industry to Norton Simon's take-over of Wheeling Steel was in part an example of industrial provincialism. And it took LTV a tender offer approximating 180 percent of market price to break through Jones & Laughlin's resistance.

The reasons for these reactions are understandable. It is natural to prefer joining up with someone you know, someone who will keep the power center close to your operation and who will be sensitive to the political and economic needs of the local community. These considerations are not likely to change much over the next ten years. And if they continue to dominate the thinking of management in many regional companies in the $100 million to $500 million sales category, these attitudes could pose a continuing, perhaps rising, barrier to conglomerate growth.

Perhaps the factor that most severely threatens the future of the conglomerate movement is the decline in stock prices since mid-1968. Even before the depressing effect of recent government regulation activity, the market prices for many conglomerates had already fallen substantially below their 1968 highs. This is best illustrated in Table 1, which compares price trends of ten randomly selected conglomerates to the Dow Jones and Standard & Poor's industrial averages.

Table 1. Conglomerate stock price declines

	*1968–69 High**	*Feb. 28, 1969**	*Percent Decline*
LTV	136	63	54
Litton	104	56	46
Gulf & Western	66	37	44
Whittaker	94	55	41
Monogram	76	49	36
Textron	58	37	36
TRW	60	41	31
Grace	53	40	25
ITT	62	51	19
Teledyne	45	42	6
Dow Jones Industrial Ave.	998	905	9
Standard & Poor Industrial Ave.	118	107	10

* To the nearest dollar.

As this comparison illustrates, the decline in market prices for these representative conglomerate stocks greatly exceed the bench mark industrial averages. Part of this decline is due to specific reductions in profit levels for some conglomerates such as Litton. However, the larger factor in the decline appears to be investor unwillingness to continue to pay high price/earnings multiples based on future profits for conglomerates, regardless of attractive current profit growth rates. This reduction in current P/E ratios could prove to be the most effective constraint upon continued large-scale acquisition activity by today's major conglomerates. For without a higher P/E than its acquisitions, a company cannot realize earnings growth from a common-for-common stock exchange acquisition. When reduced P/E's are combined with possible governmental constraints on the use of convertible instruments for acquisition, or pooling of interest accounting treatment, conglomerates may well be forced to look within for continued profits and sales growth in the 1970's.

Internal Constraints

Most large conglomerates will also eventually find that their own success will not allow them to rely indefinitely upon acquisitions for a major portion of their growth. ITT is a good example. During 1968, ITT's sales reached $4.1 billion. In early 1969, further growth of 12 to 14 percent was projected for the year without benefit of additional acquisitions.[1] This internal growth will result in about $530 million in additional sales for ITT in 1969. The fact that this increment would exceed the *total* 1967 sales of all but 161 U.S. industrial corporations suggests why ITT cannot long continue to rely on new acquisitions to attain its annual growth.

Beyond this difficulty, however, lies a more critical issue: how much of top management's time and energy should be allocated to an acquisition program when internal growth is becoming so significant for large corporations? Selecting and negotiating an acquisition, let alone integrating it into the acquiring company, can be a major drain on top management resources. Unless conglomerate management is content with running a financial holding company, the true test of superior management typically comes after the acquisition, along with a heavy managerial work load. Over the coming years, then, in response both to external constraints and to the diminishing returns from acquisition programs, the major acquirers of the past decade will increasingly turn their attention to internal growth.

The Challenge of Managing Assets

The professional managers of today's conglomerates have surely sensed that acquisition barriers stand ahead of them. Already, in all probability, they are quietly changing their strategies for continued growth. Not that all acquisition activity by these companies will cease forthwith; regardless of the hurdles, some additional acquisitions will be appropriate and successful. But the real challenge and opportunity facing the managements of today's big growth-minded companies will be to effectively use the vast assets already under their control.

[1] H. S. Geneen addressing the Boston Security Analysts Society, reported in *Electronic News* (March 24, 1969).

This is not a totally new concept to conglomerate management; for many it is just a change in emphasis. Since the early 1960's and even before, some corporations have shown their keen awareness of the value of monitoring and directing the deployment of assets beyond an acquisition program. An example is W. R. Grace, which has maintained an impressive objectivity toward management of its acquisitions. This approach has coupled capital budgeting, internal cost redirection, and divestiture with a determined effort to make additional acquisitions. Similarly, Textron has kept an eye on the continued attractiveness of its acquisitions; the company has not hesitated to manage newly acquired assets to the point of divestiture if it decided it had made a mistake, or could more effectively use its assets elsewhere.

An interesting contrast to these two companies is ITT, one of the better managed of today's conglomerates. No less concerned to maximize its return on assets, ITT has favored internal channeling of capital rather than making major use of divestiture. Table 2 illustrates this contrasting use of divestiture by ITT, Textron, W. R. Grace, and seven other conglomerates. The data raise a question beyond the scope of this article: when has divestiture been necessitated by poor selection and subsequent mismanagement of acquisitions, and when has it resulted from tough-minded management recognition that corporate goals for return on assets could no longer be met by some operating units, despite proper initial acquisition and subsequent effective management? To answer this question would require detailed analysis of individual companies, and the answer would still be subject to personal interpretation. But the basic point is clear: some corporations, by taking a broader approach to asset deployment, have developed a management style and perspective that may well be better suited to the demands of the coming decade.

Table 2. Use of divestiture by conglomerates

	1958–68	
	Number of Acquisitions	*Number of Divestitures**
Textron	51	10
LTV	21	9
Grace	42	3
ITT	44	1
Whittaker	38	1
TRW	25	1
Gulf & Western	87	0
Teledyne	78	0
Litton	77	0
Monogram	13	0

* Divestiture is defined as the sale of total or majority control of an operating unit or its liquidation.

Willingness to give divestiture an important role in asset management, alongside capital budgeting and profit improvement, is the hallmark of this style. Capital budgeting is likely to retain the principal role, but it will best serve those managements that have the courage to allocate funds according to company-wide return-on-investment criteria, rather than simply plowing most of the money back into the operations that generated it—and this implies occasional use of divestiture. As the barriers to acquisitions continue to rise, it seems likely that more and more conglomerates will awake to these implications. Let us take a closer look at this possibility.

Divestiture As a Management Tool

As commonly understood, divestiture means the sale of an operating unit of a company for cash, stock, or some other medium of exchange. For the purposes of this discussion I shall use the term to include the liquidation of an operating unit, the sale of a majority interest in a business, or a spin-off. The administrative details of planning or consummating such transactions have been adequately covered by Bettauer and others.[2] I shall be concerned only with the development of divestiture as a management tool and the factors influencing its effective use.

A Brief History. For many, perhaps, the earliest use of divestiture is associated with the antitrust divestments in the oil industry in the early 1900's. Undoubtedly, Teddy Roosevelt and his trust-busting colleagues gave special force to the term "divestiture," though transactions of this kind were not unprecedented even then. With the rising level of acquisitions in the 1920's the use of voluntary divestiture increased as one company acquired what another was willing to divest. Finally, divestments in the form of liquidations rose to a peak in the grim Depression years, ending with World War II. By and large, however, management used divestitures during this period not so much to upgrade the use of its assets as to comply with the economic needs of the times.

Recent Divestiture Trends. Shortly following the end of the Korean conflict, however, a new breed of entrepreneurs and investment analysts came on the scene, bringing fresh ideas about corporate form, purpose, and operation. From these men and their ideas sprang the conglomerate movement with its rapid hurdling of industry barriers. Conglomerate management's lack of emotional attachment to any one industry segment or business operation implied a recognition that assets could occasionally best be deployed by selling a company, though buying was usually easier and more satisfying.

The opportunity that exists in this approach to asset deployment was recognized in LTV's imaginative reorganization of the Wilson Company in 1967. Shortly after acquiring Wilson, LTV divided it into three separate corporations: Wilson Sporting Goods, Wilson Pharmaceutical and Chemical,

[2] See Arthur Bettauer, "Strategy for Divestments," *Harvard Business Review* (March–April, 1967), p. 116.

and Wilson and Company (meat and food products). LTV then sold a substantial minority portion of the stock of each of the new companies to outside interests at P/E ratios higher than it had paid initially for the total Wilson operation. This allowed LTV to improve its return from Wilson by recovering part of its initial investment, while retaining control of a disproportionately large share of Wilson's earning power. Table 3 illustrates a simplified and generalized example of this profitable approach to asset deployment.

Table 3. Divesting to improve earnings per share

XYZ Corporation is a diversified growth-oriented company with three operating units, A, B, and C.

Assume

1. A, B, and C each represent an investment of $10 million, and each will generate $1 million in profits during the year.
2. XYZ has a 15.0 price/earnings ratio.
3. Stock of companies in C's business typically sells for 30 times earnings.

Decision

1. XYZ establishes C as a separate corporation and sells 50 percent of stock to outside interests at 30 times projected earnings.
2. The proceeds of this stock sale are used by XYZ to gradually buy back its own stock from the open market with no appreciable change in stock price.

Benefit to XYZ

This transaction increases earnings per share of XYZ by 25 percent:

$$\frac{\dfrac{1.5\ P/E \times \$2.5\ MM\ profit}{2/3\ (stock\ remaining)}}{1.5\ P/E \times \$3.0\ MM\ profit} = 1.25$$

While LTV was taking this unconventional approach to its assets, most other conglomerates appeared to feel considerable loyalty to their acquisitions, as Table 2 suggests. A broader sample of conglomerates would probably confirm that over the past ten years most gave little emphasis to divestiture, allocating most of their management effort to acquiring companies and trying to operate them effectively. Group and operating-level managers in many conglomerates, ITT and Litton among them, typically felt committed to making an acquisition work once it was consummated. They had little time, and little encouragement from the top, to worry about whether the business was really a good use of company resources. The "can do and will do" spirit then prevailing was admirable in many ways, and perhaps necessary at the time to prevent these companies from turning into mutual funds. Now, however, the time may be at hand for a more objective, balanced perspective, at least at the corporate planning level.

Some companies are already moving in this direction. North American Rockwell is redefining its corporate development function to give more attention to asset deployment at the expense of acquisitions. ITT has recently established a corporate-level planning function; in the past, planning was delegated primarily to operating levels. W. R. Grace has established within the year a corporate vice-presidential function, intended to be concerned with divestments as well as acquisitions. These are signs of the times, signs that some conglomerate managements are aware of the changes going on about them and possible tax changes ahead.

How About You?

Should managements of all growth-minded diversified companies consider divestiture to channel asset deployment? This can probably be best decided by the management of each company taking a hard look at such questions as:

Are some operating units in the company consistently below the company average in their returns on assets and growth? Is diversification in itself sufficient justification for continuing to live with this performance?

Are superior incremental growth prospects in certain of the company's businesses currently being hampered by insufficient capital, management, or technological resources?

Are the chief executive officer and other senior executives constantly getting bogged down in problem areas instead of spending their time on operations with the greatest prospects for growth?

Affirmative answers to questions such as these, of course, do not in themselves dictate the use of divestiture, but they could indicate that serious consideration should be given to the option. For managers interested in stockholder return and earnings per share, this option would be particularly appropriate if a divestiture candidate were in a business with a higher price/earnings ratio than the parent company's, as illustrated in Table 3.

This reversal of the customary acquisition game, however, is not usually an option. More frequently, a company may find that all or part of one of its operating units can be divested at a price that allows the proceeds to be employed more effectively in the remaining business activities. Regardless of the approach taken, however, the divestiture option requires management vision, decisiveness, and courage. It is these characteristics that will distinguish the successful growth-minded companies of the next decade.

36

The Conglomerate—Corporate Form of the Future

David N. Judelson

Conglomerates are referred to as diversified companies, multi-market or multi-industry companies, and "free-form" corporations. One hears of "emerging conglomerates," "mature conglomerates," and there is at least one "mini-conglomerate." There is even a company now that calls itself Conglomerate Incorporated.

The truth is, there is a lot about conglomerates that is not really new.

Years before Gulf & Western and other present-day conglomerates came along, General Motors showed directions toward conglomeration as a manufacturer of refrigerators, household appliances, and locomotives, as well as automobiles.

General Electric has long been in varied markets including some 100 different fields ranging from light bulbs to aircraft engines.

Uniroyal was formed way back in 1893 through the merger of six companies. Since that time Uniroyal has been involved in no fewer than 93 mergers.

Ford Motor Company, through its Philco Division, produces television sets, as well as its line of cars.

In the past several years we have witnessed such phenomena as the entry of RCA into the book business, U.S. Steel into the chemical fertilizer business, the American Tobacco Company into the liquor business, Time & Life into the motion picture business, and CBS into the guitar, toy, and baseball businesses.

Even bankers are following the acquisition, merger, and diversification route. They are seeking alternatives in the allocation of their resources through the formation of holding companies that are free of the legal restrictions under which bankers themselves must operate.

In some instances, firms are even *trying* to gain recognition as conglomerates, hoping to attract market attention.

Growth of Conglomerates

On the *Fortune* list of the top 500 industries in the United States, some 398 are classified as "truly diversified" or "truly conglomerate." Only 102 still do business in what the magazine calls "single category." There are more than a dozen conglomerates now in the billion dollar class.

Conglomerates grow by mergers, but I should point out that all the recent merger activity is by no means limited to the conglomerates.

Of the 3,158 mergers in the first nine months of last year, the ten most-active conglomerates accounted for only 78 mergers—only two per cent of the total number of mergers during this period.

Reprinted by permission from the July 1969 issue of the *Michigan Business Review*, pp. 8–12. Published by the Graduate School of Business Administration, The University of Michigan.

Fortune magazine more or less arbitrarily, sets *eight* as the minimum number of different fields in which a corporation must be involved to qualify as a conglomerate. The *Fortune* list of conglomerates includes such traditionalists as Borden, Chrysler, and Firestone.

One of the findings of a recent *Fortune* survey is that the most successful of the conglomerates are the relatively new companies that became conglomerates at an early stage in their development *by design,* rather than the older companies that began diversifying only *in response* to problems and anxieties about their original corporate operations.

Characteristics of a Conglomerate

One definition of a conglomerate might be "a group of companies in diverse and apparently unrelated fields, coordinated and controlled to varying degrees by a central management group."

In a sense the University is a conglomerate with its many different faculties, each contributing its own particular discipline to a single goal—education.

In a like manner, the various companies of a conglomerate contribute their specific strengths synergistically to the parent company.

The conglomerate represents changes in corporate form, behavior, and purposes in three areas that we can, for the sake of convenient reference, call the "three M's," These are Management, Markets, and Money.

In my opinion, *management* comes first.

The Managerial Revolution

The general business revolution we have been experiencing is primarily the result of the Managerial Revolution that, in the decades since World War II, has brought a tremendous expansion in the capabilities of management.

I have said there is a lot about conglomerates that is not really new. But the management techniques necessary to direct the modern conglomerate, with all its complexity and range, are very new. There is a vast difference between modern managers of multi-market companies and the diversifiers of thirty, twenty, or even ten years ago.

Without the high degree of sophistication, skill, and effectiveness that management has developed only in the last two decades, the conglomerate could not exist. These management techniques provide the necessary unity and compatibility among a diversity of operations and acquisitions.

An absolutely indispensable characteristic of today's new kind of corporation is what might be referred to as the *entrepreneurial spirit.* It is not only characteristic of all members of top management, but is also transferable to the managements of the acquired companies. As a result, they, in turn, expand their efforts, ambitions, and accomplishments beyond what they had once thought were their natural limitations.

Today's corporate management must provide both a rationale and an operational pattern in directing a multi-market company. It must provide new operations with very real assistance in the way of necessary funds for expansion *plus* managerial and technical talents that otherwise would not be available to it. In other words, management must be able to produce substantially greater internal growth for an acquired company than it can achieve on its own.

An Example of Internal Growth

One of the best examples of internal growth is how G&W built its automotive manufacturing division from a single product company—automobile bumpers—to a broadly diversified multi-product manufacturer for the automotive and appliance industries.

Through a carefully planned acquisition and internal growth program G&W added new and logical product lines to the original bumper company.

In 1964 we added decorative die castings for automobiles. Later the same year we entered the Canadian market by building another bumper producing facility. We also added precision stamping facilities for automotive and appliance components. In 1965, production of chrome plated plastics was added. To maintain a balance and blend of product line we expanded into heavy stampings and large die-casting. We also entered the related field of heavy bearings.

The total sales volume at the time of acquisition of all of these acquired companies was $46 million. By applying management techniques and financial controls, G&W has given them the resources and incentives to grow to a present level of $83 million. This is an increase of 80 per cent.

What I am saying here is that a well managed conglomerate contributes substantially to the economy through the internal growth of its subsidiaries—growth that occurs after the acquisition and as a result of the contribution the conglomerate itself makes to the merger.

Starting from Scratch

I don't mean that we have to always acquire a company in order to grow and enter new markets, Gulf & Western's cable television operations are an example of new market opportunities exploited solely by internal growth. One and a half years ago when G&W decided to enter the CATV field, we started from virtually zero. Today G&W has franchises and operating systems in 19 cities and seven states, stretching from Berkeley, California, to Daytona Beach, Florida, and is well on its way to becoming the largest CATV operator in the United States.

In four years we shall have invested $13 million in CATV. At present market evaluation, this $13 million represents a market potential of $100 million—and $100 million is what it would have cost us to reach this position had we attempted to enter the CATV market by acquisition.

The conglomerate approach, as opposed to the traditional corporate "one product" or "one industry" approach, fills the needs of this volatile marketplace.

Expansion Around a Central Core

The modern multi-market corporation, using the Gulf & Western form, expands in a series of concentric circles around its central core—rather than vertically on a one-product line or horizontally on a one-industry line. The conglomerate is in a number of markets at once. It should have the ability—through a balanced and tightly knit staff—to coordinate the activities of its subsidiaries in different geographical or industry markets.

Under the conglomerate structure, it should be possible for one subsidiary to profit from the experiences of another, and for all subsidiaries to draw on the general, overall financial and marketing expertise of the corporate headquarters, the central core.

Technological Change the Crucial Factor

The *Marketplace* is where the most important influences occur with the greatest frequency and force. The crucial factor in the marketplace is, in turn, technological change—change that takes place with incredible speed.

Technological change has time and again brought overnight obsolescence to products, whole product lines, and even entire industries. At the same time, it has just as suddenly created vast new "instant" markets for other products and industries.

Technological change has brought much faster communication and transportation. It has produced the computer and data processing. It has broadened consumer sophistication and demand. The result of these changes has been that the world has become almost one vast marketplace, rather than a number of fragmented, individual, and insulated markets.

Given this "one world" market, it is apparent that a company—if it is going to prosper in today's economy—must be able to act with the speed necessary to keep up with the rapid rate of change that is taking place in today's marketplace.

Role of Market Substitution

An even more important advantage of the conglomerate approach in today's marketplace is the vital question of *market substitution.* Market substitution is vital for two reasons: (1) The rapid change in modern markets; and (2) The great capital outlay and the years of time required to enter a market in the traditional manner. The bigger and more entrenched a corporation is in a given marketplace, the harder it is for it to enter a substitute market when its original major market has begun to fail.

The advantages of the conglomerate under these conditions are obvious. The conglomerate, by definition, is not in one market, but in many. When the outlook for one market is unpromising, the resources can be pulled out of that market and transferred to another. Should one market go completely bad, the subsidiary operating in that market can be transformed in character or product without significant damage to the overall performance.

A conglomerate should be like a partitioned ship. A hole in one section, thanks to the dividing water-tight bulkheads, is not going to sink the entire vessel. On the other hand, a damaging blow to the major market of a traditional corporation could very well send the entire corporation to the bottom of the economic sea.

I have mentioned some of the defensive aspects. However, the question of market substitution becomes even more important when we consider the *growth potential* of traditional single-market corporations and the more flexible multi-market approach of the conglomerate.

When the traditional corporation stops growing because technological obsolescence has slowed or reversed the growth in its major market, the company is in trouble.

The conglomerate is flexible. Its capital investment is not concentrated in any one industry. Because of its structure, its management philosophy, and its experience, the conglomerate is able to move while the traditional corporation is often forced to sit and wish that it *could* move.

Raising Capital

The third "M" is *money*—and more specifically, the high cost of *borrowing* money and the high cost of capital. As we all know, it takes money to grow, and you need funds if you are going to exploit either internal or external growth opportunities. Yet, where the markets for products have become more fluid and flexible, the money market has become increasingly tight, and the equity market is expensive for many kinds of businesses.

As a result, if any corporation is going to grow at all, it will have to grow in the marketplace, and if it is frustrated in the marketplace because of its inability or reluctance to take advantage of rapidly developing situations, it again, is in a disadvantageous position. For a company in this situation finds itself trapped between two immovable obstacles that block action in either direction; caught between the devil of decline in demand and the deep blue sea of tight money.

With the money market what it has been, the only *real* alternative for traditional companies in traditional fields is to bring down the cost of their capital and make various investment opportunities more attractive.

This means: (1) Expanding into growth markets in order to achieve real and productive alternatives for their allocation of resources; and (2) Accomplishing this expansion through acquisitions that will not only provide an immediate foothold—and an immediate return—in a given market, but will hopefully increase the value of the acquiring company's stock over a period of time. In this way a company has the best opportunity to reduce its cost of capital.

The conglomerate form can be considered to have passed through the initial stage of its development. It is out of the novelty category. It has come of age. From now on, performance, rather than flair, will be the chief factor by which it is judged.

Outlook for Conglomerates

Moving into this new era of maturity, the conglomerate has become, even more than before, the center of speculation as to its capabilities. Can a conglomerate be effectively managed? Can it withstand recession or other forms of economic set-back? Can it grow and diversify internally?

These are some of the questions you hear and read about conglomerates today. In considering them, you have to start with the premise that there are conglomerates and there are conglomerates. I can answer only for Gulf & Western; and I think that some of the points made here are applicable to other firms.

The well-managed conglomerate can establish strong positions in a number of different market areas. This diversity provides a built-in protection against recession. The sectors of the economy that Gulf & Western serves—distribution, manufacturing, metals and chemicals, leisure-time activities, agriculture, consumer and paper products, and financial services—offer a balance and blend of product mix. These are products and services that have a history of growth consistency and they are in markets that will not disintegrate.

Most important of all, the forces that have shaped Gulf & Western and other conglomerates—speed of technological change, the variety of products, the tremendous and varied demand, the increasing complexities of modern business, the conditions in the world money market, the need for major resources to achieve growth, the erasure of the boundaries of markets and nations, the increasing interdependence of peoples, institutions and industries—all of these promise to be with us, and will increase in impact for decades to come.

To cope with them, we must rely on a business organization that can handle change. The conglomerate—because it is, in itself, a product of change—is this kind of organization. Shaped by change, it responds to change, and will continue to meet its challenges. Today, it is already the corporate form of tomorrow.

new dimensions for corporate strategy

part four

The previous sections have dealt with a concept of corporate strategy, the decision process for strategy formulation, and problems of implementation. Emphasis has been placed on the economic mission of the firm. Although the approach has been to urge new ways of looking at corporate problems, the basic role of the corporation and values of executives have been identified and discussed but have not been greatly challenged. Part Four is designed to challenge conventional assumptions about the role of the corporation both domestically and internationally.

New demands are being made on corporations almost daily. On the international scene, political developments, both foreign and domestic, are causing executives to re-evaluate their strategies. The United States government and foreign governments increasingly have a voice in how the United States firm operates internationally. Peoples of all countries are becoming more sophisticated and in some cases more nationalistic. Corporate operations in some foreign countries are being challenged at home by those who disagree with policies of those countries for political or moral reasons. These developments require a continual evaluation of operations in widely varying cultures.

On the domestic scene, new demands are being made on the role of the corporation as well. Groups that did not exist a few years ago are now demanding an influence on corporate policy. Stockholders and employees have long made major claims on the corporation. Additional groups are now claiming consideration in the allocation of resources. Conservationists, consumer groups, civil rights advocates, and charitable organizations are urging executives to expand their concepts of the role of the corporation.

The readings in these last two sections deal with added dimensions to the entire strategic decision process. In most instances the variables have been identified in Part Two, but the new dimensions may change the magnitudes and priorities of the variables, increase the complexity of their interrelationships, and alter the assessment of environmental and competitive factors. In short, these added dimensions will modify existing viewpoints on the over-all corporate perspective and the decisions for strategy formulation and implementation.

International Operations

Although many United States firms have operated on an international basis for decades, only in recent years have the pace of international business activity and the experience of truly world-wide operations been sufficient to generate research and develop concepts appropriate to study the policy implications and problems attendant with international operations. Business organizations have learned, often by bitter experience, that operating in foreign environments involves much more than merely extending strategies appropriate to domestic operations.

In situation analysis for strategic decision making, another dimension (the foreign environment) is added, but the increase in complexity of variables and their interrelationships is magnified. The types of environmental information inputs are basically those described in Section 3; however, the dimensions and priorities are quite different. Factors taken for granted in a domestic situation cannot be assumed in a foreign situation. Analysis of relevant variables is necessary for each foreign location, at least for each country where foreign operations are undertaken. As competition increases and new demands occur for the firm's resources, analysis of resource capability and allocation presents new challenges. The very mission of the organization may require revision, and objectives may take on new dimensions and priorities. Implementation strategies will change. And, finally, the perspective and values of decision makers may undergo change.

The first three articles deal with major strategic considerations for formulating international business strategy. M. Y. Yoshino focuses on the identification of variables relating to decisions regarding entry into foreign markets and the integration of the variables into the firm's international business policy. P. J. Hovell focuses on the development of a conceptual planning framework for global operations. Both authors utilize empirical research findings from a broad range of companies. Richard Eels discusses the corporate intelligence function for international strategic decisions and some trends and issues which confront many international corporate managers.

The remaining articles deal with more specific managerial problems in formulating and implementing international corporate strategy. David Rutenberg focuses on organizational relationships between a headquarters and its international subsidiaries and presents planning guidelines for dealing with specific types of decisions. The second article by M. Y. Yoshino deals with managerial control for a world enterprise. Participation in international operations requires functioning in different cultures; the article by Donald Stone discusses that topic in the context of interpersonal and intercultural communication.

Social and Political Involvement

Social issues have become sufficiently critical that a concerted effort is required to alleviate them. Social pressures by government and the public are fostering a reappraisal of the role of business in American society. The primary goal of business to provide a good or service at a profit may be insufficient orientation for operating in today's, and certainly tomorrow's, environment. Business is being called upon to direct some of its vast resources to the solution of broader problems.

The most crucial challenge facing business is to redefine its relationships to its many publics using the concepts of systems theory. Business leaders are being asked to recognize that large corporations have a far-reaching social impact on employees and communities and to consider that many of these social outputs from their operations are subject to little or no regulation by any market-place mechanism.

The question of the social responsibility of business can be argued in many ways. Whatever the specific direction, it is clear that the environment of business is becoming increasingly complex and interdependent with the decisions of the businessman. Both on and off the job, the quality of life in the United States and in the world can be significantly affected by the way in which managers view their responsibility and discharge it. This "view" is a major input into the policy-making activities of the firm. It is also a direct manifestation of the personal values of the executive, discussed in Part One.

The readings in this section focus on the opportunities and problems presented by some major political and social problems. These selections are not exhaustive of the areas of concern, but they do generally outline the major issues. Most of these readings contain less guidance and conceptualization for decision making than those in previous sections. The emphasis here is on issues, problems, and ideas to stimulate thoughtful and innovative approaches toward the solutions of the issues raised.

Edward Cole leads off the section with an identification of major challenges and opportunities facing the business enterprise in the 1970's and a discussion of some of the ways these challenges may shape the role of the manager. Alvar Elbing presents a case for a social model of the business organization as a means for meeting the social responsibility role of the businessman. Frank Cassell extends the social issue by looking at business support of community action programs. Another challenge to business is examined by David Cravens and Gerald Hills in their article in which they describe the nature and scope of consumerism, develop a perspective toward it, and discuss implications for corporate decision making. Leslie Dawson challenges the adequacy of the marketing concept to deal with today's and tomorrow's business problems and presents a new and broader philosophy for business. One of the areas where business feels specific pressures outside of its economic activities is in the area of cultural contributions. The demands of educational, charitable, and cultural groups for substantial monetary support are growing and at times conflict with stockholders who question philanthropic activities. Some thoughts on this topic are presented by Peter Bone.

The readings in this section all urge an increased role for business in the social and political environment. Yet business must survive if it is to be of service to anyone. The tasks of adjusting these demands to the realities of economic life and of integrating these ideas with the development and implementation of strategy are left to the manager and the student.

Part Four. References for Further Study

Section 7: International Operations

Behrman, Jack N. "Multinational Corporations, Transnational Interests and National Sovereignty." *Columbia Journal of World Business,* **IV**, 2 (March–April 1969), 15–21.
Identifies and discusses problems of intervention, authority, interference, responsibility, and allegiance among the managers of multinational corporations, parent countries, and host countries.

Butler, W. Jack, and John Dearden. "Managing a Worldwide Business." *Harvard Business Review*, **43**, 3 (May–June 1965), 93–102.
Highlights some of the principal management problems confronting international companies and develops guidelines for a more effective management approach. Discusses problems of local profit distortion, multiproduct difficulty, incremental investment flow, political-economic risk, communications roadblocks, staff contributions, and key-man obstacles. Develops concepts of wide-angle accountability and product-stream management.

Clee, Gilbert H., and Wilbur M. Sachtjen. "Organizing a Worldwide Business." *Harvard Business Review*, **42**, 6 (November–December 1964), 55–67.
Describes dominant organizational patterns (international division, geographic, and product) and explores advantages and problems each raises for top management.

Keegan, Warren J. "Multinational Product Planning: Strategic Alternatives." *Journal of Marketing,* **33**, 1 (January 1969), 58–62.
Identifies five strategic alternatives available to international marketers and factors that determine the strategy that should be used.

Kendall, Donald. "Corporate Ownership: The International Dimension." *Columbia Journal of World Business.* **IV**, 4 (July–August 1969), 59–65.
Discusses issues related to the development of a new variety of stockholders – truly multinational owners of multinational companies.

Martyn, Howe. "Effects of Multinational Affiliation on Local Management." *Michigan Business Review*, **XIX**, 2 (March 1967), 15–20.
Discusses management problems in a foreign subsidiary from the viewpoint of the subsidiary management. Includes the topics of budgeting, accounting, purchasing, records of decisions, market research, and personal contacts.

Moyer, Reed. "International Market Analysis." *Journal of Marketing Research,* **V**, 4 (November 1968), 353–60.
Discusses and analyzes market research techniques appropriate for international markets with particular emphasis on the less developed countries.

Pryor, Millard H., Jr. "Planning in a Worldwide Business." *Harvard Business Review,* **43**, 1 (January–February 1965), 130–139.
Points out common mistakes made in planning worldwide operations and discusses steps that can be taken to assure effective planning of the major business functions. Includes long-range strategic plans, information flows, financial objectives, supply

strategy, management mobilization, marketing strategy, and product specifications.

Root, Franklin R. "U.S. Business Abroad and the Political Risks." *MSU Business Topics,* **16**, 1 (Winter 1968), 73–80.
A research report on the ways American managers respond to political risks in international business and a discussion of the implications of the responses.

Waterman, Merwin H. "Financial Management in Multinational Corporations: I. "*Michigan Business Review,* **XX**, 1 (January 1968), 10–15.

———. "Financial Management in Multinational Corporations: II. "*Michigan Business Review,* **XX**, 2 (March 1968), 26–32.
These two articles deal with a number of variables and problems, inside and outside the company, that a financial manager may expect to encounter in foreign business operations.

Yoshino, M. Y. "Administrative Attitudes and Relationships in a Foreign Culture." *MSU Business Topics*, **16**, 1 (Winter 1968), 58–66.
Sets forth major problems and guidelines for administrative effectiveness for rapport between the American executive overseas and his foreign counterpart.

Section 8: Social and Political Involvement

Davis, Keith. "Understanding the Social Responsibility Puzzle." *Business Horizons,* **10**, 4 (Winter 1967), 45–50.
Develops a model of balanced power and responsibility for assisting the manager in understanding and dealing with the social responsibility dilemma.

Doctors, Samuel I. "Project Management in Urban Development." *MSU Business Topics*, **16**, 3 (Summer 1968), 19–23.
Suggests an approach to uniting government resources with those of private industry to find and implement solutions to problems of the cities.

Gingrich, Arnold. "The Arts and the Corporation." *The Conference Board Record,* March 1969, 29–32.
Discusses interactions between the corporation and the arts and the role of business in cultural activities.

Henderson, Hazel. "Should Business Tackle Society's Problems?" *Harvard Business Review,* **46**, 4 (July–August 1968), 77–85.
Examines and analyzes the trend of turning to business in seeking workable solutions to massive public problems and the effects on businessmen, voters, consumers, stockholders, and employees as well as probable effects on future generations.

Levitt, Theodore. "The Dangers of Social Responsibility." *Harvard Business Review,* **36**, 5 (September–October 1958), 41–50.
Develops a case for business concentrating on its principal task of pursuing its dominant objective of long-run profit maximization.

Pearson, Henry G. "A New Co-aim for Business." *MSU Business Topics,* **16**, 2 (Spring 1968), 51–56.
Presents the argument that the development of people is a corporate aim coequal to product and profit as the ultimate purpose of business.

Staats, Elmer B. "Industry-Government Relationships." *California Management Review,* **XII**, 1 (Fall 1969), 83–90.
Discusses ways in which benefits can be achieved through cooperation and joint effort of business and government toward the solution of some major social and economic problems.

international operations

37

International Business: What Is the Best Strategy?

M. Y. Yoshino

One of the most significant business trends today in advanced industrial nations is an increasing internationalization of business activities. A number of major corporations throughout the world are now committed to full-scale, long-term participation in the intense, sophisticated rivalry of world enterprise. Far-sighted business executives no longer limit their horizons to opportunities in the domestic market; they have begun to evaluate alternative opportunities for development of their corporate resources on a global basis.

In the last decade, a basic change has occurred in the character of international business, which up to that time had been traditionally an export-import type of operation. An increasing number of firms are undertaking local manufacturing either through licensing arrangements or through direct investments. This development has created new opportunities as well as problems for top management. International business now accounts for an important share of the business of many large corporations throughout the world and requires the full-time attention of first-rate executives and staff. It can no longer be managed successfully by second-rate executives nor can it be treated as an adjunct by executives whose responsibilities lie elsewhere.

Recently I undertook a study to investigate the process whereby a firm evolves from a domestic organization, serving a relatively homogeneous home market, to an international corporation, serving a large number of diverse multinational and cultural markets. The study sought to examine the degree to which a firm's expansions into international markets are deliberately planned as an integral part of the firm's long-range corporate goals and strategy.

The main objectives of the study were to identify patterns and recurring problems in current practices in this area and to suggest some useful guidelines to those firms that are contemplating expansion overseas. Data were gathered through intensive interviews with executives of twenty-five major North American corporations with large international commitments. These firms represented the following industries: chemical, automobile, pharmaceutical, home appliance, electronics, food and farm equipment.

The study has revealed that:

- *In spite of much current interest in international business, an overall policy to guide a firm's entry into foreign markets has been generally lacking. The failure to develop long-range international objectives prior to moving overseas has resulted in many unsuccessful foreign ventures.*
- *Decisions relating to entry into foreign markets are complicated by many variables, the counterparts of which are not found in decisions relating to entry into new domestic markets. These variables must be explicitly recognized and reflected in the firm's international business policy.*

Consequences of Lack of Planning in Entering Foreign Markets. In the majority of firms studied, international business has evolved over a period of time without a deliberate policy guidance established by top management. Typically, a firm's foreign business began in the form of export sales in response to inquiries from distributors overseas. Export sales were traditionally handled by export managers, whose status in most organizations was nothing more than that of glorified shipping clerks. As the firm's foreign markets grew, it began to encounter difficulties in supplying these markets through export operations because of a variety of import restrictions imposed by the foreign governments. Management, faced with the alternatives of abandoning the market or undertaking local production, usually chose the latter course. In most cases, this decision was delayed as long as possible because of management's reluctance to make a large commitment overseas.

In some cases, the initial inducement for direct investment overseas came from a local distributor who saw the benefits of establishing a more permanent tie with the foreign firm in the form of a joint venture. Occasionally a local distributor may have been motivated by fear of losing the market if a competitor succeeded in persuading his foreign supplier to establish local production facilities first.

What are the consequences of a lack of overall planning for entry into foreign markets? First, lack of planning usually leads to sub-optimum deployment of corporate resources overseas and a consequent loss of the potential benefits of multinational operations. An important advantage of multinational business as contrasted with purely domestic operations is that it provides management with the broadest possible dimension of enterprise in which to take full advantage of worldwide investment opportunities that offer the highest returns. However, this strength can be realized only when alternatives are systematically examined and compared on a global basis. For example:

Senior executives of a large pharmaceutical firm still held an opinion that foreign investment projects were inherently riskier than domestic ones. Thus they favored domestic investment projects over their international counterparts. The firm's International Division was allocated every year a certain percentage of the total fund available for new investments, so that, according to one senior executive, "safer" domestic investments did not have to compete against "glamorous" but "riskier" international projects. Furthermore, International Division lacked a clear-cut policy to guide allocation of its fund between projects for expanding existing facilities and those for entering new markets. Thus, decisions concerning allocation of corporate resources within International Division were reached primarily through "negotiations" among various interest groups. One executive, having noted the inadequacy of this method, commented, "We take a great pride in being an international company, but we are far from achieving optimum allocation of our resources on a global basis."

Secondly, lack of planning indicates ignorance of timing as a critical element in achieving successful entry into foreign markets. Unless a firm can time its entry properly, there is a possibility that it will be excluded from certain promising markets permanently. The reason for this exclusion is that the first firm which undertakes local production can often negotiate with the host government for preferred treatments and special concessions, including a provision to make subsequent entry into the market by competitors extremely difficult, if not impossible.

Even without these negotiated benefits, the first entrant can often enjoy decided advantages over potential competitors because of the need for a long lead time to initiate a foreign venture and to build a viable position in the market. The following example is illuminating:

A manufacturer of industrial equipment had for a long time followed implicitly a policy of undertaking local production only when it was forced upon it by competitive pressure or actions of the host government. When the management became aware that the company was being squeezed out of some promising markets because of this policy, it reversed its position and began to seek actively opportunities for direct investment overseas. A senior executive of the firm noted that the company was experiencing considerable difficulties in regaining the lost ground because it was virtually locked out of some markets due to governments' concessions granted to earlier entrants, while in others competition was too entrenched for the firm to develop a viable position.

The fact that a firm cannot simultaneously enter every promising market in the world creates a need for establishing a priority ranking to allow a systematic approach to develop these markets over a period of time.

Thirdly, lack of planning tends to restrict the flexibility of a firm's subsequent operations. For example, in some firms studied, earlier licensing agreements or exclusive distribution rights had seriously hampered their subsequent expansions overseas. Such firms have found it impossible to establish their own production facilities in certain markets to take advantage of rapidly growing opportunities because of exclusive licensing agreements made earlier without careful examination of their consequences. It is no comfort to the management of these firms to know that their licensees are developing a highly profitable business in these markets, while their own returns are limited to a small royalty.[1]

A large manufacturing firm had relied exclusively on licensing route to enter rapidly growing markets in Western Europe and Japan because top management of the firm believed that licensing allowed the firm to enter foreign markets with minimum commitment of resources, while enjoying a guaranteed level of return. As time went on, however, the management became aware that many licensees overseas had developed extremely profitable business based on the licensed know-how, while the licensor's participation was limited to only a negligible royalty. The management belatedly realized that direct investment route would have been much more suitable in entering these growth markets. The firm's position would have substantially improved, even under licensing agreements, had it insisted on equity participation rather than a straight royalty arrangement, in return for its technical know-how.

A related difficulty to lack of planning is the selection of partners, if the ownership of a contemplated venture is to be shared with local interests. If a firm undertakes direct investment as a result of continuing pressure from a particular local interest, such as a distributor or licensee, it becomes in a sense a captive of that local group and loses the freedom to search for alternative candidates for partnership. Many firms have learned at considerable expense that a satisfactory relationship in one form of collaboration does not guarantee success under a different type of arrangement. For example, a distributor who has had outstanding success in export operations has not necessarily proved to be an effective partner in manufacturing ventures.

Finally, ill-planned market entry is likely to lead to numerous operating problems after the foreign venture gets under way. Lacking a policy to guide its move overseas, a firm may postpone the decision to enter a given market until the last moment, thereby creating further problems.

[1] Michael Y. Yoshino, "Marketing Orientation in International Business," *Business Topics*, Vol. 13, No. 3, Summer 1965, p. 61.

Host of Problems Face Management. Once a decision is made to enter a foreign market, management faces a host of complex problems: it must investigate the political climate, satisfy legal requirement, undertake complicated financial transactions, or negotiate with the local government. Being preoccupied with these problems, management is often tempted to postpone examination of such important considerations as cost structure, competitive strength, distribution program, product policy, and capital requirements of a new venture until the operations get under way. Frequently, management assumes that each of these problems can be resolved as it arises *after* the overseas venture is in operation. Unfortunately, this assumption has proved false on many occasions. For example:

A leading manufacturer of consumer durable goods became impressed with rapid postwar growth in the Japanese market and was anxious to beat its competitors in establishing its operations there. The firm hurriedly negotiated with a local firm to form a joint venture, sought successfully an approval of the Japanese Government and immediately began constructing a new plant. The management felt that once it established its foothold in the market it could then devote its attention to various operating problems. When the operations got underway, the management was surprised to learn that it faced serious operating problems resulting from stiff local competition, intricate web of business relationship governed by tradition and difficulties of breaking into the well entrenched distribution system. The management found it difficult to correct these problems and was forced simply to live with them. The performance of the subsidiary remained at a level substantially below what the parent company had expected it to be.

Developing a Policy for International Operations

The foregoing considerations indicate an acute need for establishing a policy to guide a firm's entry into international markets. Given diverse and rapidly changing conditions overseas and the risks inherent in international ventures, this need cannot be overemphasized. The policy must clearly identify the firm's international goals and how these goals are to be achieved. How, then, can a firm formulate such a policy? What important considerations must a firm weigh prior to moving abroad? The most basic question that top management must consider can be stated simply, "Should the firm go 'international'?" Only when this question is satisfactorily answered is management ready to proceed to examine the "where," "when," and "how" aspects of entry into foreign markets. In view of the abundant opportunities existing in many foreign markets, such a question may seem irrelevant. However, it is important to recognize that attractiveness of market opportunities overseas varies widely among industries as well as among individual firms. There is also a wide variation in the abilities of individual firms to exploit foreign markets successfully. Not every firm can build successful operations abroad. Some are likely to find it more profitable to deploy their limited resources in more intensive development of familiar domestic markets than to make extensive commitments overseas. In evaluating the appropriateness of entry into foreign markets, a management should:

1. Assess opportunities in international markets for its products and technology as well as the potential risks associated with these opportunities.
2. Examine the degree to which the firm can develop potential opportunities abroad in the light of its own organizational and managerial competence.

In assessing the opportunites and threats posed by foreign markets, management is faced with a vast array of nations and societies. An accurate analysis is hampered by the unreliability, or total absence, of critical statistical information in many parts of the world. Management, being unfamiliar with conditions overseas, may find it difficult to understand the true implications and significance of whatever data are available. The task is further complicated by rapid changes occurring in economic and social environments throughout the world.

Despite these apparent difficulties, three alternative methods of making organized, objective country-by-country surveys of opportunities exist. One method is to require each domestic product division or group to identify opportunities overseas for its respective sphere of activities. This method is particularly useful for a firm whose operation consists of technically oriented product lines, where technical knowledge is essential in recognizing and assessing market opportunities. The limitations of this method are that domestic executives may be too preoccupied with managing existing operations, or that that they may lack familiarity with foreign market conditions.

Another method of surveying foreign markets is to organize a company-wide committee or task force for this specific purpose. The committee is usually headed by a senior executive and consists of men from various functional and product groups. This method makes it possible to provide coordinated direction and a company-wide view in identifying opportunities overseas.

Finally, it is possible to enlist the services of an outside consultant to undertake a survey. The advantages and limitations that are usually associated with employment of outside consultants apply equally well in this case.

If a well-directed search reveals promising potential markets overseas for the company's products and technology, management must then determine if the existing organization has the real or potential capacity to capitalize on these opportunities. Unfortunately, there is a widespread assumption that any sizable firm possesses the necessary skills for dealing with international business problems or that it can readily obtain the needed skills and resources. When the complexity of international business is understood, the fallacy of this assumption will be readily seen. In multinational operations, the managerial task must be performed in diverse economic, cultural, political, technological and legal systems. Far-flung foreign affiliates must be continuously supported by the financial, technological, and human resources of the corporate headquarters. Time-consuming and often frustrating negotiations with foreign governmental officials must be conducted. Top management must also establish and maintain long-term collaborative relationships with foreign executives whose cultural backgrounds, ethical standards and value systems may differ substantially from their own view.[2]

In view of these complexities, it is well for management to examine objectively its own competence. Furthermore, risks inherent in international ventures must be clearly recognized. Since the ability and willingness to take risks varies widely among executives, management should carefully assess the degree of risk associated with opportunities abroad and determine if it is acceptable in terms of both the organizational goals and personal orientations of top management.

Developing an International Business Strategy. If a firm decides to "go international" based on the preceding analysis, management must develop a strategy to meet this objective. At the risk of oversimplification, I shall single out five major issues that top management must consider in formulating a strategy to achieve successful entry into foreign markets. These considerations are: (1) definition of the basic perimeter of the firm's international activities, (2) selection of markets, (3) alternative routes of entry into foreign markets, (4) alternative methods of market entry, and (5) ownership policy of foreign ventures.

1. Definition of the Basic Perimeter. Each of the market opportunities identified by the initial survey must now be reviewed carefully to measure its relative attractiveness and risks. Thorough investigation of a foreign market is time-consuming and costly. Thus, before undertaking a comprehensive study of each potential market, the basic perimeter of the firm's international business must be clearly established by top management.

The two major steps discussed earlier—survey of opportunities and assessment of internal resources and competence—should provide useful guidelines in this attempt. In defining the character of the firm's international business, the following questions must be answered.

- Regional Specialization: Should the firm limit its international activities to certain geographic regions of the world? Or should it become truly global, as long as entry is justified by market opportunities?
- Time Span: Over what time period should the firm plan its strategies for foreign market entry? Can the firm effectively time-phase its entry into various markets? The decision is complicated by two basically conflicting pressures—rapidly changing conditions overseas, and the need for a long lead time to implement entry into a foreign market.
- Relative Extent of Foreign Commitments: Should the management impose some restrictions on the extent of commitments it is willing to consider in a given market? A project below a certain economic size is not worth undertaking, yet it may be wise to place some limit on the size of the firm's commitment in each market in order to diversify the risks.

[2] For illuminating discussion of intercultural administrative problems, see John Fayerweather, *The Executive Overseas* (Syracuse, N.Y.: Syracuse University Press, 1959) p. 182.

• Degree of Operating Flexibility. To what extent is the management willing to adjust the firm's product designs or processing to differing requirements of foreign markets? To what extent is the management willing to deviate in its overseas ventures from the basic character of its domestic business?

Careful examination of each of these issues would considerably limit the scope of potential opportunities to be investigated in detail. For example, one firm included in this study concluded from a similar analysis that it should concentrate its initial overseas efforts in establishing itself firmly in the countries of the European Common Market. Another firm has discovered that opportunities for its products existed practically all over the world. To facilitate further analysis, however, the firm divided those potential markets into three categories, according to levels of economic development and of political stability. The first group consisted of those markets that are found in industrial countries with stable political conditions. The second group included markets in underdeveloped but politically stable countries. The third group represented economically underdeveloped and politically unstable markets. The firm has subsequently decided to time-phase its approach to these markets by beginning with those in the first category. Meantime, the management is closely watching dynamic developments in markets of the second and third categories.

2. *Selection of the Markets.* In investigating the relative attractiveness of potential markets, four considerations are important: (1) the size of the market, (2) conditions and structure of a particular industry in each market, (3) the degree of risk associated with each, and (4) the attitude and policy of the host government toward foreign ventures.

The procedure involved in estimating the potential size of a foreign market is basically the same as the one commonly followed in domestic operations, allowing for extra complications introduced by the absence of accurate data and rapid environmental changes.[3] Though the desired level of precision and accuracy may be difficult to achieve, it is usually possible to obtain useful benchmarks to allow meaningful comparisons among various alternatives.

Management must then analyze the environment in which a particular industry operates in each country. In entering a foreign market, a firm faces a new industrial constellation where competitive conditions are likely to differ from those found in the home market. Thus, a new entrant must carefully examine the limits within which it must operate in a particular industrial environment, and must identify the means of competition. Management can then assess the degree to which the firm as a new entrant can satisfy the requirements imposed by the adapted industrial environment and what strategy it should pursue to compete effectively with those domestic and foreign firms which already possess broad established bases of operations.[4]

[3] Boyd, Frank, Massy and Zoheir, "Marketing Research in Emerging Economies," *Journal of Marketing Research,* Vol. 1, No. 4, pp. 20–23.

[4] Ralph Hodgson and Hugo Uyterhoeven, "Analyzing Foreign Opportunities," *Harvard Business Review*, Vol. 40, No. 2 (March–April, 1962) pp. 60–79.

The third variable to be examined is the degree of risk associated with each alternative market. Because of a wide diversity in environmental forces, the risk level is likely to differ substantially among various markets. Consequently, the attractiveness of a particular market becomes meaningful only when the risk level is properly considered. Basically, risks in international operations can be classified into four categories—political, economic, operational, and ownership. Political risks range from minor bureaucratic harrassment to outright expropriation. Economic risks, though often difficult to separate from political risks, may take the form of unstable currency, a poor foreign exchange position, a galloping inflationary trend, or a shifting government economic policy.

Operational risks arise from certain inadequacies in indigenous technological and institutional systems and from the scarcity of essential resources needed for the smooth functioning of an industrial enterprise. Such risks include the absence of various forms of economic and financial institutions, of reliable sources of supply of raw materials, and of local managerial and technical talents.

In some countries ownership of a foreign venture must be shared with a local interest, which also has elements of risk. Though participation of local interests in a foreign venture decreases the political vulnerability of the enterprise, it results in dilution of control over key managerial decisions.

Some of the risks mentioned above, particularly those of a political nature, can be reduced substantially by deliberate action on the part of management. Here, the fourth consideration, the attitude of the host government toward foreign ventures must be examined. It is possible to reduce potential risks by negotiating for specific guarantees and concessions from the host government at the time of entry into the foreign market. Some governments are willing to grant special considerations to foreign firms if their activities are deemed beneficial to the welfare of the host country.

A more permanent way to reduce political and economic vulnerability is to so structure and manage a foreign venture that the long-term interest of the host country is integrated with that of the investing firm. In any case, the attitude of the host government toward foreign investments is the decisive factor. Thus, the government's real attitude as well as its proclaimed position toward foreign investment should be carefully studied.

Having considered these four elements in each of the potential markets, management can now assign a rough priority ranking to each one. By this means, the potential foreign markets may be surveyed in order of importance. However, this ranking must be adjusted by competitive conditions. The real or potential threat of actions by competitors in certain markets may force management to consider shifting the priority among the potential markets, whenever there is a danger that the first entrant into a specific foreign market can effectively block the subsequent entry of others.

3. Exploring Alternative Routes of Market Entry. When a market is selected for entry, management must decide how to enter this market most effectively.

Basically, entry into a foreign market can be achieved by three alternatives—exporting, contractual arrangements and direct investment. An understanding of the advantages and potential hazards of each alternative and flexibility in using each are vital to the long-term success of an international business.

Traditionally, export has been used most frequently in reaching foreign markets. It involves less risk and a smaller managerial and financial commitment than either of the other two methods. Furthermore, for certain types of products where economy of scale is critical in the production process, an exporter may conceivably enjoy competitive advantages over local producers despite transportation charges and tariffs.

Exporting, however, has several decided disadvantages. It is impossible to reach many parts of the world through the export route because of various import restrictions. The method is most vulnerable to restrictive measures if a competitor decides to undertake local production in a given market. In fact, under some circumstances, exporters may be completely frozen out of the market. Another disadvantage is that exporting offers limited potential for those products that require intensive marketing effort, product adaptation, promotions, and customer services.

A popular alternative to exporting is contractual arrangements of various types, such as licensing, contract manufacturing and management contract. While they cover a wide spectrum of activities, there is one common feature, that is the scope and coverage of a given arrangement is specified by a contract both in terms of time period and services rendered. Licensing allows a firm to enter a foreign market quickly, and to take advantage of the existing organization, managerial and technical personnel, and marketing organization of a licensee. As a rule, approval of the host government can be obtained much more quickly for licensing than for direct investment. Licensing also requires relatively little financial and managerial commitment from the licensor. Furthermore, it helps overcome those nationalistic barriers commonly raised against exporting operations.

Licensing, however, has several major limitations. Because of its contractual nature, licensing limits the time period during which a firm can operate in a given market. If a firm wants to renew licensing arrangements indefinitely, it should realize that a continued representation in a foreign market depends upon its ability to generate new technology. There is a potential danger that a licensee may become a strong competitor in the market when the agreement expires. Practical considerations often prevent a licensor from exercising control over production and marketing of licensed products. Perhaps the most serious limitation is that straight licensing, by its very nature, is not suited to long-term development of a foreign market.[5]

Manufacturing contract allows a firm to undertake local manufacturing by using existing facilities of a local firm through contractual agreements. There are

[5] Charles Henry Lee, "How to Reach the Overseas Market by Licensing," *Harvard Business Review*, Vol. 36, No. 1, (January–February, 1958). pp. 77–80.

some obvious advantages to this method of operations. The contracting firm can avoid a heavy investment in establishing its own manufacturing facilities. It also enables the firm to enter a foreign market quickly. For this reason, some firms have used it as a temporary measure, while their own plants are being constructed in the market. Moreover, unlike licensing where both production and marketing aspects are tied in a package, manufacturing contract allows the firm to undertake its own distribution in the country. In some cases, the contracting firm can negotiate an extremely attractive arrangement because a local firm may have excess capacity it is anxious to utilize or it can benefit from a greater scale of production. There are, however, several major disadvantages. The firm may find it difficult to locate a suitable manufacturer who is not only willing but also capable of manufacturing the firm's products under its specification. Quality standard has been found particularly difficult to enforce. Furthermore, the firm may be reluctant to share its manufacturing know-how with a foreign firm.

Management contract makes it possible to capitalize on firm's managerial know-how by agreeing to provide a foreign venture with managerial talents. It enables the firm to obtain operating control of a venture without making large equity investment. Moreover, the contractual nature of this arrangement tends to ease local resentments which may otherwise result from an attempt to assume managerial control of a foreign venture through other means.

Management contract is frequently welcomed by a foreign firm as well as the government of the host country, inasmuch as it brings to the country managerial know-how, one of the most critical and scarce resources in most developing countries. Management contract can provide needed managerial support to a new venture until the local management is trained. From the point of view of a contracting firm, however, management contract has two main limitations. First, since managerial effectiveness depends, in part, upon local environments, there is no guarantee that managerial practices developed in one country can be applied in another with equal effectiveness.[6] Secondly, managerial talents are scarce in almost any parent corporation, thus providing a foreign firm with managerial support for a fixed fee may not be the best use of the firm's scarce resources.

The third method of entering a foreign market is by direct investment. While the specific nature of commitment may vary from simple assembly set-up to fully integrated manufacturing operations, the direct investment route enables a firm to combine its technical, managerial, and financial resources for a long-term development of a foreign market. Only in this way can profits be earned on the full range of operations involved, and full advantage be taken of the local wage and salary level. Furthermore, the firm can benefit from various incentives made available by the host country. It must be recognized that the direct investment route requires an extensive commitment of corporate re-

[6] Richard N. Farmer and Barry M. Richman, *Comparative Management and Economic Progress* (Homewood, Illinios: Richard D. Irwin, Inc., 1965) pp. 1–24.

sources, thereby making the firm more vulnerable to economic and political risks. Furthermore, a long lead time and much development effort are usually required before the operations become profitable.

The suitability of each form of entry must be analyzed carefully in terms of the conditions of a particular market. There are, however, general guidelines in selecting a particular form of market entry. First, the three routes should be viewed as alternatives rather than a sequence of developments to be followed. Some firms pursue implicitly the practice of a step-by-step approach in developing a foreign market. They begin supplying a market through the export route first and consider local production only when export sales have reached a sufficient volume or when the market can no longer be supplied through exporting.

While this practice has the advantage of minimizing risks, it has often resulted in the loss of promising markets or in forfeiture of rapid growth opportunities. There is no reason why a firm should pursue the policy of a stage-by-stage development, when direct investment is justified right from the start by the local investment climate and the capacity and commitment of a particular firm. In fact, at times an early and large scale entry in the form of direct investment is the only way a firm can build a viable position in a foreign market. This is particularly true for those industries manufacturing capital intensive products.

Thus, if any firm confines itself, by default, to any one of the three routes, it is severely limiting its opportunities in a foreign market. There is, however, perceptibly inflexible attitude among the firms studied toward devising an appropriate entry strategy to meet the particular requirements of the market under consideration.

Secondly, these three routes of market entry are by no means mutually exclusive. Frequently they must be integrated to enable a firm to penetrate a foreign market. Such an integrated approach is particularly applicable for a diversified firm whose multiple product lines are likely to require different entry strategies. For example, a firm may follow the licensing route of entry for products with a limited or specialized market, or for products or processes expected to have a relatively short economic life. It can simultaneously establish a local base of production in the market for its major product lines. Furthermore, the firm can export certain types of products to the market to supplement the product lines of the local manufacturing or licensing operations.

Another important consideration in choosing among alternative routes of market entry is to examine the firm's objectives with respect to a market under consideration. As has been pointed out earlier, the initial decision on the form of entry has far-reaching implications on subsequent operations in the market.

Finally, it is important to review periodically the suitability of a particular form of operation in a given market because changes in the operating climate and regulations governing the activity of foreign companies can rapidly alter the applicability of any one of the alternatives for a given company or a category of products.

4. Evaluating Alternative Methods of Entry—Acquisition vs. Initiating New

Ventures. If a direct investment route is chosen, management has the choice of either initiating its own venture or acquiring an existing foreign concern. Some quite successful multinational firms rely almost exclusively on acquisition in entering foreign markets.

The proponents of acquisition claim that it allows timely entry into a market with relative ease. If a firm has to initiate its own venture, a year or two of intensive developmental effort is usually required before the affiliate becomes productive. Through acquisition, however, the investing firm can take advantage of managerial talents, technical resources, and the labor force of the acquired company, thus avoiding some of the major difficulties of starting a foreign venture. Qualified experienced managers and technicians are extremely scarce overseas. The labor market for non-managerial personnel is becoming increasingly tight also in most highly industrialized countries, and in underdeveloped areas much initial investment is needed to train the indigenous labor force. An acquiring firm can also take over the existing distribution network and goodwill among distributors and ultimate customers cultivated by acquired firm over a period of time. Acquisition also can reduce high risks usually associated with foreign ventures because an acquired firm possesses familiarity with the particular industrial environment and competitive conditions in the market.

The limitations of acquisition are as follows: First, the potential firms to be acquired may be non-existent or alternatives may be severely limited. Second, acquisition may arouse nationalistic resentment in the host country against the investing firm because the action may be interpreted as a local firm being taken over by a foreign interest. Aside from the emotional overtones connected with acquisition, some foreign governments that are anxious to obtain *new* manufacturing facilities and technology through foreign investment may take discriminatory actions against the firms choosing this manner of entry. Thus, a firm considering entry into foreign markets through acquisition is usually in a weaker position to negotiate with the host government than one planning to establish a new operation.

Some of the frequently cited advantages of acquisition should be examined carefully. For example, the time-saving feature of acquisition is not universally applicable. Location and evaluation of potential candidates for acquisition are often time-consuming processes. Negotiations may extend over a long period of time.

Advantages associated with taking over an existing organization and managerial personnel are, in part, offset by the problems of integrating the acquired firm and its management personnel into the parent organization. The process of integration is complicated by basic differences in managerial philosophy and orientation arising from cultural and environmental variations, and the climate of insecurity found in most acquired firms. In choosing between the two alternative methods of undertaking direct investment, the general considerations presented here should be used as guidelines for careful analysis of each specific case.

5. Determining Ownership Policy. In making direct investments overseas, management faces another important decision, that is, it must determine the firm's policy toward ownership of foreign ventures. The ownership pattern of a foreign venture can range from no equity (i.e. only a contractual relationship and/or debt financing), minority ownership, 50–50 split, majority to one hundred percent ownership. An investment firm can obtain equity participation in a foreign venture through a variety of ways, such as through contributions in cash, technical assistance, used equipment, brand names, managerial know-how, and stock of the investing firm. Combinations of any one of these alternatives is entirely possible. In fact, some of the most intricate financial arrangements are known to have been employed in acquiring equity in a new foreign venture.

Though the participation of local interest in foreign ventures is required in some countries such as India, Mexico and Japan, management has considerable flexibility in determining ownership patterns in other important markets, including those in the European Common Market.

There is a wide diversity in managerial attitudes toward ownership of foreign ventures. Some firms insist on, or at least prefer, complete ownership of their ventures, while others actively seek the participation of local interests in theirs. Although there are various ramifications to the ownership issue, the basic choice lies between total ownership and joint ventures. The advantages and limitations of each choice deserve careful attention.

The chief advantage of total ownership is that it assures a greater degree of managerial control over a foreign venture than is possible under a joint venture arrangement. The firm can enforce its own policy and standards in such key areas as financial management, product quality, selection of managerial personnel, and disposition of profit. With total ownership, the basic conflicts of interests often found in joint ventures are avoided.

Under joint ownership, differences in managerial orientation and corporate objectives often cause disagreements over basic policy. Such disagreements may lead to vacillation and inability to develop a unified policy or to the emergence of a dominant partner. Joint ventures, particularly those with evenly divided ownership, are inherently difficult to manage. There is also a risk in associating with a local firm in a politically unstable country. When a political upheaval occurs, it is possible that the chosen partner may fall out of favor with a new government, thereby damaging the investing firm.

What then are the potential benefits of a joint venture? One important benefit is the reduction of risk. The arrangement allows a firm to enter a foreign market with a substantially smaller initial capital outlay than would be possible otherwise. Furthermore, by working with a local partner the investing company can realize a threefold benefit. First, it would acquire a staff that would otherwise take a long time to develop. Second, it would acquire knowledge of local business practices that could otherwise be obtained only by costly trial and error or time-consuming analyses. Finally, it would gain ready access to the government and business community. The investing firm can benefit from the local partner's carefully developed associations in such areas as government relations and banking connections. Thus, the system of joint ventures provides, at least in theory, an effective combination of the managerial and technological resources of the investing firm with the distinctive competence of the local partner. Moreover, joint ventures are likely to be favored by the host government as well as by the industrial community in the host country.

If the firm chooses to pursue the policy of one hundred percent ownership of its foreign ventures, it must be aware that such a venture is likely to be vulnerable to pressures and resentments of various sorts in the host country. This is particularly true in developing nations, where the past record of Western enterprises has been far from impeccable. Thus, the firm must be prepared to reduce this vulnerability and conflicts by finding a mutuality of interest between the host country and the firm through deliberate managerial planning and actions.[7]

There are several ways that a firm can effectively contribute to the interest of the host country other than by sharing ownership of an enterprise with indigenous interests. The investing firm can turn over a considerable share of management responsibility to local nationals; it can continuously support the venture by feeding new technical knowledge and discoveries; it can develop local managerial skills and reinvest savings in the host country.

If the firm chooses to pursue the joint venture route, it must determine with whom ownership is to be shared. The most common way is to share ownership of a contemplated venture with an established local firm (or firms). In this case, choice of a local partner (or partners) becomes an extremely important decision. In evaluating a potential partner firm, management should go far beyond examination of its financial, technical and managerial capacities. The investing firm should analyze the local firm's hidden commitments to other firms through banking connections, cartel arrangements, or family relations. Most importantly, the investing firm should understand clearly what objectives the local firm wants to pursue and what it expects out of the contemplated venture.

Another way to share ownership is to obtain a part of the equity in a new venture from the local capital market in the host country. For example, when Kaiser Motors established its venture in Argentina, it sold approximately a third of its equity to private investors in the country.[8] This method has an advantage of diffusing benefits derived from the venture directly among a wider segment of the population. A broader ownership participation also tends to reduce political vulnerability of a foreign venture. Moreover, it enables the investing firm to obtain operating control with relatively limited equity participation. There are some basic problems, however. Frictions may arise between

[7] Richard D. Robinson, *International Business Policy*, (New York: Holt, Rinehart and Winston, 1964) pp. 99–145.

[8] John E. Ewing and Frank Meissner, *International Business Management: Readings and Cases* (Belmont, California: Wadsworth Publishing Co., 1964) p. 506.

the management and local stockholders because expectations of local stockholders may differ rather markedly from those of the management. More basically, this method is impractical in many countries where an adequate capital market is yet to be developed.

The concept of shared ownership can be carried to the ultimate form by offering local investors opportunities to buy equity in the parent firm, thus creating a truly internationally owned corporation. While this represents the idealized form of a true multinational corporation, there are a number of practical constraints to prevent immediate application of this concept to a significant degree.[9]

[9] John Fayerweather, "LRP for International Operations," *California Management Review*, Vol. 3, No. 2, (Fall, 1960) p. 24.

38

International Operations and Corporate Planning[1]

P. J. Hovell

The attitudes of businessmen towards import substitution, exporting, and direct foreign investment are at present attracting widespread attention. Most of the studies which have been made tend to concentrate on one or other of these. However, these three areas are not mutually exclusive. Together they form a range of operations which must be viewed in an international context. Since not every company will have the resources to be concerned directly and immediately with all aspects, there is a need for a corporate planning approach which will supply direction and focus for appropriate profit alternatives in domestic and foreign markets to be evaluated in terms of current and planned capabilities.

The aims of this paper are threefold. Firstly, to establish the need for this wider perspective by referring to the international business environment. Secondly, to suggest a conceptual corporate planning framework for international operations. Thirdly, to examine this in the light of the findings of research into the management of selected firms in the agricultural, mechanical handling and textile machinery industries.[2]

Reprinted with permission from *Journal of Management Studies*, Vol. 6, No. 3, October 1969, pp. 302–317.

[1] I should like to thank Professor W. H. Scott and Mr. J. D. Froggatt of the University of Salford for the helpful comments they made when reviewing the draft version of this paper.

[2] This research has arisen out of an earlier project carried out at the University of Salford by Dr. H. G. Hunt, J. D. Froggatt and P. J. Hovell. The analysis is derived from information obtained in two series of interviews with top executives in 50 companies. The first series of inter-

1. The International Business Environment

In the contemporary world few companies of significant size, pursuing long-term profitable growth objectives, can safely base their plans on the assumption that the major sources of supply, income and competition will be found in the domestic market. The cogency of this argument rests on the need for a company to be strategically placed to seize the opportunities provided by, and to withstand the strong competitive pressures operating within, the international business environment.

Between 1953 and 1966 the value of world exports rose from U.S. $78.3 billion to U.S. $200.7 billion.[3] Within this broad outline of expansion a number of important trends emerge.

The Growth of Trade Between the Industrial Nations. Firstly, by far the greater proportion of the growth in world exports is attributable to the accretion of trade between the industrial nations. In 1953 sales to other industrial countries accounted for 63 percent of the industrial countries' exports, by 1966 the proportion was nearly 72 per cent.[4] A powerful factor in bringing about this increase has been the economic expansion of West European countries. An important facet of their "foreign trade" lead growth has been the notable increase in international specialization which seems to be characterized more by intra-industry than inter-industry specialization. Intra-industry specialization can stem from the production policies of dominant manufacturers, consciously based on international comparative advantage. In this respect domestic producers, wanting to increase their economies of scale, may concentrate on a narrower range of products which meets the modal customer requirements, assuming that these represent a sufficiently large share of the home and traditional export markets. In addition to these positive supply considerations another important factor promoting this type of specialization has been the dissatisfaction of some home-buyers with, for example, lack of sophistication in basic design and end-use suitability of domestic products. Shortcomings in the former may be due to home producers neglecting research and development associated with the more dynamic and advanced sectors of the industry's technology. This in turn may have been exacerbated by insufficient contact with the faster growing centres of demand. Weaknesses in end-use suitability often result from an absence of marketing orientation.

In spite of there being some uncertainty about the anticipated development

---

views was conducted during the period September 1966 to April 1967. The original sample included small firms with under 500 employees, medium-sized firms 500–1500 employees, and large firms with over 1500 employees and companies with foreign parents and British companies with overseas subsidiaries.

A second series of interviews was carried out between July and September (inclusive) 1968. On this occasion the firms with over 1500 employees were concentrated on (30 per cent of the original sample).

[3] *International Trade* 1966, General Agreement on Tariffs and Trade publication, Geneva, 1967.

[4] Balassa, B., "Tariff reductions and trade in manufactures," *American Economic Review*, June 1966; pp. 466–72.

of the trading policies of some of the major countries, notably that of the U.S., there is every reason to believe the expansion of world exports will continue. However, and regardless of the future rate of this growth, it is probably safe to forecast an intensification of international competition between companies.

The Developing Countries and Protectionism. Secondly, many of the developing countries in complementing their industrial development programmes have, increasingly, resorted to the use of import controls on the one hand and incentives to attract foreign private investment on the other. A typical pattern which has been adopted in building up particular industries is, in the first instance, to prohibit the imports of products in specified categories and to substitute these with imported kits of components for local assembly. Since the tendency is to reduce the unit value of the kits by decreeing that designated components are to be obtained locally, foreign suppliers may find that they are, ultimately, providing only a few technically advanced parts and know-how. This is not to suggest that many of the traditional markets concerned will shortly be denied to exporters. In the first place, product exports most likely to be affected by industrialization programmes will be those which are relatively standard and which lend themselves to assembly line techniques. Secondly, the promotion of industries in particular economies will stimulate the demand for plant and machinery. Thirdly, the diversity existing among the developing countries is extreme and this is reflected in their widely differing patterns of importation.

Private Foreign Direct Investment. The third major trend discernible is the rapid expansion of private direct foreign investments which have been growing at about 10 per cent per annum. The main supplier has been the U.S. which in 1961–64 accounted for about 70 per cent of the total flow; the proportions for the U.K. and the E.E.C. were nearly 15 per cent and 13 per cent respectively.[5] By 1966 the combined book values of U.S. and U.K. corporate investments abroad stood at U.S. $67.1 billion.[6] Most of the recent investment activity has taken place within the advanced industrial countries, with the U.K. and the E.E.C. attracting much of the inflow. Among the chief pace-setters are the large U.S. international companies who have been quick to seize the opportunities offered by inter-country profit differentials and to exploit fast-growing markets by circumventing such impediments as transport costs and tariffs. Although the U.K. has international companies second in number and size to the U.S.A.,[7] continental European companies are now taking large strides in building up their foreign interests. Ten years ago these were negligible. For example, West German firms, in spite of the distractions of very high domestic investment returns increased their average annual direct investments

[5] Diamond, M., "Trends in the flow of international private capital," *I.M.F. Staff Papers*, Vol. XII, No. 1, March 1967.

[6] *Survey of Current Business*, U.S. Department of Commerce and *Board of Trade Journal*, 26th January 1968.

[7] See the *Fortune Directory*, 1966, of the 200 largest international companies outside the U.S.A.

abroad by 33 per cent between 1959–62 and 1962–65. The increase for U.K. companies was 19 per cent.[8] This last example throws some light on the corporate view on international investment. There is a tendency when concentrating, as did the Reddaway Report, on quantitative cost benefit models of foreign investments to not fully accommodate this view. Such analyses usually have relatively short-term horizons and their concepts of profitability tend to avoid some of the wider and more qualitative factors influencing investment decision objectives.[9] Important as specific profitability considerations are, or should be, they do not in themselves represent the prime mover behind overseas investment. For large companies, an important motivation often is, that if an insufficient scale of foreign investment is undertaken they are unlikely to remain in, or gain promotion to, the "big-time league."

Another, yet more positive, inducement is the realization that a wider range of products can be produced at an optimum volume and also, financial, marketing and research economies can only be exploited to the full, where the operation is mounted on a global scale.

2. The Corporate Planning Approach to International Operations

Having made a brief review of international business trends, we are now in a position to draw on some of the more salient conclusions which appear to have emerged and which have a direct bearing on the corporate planning function.

Managerial Attitudes, the Global Concept and Global Strategies. A firm depends on its survival, in the last analysis, on achieving some measure of profit. This measure and its growth will be conditioned externally by such factors as shareholders' expectations, the level and growth of demand, the rate of product and plant obsolescence and, especially, the intensity and scope of competitive activity. Set in the international context, survival as a business goal is unlikely to be maintained in the long term through passive and defensive managerial attitudes. Of course, sectors of industries are exposed differentially to international competition. This is evident from the examination of the survey industries. However, it was recognizable, even from the most sheltered sector studied, that the number of firms which can rely indefinitely on domestic customer loyalty and tariff protection is becoming smaller.

Therefore, it would not appear unreasonable to assume throughout this section that the firm's exposure to international competitive forces is not partial but complete. As a consequence, the achievement of long-term survival requires that the top management, (a) exercises acute perception in understanding the company's environment and being able to project its trends, (b) adopts dynamic attitudes which should reflect themselves in the choice of

[8] *Economic Bulletin for Europe*, Vol. 19, No. 1, New York: U.N.; November 1967.

[9] Reddaway, W. B. et al., *Effects of the U.K. Direct Investment Overseas*, Interim Report, Cambridge University Press, 1967.

specific growth and profitability goals, and (c) employs skills necessary to establish and implement strategies and policies which will bring about desired performances. In these respects, planning for, and the pursuit of, growth will be through a multi-dimensional strategy, based on targets set for profits, sales and market share levels, and on programmes for adding new products, customer segments, geographical markets and technologies, yet conditioned by the strengths and weaknesses inherent in the company's product-market scope.[10]

It can be postulated that managements possessing these dynamic attitudes will decide on given global strategies corresponding to the size and nature of the resources at their disposal and related to the anticipated returns and risks associated with each opportunity. Therefore, for a particular set of company, product range and market circumstances, there is a complementary group of profit options. The dimension dealing with market penetration and development will include securing and developing the home base, product, project, and component exports, licensing and foreign manufacture. Permutated with these will be a range of distribution channels and investment ownership media. In relation to the more long-term strategic elements of corporate planning, the company will have to resist organizational pressures tending to maintain the *status quo,* so that its choice is not restricted to opportunities available only in the home market and those too closely connected with the existing and perhaps too narrowly defined product areas. Therefore, when a company is considering a major extension of its existing research or corporate acquisitions to add new technologies and market outlets or long-term capital raising, the search and screening process should extend, wherever possible, beyond national boundaries. As with all the other profit alternatives, the assumption is still that dynamic managerial attitudes and skills and corporate capabilities are inseparable prerequisites.

Companies which are planning the long-term development of international strategies need to make the distinction between the managerial adoption of a global concept and the achievement of a global coverage, in the sense that the former must precede the latter.

Deciding on the Scale and Mix of International Operations. A company when deciding what scale and mix of overseas operations, if any, it should undertake will obviously be constrained by its current level of resources. Some companies might conclude that their present capability, in relation to the competition they would have to encounter abroad and to the cost of overseas distribution and of designing products for specific foreign customer requirements, could be more profitably employed in the domestic market.

While the absolute size of resources is clearly a significant consideration in itself, expectations about domestic demand will be an important element. A firm might have the resources and skills normally required for foreign business but it may rationally preclude this from its present range of options.

[10] Ansoff, H. I., *Corporate Strategy*, New York: McGraw-Hill, 1965.

The expectations about the growth in long-term domestic demand may be so promising that the firm feels it can rely on the home market to provide the opportunity for high corporate growth rates to be obtained. In practice, not many firms face such clear-cut prospects. Given a high level of demand, the realization of the profitability goals will also depend on no unexpected and major changes in competitive and technological activity taking place. Here it should be noted once more, that however good a domestic firm might be it will be prone to international competition. Furthermore, secular demand trends, however encouraging, may not compensate some firms, sufficiently, for the shorter term fluctuations in growth that might come about because of, say, cyclical factors and changes in government economic policy. Hence, in most cases there will be a point in time when a developing company will find its growth aspirations hampered if it continues to concentrate only on its present product field or on domestic outlets. Assuming that the company has a comparative advantage in its technology and that international demand offers good opportunities, then when this point has been reached it will probably seek a proportion of its total business abroad. Therefore, deciding when the company should "go foreign" will rest on the management's assessment of when and to what degree domestic performances will fall short of desired targets. The attainment of overall profitability goals is the principal criterion rather than whether home as opposed to foreign orders are more profitable. It will become worthwhile cultivating overseas business as long as it can increase aggregate net revenue and is seen as a means of optimizing long-term profitability.[11]

Once the company is committed to foreign operations it will probably want to revise its specific performance objectives upwards; faced with the enlarged opportunities that are seen to emerge from a detailed analysis of those selected markets abroad which are within its range to develop. Consequently, the amount it will want to appropriate to its foreign operations will depend largely on the resources required to realize the levels of domestic and overseas business which the company feels are there to exploit and which will achieve the revised targets. The actual market and distribution mix of the firm's foreign activities will, within the limitations of the global resources allocation, be influenced by a number of market, product range and competitive constraints.

A company's decision to select a given market abroad for development will be conditioned, among other things by, (a) relative transport costs, (b) relative tariff differentials and the existence and strength of local industry, (c) the size and growth potential of demand; here the important issues are likely to be the penetration gained by other firms, the way demand requirements differ from those of other major markets and the long-term profitability to be earned relative to alternative sources of foreign income, and (d) the manner in which the market will assist in the future development of a global logistical network.

[11] See Hovell, P.J., "Export Pricing Policies," *District Bank Review*, September 1968; pp. 42–5.

If the last two conditions are satisfied, adverse landed costs might provide the incentive for the firm to carry out local assembly or manufacture. Alternatively if the company does not wish either to make direct shipments or to undertake local assembly/manufacture, thought can be given to a licensing agreement which will not prevent the licensor from being able to exercise the option of controlling the market later.

The range of distribution media open to a company in a particular market will depend on the inter-relationship of such variables as (a) the number of end-users and (b) the demand for pre- and after-sales services. For example, standard products, purchased frequently and requiring technical and commercial service support, will meet with little success if they are handled by agents whose responsibilities generally end when they have brought together principal and prospective buyers. Such products require a permanent and extensive distribution system which provides for selling, promoting, display, stocking and servicing facilities. If because of low-brand acceptance, weak market penetration and the lack of uncommitted distributors which could overcome these difficulties the company has to take on the distribution function itself, then the costs of reaching the customer can be high. A consideration of this order will certainly limit the number of markets a firm could effectively choose to penetrate.

In international business the timing of investment decisions cannot always be ordered to meet the convenience of the company. Decisions taken, or likely to be taken, by competitors and foreign governments often force the pace of specific strategic investment decisions. For example, in markets which the firm considers to be of long-term significance, it must try not to be overtaken, suddenly, by changed import control conditions. It might be in the firm's forward interests to take the initiative on local assembly or manufacture, especially in a developing country, if by so doing it can obtain such preferential terms which would not only bar product imports but provide the firm with a considerable competitive edge over latecomers to the field.[12] As Drucker points out, in addition to the hazards that a company's resources can support and those which it cannot, there are risks which a company "cannot afford *not* to take."[13] This means that a company needs to draw up well in advance, the anticipated returns and risks associated with each main opportunity and have a clear idea about ranking these but nevertheless be prepared to reappraise its list of priorities as and when external stimuli change. These circumstances underline the rationale for taking decisions within a corporate planning framework.

A Global Strategy Continuum. In some respects the strategic approach described in this section suggests a time continuum. At one end there will be the firm, which because its resources are as yet inadequately developed, will consciously decide to postpone taking on overseas commitments. At the other

[12] See Yoshino, M. Y., "International Business. What Is the Best Strategy?" *The Business Quarterly,* Fall 1966; pp. 46–55.

[13] Drucker, P. F., *Managing for Results*, Heinemann, 1964: pp. 190–5.

end there will be the truly international company,[14] whose large capability permits it to make decisions regarding markets, products, techniques and processes, personnel and capital in terms of the alternatives available to it throughout the world. For example, when formulating its product-market strategy it will be expected to resort to logistical systems of world-wide distribution which seek to reconcile minimum supply-distance-input costs with maximum economies of scale and which in turn have to take into account the facts that international demand within given product segments is not necessarily homogeneous and that there exist political impediments in the flows of international trade. Between these bipolar models there will be a number of corporate situations where because of limited resources it is not currently possible to bring about a full integration of an internationally oriented managerial perspective and a world-wide market coverage. It can be expected that these firms in varying stages will have strategies which, although restricted as to what profit alternatives and national markets can be dealt with, nevertheless are capable of future development.

Even assuming, in conceptual terms, that it is possible to exclude such factors as self-imposed and external restraints on financial and organizational growth, the notion of such a continuum requires some qualification. It does not necessarily follow that each company can be viewed as a potential to progress as resources allow, from domestic through to foreign manufacture and marketing. Those that can be expected to follow this path in selected markets probably will have limited themselves to a particular range of product technology. That is to say, either to one product range or to product groups where there is a high degree of design, production and/or distribution commonality. Other firms may decide against committing additional resources to more "ultimate" forms of control over given overseas markets in favour of seeking what are, for them, higher returns from developing new aspects of their skills. It is recognized here that it is also possible for some firms to have hybrid strategies; one product division may be operating on a global scale, while others are either being developed for this or because of special demand and technological reasons never will be.

3. The Empirical Findings—Managerial Attitudes, Corporate Objectives and International Policies of the Survey Firms

It is one thing for firms to have basic objectives, such as the desire to survive, but it is, of course, another matter for their managements to have the ability to achieve these. The personal differences in managerial perceptions, attitudes and skills help to explain why, even within a given sector of an industry,

[14] These are frequently referred to as multinational, global, transnational or supranational companies. However, because different connotations are attached to these respective terms, about which there is no general agreement, it has been decided to use the more simple term "international company." Moreover, as will be amplified below, there are still very few companies operating on a global basis which come close to demonstrating the various qualities implied by these special descriptions.

there are considerable variations in emphasis accorded to growth and profitability objectives, not to speak of the diversity of policies and procedures. Nevertheless, managerial objectives (and the attitudes which underlie them), however imprecisely and implicitly expressed, declare themselves through company policies, procedures, performances and reactions to financial results and external pressures.

In our research we attempted to work back from such corporate frames of reference towards explanations of the principal managerial attitudes which give rise to the survey firm's international strategies and operations. Reference can be made to some of the attitudes and policies which were seen to emerge from the research.

Passive Attitudes and Policies. Several of the smaller and medium-sized survey firms have domestic market preoccupations and although nearly all of them have acquired foreign trade experience (without exception the medium being product exports) their attitudes towards exporting are passive. They do not solicit orders. Quite frequently these are received through, for example, parent companies, consortia relationships and fortuitous contacts with foreign buyers. Alternatively, there are managements which tolerate a small but continuing export sideline as long as this does not interfere with home market business. In themselves, passive attitudes and policies on exporting are not incompatible with the model. But in the majority of cases this passivity stems not from any attempt to plan growth by employing limited resources in the most effective way. Many are old-established firms which can hardly lay claim to being in a transitionary development stage. Several of them having faced a decline in demand are now content to rely on some niche or traditional foothold of the domestic market which they had created in the past. A large number of the companies meeting highly specialized demands in the custom-built sectors of the three survey industries typify such behavior.

Other Attitudes and Policies. The incidence of these passive export practices should not be over-emphasized. In relation to the total output of their particular industrial sectors, the firms involved are, with a few exceptions, not very significant. The managements of many of the sample firms are not indifferent to the value of maintaining a permanent level of organizational infra-structure for obtaining overseas business. Among the most frequent reasons given for this approach are, exporting provides a good hedge against too great a dependence on the home market and it affords the opportunity of utilizing plant to the full.

However, apart from the few notable exceptions (which admittedly have an importance out of all relation to their number), many of the firms have been slow to exploit their international opportunities.[15] It is not so much that they

[15] It is not proposed to describe in any great detail the policies and practices and their implications. These have been reported on in previous articles, namely Hunt, H. G., Froggatt, J. D., and Hovell, P. J., "The Management of Export Marketing in the Engineering Industries," *British Journal of Marketing*, Spring 1967; pp. 10–24, and Hovell P. J., "Export Pricing Policies," *District Bank Review*, September 1968; pp. 34–55.

fail to export in reasonable volume; many of them have a substantial foreign sale; it is more the way they go about their overseas business. In those sectors where secular domestic demand is neither declining nor likely to become static, most of the companies only attempt to slip their exporting activity into a higher gear when the home market becomes temporarily depressed; primarily it is said, because in normal times orders taken abroad are relatively unprofitable. Even where there is a permanent export organization it is often impracticable to expect the tempo of its operation to correspond with the state of the home order book. Therefore, and in line with earlier comments, short term profitability comparisons between domestic and foreign business should not form the main criterion when deciding how much effort should be applied to exporting. A large number of the firms' products compared with their principal foreign counterparts are often less technically sophisticated. For many of the textile machinery and mechanical handling products, these factors combined with adverse tariff and transport cost differentials make them uncompetitive in some of the faster growing markets of Western Europe.[16] There is an overwhelming emphasis on direct exports as opposed to other forms of international operation. In the field of distribution, there are a few deviations from traditional methods. For example, there is little attempt to set up marketing subsidiaries which might, in given product and demand circumstances, compensate for low-brand acceptances and weak market penetrations while at the same time providing that degree of pre- and after-sales service which better established companies can extract from their franchised distributorships. Several firms are restricted in their selection of overseas markets by licensing arrangements with foreign companies. The incidence of this is not altogether confined to the smaller and medium sized firms.

Many of these practices are the defensive outcome of corporate objectives which have been constrained by limitations imposed by the senior management on the growth of the financial and organizational structures of the

[16] The figures below underscore the competitiveness of the U.K. textile machinery industry relative to that of the other two leading exporting nations concerned.

	Export values (U.S. $'000 m.)				*Growth Rate 1959–60*	*Export/ Import Ratios*			*Proportion of Exports to: (%)*					
									(1) O.E.C.D. Europe			*(2) Non-ind Cos.**		
Country	'55	'64	'65	'66	(%)	'64	'65	'66	'64	'65	'66	'64	'65	'66
West Germany	95	327	350	401	204	2.4	2.1	2.4	56.4	50.4	51.7	26.9	30.9	26.3
United Kingdom	130	188	199	230	95	1.7	1.6	1.8	32.1	29.5	28.0	45.8	50.9	48.5
Switzerland	†	157	175	191	170	3.0	3.4	3.2	67.2	61.7	57.8	21.5	22.5	23.4

* Total Exports less (O.E.C.D. Europe + North America + Japan + Sino-Soviet Bloc).
† The first available figure for Switzerland is for 1959 when the figure was $70.6 million.
Source: O.E.C.D. Commodity Series C 1966, 1965 and 1964.
The figures for the mechanical handling equipment industry convey a similar pattern.

companies concerned. These constraints are not only limited to the smaller and medium sized firms. Several of the larger groups of companies, while they have based their diversified interests on a considerable degree of technological linkage, have in most cases brought about surprisingly little organizational integration on the research, production, financial and marketing fronts. Often a new branch of engineering has been turned to in order to offset some product strategy weakness such as an all too apparent decline in long-term demand, rather than to exploit a main strength which would have probably led to increased competitiveness. The defensive character of some of the sample firms' diversification patterns is frequently borne out by their group financial results.

It is when attention is turned to the few more impressive company performances that the role of top managerial attitudes becomes really apparent. Aside from the international agricultural tractor firms referred to later, the examples observed can be divided in two categories. The first concerns companies which have centred the major share of total resources on a specialized product range. They are fairly large sized firms having between 1500 and 4000 employees and are product leaders at home as well as being to the forefront in world markets. One produces man-made fibre machinery, a second, hosiery machines, a third mobile cranes and a fourth manufactures industrial trucks (e.g. fork-lift trucks). Two of these, supplying mobile cranes and industrial trucks respectively, have because of the nature of their products' distribution requirements, recently appraised their selection of overseas markets. They have decided to concentrate effort on building up "first order" distribution systems, in growth markets (mainly in Europe). This has led to a number of assembly and marketing subsidiaries being created and in some instances actually withdrawing from markets where the return on maintaining expensive servicing arrangements is insufficient. In addition to these policies all four companies, because of product specialization, have been able to derive R & D and production economies of scale. However, while dynamic attitudes and policies undoubtedly prevail, it must not be overlooked that some measure of their success rests on the four product groups each having fast growing international demands. This is seen as justifying the high degree of dependence on a particular product technology.

The second category of firms are those that have not limited their growth in this way. They have diversified into a number of product fields. In doing so they have built on their more basic strengths and by integrating their several interests through efficient managerial control systems they have been able to achieve increased economies. One example can be mentioned. It concerns a diversification based on a strong design and engineering capability. The group of companies forms an organization of about 10,000 employees and is a specialist in a wide range of advanced chemical and mechanical engineering technologies. Its financial performance is well above the average for the engineering industry which is partly a reflection of two important strategies pursued. Firstly, the company being heavily committed to contract business, is able to buy in a large proportion of its components, estimated at some 75 per cent of prime cost. Therefore, not having the distractions associated with a large production capacity it can intensify the development of its main skills of design and engineering. Secondly, before it allocates any sizeable scale of resources to a new technology it attempts to evaluate world demand because an insufficient and irregular domestic sales pattern is normally related to a specialist technology. Stemming from this, the company derives about 65 per cent of its income from international operations and has about a third of its labour force abroad. Although the majority of its foreign investment is in such markets as Australia, South Africa, Canada and India, through the aegis of a recently formed corporate planning department, the company is proposing to set up a European division by taking over specialist Continental firms, especially within the E.E.C. In doing this it is both seeking a good foothold in Europe and is buying its way into areas of technology which although related to its own are considered to be more advanced. This particular company example has been given in some detail because it contrasts sharply with the defensive models of diversification referred to earlier. Furthermore, the example does provide a demonstration of how it is possible for a company, albeit large by national standards, to plan a limited global strategy that has, probably, the potential for developing into a full one.

The International Companies. The other major industrial sector covered by the research project concerns the agricultural tractors. Several leading North American multi-product corporations dominate this and cause it to be very internationally oriented.

These companies, by being able to draw on massive resources have established large production and marketing subsidiaries in many countries. Although by no means with equal success, the companies endeavour to co-ordinate their operations so that they form integral parts of multi-national organizations. The essential media adopted to try to bring about this integration are, the product-logistical strategy, the organizational structure and a managerial control system, a prerequisite of which is the planning mechanism.

In many ways, the tractor lends itself very well to a *world-wide logistical system.* International demand is large and, especially outside North America and Western Europe, growth potential is considerable. Customer choice is strongly motivated by end-use functionality. While end-use differentials, corresponding to major crop and farming conditions prevailing in particular regions of the world, call for a certain amount of obvious product heterogeneity, the categories involved are broad enough, in themselves, to permit large economies of scale to be obtained. Attractive as these economies can be for any one production location, there reaches a point when, because of a combination of the demand differences referred to, rising transport costs, tariffs and competition, a selective multi-plant-multi-national policy becomes an imperative. Some of the companies have shaped their global strategies—and organizational structure—to take full advantage of these general conditions. Firstly, most of the companies have found it relatively easy to reconcile many of the requirements of logistics and demand, in that standard tractors can with quite simple modifications and/or attachments serve a wide range of market segments, not all of them confined to farming. Secondly, some companies source "open" world markets from manufacturing plants grouped largely on a product type and market segment basis. The British plants of two international organizations, which account for about 70 per cent of the of the total U.K. tractor output, have been selected as main supply sources of medium-range wheeled tractors for the rest of the world. Thirdly, another important facet of the logistical systems of three of the companies studied, is their "common component" policies. These are designed to ensure that a high ratio of standard sub-assemblies exists between multi-national plants, tractor ranges and, also where feasible between, product divisions. Commonality not only makes inventory control simpler and less costly to operate but it allows designated plants to concentrate on extensive production runs of particular sub-assemblies, which are then interchanged between plants.

At the present time, various aspects of *global organizational structure* are receiving widespread attention. Several classifications have been coined to describe the interdependent configurations of headquarters and subsidiary company relationships with special reference to (1) domestic–overseas operations integration, (2) multi-national plant integration, (3) decision-making delegation, and (4) the staffing of key executive positions. These are special problems which most large international companies have had to encounter. In an attempt to describe the way the organization evolves structures to cope with these issues, H. V. Perlmutter has coined his "ethnocentric, polycentric and geocentric" conceptual models.[17] These have gained much currency recently and they provide a useful framework, but three such broad classifications must not be taken too literally since they cannot hope to accommodate the many permutations of constraints which influence the strategies and structures of particular international companies. Some of these constraints, which do not necessarily introduce dysfunctional elements, are those which arise out of product technology, nature of demand, the degree of commonality between a company's product divisions, the deployment mix of a company's overseas

[17] Perlmutter, H.V., "L'enterprise, internationale—Trois Conceptions," *Revue economique et sociale*, Lausanne, Mai 1965, and "Social Architectural Problems of the Multi-national Firm," *The Journal of Social Issues*, 1966. The ethnocentric international company has a powerful headquarters and manufacturing and marketing organization in the "home" country. All the important decisions are taken centrally. Overseas subsidiaries typically conduct no R & D and manufacturing as such and expatriate executives hold key posts in these. The polycentric model differs from the last in that while the expatriate executives are still very much in evidence, they are given more individual decision-making authority, primarily because of the complexity of foreign operations. The geocentric organization can be equated with the truly international company. There is a complex and interdependent collaboration between foreign subsidiaries and headquarters in decision making. The country of origin is just another market and there is, therefore, no distinction between domestic and foreign operations. Senior executive positions in both the headquarters and in the subsidiary companies are filled on the basis of merit, regardless of the nationality background of potentials.

investments (as to legal, product and functional type, degree of maturity and country locations) and the company's country of origin.

It is important that the organizational structure (and its management control system) is fashioned to serve the corporate strategy.[18] Normally any decision which impinges on the long-term development of the global strategy requires to be taken centrally. It has been seen how tractor technology, demand and supply combined with political and competitive factors have a dominating influence on the overall strategies of some of the companies concerned. These features indicate the need for a considerable amount of control and co-ordination by headquarters if the full logistical advantages are to be extracted. In the circumstances, for example, it would not appear to be incompatible with good international management for the companies (as so many of them do) to retain central responsibility for the R & D function and perhaps only delegate its engineering facets to the overseas production centres.

One survey company is in the process of developing an organization which would appear to have the potential for taking on the form of a structure that could compare with an appropriate truly international model for this industry. In this respect it has probably been assisted, organizationally, by the high design, production and distribution linkage between its product divisions and also by the fact that its country of origin is not the U.S., the world's largest single tractor market. This company has established what represents, in part, a product division–geographical regional structure. Corporate management, comprising the staff and the product division directorate are hierarchically and geographically separate from the main operating divisions. For two of its three main product groups, there are a number of joint marketing and production divisions based on North America and major markets such as the U.K., France and West Germany. Another division, based on the U.K. but reporting directly to corporate headquarters, is responsible for marketing both product groups in all the other countries and for sourcing these from the company's principal manufacturing-units located around the world. Within this structure headquarters has the ultimate responsibility for planning. However, in the formulation stage, especially for the short (1 year) and medium (5 years) term plans, there exists adequate machinery for two-way communication. This is not only confined to the plans themselves but also includes certain of the planning guide-lines and targets. The plans, when established, thus reflect what headquarters expects and what the product and geographical divisions think they can accomplish. As such, they provide a reasonably flexible basis for a management control system. Several of these organizational elements are also to be found in the other international companies examined. Nevertheless, and taking account of some of the special constraints involved, there would seem to be less integration between domestic and foreign strategic planning, more detailed supervision of production and marketing programmes from the centre

[18] See Chandler, A. D., Jr., *Strategy and Structure,* M.I.T. Press, 1962.

and a greater predominance of expatriates filling senior executive positions in the major overseas divisions.

4. Summary and Conclusions

The suggestion has been made in this paper that a firm should consider its international operations as an integral part of its overall strategy and that this should be cast in a corporate planning mould.

The proposal presented is more in the nature of a prescriptive one, in the sense that it purports to prescribe an efficient and dynamic approach to all facets of international business. But it does claim to contain descriptive elements. Firstly, it is based on one of the main corporate motivations, survival. Secondly, the survival goal has been set in the global context and, therefore, it is unlikely that it can be sought in the long term through passive and defensive managerial attitudes.

Being largely a prescriptive model it is not surprising why so many of the empirical research findings deviate from it. These findings suggest how a large number of, especially, small and medium sized, but also in some cases, large firms are engaged in low return exporting activities. It is felt that a significant proportion of these would find the opportunity costs involved justifying a diversion of resources to secure their domestic markets and/or where feasible, to take on less defensive forms of diversification. It was seen how several firms, while regarding the maintenance of an export trade as a necessity, have been loath to experiment with alternative means of supplying and servicing foreign markets. The most salutary aspect of the research was to find how several of the main British exporters had during the eighteen months interval between the two series of interviewing programmes, made many adjustments to their overall marketing policies. Some had tried, successfully, new forms of penetrating and developing selected overseas markets. In three cases it was apparent that, even if limited in resource support, a global strategy is being conceived and acted on. These are large sized companies (but small compared with the international organizations included in the sample) having between 2500 and 10,000 employees. Their dynamism and skills should not be underestimated seeing that they have consciously accepted the challenges of increased competition on an international scale and are having to follow strategies which, for them, involve relatively slim margins for error. It is also significant that these firms have comparatively good financial performance records.

The role of the large international tractor companies was studied. It is no exaggeration to say that the increasing dominance of these companies during the last ten years has radically transformed this sector.

Taking a general view of industry and without having to rely on some of the several forecasts bandied about, it is reasonable to predict that the international company as a unit of commercial organization will, increasingly, predominate the economic scene. The trends outlined in the first part of this paper underscore this view. Scientific advances in communications, automation, new materials and processes, requiring a large R & D expenditure by individual companies are compelling firms not only to seek technology abroad but to establish and develop markets for the resulting products.

39

Multinational Corporations: The Intelligence Function

Richard Eells

The modern corporation is one of the major social institutions of our time. It is not simply a device for doing business, nor can its social role be properly assessed in terms of size and business "bigness." More interesting is the fact that the modern corporation represents a new system of cooperative social organization, the bringing together of the intelligence, the labor and the investment of large numbers of men. The old combative individualism, so often idealized in classical economic theory, recedes before the advance of this cooperative effort. Sometimes denounced in outworn nineteenth-century ideological terms as a monster spawned by finance capitalism and "imperialism," the modern corporation in fact has emerged in the twentieth century as a positive social force. It has become a nearly indispensable organizational form in a world of rapid social change.

A necessary link in industrial development and an invaluable source of strength for a modernized nation, the corporation is now being assessed in new philosophical terms. The issue of the role of the modern corporation within a single nation, and its place in the structure and dynamics of that nation, arises not only in the United States but also in every developed and developing nation. It arises, too, in one of the great debates of our age: how to bring into being on our violent planet a civil society that assures a "minimum public order"[1] under a regime of law. It is in the context of this larger global community that we must also ask what the role of the modern corporation is.

With the vast expansion of international business by the great corporations of Europe, the Americas, the Far East and Africa, the modern corporation has become multinational. Its institutional significance, both actual and potential, is often unrecognized. It is capable of active collaboration with states and public international organizations. It can and does undertake cooperative

Reprinted with permission from the November–December 1969 issue of the *Columbia Journal of World Business*, pp. 15–24.

[1] This term derives from Myres S. McDougal and Florentino P. Feliciano, *Law and Minimum World Public Order*, New Haven and London: Yale University Press, 1961.

tasks as great as the industrialization of Asia and Africa. It can provide cultural interchange on a worldwide scale through the cumulative effects of its social activities in thousands of localities.

Multinational corporations, simply as business enterprises, have a major part to play in lifting world living standards to a higher level. They scan the world for investment opportunities to maximize the results obtainable from their research facilities, technical skills, patents, equipment, capital and experience. They are perhaps indispensable catalysts in the process of economic development.

Beyond the economic function, the multinational corporation in its most highly developed form offers a type of organization that can be turned to many other tasks, regionally and for the world at large. Minimum public order might possibly be supplied by some form of government at an international or supranational level, sufficiently powerful to effect a reduction in conflict. But in most of the world arena, a public order based upon norms of mutual respect does not seem to be achievable without the collaboration of the ablest private-sector organizations.

The multinational corporation at its best is the servant of no one group or country. Its constituencies include all the interests that must be balanced in a good corporate constitutional government.[2] The essential characteristics of such an organization have only recently begun to be comprehended. One specific aspect is especially interesting: the systems and strategies involved in the use of information for survival and growth and for meeting its social responsibilities in the world arena. Any organization, however large in size or great in purpose, depends upon effective means of knowing what is going on, both within and without its walls, as a prerequisite to wise policy. Workable methods of receiving messages from outside the organization, integrating these messages with already accumulated knowledge, and using the combined intelligence as input for formulating the policy of the organization as a whole; then sending out the necessary messages to external receivers—these methods are standard requirements for survival and growth as well as for meeting responsibilities. In the multinational corporation, however, there are special problems related to the environment in which it functions.

International Systems

There are conflicting theories about the international system as it operates today. There are, in fact, many rival views of "international systems"—in the plural. Nor is this only because the political map of the world arena has changed radically since World Wars I and II. Historically, there have been

[2] This subject is discussed in: Richard Eells, *The Government of Corporations*, New York: The Free Press of Glencoe, 1962; R. Eells & Clarence Walton, *Conceptual Foundations of Business*, Revised Edition, Homewood, Illinois: Richard D. Irwin, Inc., 1969; and Sanford A. Lakoff, "Private Government in the Managed Society" in Roland J. Pennock & John W. Chapman, *Voluntary Associations*, New York: Atherton Press, 1969.

many kinds of international systems. Even the future of the so-called state system, inherited from the treaties of the early modern period in Europe, is in doubt. No one knows whether the system of 150-odd sovereign states will survive both the rush of new knowledge and revolutionary technology—especially technology affecting the art and science of war, and the ecological crises precipitated by logarithmic population growth and perhaps irreversible pollution of air, land and sea resources. Are we moving toward a new age of regional or supranational government in the world arena; possibly toward an age of "world peace under world law"? Are we headed toward the breakdown of the state system under the weight of numerous ministates that cannot conceivably bear their share of the responsibility for preserving peace and and order? Models for "the international system" vary all the way from extreme monism to extreme pluralism. Who knows what units of government will at length prevail in a series of reconstructed international systems—if, indeed, one is justified in using the term "international" when the very survival of nations as major participants in the system remains in question.

There is little doubt about the prevailing theory of the international system. In formal, legalistic and conventional terms it is a system of 126 sovereign states represented in the United Nations together with some thirty or more entities—usually national in one sense or another—that are or claim to be sovereign participants in the system. These are the major "actors" of international law. All other entities on the scene are "minor actors" in the process of making and applying the rules of international jurisprudence. The major actors, the nation states and other public entities (including public international organizations) are the principals in the use of instruments of national and international policy: diplomacy, economics, the use of force, and communicational or ideological strategy. The international system, so conceived, is pluralistic in a limited sense. It is not a monistic system of supranational authority. On the other hand, it excludes numerous nongovernmental organizations (NGOs) and the innumerable private-sector organizations in the world which engage in significant transnational activities. Recognition of this larger and more complex plural structure of the world arena demands new ways of viewing "the international system" that depart from the traditional and conventional maps.

Both public international organizations and the NGOs pose difficult problems for those who rely on simplistic models of the world arena. Traditionalism has required that the world be divided up into territorially defined nation-states with fixed frontiers that mark jurisdictional boundaries. In addition, there are the open seas, the beds in which they rest and the undivided realm of space. Otherwise, the world arena is patterned as a flat mosaic. Yet public international organizations at a higher level have proliferated since World War II along with an increase in the numbers of sovereign states. At the same time private-sector organizations (often called "international" for want of a better term) have also greatly increased both in numbers and in the scope and importance of their activities in the world arena.

Furthermore, the public international organizations—notably in the common markets—have moved appreciably toward supranational status with consequent undermining of claims to absolute sovereignty on the part of member states. All of these developments may foreshadow the dominance of functionalism[3] over traditional legalism in the structure of the world arena. They also serve to remind us of the shadowy line that separates, or seems to separate, the public from the private character of organizations in this arena. One has to talk of "quasi-public" and "quasi-private" organizations and activities and to abandon the black-and-white distinctions of pure theory.

The pluralistic structure of the world arena reflects the many functions that have to be organized and carried on in response to mankind's expectations. In religion, in education, in the arts, the sciences, in the press and other communications, in transport, in health and hygiene, in sports and recreation, as well as for the economic purposes of industry, agriculture and commerce, the multinational corporation—like the nation-state—finds itself one among many. Some of these entities approach public status. Many of the NGOs, which lie within the penumbra of quasi-public institutions between state and private associations, have consultative status at the United Nations Economic and Social Council. The International Labor Organization is one example. A more recent example is the International Telecommunications Satellite Consortium (INTELSAT), a 68-nation network which relies upon various mixes of public and private ownership in the national user organizations. The interweave and interplay of state and privately owned facilities in INTELSAT is characteristic of many of the new transnational functional devices.

Transnational Trends

This trend, heightened during the past half-century, is a response to many regional and worldwide needs that the conventional international system of sovereign states could not meet effectively. The multiplication of organizations and other devices for meeting these needs is often referred to as the "internationalization" of undertakings. The word is misleading. Some of these efforts are truly international—that is to say, undertaken by the joint action of sovereign states. Others are more properly designated as "transnational," transcending to a degree the political boundaries of states and independent of state action.

Transnational action is required because the forces of life on this planet are increasingly transnational. The reach of world commerce, of all science and art and of the human spirit goes beyond transient political boundary lines.

[3] See Ernest B. Haas, *Beyond the Nation-State: Functionalism and International Organization*, Stanford: Stanford University Press, 1964; Charles A. McClelland, *Theory and the International System*, New York: The Macmillan Co., 1964; James P. Sewell, *Functionalism and World Politics*, Princeton: Princeton University Press, 1966.

The growing incongruence of parochial political jurisdictions in the face of these more expansive life forces is everywhere evident—in metropolitan government, in a still Balkanized Europe, in a world of nation-states that, like other anachronistic political institutions, may at length be swept into the scrap heap of historic curiosities.

World commerce and industry call for new institutions. One response to this demand is the mutinational corporation, which is essentially a cross-boundary operation involving "home" and "host" nations (or "sending" and "receiving" states). Actually, the multinational corporation may take the form of a group of corporate entities acting in unison from numerous home bases, "home" meaning variously the locus of the originating or creating or certifying sovereignty. Eventually we may come to speak of these new institutions of industry and commerce in more appropriately ecological terms, relating them in the usages of language to natural zones or eco-systems of our global biosphere, such as regions, continents and the oceans. Oceanography, in particular, will turn up opportunities for extractive and other industries that will make new demands on our powers of conceptualization. As we turn to agribusiness, aquaculture and space-dimensioned corporate efforts, the "multinationality" of these efforts will probably recede in importance as other units of political integration rise to prominence. Think, for example, of corporations organized for the development of the seabed under an ocean regime that may be neither national nor international. The ocean regime of the future may be a new kind of political form not known to the traditional international system.[4]

There is also the darker side of transnational forces. The problem of pollution, like the problem of bacterial and parasitical disease, does not stop at national borders. As Margaret Mead writes, "We are altering man's environment in ways we do not understand and in ways that may be disastrous." Since this planet is hopefully to be the chief habitat of the human race for generations to come, despite the major advances in space exploration, there is a pressing need for a worldwide analysis of all the means by which man is befouling his environment and an equally comprehensive program for halting this menace. Even if international machinery is devised for making this effort, transnational organization must be used to supplement it.

The hard fact is that the modern state stands stubbornly in the way of many vital transnational efforts. It might be said that it stands in its own way. Professor Frank Tannenbaum once declared that the old nationalistic system of sovereign states is ending because it cannot protect the human race from annihilation. Wars and threats of wars traditionally used to protect the state

[4] See Myres S. McDougal and William T. Burke, *The Public Order of the Oceans: A Contemporary International Law of the Sea,* New Haven and London: Yale University Press, 1962; and Elizabeth Mann Borgese, "The Ocean Regime: A Suggested Statute for the Peaceful Uses of the High Seas and the Sea-Bed Beyond the Limits of National Jurisdiction," Santa Barbara, California: The Center for the Study of Democratic Institutions, October 1968.

and its citizenry are of little use when war becomes indiscriminatingly destructive. "The peace of the world," Tannenbaum wrote, "must rest on an institutional base indifferent to the idea of national security." He observed that over the centuries political entities rise and fall while trade and commerce go on and on. "If the nation-state goes the way of its feudal predecessor," he believed, "the extra-national corporation may well take over."[5]

Polarities in the World Arena

For the present, however, corporate managers must plan their tasks in a world arena of sovereign states which wield coercive powers based on heavy sanctions. This environment is hardly predictable with certainty. Alternative hypotheses, if only for the purpose of short-range corporate planning, to say nothing of twenty- or thirty-year perspectives, are essential. Some observers suggest that only four political powers will count in the future: the United States, the Soviet Union, a united Europe and Japan. Others say that the age of superstates is nearing its end and we are entering upon an era of functional pluralism in which entities of different kinds can be expected to proliferate in the world arena, some nationalistic, some local, others functional.

Meanwhile, the course of the multinational corporation has to be charted amid the bipolarities and the multipolarities of the world arena, amid the economic overlordships of the countries, large or small, in which it does business, and in that vast realm beyond the "open" frontiers with attendant problems of the public order of the oceans and space.

Charting a course in this complex world arena demands certain specific capabilities: knowledge of the decision-making processes and of the strategies of states and other participants in the world arena, and the ability so to define corporate goals that corporate policies can be stated as preferred outcomes and the strategies to achieve these outcomes can be designed.

Decision Strategies

Decision making, whether by nations, groups or individuals, can be regarded in part as a continuous process of combining the informational streams that come to the decision maker from the outside world and from within the organization. And there is a stream of messages moving from the subliminal to the conscious levels of the mind, made up of memories, experiences apparently forgotten and all the psychological events that shape and condition the human personality.

The world arena, because it is not a regime of law, is a place where all participants at times fall back on four types of strategies: coercion, negotiation, use of economic resources and persuasion. It is not realistic to expect that these strategies will be in fact (although in theory they may be) monopolized by

[5] Frank Tannenbaum, *The Balance of Power in Society,* New York: The Macmillan Co., 1969.

sovereign states so long as nonstate claimants can command large powers. Yet there are important differences which relate to any discussion of the strategies of multinational corporations. This is apparent in an examination of the parallel strategies of corporations and states.

Force can seldom be used by corporations directly, except for local police purposes in industrial plants and communities. With multinational corporations in host or receiving countries, it is always questionable whether corporate policy can or should be pursued by means of supportive strategies—military or other—of the home or sending country. A full spectrum of possibilities has to be considered. At one end the citizen, organization or corporation of any nation can hypothetically be left entirely on its own, with no support whatsoever from the home or host governments. At the other end of the spectrum one would postulate unlimited intervention by sovereign governments on behalf of or hostile to a corporation. Neither extreme is realistic. In practice, all corporations make direct and indirect use of the powers and strategies of public governments.

The strategy of negotiation is an essential tool of both corporate and national policy, not only for economic advantage but more importantly for status in the world arena. Status as a matter of law, of prestige or rank, of preferred position in a given situation is an outcome that depends as much on negotiating capability as it does on economic assets. Corporations, which are not among the major "actors" of international law and diplomacy, are nevertheless frequently represented in national capitals and other power centers. Their representatives may be received with more consideration, if less pomp and circumstance, than ambassadors, and the weight of their words may be far more persuasive if for no other reason than corporate command of valuable informational flow.

Economic power is often regarded as the sole key to the role of multinational corporations in world affairs. But the economic instruments of corporate policy are only part of the story. Economics, in national strategy, involves the effective allocation and use of scarce resources, as it does in corporate strategy. But the assets of nation and corporation include all resources that can be sold or withheld from the market. Insofar as these resources include land (the title to which is controlled by sovereign states), minerals, money and other negotiable instruments (the value of which is subject to legal regulation), it seems that economic strategy is heavily derivative of national policy. The dependence of multinational corporations (operating as they do in an arena without an over-arching regime of world law) upon the laws of many different—and sometimes hostile—regimes makes economic strategy in the world arena something different in kind from that of a corporation operating entirely within the home nation. For the multinational corporation, as for the modern corporation generally, the strategy of economics always has to be aligned with the public interest. The economic goals of the corporation cannot safely be at odds for extended periods with the goals of national communities in home and host countries.

The use of persuasion and ideas also has its special character in the multinational corporation. The use of communicational and informational systems is of paramount importance in this type of strategy, since it involves both input and output. The concern is mainly with input. In national governments this is ordinarily called intelligence. One can also speak of corporate intelligence. However, this is but one aspect of communications strategy in general. Intelligence, narrowly viewed is the knowledge that highly placed government officers and military men must possess to safeguard the welfare of a nation. Intelligence, broadly viewed, is the knowledge that any person or group must have to safeguard the welfare of that person or group.

Corporate Intelligence

As regards corporations, intelligence[6] deals in certain kinds of knowledge. It is produced by the activity of a special kind of organization. It has three principal aspects. The knowledge essential for intelligence of any sort includes: (1) basic descriptive content, (2) current reportorial content and (3) speculative-evaluative content.

Descriptive knowledge is needed of all of the geographic regions where a multinational corporation operates and where social, political, economic or military developments may affect company operations adversely or favorably. Current reportorial content is needed, of course, to keep the basic content up to date. The speculative-evaluative element in corporate intelligence necessarily includes studies of the strategies of both nations and the private-sector groups. It is noteworthy that strategy in this wider sense is a rapidly growing field of the social sciences, in which there are such new topics as conflict-resolution and such new areas of study as the policy sciences.

A special kind of organization is needed to produce such knowledge. Its nature is suggested by the observations of two students of the art and science of intelligence, one of whom (Sherman Kent) specialized in national intelligence, the other (Harold L. Wilensky) in corporate intelligence. The former has observed the intelligence organization of a national government. National intelligence organizations require certain of the characteristics of good business organizations. Kent finds it natural that the language of intelligence organizations should be weighted with words from business. These organizations are engaged in "the manufacture of a product (knowledge) out of raw materials (all manner of data) and labor (highly skilled, but not practical in the business sense of the word)."

The resultant product has to be packaged in ways to suit the diversities of consumer demand, namely in governmental bureaus that use the intelligence

[6] A basic work on this subject is Sherman Kent, *Strategic Intelligence for American World Policy*, Princeton: Princeton University Press, 1951, which I follow here to some extent. See also Roger Hilsman, *Strategic Intelligence and National Decisions*, Glencoe, Illinois: The Free Press, 1956.

output. Some consumers want this output in semi-finished form, for example, as field notes with accompanying comments. Others want it finished, in bulk and in encyclopedic form. The most demanding want it "in small amounts done up in gift wrapping (the one-page summary of the world situation in words of two syllables or less)." In its packaging, the product must both direct and reflect the fluctuations of consumer requirements, the consumer in this case being the receiving corporation.

If a country threatens to go Communist, the intelligence on that country must be stepped up. If another country gets ready to take a stand against the intelligence-gathering nation in the matter of bases, then information on that country will have to be increased. Like many a producer of consumer goods, an intelligence organization will have "its greatest marketing success when its product bears the unmistakable signs of superior research, cautious development, sound design and careful production."[7]

Attention can be profitably given to the proper organization of the intelligence function in industry. Harold L. Wilensky, in his study[8] of the way in which knowledge shapes policy, suggests that while some gains in the quality of intelligence are possible from a reorganization of the intelligence function, two points need to be kept in mind to avoid "information pathologies." First, the attitude of the top executive toward knowledge is crucial. This attitude is "a product of his own education and orientation, his exposure to independent sources, his capacity to break through the wall of conventional wisdom." Secondly, the intelligence specialist himself can affect the general tone of policy discourse. This sound advice bypasses excessively elaborate discussions focussed solely on intelligence organization and gets to the heart of the matter: an appreciation by corporate leaders of the need for new knowledge and their respect for its uses in shaping policy.

This may seem elementary advice at a time when science and technology are recognized as major keys to economic growth and development and to the modernization of societies. Yet there is far less recognition of this fact with respect to social sciences than in those branches of knowledge that produce hardware. Wilensky speaks of "structural and doctrinal distortions of information" that seem less likely to occur in rapidly growing organizations that are in contact with a fluid environment, as against dangers that appear in the more established and slower-growing organizations. The alert executive has to know how, in any case, to reach out into a population of "unofficial intelligence agents" as well as to tap often unused sources within the organization itself. The more imaginative administrative leaders "looking toward the bottom, rely on internal communications specialists such as education directors and auditors; looking outward, they rely on contact men such as press officers, lobbyists, mediators. They talk to reporters and researchers investigating

[7] Kent, op. cit.

[8] Harold L. Wilensky, *Organizational Intelligence: Knowledge and Policy in Government and Industry,* New York and London: Basic Books, Inc., 1967.

their organizations; they establish study commissions or review boards comprised entirely of outsiders, like the members of British Royal Commissions; they institutionalize complaints procedures and thereby subject themselves to systematic, independent criticism from below, as in the case of the ombudsman; they assemble ad hoc committees, kitchen cabinets, general advisors, personal representatives." The unofficial intelligence agents Wilensky regards as independent enough to provide detached judgment yet sufficiently sensitive to the culture of the executive to communicate. He sees them as bringing to bear "the multiple perspectives of marginal men."

This counsel against undue emphasis upon intelligence organization at the expense of sound top executive attitudes toward knowledge—its sources, its substance, its uses—is undoubtedly a counsel of wisdom, and it may be needed in corporations even more than in government bureaus.

One has to be on guard against what Wilensky calls "the anti-intellectual spirit and crude empiricism" that one may encounter not only in unofficial intelligence agents but in intelligence specialists themselves. There remain, however, hard issues of organization of the intelligence function of multinational corporations, and there is little evidence that these issues are sufficiently visible today. Does the new information technology, with the advent of whole staffs of specialists in linear programming, simulation, operations research, electronic data processing and systems analysis, lead to disruptive developments in the authority structure of a company? The new technology is here to stay, but the new specialists are suspect by the old guard in gold braid or in mufti. The old guard fears a take-over by the "Whiz Kids." In corporations, the parallel may be seen in old-guard resistance to the idea of new knowledge as against the "wisdom of the ages" and rejection of the input of a radically revised intelligence function as against the received dogmas of conventional wisdom about trade and commerce.

The fact is that the multinational corporation of today and tomorrow is not adequately conceptualized in the conventional wisdom of economics and politics for effective use of communicational strategy. The intelligence component in the multinational corporate organization must be fitted for use in a new kind of transnational entity vying for place and meaning in the world arena, an arena that is neither an "international market" (whatever that means) nor an "international system" (again a doubtful term).

The world arena is a condition, as well as a place of contention for power, for wealth, indeed for a wide range of goal values. The range of values is not perceived, typically, either in board rooms or in top executive levels of many multinational corporations. How to introduce a modern intelligence function into these corporations, with attitudes and an organization that meet the the onrush of change in the world arena, is one of the most challenging tasks of business management today.

Lest anyone think that organization of the intelligence function in the multinational corporation is merely desirable but not vitally important, it is well to consider some of the substantive issues that now confront many multinational corporate managers.

To Whom Does It Belong?

1. Whose instrument is the multinational corporation? The stockholders'? The home country's? The host country's? Is it perhaps an indispensable instrument of mankind in its search for a viable structure of world economy and, more basically, man's search for a way to preserve our invaluable biosphere?

For several generations managers have not thought of multinational companies as the instrument of any group. They have sought, in theory, to be impartially responsive to stockholders, consumers, workers and suppliers. They claim to be responsive also to the requests of the government of whatever country they are working in. But what would the working policy of the company be if it referred these received doctrines to the hard-nosed analysis of its intelligence staff? Does that staff insist upon balance in the intelligence input? The intelligence files of the company now contain far more intelligence about consumers of its products than about any other group. This preponderance of data may reflect the doctrine that by reason of the economic votes consumers cast when making market choices, they will affect the future of the company immediately and directly, as though all mankind were made up of consumers. Intelligence input might well correct this perilous imbalance.

Responsibilities

2. What, if any, are the economic, social and political responsibilities of a multinational corporation to the home country and the host countries? Let us assume that established policies include the following general features: (a) good products at fair prices, (b) the rights of employees, (c) economic and social cooperation with the government when requested, (d) initiative in local and transnational community problems, (e) conservation of natural resources, (f) better international communication and understanding, (g) support of cultural traditions and popular aspirations. Is this a complete and timely list?

The intelligence organization of the company should systematically collect data pertinent to all of these but should not stop there. It should ask how these responsibilities are to be exercised, on whose behalf and with what measures of accountability. Most importantly it should ask whether the very concept of corporate responsibility requires complete revision in the light of conditions that prevail in the world arena. Only in the local community does the company take initiative, and even there it strives to keep its role inconspicuous. In several underdeveloped countries, for instance, the local school system developed out of the company's training programs, and company managers are in effect the directors of that system, but they never admit to being anything more than consultants.

Sanctions

3. What sanctions, if any, are available to enforce the economic, social and political responsibilities of the multinational corporation?

Apart from commercial codes and antitrust laws, which the company strictly obeys, there would appear at first to be few formal sanctions. The effective sanctions seem to be informal and popular. The general public is made up of consumers. If only a small percentage of them were to take offense at the company or any of its corporate colleagues, sales could suffer severely. The company believes it is guided by "public opinion." For more than a generation it has been gathering intelligence about public opinion in all parts of the world. Updating its intelligence function, the company now finds that there is a wide range of formal and severe sanctions that both home and host governments command and can use to the disadvantage, as well as the advantage, of the company. The "public," moreover, which had appeared to be essentially a public of consumers, now turns out to be strongly imbued with nationalistic drives.

In some sectors public opinion reflects Third-World commitments of of nonalignment in the epochal struggle between East and West. Does this indicate the need for corporate policy that is explicitly "geocentric," avoiding either the Scylla of "ethnocentrism" (home-country orientation) or the Charybdis of "polycentrism" (host-country orientation)? The "ultimate goal of geocentrism" in multinational corporations "is a worldwide approach in both headquarters and subsidiaries" in the constructs of Howard V. Perlmutter, and this geocentrism is "expressed by function, product and geography."[9] The intelligence work of a company will necessarily be geared to meet one or the other of these orientations.

Sovereignty

4. Would it be possible or desirable in the future to have large multinational corporations assume some of the powers and responsibilities of the sovereign state?

We have been discussing a type of organization that operates on a scale as vast as that of many states. It can, and indeed must, define strategy and gather intelligence by means that are comparable to those of many states. But can it or should it assume the right to use all of the strategies and instruments of policy of sovereign states? It functions both internally and externally more as a voluntary association with its own private government than as a sovereign nation with a public government.

The large multinational corporation is basically an instrument for bringing together very large numbers of men and women in a coordinated productive enterprise. But is it not more than a productive business enterprise? Must it

[9] Howard V. Perlmutter, "The Tortuous Evolution of the Multinational Corporation," *Columbia Journal of World Business*, January–February 1969.

not also try to satisfy so far as possible the totality of social, cultural and economic expectations of its many constituencies? The multinational corporation is coming to act more and more like an entity on which people can center their loyalties and their lives. The intelligence function will undergo profound change as multinational corporate managers adopt, operationally as well as theoretically, the position that their organization is a major social institution in the world arena.

What Is It?

5. What, precisely, is the definition of the multinational corporation in the world arena? There are antithetical views. On one side there is the view that corporate enterprise moving into this arena is simply a profit-seeker in a far more hazardous environment than the domestic corporation that stays at home. On the other is the view that the venture into the world marketplace is inevitable and that this inevitability carries with it important implications. Among those who take this latter position, there are further divergencies.

One may assume that multinational corporate enterprise in the world arena is simply enterprise but that, because of the disorder which now prevails in that marketplace, managers of such enterprises must do all that they reasonably can to work toward a regime of minimum public order there. This means heavy involvement of the corporate intelligence function in both public and private efforts toward the organization of world peace. Or one may assume that the mutinational corporation should go much further than this and contribute actively and systematically toward a world regime of optimum public order: embracing, that is to say, "the totality of a community's legally protected goal values and implementing institutions" and a public order which seeks "beyond an effective community monopolization of force, the richest production and widest sharing of all values."[10]

The relevant community, in the latter case, may not be worldwide for a given corporation; it may be regional or confined to a noncontiguous group of countries. In any case, it is clear that the future of the intelligence function in multinational corporations will vary greatly, depending upon which of these positions is taken by those who govern them.

[10] McDougal and Feliciano, op. cit.

40

Organizational Archetypes of a Multi-National Company*

David P. Rutenberg

Introduction

A multi-national company does more than import and export from its U.S. home plant. It may do research in Germany, engineering design in Japan, and then manufacture in Taiwan, Italy, and Mexico to supply a hundred national markets, including the U.S. market in which its headquarters may be located. A number of multi-national companies already move products, managers, capital, and research around the world, adjusting the rates of flow as local environments change. The ideal is to be rational on a global basis.

Current international management practice falls short of this ideal. There is very little sophisticated mathematical planning for international operations. For example, surprisingly few operations research models have been developed for international planning and coordination. Operations researchers object to the risks and uncertainties that cannot be assumed away, and to the confused problem statements. Risks and uncertainties constitute a weak excuse when one realizes that military planning is undertaken despite risks and uncertainties far greater than those ever encountered within a multi-national company. In fact, mathematical analysis should offer a unique contribution in environments of rapid inflation and great uncertainty, where U.S. business intuition may be quite inappropriate. Nevertheless there remains the objection to confused and contradictory problem statements.

One might conjecture that the degree of confusion in problem formulation would be linked to the industry and the formal organizational structure. Fouraker and Stopford [9] found a significant correlation between the extent of expansion abroad and Chandler's [2] organizational structure. Corporations with few related products (steel and nonferrous metals), organized by function, have not expanded to integrated operations abroad. Corporations with many product lines (electrical, transportation, power machinery, chemicals) generally have a product divisional structure, and have undertaken substantial expansion abroad. Chandler noted that some industries lay between these two clear cut cases (agricultural processing, oil, rubber, mass merchandising) and are laced with dotted line relationships between functional and product organization which, one might conjecture, would add ambiguity to problem definitions.

This may well be true, but there are ambiguous problem statements even in

Reprinted with permission from *Management Science*, February 1970, pp. B337–B349.

* This report was prepared as part of the activities of the Management Science Research Group, Carnegie-Mellon University, under Contract NONR 760 (24) NR 047-048 with the U.S. Office of Naval Research.

Chandler's clear cut industries. In fact, unique statements of problems appear less possible as one looks in more microscopic detail at the statutory organization of a real company. There are technical licensing agreements with autonomous partners, intimate cross licensing in which know-how has been exchanged for some equity and the aspiration of more various species of joint ventures, even management service contracts. Nor is there aesthetic refuge even among the wholly owned subsidiaries, for most have grown too fast and too unevenly. According to Lovell ([18], p. 85) "the lack of system in the organization charts of international management units is simply a reflection of the existing uneven state of development, and the different volume of activity within the various geographical areas, functions, and product lines." In an international company one might expect the formal organization to have even less relevance to the informal organization than in a domestic company subject to one set of laws. The reasons were explained a decade ago by Clee and diScipio [4].

> For a number of reasons (e.g. local legal requirements, tax advantages, or need for financial control), a company creating a world enterprise often sets up a statutory corporate structure that differs from the more fluid and informal (though very real) lines of communication followed in the day-to-day operations of the business. The *statutory organization* is designed to put the pieces of the company together into a legal structure that optimizes cash flow for the overall corporation. The manner in which the company is actually coordinated and run involves a set of working relationships that are constructed to fit the managerial requirements of the company . . . . Recognizing the distinction between the formal statutory organization and the manner in which the total business is coordinated and managed dispels much of the fog that often surrounds all foreign operations.

The theme of this paper is that planning guidelines emerge as one studies the convictions of headquarters executives. Such men usually have firm convictions about the working relationships they shall have with foreign subsidiaries, and how the subsidiaries should regard headquarters. Clearly if two such executives have different convictions they will provide the planner with different (probably contradictory) decision premises within which to develop optimal plans. In this paper we shall delve into headquarters' behavioral patterns that appear to foster different convictions as to headquarters-subsidiary relationships. It is asserted that an appropriate combination of four archetypal patterns is very helpful in comprehending real problems, though naturally no archetype can encapsule the whole of reality. Thus an operations researcher could work through the implications of four sets of decision premises by formulating and solving his problem for each, and thereby gauge the significance of the political choice of premises being made around him.

To launch the taxonomy, we shall temporarily use a gross simplification of reality. We shall interpret headquarters as one person, and a subsidiary as another person. We can then invoke research into the interpersonal relationships between people two at a time. Clearly this is too gross a simplification, so we shall enrich each of the four archetypes with the insight of past investigators of organizational theory.

Leavitt ([16], Chapters 11–13) analyzing relationships between people two at a time, focused on a person intervening in the affairs of another, both directly and indirectly. He devoted a chapter to each of authority, manipulation, and collaboration. Churchman and Schainblatt [3] analyzed the process one person might use to affect another, focusing on the question of whether each understood the other (understand was given the strong definition of ability to anticipate, teleologically, the other person's response). Churchman and Schainblatt devoted a section to each of communication, persuasion, and mutual understanding. Both taxonomies deal with people two at a time. Let one person be the headquarters, the other a subsidiary.

		Indirect intervention by headquarters? Headquarters understands subsidiaries?	
		NO	YES
Direct Intervention by headquarters?	No	*Archetype 1* No intervention Separate function	*Archetype 2* Manipulation Persuasion
Subsidiaries urged to understand headquarters?	Yes	*Archetype 3* Authority Communication	*Archetype 4* Collaboration Mutual understanding

Figure 1. Multi-national Corporate Interpretation of the Taxonomies of Leavitt, and of Churchman and Schainblatt

Clearly a specific problem must be in mind if these questions are to be answerable. Most headquarters intervene in major capital expansions of their subsidiaries, but few require central coordination of minor office supplies. Thus one company can occupy all four archetypes simultaneously, but on different problems. For a *given* planning problem, at a given time, this poses no problem. However, problems arise because different subsidiaries are treated differently. There is then a conflict between standardizing all subsidiaries, allowing a few exceptions, or grouping subsidiaries as to their most suitable archetype for the problem under consideration.

Easing people's transition between archetypes is central to the work of Perlmutter [22], [23], a social psychologist concerned with the way international managers impose boundaries upon the range of their awareness. Perlmutter's terminology has become popular in European discussions of multi-national companies. Archetype 1 would be described as a polycentric headquarters with ethnocentric subsidiaries; there is no headquarters intervention, so there become as many corporate strategies as there are subsidiaries, and the awareness of each subsidiary is circumscribed by the borders of its nation. In Perlmutter's terminology Archetype 2 has a geocentric headquarters and ethnocentric subsidiaries as the headquarters manipulates and persuades the subsidiaries. In Archetype 3 the headquarters is ethnocentric and authoritarian, so the subsidiaries react by becoming xenophobic and resent the one-way stream of communication from headquarters. In Archetype 4 collaboration and mutual understanding are possible because both headquarters and its subsidiaries maintain geocentric world views. The focus is on interpersonal relations and convictions, rather than organizational structure.

The purpose of this paper is to evaluate the literature that might justify different planning decision premises within different archetypes of multi-national companies. Decision premises are an acknowledgement of bounded rationality, a concept fundamental to the organization theory of Simon [26] and March and Simon [19].

Archetype 1

The separate function position, in which each subsidiary is a center of decision making for itself, occurs when:

1. The legal owner is a holding company which has diversified its holdings over many countries.
2. The legal owner of subsidiaries is a large U.S. company. Its headquarters International Division has not grown as subsidiaries evolved abroad, and it is clogged with work.

A corporation engaged primarily in domestic business cannot afford to have all of its executives keep up to date about changes in tariffs, foreign exchange regulations, and political ideologies. Howe Martyn ([20], p. 135) has described the evolution of ethnocentric subsidiaries when headquarters control is weak:

> ... The theory has been that [presidents of subsidiaries] need almost complete freedom to make the best use of their knowledge of local conditions and to take prompt actions. There has also been an unacknowledged readiness to shift some of the heavy weight of responsibility that burdens the top management of a large concern. Why should the parent company look for trouble? Let Jones, who is on the spot, follow his own way, which he says is the African or Australian way, so long as he makes profits.

The multi-national company has a geographically diversified portfolio of investments, whose stream of total income should therefore be quite steady. Unfortunately, as relative business conditions change around the world, there is no adjustment mechanism to reallocate markets to plants, or otherwise to change the rate of flow of resources. Furthermore, because there is no strong central coordination, the bottom-up nature of planning in this archetype will likely result in many small investments which otherwise might have been combined for economics of scale.

For the twenty years preceding 1948, the Ford Motor Corporation had a separate function relationship with its subsidiaries abroad. The stronger ones, such as British Ford, spawned subsidiaries of their own, adopted a local identity, and became entrenched in their independence. In the years after 1948 Ford gradually assumed control of these subsidiaries. The consequences at British Ford are criticized by Simmonds [28].

In this archetype no planning guidelines can be presented, for no operations planning is performed by the headquarters. The four illustrative problem areas that will be used for all archetypes are:

A. *Cost of Capital.* Each subsidiary will undertake its own capital expansions, using its own decision criteria. The marginal cost of capital will be the cost of any local borrowing that does not require headquarters approval.

B. *Pricing Policy.* Each subsidiary will set its own prices, bargaining for transfer prices on intercorporate imports without cognizance of worldwide production interdependence.

C. *Product Design*: Design standardization will be rare, and headquarters attempts to issue guidelines will be thwarted; such guidelines would impinge upon the autonomy of the subsidiary.

D. *Managerial Rotation*: Although individual subsidiaries may plan managerial development through rotation, there will be no intersubsidiary movement of managers nor will there be rotation to or from the headquarters.

E. *Liquid Assets:* Each subsidiary will manage its own portfolio of liquid assets, and there will be no mechanism by which a subsidiary in need of funds can obtain them from other subsidiaries.

Archetype 2

This archetype corresponds to Churchman and Schainblatt's [3] persuasion position. The headquarters has a geocentric viewpoint, understands the details of its subsidiaries, and how the subsidiaries interact. The subsidiaries are not urged to attain a similar geocentric understanding. In fact, as Leavitt ([16], Chapter 12) would see the interrelationship, the myopic ethnocentricity of the subsidiaries leaves them open to manipulation by headquarters.

Headquarters would be most likely to understand each national subsidiary if it is arranged into geographical divisions of formal responsibility. A contact officer mans a national desk, and all communication to the subsidiary is channelled through him. Clee and Sachtjen [5] have suggested that a geographical structure of formal responsibility is especially viable if only a narrow range of products is manufactured and marketed. It is also appropriate if the products are sold to nationalistic local governments. Robinson ([24], Chapter 8) calls this structure a multi-national firm and emphasizes that it is psychologically viable only when more than 50 percent of sales are outside the headquarters nation. It may appear a little ironical to recommend gaining control over ethnocentric subsidiaries by creating a geographically organized headquarters. Yet this seems necessary if understanding (such that headquarters can teleologically anticipate the reactions of each subsidiary) is deemed a prerequisite for control.

The danger inherent in a geographically structured headquarters is that the contact officers may identify too closely with the subsidiary they are supposed to be controlling and become its proponent with headquarters. Some of the factors affecting group identification have been discussed by March and Simon ([19], Chapter 3).

March and Simon ([19], p. 68) suggest that similarity of background and similarity of position increase the perception of shared goals. Headquarters could recruit contact officers from the same graduate school of business, and by small group pressure encourage them to dress alike. On the other hand, the contact officer has some prior knowledge of, and probably empathy for, the nation he is supposed to control, and will identify with it.

The sharing of common goals and the satisfaction of an individual's needs within the headquarters group will tend to increase the frequency of his interaction with the group. This also works in reverse, and at a superficial level calls for company dining rooms, cocktail parties, and social pressure to live in the same suburb. But if meaningfulness of interaction leads to group identification, there has to be a common language or planning framework in which to converse about the nebulous uncertainties of international business. On the other hand, the contact officer interacts with his subsidiary. He is exposed to a deluge of communication about the subsidiary, about government balance of payments policies, growth policies, commercial risks, and general political and social movements of the nation. His visits abroad are to the nation, and, in turn, he acts as host for visitors from the nation.

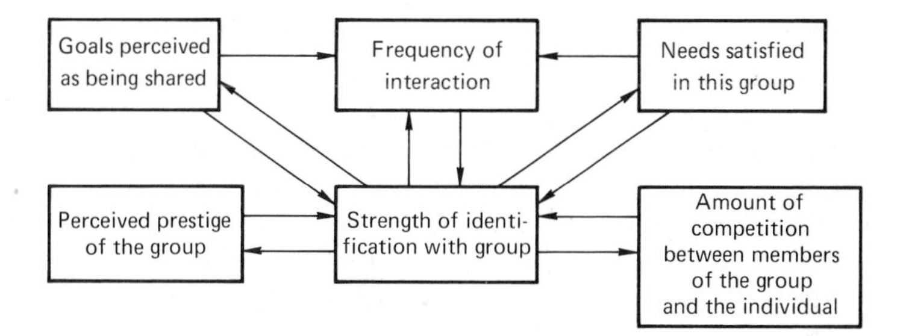

Figure 2. Basic Factors Affecting Group Identification (Source: Rearranged from March and Simon [19], Figure 3–8)

The more needs satisfied by a group, the closer a person identifies with it. A number of psychologists such as Maslow [21] have proposed hierarchies of human needs. The contact officer occupying a national desk in headquarters will have his physical and social needs satisfied by his pay check, fellow employees and family. Once these have been gratified, then a failure to achieve his ego ideal or his self-actualization in headquarters will appear most acute. He will identify with the subsidiary, and any desire for power in his ego ideal may well be satisfied by his relationship with it. He dominates the subsidiary and has autonomy of action to veto or censor messages sent to it. By linking this autonomy with the artistic subtlety of his job he can even satisfy his needs for self-actualization as he tries to make his part of the world into the image he desires.

There is a self-fulfilling prophesy to the contact officer's perception of the prestige of his headquarters. If the headquarters intervenes in the affairs of the subsidiaries then the contact officer will see the importance of headquarters, will tend to identify with it, and will therefore be more willing to intervene in the affairs of his subsidiary. Furthermore, he will likely strive to get promoted within headquarters, and this aspiration will weaken his identification with his subsidiary. The subsidiary itself may be prestigious. Prestige accrues to a subsidiary because of its size and its importance to the multinational corporation. But the general political prestige of the country will also influence the perceptions of the contact officer.

If an individual is in competition with other members of a group, then "in making a decision, he evaluates the several alternatives of choice in terms of their consequences for the specified group." (Simon [26], p. 205). Competition helps him identify with the group; of course he will be scheming against the group if the competition becomes more serious than sporting. Each contact officer will identify with headquarters to the extent that he has an adequate conceptual framework to see that he is competing against other national desks for corporate resources. However, the contact officer is also in competition with his subsidiary. If the subsidiary employees are intelligent, an element of gaming in their responses is inevitable. So long as the contact officer retains his feeling of superiority then the more cunningly responsive the subsidiary the more he will be engrossed with it. There are a number of geographically organized companies depicted in Lovell [18]. Generally they are mature companies with mature product lines, so that marketing is their most important function. Clee and Sachtjen [5] describe a Massey-Ferguson like Gamma, Ltd.

> Some years ago Gamma, Ltd., a huge international farm equipment manufacturer whose operations had been organized along regional lines adopted an organizational structure built around a series of largely self-contained marketing and manufacturing operations units. These are centered on important individual markets (the United Kingdom, France, Germany, the United States, and Canada). Supplementing these units is an export marketing unit to cover sales in parts of the world where Gamma has no manufacturing operations.
>
> Longer-range corporate strategy—determination of the basic world-wide product line, decisions on major facilities, and changes in the logistic product flow from production sources to markets—is set at corporate headquarters. But these decisions are heavily influenced by operations unit judgments and recommendations. Each unit is responsible for determining the product lines best suited to its local markets.

In an extreme example of this archetype the pattern of interaction within the headquarters, and the relationships with the subsidiaries, would result in unambiguous planning guidelines within which a problem would be formulated and optimized. In a real geographically organized company, other views might prevail, but one would expect as strong sentiment for the following guidelines:

A. *Cost of Capital:* Especially if shares of each subsidiary are listed on its nation's stock exchange will each subsidiary remit a standard dividend to headquarters. This dividend will be adjusted only if inequities appear in the use to which retained earnings can be put. Thus the discount rate used in capital budgeting need not be identical in all subsidiaries, nor will it include the cost of taxes of repatriation back to headquarters.

B. *Pricing Policy:* Though joint production costs will be recognized in setting national prices, no pricing system will be imposed on the subsidiaries.

C. *Product Design:* Products will be designed or chosen to best suit each national subsidiary. If the company tailors design to each national requirement, it can get its products reclassified by customs inspectors so that they pay lower rates of import duty, can meet local safety and engineering standards, can use local grades and types of raw materials inputs, and can cater to local customer tastes. Tempering this on an *ad hoc* basis will be efforts to standardize some components so as to ease trans-shipments. Nevertheless the total number of designs will be quite high.

D. *Managerial Rotation:* Nationals will be employed in each subsidiary to the greatest extent possible, and only bilateral movements of managers will be planned. Nationals will be brought to headquarters to learn technical positions so that they can return to their homeland. In their temporary absence, Americans may fill their position.

E. *Liquid Assets:* Although each subsidiary will manage its own portfolio of liquid assets, dividend payments will be manipulated to get liquidity to subsidiaries in need. Some intersubsidiary loans may be arranged by the headquarters, but transfer prices and fee payments will remain unmanipulated.

Archetype 3

It sometimes happens that a prominent domestic company decides to expand abroad by building subsidiaries. It may have had an international division before, but its product managers were insulated from foreign business, and are now openly concerned about the instability of each foreign country, and suspicious of nationals as potential employees. They are ethnocentric. With the self assurance of missionaries, their attitude is that "we (people of country *A*) are superior, and have greater resources, facilities and competence than you (people of country *B*). We will build facilities in your country if you accept our inherent superiority, and our methods and procedures for doing the job." (Perlmutter, [22]). Especially if the company has been successful domestically will it feel that its standard methods and procedures for problem solving represent a unique contribution that the alien company can make to the economy of the host country. The headquarters, therefore, requires that these standards and procedures be used by the subsidiaries. Product and professional specialists fly about the world educating their subsidiary counterparts.

The headquarters may not understand the environmental details of its subsidiaries. If it does not, it cannot tailor communications to the subsidiary but instead must urge the subsidiary to understand the way headquarters perceives the world, and implement communications in that way. Churchman and Schainblatt [3] call this the communications position, emphasizing its one way flow. Leavitt ([16], Chapter 11) would describe the behavior of the headquarters as authoritarian, for its intervention in the affairs of its subsidiaries is direct, rather than manipulatively indirect. If there are few products, the company can be organized by function: worldwide marketing, worldwide production, worldwide accounting, etc. Usually there are more products, and each product division can be given worldwide line responsibility, backed by functional staffs.

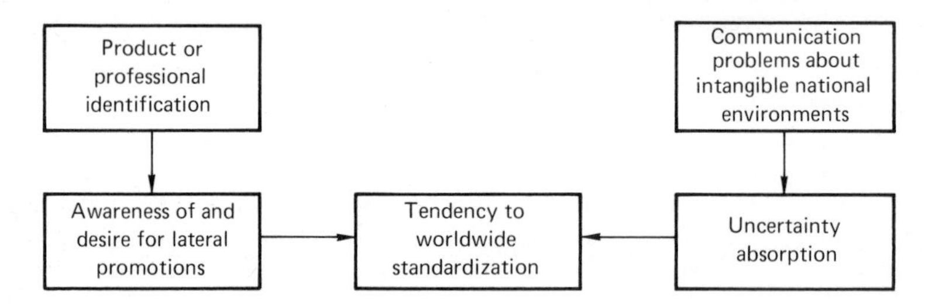

Figure 3. Forces Leading to Standardization

If the production process for a product is complex, each subsidiary production manager will tend to identify with his worldwide product. He will probably develop a loyalty to his product division and may view himself as only temporarily stationed in some particular subsidiary. Furthermore, his advancement is likely to be in the form of lateral moves, in the same product division, to larger subsidiaries. As a member of a group of professionals or product specialists, whether in headquarters or in the subsidiaries, he will be affected by norms of behavior. An individual whose recommendations transcend group norms will be eased out of the group. If a production manager recommends a non-standard design, tailoring products to a certain nation, he may find himself stuck at that plant for the rest of his working life. Perhaps this group identification is the basis for Martyn's observation ([20], p. 139) that:

> It is a strict rule among the long-established international firms to manufacture the same products or to deliver the same services on which their home success was founded in as many countries as possible. If one of these products will not sell in a country for peculiar national reasons (soap with a carbolic smell was associated with brothels in France), the international concern prefers to withdraw rather than modify the product. Accepting variations would leave the company without consistent standards, which could disturb its accounting and its marketing, as well as its production arrangements.

A number of companies have been organized along product and professional lines so as to assure that the local subsidiaries will be run well but have then selected a local national president. The local president, assured that business is being well taken care of, is expected to make public appearances to refute the negative impression his (host) nation has of foreign corporations. He may not understand the language of each product and professional group, but he is likely to develop a well-founded suspicion that their decisions are not in the best interests of his subsidiary. But he can do little about it, because though he has formal authority he lacks professional authority (Etzioni, [7], Chapter 8). His reaction will probably be that of xenophobia—distrustful fear of foreigners, and their machinations.

One might expect the most vivid examples of product divisionalization to occur in the electrical manufacturing industry. Unfortunately, the example of General Electric is complicated by the indigestibility of Machines Bull of France, and the example of Westinghouse by its history of licensing agreements so that until recently foreign operations were minimal. Thus we shall use a Cellanese-like example that Clee and Sachtjen [5] named Epsilon. This is a mature company that still maintains traces of its former geographical organization.

> Since Epsilon's large and diversified domestic operations overshadow their foreign counterparts, the [product] group organizations are built around the existing domestic operation . . . . Each product group has a vice-president-international, who acts as a deputy for international matters, with as much responsibility for managing the group's foreign operations as his group executive chooses to assign. Functional and technical advice are provided by appropriate staff at the domestic operating company level or the corporate level.
>
> To coordinate the various product-group activities in major world markets, Epsilon has established area managers at the corporate staff level. Each area manager is responsible for keeping corporate management and the product groups informed about economic, political, and social developments in his assigned area . . . .

In a pure Archetype 3 relationship certain planning guidelines would rarely be questioned.

A. *Cost of Capital:* Financial resources are directed by the headquarters which is the only source of expansion capital. The discount rate used for capital budgeting will have to include the cost of taxes of repatriation. For reasons of control (though at an incredible tax cost) a few companies actually do repatriate profits each year, but most suffice with tight administrative control.

B. *Pricing Policy:* An item is sold at its U.S. price around the world, though the customer pays freight plus import duty. Performance evaluation is then more direct, and customers which are other multi-national companies cannot buy in low-price nations for use in high-price nations.

C. *Product Design:* The U.S. design will be sold in all nations, except where some law necessitates minor modifications. This policy will be justified by the cost of research and development, and thus the fixed cost of introducing another product. At a more sophisticated level, if a company manufactures identical products around the world it can achieve economies of scale, can benefit from the reliability of multiple manufacturing plants, can enjoy easier maintenance and can consider standardized marketing campaigns.

D. *Managerial Rotation:* Planning guidelines for managerial rotation will be quite explicit for Americans, who will be moved between subsidiaries and then back to headquarters. The acute shortage of local managerial talent will necessitate all local nationals staying within their subsidiaries, where their contribution is greatest.

E. *Liquid Assets:* The dividend rate will be set equal to earnings minus capital required for approved expansions. Any excess liquidity will be managed by the headquarters. If a currency is blocked, transfer prices and fee payments will be manipulated to get money out.

If the planning group can convince headquarters product executives of the appropriateness of their work, worldwide implementation is probable; the subsidiaries will succumb. This stands in contrast to Archetype 2 where implementation of a plan would be less likely.

Archetype 4

In the theory of this archetype of mutual understanding, headquarters not only understands the subsidiaries but also realizes that its maneuvers are understood by each subsidiary. Furthermore, it tries to encourage this understanding, for headquarters' ability so to encourage the subsidiaries is one measure of its own understanding of them. Leavitt ([16], Chapter 13), discussing collaboration, would have headquarters intervene indirectly in the affairs of a subsidiary so that the latter would recognize its areas of weakness and call in the headquarters for direct help.

Churchman and Schainblatt [3] eulogized mutual understanding, then described it in less than two pages. Leavitt ([16], Chapter 13) was reduced to using Alcoholics Anonymous as his example of collaborative organization. Similarly, Howard Perlmutter [22] depicted only the goal of a geocentric-geocentric organization, not the means. Although the previous archetypes have been descriptive of real companies, this fourth and final archetype is more conjectural. The first step to organizational design is to draw clear distinction between employees destined to remain always in their subsidiary (or their headquarters) and employees who will travel and live around all their lives. The latter group, the cadre of international managers, cannot be expected to accept pay differentials based on their original nationality. A pool of mobile managers is desirable for two reasons. First, the company would like to be able to adapt quickly to changes in business environments, and be able to move *some* people from a slack nation to a booming nation (this is in addition to the effective movement of people by the ability to have a worldwide engineering staff, in Japan perhaps, stop working on projects in the slack nation and turn to projects for the booming nation). The second reason for having this cadre is that they act as link pins ([17], 1961) to effect responsive communication and coordination between the following four dimensions of an organizational grid:

—Area.
—Product.
—Function.
—Planning time horizon.

The dimension of different planning horizons is implicit in the ability to respond flexibly to environmental changes. The need for long-range planning is accentuated by the nationalistic reactions of host governments, and of local partners in joint ventures which make it difficult to back out of ventures. In this hypothetical geocentric–geocentric organizational design, the formal structure of authority shall be based on planning time horizon.

The multi-national headquarters as a group is primarily engaged in strategic and entrepreneurial planning. This has been described for domestic companies by Ansoff ([1], p. 8), and must be done globally.

> Extrapolative projections of the firm's present product-market position are supplemented by probing and far-ranging analyses of the firm's environment to discover threats and opportunities which may produce major departures from the extrapolative projections of performance and resources . . . .
>
> The analysis involves studies of: economic and social forces which determine demand for the firm's products; the nature of the competitive forces which operate in its markets; and prospects for political and social changes which will affect the company and its environment.
>
> Another new activity is a "strengths and weaknesses" analysis, which attempts to determine and project the firm's capabilities and skills. This includes estimates of both reserve and excess capabilities as well as distinctive capabilities possessed by the firm.

Massive information flows are implied, especially for information that cannot readily be reduced to unambiguous technical terms—reporting on possible government actions to further national development is appreciably more complex than reporting last month's production rate. March and Simon ([19], p. 164) emphasize that:

> It is extremely difficult to communicate about intangible objects and non-standard objects. Hence, the heaviest burdens are placed on the communications system by the less-structured aspects of the organization's tasks, particularly by activity directed toward the explanation of problems that are not well defined.

Because a multi-national company operates in many environments, and can thereby move resources from an adverse to a favorable national environment, it is all the more important that some groups compare environments. This will not occur automatically. As Leavitt ([16], p. 33) so clearly states: "People perceive what they think will help satisfy needs; ignore what is disturbing; and again perceive disturbances that persist and increase."

The various Area headquarters perform tactical planning and establish controls for the subsidiaries. There must be procedures and controls if production is to be coordinated, for this implies cross shipments of parts and subassemblies, coordinated inventories and production smoothing over all nations in the Area. Strongly centralized procedures and controls are also vital if transfer pricing between subsidiaries is to be used as an instrument of corporate financial-tax policy rather than be a hotbed of bitter acrimony. But the key difference between this and Archetype 3 is that now there are several Area headquarters. As soon as one Area adopts different norms and standards, an aware subsidiary elsewhere in the world realizes that it no longer faces an invincible wall of a single worldwide standard and is more likely to get procedures tailored to its local conditions. This possibility encourages a geocentric awareness by the subsidiary.

Though several corporations are close, there are not yet any examples of truly multi-national, trans-national, or global corporations illustrating Archetype 4. Shell Oil, and Standard Oil of New Jersey have historically developed very capable local managements in each subsidiary. These managements are now being urged to think globally and the use of third country nationals is becoming common. Nevertheless, perhaps Unilever is even closer to being geocentric except for its subsidiaries in the U.S.A. and in underdeveloped nations.

Most routine O. R. problems will occur in the Area headquarters, although their initial conception probably occurred in the planning group of the multinational headquarters. Thus it is still possible to propose guidelines consistent with the archetype.

A. *Cost of Capital:* Capital can be raised in many nations of the world, especially if it is to be used locally, though capital can be moved between some nations. Thus the appropriate discount rate for a project in one nation depends on the strategic plans of the multi-national company, for they determine the interest rates and tax liabilities.

B. *Pricing Policy:* In pricing a line of products for Archetype 4, an appropriate guideline would be to optimally determine the vector of one benchmark country (e.g. U.S.A.), and simultaneously calculate an optimal scale factor for each nation by which to multiply the vector of benchmark prices to obtain local prices. This scheme is simple enough to permit central coordination, yet is also responsive to overall market conditions in each nation.

C. *Product Design:* Non-price marketing considerations lead to a proliferation of tailored designs as described in Archetype 2. Product considerations tend to a single design to be marketed throughout the world. One rational approach to an optimum would be to modularize the design by subassemblies (and styling panels). Some modules would be standard around the world.

D. *Managerial Rotation:* In Archetype 4, multilateral moves, the use of "third country nationals" must be analyzed. The number of Americans and other foreigners who can hold executive positions in a subsidiary may be restricted by a host government, so it would seem that these slots should be allocated with care, being viewed as an opportunity to gain familiarity with that nation. The emphasis upon linking pins implies selecting personnel who can tolerate the role ambiguity such a position implies.

E. *Liquid Assets:* Dividends, intersubsidiary loans, transfer prices and managerial fee payments will be manipulated to get liquidity to subsidiaries when they need it, but in such a way as to minimize taxes paid to the world minus interest earned [25].

Conclusions

Once it has made a commitment in some nation, the foreignness of a multi-national company may result in its having less flexibility than a native company. On the other hand, at the planning stage, until a commitment is made to a market name, a plant, or a work force, the multi-national company has exceptional flexibility to set patterns for the movement of products, managers, money, and know-how. For example, the multi-national company can establish a market in a nation long before it builds a plant, and then it can size that plant according to the number of national markets it is to serve. If the company is growing in a hundred nations, it faces many possible combinations of resource deployment patterns. The role of a headquarters planning group is to sift for the most promising ones.

On the other hand, it is not easy to plan in a multi-national company. Data is lacking or irrelevant to the problem at hand, even for deterministic models, yet surely flexibility in the face of uncertainty should be achieved. Different interest groups have different perceptions of the same problems. Plans are not implemented, and planners become frustrated. Implicit throughout the paper is the viewpoint that to be effective a planning group must understand the positions within the multi-national company, so as to implement from a Churchman-Schainblatt [3] persuasion position.

Four archetypes have been described, and for each appropriate planning guidelines have been put forth for a few problems. No archetypes encapsule the whole of reality; they merely provide a conceptual framework in which to hold problems of setting decision premises. At the very least, one has a mental check list to guide the discussion of ways to tackle a problem.

References

1. Ansoff, H. Igor, *The Evolution of Corporate Planning*, Stanford Research Institute, Long Range Planning Service Report No. 329, Menlo Park, California, September 1967.
2. Chandler, A. D., Jr. *Strategy and Structure*, Doubleday and Company, Inc., Garden City, New York, 1966.
3. Churchman, C. West, and A. H. Schainblatt, "The Researcher and the Manager: A Dialectic of Implementation," *Management Science*, Vol. 11, No. 4, (February 1965).

4. Clee, Gilbert H., and Alfred diScipio, "Creating a World Enterprise," *Harvard Business Review* (November–December 1959).
5. ——— and W. M. Sachtjen, "Organizing a Worldwide Business," *Harvard Business Review*, (November–December 1966).
6. Creelman, G. D., and R. W. Wallen, "The Place of Psychology in Operations Research," *Operations Research* (January–February 1958).
7. Etzioni, Amitai, *Modern Organizations*, Prentice-Hall, Englewood Cliffs, 1964.
8. Faltermayer, Edmund K., "It's a Spryer Singer," *Fortune* (December 1963), pp. 145–167.
9. Fouraker, Lawrence E., and John M. Stopford, "Organizational Structure and the Multi-national Strategy," *Administrative Science Quarterly* (June 1968), pp. 47–64.
10. Gulick, Luther, and L. Urwick (eds.), *Papers on the Science of Administration*, Institute of Public Administration, New York, 1937.
11. Haire, Mason (ed.), *Modern Organization Theory*, Wiley, New York, 1959.
12. ———, E. E. Ghisselli, and L. W. Porter "Cultural Patterns in the Role of the Manager," *Industrial Relations*, Vol. 2, No. 2 (February 1963), pp. 96–117.
13. ———, ———, and———, *Managerial Thinking*, Wiley, New York, 1966.
14. Hall, Edward T., *The Silent Language*, Fawcett, New York, 1959.
15. Kolde, Endel, *International Business Enterprise*, Prentice-Hall, Englewood Cliffs, 1968.
16. Leavitt, Harold J., *Managerial Psychology* (2nd. ed.), The University of Chicago Press, Chicago, 1964.
17. Likert, Rensis, *New Patterns of Management*, McGraw-Hill, New York, 1961.
18. Lovell, Enid B., *The Changing Role of the International Executive*, National Industrial Conference Board, New York, 1966.
19. March, James G., and Herbert A. Simon, *Organizations*, Wiley, New York, 1958.
20. Martyn, Howe, *International Business*, Free Press of Glencoe, New York, 1964.
21. Maslow, Abraham H., *Motivation and Personality*, Harper and Row Bros, New York, 1954.
22. Perlmutter, Howard V., "L'Enterprise International–Trois Conceptions," *Review Economic et Social*, (May 1965), a translation appeared in the *Quarterly Journal of AIESEC International*, Vol. III, No. 3 (August 1967).
23. ———, "The Tortuous Evolution of the Multinational Corporation," *Columbia Journal of World Business*, Vol. IV, No. 1 (January–February 1969).
24. Robinson, Richard D., *International Management*, Holt, Rinehart & Winston, New York, 1967.
25. Rutenberg, David P., "Maneuvering Liquid Assets in a Multi-National Company," *Management Science*, Vol. XVI, No. 10 (June 1970), pp. B671–B684.
26. Simon, Herbert, *Administrative Behavior: A Study of Decision Making Processes in Administrative Organization*, Macmillan, New York, 1957.
27. Steiner, George, and W. M. Cannon, *Multi-National Corporate Planning*, Macmillan, New York, 1966.
28. Simmonds, Kenneth, "Multinational, Well, Not Quite," *Columbia Journal of World Business*, Vol. I (Fall, 1966).
29. Watkins, Melville H., *Foreign Ownership and the Structure of Canadian Industry*, Queen's Printer, Ottawa, 1968.

41

Toward a Concept of Managerial Control for a World Enterprise

M. Y. Yoshino

One of the most significant business trends today is the emergence of many American firms in the world market. The United States Department of Commerce reports that direct private investments overseas have almost tripled in the last decade, reaching $44 billion in 1964. In the same year, moreover, these investments earned $5.1 billion, of which $3.7 billion has been repatriated to the United States.[1] Over 3,300 American firms have some interest in overseas production either through licensing agreements or direct investments. For a substantial number of these firms, international business represents over 50 percent of earnings.

High profit potentials in the world market have also drawn a large number of firms from other industrially advanced nations into international business. As a result, competition in promising markets throughout the world is rapidly taking on a multinational character. Though international business continues to offer good profit potentials, there is mounting evidence that the return on foreign investment for many leading American firms, though still higher than on domestic investment, has been continuously declining over the last several years.[2] The increasing competitive pressure, coupled with the inherent difficulties in managing a worldwide enterprise, points to a need for ensuring effective managerial arrangements.

One of the critical tasks of managing multi-national operations is to design an effective managerial control system to allow top management to coordinate and guide activities of a large number of far-flung foreign affiliates into a unified whole. Since entirely new variables enter into the calculus of decision-making in international business, the mere extension of a domestic control system is inadequate in meeting the demands of multinational operations.

This article seeks to identify major problems faced by corporate management in exercising managerial control over foreign operations and to offer some basic suggestions toward development of a more meaningful way of viewing managerial control in multinational and cultural contexts.

Reprinted by permission from the March 1966 issue of the *Michigan Business Review*, pp. 25–31. Published by the Graduate School of Business Administration, The University of Michigan.

[1] U.S. Department of Commerce, Office of Business Economics, *Survey of Current Business*, September 1965, p. 24.

[2] For example, see Walter P. Stern, "U.S. Direct Investment Abroad," *Financial Analysts Journal*, January–February 1965, p. 98.

C. Wickham Skinner, "Management of International Production," *Harvard Business Review*, September–October 1964, p. 125.

Allocation of Decision-making Authority

Though it is by no means unique to international business, one of the recurring issues raised by corporate management is the division of authority between headquarters and foreign affiliates. Some firms choose to centralize practically all decision-making at corporate headquarters and to require from foreign units extremely detailed operating plans and reports with great frequency. As one would expect, this arrangement tends to dampen the enthusiasm and initiative of the management overseas and to limit its flexibility and freedom in meeting local problems and opportunities.

Excessive demand for information and reports not only has a demoralizing effect upon local executives, but it also diverts them from more pressing operating problems. Frequently, the headquarters staff are paralyzed by the sheer volume of information coming from foreign affiliates and fail to make effective use of it. Decisions are likely to be delayed, leading to losses in operating effectiveness.

Interestingly, tight control does not necessarily guarantee that local management will adhere strictly to the policies of the home office. I have observed some local executives who ostensibly comply with the requirements of headquarters but in reality deviate substantially from the policy directives of the home office.

Some firms go to the other extreme by almost completely delegating decision-making authority to local management. My recent field research has revealed that corporate headquarters of some international firms exercise virtually no control over their foreign operations, as long as the foreign units somehow meet the minimum sales or profit goal established by the headquarters. This approach is observed to be particularly prevalent among manufacturers of consumer products with many years of international experience. Some do it out of a conviction that it is impossible to manage daily affairs of overseas units from a headquarters located several thousand miles away, while others follow this practice out of negligence.

Weaknesses of Laissez Faire Approach

Though the laissez faire approach gives maximum flexibility and freedom to local management, it suffers from two major weaknesses. Foreign affiliates which are virtually autonomous tend to generate subgoals not necessarily consistent with those of the headquarters. Also, extreme decentralization limits use of a wide variety of resources and experiences available at headquarters which are of potential value to foreign units. There seem to be nearly always some elements of a company's managerial competence that can be applied overseas. The latter point is particularly important inasmuch as the real strength of a world enterprise derives from its ability to integrate the activities of widely scattered affiliates.

Obviously, the optimum pattern lies somewhere between the two extremes described. Since the effectiveness of a particular pattern depends on such factors as nature of products, stage of organizational evolvement, size of the company, and availability of executive talents, it is impossible to prescribe a pattern that is equally suitable under any circumstances. However, it appears that distance, complexity, and instability in operating environments overseas tend to favor maximum decentralization of decision-making. Only the very critical decisions should be reserved for corporate management. These are likely to be decisions involving such elements as major capital investments, selection of top managerial personnel, important government negotiations, and introduction of new products. This approach tends to maximize contributions that both headquarters and local management are best qualified to make. It must be noted, however, that such an approach is effective only when the following conditions are satisfied: (1) The headquarters-foreign affiliates relationship must be examined in terms of the allocation of specific responsibilities. (2) Corporate headquarters must be properly informed by local units on major decisions that are made by the latter. (3) Finally, headquarters must design an effective system of control over those areas of responsibility that are delegated to the local units.

Establishing Meaningful Standards of Performance

A critical problem in planning managerial control for multinational operations is the determination of standards against which to evaluate the performance of foreign affiliates. In this regard, two points deserve careful consideration. They are (1) the appropriateness of reported profits as a measurement criterion, and (2) the need for multiple performance criteria. In multidivisional domestic operations, reported profit is generally accepted as the critical measure of managerial effectiveness. Each division is relatively self-contained, and interdivisional transactions can be adjusted through the mechanism of transfer pricing. Since general operating environments among various divisions are relatively homogeneous, top management can make some meaningful comparisons. In multinational operations, however, reported profit alone is quite inadequate as the measure of performance.

In the first place, the reported profit of a foreign operating unit is likely to be distorted by a number of external and internal variables that are absent in domestic operations. Because political and economic risks vary widely from country to country, what appears superficially to be high profit may, in fact, be quite unsatisfactory when risk factors are properly weighed. Foreign exchange regulations, legal restrictions, foreign tax structures, or unexpected political developments can have a decided impact upon the profit performance of a foreign affiliate. Yet the local management has virtually no control over these external factors.

Profit performance of a foreign affiliate can also be affected by intra-firm decisions that are beyond the control of local management. A worldwide enterprise has a wide range of alternatives in allocating its corporate resources. Hence, within the broad constraints of political and economic risk, a network of logistics can be developed on a global basis to maximize comparative advantages of each area. Obviously, company-wide logistics decisions can only be made at headquarters. Nevertheless, these decisions can affect profitability of foreign units rather markedly. Some financial decisions made centrally to expand worldwide profits may also lead to an increase of profits in one or more individual country affiliates and a decrease in others. These factors provide convincing evidence that the reported profit-and-loss data must be carefully scrutinized and adjusted by removing various extraneous influences on the operations of a local unit. In so doing the following guidelines are important.

Environmental Variables

The most serious problem is determining the degree of controllability of the environmental variables. It is evident that local management can exercise no control over such developments as galloping inflation in a foreign economy or a surge of nationalistic feelings. However, it is possible to minimize the impact of these developments on the particular firm through careful planning and judicious actions. Corporate management must somehow determine the degree to which local management should be held accountable for these environmental variables.

Obviously, there is no hard-and-fast rule that is applicable to every situation. It must be noted that there is an inherent tendency for management of most foreign affiliates to attribute poor performance mainly to hard-to-measure environmental variables or arbitrary decisions made by headquarters. Hence, each case must be reviewed carefully. Careless or arbitrary decisions in this respect contribute to poor morale among local management and relaxed control.

The next step involves technical adjustments of reported data. Here, two considerations are important. Since adjustments of profit-loss data of a host of foreign affiliates are highly complicated, time-consuming, and costly, they should be limited to major items large enough to make significant differences. Also, adjustments should be made only on a memorandum basis without entering into the formal accounting records.[3] Furthermore, it is important that the criteria and methods of adjustments be explicitly defined and understood by the management of foreign affiliates.

Evaluating Performance

Removing distortions from the reported profit is only one step. Performance of all foreign units must be evaluated on a comparative basis. This is essential not only for the purpose of managerial control but for future decisions on

[3] *International Enterprise: A New Dimension of American Business,* New York: McKinsey & Company, Inc., 1962, p. 30.

allocation of corporate resources on a global basis. Establishing a comparative criterion of profit performance is extremely difficult because of a wide diversity in operating environments overseas. It is obvious that an investment in a high-risk country should earn a greater return than one in a stable economy. But is it possible to quantify the rather elusive political and economic risks?

One solution has been suggested by Millard Pryor, Jr., in a recent article in the *Harvard Business Review*. Pryor proposes to establish "compensatory" financial goals for operations outside the United States. Such goals are constructed by adding to the basic financial goals established for domestic operations factors which quantify the long-range overseas political and monetary risks and the extra costs of absentee management.[4]

Another promising concept that needs further exploration is the development of a classification scheme to group various operations into a number of clusters on the basis of key environmental variables. Common performance criteria may then be set for these operations in the same classification. For example, an important variable for a particular type of business may be the level of economic development. The firm's operations throughout the world may be classified into several categories on this basis, regardless of their geographic locations; and common performance criteria may be set within each level. Relative homogeneity in operating environments would presumably allow more meaningful comparison.

Performance Criteria

Now let us turn to the second basic issue. This involves the question of the relative importance to be attached to profitability as a performance criterion. Though other standards are by no means insignificant, profitability is widely accepted as the final performance standard in multidivisional domestic operations. In view of added environmental dimensions, should the management of multinational operations rely predominantly or even exclusively on this single criterion in measuring managerial effectiveness of foreign affiliates? The answer is clearly negative when the following factors are considered. (1) Multinational operations are conducted in sovereign nations with diverse national goals and interests. (2) Foreign enterprise induces a potential conflict of interest between the American parent company, its local associates, and the governments of the host countries.

Any foreign enterprise that must rely heavily on local resources cannot expect to survive, let alone succeed, over the long run unless it is so structured and managed as to make the maximum contributions to the host country. This is particularly true in developing countries where productive resources are scarce and nationalistic feelings are rampant. Satisfaction of this requirement, however, may well conflict with the profitability criterion, at least in

[4] Millard Pryor, Jr., "Planning in a World Business," *Harvard Business Review,* January-February 1965, p. 134.

the short run. This conflict of interests must be recognized by top management in setting performance criteria for foreign affiliates.

Some may object to inclusion of such a consideration in performance criteria on the ground that it is beyond precise measurement. While very precise measurement is admittedly difficult, some imaginative approaches are being developed. For example, Professor Robinson has developed a conceptual framework to approximate the political and economic impact of a foreign enterprise on the host country.[5]

There is another area of potential conflict that must be recognized in establishing performance criteria. Many multinational operations involve joint ownership with local interests. Local investors can participate only in profits of the foreign enterprise, not those of the parent company located in the United States. Hence, performance criteria must be established in such a manner as to optimize the interests of different ownership groups. Otherwise, local management is likely to find itself subject to conflicting pressure groups in an atmosphere of indecision and confusion. Such a situation may lead to the ultimate emergence of one dominant group, which in turn enforces its own performance standards.

Designing an Effective Information System

The critical role of information in planning a managerial control system has been repeatedly emphasized in management literature. Distance, diversity, and instability in environments overseas place a premium on an effective information system in multinational operations. Information processing and analysis are much more complex and, correspondingly, more expensive in international business than in domestic operations. Top management, therefore, must balance comprehensiveness and speed on the one hand and the cost of information on the other.

Three basic considerations are important in designing an information system for a world enterprise. They are (1) the types of information sought, (2) the flow of information between headquarters and foreign affiliates, and (3) analysis of information for managerial planning and control.

The types of information sought must be determined by careful examination of the requirements of planning and control. The informational needs of a firm ultimately depend on corporate strategies and goals. This basic consideration, however, is often ignored. Though the exact requirements vary from company to company, basically three types of information are needed by the management of multinational operations. They are environmental data (political, social, and economic), competitive data (real and potential), and internal operating data (both quantitative and qualitative). In many multinational firms, the only type of data systematically and regularly gathered is

[5] Richard D. Robinson, *International Business Policy*, New York: Holt, Rinehart and Winston, 1964, pp. 99–145.

that related to internal operations. Even those data are primarily designed for accounting purposes rather than for decision-making.

Since international operations are much more vulnerable to external variables than domestic operations, data on environmental and competitive conditions become all the more critical. Moreover, much internal data is meaningful only in the perspective of the general environment and in the light of competitive activity.

In view of their importance, it is dangerous to delegate overall intelligence functions solely to foreign affiliates. Though foreign affiliates are unquestionably an important source of vital information for management, local executives are usually preoccupied with daily operating problems, and they may overlook subtle developments with far-reaching implications. Furthermore, there are other equally important sources of environmental and competitive data available to headquarters. For example, United Nations, United States Government agencies, and trade associations can provide useful information.

The Flow of Information

The second factor in designing a global information system is facilitating the flow of information between corporate headquarters and foreign affiliates. Two media of communication—written reports and personal visits—are available for this purpose. Though both serve useful functions, the balance between the two must be carefully considered. As noted earlier, excessive reliance on written reports tends to aggravate the already difficult and sometimes strained headquarters–foreign affiliates relationship. Action-oriented local executives find it time-consuming and difficult to prepare reports. Furthermore, foreign nationals are placed at a disadvantage because of language and cultural barriers. For these reasons, written communication should be kept to the minimum level. Headquarters must also standardize reporting procedures and methods to facilitate reporting and subsequent analysis.

Personal visits are used extensively by the management of most multinational corporations, though the character of personal visits varies widely as does their effectiveness. Too frequently, personal visits are used as a tool for trouble-shooting—to solve immediate problems occurring unexpectedly. Viewed in this fashion, personal visits have very limited educational value. Since face-to-face contacts can be useful in bridging the distance and cultural gaps that exist between headquarters and foreign affiliates, they must be well planned and made on a regular basis. Personal visits, if appropriately conducted, are useful in developing an insight into local problems, communicating policies of headquarters, discussing long-term plans, and sharing valuable experiences.

The most challenging area in designing an international intelligence system lies in analysis of data by headquarters staff for effective control and planning. Thus far, in many international firms relatively little has been done beyond the traditional accounting analysis. Comparative analysis of internal data is complicated by diverse environmental factors, as noted earlier; but this step is critical in identifying weak spots and unrealized opportunities. Some progressive firms have begun to make imaginative use of these ideas. For example, labor productivity, efficiency of logistics system, and effectiveness of a given marketing mix are analyzed and evaluated on a global basis.

Understanding Cultural Variables

Perhaps the most difficult and elusive aspect of managerial control in international operations is that control functions must be performed in a multicultural context. This is particularly significant when affiliates are managed by foreign nationals. Cultural variables affect managerial control in several ways.

First, culture may block effective communication between foreign affiliates and headquarters. Particularly serious from the viewpoint of managerial control are distortions introduced in reporting as a result of certain cultural values prevalent in some societies. Some cultures tend to emphasize politeness and agreeableness in superior-subordinate reporting relationships, even at the expense of accuracy and directness. Thus, local management may ignore or distort data deemed unpleasant to corporate headquarters.

Secondly, to a large degree culture prescribes the standard of achievement and dictates the concomitant system of rewards. Not every culture rewards what is considered to be productive achievement in advanced industrial societies, nor is the reward for similar achievements the same. For example, some traditional cultures place the ultimate reward upon loyalty, devotion, and contribution to the group rather than upon outstanding individual achievement. Thus, a system of motivations and incentives—an essential ingredient in managerial control—must be meaningful in terms of the local culture.

Culture also affects superior-subordinate relationships in an organization. As Professor Fayerweather concludes from his pioneering research, some cultures are prone to produce interpersonal relationships characterized by distance, distrust, and hostility; while others are more conducive to group-oriented, collaborative interpersonal relationships.[6] He further notes that the former type is relatively prevalent in more traditional societies, whereas the latter is predominant in Western societies, particularly in American culture. Though each pattern is meaningful and effective in its own cultural environments, difficulties are likely to emerge when control functions must be performed among men of diverse cultural backgrounds and orientations.

Finally, there is the problem of sensitivity often manifested by national executives toward control exercised by American executives. This is particularly prevalent among those in underdeveloped and former colonial countries.

The only permanently effective way to overcome these cultural gaps is to

[6] John Fayerweather, *The Executive Overseas,* Syracuse, New York: Syracuse University Press, 1959, pp. 15–40.

view managerial control as an educational process rather than a superior-subordinate authority relationship. Continuous educational effort is the only feasible way to provide management of foreign affiliates with the necessary background to understand the headquarters' points of view. With this background, local management could intelligently interpret policy directives from the home office as well as effectively participate in the formation of such policies. Such an educational approach would also minimize the sensitivity problem mentioned above.

Conclusion

Managerial control in multinational operations is complicated by a number of external as well as internal variables unique to multinational operations. Clearly, it is impossible to rely solely on comfortable assumptions and generalizations developed out of domestic experience. A need is apparent for developing a conceptual framework for managerial control of multinational operations.

At the risk of oversimplification, this article has singled out four basic considerations as a step toward development of a useful way of viewing managerial control for a world enterprise. The task is by no means easy, but the undeniable facts of the tremendous potential of the expanding world market and increasing competition should provide sufficient incentive for American management to meet this challenge effectively.

42

Bridging Cultural Barriers in International Management

Donald C. Stone

Cultural shock takes place in Americans assigned to overseas positions when they feel anxiety or inadequacy as a result of losing familiar signs and symbols of social intercourse. Some experts in cultural adjustment and adaptation point out that there are three distinctive patterns of response to "culture shock." They refer to "flight," "fight," and "adaptation."

When a person adjusts to a new situation through *flight*, he rejects those people and things around him which cause his discomfort, and he withdraws from interaction with them. He places "blame" on other people for lack of understanding, or on himself for inadequacy in handling the new experience.

Reprinted with permission from *S.A.M. Advanced Management Journal*, January 1969, pp. 56–62.

The result is defensiveness such as flight to fellow nationals in a foreign enclave or regressive action by withdrawing into the security of the familiar.

Or, alternatively, his response may result in flight into opposite behavior. He flees from his own cultural identity by joining the host culture. He may "go native." The effect of denying one's own culture is usually harmful.

Persons in the second, or "fight," category become hostile and aggressive. They become obsessed with telling how we do it at home. How often in meetings of Americans with foreigners we find preoccupation in reporting on how we fry fish in Keokuk, Iowa.

A third and all too rare type of American assigned abroad concerns himself with the slow and painstaking process of *cultural adjustment*. He neither rejects himself nor others, but tries to adapt through constant openness to learning and behavioral growth. He develops an awareness of the behavioral as well as verbal messages he is transmitting, and the interpretations he is receiving. He works seriously in acquiring skills of interpersonal communication which can hurdle cultural barriers.

This skill is not something that comes naturally, or that one necessarily acquires by contact or by reading books. Long ago I came to the conclusion that a person could study international relations for 25 years and never become skillful in international negotiation or in the conduct of intercultural relations. Through intensive training and orientation, some persons can learn to avoid both "flight" and "fight" patterns, and become skillful in such interpersonal adaptation.

Disappointing Results

All of us engaged in operations abroad have frustrations and disappointments. People with whom we are dealing do not seem to respond sensibly. We begin to view them as inferior, unappreciative people, or we may wonder if there is something wrong with us. Let me give a couple of illustrations.

A group of American management consultants made a lengthy presentation to the head of a French shoe factory. They described how the adoption of their plan would increase the owner's personal income and that of his employees. Their proposal produced merely a shrug of the owner's shoulders. The factory had been in his family for three generations. To install new machinery and bring in fast working young men and women would upset everything. His faithful employees would be distraught. He himself would have to put in much more work and have less time for vacations. His wife would object to his longer work day. Why disrupt everything for an uncertain amount of increased income when he had sufficient already for his needs?

In the Middle East I learned of an American oil refinery concerned with the lack of protein in the workers' diet which impaired their energy and hence productivity. They company installed a canteen and asked the workers to bring their cups and plates to secure an enriched noonday meal. Managers were perplexed when only a few workers responded. A visiting sociologist discovered the reason. The holding up of a cup and plate for a handout was viewed as a symbol of begging. The management secured trays on which food could be placed and arranged for the dignitaries to engage in a meal. The workers fell in line.

In Europe a business group broke off a profitable sale to an American corporation because its overseas manager continuously referred detailed legal questions to the company's lawyers. This was interpreted by the Europeans as a lack of trust and an inability of the executive to fulfill an oral agreement. The problem was solved when the executive grounded himself in the legal details and was granted authority to act. How often words or personal motions mean different things in different places.

Behavior of Local Employees

Obviously the greater the difference in cultures, the more likely is the manager to encounter failures and frustrations. In an agrarian culture, the habits and values of workers may conflict seriously with the requisites of efficiency and effective industrial production. Traditional modes create a personality structure that differs from the one produced by and essential to an industrial way of life. Having no concept of a system of impersonal assignment of responsibility to positions and of the evaluation of performance according to work standards, the local worker does not understand a system under which a supervisor evaluates performance to indicate satisfaction and provide rewards. Rather, he assumes that personal relations determine one's welfare. How he gets along depends on how much his superior likes him.

The reluctance of local supervisors to take responsibility is another common problem. They fear that subordinates will resent anyone in a supervisory position who does not occupy a superior role in the social structure outside of the factory. Or, if they assume responsibility, they may refuse to share knowledge about the work for fear that employees will become qualified to take over their jobs.

Larger salaries may be no inducement as this may only increase the worker's obligations to his extended family or social group with whom he must share his income. Indeed, social pressures to share the company's wealth with relatives may take precedence over the necessity of a supervisor's responsibility for efficient performance.

Devoid of understanding of what constitutes costs of production, income, and profits, workers in a non-industrialized society may respond as Professors Brannen and Hodgson describe the reaction of a local supervisor. When asked about his inefficient operation and if better results could be obtained at lower costs, the reply was "oh, that does not make any difference. We do not worry about what anything costs; this company has plenty of money."[1]

I have found on overseas assignments that the task of achieving development programs is beset by the same difficulties. Value patterns and traditional

[1] *Overseas Management,* published by McGraw-Hill.

social structures incompatible with the requirements of modern management may serve as an impenetrable barrier to productive effort unless major reorientation of employees takes place. U.S. technical and economic assistance advisors require special skill in interpersonal communication in contributing to such an institution building process.

Cultures vary from country to country, from one ethnic group to another, and among organizations. Interpersonal and intercultural communication must be adapted to each circumstance.

Changing Cultures?

Often the issue is whether to accept and adapt to the culture or whether the objective should be to change the culture. I am not referring here to personal or family adjustment, to whether one lives in an American colony or goes native, or whether one maintains his own values and standards. What I am referring to is the legitimacy of efforts to change another culture.

U.S. foreign policy, for example, is committed to cooperation with Latin American countries under the Alliance for Progress in the development of the Western Hemisphere. Progress in most countries is slow in part because of resistances to social, economic, and political change. The patterns of land ownership and land use are inimical both to higher agricultural output and productivity and to more broadly based consumption. To achieve mutually committed objectives, there must be cultural penetration and intervention.

The legitimacy of efforts to bring about cultural change depends upon the moral validity of objectives and the extent to which the effort is a cooperative one. This underlines the principle of mutual help and self-help, with maximum reliance on multilateral rather than unilateral approaches. Mutual respect and cooperation are the foundation for not only the success of international business activities, but also for church missions and interchurch unity, educational exchange, economic and social development, and military security.

A first requisite in gaining respect and cooperation is integrity of policy and use of humane methods. Do our objectives and policies help fulfill the legitimate aspirations of the people of another country, improve their well-being and conditions? In operations do we espouse individual and group behavior based upon universal moral concepts—such as brotherhood, integrity, and humility?

Throughout history, most of man's foreign activities have not been dominated by high motives. Even under enlightened colonial policies, the human tendency towards ethnocentrism has resulted in transplanting what a person learned in another culture without suitable adaptation. Government systems, education, and business methods have been imposed without regard to their suitability.

American businessmen often have imposed inappropriate practices, or tried to sell products which did not fit local situations. Establishment of a mine or factory in a foreign area may be a traumatic experience, many aspects might be avoided by better corporate training programs.

Personal Adjustments

Today's international manager must be a semi-superman. He requires abilities and skills no one thought about a few years ago.

Estimates from international corporations suggest that a majority of persons sent overseas have to return prior to completion of their assignment. The financial costs are enormous. Direct out-of-pocket expense entailed in recruitment, preparation, travel, moving expenses, and reassignment of a family are reported in terms of up to $50,000. Some years ago I calculated the cost to the government as being around $25,000 to $30,000. Such costs do not take into account the lack of accomplishment of the individual's mission or the public relations and political cost to the organization or to the U.S.A.

The reason for failure in managerial assignments is seldom lack of technical and professional competence. Rather it is the inability to apply administrative and technical skills in a new cultural framework. The individual can't again forget how he used to fry fish in Keokuk.

Americans abroad need to consider what there is about the U.S. worth communicating and what aspects of American behavior create suspicion, and lack of credibility.

We need to know enough about Marxism, on the one hand, and social injustice, on the other, to appreciate why Communism has appeal. We must understand why "Capitalism" is not viewed with favor in many countries, and that much exploitation and injustice has taken place in the name of Capitalism.

How many American businessmen and government representatives can explain in simple terms their own philosophy of life, the concepts of free society and free enterprise or democratic government in a manner which has relevance and appeal in another culture? Few persons are able to do more than describe some of the structure and details of what goes on, little of which is relevant.

A person sensitively capable in cultural, ideological, and spiritual as well as professional matters will find many doors open to him. I emphasize spiritual, because I believe that interest in and appreciation of religious concerns is the best bridge to understanding—a bridge which most Americans abroad ignore. In our ignorance, we view religion as divisive—as its practice often is, but a mutual appreciation of the teachings and values of other religions is cohesive.

A Plan of Action

Every organization operating abroad needs a formal plan and assigned responsibilities in coping with these intercultural problems.

First, is the recruitment and assignment of persons on the basis of personal traits and aptitudes for overseas adjustment.

Second, is equal attention to the prospect of a wife proving an asset.

Third, is formal training in intercultural operations, including the screening out of persons at this stage.

Fourth, is the preparation and conduct by each overseas office or installation of an orientation and intercultural bridge building program.

Fifth, is a plan of evaluation, and sustained assistance by the home office on these matters to overseas offices.

Sixth, a system of rewards for effective work.

Unsuitable persons can be eliminated in the recruitment and assignment stages by securing exceedingly thorough evaluations of both the man and wife. An individual prone to considerable drinking in the U.S.A. easily becomes alcoholic abroad. A wife—domineering and rigid in her social and civic relations—would probably mistreat her servants. An individual who seems to enjoy attention and personalized service at home often develops delusions of grandeur on a foreign assignment. Each additional servant increases the delusion.

One of the great values of a rigorous training program in intercultural operations is the opportunity to evaluate the individual on behavioral and interpersonal factors. Enough savings can be made by weeding out a couple of misfits to pay for the whole program.

Learning Abroad

If it were not for the high percentage of persons who have to be brought home before the optimum period has been served, we might conclude that the way to master competence in intercultural operations is to engage in them. There is little evident correlation between service abroad and intercultural skill and understanding. A lot of persons do gain knowledge and skill this way, like learning to play a piano or swimming without formal instruction. True you may eliminate discordant notes, and you may even keep from drowning.

One positive result of overseas living is a more objective understanding of American culture, but not necessarily understanding of the foreign culture. However, persons working in an internationalized subculture develop common attitudes and understandings. Protocol in diplomatic service helps to bridge the gap between national cultures.

Likewise, in the field of business, the world-wide dissemination of concepts about organization and management, mass production, marketing, efficiency, employee incentives, shared benefits, personnel and training provides a common language for the American businessman whether he is in Lagos, Calcutta, Tokyo, or Lima. Such international concepts are not of much help once the businessman leaves the big cities, any more than the rules of protocol are of much help to the diplomat trying to communicate in the provinces. Nor does it help the wife once she steps out of the security of the American colony.

Experience indicates that training can be very effective if it fully utilizes new knowledge of educational methods, human motivation and behavior, culture and communication.

Therefore, it is important to stress the development of:

One. *Cultural self-awareness*—to know how we as members of a technological culture behave and how the other person responds to our normal methods of conducting business.

Two. *An attitude of cultural objectivity*—to discover why people act the way they do. To understand that their way of behaving may be best for them and that we may have to adapt to their needs if we are to succeed in working with them.

Three. *An appreciation of American cultural strengths and weaknesses for working abroad*—we do some things well and others not so well. It is important for Americans to know this and to stress our positive aspects.

Four. *Construction of bridges from American to other cultures*—by helping us to understand ourselves within the American culture and learning how other people behave in their cultures. For instance, we usually distinguish rather clearly among work, play, and social activities. In other cultures these activities may be intertwined, not compartmentalized. If a foreign manager combines work, play, and social activities, this does not mean that he is lazy or irresponsible.

In-House Measures

In setting up an operating plan to improve intercultural competence, an organization should utilize all of the instruments that training experts find useful in improving supervision, attitudes, skills, circulation of ideas, inducements, rewards and punishments.

Beyond this the officers of the organization should request every overseas office or installation to develop an approved program consisting of a plan for welcoming and installing new employees, orientation to the life and institutions of the country, language training, maintenance of a circulating library of materials about the country and intercultural operations, a "wives committee" to foster contacts and voluntary services, dissemination of information on local cultural, religious, welfare, and sporting activities, arrangements for contacts and discussions with foreign nationals, staff meetings and training sessions on interpersonal communication problems within the country, and linkage with other U.S. agencies and with the Embassy. To get started I propose that managements send some of their Training Division Staff to the few universities concerned with these matters for graduate work and enroll them in training institutes.

Citizenship Overseas

U.S. business has a most challenging opportunity to contribute to the enhancement of the communities and nations in which it serves. Whenever I discuss with a group of foreign visitors what I feel to be significant about the U.S., I describe the high degree of social responsibility, accountability, and ethics which has developed in American business. I mention the leadership provided in community affairs, support of education, civil rights, good citizenship, and labor relations.

However, I feel that U.S. business has lagged in achieving an equivalent contribution abroad. Its relations with employees tend to be more patronizing. It usually functions in a more permissive society and is thus freer of ethical constraints. It has less linkage on a mutual basis with indigenous institutions. The more limited opportunities for community relations overseas only underline the need for sustained effort by each company in finding ways to maximize its contribution. Here again we see the role of training in intercultural operations in opening up many constructive possibilities.

We live in a world of conflicting ideologies, racial antagonisms, national rivalries, and economic inequities. It is far easier to create dissension, and conflict, than good will. Through ignorance and false self-assurance in intercultural relationships, we unwittingly contribute to resentments and suspicions. Through commitment, development of knowledge and skill, and sustained effort we can consciously build a world-wide culture in which cooperation and international well being can be achieved.

social and political involvement

section **8**

43

Managing for Progress in the 1970s

Edward N. Cole

More effective management of the nation's physical and human resources becomes increasingly critical as our society grows more complex and places heavier responsibilities on all sectors of our economy—particularly on business and industry. Several major trends will significantly affect the course of the business world not only in the 1970s but also during the remainder of the twentieth century. There are challenges ahead for those who will be managing the business enterprise in the future decades.

As we look forward to the next thirty years, we can see four major trends which will have an important influence on American business.

First, barring some unforeseen catastrophe, business in the next three decades faces the greatest opportunity for growth in its history. During this period, our population increase is estimated to produce 100 million new consumers and 45 million new participants in the labor force.

Second, the people of this country will be more affluent, better educated, more sophisticated, more demanding, and more articulate. To us as businessmen, this means they will be more discriminating as buyers and they will

Edward N. Cole, "Managing for Progress in the 1970s," pp. 7–12, *MSU Business Topics*, Autumn 1969. Reprinted by the permission of the publisher, Division of Research, Graduate School of Business Administration, Michigan State University.

want more variety, newness, and excitement in the products available. They will demand a good return on their investment in terms of quality, dependability, durability, and—very important—in terms of service.

The third trend will be the impact of technological progress. Thus far in the twentieth century, we have witnessed not only giant steps into space, in the skies and under the seas, but also great advances in nuclear physics, medicine, communications, manufacturing processes and methods, computers, and in other fields. In the next thirty years, however, our over-all technological progress should surpass that of the first seventy years of this century.

The fourth trend will be the increasing attention to improvements in social and environmental fields, with particular emphasis on urban areas. Maximum use of natural resources—land, air, and water—will be a critical requirement. Improved transportation systems must be given prime consideration. Because of the increased density of population, greatly enlarged investments in public utilities, recreational facilities, housing, and similar fields will be required in our cities.

Certainly, these are trends of challenge and opportunity. They point to a society which will continue to grow in size and complexity, a people which will continue to seek higher and higher standards of living, an economic opportunity for business unequalled in American history.

There are days when many of us would welcome a return of the good old days when business—it is said—was simpler and less demanding; when change was an infrequent necessity. Now and in the future, we must recognize change not only as a fact of life but as a way of life.

While change itself is a major challenge, it is the speed of change which constitutes the element of greatest demand. This rapidity of change is reflected in population trends, consumer demand, technology, and the impatience of society for progress. It is not *change*, but *time*—our ability to adapt quickly—which is the critical requirement of acceptable progress.

Growth in Urban Areas

Consider our metropolitan areas, for example, where during the past fifty years population increased by 100 million. While admittedly our nation faced major wars and economic crises during this period, the fact remains that we were not able to accommodate our expanding population as well as we desired, particularly in the urban areas. Looking ahead, the population of the United States is expected to increase by another 100 million people—not in fifty years, but in thirty years. And all of this increase, and more, will occur in the urban areas. The challenge is to provide for an additional 100 million people in a shorter time span and to do it more adequately than in the past.

Our nation will face similar problems of accelerating change in other areas, too. Responding to these challenges will not be enough. What is really needed is leadership—leadership in anticipating, directing, and in helping to create the forces of change. In short, we must learn how to manage change more effectively than we have in the past so that we are the beneficiaries rather than the victims of change.

This is the real challenge for tomorrow's managers, including those who will have the responsibilities for both the private and public resources of our nation. We must learn how to manage accelerated change so it can be more effectively assimilated into our businesses and into our society.

Of critical importance will be the need to make maximum use of the expanding storehouse of knowledge which will become available, particularly in the technical fields. The magnitude of this assignment can be demonstrated by indicating what I believe will be some of the areas of greatest change in the automobile field during the next few decades.

Accelerating technological advances will bring new materials and processes, design concepts, and products. We expect greater use of electronics to monitor or control functions of the automobile, its route of travel, and its safety.

Computer technology should see its biggest growth in the operations end of our business, including marketing. Many people think of the computer in terms of repetitive mechanical tasks and as an information aid to decision making. However, it is already being used for highly complex assignments in many fields.

In the future, we will place much greater reliance on the computer to perform complicated tasks. These will include the ability to discriminate between different types of functions, to monitor its own performance, and to signal when tools need replacement. All of this will be done with no human action once the equipment has been programmed.

The computer is a tool of fabulous potential. But we must remember that it is man who must control the machine. We must not allow ourselves to become so mesmerized by the computer's capabilities that we allow it to carry us to levels of complexity beyond the capability of our human resources.

The automotive vehicle of the future will benefit from more sophisticated technology—including reduced pollution and further improvements in vehicle safety.

While automotive engineers will extend the frontiers of technological competence in building even safer automobiles, the next few decades will see much greater emphasis on improving the quality of both roads and drivers. These are by far the greatest areas of potential improvement and this will be increasingly so in the years ahead if we expect to make significant gains in reducing highway deaths and injuries.

Automotive engineers and scientists also will be seeking ways to design cars with greater simplicity in many areas. This will make them easier to build, less dependent on periodic maintenance to retain a high level of performance, and easier and less costly to maintain and service.

Of all fields of advancing technology, none is more important to the automobile industry than that of materials and fabricating processes. The next few decades will see the birth of new alloys and non-metallic materials with performance far surpassing that of traditional metals—and, hopefully, at lower costs.

Some of the most critical problems facing the automobile industry today (such as vehicle safety, automotive emissions, quality, durability, repairability, and rising costs) could be resolved or eased substantially with breakthroughs in the materials field. Accelerated advances in material technology during the next few decades will open up new avenues for improving the automobile and for developing new concepts encompassing both design and propulsion.

Transportation Needs

With respect to the over-all transportation system in which the automobile operates, we must recognize that America is a nation of massive transportation requirements, and these needs will become even greater in the future. Our total transportation system must be able to handle a large number of people and a large volume of goods—and in our metropolitan areas this must be handled in a comparatively limited space.

More effective urban transportation systems are a particularly critical challenge. The engineer-manager has the problem of deciding the proper mix of transportation modes to fit the future needs of his city, and no two cities have the same requirements. He also must consider the factors of speed and cost, as well as such additional items as land use, noise, air pollution, visual aesthetics and, highly important, the convenience and desires of passengers.

In analyzing our transportation needs of the future, we cannot limit our thinking to the metropolitan areas of today. We must also take into account those medium-sized cities which will be growing to full metropolitan status during the next twenty or thirty years.

We also must have the vision to dream of completely new concepts of planning for the future. In the past, cities generally grew up like Topsy, with all of the problems associated with add-on and piecemeal solutions. Some experts have proposed that we start new cities from scratch out away from present urban areas—cities designed for systematic and orderly expansion.

The Future Megalopolis

We should be giving serious consideration to the megalopolis: the population concentrations which soon will stretch almost solidly, for example, from Washington to Boston; and from Milwaukee to Chicago, Detroit and Cleveland. Providing the needs of these areas for high-speed transportation both on the ground and in the air will require the best talent and ingenuity that the transportation industry and society can command.

These are some of the technological changes in which we expect the motor vehicle industry to play a key role.

The future effects of technology will be most obvious in such areas as products, materials, and processes. Even more significant will be the impact on management attitudes as they relate both to the management of physical resources and of people.

We must recognize that management skills and concepts are under the same pressures for change as activities in technical, economic, political, and social fields. It is imperative, therefore, that advances in management stay ahead of the rapidly changing forces of our society if business and industry are to achieve maximum efficiency. Managers must be kept abreast of these changes and of the evolving tools of their profession.

In addition to technological change, there are other major factors with which the professional manager will have to contend in the years ahead—not only in our industry, but also in other areas of the business world.

American business will continue to operate in a highly volatile and dynamic environment. We can expect even tougher competition for the consumer dollar from an increasing variety of goods and services produced both here and overseas. Maintaining a satisfactory cost-price-profit balance will continue to be a crucial issue facing business management in the years ahead.

Perhaps the most severe discipline faced by American business, however, comes from the consumer. The traditional concepts of what the consumer is, what he wants, and what he will accept in terms of a product, must undergo continuing analysis and modification.

Greater professionalism in marketing is an absolute must. Marketing must be viewed not only as the end result of our efforts but, more important, as a critical element in the original planning of product programs. We must be as sophisticated in the art of marketing as we are in the areas of science, engineering, and finance.

Managers must learn to read the future more accurately and to anticipate the trends of business and the changing preferences of customers. The rewards for right decisions and the penalties for wrong ones continue to increase.

In working toward this objective, it is particularly important that businesses look at every phase of their operations from the other end of the horn—in terms of what the customer really wants, needs, and expects from his product. Such a continuing and accurate reading of the consumer voice is a vital requirement for designing and building that product or creating that service which provides the customer with a good return on *his* investment and, in turn, provides the company with a good return on *its* investment.

Physical Distribution

An area with great potential for increasing customer satisfaction and reducing costs is that of physical distribution. This has been a neglected stepchild of business administration, yet it probably constitutes the largest single item of cost in modern business. This includes much more than the base cost of transportation, from raw materials to finished products. It also involves such items as the cost of transit damage, as well as excessive inventories and storage facilities which must be maintained at plants and dealerships if the distribution system is not highly efficient. Physical distribution will be a major area of attention for business managers in the years ahead.

The growing trend toward more government regulation will be another key pressure point for the manager of tomorrow's business. In our increasingly complex society, there are many problem fields in which the full cooperation of business and government are required. At the same time, there are many areas in which the competitive and profit-motivated free enterprise system continues to offer substantially more potential for progress than could be provided by government.

Unnecessary government regulations tend to reduce incentives for new ideas, efficient operations and progress. The challenge is to develop a cooperative, workable relationship which will allow these two important segments of our society to contribute most effectively, whether separately or in partnership, to the continuing progress of the nation.

Role of the Manager

I have attempted to outline some of the challenges and opportunities facing the business enterprise. To a large degree, these challenges provide shape and substance to the role which the manager will play in the operation of the business world of tomorrow.

The future of American business, however, will not be based primarily on more sophisticated technology or improved marketing or financial competence. Success, in the final analysis, will depend on people. We will need better trained people for the more complex tasks of tomorrow, better trained people to insure a continued flow of new ideas and improvements, better trained people to manage most effectively both our physical and human resources.

Of paramount importance is the need for a new language of communications—a more effective language of motivation and common purpose—between management and employee. The industrial employee today is vastly different from his counterpart of even a few years ago. He is more affluent and independent. But, there has been a loss in pride of workmanship among some industrial employees. All of these changes have been reflected in a dramatic recent rise in absenteeism and turnover rates.

We must find new ways of reinstilling in the minds of each employee his importance as an individual and his importance to the success of the business. Individual creativity and initiative are valuable assets. They must be stimulated and challenged productively.

By far our most important priority in seeking further efficiency is the develop- of capable management personnel. These are the men and women who must decide which ideas and which innovations hold the greatest potential. These are the men and women who, through their knowledge and their example, can motivate, inspire, and lead people to accomplish the great tasks which lie ahead.

Management Decisions

Not too many years ago, many management decisions were made on the basis of experience—or as we used to say, by the seat of our pants. Those days are gone forever. The rapidity of change which is taking place from one generation to another, literally from one year to another, makes reliance on past history for management decisions almost as treacherous as quicksand.

More of the changes we will experience will not be of the traditional, predictable type which flow logically from past experience. Rather, they will be what Peter Drucker has called "discontinuities"—striking disruptions to an otherwise orderly state of affairs.

Certainly, experience is a valuable guide but the status quo deserves no reverence. Rather, it should be viewed as the starting point from which to move to higher plateaus of accomplishment.

It should be emphasized that sound and efficient management of American business is the foundation for the future progress of this nation. More than at any time in our history, the manager of tomorrow must be a professional—both in terms of technical competence and human understanding.

As he moves up the ladder of responsibility, the manager must develop an increasing understanding of the interrelationships of the many disciplines of his business. These include such areas as engineering, manufacturing feasibility, costs, trends in consumer preferences and market potential, legal and public relations implications and, increasingly important, the effects of government policies on the operations of our business. We need managers who perform their assignments within a framework of understanding of the effects of the use of their products on the total environment. In addition, we need managers who have a social consciousness which leads them to participate in seeking solutions to the major challenges of our society.

Tomorrow's manager must have the ability to understand and stimulate change. He must be receptive to new ideas and methods. He must have not only the ability to manage change, but also the ability and flexibility to adapt to the effects of change more quickly.

Change is the essence of progress. But its magnitude—the sheer speed with with which change is rushing toward us—can overwhelm us unless we are prepared for it intellectually and emotionally. To meet this challenge will require a philosophy of business and technical progress which is compatible with the clearly emerging economic, political, social, and human requirements of our future society.

America has demonstrated the capability and the vision to send man out among the stars. We have equally exciting and formidable tasks to perform in creating an even better way of life for people here on earth. As it has in the past, American business will be a dynamic, driving force in moving this nation forward to new levels of accomplishment in the decades ahead.

44

The Value Issue of Business

Alvar O. Elbing, Jr.

Perhaps more than at any time in its economic history, the United States is faced with what can be called "the value issue of business." Questions are regularly raised in the public forum concerning business and its relationship to problems such as unemployment, racial discrimination, social conformity, automobile safety, air and water pollution, and collusion. The very raising of these questions, however, brings with it some explicit or implicit theoretical concept of the nature of the relationship between man's values and his economic activity. To understand the value issue of business, it is necessary to understand what concepts the businessman brings to these problems.

Economics As a Value System

The basic concepts which are commonly accepted today of the relationship between economic activity and values are a direct outgrowth of a formulation laid down by Adam Smith some 200 years ago. "Capitalism," "free enterprise," or, as it is commonly labeled, "the classical economic model," is the basic philosophical rationale to which most businessmen turn when faced with social value questions. To understand the businessman's approach to "the value issue," we need to understand the relationship between the classical economic rationale and social value questions.

From its inception, the classical economic model has combined a "scientific" theory—a descriptive-predictive theory about the exchange of economic units—and an ethical theory—a theory of social values. Moreover, from its inception, it has offered both its scientific and social value theories not only as theories of how economic activity and social values *ought* to be worked out, but as theories of how they *will,* more or less automatically, be worked out. The model presents the economic marketplace as a self-regulating device, at both the scientific and ethical levels.

Briefly, the important assumptions of this economic model are that the production of goods and services in the pursuit of self-interest are automatically regulated by the interactions of the marketplace. Those items which are "best," "most wanted," "least expensive," and so on will prevail, driving the others from the market. The ultimate result of such competition is the economic good of the nation. This is the mechanism behind the descriptive-predictive aspect of the economic model. The workings of this system have been the

"The Value Issue of Business" from *Behavioral Decisions in Organizations,* pp. 781–789. Copyright 1970 by Scott, Foresman and Company. Reprinted by permission of the publisher and Alvar O. Elbing, Jr. This chapter was prepared with Carol J. Elbing. It is a summary of some of the major arguments which are fully developed in Elbing, Alvar O., Jr., and Carol J. Elbing, *The Value Issue of Business,* McGraw-Hill Book Company, 1967.

subject of continuing discussion among economists and, indeed, is a topic basic to their discipline. It is to this rationale that the businessman tends to turn when confronted with questions about the relationship of his actions to social values.

Confusion about the two aspects of the economic model—the scientific and the ethical—underlies many of the difficulties facing businessmen as they attempt to deal with the value issue of business. Social value problems are frequently taken for granted, on the assumption that they are worked out automatically in the economic exchange of goods and services. How does the economic model stand as a social value rationale as well as a descriptive-predictive model?

Economics As "Moral"

One rationale for dealing with the relationship between economic activity and social values is the notion that greater social good is directly concomitant with greater economic good. As Charles Wilson, former Secretary of Defense, is so often quoted as having said, "What is good for business is good for the country." The implicit social value theory here is that the value issue of business is dealt with automatically by the marketplace, in the same manner by which it works out the problems of economic exchange. This rationale thus posits economics as a moral system.

The difficulty with this argument is that, of course, the marketplace does not arbitrate all values optimally in the same sense that it optimally arbitrates the exchange of goods. The marketplace is neither democratic, objective, scientific, or rational. Furthermore, it cannot be assumed that the marketplace even touches on all social value problems: many important business value issues are not affected by marketplace exchange. The quality of life in an organization, for example, is one value issue of business not directly arbitrated by the marketplace. The effects of multinational firms on the cultures of the world is another. Thus, whatever the usefulness of the marketplace as an optimum economic regulator, it is no guaranteed device for the automatic working out of social value problems. The assumption does not stand up to critical analysis that any economic system insures moral or social values by its very nature, so that value issues need not be of active and direct concern.

Thus, even if we could substantiate that the greatest profit to business brought about the greatest national wealth and the greatest *economic* well-being to the greatest number of individuals, the value issue is not thereby disposed. It is not justifiable to treat the entire value issue of business only by pointing to some standard of economic well-being. Although the economic model is a useful explanation of the exchange of economic units, it must be concluded that it is inadequate if taken as a social or moral value rationale for business. The surface of the value issue is barely scratched by application of the rationale of the nonobjective and nonrepresentative marketplace arbitrating the production of goods and services, or by reference to a broad general index of national economic level of activity.

Economics As "Amoral"

One way of attempting to dispose of the logical difficulties of the economic model as a social value rationale is to disengage it from all claims to its being a moral philosophy, and define it as amoral, having no reference to value issues. It is advised by some that the economic model should claim only technical or scientific utility and be judged in such terms only. Far from purporting to deal with behavior, values, or with the general relationship of economic activity to values, the economic model, conceived as amoral, claims to deal solely with economic man, economic events, and economic ends, and to take as given the relationship of economic activity to social values. The economist Frank Knight (1965), for example, has said: "The science (of economics) abstracts from *error* much as mechanics does from friction. . . . Analysis must begin with individual economic conduct, hence, with the man isolated from society. . . ."

Economic data of all kinds are thus declared to be separate from any value connotations. Whenever "man" is referred to in such a model, it is not social man or moral man or the total man, but an abstract "economic" man, who is presumed, for the purposes of economic discussion, to operate rationally in terms of purely economic factors. Similarly, in terms of this amoral model, economic activity is abstracted from the complex of human and social moral actions and viewed narrowly as a purely economic or technical pursuit. The implicit claim is merely that, *given* the economic system, the model serves a descriptive-predictive function.

It is commonly assumed that such a model of economic activity, claiming only technical or scientific utility and asking to be judged in such terms only, is entirely value free. But however much an amoral model of economic activity may be desired, such a model is as fraught with value assumptions as a broad social philosophy. At first it may seem that such an amoral model has narrowed itself to a strictly scientific theory, has avoided entanglements with value issues, and has placed value questions in a realm separate from economics and business, presumably to be dealt with by other disciplines. In actuality, it has not accomplished those feats at all. Inherent in such a model is the assumption that economic actions lead to consequences which are, if not positively good, at least socially or morally harmless. Thus, far from being value-free, the model fosters an assumption about the relationship between economic activities and values—the assumption that the two can, with impunity, be considered in isolation.

This value assumption is the most undermining of the value issue of business. While it is conceivable that we might generally isolate, with social and moral impunity, a concept of mechanics from a concept of friction, it is not conceivable that we could generally isolate economics from social value issues. Economic action does not in fact exist separately from social or moral action, any more than mechanical action exists separately from friction. Economic value is always a social value, always interacting with other values in the arena of human action, and strongly affected by and affecting other social values. Obviously it is legitimate to declare—in any field—that for certain technical problems it is useful to artifically set aside social value considerations as given. In a value context, however, any attempt to isolate economic and social considerations is not realistic.

The Shortcomings of Economics As a Value System

The economic model blocks active work on vital business value issues in that it fosters a groundless optimism. In the moral version of the model, the marketplace is imagined to be an automatic device for working out not only economic but social value questions and for insuring not only material but social progress. In the amoral model, the abstraction of social value issues from economic considerations fosters another sort of optimism, the optimism that somehow economic processes are of such nature that they can go on revolutionizing society without disrupting human values.

Both the moral and amoral economic models foster the attitude that the value issue of business is of merely peripheral concern. When business processes are broadly considered as automatically worked out in the marketplace or as inherently morally justifiable or legitimately amoral, value problems are seen as a mere side issue. Once social value is conceived as a side issue, an over-simplified formula may seem adequate to the magnitude of the social value problem. Values and business can then be discussed in terms of easy platitudes, or the entire issue can be reduced to a strictly legal matter, or it can be set aside as a matter for personal conscience.

Business As a Social System

The fundamental reason why the value issue cannot be satisfactorily formulated within a purely economic model is that the business institution is not merely an economic-technical system. It is a social system as well. Indeed, economic activity *is* social activity. Every business act, whether or not it has direct economic connotations and ramifications, is a social act in that it is a social response to other human beings. Even purely "technical" and "economic" acts have their social dimension. Business produces not only economic consequences—goods and services, profit and wealth (and the social ramifications of these economic consequences)—it also produces a great variety of important social consequences. Its moral nature derives from that fact. The value issue of business derives from the pervasive social (hence moral) nature of business, and cannot be extrapolated merely from its abstracted economic functions. Thus the full scope of the value issue of business can be understood and formulated adequately only when it is viewed within a social framework which includes all the social effects of business action.

Business and the Individual

Because the firm is a social system, its effect on the individual goes well beyond economics, influencing the individual's sense of self and his functioning in the firm, family, and community. When the firm is recognized as a social system as well as a technical-economic system, the values of individuals are seen as growing, in part, out of social interaction within that system. The firm is thus recognized as a basic *source* of individual values as well as an arena for their enactment, affecting the individual's own evaluation of himself, his value outlook toward his world, and in turn, the sort of influence he will have on the values of that world.

Business and Other Groups

The relationships among various business groups—managers, workers, unions, stockholders, consumers, government agencies, schools of business, and so on—generate intergroup attitudes, social trends, and values far beyond those of merely economic import. Norms, goals, and values are formed within groups and solidified through intergroup action. Group action thus results not only in economic change but change in the social groups themselves. When business is viewed solely as an economic system in terms of the traditional economic model, it appears logical that its only responsibility is toward one group, its capital investors. However, when the various groups within the business institution are also recognized as claimants, all intergroup action, being social action, is seen to involve *reciprocal* social responsibility.

Business and Society in the United States

The influence of business on society as a whole in the United States extends so far beyond merely economic considerations that the United States is often characterized as a distinctly business culture. The relationship between business and society is not primarily economic, nor is it primarily determined by the marketplace. When business is recognized as a vast social system, it is also recognized that a vast array of its social transactions, little affected by the marketplace, is as primary a function of business as its economic transactions. The social value implications of this cultural climate go far beyond what can be formulated in terms of the classical economic framework. The climate of this vast network of social transactions is a significant aspect of the characteristically American culture.

Business and Foreign Societies

The relationship of business to foreign societies must also be viewed within a social framework. American business in foreign countries influences not only the economic life of the world, but the entire social-political climate of a precarious international scene. Foreign trade today is often justified—as it was in the eighteenth century—in terms of national wealth and power, with the added boon of economic development for other nations. Now, as then, economic progress is equated with social progress. Yet the relationship between social values and economic forces should not be assumed *a priori,* but should be subjected to broad social analysis, in keeping with the fact that business abroad does have critical social impact beyond its economic impact. Only by examining within a social framework our business relationships with other countries can we begin to assess how economic values relate to other crucial social values.

In summary, any attempt to deal with the *value* issue of business on any level—at the level of the individual, of groups, of domestic society, or at the level of the broad international scene—must begin by placing business in a social framework, rather than in the traditional economic framework. Whatever the utility may be of viewing the social relationships of business in narrowly economic terms for specified technical purposes, the traditional economic framework is useless for the purpose of formulating values. It merely distorts and reduces the value issue. The relationship between economic and other social values in society requires broad social analysis, rather than mere economic analysis, in keeping with the broad social influence of business.

A New Social Value Theory for Business

We have concluded that the value issue of business is distorted and reduced when formulated in terms of the economic model. Let us now state explicitly the fundamentals of a *new social value theory* to replace the social value theory of the economic model. All of the foregoing discussion, of course, has been an implicit reformulation of theory, but a concise statement of basic principles is now possible on the basis of the foregoing discussion, and may serve as a useful reference point.

The first principle of a social value theory based on a recognition of business as a social system is that the moral nature of business inheres in all of its social acts, and is therefore pervasive. The social value rationale of the economic model is a claim that the moral nature of business inheres in its production of economic goods, services, and national wealth (and in directly resulting social goods). A value rationale derived from a social model is a recognition that the moral nature of business inheres in all of its social, not merely economic, acts and effects. The social influence of business is seen to be truly extensive when it is recognized that every act—even every "economic" act of business—is a social act. When it is recognized that every social act implies moral value, it can be seen that the value issue of business is pervasive.

The second principle of the theory is that business-social transactions at all levels are value arbitrations. The social value rationale of the economic model assumes the marketplace to be the arbiter of social values, but it has been demonstrated that the marketplace does not and cannot achieve such a role. It is clear that the social values of business are, in fact, worked out by all of the social actions and transactions of the entire business system, not merely those of the marketplace. All choices and acts regarding production, finance, advertising, marketing—all relationships with workers, stockholders, buyers, sellers, consumers, government—work out the value issue, not merely marketplace choices and acts.

The third principle of the theory is that because the social effects of business go beyond the economic, economic measures cannot be used as indexes for other social values. The social value rationale of the economic model makes the implicit claim that it is feasible to measure the social value of business in economic terms, and to take for granted all other social values as parallel; and it makes only economic factors explicit while all other social factors are implicit or taken as given. A value theory based on a social model recognizes that, in order to assess the social effects of business, it is essential to measure them explicitly.

The fourth principle of the theory is that the social value issue is as important as the economic issue of business. The social value rationale of the economic model assumes business to be an economic-technical system and the social value issue to be peripheral. A value rationale based on a social model recognizes that business inescapably functions as a social system, and that social value issues cannot be subordinated. Recognized as a social system with pervasive social and moral influence, business cannot be written off as amoral, nor can economic considerations be said to be the main issue of business and social and moral value concerns as side issues. While it is perfectly true that the economic profitability of the firm is essential to its ability to function at all, it is just as true that its overall "social" profitability is what justifies its existence in the first place.

Conclusions

Two hundred years after the first Industrial Revolution, business has become a continual revolutionizing force in U. S. society and in those societies with whom the U. S. does business. The danger is that so long as the rationale of the economic model is the working social value theory, economic value will continue to be the driving revolutionary force, and technological means will determine social ends. If we are interested in social values, we are concerned that the growth and development of society and of the individuals within it be commensurate with technological revolution and business advance. Business being a social system, a social value framework which includes criteria from all of the social sciences, not just economics, must be used to assess the social growth of business.

If we are concerned with the value issue of business, we are concerned that it be an active field of direct inquiry, and we are also concerned that the best methods available be used in the pursuit of such inquiry. Once freed from the assumptions of the economic model, which attempts to guarantee that values will be worked out automatically, the value issue of business is seen as a matter *requiring* investigation. Yet the concept of objective systematic investigation, of "method," in the value realm is not a commonly accepted one.

There has been skepticism about the actual feasibility of "method" in the value realm. Certainly if by "method" we mean such popular concepts of method as those of the physical sciences, technology, mathematics, or computer programming, it may well be that the concept of method for social value inquiry is inappropriate. However, if by "method" we mean the most critical procedures available pertinent to the question of concern, the concept of method is not only appropriate but essential to value inquiry.

Some method is bound to be used in every inevitable encounter with the value issue of business. Insofar as our moral aspirations are high, our standards for methods of pursuing them must also be high. Certainly, business being a social system, methods from all of the social sciences, not just economics, must be used to deal with business value questions. They are essential if the value issue of business is to become an active field of study commensurate with its significance. If our most rigorous critical methods are merely harnessed to technological means and to the market, they will assuredly run away with ultimate ends.

Not only must interest in the social value issue of business be translated into direct critical inquiry, it must be translated into the very practical process of decision making. Values inhere in every stage of that process, so that the question is not whether we deal with value issues in decision making, but whether we deal with them by design or default. Viewed in a social framework, however, it is clear that the inherent value issue in decision making is by no means vital only to the business manager. It is through the decision making of all citizens that social values are made concrete in a business society.

References

Elbing, Alvar O. Jr., and Carol J. Elbing. *The Value Issue of Business*. McGraw-Hill, 1967.

England, George W. "Personal Value Systems of American Managers." *Academy of Management Journal,* March 1967.

Freedman, Robert. "The Challenge of Business Ethics." *Atlanta Economic Review,* May 1962.

Galbraith, John K. *The Affluent Society*. Houghton Mifflin, 1958.

Heilbroner, Robert. "The Future of Capitalism." *Commentary,* April 1966.

Knight, Frank H. "Understanding Society through Economics." *American Behavioral Scientist,* September 1965.

Leighton, Dorothea, *et al. The Character of Danger*. Basic Books, 1963.

Parsons, Talcott, and Edward A. Shils, eds. *Toward a General Theory of Action*. Harvard University Press, 1951.

Schein, Edgar H. "Organizational Socialization and the Profession of Management." *Industrial Management Review,* Winter 1968.

Whyte, William F. Jr. *The Organization Man*. Doubleday, 1956.

45

The Corporation and the Community: Realities and Myths

Frank H. Cassell

It is now twenty years since a board member of one of the largest Chicago banks proposed that the bank employ some Negroes. The board chairman, aghast at the suggestion, asked if the director didn't realize that then *they* would be sitting on the same toilet seats. The board turned down the proposal.

At the close of the decade of the 1960s the Chicago banks, including the one involved in that incident, passed that hat for $815,000 to finance a black "think tank," originated and headed by some of the most militant black leaders in Chicago.

That is change. It is change perhaps even broader in its implications than some of the contributing businessmen may yet realize, for it departs radically from the usual "safe" participations of business symbolized by Junior Chamber of Commerce man-of-the-year contests and the Community Fund charities administered by whites for blacks. It would be incorrect to interpret the support of the think tank as reflecting a trend in business in general. But its structure and support does imply that a number of businessmen, among them men considered leaders of the Chicago business community, have had their community stance affected by profound social changes in the city. And it is significant that it is in the historically conservative banking industry that such a change comes into focus.

Chicago, like other large American cities, is undergoing a painful metamorphosis. On the one hand, it is engaged in a vast effort to rebuild the central city. Billions of dollars worth of new steel and glass high-rise office and apartment buildings are going up. The banking and insurance industries have been in the forefront of this building boom.

Simultaneously, great changes are taking place in the character of life in the city. Chicago lost population during the 1960s and the rate was speeded in the last half of the decade; its population has decreased to pre-depression levels. A third of the remaining population is black; 56 percent of elementary school pupils and 48 percent of the high school pupils are black, many of them increasingly angry at the system which they see as designed to keep them in second class roles. Black unemployment figures continue to be more than twice as high as white, and far higher than that among the young people. The jobs which the burgeoning black population might fill are fleeing to the suburbs; the metropolitan area outside the city gained 277,000 jobs from 1957 to 1966, but the city of Chicago lost 48,000 jobs. It is difficult or impossible for

Frank H. Cassell, "The Corporation and Community: Realities and Myths," pp. 11–20. *MSU Business Topics*, Autumn 1970. Reprinted by permission of the publisher, Division of Research, Graduate School of Business Administration, Michigan State University.

many blacks to follow the jobs because of housing discrimination in the suburbs and the great costs of commuting long distances.

These economic facts, plus a profound change in the feelings of the black community—growth in black consciousness, search for a black identity, regard for one's heritage, and reaction to white rejection in housing and school patterns—are making for a qualitative difference in the problems of the city. The Kerner Commission warning that we are drifting toward two separate societies, one white and one black, a sort of indigenous apartheid, has not altered the drift. Some say, including both white leaders and black militants, that it is only a matter of time.

Separateness may be much further advanced than many of us are willing to admit. Separateness has gone a long way when a militant black leader in Chicago attempts to roll down the curtain and not permit whites to enter black neighborhoods at night. The suggestion was made by the Rev. C. T. Vivian, Executive Director of "Think Tank," at a moment of deep fury in the black communities over a raid by district attorney's police on a Black Panther apartment, a raid in which two Panther leaders were killed. The Rev. Vivian withdrew his angry proposal for a curfew, but not before the whites got the message.

The political ferment is reflected in the high schools, too, where black students are increasingly strident—and sometimes threatening—about the lack of quality of their schools, about what they call irrelevancy of the traditional school program, and about the shortage of black teachers and administrators who, they believe, can understand the black perspective better than whites. In some areas this has led to demands for community control of schools, through little boards of education responsible to the people of an area rather than to a central hierarchy. In other areas, it has meant turmoil in the schools, particularly at times when community tension is high. In most areas, disillusion with school leads many black young people to drop out (or to be pushed out), which increases the unemployment problem, already a staggering one among poorly trained young blacks. White-managed industries in and near the ghettos feel the effects of this kind of unrest. If they fill their work forces from the area, they find the discontent transplanted into factories; some first-line white supervisors leave because they fear for their own safety.

These forces add impetus to the flight of higher income whites from the city. Those who stay behind are more and more determined to preserve their turf and not let the blacks cross over from "the other side"—the other side of the city, or the neighborhood, or the street that has been a traditional dividing line between white homes and black. Where this has occurred in other smaller cities the remaining whites have sought to preserve their political power, giving only token appointments to blacks. This too has heightened political tension. The whites don't see the fact that the vital, pulsating new force of the cities is a rapid increase in determination by blacks to have a say in their own destiny. There is an increase in strong, savvy black leadership, including men of education and experience in coping with both the militants and with recalcitrant white leadership. They want a share of the power, and they are going to get it. The choice as to how they get it is pretty much up to the whites.

An Example of Business Response

It is in this context that Chicago's Strategy Center, the think tank, was born. Basically it provides business support for "the black communities to establish its own priorities," in the words of one of its supporters. At the Center, staff will be all black. It will use the funds for research and training, conducting surveys to establish needs, assisting with budgets, and taking packaged proposals to the city and federal government and to foundations for funding. There seem to be no grandiose ideas about training for the use of power; instead, the focus will be on the economic, educational, and health problems that plague the ghetto. Presumably the Center will not engage in politics, although some of the programs it devises will have to be promoted politically by someone.

The Center is being supported for a variety of motives—some lofty, some not. One of the motives is the hard-headed practical need to face reality. Planners think that by 1980 blacks will have the majority vote in Chicago and that a black mayor may be elected in that year.

Some of the most influential of the white contributors probably clearly perceive the need for an avenue for sharing power with the black community and would like it to be an avenue where they can erect some of the traffic signals. The Center, if it works well, can be a valuable training locale for black leaders. Leadership has been diffuse in the black community; it has been hard to know who to listen to. There is some feeling that the Center can be a structure for the white power structure to deal with.

Others are perhaps more concerned with safeguarding their investment in the city and are thinking about the business climate of Chicago under a black administration. Business has no intention of abandoning its home base, and there are those new buildings to prove it. Some business supporters of the think tank see their contributions as sort of an insurance policy for all that plate glass.

Those are some of the white views of the Strategy Center, and they are a mixed bag, indeed. The black views may be just as mixed. There is no consensus that the people running the Center really are Chicago's black leaders. Some say the Center people are just being paid off by whites. There is much skepticism about the nature of business support. (One old-line black leader, not involved in the Strategy Center, wondered, for example, if the whites were "doing the right thing for the wrong reasons.") They wonder what will happen when the black-proposed solutions to problems don't coincide with white solutions.

There are, indeed, many pitfalls, and we don't know whether the Strategy Center will ever be able to change any of these facts the banker-supporter was talking about. Among the pitfalls are several financial ones: the Center still has not been given tax exempt status because it is not clear how it can avoid political action entirely, the businessmen have set up "fiscal safeguards for the disbursement of money" although they say they are not policing the programs, and there is no present provision for continued business support of the Center once the initial funds run out. There are other pitfalls, too; it seems inevitable that there will be considerable infighting, a good deal of rhetoric, and the destruction of some false hopes. One big question mark centers around Mayor Daley, without whom nothing much happens in Chicago, but who has taken a "hands off" approach to the Center.

Real Significance

But despite the conflicting views about the things that can go wrong, the establishment of the Center has real significance. It is a facing of the reality that blacks do have problems that concern us all and that blacks want a greater share in decision making to solve them. It is a recognition of the need for thinking and planning and understanding that you can't operate a society in change on an ad hoc basis. At the very least, the Center does give status to a point of view, a black perspective which black leaders have always insisted is simply not being heard. If the Center works, it can be a step toward an orderly transference of power to a soon-to-be-realized black majority in the city. If it doesn't work, the inevitable changes will be less orderly. Either way, it is a dramatic departure from the traditional business method of dealing with community problems, one very much out of character for conventional business organization and operation.

Traditional Business Response to Change

The mechanisms of business, like all authoritarian institutions, are not well suited for coping with basic change outside its product markets. Business has no strong internal mechanism for criticism of its performance in the community. Unlike an institution like Congress, it has no constituency that votes it in or out on the basis of its success in community life. Its organization is designed for stability, for continuity, not for change.

The conventional business policy has been to place the bets on those in power, people like Mayor Daley, because they seem to give the best promise of stability as against the more menacing leaders who want to change the status quo. Where the power structure has had to give way before powerful underlying forces, the strategy has usually consisted of participating in the least risky ventures, minimizing the risk with strings attached to the money contributed in order to control the speed and direction of the advance, and supporting politically only those dissidents who could be counted upon to merge with the establishment. (Martin Luther King was invited by business executives to talk in Winnetka, Illinois, not before Selma and Bull Connor's cattle prods, but after his "I have a dream" sermon at the March on Washington, a march the executives did not make.) However, the conventional business policy for action in the community has led to supporting the forces of reaction, the establishment, the entrenched political forces rather than the forces which accommodate change and prepare the way for new leadership. The Chicago Urban League is an interesting case in point. It is only a few years ago that business supporters of the League could have met in a telephone booth; the League was trying to cause the schools to change. But in 1970, 2,500 business leaders and others attended a luncheon to pay homage to the retiring Urban League director. A very safe event.

The interpretation of this by the underclass could hardly be that the establishment was in their favor. And when company policies began to change, it was to support organizations which, though useful, had themselves sometimes lost touch with the times and the realities and the people. The old-line groups working for change got support only when newer, much more radical groups appeared and threatened.

Conventional corporate policy is based essentially upon a stable environment with change occurring only at a rate sufficient to be easily absorbed. Because business mistrusts unorthodoxy, it also mistrusts the "bubble up" theory of participative democracy, of community action programs which have been spawned in the cities under the sponsorship of the Office of Economic Opportunity. (This policy began to be abandoned in the closing months of the Johnson administration and has been buried by the Nixon administration.)

The businessman is a top-down person. That is how he is selected, how he is trained, and how he is developed in an environment which is essentially authoritarian and carefully structured. Important decision making is limited to the few at the top (despite the years of effort by Peter Drucker and Douglas MacGregor to change things); and those at the bottom are expected to comply. In some magical way hierarchical position seems to confer wisdom regardless of knowledge or experience; those down the line with less status have less wisdom and competence.

The Conventional Stand

The conventional business stand is in favor of strong top-down government as against grass roots neighborhood decision making because the former is perceived as the most "efficient" way to govern. This concept leads the businessman to work through established organizations which are essentially top-down, such as the charity and settlement house boards. The typical structure of a Community Fund parallels the business organization; in fact, it is often designed by business consultants whose object is efficiency, not necessarily relevancy. Attempts of black people and poor people to participate in the fund allocation process are resisted bitterly, much as some school superintendents resent meddling by "outsiders" in the affairs of the schools. Most important, these money allocations are directed to preserving the structure and the underlying assumptions of those who control it; they are steered away from those in the black or Spanish-speaking community who would use the money to develop political power to challenge the establishment and change the system.

This is similar to the Community Action Organizations which were converted into nodules of political power and were opposed alike by northern big city mayors, southern governors, businessmen, and the established federal bureaucracies. The Community Action Program (CAP) was designed deliberately to skirt the established organizations because they had shown no particular talent or interest in solving the problems of hard core poverty or unemployment. It was thought that those experienced in the condition of poverty might contribute to its solution. No more upsetting measure could have been devised, and before the nodules could grow into power centers they were effectively squelched by the passage of the Green Amendment. And order has been restored with the new (or old) federalism so that poverty funds and other funds for relieving the condition of the poor are channeled through the offices of the governors, from there to the mayors, and from there to the neighborhoods—the trickle down theory.

The distaste of the businessmen for doing business with those outside the established organizations is represented by the virtual failure of the Concentrated Employment Program of the U.S. Department of Labor which began in the latter part of the 1960s. The object of this effort was to link up indigenous leadership of the ghetto with other organizations both public and private to provide a job delivery system including outreach, job readiness training, remedial health care, not job survival skills leading to a job in private enterprise.

It was believed that if those who needed jobs, those who operated the employment market, and those who had the jobs to give, were put under one administrative tent, the whole operation would be more efficient, duplication of functions would be reduced, and understandings would be developed among employers, government, and the poor which would lead to productive and cooperative relationships. Nothing of the kind happened. The Community Action Programs at the grass roots let the employers know in no uncertain terms that they were not liked in the slums; nor did they think private enterprise had much to offer in the line of social improvement. The employer reciprocated. He was not interested in revolutionaries and incompetents; furthermore, he didn't want to get mixed up with government bureaucracy—meaning the federal government.

About the same time the Labor Department developed the idea of contracting out to private enterprises the complete package of training and job development, with the exception that the community action people would refer unemployed people to the job or training openings. And this didn't really work either. An example serves to illustrate this point. In a large city in Connecticut, a defense contractor received a contract under a Manpower Administration grant from the Labor Department to train ghetto people for employment in the various industries in the town. The defense contractor's office was located at one end of a large building in the slum area. At the other end of the building was the Community Action Program. A door between the two ends of the building was locked, having never been opened during the tenure of the tenants despite the fact that the CAP and the defense contractor were supposed to cooperate in putting people into the training program and to work.

In city after city this is the case. The employer prefers to do the job himself even if he does not have the expertise or the relationship with the slum. This he is doing under the National Alliance of Businessmen. No doubt he is more efficient in organizing to do the job of employment than the people at the bottom of the job scale. This reluctance of the businessman to share authority with others in the community represents a deep desire for order, the need to control his situation (as he has been taught in business schools), and the need to assure the continuity of the firm. It reflects also the public relations man's approach to things to make sure the numbers are counted and the credit goes where it belongs—to the company, as in the case of the National Alliance of Businessmen.

A Philosophical Gap

More importantly the inability of community action people, ghetto militants, and business to work together represents more than political differences, although this is a factor; more than the businessman's distaste for long hair and blue jeans, more than his resentment of having to share power with people he feels have not earned the honor by hard work. It represents a huge philosophical gulf. In the Connecticut situation the employer said that he did not cooperate with the CAP because the people whom the CAP sent for training did not fit the jobs and that they (the CAP) raised their expectations too high. The CAP people said that the employers did not have jobs which fit their people. Here is a conflict of tradition and of philosophy. The employer expects to reject people who are not qualified according to his standards. The individual, if not qualified, should adjust. This is the expectation of free private enterprise. The CAP people, however, expect the enterprise system to adjust to the people, that is, if they have no qualifications, make a job of some kind or redesign it and train the person to fill it. The enterprise system should help people realize their ambitions, even the lowliest of them. The company should serve people, not vice versa.

If one looks particularly closely at these arguments he will find that the CAP people are challenging the legitimacy of the private enterprise system. How can it be justified solely on the basis of profits? What about the welfare of people and the good of society? Does not business exist at the pleasure of the people? Should it not serve them? Would it not be better if business had a social purpose as its prime goal? Whether or not the businessman has sensed this, he has kept away from these people as much as possible.

A Corporate Dichotomy

The corporate ethos, regardless of the imperatives of community, is to make profits and not to produce social uplift. Social responsibility must always be an adjunct. Consequently, it is not reasonable to expect community relations to be the firm's specialization. It is equally unreasonable to expect the corporation to take the load of the community on its shoulders, or to expect it to be expert in solving such problems. Furthermore, if the corporation assumes this function it must then expect to live with the criticism which inevitably comes to all who would attempt to lead and influence social change, criticism which may affect it adversely in its product markets.

The realities are that the corporation faces two ways, inward and outward. Its inner core capitalizes upon the specialized skills of its managers and other employees to exploit markets. It is beyond the range of normal expectation that men expert in manufacturing and marketing will be equally expert in the political and social milieu of the outer environment. If the chairman of the firm is skilled in his ability to be persuasive with the commerce commission or relates well to black militants this is a bonus for the firm, but he is paid to make a profit. No matter how successful his community relations, he will not survive too many poor profit years.

Having to face both outward and inward leads to a dichotomizing of management. Over time individuals emerge who develop the characteristics which bring success in the outer environment, including interest in human beings, a capacity to understand political and social complexities, and above all the ability to exist in ambiguous situations. In contrast, those who live on the inside tend to work by plan, are often uneasy with politics, and are uncomfortable with ambiguity. In other words, specialization exerts itself to lead people either toward the inside of the corporation or toward the outside.

As time goes by a gap develops between the external and the internal people, much in the manner of the "growing apart" of the corporate labor relations people and the line operating people. In both cases there develop differences in viewpoint. The corporate labor relations people come to view the politics of elective leadership as they affect corporate collective bargaining strategy. This often places the labor relations people at odds with the internally oriented people whose lack of contact with the outside preserves a parochial view, often times a hard line which ignores the politics of power over which the firm has limited control.

In much the same way the corporation executives who face toward the community inevitably are confronted with the realities of a world which they cannot control. Employees can be fired, but not the community. Such executives often find themselves interpreting the outside to an unsympathetic internal management.

The people inside are often impatient with the tools of diplomacy and the complexities of social and political organization. The results of community activities cannot be chalked up neatly on the blackboard in the manner of so many automobiles produced per hour. The people operating on the inside, accustomed to operating within a structured and controlled environment, as contrasted to the uncontrolled community, have difficulty understanding why this outer world cannot be put in order.

Sufficient time has passed since business and industry have employed labor relations and community relations experts to suggest that these careers are not the roads to the top of the firm. When the promotion decisions are made, it is the person who has attended to the nitty gritty of selling, producing, or financing who gets the job. And this is entirely consistent with the object of the corporation, namely to make profits. As long as the goal of the firm is so perceived, the community relations function is likely to be secondary and correspondingly the level of skill and effort applied to it will lag behind the skill and effort devoted to the operation of the firm. In addition the evidence seems to be that men allocated by the corporation to handle the community relations of the corporation are not "main line" executives and consequently lack the prestige or power within the corporation to materially influence corporate policy. (In the case of companies which have taken on government contracts to train the hard core or to administer the Job Corps camps, the men assigned have not generally been main liners, and furthermore when cutbacks have occurred their reintegration into the main organization has either been accomplished with maximum difficulty or not at all. One large eastern firm which had held large government contracts to improve the skills of the poor was unable to effect the reintegration and tried to convert the government contracts division into an internal human-relations consulting division. It was not a success. The main divisions felt they could get along without internal human-relations consultants.)

Calculating the Riskiness of Community Involvement

Although the financing of the black "think tank" may be a portent of things to come insofar as corporate policy toward the community is concerned, business today is not generally geared to engaging in such high risk community relations. The businessman is sophisticated in the things he does well, namely managing financial and entrepreneurial risk. Community risk, however, is another matter. Typically he ranks his risk from high to low in a sort of cost-benefits relationship. At the low risk end of the community activity scale (high prestige) is the Community Fund, the settlement house, or a liaison relationship between his suburban church and a community organization in the city. He has substantial control; the results, being based upon the past, are predictable; the assignment is not overly time consuming; and he is not likely to find his name in the newspaper because of some rash act of the staff. But in today's terms the organization is not likely to be particularly relevant either.

At the high risk end of the scale, he might find himself participating in a privately financed, slum based and led model city-type program which challenges the established political and economic institutions to which the company he represents is linked. This is a situation which exists in Chicago today. A number of firms are supporting a community based program called Towards Responsible Freedom. The program is located in the Kenwood-Oakland section of the city. It is a self-help effort to create community structure and machinery to cope with the problems left untouched by the established political structure and government programs—including preparation for better jobs, improvement of the local schools, elimination of garbage in the streets, better law and order—and justice for the residents, renovation and improvement of housing, and self-developed local businesses. No money was allocated to the area by the federal Model Cities program.

The community organization known as KOCO includes just about everybody in the area including the leaders of the Black P Stone Nation, a street gang. It does not, however, include the local alderman. It does not include the local school people. Many of its leaders have at one time or another been in jail or prison. A chief organizer of KOCO, who is also a leader of the Black P Stone Nation, was charged with murder but later acquitted. KOCO is financed through the Community Renewal Society from the contributions of foundations, individual givers, and a few corporations—referred to collectively by the Chicago police as softheaded liberals who are financing revolution. The strings attached are minimal. During the past two years as KOCO has been getting under way, repeated police harassment of the organization generally has not frightened supporters into withholding their funds. But the police efforts have not helped to broaden the financial support either.

It is indeed significant that in the range of risk value, many Chicago corporations seem more willing to finance a "think tank" despite its often violent rhetoric than a community self development and self determination effort. Perhaps community action ranks higher on the risk scale than revolutionary speech, especially when the condition is that the speech must be non-political, in order to get tax deductible corporate contributions. After all, community self development effort may produce fundamental changes in the community.

The basic difference between the community fund and KOCO is that the businessman who supports KOCO does not have strings which he can pull if the neighborhood people get out of line. He has essentially given up his right to control as to how the money will be spent, and who will be employed. This is alien to the prudent businessman or the politician who needs to maintain control.

Whether it is the businessman or the established political structure, or old line unions, this kind of community activity is the ultimate in risk—though it may turn out that this is one of the few ways slum and ghetto people can be aided to enter the mainstream of American society through self-government and breaking down of colonialist control.

The evidence so far is that businessmen in general are not yet ready for this kind of long range political planning. Support of rhetoric, yes, as long as it is apolitical—action no. And in this they are joined by practically everybody in the organized structure from the president of the United States on down. The burgeoning black and brown communities, however, will continue to militate for involvement in the action. The "think tank" and the Community Renewal Society efforts in Kenwood-Oakland are among the very few efforts remaining where the underclass can have a say and can develop community experience in leadership.

It seems to be that business efficiency can be brought to bear on solving unemployment, housing, and urban planning programs, as long as it is through the established structure. It can solve problems as long as the people of the slums have no effective say to change the plans, or to obstruct them. This is how the model cities program seems to be proceeding. Without the grass roots, business participation is easier to get. Without the CAP community action activities, the National Alliance of Businessmen is willing to exercise its talents in finding jobs for people.

Their efforts can be brought to bear best upon those things that cannot talk back—such as pollution. Maybe, as Tom Wicker observes rather cynically, Mr. Nixon's state of the Union message was a clever flank movement into the environment and away from the ghetto. Suddenly almost everyone rich and poor and in between is concerned about choking to death. These quite legitimate concerns represent finite challenges which can be met (unlike the ghetto) by energy, technology, and money without challenging the system.

That is the word: finite, certain, planned, order, continuity, those are the needs of business. And it attempts to shape the environment around it to fill those requirements. It can do that with the physical environment to some extent, it cannot do it with people.

This should be a troublesome concern for the educator, especially business school deans and faculties. How does one train a businessman to cope with a world in profound change where values are shifting, and the environment is quite uncertain? The business school training equips the individual with the tools to take the risk out of taking risks. It teaches him about controls so that he can operate with greater certainty that error will not creep in. He is given knowledge about systems planning so that he can account for every last item in his planning. He is taught supervisory skills which work when the work force is docile, or when it is organized and follows carefully designed procedures to settle differences. But he is not equipped or even selected because he has the capacity to cope with risk and uncertainty and revolutionary forces. There is nothing in the business school which lets him know that his tools will seldom if ever help him solve the problems of the community. It is a peculiar fact of life which also affects the business school that we believe we can manage the most difficult of all endeavors, namely, human affairs, by ear, without training, without knowledge, without experience. Perhaps that is why we do it so badly.

It is human qualities—generosity and selfishness, loving and hating, cooperativeness and perverseness—which make molasses out of the best designed procedures either inside or outside the organization. We teach people to delegate responsibility when they are not psychologically able to relinquish it. We skip over political concepts that have much to do with how people are governed and govern. We say very little about how authoritarian organizations such as business clash with the underlying notions of democracy.

We must ask whether business should be socially responsible. Can it have multiple and even contradictory objectives? Should it exist to serve the society or to make profits; what really is its ultimate objective? Does the man attracted to business have the special talents and the capacity to be a leader in a world of change and uncertainty which is characteristic of the community? Will businesses and businessmen respond constructively to increasingly harsh criticism, or will their response exacerbate the already wide gulf between the corporation and a large portion of the community?

46

Consumerism: A Perspective for Business

David W. Cravens and Gerald E. Hills

The consumer self-interest movement will assert itself as a powerful and pervasive influence on business decision making in the decade ahead. The implications of consumerism span virtually every type of firm that produces or distributes consumer goods and services; moreover, firms producing and marketing industrial goods may find that certain aspects of the movement will influence their marketing strategies. Although some of the origins and causes of this movement can be traced back many years, it is more realistic to view it as a product of the sixties.

In general, consumerism expresses itself in efforts to bring pressure on business firms as well as government to correct business conduct thought unethical. Its main thrust encompasses a multitude of group actions concerned with such issues as consumer protection laws, the availability of product and price information, fraudulent and deceptive business practices, and product safety.

Consumer coalitions have focused their actions on the business community, which suggests that major responsibility for the current state of consumer unrest should fall upon business. Although instances of insensitivity of business to consumers may be identified, analysis indicates that the problem is far more complex than the simple failure of firms to respond appropriately to consumer needs and wants. It is clear that all groups—whether consumers, the government, or others—must share with the business community the task of both identifying the issues and problems erupting in our society and carefully formulating and implementing actions for responding to them.

Business leaders must develop appropriate strategies for the decade ahead. Neither panic actions nor violent attack are realistic courses, and unconcern and nonresponse are, at best, naive in view of the growing momentum of the

Reprinted from *Business Horizons*, August 1970, pp. 21–28.

consumer movement. Analysis of the origins of consumerism and an assessment of its nature and scope will provide the businessman with the foundation for developing an objective perspective. Such a perspective must include an examination of social goals, the parties involved, their interrelationships, and identification of the emerging issues.

Consumerism—Background and Scope

Origins. Why did the consumer movement come into sharp focus at the end of the sixties rather than before? During the decade of the forties, the nation was preoccupied with World War II. After the war, effects of accumulated demand, reinforced by the economic impact of the Korean conflict, extended well into the fifties. Consumers were primarily concerned with *obtaining* desired goods and services, and their inattention to issues that now underlie the consumerism movement is not surprising. As supplies of goods and services became plentiful in the late fifties, however, other factors began to influence consumer behavior in the market place.

The consumers of the sixties were better educated, more affluent, and had more leisure time than consumers at any other point in the history of the nation. Moreover, they were offered complex assortments of goods and services, one result of postwar technology. Mass communications, particularly television, made the buyer more aware of the proliferation of economic goods as well as, eventually, the existence of problems related to products and services. Although reports of fraud, deception, and disregard for safety were infrequent, the publicity they received invited consumer reactions.

High levels of demand combined with highly efficient production processes introduced and established the mass marketing concept. The attention of firms was focused on utilizing their increased productivity and moving goods and services in unprecedented volumes. Marketing institutions became less labor intensive, and retailing became more impersonal in nature. Consider, for example, the growth of the self-service supermarket and the commercial success of the discount house as alternatives to the neighborhood grocery store and the full-service department store. Similar trends developed in virtually all aspects of retailing.

During this period, an integrated consumer-oriented marketing effort was advocated by certain leaders in the business and academic communities. In many firms, however, the concept of an integrated marketing effort was never fully implemented. While the consumer was acknowledged as the focal point of the marketing thrust, not enough research was aimed at understanding buyer behavior as a guide to marketing strategy. Much of the consumer dissatisfaction with products and services could have been avoided if marketers had obtained appropriate intelligence from the market place and truly implemented the marketing concept.

As a result of all these factors, the sophisticated consumers of the sixties were confronted with a complex, impersonal, and, on occasion, deceptive marketing system designed to serve their needs and wants in a highly efficient manner. Clearly contributing to the development of this system was the consumer's increasing demand for goods and services of better quality and at lower prices.

Therefore, the stage was set for an assessment of consumer problems. Rumblings of discontent over business insensitivity to consumers led to formal government recognition of consumers and their role in our economy:

> On March 15, 1962, President John F. Kennedy sent to the Congress a Special Message on Protecting the Consumer Interest. In this message, the first ever delivered by a President on this topic, President Kennedy took note of the important role played by consumers in the American economy and the challenging problems that confront them.[1]

From this point forward the consumerism movement developed rapidly. Although laws and regulatory actions designed to protect the consumer emerged during the first half of this century, many new aspects of consumer protection were supported in the sixties at both the national and state levels by an increasing number of political representatives. Tight federal budget constraints spurred the search for inexpensive but popular bills. Motives aside, however, certain political figures have contributed significantly to the attention given the consumer's role in our society. Their efforts are perhaps best illustrated by Senator Warren D. Magnuson, chairman of the Senate Commerce Committee and long acknowledged consumer champion on Capitol Hill.

The continuing impact of individual crusaders is best illustrated by the highly publicized efforts of Ralph Nader to spearhead improvement, through legislation and public pressure, in such areas as automobile safety standards, pipeline hazards, and radiation standards. In addition to individual crusaders in government and private life, consumers in their role as consumers have become active; coalition formation and demonstration for the purpose of seeking change were popular tactics in the sixties.

A pervasive force underlying the social issues that emerged in the sixties (including consumerism) was a general atmosphere of questioning on the part of many groups. Environment and the quality of life became important issues, and both government and business were criticized. Questioning of the system or the Establishment by intellectuals, popular journalists, and students spread to the man on the street. Many criticisms directed toward large corporations alleged misuse of power, lack of social responsibility, and the adherence to questionable goals. Social critics like Vance Packard increased public interest and social awareness.

A final accelerating force underlying the development of consumerism in the late sixties was the pace of inflation. This was particularly effective in the development of store boycotts and demonstrations by housewives, who tend to blame retail food stores for high prices.

[1] "Consumer Advisory Council, First Report," Executive Office of the President (Washington: U.S. Govt. Printing Office, October, 1963), p. 5.

Thus, the consumerism movement was perhaps an inevitable response to the increasingly complex and impersonal society of our times. Analysis of the contributing factors and accelerating forces suggests that our socioeconomic system is seeking a new level of maturity in moving from a preoccupation with mass needs and wants toward a reassessment of social goals and the means necessary to achieve them.

Nature and Scope. The developing thrust of consumerism is difficult to describe in terms of specific objectives and issues, but identification and analysis of the myriad of activities under way provide a partial description of the nature and scope of the movement. In addition to the actions of elected officials, consumer boycotts, and consumer crusaders, other activities include:

The widely publicized efforts of Mrs. Virginia Knauer, President Nixon's Special Assistant for Consumer Affairs.

Product testing and information services such as the Consumers Union; efforts have been expanded beyond product evaluation to include attempts to influence both the business community and government on the behalf of the consumer.

Student involvement with socioeconomic issues (including consumer affairs) reflected in the magazine *Business Today*, published by students for students.

Increased interest on the part of state and local governments in establishing consumer units and advisory groups, for example, New York City's Department of Consumer Affairs, headed by television personality Bess Myerson Grant.

Popularity of consumer cooperatives and organized groups such as the Consumer Federation of America, which sponsored Consumer Assembly '70, attended by over 600 delegates representing 100 consumer organizations.

The developing interest in consumer affairs by labor unions and related groups as reflected by the consumer education program recently implemented by the Central Labor Council in Washington.

Although the term "consumerism" is increasingly used, it has apparently never been operationally defined. The various actions and concerns associated with the movement provide a basis for defining consumerism—recognizing that it is presently loosely structured and is likely to change as the parties involved develop more explicit statements of their goals and positions. Our definition is that *consumerism is a social force within the environment designed to aid and protect the consumer by exerting legal, moral, and economic pressure on business.*

The fact that private individuals, politicians, and groups engage in consumerism-related actions to generate public opinion and, ultimately, public pressure makes consumerism a social force. It is also an environmental force in that it is pervasive and surrounds business. Furthermore, the examples that have been cited illustrate attempts to either protect the consumer from business (for example, product safety and cases of fraudulent sales practices) or to aid him in processing information as a basis for allocating his income (for example, the "truth-in" laws).

Finally, a critical part of the definition is recognition of the tactics employed. Private individuals and groups utilize existing laws as well as generate pressure at all levels of government for new legal constraints. They also apply coalition tactics to generate public opinion and pressure not only on government, but directly on business. This is primarily moral pressure, but it may be translated into economic pressure if customers respond to the negative publicity. The role of government in this process is as both initiator and responder. Individuals within government may generate support in and out of government for issues that may result in legislative action, and government will, of course, respond to issues that have the support of the public.

A Systems Perspective

It is helpful to view the business firm as an element in a large complex system comprised of various organizations, groups, and institutions, all concerned with various aspects of consumer welfare. The accompanying figure shows the primary groups involved in the consumerism movement and the flows of information and influence that bind the system together. Analysis of the movement is complicated by the large number of consumer interest groups and their interrelationships with government agencies, the business community, and the individuals who comprise the markets for goods and services.

Goals. Apparently, all of these groups hope to advance the welfare of the consumer. Business provides much of the income with which consumers can advance their material well-being; business also produces and distributes the multitude of goods and services which provide the consumer with alternatives

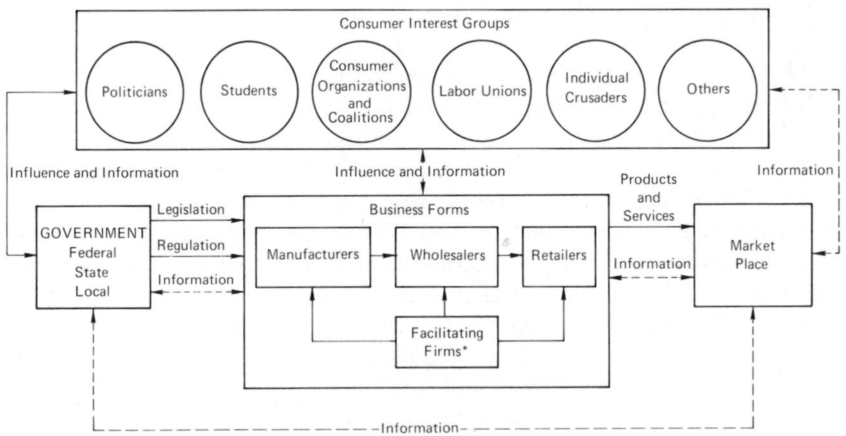

*Financial institutions, transportation firms, and advertising agencies, for example.

The Consumerism System—Group and Information Flows

for allocating his income. If we assume that the consumer allocates his income to maximize his satisfaction, can we further assume that this objective is achieved the same way by all people? Obviously not. Yet assumptions are implicitly made by many who undertake crusades that all consumers desire more and better information so they can make more "rational" decisions. Although less applicable, the same may be true of certain product safety crusades where the cost is ultimately borne by the consumer.

This is not to condone negligence but rather to suggest that an understanding of consumer decision processes and desires is basic to a true understanding and evaluation of the consumerism movement. The informational needs and desires of consumers vary from person to person. For some, the economic and/or psychological costs of additional information may be exorbitant when related to the "returns." For example, a person who values his time highly and finds the shopping process annoying will be unlikely to incur these "costs" to obtain information that would help him make a slightly better purchase decision. A shopper who enjoys the process (no costs) may desire and seek such information.

These questions should be reflected in the actions of consumer interest groups. The obvious issues have gained overwhelming support, but as these are exhausted, it will be necessary to make explicit the costs involved in certain consumer actions. Moreover, curtailment of competition in certain industries could result, which would depress rather than improve the welfare of consumers in society.

The potential impact and possible danger to our society in continuing these fragmented approaches to improving consumer welfare must be assessed. Increased government legislation and control are likely by-products, leading to further constraints for the business decision maker and possibly hampering our pursuit of socioeconomic progress. The flow of new products and services could also be constrained; buyer-seller relationships are likely to become even more impersonal than they are today. In sum, it is clear that if the goal of consumerism is to improve the welfare of consumers, then many factors must be considered. Consumers may be willing to incur more costs for higher levels of satisfaction—but the balance is critical.

Interrelationships. Flows of information and influence provide the basis for examining interrelationships between major components of the system. The complexity of our socioeconomic system makes the economist's dream of perfect information flows unattainable. Yet development of effective macro-information systems is likely to become a central consideration in helping the consumer voice his opinions and preferences and achieve his goals. Actions taken on his behalf without this intelligence from the market place can easily lead to an imbalance in control and regulation with a possible delay in moving the consumer toward higher levels of satisfaction.

The primary information flows to consumers include promotional efforts of business (as well as varying responses to the consumerism movement); activities of government officials as reported by the news media; communication and interaction among consumers and their "representatives" (both interpersonal and by the media); and the availability of published consumer product ratings. These flows provide the basis for consumers' evaluation of products, as well as for their assessment of the consumerism movement, and indicate the crucial need for effective information flows to and from the consumer. "Noise" and distortion in the system (for example, misleading advertising or unfounded charges by consumer leaders) only serve to impair the ability of the customer to intelligently compare his alternatives.

Government also depends on flows of information and influence. Although government is responsive to voters, many elected representatives are involved in *creating* public opinion; therefore, a two-way flow of information exists. Testimony (state and federal), communications from consumer-interest leaders (as translated by the media), and public opinion polls serve as critical inputs to government leaders. Once again, however, biased and distorted information flowing to and away from government can only serve to impair decision making. Lobbying by business is a particularly influential information flow, which may balance countervailing charges from consumer groups. It also typically reflects the vested interests of certain industries. Rather direct information flows from government include the passage of additional laws and establishment (or strengthening) of regulatory agencies. Unfortunately, these typically reflect the failure of business.

All groups should recognize the desirability of reducing the noise generated by superficial and biased treatment of issues. This is not to suggest, however, that bias can be eliminated from the information flows or that people (consumers, politicians, and businessmen) believe all (or even most) distorted information. Nevertheless, a critical self-examination is in order for all groups, particularly with regard to their role in this system.

Implications for Decision Making

Several specific guides on action for business firms have been developed by a task force of business, academic, professional, and association leaders.[2] In addition, more fundamental implications for business decision making are clear.

Understanding Consumer Behavior. The rise of the consumerism movement raises serious question as to the effectiveness of business firms in assessing customer attitudes and preferences; therefore, a better understanding of consumer behavior is a basic requirement for designing effective business response. Over the past ten years, progress has been made in developing both concepts and methods to guide the analysis of buyer behavior, and an increasing number of business firms are beginning to allocate substantial resources to various types of consumer research. Thus, business firms have

[2] Chamber of Commerce of the United States, "Business and the Consumer—a Program for the Seventies" (1970), pp. 12–13.

available or can obtain the assistance needed to increase their understanding of buyer behavior. The question then becomes one of resource allocation.

Product research and development, advertising, and other parts of marketing programs have for many years commanded large amounts of corporate resources. Yet the use of corporate resources for consumer research has been relatively limited. Business managers should carefully assess their need for a better understanding of their consumers.

Organizational Design. The importance of assembling marketing resources into a coordinated and integrated program aimed at seeking favorable responses in the market place has been emphasized for the past two decades. Although a number of highly successful firms have organized and implemented these resources in terms of the marketing concept, many continue to manage their activities in a fragmented manner.

A proposal has been made that companies establish a position of "vice-president, consumerism" in order to more closely coordinate strategies.[3] While creation of top-level staff positions for coping with emerging problems and issues fails to recognize many of the more basic considerations in designing effective organizations, the proposal does clearly indicate the need to identify appropriate responsibility for assessing and responding to the consumer movement. The executive responsible for managing the firm's over-all marketing effort is a logical candidate for this assignment. Of course, the absence of an integrated company marketing effort suggests the need for a more viable marketing organizational design for interpreting issues and determining needed actions.

Involvement in Consumer Affairs. Business must look beyond the direct relationship between the firm and the consumer. Executives can participate through trade associations and industry organizations in various aspects of the consumer movement. Involvement in consumer affairs may require reassessment of the goals and policies of these organizations, including the support of needed projects and programs. Jointly funded consumer research studies would enable many small firms to obtain information for decision making. Moreover, measures of attitudes and preferences of consumers will provide these business groups with needed intelligence for more effectively assessing and participating in public policy issues associated with the consumer movement.

Trade organizations also should consider the possibility of social benefit of certain laws—particularly where they would facilitate the compliance of all competitors to certain desirable standards. In addition, more communication within the business community and the strengthening of self-enforcement organizations is in order.

The first response of business to the consumer movement was skepticism and condemnation; increasingly, however, business is acknowledging this

[3] E.B.Weiss, "Marketers Fiddle While Consumers Burn," *Harvard Business Review* (July–August, 1968), p. 51.

countervailing power. Not only must business respond, but business must communicate this response to the appropriate parties. For some time, in fact, this communication may offer a competitive advantage. Let consumers perceive desirable changes being made before demands are made.

Businessmen should also recognize the commercial opportunities presented by the increasing complexity of purchase decisions and the limited capacity of people to process information. At least one retailer now offers a computer for home installation complete with a standard software (programs) package. Although this alternative is open only to the most affluent, the demand for consumer information services will grow. One company now franchises computerized information centers that provide real estate, automobile, employment, and college search information services.

The Role of Top Management. One of the major responsibilities of top management is to chart the course of the enterprise through the uncertain future. This requires an assessment of both the importance and nature of various environmental forces. Middle management, however, given certain achievement targets, is primarily concerned with efficiency of internal operations, yet many of their tasks are performed at the interface between the firm and its consumers.

This is particularly true of persons with responsibilities for various marketing tasks such as advertising, sales force management, pricing, and distribution. In these areas, top management must achieve highly effective communications and feedback with middle management, encouraging careful assessment of both efficiency and customer satisfaction goals. Appointment of a top executive for consumer affairs, suggested previously, recognizes this need.

Active participation by top management in the consumerism movement is needed. The business community can provide an important point of view in developing an appropriate perspective toward the consumer. Moreover, the continuing commentary on the proper balance between business and government demands that businessmen respond to the challenge for leadership.

The problems and issues concerning the consumer that have emerged in the past ten years must be viewed as a challenge rather than as an indication of failure. Careful assessment of corporate goals and required action can provide a stong foundation for moving the business community toward higher levels of social responsibility and achievement.

The need is clear for improved communication and information feedback among all parties involved in the consumerism movement. Debate has been based far too often on superficial response and emotion rather than on an objective assessment resulting from carefully formulated and executed research. Fragmented actions on the part of consumer interest groups without the benefit of information concerning their effects could result in over-control and a hampering of the important forces and influences that comprise our socio-economic system. At the same time, however, all groups should be aware of the potential value of achieving certain consumerism goals. The trade-offs must be weighed carefully for each specific issue and action taken which will tend to benefit both business and consumers over the long run.

47

The Human Concept: New Philosophy for Business

Leslie M. Dawson

One of the more intriguing examples of graffiti reported in recent years is the scrawl on a New York City sidewalk, "Marvin Can't Relate to His Environment." While it is unlikely that Marvin was a business executive at the time of his immortalization in cement, a growing number of businessmen nonetheless share his problem. Certainly the business professional, in common with everyone else, has a vital need for *some* orientation to a world that daily grows more complex, convulsive, and confounding. To lack such a sense of relationships is to be "disoriented" or, according to *Webster's*, "to lose an appreciation of place and time or of one's own identity." Much of the literature of business since the end of World War II has harped on the idea that we live in a "marketing era" and that firms ought to adopt a marketing orientation or a marketing concept as the cornerstone of their corporate philosophy. A crucial question to be asked today, however, is whether a marketing orientation remains the correct orientation for the business executive.

Irwin Miller, chairman of Cummins Engine, observed recently that we are living in a remarkable and perplexing time; despite the long list of accomplishments of American business and the unprecedented prosperity of the nation, the businessman feels insecure and under attack from many groups: workers, customers, government, children, education, and even the church.[1] While the marketing concept may indeed have been ideally attuned to a marketing era, the evidence builds that we are well on the way into an era that must be described in some other way. The eminent sociologist, Pitirim A. Sorokin, has identified the decay of the sensate culture, with its emphasis upon materialism, and a movement toward an ideational, spiritually based form of culture as one of the basic trends of our time.

In the past several years, a number of institutions and foundations have undertaken serious research projects involving speculation as to the future. The Ford Foundation, the Rand Corporation, and the Hudson Institute have

Reprinted from *Business Horizons*, December 1969, pp. 29–38. Copyright, 1969 by the Foundation for the School of Business, at Indiana University. Reprinted by permission.

[1] Irwin Miller, "Business Has a War to Win," *Harvard Business Review*, XLVII (March–April, 1969), p. 4.

sponsored such studies, and the American Academy of Arts and Sciences has created the Committee on the Year 2000. A general theme of agreement in their published reports is that a strong accentuation of human values is likely to dominate the last third of this century. The committee makes this statement:

> Let it be added that in this 'super-affluent' society of year 2000, it is not likely that efficiency (defined by the criteria of maximizing profit or income) will still be primary, though it will doubtless remain important . . . . We could think of this phenomenon as a shift to humanistic rather than vocational or advancement-oriented values, and conjecture that this tendency will increase over the next 33 years.[2]

This article suggests that, *first*, we are no longer living in a marketing era and are witnessing the start of what may ultimately be termed the human era; *second*, today's executive must cope with a variety of issues, many vaguely or directly threatening, which extend far beyond mere market considerations; *third*, a marketing concept is of little help in coping with such problems; and *fourth*, the actions of many leading corporations today do in fact testify to the gradual replacement of the marketing concept with a more embracing philosophy which, for want of a better term, may be called the human concept.

Historical-Ecological Perspective

At least one business scholar has suggested that cultural ecology, the study of the adaptation of a social system to its environment, provides a more meaningful perspective from which to study business activity than economics or any other social science.[3] Cultural ecology focuses upon the capacity of an organized behavior system to sustain itself by drawing upon the resources of its environment, in terms analogous to the capacity of a living creature to utilize life-sustaining resources. Survival and equilibrium are critical concepts in cultural ecology. Survival is the ultimate goal of the organized behavior system, but the system can exist only by adapting to environmental change and maintaining a dynamic ecological equilibrium.

It can be argued that the main thrust of business thought and action has always tended to reflect the basic orientation that top management believes to be most compatible with perceived contemporary environmental conditions. For example, three distinct phases of managerial orientation in twentieth century American business have been observed:[4]

> *Production orientation (1900–30)*—An emphasis upon production volume and plant efficiency, in response to newly developed technology for mass production and expanded markets combined with a steady rise in consumer affluence and spending.

[2] Herman Kahn and Anthony J. Weiner, *The Year 2000: A Framework for Speculation on the Next Thirty-Three Years* (New York: The Macmillan Co., 1967), pp. 214–15.

[3] Wroe Alderson, *Dynamic Marketing Behavior* (Homewood, Ill.: Richard D. Irwin, Inc., 1965), Ch. 13.

[4] Robert J. Keith, "The Marketing Revolution," *Journal of Marketing*, XXIV (January, 1960), pp. 35–38.

Sales orientation (1930–50)—An emphasis upon aggressive sales and distributive practices in response to mounting production saturation combined with new caution and moderation in consumer spending and business investment.

Marketing orientation (1950–?)—An emphasis upon consumer satisfaction, crystallized in the marketing concept, in response to new competitive interfaces among products and industries, an unprecedented level of consumer affluence, and a volatile mixture of other new postwar pressures.

Wroe Alderson has called attention to two crucial environmental levels in the cultural ecology of business: first, the proximate environment, the external domain with which a system is in direct and continuous contact (for a marketing firm, the markets in which it buys and sells and competes) and, second, the more embracing ultimate environment, composed of the technological, ideological, moral, and social dimensions of the culture. The figure illustrates this environmental perspective. In the long run the business enterprise must maintain dynamic ecological equilibrium with *both* environments. A system that fails to do so may fall into an "extinction mode."

None of the basic orientations described has been especially attuned to the relationship of the firm to its ultimate environment. Even the ubiquitous marketing concept, relevant and valuable as it has been in an era of marketing emphasis, has serious weaknesses as a management guide in an era reflecting deepened human concern. A fuller consideration of the marketing concept and the environmental conditions that spawned it may be helpful as a prelude to discussing these weaknesses.

The Marketing Concept—Yesterday and Today

In the post-World War II years, the nation's economy not only recovered from the effects of the Depression, but swiftly advanced well beyond the highest prewar levels. Postwar prosperity ushered in the age of the affluent society in the United States. The postwar consumer not only was economically better off, better educated, and more sophisticated, but before long more saturated with goods as well. The notion of a limit to the "capacity to consume" became more than a mere theoretical concern, and the survival of the business enterprise depended largely upon its skill in determining, and flexibility in adjusting to, shifts in consumer tastes. An all-out commitment to market considerations—expressed as the "marketing concept"—became vital. A typical definition of this concept is the following:

> A managerial philosophy concerned with the mobilization, utilization, and control of total corporate effort for the purpose of helping consumers solve selected problems, in ways compatible with planned enhancement of the profit position of the firm.[5]

[5] Robert L. King, "The Marketing Concept," in George Schwartz, ed., *Science in Marketing* (New York: John Wiley & Sons, 1965), pp. 70–97.

The implementation of a marketing concept often necessitates major organizational and operational changes for the firm. At the very least a new accentuation is placed upon interdepartmental consultation and synchronization (the "systems approach"). Reversal of the "normal" planning sequence is emphasized, so that plans and strategies are formulated first with a view to the marketplace and then translated "backwards" into the development of a profitable market offering. But in its essence the marketing concept represents a basic corporate philosophy, a rationale for the existence of the enterprise. The rationale is not the production of a particular product or service, but the fulfillment of a selected consumer need category, and thus the attention of management is redirected from precedent to potential.

The marketing concept has been one of the most plausible and useful concepts to emerge from business literature, and it has gained virtually universal acceptance in principle. In the context of the figure, the marketing concept represents an outward extension of environmental awareness and sensitivity in contrast to the more inward-looking production and sales orientations. Yet the perspective of the marketing concept remains essentially confined to the proximate environment. Preoccupied as it is with consumers and competitors, the concept is not especially attentive to the healthfulness of a firm's relationship to the various dimensions of the ultimate environment.

New Pressures on Business. It seems clear that the environmental forces which resulted in a greater focus on the marketplace will endure and intensify. Rapid technological progress, increased production efficiency, growing consumer affluence, a broader range of competitive interfaces among industries, the profit squeeze—these and similar pressures, which evoked the marketing orientation, are not likely to let up.

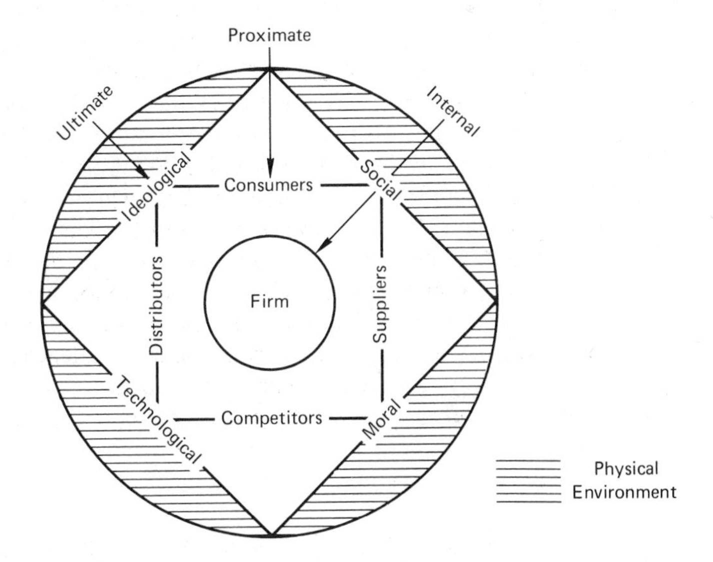

An Environmental Perspective of the Firm

At the same time, the tumultuous events ushering in the last third of this century suggest that powerful new currents of change have begun to flow through the ultimate environment—currents that will profoundly affect the future of business in America. Consistent with the prediction of Sorokin and others, a great share of the pressures emanating from this environmental realm, ideological, moral, and social in nature, revolve around a deepening concern over the "human condition." The demand has been made for a far deeper commitment by business interests to the solution of the social problems which plague America, and for that matter, the entire world. Pressures are being brought upon business to exercise its vast power in such missions as the elimination of poverty, the cleansing of the atmosphere and waterways, and the eradication of social injustice in all its manifestations. Demands are made upon business to provide more genuine opportunities for individual development within the industrial organization. Business leaders are mandated to adopt roles of leadership in the advancement of our society to new levels of moral conduct.

It is significant that these pressures and demands are prominently associated with the brightest and best of the nation's youth. The business image among college students has ramifications for the future which extend far beyond the special (and worsening) problem of attracting a sufficient number of college graduates to business careers. The available evidence leaves room for disagreement as to the depth and breadth of student disenchantment with business, but it does show that the criticism of business is not limited to a vocal minority of young radicals whose value orientation is out of the mainstream of American life. *Fortune's* recent report on the present college generation indicates that fully 40 percent of the nation's college students can be included in a group characterized by a notable "lack of concern for making money" and "an extraordinary rejection of traditional American values."[6] Significantly, *Fortune* refers to this group as the "forerunners," believing that as our society grows more affluent their percentage of the total college population will increase.

The Harris poll of the attitudes of the general public toward business, undertaken for *Newsweek* in 1966, covered 2,000 Americans in all age and income brackets.[7] The results led *Newsweek* to conclude that business faces a "clear and cogent mandate" to adopt a new and broader set of social goals.

The Marketing Concept Falters. In an environment that exerts upon the business enterprise a new milieu of pressures, predominantly oriented to humanistic values, the marketing concept appears unsuitable for providing the executive with a meaningful and viable sense of identity and direction. Several of its weaknesses become clear when thought is given to some new developments that are, or should be, of concern to several major industries.

1. The marketing concept stresses a *consumer* orientation. In one definition, the consumer is said to become "the absolute dead center of the universe"

[6] Daniel Seligman, "A Special Kind of Rebellion," *Fortune*, LXXIX (January, 1969), p. 67.

[7] "Speak Now . . . a Newsweek Report," *Newsweek* (1966).

for the business firm. A consumer orientation directs the attention of the firm only to some fraction of the population of the society which supports it. Moreover, insofar as present or potential consumers are concerned, the consumer orientation generates concern only with the individual's role as a buyer or consumer of a particular product or service. Thus, the consumer orientation is limited in scope and one-dimensional in nature.

The tobacco industry has certainly been consumer oriented in postwar years. Playing a fine tune of market segmentation and product differentiation, the industry has adapted skillfully to changing consumer preferences as the major prewar brands have yielded to a proliferation of new shapes and styles. Industry sales and per capita cigarette consumption have gained steadily. Do we conclude that a consumer orientation is enabling this industry to adapt with perfect harmony to environmental change? Hardly. A powerful and growing array of forces are united in an effort to erase the industry altogether. These forces emanate from state and federal government, the medical profession, and concerned citizens at large. They are generated by persons whose most likely common bond is that they are *not* consumers of the product. The individuals have managed to create a steady stream of woe for the tobacco industry over the past five years.

It is irrelevant to speculate as to whether these forces will succeed (though it is worth noting that per capita cigarette consumption showed declines both in 1967 and 1968). The important point is that a consumer orientation can help not at all in eliminating what is unquestionably the major threat to the survival of this industry, because the threat specifically emanates from nonsmoking sectors of society. What has made the future of this industry in the coming decades a question-mark is not its failure to provide consumers with a pleasant, satisfying product, but rather the product's vulnerability to society's deepening concern over human well-being.

Small firearms are another example of this vulnerability. Obviously, manufacturers are satisfying consumers with their product array of pistols, high-powered rifles, and shotguns; in fact, few industries can count upon a similar degree of consumer loyalty and dedication. The gun lobby, spearheaded by the National Rifle Association, has successfully fought off Presidents, senators, judges, public safety officials, and the FBI in their efforts to curb the sale and possession of guns. The cultural and constitutional aspects of gun ownership in a country with a revolutionary and pioneering heritage are complicated and fraught with emotion. But surely such vestiges of the frontier spirit are being wiped out by the slaughter of political leaders and by rising crime rates. The *Wall Street Journal* recently editorialized as follows:

> It seems predictable that in an urbanized and crowded America the gun lobby will in the end, for good or ill, find itself overwhelmed—much as the equally competent doctors' lobby eventually was in its fight against Medicare. Like civil rights legislation, domestic disarmament is likely to be voted in successive and increasing doses.[8]

[8] "Domestic Disarmament," *Wall Street Journal*, July 3, 1968.

Should the environmental clouds swirling about this industry continue to darken, a consumer orientation would be of little help to a member firm in clearing the way to a healthy long-run ecological balance.

2. The marketing concept emphasizes research and long-range planning, but with an almost exclusive stress on technological trends and product improvement. To be sure, a consumer orientation seeks to alert management to possible long-run shifts in tastes and preferences. But neither the technological nor the consumer perspective calls attention to a much broader form of "cultural obsolescence" which may occur in a world of rapidly changing values and priorities.

However naive and futile the peace demonstrator may appear amidst the violence and tensions which mark the international scene, industries that depend heavily upon military and defense contracts might do well to ponder their long-term prospects. From the M-1 rifle to the multimegaton neutron bomb the applied science of death and destruction represents a high degree of technological perfection. Yet throughout the world the clamor for arms control and ultimate disarmament grows louder. An expenditure in the billions is proposed in this nation for a thin antiballistic missile system, and yet the experts admit that it may well be obsolete before it is completed. Nations which cannot afford to feed their people adequately pour a steady stream of their national incomes into armaments.

Well-founded mistrust and caution certainly make genuine disarmament a long-range prospect at best. What is important here, however, is that the marketing concept is not very effective in alerting management of a firm heavily involved in armament production to the fact that the habitability of the environment may ultimately be in question, and that, indeed, society is trying to make the environment unsuitable for the continuation of such production.

The clamor against war and violence has even spilled over into the children's toy industry. In recent years the New York City toy fair has been picketed by mothers and children protesting the manufacture and sale of war-like toys. In a recent address to European toy manufacturers, Pope Paul VI added his voice to the outcry against toys that encourage antisocial behavior. This industry may find its future influenced far more by cultural acceptance than by mere consumer preferences or technical product improvements.

In fact, all manufacturers of consumer durable goods would be well-advised to raise their long-range planning sights above the levels of technology and taste to the more fundamental changes in life styles that may accompany the maturation of the next generation of young Americans. *Fortune* raises a crucial question in commenting upon the current "youthquake" in our culture:

> In its visible and audible impact on styles and tastes, the youthquake has been mostly fun so far . . . . Still, there is something a bit spooky, from a business point of view, about some implications that can be found in youth's widespread rejection of middle-class life styles ("Cheap is in"). Like so much else among the young that rejection may prove to be transient, but if it persists and becomes a dominant orienta-

tion, will these children of affluence grow up to be consumers on quite the economy-moving scale of their parents?[9]

3. Perhaps the most fundamental weakness of the marketing concept is that it satisfies selfish interest, thereby becoming incompatible with an age in which society demands a higher degree of selfless sacrifice on the part of its institutions and constituents. A marketing concept inevitably casts the industrial organization in the role of one of society's more predatory creatures, a giant corporation stealthily and eagerly stalking the marketplace, always at the ready to leap upon a new market opportunity or to devour a competitor. We can dust the cobwebs off models of pure competition and insist that the persistent search for commercial self-gain somehow, sometimes leads to ultimate good for all.

But indications mount that insofar as social and human progress is concerned, our society is becoming impatient and intolerant—unwilling to settle for the accidental by-products generated by business' self-centered pursuit of greater market opportunities and profit. Because of the market focus, the involvement of major corporations in social reform projects is more often than not met with skepticism and cynicism by the public. The young, in particular, are inclined to dismiss such activities as conniving public relations gestures, financed by otherwise-taxable profits, and all aimed ultimately toward enhancing market position. Indeed, the marketing concept certainly does imply that the justification for social pursuits by business must ultimately rest upon market considerations.

Certainly it can be argued that it is a matter of self-interest, if not selfish interest, for business to lead in the fight against the grave weaknesses which beset our society, and thus such actions are not inconsistent with a marketing concept. But semantic confusion, if nothing else, renders the marketing concept useful in a contemporary environmental context, simply because market considerations alone, even long run, can no longer determine what is good or bad, right or wrong, prudent or imprudent, urgent or nonurgent in the business community.

The Human Concept

We have only to look at the actions of major business firms in recent years to recognize that many progressive organizations already are operating under some concept far more broad and meaningful for today's conditions than the marketing concept. These news stories have appeared during the last few years:

> Detroit's Big Three automakers take on tens of thousands of hard-core unemployables in massive retraining effort.

[9] Sheldon Zaleznick, "The Youthquake in Pop Culture," *Fortune*, LXXIX (January, 1969), p. 134.

Lockheed Space and Missile inaugurates new vocation improvement program with hiring limited to dropouts, welfare recipients, ex-convicts, and others with entirely unsatisfactory work records.

Control Data opens new plants in black slums of Washington, D.C. and Minneapolis; AVCO opens new plant in Boston ghetto.

SK&F Laboratories establishes information center to advise its black neighbors in Philadelphia ghetto on wide variety of employment, housing, health, education problems; Quaker Oats has similar program in Chicago slum area.

U.S. Gypsum turns tenements into pleasant living units in pioneer private industry slum rehabilitation projects in New York, Cleveland, and Chicago ghetto areas.

Life insurance industry pledges $1 billion investment in housing and industry in massive effort to reclaim slum areas.

Such actions are hardly more understandable under a marketing concept than under the economists' anachronism of profit maximization; therefore, the author suggests that they are manifestations of the gradual evolution of a new concept influencing the thoughts and actions of progressive business leaders. Far more responsive to human needs and values in their totality than the marketing concept, this is perhaps best described as the "human concept." An appraisal of the current range of concerns and activities of prominent business corporations indicates that a business enterprise, operating under a human concept, directs its attention, resources, and energies toward the fulfillment of human needs at three levels.

The *first* level is internal in nature, and pertains to the role of the enterprise as a developer of human resources within the organization. The benefits and security commonly provided for all levels of employees today testify to the gradual assumption by American business of a responsibility for employee welfare that transcends short-run profit goals. As indicated in the preceding examples, a number of corporations have now taken on the tremendous challenge of transforming the hard-core unemployables of our society into productive members of the work force.

This may be the beginning of an all-out commitment by private industry to a massive program of reclaiming the lost human resources of our society. But the interest of progressive management in human welfare has not been limited to the disadvantaged. All managerial levels are more interested in creating work opportunities that allow individuals to develop their full potentials and that genuinely meet the need of workers for occupational self-fulfillment. Private industry has become increasingly aware of the importance of recognition, esteem, and perceived contribution as complements to material rewards in producing job satisfaction.

Dr. Edwin H. Land, president of Polaroid, has said that the function of industry is the development of people. When Charles H. Percy headed Bell and Howell, he stated that "our basic objective is the development of individuals."[10] The fulfillment of such objectives thrusts upon management a vastly

[10] Quoted by Henry G. Pearson, "A New Co-Aim for Business," *MSU Business Topics*, XVI (Spring, 1968), pp. 51–56.

enlarged responsibility in the design and redesign of jobs and job relationships, refinements in selection and placement techniques, and advances in the provision of necessary education and training.

The *second* level of the human concept concerns the relationship of the enterprise to its consumers, competitors, suppliers, and distributors, that is, the proximate environment. It is primarily at this level where profit, the lifeblood of the enterprise, is generated. The human concept implies no lessening in the need for the business organization to remain in dynamic ecological equilibrium with its proximate environment. The consumer orientation and need fulfillment imperatives, so well expounded and thoroughly developed under the doctrine of the marketing concept, remain vital to the firm under the human concept.

The *third* level concerns the relationship of the enterprise to society in general, that is, the ultimate environment. At this level the human concept commits the firm to involvement in a "market" far more significant and vast than the markets for toothpaste, television sets, or cars. This is the market for human fulfillment.

J. Wilson Newman, chairman of Dun & Bradstreet, argues that the purpose of business has always been to answer human wants, and that the American market is now undergoing a transformation wherein the predominant wants are not material but psychological and social.[11] He foresees a total market averaging as much as $100 billion a year over the rest of the century to lift the smog, clean the rivers, rebuild the cities, unsnarl the traffic, and educate and reeducate the young and old. Marketing expert William Lazer has stated that "one of the next marketing frontiers may well be related to markets that extend beyond mere profit considerations to intrinsic values—to markets based on social concern, markets of the mind, and markets concerned with the development of people to the fullest extent of their capabilities."[12]

At the third level the human concept establishes an external social purpose for the business enterprise by linking its energies to the efforts of mankind to achieve a way of life that fulfills the human yearning not only for material comforts, but for security, dignity, and spiritual solace. Clearly the capacity of every business enterprise to contribute to this effort must be evaluated individually. By virtue of size, product category, or other unique attributes, some organizations have a far greater potential for such contributions than others. But the most important attributes undoubtedly are will and vision. A number of the corporate projects mentioned above are partially funded by public agencies. In some instances, modest profits have even been realized, though naturally less than could have been earned in alternative capital expenditures. The smaller enterprise should be able to participate too, whether on its own or in cooperation with state and local agencies and foundations.

[11] J. Wilson Newman, "Does Business Have a Future?" *MSU Business Topics*, XV (Autumn, 1967), pp. 16–20.

[12] William Lazer, "Marketing's Changing Social Relationships," *Journal of Marketing*, XXXIII (January, 1969), p. 4.

The following is offered as a tentative attempt to summarize the meaning and scope of the human concept in definitional form:

A managerial philosophy centered upon the continuous search for and evaluation of opportunities for the mobilization, utilization, and control of total corporate effort in: (1) achieving a genuine internal social purpose in the development of organization members to their fullest potential; (2) generating the necessary profit input within the proximate environment by devising solutions to selected consumer problems; (3) achieving a genuine external social purpose within the ultimate environment by contributing to the identification and fulfillment of the real human needs of our time.

Implementation of a human concept may involve organizational role and structure change, particularly in larger organizations, at least as fundamental as those called for under a marketing concept. For instance, the sales management position may have to be redefined to accentuate responsibility for the total development of the members of the selling force, constituting an important share of the firm's human resources. Whereas this objective has traditionally been secondary to volume, or more recently profit, it is doubtful that such should be the case for an enterprise committed to a human concept. In a number of progressive firms the old-line public relations department has been supplanted, or at least supplemented, by such new departments as "community relations" and "college relations." These are surely reflections of increased awareness by business of the need for more links to the ultimate environment.

The Concept, Profits, the Future

Change in the ultimate environment is likely to assume special significance to the firm's destiny in the last third of the century. A marketing concept is not adequate to help business retain healthy ecological balance with an environment characterized by an increasing shift from sensate values to human, social, and moral values. A broader human concept can provide management with a sense of direction in an era of increased concern over the human condition by committing the business organization to the service of an internal and an external social purpose concurrent with the service of profit.

It is not suggested that the human concept offers, at last, an easy solution to the classic management conundrum of profit maximization versus social responsibility. At the one extreme, the private corporation clearly cannot be expected to become a philanthropic institution so long as its survival is in large measure determined in a competitive marketplace. At the other extreme, over several generations the will of the nation has been expressed, legally and otherwise, to restrain unbridled competition for maximum profits on the part of big business. Countless efforts have been made to apply a semantic crowbar to force a convergence of the two goals. For example, if profit is defined in sufficiently long-run and indirect terms, it can justifiably be argued that slum clearance maximizes profits by forestalling destructive riots, or that purification of the atmosphere maximizes profits by preventing customers (and everyone else) from being poisoned. What emerges from such arguments is a compromise goal of "enlightened profit maximization," wherein recognition is given to some socially determined limit on what the maximum can be.

The point is, simply, that the firm concerned only with profit performance may find its lack of other internal or external social purpose to be a growing threat to its survival in an increasingly humanistic world. To borrow from the lexicon of economics, profit may become the necessary, but not sufficient, condition for the survival of the firm. There is no need to remind the business executive of the sanctions imposed within the proximate environment for profit failure. But there *is* need to point out that the ultimate environment can impose very real sanctions too for a failure in social purpose. One of the more familiar of these is restrictive legislation. But such sanctions may take other forms as well: the drying up of the wellspring of new business recruits from the colleges; turmoil for the corporate headquarters not unlike contemporary campus disorders (Dow Chemical has already suffered through some relatively minor experiences); work-interfering demonstrations such as those recently conducted by blacks against the construction unions and steel producers in Pittsburgh.

The contribution of the human concept lies in focus and commitment; it can extend the vision of management into those areas of corporate involvement where social purpose beyond profit can be found. Every business organization, regardless of size, can find genuine social purpose in its attitudes and actions concerning employees. Most firms, in alliance with local, state, and federal agencies and institutions, can find genuine external social purpose.

The human concept is not an easy cure for the managerial schizophrenia that may result from the attempt to reconcile profit with social responsibility. The human concept can no more supply the kind of executive judgment, sensitivity, creativity, and courage required for its successful implementation than could the marketing concept. It is for this very reason that business has an answer to the bright young people who turn away from a business career because they believe it offers no challenge and serves no lasting purpose. Challenge of the highest order is implicit in the human concept, and so is purpose of the utmost significance to human progress.

In considering the real value of the human concept as a basic corporate philosophy, one is reminded of the classic anecdote of the two bricklayers at a construction site. Each was asked what he was doing. The first replied, "I am laying bricks." The second answered, "I am building a cathedral." Business can answer its critics, revitalize its ranks, and provide itself with an unlimited future through acceptance of the spirit of the human concept. Such acceptance could be one of history's momentous turning points.

48

What Has Business to Do with the Arts?

Peter Bone

What has business to do with the arts? At first glance it would appear that business and the arts have very little in common. The prime purpose of most corporations is to earn the maximum profit for their shareholders. After all a business is *in* business. Its first responsibility is to remain that way for the sake of its investors, its employees and its customers all of whom presumably benefit from the association. Certainly most businesses want to be good corporate citizens but, surely, by definition they must be practical and hardheaded.

Art on the other hand is in a much vaguer realm. As Tolstoy remarked, "Art is not a handicraft, it is the transmission of feeling an artist has experienced." It is the expression of any ideal which the artist can realize. By definition, money and the muse would seem miles apart.

Throughout the history of the world, the dominant centre of power has always been the main stimulus to art. Kings, emperors, the church, and merchant princes were patrons to some of the greatest artists and artisans whose heritage we enjoy today. The most recent period in history is the one exception. Although barons of industry amassed huge collections of art, much of which has now made its way into public institutions, little concern was given to the support or sponsorship of contemporary artists. For the most part, their struggle remained their own. State support of the arts in many countries was minimal. When money needed to be spent, education and welfare first made their demands on the national coffers. (A notable exception was the priority given by the citizens of Vienna to the rebuilding of their opera house after the Second World War.) With the disappearance of the wealthy patron and the absence of substantial government support, the arts were plainly in trouble.

Until the middle of this century corporate concern for the arts has been negligible. Industry was little concerned with anything but showing a profitable balance sheet. At the board of directors meeting for the Grand Trunk Pacific Railway in 1922 it was declared, "We will now get all we can out of the people of Canada." This was a bold statement indicative of the solitary goal of one business. A dozen years later a Royal Commission report declared that "It had been difficult not to be impressed by the fact that the corporate form of business not only gives freedom from legal liability, but also facilitates the evasion of moral responsibility." The charge of a lack of moral responsibility as a corporate citizen has often been levelled at business. In the field of support for the arts it would appear that the criticism is not without foundation. In a recent Rockefeller Brothers Fund survey it was shown that 3% of the corpora-

Reprinted with permission from *The Business Quarterly*, Summer 1970, pp. 60–63.

tions polled had only *studied*, directly or through company foundations, the possible role of corporate giving to the arts.

Profit Not the Only Role

The more astute leaders in business are realizing that showing a healthy profit for their companies is not their only role. An economic responsibility is of course mandatory but the role of the company in the society in which it flourishes has broadened beyond the single motive of making a profit. As a corporate citizen business has a major share in the responsibility for creating a more meaningful society. Business is the natural successor to the wealthy patrons of the past. Indeed, if private enterprise is to continue to be a major force in the society in which we live, private enterprise—in all its varied forms—has a responsibility to improve the quality of life in this society. But profit can manifest itself in many ways.

At the outcome of the UNESCO meeting held in Ottawa in February 1970, it was recommended that the organization through its Member States, " . . . encourage the decentralization of the resources and means to art education for the general public through the creation of regional and local cultural centres; the organization and distribution of programs in all the arts to regional and local centres, including original materials in the visual and plastic arts . . . either within the Member States or through international exchange." The object is to get a greater support for the arts in areas where opportunities for enjoyment of all forms of art have received too little attention in the past—to offer grass roots support for the arts. This is no easy task in this vast country of more than three and one-half million square miles; a country where the Trans-Canada highway from St. John's, Newfoundland to Victoria on Vancouver Island covers no less than 4,860 miles.

Rothmans of Pall Mall Canada Limited has been helping to implement the recommendations of the UNESCO report for several years. But, why should a manufacturer of cigarettes have chosen this role?

Any successful company succeeds simply because it supplies a product that the consumer wants and, at the same time, makes a profit. A manufacturer of cigarettes is no different. This corporate business is a success and allied with its prominence in this field it chose, as a corporate citizen, to return to the community in which it functions a measure of its financial success in support of the arts.

How the Support of the Arts Began

Rothmans of Pall Mall Canada Limited, like other companies, was asked by many art organizations to buy advertising in various concert programs. This form of token support of the arts had been a standard and time-honoured but not too pragmatic way of offering support to the arts.

It was suggested that it would be far more efficient for the company to take over the responsibility for the complete production of the programs. All costs are underwritten by Rothmans and the requested number of programs are given to the organization to sell at their own price for their *own* benefit.

What would the company get in return for this generous offer? A statement on the inside front cover that the program was contributed by them, a single ad—the only one in the program on the back cover, and sampling rights. This was the beginning of one corporation's contribution to the arts. It was by no means the end.

The enthusiasm and success which accompanied this venture saw the company expand its community involvement in the field of arts, sports and leisure. It became increasingly evident that the long-range survival of a corporation was directly linked to all the environmental factors which affected its future. The obligation to help build a better society was apparent. To build a successful business in a culturally barren environment is becoming less and less acceptable. Rothmans has recognized this and has become a forerunner in the support of the arts in Canada.

This company's efforts to support the arts do not stop at the printing of programs. From other members of the Rothmans World Group of companies it introduced to Canadians from Victoria to Saskatoon, from Rimouski to St. John's, Newfoundland a series of travelling art exhibitions. People in communities who had never seen a Rodin sculpture, a Riopelle painting or a Lurcat tapestry were offered their first taste of art from these contemporary masters.

In 1970 three travelling exhibitions, *Scultura Italiana, Rodin and His Contemporaries,* and *Contemporary French Tapestry* will be shown in twenty centres throughout Canada. The company pays all the costs of shipping, installation and promotion including the official opening night reception. Catalogues are supplied to the gallery free of charge to sell at any price it chooses with the proceeds being used for a worthwhile purpose such as local charities or art crafts. For example, the sale of Rodin catalogues at the National Arts Centre in Ottawa during February benefited the Canadian Association for Mentally Retarded Children.

The town of Stratford, Ontario for its Centennial project decided to convert the old town pumphouse and another building into an art gallery. Money became a problem and Rothmans were approached for financial assistance. Using the same philosophy they found worked so well with their programs, the company decided to take over the whole project. Rothmans completed the entire gallery and turned it over to Stratford replete in every detail from stationery to a landscaped sculpture court. The gallery has become an important addition to the town. Like the Stratford Festival itself, the gallery could influence the whole cultural scene in Canada.

Still another means of the corporation's community involvement are eight special events caravans or mobile sound units spotted around the country for use—without charge—at exhibitions, fairs, horse shows and sporting events.

Each is essentially a committee room on location fitted with public address facilities serving as a broadcasting centre. These mobile units are in constant use throughout Canada and are heavily booked in both summer and winter.

Dr. Frank Stanton, president of the Columbia Broadcasting System, declared before the Arts Council at Columbus, Ohio in 1967 that, "It is inevitable that the rise of business support for the arts will be no less dramatic than has been the case with education. This has been brought about by many factors—among them, modern communications; increased travel, the irrepressible growth in the number of museums and performing art centres; the rise of arts centres that channel, both outwardly and inwardly, activities in the arts; and the restless search, in an era of rapidly increasing leisure, for new meaning and new experience." To understand the human context of a healthy business life, a continuing awareness of the arts is essential to wise business leadership as it is to any other kind of leadership, spiritual, intellectual or social.

Art is not an isolated oddity in life. It is not something that can be tucked away in a remote corner and dusted occasionally. Art is something that must be nurtured and be made to flourish. In our complicated and often tortured world where communications bring us together and conflicts keep us apart it supplies a human element that is desperately needed today. As Dr. Stanton stated, "It is the thing that preserves for all life—including business life and, perhaps, in a complex industrial society, especially business life—the human scale." The wisdom of the increased support of art by business is apparent.

What Do the Arts and Business Have in Common?

What then do the arts and business have in common? It is becoming increasingly apparent that an interdependence exists albeit support for this interdependence is still in its developing stage. The liberalized youth of today which is getting a more massive exposure to the arts, greater than we have ever seen in the past, will be going into business or will have a profound influence upon the society in which business flourishes. If business is going to attract the best young graduates it must be cognizant of these facts and be more imaginative, more creative and more enterprising than it has in the past.

To describe the mobile society in which we now live, E. M. Forster coined the phrase "baggage civilization" at the beginning of this century. Today satellite communications can instantly bring us verbally or visually to any part of our world—and even beyond as witnessed by telecasts from the moon. This increased mobility is a reflection of our own changing communities. In 1968 one out of five families in North America moved from one location to another. Man's mobility cannot help but increase his perception of the world in which he lives and sharpen his awareness of values. Tougher demands are going to be made by managers and employees who find themselves uprooted and transplanted into new communities. With an increased exposure to the arts these citizens are going to expect a greater role from the business community as corporate citizens. Art in all its manifestations will play an increasingly important role in our lives as we move toward the year 2000—less than thirty years away.

By the beginning of the next century it has been predicted that North Americans will have 213 days free from work each year. This leisure time gap will have to be filled. Healthy communities in a meaningful society will become more and more attuned to the values of the arts. It would appear that business and the arts have much more in common than we have so far recognized. The challenge is obvious. If business is to play its part as a full-fledged corporate citizen, it must become increasingly involved in the society in which it functions and serves.

author
index

subject index